HANDBOOK OF PERCEPTION

Volume III

Biology of Perceptual Systems

This is Volume III of

HANDBOOK OF PERCEPTION

EDITORS: *Edward C. Carterette and Morton P. Friedman*

A complete list of the books in this series appears at the end of this volume.

HANDBOOK
OF PERCEPTION

VOLUME III

BIOLOGY OF PERCEPTUAL SYSTEMS

EDITED BY

Edward C. Carterette and Morton P. Friedman

Department of Psychology
University of California
Los Angeles, California

ACADEMIC PRESS   New York   San Francisco   London   1974
A Subsidiary of Harcourt Brace Jovanovich, Publishers

ACADEMIC PRESS, INC.
111 Fifth Avenue, New York, New York 10003

United Kingdom Edition published by
ACADEMIC PRESS, INC. (LONDON) LTD.
24/28 Oval Road, London NW1

Library of Congress Cataloging in Publication Data

Carterette, Edward C
    Biology of perceptual systems.

    (His Handbook of perception, 3)
    Includes bibliographies.
    1. Perception.   2.   Senses and sensation.
I.   Friedman, Morton P., joint author.   II.   Title.
[DNLM: 1.   Perception.   2.   Sensation. WL700 C325h]
QP441.C37   612'.8   72-9323
ISBN 0–12–161903–6

PRINTED IN THE UNITED STATES OF AMERICA

CONTENTS

Chapter 1.   Energy, Transducers, and Sensory Discrimination

T. D. M. Roberts

Chapter 2.   Neuronal Properties

Charles F. Stevens

Chapter 11.   Cutaneous Mechanoreceptors

Paul R. Burgess

Chapter 12.   Tactual Perception of Texture

*M. M. Taylor, S. J. Lederman,
and R. H. Gibson*

Chapter 13.   The Spatial Senses

I. P. Howard

Chapter 14.   Orientation and Motion in Space

I. P. Howard

Chapter 15.   Temperature Reception

Herbert Hensel

Chapter 16.   Vision

Israel Abramov and James Gordon

Chapter 17.   Seeing

Israel Abramov and James Gordon

Chapter 18.   Hearing: Central Neural Mechanisms

Bruce Masterton and Irving T. Diamond

LIST OF CONTRIBUTORS

Numbers in parentheses indicate the pages on which the authors' contributions begin.

ISRAEL ABRAMOV* (327, 359), The Rockefeller University, New York, New York

PAUL R. BURGESS (219), Department of Physiology, University of Utah, College of Medicine, Salt Lake City, Utah

IRVING T. DIAMOND (407), Department of Psychology, Duke University, Durham, North Carolina

R. H. GIBSON (251), University of Guelph, Guelph, Canada

JAMES GORDON (327, 359), Hunter College, CUNY and The Rockefeller University, New York, New York

HERBERT HENSEL (317), Institute of Physiology, University of Marburg/Lahn, Germany

G. ADRIAN HORRIDGE (39), The Australian National University, Canberra, Australia

I. P. HOWARD (273, 291), Department of Psychology, York University, Toronto, Canada

LAWRENCE KRUGER (73), Department of Anatomy, UCLA School of Medicine, Los Angeles, California

S. J. LEDERMAN† (251), Defence and Civil Institute of Environmental Medicine, University of Toronto, Toronto, Canada

BRUCE MASTERTON (407), Department of Psychology, Florida State University, Tallahassee, Florida

* *Present address:* Brooklyn College, CUNY, Brooklyn, New York
† *Present address:* Department of Psychology, Sir George Williams University, Montreal, Canada

T. D. M. ROBERTS (1), Institute of Physiology, University of Glasgow, Glasgow, Scotland

WOLFGANG M. SCHLEIDT (119), Department of Zoology, University of Maryland, College Park, Maryland

BARRY E. STEIN (63), Department of Anatomy, UCLA School of Medicine, Los Angeles, California

CHARLES F. STEVENS (21), Department of Physiology and Biophysics, University of Washington, Seattle, Washington

N. S. SUTHERLAND (157), Laboratory of Experimental Psychology, University of Sussex, Brighton, Sussex, England

M. M. TAYLOR (251), Defence and Civil Institute of Environmental Medicine, Downsview, Ontario, Canada

KARLA BUTLER THOMAS (139), Department of Psychology, California State University, Northridge, California

COLWYN B. TREVARTHEN (89), Department of Psychology, University of Edinburgh, Edinburgh, Scotland

DOUGLAS B. WEBSTER* (449), Department of Biology, New York University, Bronx, New York

BERNICE M. WENZEL (187, 207), Departments of Physiology and Psychiatry, and Brain Research Institute, UCLA School of Medicine, Los Angeles, California

* *Present address:* Louisiana State University, Medical Center, Kresge Hearing Research Laboratory, Department of Otolaryngology, New Orleans, Louisiana

FOREWORD

The problem of perception is one of understanding the way in which the organism transforms, organizes, and structures information arising from the world in sense data or memory. With this definition of perception in mind, the aims of this treatise are to bring together essential aspects of the very large, diverse, and widely scattered literature on human perception and to give a précis of the state of knowledge in every area of perception. It is aimed at the psychologist in particular and at the natural scientist in general. A given topic is covered in a comprehensive survey in which fundamental facts and concepts are presented and important leads to journals and monographs of the specialized literature are provided. Perception is considered in its broadest sense. Therefore, the work will treat a wide range of experimental and theoretical work.

The first part of the treatise deals with the fundamentals of perceptual systems. It is comprised of six volumes covering (1) historical and philosophical roots of perception, (2) psychophysical judgment and measurement, (3) the biology of perceptual systems, (4) hearing, (5) seeing, and (6) feeling, tasting, smelling, and hurting.

Another six volumes will cover the perceiving organism, which takes up the wider view and generally ignores specialty boundaries. The major areas will include speech and language, perception of space and objects, perception of form and pattern, cognitive performance, information processing, perceptual memory, perceptual aspects of thinking and problem solving, esthetics, and the ecology of the perceiver. Coverage will be given to theoretical issues and models of perceptual processes and also to central topics in perceptual judgment and decision.

The "Handbook of Perception" should serve as a basic source and reference work for all in the arts or sciences, indeed for all who are interested in human perception.

EDWARD C. CARTERETTE
MORTON P. FRIEDMAN

PREFACE

. . . some of the flexibility of the perceptual process—for instance, the recognition of relational rather than of absolute properties and of changes rather than of constant stimulation, and a primitive type of abstraction— follows from the known properties of the physiological structure and can be imitated by physical mechanisms. While not underestimating the degree to which sensory qualities consciously apprehended differ from and transcend anything known in the physical world, it seems legitimate in view of all this to treat the two in conjunction and to ask how far the unknown can be explained in terms of the known.

K. J. W. CRAIK
(Epilogue, Ph.D. Thesis
on Visual Adaptation,
Cambridge University, 1940)

Sensory physiology has in the past neglected to deal with many of the properties of perception that any physiological theory must consider. Some of these properties involve the perception of physically different patterns as similar. Similarity is itself based on perhaps more primitive aspects of perception: patterning, selectivity, and the equivalence of some spatial and temporal sequences. The last is crucial in the decoding of signals of all sensory modes. The role of serial order is very large in such perceptual activities as reading, listening, and speaking.

This volume aims to provide the elements of sensory physiology, with special attention being given to the basic properties of perception. The authors have tried to be alert to the significance for perception of a physiological function, of a striking neural net, or of special features of a sensory structure.

The first five chapters deal with the general problems of energy transduction, detection, and discrimination; the properties of neurons alone and as conjoined in nets; the natural diversity and evolutionary divergence of sensory systems; and "*psychogenesis*—the maturation of a system prefabricated to become an intelligent, conscious individual who will assimilate knowledge of objects and beings according to inherent rules" (Trevarthen, in Chapter 5).

A chapter on the relatively new field of ethology and a chapter on the genetics of behavior are followed by a treatment of the facts and theories about the way in which animals and men construct patterned stimulation of receptors into significant objects.

The second half of the volume deals with the structure and function of sensory systems on which vertebrates depend for their construction of the varieties of experience. Chemoreception, tasting and smelling, cutaneous mechanoreception (of position, velocity, transients), active texture perception, mechanisms of spatial orientation and of motion in space, thermoreception, vision, and audition are all considered. In almost every case the underlying physiological mechanisms are related to the psychophysical or perceptual observations. However, the reader must keep constantly in mind that it is the more primitive sensory and perceptual acts which are dealt with in this volume.

The aim of the material in this volume is to provide a foundation for understanding the more complex aspects of human perception which are to be covered in considerable detail in volumes now in preparation. Full treatment of hearing will be given in Volume IV, of seeing in Volume V, of feeling, tasting, smelling, and hurting in Volume VI. Each volume ranges over the appropriate history, stimulus measurement, biophysics, neural coding, central neural mechanisms, the perceptual phenomena themselves, explanatory models, and theoretical issues.

We are grateful to Mrs. Claudia Seapy and Mrs. Cheryl Grossman for their substantial help with myriad editorial details. The very difficult and important task of preparing the Subject Index was done by Mrs. Patricia Blum Carterette, and we are deeply in her debt for this.

Financial support has come from The Regents of the University of California and from The National Institute of Mental Health. Intellectual support has come from our colleagues, friends, former teachers, and students. They will understand that we cannot list them all here but they should know too that we thank them very, very much for their counsel.

EDWARD C. CARTERETTE
MORTON P. FRIEDMAN

CONTENTS OF OTHER VOLUMES

Volume II: Psychophysical Judgment and Measurement

I.   Introduction and Overview

II.   Perceptual Choice and Judgment

Chapter 1

ENERGY, TRANSDUCERS, AND SENSORY DISCRIMINATION

T. D. M. ROBERTS

I. INTRODUCTORY SUMMARY

In this chapter we consider some of the general principles that have to be taken into account in a study of the relationship between sensory experience on the one hand and the neurophysiological properties of sensory receptors on the other. We examine the implications of the nature of the signalling system, how receptor specificity can be related to sensory discriminations, and how interactions between the effects of change and the effects of rate-of-change introduce ambiguities into the signalling of stimulus intensity. The factors brought to light in this discussion should be continually borne in mind when reviewing the details of the individual receptor systems as they are presented in later chapters.

II. SENSORY EXPERIENCE

A. The Function of a Sense Organ

We start with the elementary concept that each living organism is continuously engaged in interchange with its environment: in uptake of nutriment, in disposal of wastes, and in exchanges of energy. The composition of the immediate environment cannot therefore be regarded as unchanging. Consequently it may become important to the survival of an organism that it should detect and respond to certain crucial aspects of environmental change. It is in this context that the specialized organs of sensory reception have been evolved.

The function of each particular sense organ is to focus upon one specific feature of environmental change and to signal the current value of the intensity of that change. The organism then puts together all the signals it is receiving from whatever sense organs it happens to possess and "draws conclusions," so to speak, about the significant trends in the environment as a whole.

A generalized statement such as this may tempt one to suppose the situation to be rather more simple than it is. We are accustomed to describing the features of our environment in words but we must be careful to avoid the notion that the messages sent by the sense organs to an animal's central nervous system have something in common with the messages we might ourselves use to convey to someone else our impressions of what is happening around us. Consider the following two situations: in one there is a flickering blue spot somewhere in the left visual field; in the other, a moving limb suddenly encounters a solid object, as when we accidentally bang our knee against a chair. Any verbal message about these happenings is likely to contain unambiguous information about the nature of the environmental change that acted as a "stimulus," and we may be tempted to suppose that some information about the nature of the stimulus will also be present in the messages from the relevant sense organs. The evidence from neurophysiological experiments shows that this is definitely not the case. Nervous messages do not contain information about the nature of the process that initiated the sending of the message.

B. A Simple Experiment

The reader may carry out a simple experiment to illustrate this point. Direct the gaze to the far left, close the eyes, and tap gently with the fingertip at the extreme outer edge of the right eyelid close against the bony rim of the orbit. A flash of "light" will be seen in the left visual field. In fact, of course, no such flash of light occurs in this experiment.

What happens is that the receptors in the eye can be activated by mechanical deformation as well as by light. When they are active they initiate nervous messages which of necessity pass only in those nerve fibers that are anatomically connected to these receptors. Now these particular receptors are structurally adapted to be exquisitely sensitive to electromagnetic radiation (light); they are also so placed that light can fall on them and that they are relatively well protected from mechanical deformations. In consequence, there is a high probability that a message received by the nervous system along a nerve fiber connected to one of these receptors will have been initiated by the incidence of light. We classify the resulting experience as "a flash of light," and, because the nervous message is no different when the receptors have been activated mechanically, we persist in the classification and report a flash of light even when the relevant environmental change was, in fact, a mechanical tap.

C. Experience and Interpretation

It can be seen from this argument that our subjective sensory experience involves a process of interpretation of the messages in sensory nerves. The nature of our interpretations depends on a number of factors. Previous experience, even including prenatal experiences, appears to play a dominant role (Melzack, 1965) and it is correspondingly difficult to establish whether or not there is any innate component at all.

It cannot be too much stressed that sensory experience is a subjective, personal matter, and that we can have no direct knowledge about the sensory experiences of anybody else. The nature of the interpretations carried out by other people can be conveyed to us through language, but here again the significance of the words depends on the individual's earlier training and it may not be the same for the listener as it is for the speaker.

D. Sensory Discrimination

We are on safer ground when we consider sensory discrimination. We can set up test situations in which another person, or even an animal, is called upon to make a choice on the basis of his classification of a sensory signal when presented with one of a variety of signals which differ in known ways. We can then determine whether or not the experimental subject shows a difference in behavior that we can correlate with what we know of the differences between the signals. By such a routine we can demonstrate, for example, that an individual differs from "normal" in his color vision. We may describe him as "color blind" because of the confusions we have been able to demonstrate, by specially constructed tests, even though he was not previously aware of anything at all unusual in his capacity for visual experience.

Even this procedure is not without its pitfalls, as we may not know the basis on which he makes his discriminations. This is a particular difficulty in the design of animal experiments on sensory discrimination where an animal may be attending to some feature of the experimental set-up that is completely ignored by the experimenter. We need to bear in mind also in human experiments that an individual's basis for sensory discriminations may be markedly altered by suggestion under hypnosis. After suitable indoctrination in the trance state as to the ways in which colored dots can and can not be distinguished, a subject with otherwise normal color vision may be induced to respond consistently to the Ishihara test charts as though he were red-green color blind (Erickson, 1939). Surgical procedures which would not otherwise be undertaken without deep anaesthesia can be carried out successfully on the relaxed, conscious patient after he has been prepared, under hypnosis, by the suggestion that he will feel no pain (Mason, 1960). Such observations have important implications for any theory about the relationship between the characteristics of sensory experience on the one hand and the facts of neurophysiology and histology on the other. However, this is not the place to do more than simply draw attention to the presence of difficulties of this kind before passing on to consider the action of the sensory receptors themselves.

E. The Kinds of Information Required

In relation to environmental change, we may distinguish different kinds of information that may be relevant, namely (*1*) the nature of the change, (*2*) its intensity, and (*3*) its location in relation to the body as a whole. In a discussion of the nature of the environmental change, the traditional five categories of sensation, sight, hearing, touch, taste, and smell, are rather unsatisfactory for a detailed study. In terms of experience there are many more than five categories that may be distinguished. Vision includes the senses of color, movement, and texture as well as of brightness. Flavors involve components from smell as well as taste. Touch embraces many quite distinct features: warmth, cold, pressure, vibration, pain, tickle, and itch as well as light touch, and combinations of these give rise to complex sensations such as those of roughness, wetness, heaviness and so on. Our ideas of speed and of the shape and relative positions of external objects depend on information received over several different sensory pathways taken together and interpreted in the light of conclusions from past experience.

When we come to examine the anatomic structures that might be concerned in sensory processes, we find yet another whole range of receptors whose signals do not contribute directly to conscious experience at all. Some of these have their role in the automatic control mechanisms of the body, such as the baroreceptors in the vascular system, the chemoreceptors in respiration, the organs of balance in the inner ear, and the stretch receptors in muscles and joints that are concerned in muscular movements. Others are of more uncertain function, such as the vibration receptors found in the mesentery or even in the pancreas in some animals.

III. RECEPTORS

A. The Types of Receptor

It would appear to be a logical step to try to correlate the discrete types of histological structure that are found at various sensory sites with the types of sensations to which they give rise. In practice, this exercise has proved uncommonly difficult, apart from a few very obvious generalizations, such as that the rods and cones of the retina are concerned with vision and the taste buds with savor.

There are two levels of difficulty that can be illustrated in the case of the skin. Several discrete sensations arise from stimuli applied to the skin, and it can be shown that the sensitivity is not uniformly distributed. Some small regions are more sensitive than others and these regions differ from one another in the type of sensation most readily elicited from them. Thus we can distinguish "warm spots," "cold spots," "touch spots," and so on. The locations of the various spots can be mapped with some precision (Dallenbach, 1927). In some regions, such as the lips and the fingertips, the sensitive spots lie very close together. In other regions, such as the middle of the back, the spots are very much further apart, sometimes being separated by several centimeters of relatively very insensitive skin.

Histological preparations of human skin reveal, with suitable staining, a rich profusion of elements such as Meissner's corpuscles, Merkel's disks, Krause's end bulbs, Pacinian corpuscles, peritrichial endings and others (Quilliam, 1966; Sinclair, 1967; Weddell, Palmer, & Pallie, 1955). Each is associated with the ending of at least one afferent nerve fiber, so that there is a strong presumption that these are the structures responsible for initiating sensory messages. However, the distribution of these histological "sensory" elements does not correspond with the distribution of sensitive spots as determined by sensory testing. The histological elements are in some regions much more closely packed, being separated from one another by distances measured in microns rather than in millimeters. Elements of different kinds are seen together in the same microscope field. As an added complication, skin areas can be found, such as on the back of the ear lobe, where a variety of sensations can be elicited but where many of the characteristic types of organized histological ending are entirely absent (Weddell et al., 1955).

B. Sensory Units

Part of the difficulty about the discrepancy between the distributions may perhaps be overcome by taking account of the observation that many nerve endings lie on branches of the same parent nerve fiber. Thus we speak of a "sensory unit," to refer to a single sensory nerve fiber together with all the receptor terminations that are connected to its branches. This gives a different level of organization from the histologically discrete "receptors" on the one hand and the "sense organs" on the other, where the expression "sense organ" is used to denote a specialized structure, such as the eye or the ear, containing a number of receptors and served by a number of nerve fibers.

We may map the "receptive field" of a sensory unit by exploring the skin while recording the electrical activity of a single afferent nerve fiber. This procedure reveals two new difficulties. The receptive fields turn out to be surprisingly large and they commonly show considerable overlapping

(Weddell, 1941; Mountcastle, 1961). Furthermore, it is not unusual to find that a single afferent nerve fiber can be made active by stimuli of more than one type, e.g., by temperature change as well as by mechanical deformation (Wall, 1960). When the mapping procedure is applied to single cells at higher levels in the nervous system, even larger receptive fields are found, sometimes involving both sides of the body; or there may be convergence from quite different sensory modalities, a single unit responding to visual or to acoustic stimuli as well as to various kinds of cutaneous stimulation (Bell, Sierra, Buendia, & Segundo, 1964; Jung, Kornhuber, & DaFonseca, 1963).

Another approach to the problem is to look for the sensations evoked by activating single nerve fibers, either electrically or by probing with a fine quartz needle (Murray, 1962). The results are not very helpful, as the sensory experience does not fit into any of the usual categories except perhaps those of "sharp prick" and "pain." One is forced to the conclusion that the discrimination of other types of environmental change—the discrimination of different sensory modalities—depends on central processes of interpretation using information received over numerous afferent pathways. Let us turn now to the nature of the available nervous messages.

C. Nervous Messages

The property of a nerve cell which confers the ability to convey messages resides in the specialization of its cell membrane. As with all cells, the internal fluid content of the cell—the cytoplasm—is separated from the immediate environment by a membrane which presents a barrier to the diffusion of particles. Different molecular species are hindered to different extents, while some are transported from one side of the barrier to the other as part of the activity that distinguishes live cells from dead. As a consequence of this activity the ionic composition of the cytoplasm of a live cell differs from that of its environment. Because the cell membrane is not equally permeable to all ions there is a difference in electrical potential between the two sides of the membrane.

In the nerve cell, the permeability of the membrane to certain ions can be changed by applying an electric current that alters the voltage across the membrane. The resulting changes in permeability in turn involve further changes in membrane potential in a regenerative sequence whose features and time course are independent of the originally applied stimulating current so long as this is large enough. The activity cycle is termed a "nerve impulse" and the detailed mechanisms of its generation are set out elsewhere (Chap. 2). The characteristics of a nerve impulse depend on the condition of that part of the nerve cell membrane that happens to be going through its activity cycle. Because nerve fibers are long and narrow, some parts of a nerve cell membrane can be "active" while other parts are "resting." Local electric currents pass between the resting and active regions and lead to the generation of new activity in regions that were previously resting. In this way a cycle of activity initiated at one end of a nerve fiber is propagated along the whole length of the cell.

Notice that the development of activity in a downstream region of a nerve cell thus depends on the electric currents generated by the presence of an activity cycle at an immediately neighboring upstream region and not on the nature of the events that first initiated the activity some distance further away. It follows that there is no possibility that any messages transmitted in the form of propagated nerve impulses can include information about the nature of the process, sensory or other, that generated those messages.

D. The Kinds of Information Transmitted

The whole of the information available to the central nervous system, on the basis of which judgments have to be made as to the nature, intensity, and location of specific changes in the environment, is entirely contained in a description of which afferent nerve fibers happen to be going through their activity cycles at the time in question and at what intervals the activity cycles succeed one another in particular fibers. This means that discriminations as to the nature of an environmental change, e.g., as to whether the skin has been cooled or pricked, have the same status and involve the same mechanisms as the discriminations as to the location of the stimulus, e.g., as to whether the point touched lies on the hand or on the foot. The same argument applies to the discrimination between the messages indicating a flash of light in the left visual field and those indicating that a knee has bumped into a chair.

The common mechanism for discriminating the nature of stimuli and their locations on the basis of which afferent fibers are active, is also concerned to some extent in discriminating the intensity of the environmental changes, insofar as an increase in intensity will commonly entail an increase in the amount of tissue that is affected, bringing additional sensory units into play. Recruitment of additional units may arise also from the fact that different units differ in sensitivity, so that a weak stimulus excites fewer receptors than an intense one. There is, however, another system that may be used to convey information about the intensity of the environmental change. The sequence of events comprising the activity cycle of a nerve cell, the nerve impulse, depends in detail on the condition of the active part of the cell membrane. This dependence extends both to the amplitude of the changes that take place and to their time courses. The whole of a cycle is completed within a few milliseconds, leaving the cell membrane in a condition ready to be set into a new cycle of activity. Nerve impulses can thus follow one another in rapid succession. When a receptor is subjected to sustained stimulation, a succession of impulses is generated in the corresponding afferent nerve fiber and the intervals at which the impulses follow one another reflect the intensity of the stimulus to the receptor.

E. The Interpretation as to Stimulus Intensity

One might suppose that, conversely, one could deduce the intensity of the stimulus from a knowledge of the frequency with which the impulses follow one another in the afferent nerve. However, this turns out not to be the case, for the reason that the receptors are, in general, sensitive to a number of different features of environmental change at the same time. They are also influenced by their recent history of previous stimulation. The effects of all the excitatory factors are added together at the point where their influence is converted into a stream of nerve impulses and the mixture can never be unscrambled again unambiguously into the component parts from which it was formed. If a particular nerve fiber is active to the extent of, say, 30 impulses per second, we can never distinguish the case where this is the result of two processes, each contributing respectively 10 and 20 pulses per second from that in which each has contributed 15.

IV. STIMULI

A. The Kinds of Energy Detected

In spite of the many difficulties in relating the patterns of sensory nerve impulses to the characteristics of the sensations to which they may give rise, it is nevertheless very important to try to understand as much as possible of the detailed way in which each receptor responds to those changes in the environment to which it is sensitive. There are three forms of energy involved in the environmental changes for which specialized receptors have been evolved, namely, mechanical, chemical, and electromagnetic. The corresponding receptors are classified as mechanoreceptors, chemoreceptors, and photoreceptors respectively, although, as has already been pointed out, a particular receptor may be affected by stimuli of more than one kind: the photoreceptors in the retina, for example, can be excited by mechanical deformation as well as by light.

When we say that the detection by a receptor of a change in the environment implies an exchange of energy, we mean that the structure of the receptor is changed either by mechanical work being done on it to deform it or by the uptake of a chemical substance or the absorption of electromagnetic radiation to alter the electrical configuration of the parts. In each case the essential effect is an alteration in the minute structure of a part of the cell membrane of the receptor cell, with a consequent change in its permeability to ions. The change in permeability leads to the generation of an electric current, signs of which may be observed by an experimenter, in suitably favorable instances, as a voltage change. Such a voltage change is referred to as a "receptor potential." It is the action of the associated electric current on the terminal portion of the sensory nerve fiber that eventually gives rise to the succession of nerve impulses by which the environmental change is signalled to the central nervous system.

Once the transformation has been effected between the energy exchange with the environment on the one hand and the generation of nerve impulses on the other, we cease to be concerned with the nature or magnitude of the energy changes involved in the activity cycles of the nerve cell and confine our attention to their presence or absence at particular times. We pass from the energy domain into that of signals. Energy changes are, of course, still involved in the activity of the nerve cells. The difference in emphasis is like that between the electricity supply mains and the telephone system. In each case electric currents pass along wires: in one case we are concerned with the transfer of energy; in the other with signals, i.e., with messages having semantic content. A device which converts energy changes into signals is referred to as a "transducer."

B. The Specialization of Receptors

When we come to consider the action of a specific receptor as a transducer, we have to pay particular attention to its anatomy. The various types of receptors differ from one another in the arrangement of auxiliary structures surrounding the sensitive region. These auxiliary structures perform various functions that contribute to the selectivity of the receptor apparatus as a whole. They may serve to concentrate the effects of incident energy, as the ossicles of the middle ear operating as a system of levers convert small changes in air pressure occurring at the tympanic membrane into larger pressure changes in the watery perilymph of the inner ear, or as the cornea and lens of the eye form optical images on the retina. They may serve as a filter, transmitting certain characteristics of the stimulus and attenuating others, as the concentric lamellae surrounding the core of a Pacinian corpuscle transmit only the high-frequency components of an imposed deformation, making the receptor more suitable for detecting vibrations rather than sustained pressures. They may serve to exclude the effects of certain kinds of disturbance, as the receptors of the retina and of the olfactory organ are protected from mechanical stimulation by their position. They may serve as an amplifier, as in the complexity of the organ of Corti in the ear, where energy derived from secretory cells and stored in the form of voltage gradients is used to augment the effect on the receptors of the incoming acoustic energy.

In the mechanoreceptors the auxiliary structures assume a variety of forms, as in the different types of encapsulated endings in the skin. The different arrangements appear to serve in sorting out the different ways in which the skin may be deformed. In many cases a high degree of specificity is conferred merely by the anatomic location of a receptor. Thus stretch receptors in the walls of the arteries, at the carotid sinus and elsewhere, serve as detectors of systemic arterial blood pressure (baroreceptors), while receptors of very similar structure lying in the connective tissue of a joint capsule are concerned with reporting the angle between the bones forming that joint, and again the similar though rather larger receptors found in the connective tissue of a tendon report features of the tension exerted by the muscles inserted in that tendon.

It is not always very clear which part of the histological structure of a receptor is the actual sensitive region. It is usual for the terminal portion of the sensory nerve fiber to show multiple branching in the receptor region. Often the very fine terminal branches are swollen up at intervals into small blebs. In one case (frog muscle spindle) which has been carefully examined from this point of view with the electron microscope (Katz, 1961) small tubular protrusions from the blebs were seen to come into close contact with elements of the supporting structure, and it was argued that the available deformation would need to be concentrated onto small elements of this kind in order to produce sufficient change in the membrane properties to account for the observed magnitude of the receptor potentials. However, in a search for similar electron microscope appearances at other mechano-receptors nothing comparable has so far come to light elsewhere. Little further can usefully be said, therefore, at this stage about the precise mechanism by which the mechanical deformation leads to the changes that are manifested in the receptor potential.

C. The Mechanism of Detection

There are good indications from such cases as have been studied in detail that the time course of the receptor potential corresponds closely to the time course of the repetition frequency of the impulses in the sensory nerve fiber from the receptor. It is accordingly accepted that the essential step in the detection process is the development of changes in the conductance of the cell membrane of the receptor cell, and that it is these conductance changes that lead to local electrical currents which, in turn, excite the nerve fiber repetitively.

It is usual for the individual impulses to be regularly spaced out in time and this raises a particular difficulty, not yet solved, in those cases where there is multiple branching of the terminal part of the nerve fiber. One would suppose that, if each branch is capable of carrying propagated impulses, the pattern emerging in the stem fiber should show the effect of interference between the impulse streams in the contributory branches. No such interference patterns are found. We must therefore conclude that impulse generation occurs in the stem fiber, possibly at the first node of Ranvier, rather than at the terminations of the branches. The electric currents arising from the conductance changes at the ends of the various branches presumably exert a combined effect on the membrane of that part of the stem fiber at which the impulses are first generated. The temporal pattern of the impulse-discharge thus reflects the "general climate" of excitation in the terminal spray, rather than the conditions at the end of any particular branch.

D. Receptor Cells

At some receptors the detection of the environmental change is carried out by special receptor cells, rather than by portions of the sensory nerve fibers themselves. Examples are the rods and cones of the retina, the hair cells of the inner ear, and the receptors in the taste buds and olfactory mucosa. It turns out that in all these cases, and also in many other sensory sites in lower animals, the receptor cell itself possesses fine processes that resemble modified cilia; that is to say the processes contain elements of fine structure typical of electron microscope pictures of cilia (Cordier, 1964).

Another shared feature of receptor cells revealed by the electron microscope is the organization of the junctional region of contact between the receptor cell and its sensory nerve fiber. The presence here of vesicles and membrane thickenings strongly suggests some process of chemical transmission of excitation such as occurs at the synaptic junctions between nerve cells.

V. RESPONSES

A. The Stimulus–Response Relationship

While there are still a number of mysteries about the details of the precise way in which the energy of environmental change is transduced into nerve impulses at sites involving these more specialized receptor cells, we do have enough information to make some useful generalizations. Much of the detailed information comes from studies on mechanoreceptors. Here the nature of the environmental changes can often be described in precise physical terms and it is possible to derive mathematical expressions which can be used to predict the time course of the discharge of impulses from a receptor on the basis of certain measurable parameters of the stimulus. This step has a particular importance in relation to those receptors that serve as detectors in the various servomechanisms in the body. It is of interest to analyze the behavior of these servomechanisms in engineering terms so as to understand what is happening when they become disordered in disease. In addition, the properties of the servomechanisms of muscular movement need to be understood for the design of manual control devices for the complex machines of modern civilization.

B. A Simple Mechanoreceptor

The detailed study of certain mechanoreceptors has revealed features of the transduction process that are found to be common to many other receptors also. These features must therefore be taken into account in studies of sensation as well as in relation to the servo control systems where the "sensory" signals are not themselves translated into conscious experience. We may take as an example the case of a simple deformation receptor, the spray ending of Ruffini found in the capsule of a joint and serving to report the angle between the bones at that joint. The spray is formed by multiple branching of the terminal part of a sensory nerve fiber. The fine twigs bear a number of swellings and the whole is embedded in the connective tissue of the joint capsule (see Fig. 2, inset).

When the joint moves, the disposition of the connective tissue fibers in the capsule alters, and parts of the nerve ending are distorted. A stream of impulses is set up in the sensory nerve at a repetition frequency which presumably depends on the degree of deformation of the spray. If the angle at the joint is now moved to a new position, the time course of the change in the repetition frequency of the nerve impulses does not however correspond precisely to the time course of the change in joint angle.

C. The Notion of Impulse Frequency

Where impulses follow one another at varying intervals it is not always appropriate to measure the impulse frequency in terms of a count of impulses in unit time; we need a new definition. To derive the frequency of the impulses at a particular time we measure the interval between the two most

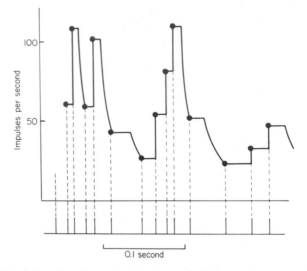

Fig. 1. Principles of reciprocal pulse interval display. Below: Impulse stream as recorded directly. Above: Plot of impulse frequency against time. The abscissa for each point corresponds to the time of arrival of an impulse. The ordinate is the reciprocal of the interval between the most recent two impulses. The full line shows that the frequency function declines along a reciprocal curve if no impulse is received by the end of a period equal to the last measured interval.

recent pulses and also the time elapsed since the last pulse; we then take the reciprocal of the longer of these two intervals (see Fig. 1). The effect of this procedure is that if the intervals between successive pulses are getting shorter, our measure of frequency is adjusted as soon as each pulse arrives. On the other hand, if the intervals are getting longer, the frequency does not continue to correspond to the reciprocal of the interval between the two most recent pulses beyond the expiry of a similar interval. If the expected next impulse does not arrive on time, we revise our estimate of the frequency. An alternative procedure is to regard the impulse frequency as a discontinuous function which has a value only at the moment of arrival of an impulse, the magnitude at that point being, as before, the reciprocal of the interval between the two most recent pulses.

D. Static and Dynamic Components in the Response

Using one of these conventions for measuring a variable frequency, we can plot the impulse frequency against time for a receptor in a joint and compare the result with the time course of the stimulus (Fig. 2). When we

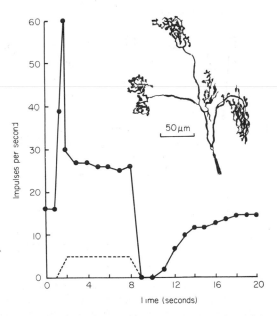

FIG. 2. The response of a deformation receptor in the knee joint of the cat to a change in joint angle from one position to another and back again. Note the exaggerated response to movement, followed by adaptation to a frequency appropriate to the new position (from Boyd & Roberts, 1953). Inset: Microscopic appearance of a similar receptor, including several planes of focus, to show the complexity of the terminal branching of the nerve fiber (from Boyd, 1954, redrawn from the specimen).

consider the change from one environmental condition to another we see that each has its associated impulse frequency, but during the change in joint angle the change in impulse frequency, though it is in the right direction, is exaggerated in degree, with the result that several seconds elapse before the discharge settles to the value appropriate to the new position. The exaggerated change during the movement is referred to as the "dynamic component" of the response, as opposed to the "static component" which reflects the relationship between impulse frequency and joint angle in sustained conditions, after the effects of movement have been allowed to die away. The gradual change in firing frequency occurring after a movement is described as "adaptation," and receptors may be classified as "slowly adapting" or "rapidly adapting" according to the time course of this change. The responses of some receptors show no static component, the discharge of impulses always adapting to zero frequency after a movement. Many tactile receptors behave in this way, so that we are usually not aware of contact with the clothes on our back until we move.

E. Ambiguities in Signalling Stimulus Intensity

The magnitude of the static component of the response may be plotted against the magnitude of some feature of the stimulus, such as the angle at the joint in the case we have just been considering. A plot obtained in this way may be thought of as describing how the intensity of the stimulus is signalled to the central nervous system. At this point we must not lose sight of the fact that the message received also includes the dynamic component of the receptor response and that there is no way of deciding, from the impulse stream itself, how much of the prevailing frequency is contributed by a static component and how much by a dynamic component. The two are inextricably confounded in the sensory message.

F. Mathematical Prediction of Responses

To study the dynamic component of the response, we may calculate what frequency of impulses we should expect at each stage if the static component were present alone, and we then deduct these amounts from the values observed experimentally. Two features emerge. The peak value of the dynamic component depends on the rate-of-change of the conditions at the receptor: the faster we move, the larger the dynamic component. Secondly, some effect persists after the end of the movement. It is the decay of this part of the dynamic component that constitutes the phenomenon of adaptation (see Fig. 3).

These two observed features of the dynamic component of the response of a deformation receptor may be combined into a mathematical statement from which we may predict the whole of its time course in any given conditions (Fig. 4). A similar formulation appears to work for a great variety of receptors, the adjustments needed to produce a good fit in a specific case affecting merely the numerical values of certain constants in the mathematical expression.

VI. SPECIAL CASES

A. Vibration

A rapidly adapting receptor with no static component in its response may be well suited to act as a vibration detector, but complications arise when we come to consider how such a receptor indicates the amplitude of the vibratory stimulus. If the vibration consists of a fluctuation in the mechani-

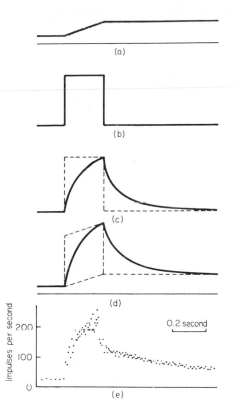

FIG. 3. Static and dynamic components in the response of a receptor (muscle spindle). Note that the dynamic component corresponds to a sluggish response to rate of change of deformation. a: Time course of stimulus and of static component of response; b: time course of rate-of-change of deformation; c: a sluggish response to (b); d: sum of (a) and (c) above; e: actual response of receptor (spindle discharge), for comparison with (d). (From Roberts, 1966.)

cal conditions repeated at relatively long intervals, the sensory discharge may consist of a group of impulses in response to each succeeding displacement in a particular direction, the number of impulses in each burst depending on the rate-of-change of deformation, i.e., giving some indication of the stimulus intensity. The intervals between the bursts will depend on the period of the imposed vibration and not on its intensity (Lowenstein & Roberts, 1951). Thus, as the vibratory frequency is increased there comes a point of confusion where the same sensory discharge may be generated either by an intense low-frequency stimulus or by a less intense stimulus at a higher frequency. Beyond this point an increase in vibratory frequency is accompanied by an increase in the frequency of the sensory discharge no matter what the intensity so long as it is above threshold.

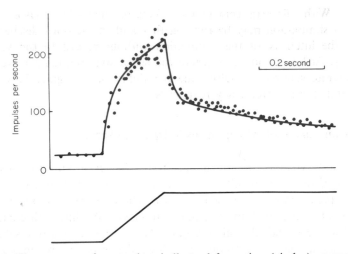

FIG. 4. The response of a muscle spindle to deformation (circles) compared with the output of an analog-computer simulation (full line) incorporating the following relations:

if x_t and y_t are the input deformation and the output signal, respectively, at time t, then

$$y_t = A\Psi(x_t) + B\Phi(x, t)_t$$

where: A and B are gain factors governing the magnitudes of the static and dynamic components,

$$\Psi(x_t) = ax_t + b \quad \text{(static component)},$$

$$\Phi(x, t)_t = y_1 + y_2 + y_3 \quad \text{(dynamic component)},$$

$$y_1 = \frac{d}{dt}(cx - dy_1),$$

$$y_2 = \frac{d}{dt}(ex - fy_2),$$

$$y_3 = \frac{d}{dt}(gx - hy_3)$$

(From Roberts & Murray-Smith, 1970.)

B. High-Frequency Vibration

A system operating in this way will not serve for the detection of high-frequency vibrations such as are involved in hearing, where the mechanical oscillations may succeed one another more rapidly than nerve impulses can follow. To meet this situation some receptors exhibit a dynamic component of response in the same sense even when the direction of the displacement is reversed. A movement in either of two opposite directions gives the same response. With this arrangement the effects of successive phases of high-frequency stimulation may be run together and the sensory discharge can indicate the intensity of the stimulation without regard to the vibratory frequency. At low frequencies where the successive mechanical cycles can each generate separate impulses, the possibility of ambiguity between intensity and stimulus frequency reappears.

C. Dynamic and Static Components in Opposite Senses

Static and dynamic components are found in varying proportions in the responses of receptors of all types. The general rule is that the two components operate in the same sense, so that the dynamic component serves to exaggerate the change in the static component. An interesting exception is found in the so-called cold receptors. These show a steady discharge in constant conditions at a frequency which depends on the temperature. There is a rounded peak in frequency near normal body temperature with lower values both above and below. On reducing the temperature the static response is a reduction in firing frequency. The dynamic response, however, is in the opposite direction; the impulse frequency increases markedly while the temperature is falling (Murray, 1962). When the temperature is held steady at the lower value, the discharge slowly adapts. Such a receptor shows a reduced discharge on warming, followed, during the adaptation phase, by a gradual increase in discharge frequency to the appropriate new static value. This increase in discharge may be responsible for the anomalous sensation of cold often experienced shortly after entering a warm room after being out in the cold

VII. CONCLUSION

From the examples indicated in this chapter it will be clear that between the apparent simplicity of sensory experience on the one hand and the precision of finely controlled neurophysiological experiment on the other there lies an important but largely unexplored territory which leaves scope for a great many ambiguities and uncertainties.

References

Bell, C., Sierra, G., Buendia, N., & Segundo, J. P. Sensory properties of neurons in the mesencephalic reticular formation. *Journal of Neurophysiology,* 1964, **27**, 961–987.

Boyd, I. A. The histological structure of the receptors in the knee-joint of the cat correlated with their physiological response. *Journal of Physiology (London)*, 1954, **124**, 476–488.

Boyd, I. A., & Roberts, T. D. M. Proprioceptive discharges from stretch-receptors in the knee-joint of the cat. *Journal of Physiology (London)*, 1953, **122**, 38–58.

Cordier, R. Sensory cells. In J. Brachet & A. E. Mirsky (Eds.), *The cell*. Vol. 6. New York: Academic Press, 1964. Pp. 313–386.

Dallenbach, K. M. The temperature spots and end-organs. *American Journal of Psychology*, 1927, **39**, 402–427.

Erickson, M. H. The induction of color blindness by a technique of hypnotic suggestion. *Journal of General Psychology*, 1939, **20**, 61–89.

Jung, R., Kornhuber, H. H., & DaFonseca, J. S. Multi-sensory convergence on cortical neurons. Neuronal effects of visual, acoustic and vestibular stimuli in the superior convolutions of the cat's cortex. *Progress in Brain Research*, 1963, **1**, 207–234.

Katz, B. The terminations of the afferent nerve fiber in the muscle spindle of the frog. *Philosophical Transactions of the Royal Society of London, Series B*, 1961, **243**, 221–240.

Lowenstein, O., & Roberts, T. D. M. The localization and analysis of the responses to vibration from the isolated elasmobranch labyrinth. A contribution to the problem of the evolution of hearing in vertebrates. *Journal of Physiology (London)*, 1951, **114**, 471–489.

Mason, A. A. *Hypnotism for medical and dental practitioners*. London: Secker & Warburg, 1960.

Melzack, R. Effects of early experience on behaviour: Experimental and conceptual considerations. In P. H. Hoch & J. Zubin (Eds.), *Psychopathology of Perception*. New York: Grune & Stratton, 1965. Pp. 271–299.

Mountcastle, V. B. Some functional properties of the somatic afferent system. In W. A. Rosenblith (Ed.), *Sensory communication*. Cambridge, Massachusetts: MIT Press, 1961. Pp. 403–436.

Murray, R. W. Temperature receptors. In O. Lowenstein (Ed.), *Advances in Comparative physiology and biochemistry*. Vol. 1. New York: Academic Press, 1962. Pp. 117–175.

Quilliam, T. A. Unit design and array patterns in receptor organs. In A. V. S. de Reuck & J. Knight (Eds.), *Touch, heat and pain*. London: Churchill, 1966. Pp. 86–112.

Roberts, T. D. M. *Basic ideas in neurophysiology*. London: Butterworth, 1966.

Roberts, T. D. M., & Murray-Smith, D. J. Method for the analysis of the neural mechanisms for postural adjustment. In H. E. von Gierke, W. E. Keidel, & H. L. Oestreicher (Eds.), *Principles and practice of bionics*. Slough, England: Technivision Services, 1970. Pp. 371–387.

Sinclair, D. *Cutaneous sensation*. London and New York: Oxford Univ. Press, 1967.

Wall, P. D. Cord cells responding to touch, damage and temperature of skin. *Journal of Neurophysiology*, 1960, **23**, 197–210.

Weddell, G. The pattern of cutaneous innervation in relation to cutaneous sensibility. *Journal of Anatomy*, 1941, **75**, 346–367.

Weddell, G., Palmer, E., & Pallie, W. Nerve endings in mammalian skin. *Biological Reviews of The Cambridge Philosophical Society*, 1955, **30**, 159–195.

Chapter 2

NEURONAL PROPERTIES

CHARLES F. STEVENS

The human central nervous system contains a vast complex of information processing circuits formed by interconnecting networks of nerve cells. This chapter describes the properties of the individual components from which these neural circuits are constructed. Because information about neuronal properties has grown so rapidly in recent years, it would be impossible in a brief article to give anything approaching a comprehensive description; thus the following discussion will focus on certain features believed to be most important in neuronal information processing.

I. STRUCTURAL BASIS FOR NERVOUS SYSTEM FUNCTIONING

Before beginning a discussion of mechanisms responsible for neuronal information processing, it will be necessary to describe the structure of the nervous system's basic anatomic unit, the nerve cell (or, equivalently, neuron). All cells are surrounded by a thin (100 Å) plasma membrane and filled with cytoplasm containing various organelles, such as mitochondria and the nucleus. Nerve cells share many properties with cells from other types of tissue, but are distinguished by a particularly complicated geometric form which is related to neuronal function. Although many various shapes and sizes of nerve cells are found in the central nervous system, three different types of structural components can be recognized in almost all neurons: the cell body (or, equivalently, soma), the dendrites, and the axon. The soma, dendrites, and axon of a typical neuron are indicated in Fig. 1, and a variety of dendritic trees from a particular cortical region are illustrated in Fig. 2 to show the range of neuronal forms typically encountered.

Neural circuits are formed by connections between neurons made at specialized structures called synapses; it is at the synapse that information flows from one nerve cell to another. A synapse, then, is a three-part structure consisting of (*1*) the axon terminals of one neuron, (*2*) the adjacent membrane of the dendrite or soma of another neuron, and (*3*) the 200–400 Å space between these two neurons (see Fig. 3). This space between the axon terminal and dendrite or soma membrane is termed the synaptic cleft and is bordered by the presynaptic membrane of the axon terminal and the postsynaptic membrane of the dendrite and soma. Synapses are

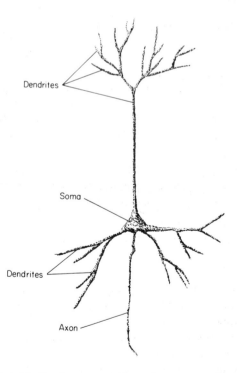

FIG. 1. Somewhat idealized representation of a neuron showing soma, dendrites, and axon. This particular type of neuron is known as a pyramidal cell, because of its pyramid-shaped soma.

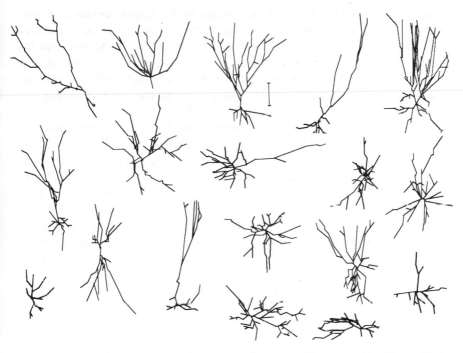

FIG. 2. Dendritic trees of eighteen neurons from cat olfactory cortex. The vertical bar adjacent to the center neuron, upper row, is a 100 μm calibration marker. The cells shown here are computer read-outs of projection drawings made from Golgi impregnated neurons; from an unpublished study by Charles Anderson and the author.

characterized by certain other structural specializations, the most prominent of which is clusters of small spheroidal objects in the axon terminal adjacent to the presynaptic membrane. These small objects are called synaptic vesicles, and are believed to contain a special chemical, termed a neurotransmitter, which participates in synaptic transmission in a manner to be described later.

The receptive surfaces of neurons—their dendrites and soma—have a high density of synaptic contacts (see Fig. 3A), approximately twenty per 100 μm². Because the surface area of a neuron varies greatly from one cell to the next, the number of synapses it receives is also highly variable; typically, the number of synaptic contacts per neuron probably ranges from about 2000 for small cells to about 16,000 for large cells, although estimates as high as 60,000 (average) per cell have been obtained in monkey motor cortex and over 200,000 per cell for cerebellar Purkinje cells. An axon does not necessarily contribute only a single synapse to a particular

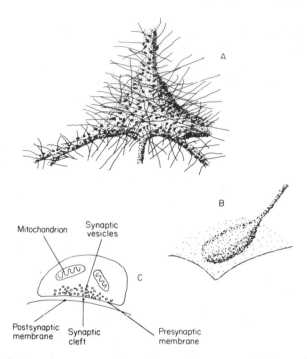

FIG. 3. Semischematic representation of synaptic contacts. A: Pyramidal neuron soma and proximal dendrites encrusted with axon terminals. B: Synapse made by axon terminals on a segment of soma membrane. C: Cross section through axon terminal containing mitochondria and synaptic vesicles, and showing the presynaptic membrane, postsynaptic membrane, and the synaptic cleft.

neuron, but may make many synaptic contacts with it, up to perhaps hundreds in special cases. The available quantitative information indicates that in many instances one axon contributes an average of about two synapses to a cell; in a special case, one particular type of axon (the climbing fiber) makes more than 250 synaptic contacts with a single Purkinje cell in the cerebellar cortex. Even allowing for large errors in the available estimates, it seems clear that each neuron receives input from hundreds, and perhaps thousands of other neurons, and, in turn, sends information to hundreds or thousands of other neurons.

II. THE NERVE IMPULSE

Information is transmitted over relatively long distances in the nervous system by nerve impulses which sweep along the axon. The nerve impulse is a complicated sequence of physicochemical changes in the axon, the most easily detected of which is a rapid change of voltage difference between the inside of the axon and the outside. This voltage transient associated with the nerve impulse (Fig. 4) is called the action potential, and it travels along the axon at velocities around 1 meter/second (range: 0.1–10 for various axons). The manner in which action potentials are generated and their properties will be briefly indicated in a later section; for the time being, it is sufficient to note that the action potential may be assumed to have uniform shape and amplitude, and that it propagates to the axon terminals where it stops without being reflected. Thus an action potential is generated in or near the soma of a neuron, and then travels over the entire axon to all of its terminals.

Because the most easily detected signs of neural activity are voltage changes, a special set of terms referring to the voltage differences across the neuron membrane has evolved (see Fig. 4). A normal resting nerve cell maintains, through the expenditure of metabolic energy, differences in ionic concentrations between the inside and outside of the cell: sodium is pumped out to maintain lower sodium concentrations within the cell than in the external medium, whereas a relatively high internal potassium concentration (relative to the external concentration) is maintained. As the result of these

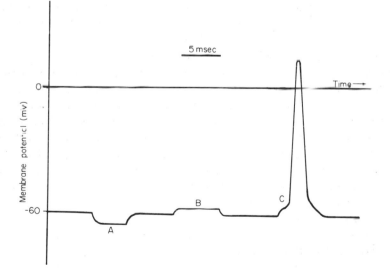

FIG. 4. Graph of membrane potential as a function of time to illustrate terms used in the text. A: A shift in membrane potential in the hyperpolarizing direction. B: A shift in membrane potential in the depolarizing direction. C: A depolarizing shift in membrane potential which has produced an action potential.

concentration differences and the specific permeability properties of the resting nerve membrane, the voltage inside a resting nerve cell is approximately 60 mV more negative than the external medium voltage. The general term for the inside–outside voltage difference is the membrane potential (because the voltage difference exists across the cell membrane), and that particular value of membrane potential seen in the resting cell is termed the resting potential. Deviations of membrane potential toward zero volts are termed depolarizations, whereas deviations away from zero are called hyperpolarizations. Thus, one could say: an action potential is a relatively large, brief depolarization of a neuron, and the membrane potential returns after the action potential to the resting potential. Although this terminology can be rather confusing, it is firmly established and invariably used in descriptions of neuron behavior.

III. SYNAPTIC FUNCTION

The sequence of events occurring in synaptic transmission is as follows: the action potential invades the axon terminal, and sets into motion a chain of steps which ultimately, after a fraction of a millisecond, causes a special chemical, a neurotransmitter, to be released from the presynaptic membrane into the synaptic cleft. The transmitter diffuses almost instantaneously (on the experimental time scale) across the synaptic cleft and interacts with the postsynaptic membrane to produce alterations in membrane properties which cause a voltage change in the dendrite, known as the postsynaptic potential (PSP). This sequence of events is illustrated in Fig. 5 where voltages recorded in a hypothetical experiment by microelectrodes inserted into the dendrite and axon terminal are displayed as a function of time.

Neurotransmitter is released in integral multiples of a common unit known as the transmitter quantum, that is, that amount of transmitter believed to be contained in a single synaptic vesicle. Transmitter quanta are released at random with an average release rate which depends on the state of the axon terminal. When an action potential invades the terminal, the probability per unit time of quantum release rises and falls rapidly over perhaps a 200 μsec time span. Current evidence indicates that the typical average quantum content of a PSP, that is, the average number of transmitter units released by one nerve impulse propagating to the terminal or terminals on a particular cell, ranges between one and ten; because the underlying release process is random, the standard deviation of the number of quanta released per nerve impulse arriving at a cell is thus between about one and three, so a considerable fluctuation occurs in the effectiveness of the nerve impulse in releasing a transmitter.

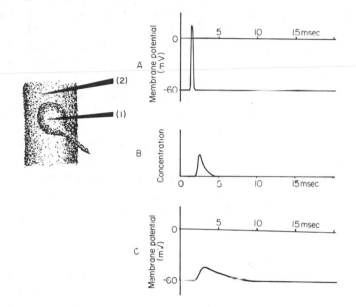

FIG. 5. Representation of the events in synaptic transmission. Semischematic representation of axon terminal (1) and dendrite (2) both impaled by recording microelectrodes. A: Voltage recording as a function of time from axon terminal (1) showing an action potential. B: Graph of resultant transmitter concentration as a function of time in the synaptic cleft. C: Graph of membrane potential as a function of time for the dendrite (2), demonstrating a postsynaptic potential. Note that the postsynaptic potential in C is much longer lasting than the action potential in A, and also of much smaller amplitude.

Considerable information about the mechanisms of transmitter release has accumulated in recent years. It now appears that depolarization of the axon terminal leads to an increase in calcium permeability of the terminal membrane; because calcium is in higher concentration outside the terminal than within (as the result of a pumping mechanism which removes calcium from the cell) calcium enters the cell and causes an increased intracellular calcium concentration. The sequestering action of various organelles within the axon terminal rapidly returns the calcium concentration toward normal, so that arrival of an action potential at a synapse produces only a transient increase in the calcium concentration within the axon terminal. While the calcium concentration is increased, however, there is, by an as yet obscure mechanism, an increase in the release probability for the transmitter quanta.

When the quanta of neurotransmitter are released into the synaptic cleft, the transmitter concentration there rapidly increases; because of diffusional loss out of the cleft as well as enzymatic degradation of the transmitter to inactive forms, the concentration of transmitter in the synaptic cleft declines toward zero in the manner shown in Fig. 5.

Transmitter in the synaptic cleft combines reversibly with special receptor molecules in the postsynaptic membrane. This receptor–transmitter complex is then thought to undergo a conformational (shape) change which causes an increased permeability of the postsynaptic membrane to one or several species of ions. Precisely what permeability changes occur depends on the properties of the postsynaptic membrane, and upon the type of neurotransmitter released. Various terminals release different sorts of neurotransmitter, although the type of transmitter a terminal releases appears not to change with time. Thus, if a terminal were observed to release acetylcholine (one of the known transmitter substances), any time an action potential invaded the terminal, acetylcholine would be released, and the acetylcholine would produce each time the same permeability change in the postsynaptic membrane.

Because the small ions typically have different concentrations inside and outside of a neuron, the permeability increase to a particular ion species generally permits it to move from the region of high concentration to low concentration.* For example, since sodium ions are in higher concentration outside of neurons than within, an increase in sodium ion permeability allows these ions to move into the cell; since the sodium ion bears a unit-positive charge, the movement of these ions from outside to inside causes the interior of the cell to become more positive, that is, to be depolarized. Thus, if a neurotransmitter causes a transient increase in sodium permeability, sodium ions will enter the cell and depolarize it. Because the cell membrane behaves like a leaky capacitor, the charge on the membrane capacitance produced by the entering sodium ions dissipates with time, and the membrane potential returns to its resting values. The transient depolarization caused, in turn, by the brief increase in sodium ion permeability constitutes a postsynaptic potential (PSP). Alternatively, if potassium ion permeability is increased, potassium ions will move out of the cell (the inside concentration exceeds the outside concentration normally), so that a brief hyperpolarization will result; this then, is a second variety of PSP, one which hyperpolarizes rather than depolarizes the neuron.

Although it appears that most information is communicated from cell to cell by the synaptic mechanisms just described, in some instances direct electrical connections, electrical synapses, occur. In these instances, an action potential in one neuron causes a PSP-like depolarization in another

---

* Voltage gradients, as well as concentration gradients, influence the movement of ions; for simplicity, however, the effect of membrane potential on ionic currents has been neglected throughout.

neuron by the direct flow of current from cell to cell through special low-resistance connections formed by small areas of close apposition or fusing of membranes. Although electrical connections between cells can have rather different properties from the chemical synapses described earlier, for our purposes it will not be necessary to distinguish between these two mechanisms for information transfer.

As has been indicated above, some PSP's are depolarizing whereas others are hyperpolarizing: the depolarizing variety of PSP is termed an excitatory postsynaptic potential (EPSP), whereas the hyperpolarizing variety is called an inhibitory postsynaptic potential (IPSP). It must be emphasized that, according to current information, a particular synapse is either excitatory or inhibitory—that is, produces either IPSP's or EPSP's—as a result of the type of transmitter released and the postsynaptic membrane properties, and that a synapse does not change from one type to another.

IV. NEURAL INTEGRATION

Each of the hundreds or thousands of synapses on a neuron surface is intermittently activated by a nerve impulse arrival, so that every neuron is being constantly bombarded by a barrage of PSP's; a typical neuron may receive an average of 10,000–100,000 PSP's/second over all of its synapses. As will be indicated later, information is carried by the rate of impulse arrivals at a given synapse, so the integration of information occurs by combining the total effects of PSP's at all of the neuron's synapses. Thus, the manner in which PSP's occurring in rapid succession at one synapse interact, and the way in which PSP's occurring at distinct synapses combine must be investigated. A simplified view of these two types of interaction, known as temporal and spatial summation, is presented in the following discussion.

To a good approximation, successive PSP's at a synapse may be assumed to add linearly, so that a second PSP occurring before the first PSP has decayed to the base line simply adds to the remaining part of the first PSP. If nerve impulses arrive at a constant frequency at a synapse, say ten impulses per second, a maintained average depolarization is produced by ongoing summation of a train of PSP's. In general, nerve impulse frequency is decoded at a synapse into an average depolarization proportional to impulse frequency by such summation of individual postsynaptic potentials; this addition of successive PSP's at a synapse is termed temporal summation (note in Fig. 6, for example, the conversion of neuron E impulse frequency into voltage in neuron N). Since, as will be seen later, many neurons encode

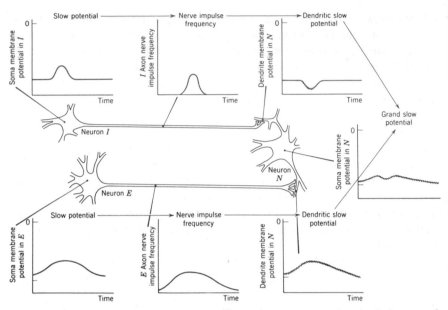

FIG. 6. Simple three neuron circuit illustrating processes involved in neural integration. Neuron *I* is inhibitory to neuron *N*, whereas neuron *E* below makes excitatory connections with neuron *N*. At the top of the figure, the slow potential in the soma of neuron *I* is translated into nerve impulse frequency and then decoded by temporal summation at the upper synapses of neuron *N* into the dendritic potential shown. In the lower part of the figure, a similar slow potential in neuron *E* is encoded for transmission and then decoded at the lower synapses of neuron *N*. By spatial summation these excitatory and inhibitory slow potentials are combined in the soma of neuron *N* to form a grand slow potential which is then encoded for transmission to another neuron (not illustrated). (After Stevens, 1966.)

messages as nerve impulse frequency, temporal summation serves to decode these messages by transforming arriving nerve impulse frequency into an average depolarization—or hyperpolarization in the case of inhibitory synapses—in a neuron. Because these depolarizations and hyperpolarizations are generally slowly changing on the time scale of a single nerve impulse, they are often called slow potentials. Thus, the nerve impulse frequency in one neuron is translated, by temporal summation of PSP's, into a slow potential in another neuron as shown in Fig. 6.

Because the generation of nerve impulses and the encoding of information for transfer to other neurons occurs in the soma, the effect that dendritic PSP's have at the soma must be investigated. As a consequence of the electrical properties of cytoplasm and nerve cell membranes, voltage changes in one part of the cell are transmitted, with attenuation, to other parts of the cell. The process by which a voltage change in one part of the cell produces smaller voltage changes in other parts is termed passive spread or electrotonic spread and has the property that, at least in certain limiting cases, the voltage change is attenuated exponentially with distance from its source. In general, smaller diameter dendrites attenuate, for a given dendritic length, more than do larger diameter dendrites; changes in the shape as well as amplitude of potentials occur, because high frequency components of voltage changes are attenuated more than are low frequency components.

Postsynaptic potentials from all of a neuron's synapses spread electrotonically to the soma where they may be assumed to sum linearly: the process by which PSP's originating at spatially separate synapses sum together is termed spatial summation. At any moment, then, there will appear in a nerve cell soma the grand sum of all postsynaptic potentials, weighted—because of the attenuation associated with electrotonic spread—according to their distance from the soma.

Figure 6 illustrates the phenomena of spatial and temporal summation in a hypothetical neuron with only two synapses, one excitatory at the bottom of the figure and one inhibitory at the top. Notice that the nerve impulse frequency is decoded into voltage changes at both of the synapses, and that the total voltage change at the soma is, in this illustration, the sum of the voltage changes produced by the separate synapses. For an actual neuron, the same type of phenomenon would be occurring at hundreds or thousands of synapses rather than just two as in this example.

V. ENCODING INFORMATION

The total voltage change produced by the temporal and spatial summation of all PSP's cannot be transmitted to other neurons by electrotonic spread because, in most instances, distances required for transmission are so large that any voltage change occurring in the first neuron would be attenuated to undetectable levels before it reached another neuron. To overcome this difficulty, the nervous system has evolved a technique for transmitting information over long distances through the use of action potentials which propagate undiminished. In the simplest case, the total synaptic potential is encoded as nerve impulse frequency with a linear relationship between magnitude of depolarization in the soma and action potential frequency. Of particular importance is the fact that a threshold for activation exists, so that action potentials are generated only when the soma membrane potential reaches or exceeds some critical value.

Although the mechanisms underlying the action potential have been understood since the classic work of Hodgkin and Huxley in 1952, the first detailed analysis of encoding mechanisms has only recently been carried out for a special type of nerve cell and the encoding process is not yet completely understood for neurons in the vertebrate central nervous system. In broad outline, however, the sequence of events underlying the repetitive discharge of nerve impulses by the encoding mechanism is understood. For the postsynaptic membrane, it will be recalled that the interaction of transmitter with receptor molecules produced increases in permeability to various ions; the axon membrane also has the capacity to increase its permeability to certain ions, but by contrast with the postsynaptic membrane, the permeability changes are produced not by a chemical transmitter but instead by depolarization. Thus, when the net effect of postsynaptic potentials is an adequate depolarization in the soma or initial part of the axon, permeability to sodium ions is increased, sodium ions enter the cell (because they are in high concentration in the external medium) and cause depolarization which in turn produces further increases in sodium permeability. This cycle continues and produces the rapid upswing of the action potential. The downward limb of the axon potential pulse is produced by two mechanisms: first, the channels which opened to increase the sodium ion permeability close in the face of continued depolarization, a process termed inactivation. Second, a depolarization produces a potassium conductance increase so that potassium channels open, but more slowly than the sodium channels. As these slowly opening potassium channels are activated, potassium, which is in high concentration within the neuron, rushes out, moving positive charges from the inside to the outside and causing the membrane potential to return toward its resting value. In the membrane responsible for encoding information, there appears to be not one but several distinct sets of potassium channels with different properties. These potassium channels are activated and inactivated at various membrane potentials, and, together with the sodium channels, open and close in such a manner as to produce the typical membrane potential trajectory between action potentials during the encoding process (see Fig. 7). Furthermore, the kinetics of activation and inactivation of these channels is such that a linear relationship between stimulus (net synaptic effect) and the response (nerve impulse frequency) is produced.

The mechanisms presented thus far which underlie neural information processing may now be summarized (see Fig. 6). In each of the axon terminals on a particular neuron, nerve impulses are arriving at a frequency which reflects the total synaptic effect in the soma giving rise to those axons; the hundreds or thousands of incoming axons thus carry frequency-coded information to the neuron in question. Through temporal summation, at each synapse this frequency-coded message is decoded into a slow potential, that is, an average depolarization (or hyperpolarization at inhibitory syn-

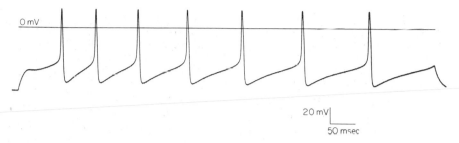

FIG. 7. Graph of membrane potential as a function of time for a neuron illustrating the phenomenon of encoding a depolarization as nerve impulse frequency. This neuron was depolarized with a constant current which produced the train of action potentials shown. (From J. A. Connor and C. F. Stevens, unpublished observations.)

apses) proportional to the frequency of action potential arrivals at the axon terminal. By spatial summation, a weighted average of all incoming messages is formed in the soma, and this average effect, as a function of time, is encoded by the soma or initial part of the axon into a train of action potentials whose frequency of occurrence is, in the simplest case, directly proportional to the net synaptic effect (assuming this is above threshold). This action potential train then propagates down the axon to terminals on hundreds or thousands of other neurons where the message is decoded and combined with messages from other neurons. Precisely how these properties are used for computations in the nervous system depends, of course, on details of neural organization, that is, on the patterns of neural interconnections.

VI. SPECIAL PROPERTIES

Many neurons in the vertebrate central nervous system appear to conform to the information processing scheme outlined in the preceding paragraphs, although the precise extent to which this picture is accurate, and the frequency and significance of deviations from it are not yet understood. Space is not available here to discuss the idealizations that have been made in the preceding presentation of neuron properties nor to survey the considerable number of alternative mechanisms known to be involved in neural information processing. To illustrate the type of variations employed by the nervous system in processing information, however, several well-documented instances of departures from the model presented above will be discussed. The view of neural information processing presented here has assumed that individual PSP's are so small that the arrival of a single impulse has practically no effect on the cell, so that the neuron's output is an average over very many inputs. Thus, the exact time of arrival of any given impulse is of little consequence, and only the average arrival rate at any moment is important. Further the encoding scheme described previously simply translates the net synaptic effect into impulse frequency, and does little to filter or abstract from the information presented to the encoder.* In the succeeding paragraphs, encoding mechanisms which filter information will be discussed, as will instances where a single impulse arrival has a large' effect on the cell's behavior. Finally, a case where the precise timing of impulse arrival is important will be considered.

Probably the most common departure from the encoding scheme described above is one in which the encoder does not continue to discharge action potentials in the face of a steady input; in this instance, the encoder filters the input information by (approximately) taking its derivative so that the output frequency is proportional to the rate of change of the total synaptic effect (see Granit, Kernell, & Shortess, 1963). An interesting instance of neural processing associated with the encoder mechanism is offered by neurons known as hippocampal pyramidal cells (Kandel, Spencer, & Brinley, 1961). These cells exhibit a mechanism which, under some circumstances, causes the frequency to increase rapidly in the face of a steady input. Although quantitative analysis is not yet available, such cells seem to integrate the signal, so that they produce a nerve impulse frequency proportional to the time integral of the net synaptic effect, at least over short time periods. A final example of encoders which differ from the type described above is provided by cells residing in the inferior olivary nucleus (Crill, 1970). The encoder of these cells appears to produce nerve impulses at a frequency proportional to the driving depolarization, but, because of special dendritic properties, the soma action potential is prolonged as illustrated in Fig. 8. This prolonged soma action potential causes the initial part of the axon to produce a burst of spikes so that every soma action potential causes perhaps four spikes to be propagated down the axon in rapid succession.

For each action potential generated in the soma of the inferior olivary neurons just mentioned, a rapid burst of action potentials is sent down the cell's axon to another type of neuron known as the cerebellar Purkinje cell. Purkinje cells offer perhaps the best example of an instance where activation of a single incoming axon produces a profound effect on the neuron's behavior (see Eccles, Ito, & Szentágothai, 1967). As a rule, each olivary neuron makes synaptic contact with only one cerebellar Purkinje cell, and, as indicated previously each discharge of the olivary neuron causes a rapid burst of action potentials to reach the synapses on a Purkinje cell.

---

* The encoding scheme indicated here does, in fact, cause some filtering of the encoded signals, but this may be neglected for present purposes.

The axon from each olivary neuron makes a large number (perhaps several hundred) of synaptic contacts with a Purkinje's cell's dendrites; these olivary cell axons are called climbing fibers. Each action potential in the olivary neuron soma then sends a rapid volley of action potentials to this massive synaptic input on the Purkinje cell, and the great number of synapses together with temporal summation from the burst produces a massive PSP in the Purkinje cell. As a result of this large PSP, the Purkinje cell responds with a prolonged depolarization, much like the olive neuron response illustrated in Fig. 8, which can produce a burst of action potentials (Martinez, Crill, & Kennedy, 1971). Because the climbing fibers evoke this behavior, it is termed the climbing fiber response. Interestingly, Purkinje cells behave as described earlier in the chapter to their other synaptic inputs, with this special type of response occurring for only one type of synaptic input. Although the exact function of the climbing fiber response is not yet clear, the olivary neuron–Purkinje cell circuit obviously is well suited for a specialized type of communication employing bursts of action potentials.

In most instances, the output of a neuron does not depend critically on the exact timing of relative inputs. A dramatic exception to this is offered by neurons in the superior olive which are believed to be responsible for sound localization (Goldberg & Brown, 1969). For low frequency tones, below approximately 1000 Hz, localization depends on the time difference between stimulation of the two ears; for example, a sound source on the left side reaches the left ear slightly before it reaches the right ear, producing

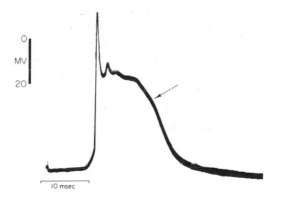

FIG. 8. Graph of membrane potential as a function of time for a neuron in the cat inferior olive. Note that after the action potential there is a prolonged (20–40 msec) depolarization indicated by the arrow. This depolarization produces a burst of action potentials in the axon of the olivary cell, but these action potentials do not invade the soma, so are not visible in this record. (Recording by W. E. Crill.)

out-of-phase signals on the two sides. Recordings from superior olivary neurons, which receive information from both ears simultaneously, show that the discharge frequency of these cells can vary over an approximately four- or fivefold range as the phase of the signal presented to one ear (relative to the other) shifts by 180 degrees. In terms of time difference, a delay in the signal to one ear of approximately 1 msec is adequate to change the firing rate of the cell by perhaps five times, and a delay of 50 or 100 μsec is adequate to cause a noticeable change in frequency. These cells, then, are specialized to detect small differences in the arrival times over various inputs, and to transform these small differences into quite considerable differences in average rate of discharging nerve impulses.

In the preceding paragraphs, several departures from or refinements of the decode-integrate-encode scheme have been described. In some types of nerve cells—how commonly they occur is not yet known—which must transmit information only over relatively short distances, the step involving encoding as nerve impulse frequencies is omitted completely. For example, a particular kind of retinal cell, the horizontal cell, transmits information solely by electrotonic spread, without the production of spikes (Kaneko, 1971). Furthermore, these horizontal cells are interconnected by electrical synapses so that information in one horizontal cell spreads over a whole chain of horizontal cells through the electrical connections.

Another similar modification of information processing without spike production has been postulated for a number of neuron types in which axons appear to be absent; in these cells synapses occur between dendrites (dendro-dendritic synapses). Since spike production is required for transmitting information only over relatively long distances, it seems reasonable that cell intercommunication should evolve which omits the spike encoding step in instances involving short-distance information transfer. Integration and transmission without intervening spike production has been observed for retinal bipolar cells (Kaneko, 1970; Werblin & Dowling, 1969), and has been suggested for olfactory bulb granule cells (Rall, Shepherd, Reese, & Brightman, 1966), ventrobasal thalamus (Ralston & Herman, 1969), and superior colliculus (Lund, 1969). Although the extent to which this mode of nervous system operation occurs is not yet clear, research in this area is currently active, and more information should be forthcoming within a few years.

VII. SUMMARY

Transmission of information between neurons by postsynaptic potentials, integration of the information through temporal and spatial summation, and encoding information—possibly combined with some processing—appear now to be the dominant properties of neurons responsible for the nervous system functions which ultimately underlie all behavior. The vast spectrum of functions performed by the nervous system, then, depends upon the way in which these properties are combined, and the complicated patterns of interconnections between vast numbers of nerve cells.

VIII. GUIDE TO THE NEUROPHYSIOLOGICAL LITERATURE

A number of books and monographs give additional information about the topics covered in this chapter. Stevens (1966) contains an elementary description of neuronal properties and principles of information processing, and contains in addition a survey chapter on quantitative theory in neurophysiology. Ochs (1965), Ruch and Patton (1965), and Mountcastle (1968) cover in a more advanced way much of the same material. The properties of individual nerve cells, and particularly synaptic transmission, are clearly presented in Katz (1966); for a more advanced treatment of synaptic transmission, Hubbard, Llinas, and Quastel (1969) may be consulted. The quantitative treatment of synaptic transmission and neural integration have been reviewed by Stevens (1968). All of the materials cited above contain references to the appropriate anatomic literature; a more systematic treatment of neuron structure and general neural anatomy may be found in Crosby, Humphrey, and Lauer (1962).

References

Crill, W. E. Unitary multiple-spiked responses in cat inferior olive nucleus. *Journal of Neurophysiology,* 1970, **33**, 199–209.

Crosby, E. C., Humphrey, T., & Lauer, E. W. *Correlative anatomy of the nervous system.* New York: Macmillan, 1962.

Eccles, J. C., Ito, M., & Szentágothai, J. *The cerebellum as a neuronal machine.* Berlin and New York: Springer-Verlag, 1967.

Goldberg, J. M., & Brown, P. B. Response of binaural neurons of dog superior olivary complex to dichotic tonal stimuli: Some physiological mechanisms of sound localization. *Journal of Neurophysiology,* 1969, **32**, 613–636.

Granit, R., Kernell, D., & Shortess, G. K. Quantitative aspects of repetitive firing of mammalian motoneurones, caused by injected currents. *Journal of Physiology (London),* 1963, **168**, 911–931.

Hodgkin, A. L., & Huxley, A. F. A quantitative description of membrane current and its application to conduction and excitation in nerve. *Journal of Physiology (London),* 1952, **117**, 500–544.

Hubbard, J. I., Llinas, R., & Quastel, D. M. J. *Electrophysiological analysis of synaptic transmission.* London: Arnold, 1969.

Kandel, E. R., Spencer, W. A., & Brinley, F. J. Electrophysiology of hippocampal neurons. I. Sequential invasion and synaptic organization. *Journal of Neurophysiology*, 1961, **24**, 225–285.

Kaneko, A. Physiological and morphological identification of horizontal, bipolar and amacrine cells in goldfish retina. *Journal of Physiology* (*London*), 1970, **207**, 623–633.

Kaneko, A. Electrical connexions between horizontal cells in the dogfish retina. *Journal of Physiology* (*London*), 1971, **213**, 95–105.

Katz, B. *Nerve, muscle and synapse*. New York: McGraw-Hill, 1966.

Lund, R. D. Synaptic patterns of the superficial layers of the superior colliculus of the rat. *Journal of Comparative Neurology*, 1969, **135**, 179–208.

Martinez, F. E., Crill, W. E., & Kennedy, T. T. Electrogenesis of cerebellar Purkinje cell responses in cats. *Journal of Neurophysiology*, 1971, **34**, 348-356.

Mountcastle, V. B. *Medical physiology*. Vol. II. St. Louis, Missouri: Mosby, 1968.

Ochs, S. *Elements of neurophysiology*. New York: Wiley, 1965.

Rall, W., Shepherd, G. M., Reese, T. S., & Brightman, M. W. Dendrodendritic synaptic pathway for inhibition in the olfactory bulb. *Experimental Neurology*, 1966, **14**, 44–56.

Ralston, H. J., III, & Herman, M. M. The fine structure of neurons and synapses in the ventrobasal thalamus of the cat. *Brain Research*, 1969, **14**, 77–98.

Ruch, T. C., & Patton, H. D. (Eds.). *Physiology and biophysics*. Philadelphia, Pennsylvania: Saunders, 1965.

Stevens, C. F. *Neurophysiology: A primer*. New York: Wiley, 1966.

Stevens, C. F. Synaptic physiology. *Proceedings of the IEEE*, 1968, **56**, 916–930.

Werblin, F. S., & Dowling, J. E. Organization of retina of the mudpuppy, *Necturus maculosus*. II. Intracellular recording. *Journal of Neurophysiology*, 1969, **32**, 339–355.

Chapter 3

INTEGRATION IN NERVOUS SYSTEMS

G. ADRIAN HORRIDGE

To cover the topic of integration in the nervous system in the space of a few pages, one must stand far back and try to discern the broadest of outlines. Most that can be said to the non-specialist has been known for several years, but some recent developments to be summarized here lead one naturally to an anticipation of trends in the analysis of behavioral mechanisms.

I. CODING

The natural way to explain the action of the nervous system is first to describe how sensory endings respond to normal stimuli. Their differences in sensitivity give us the modalities such as photo-, chemo-, mechano-receptor. Reception is basically the graded depolarization of the sensory terminal, which is well described with respect to the function of isolated receptors and is most relevant when the receptor lies in its normal anatomic setting. Mechanisms of reception are nowhere understood at the membrane level. One important generalization is that, a short distance back along the nerve fiber, nerve impulses are initiated at one, not necessarily fixed, point. The receptor potential of the sensory terminal is electrotonically propagated to this point and is converted into an impulse pattern which is coded by frequency. This separation of generator and propagator has the important result that the driving potential is not discharged to zero when an impulse is fired. The frequency code serves for distance propagation; impulse frequency is the commonest code for stimulus strength or rate of stimulus onset; however, the most important representation of the stimulus in the code lies in the identity of the destinations of the axon in which the stimulus is carried.

Every stimulus excites numerous afferent fibers, so that through the higher sensory relays, and over the watershed into the motor side, the total excitation lies in a desynchronized constellation of impulses in an excited cluster of neurons that are functionally related to each other. The main problem is how to analyze and then understand this totality.

II. SYNPASES

Axon terminals often branch and usually end at synapses upon the cell bodies or dendrites of other neurons. Synapses are sometimes considered as functional entities which explain physiological results and sometimes as recognizable anatomic structures with presumed physiological properties. The distinction is important for the separation of theory from observation. The anatomic work at EM level now gives a picture of synapses and their distribution which can be combined with the results of the physiological methods to provide mutually supporting evidence. What emerges is the anatomic framework of the physiological pathways.

At a physiological synapse (which may be correlated with a structural one) presynaptic transmitter (or sometimes presynaptic ionic currents) cause a postsynaptic response which is graded rather like the sensory response. The postsynaptic neuron is either depolarized briefly or hyperpolarized briefly [and sometimes first depolarized then hyperpolarized (Waziri & Kandel, 1969)]. The synaptic potential, of either polarity, is basically a graded local shift of membrane potential that is apparently the integrated result of the distribution and number of open channels in the postsynaptic membrane. The wide diversity of postsynaptic waveforms is certainly not correlated with the wide diversity of synaptic structures.

Recently we have had to add other normal ways of modulating neuron activity, by: (a) Synapses upon synapses (serial synapses) which permit the control of excitation at individual synapses rather than at whole neurons. They can be excitatory or inhibitory and are best known in invertebrates (Tauc, 1969). Their existence is now questioned in vertebrates, see below. (b) Low-resistance bridges between particular neurons whereby the membrane potentials of certain pairs of cells become linked electrotonically, sometimes with a rectifying junction between them (Auerbach & Bennett, 1969). (c) Current flow from active neurons can change the sensitivity of neighbors that are appropriately oriented (Nelson, 1966). (d) Causes from inside the cell itself (Strumwasser, 1967).

III. INTEGRATION

The synapse is not really the chief integrating element nor is it the only labile one; integration takes place as a result of the summation of potential changes over the neuron membrane. In impulse transmission the integration is finalized at the spike-initiating locus, at which lability is clearly crucial. Some inhibitory synapses lie closer to the spike initiating locus (and are sometimes wrapped around it).

Progressively more systems are becoming known in which some or all of the neurons have no spikes, but algebraic summation is still the rule of action. The retina of vertebrates and the retina-lamina combination of insects appear to be places where integration is wholly graded. In both these examples, graded presynaptic depolarization causes a postsynaptic hyperpolarization which is also graded.

Where spikes occur, their frequency is a measure of the probability or urgency of an appropriate stimulus. Systematic irregularities of interspike intervals are not yet clearly defined in terms of their importance to the animal except in a few cases where pairing of impulses is shown to be more effective than regularly spaced impulses. Numerous mechanisms including slow potentials and a variety of ways of timing impulses are so far little more than candidates for ways of coding in neurons (Perkel & Bullock, 1968).

IV. FIELDS OF SENSITIVITY

Consideration of pattern abstraction in sensory pathways leads to the conclusion that all neurons abstract pattern. They can do no other, because they have a particular combination of inputs impinging upon them. Numerous elegant examples are described in other chapters. As the following generalizations have emerged, the organization of sensory input has been an exciting field in the past decade.

The main explanatory concept is that of "field" defined originally for retinal ganglion cells (Kuffler, 1953). Every neuron has an excitatory field, which is the set of contours, drawn in as many dimensions as necessary, including time, to define the sensitivity of the neuron to all normal stimuli within its repertoire. Probably only the peak sensitivity matters. Sensory pathways fall into two main types in vertebrates. One type has narrow receptive fields which are topographically projected deeper into the nervous system: the other has wide receptive fields which are usually obscure in their projections. Wide field units, particularly among higher-order sensory units, are astonishingly common. Wide fields can be expected as a result of convergence of lower levels but it is surprising to find that most of the fields at all levels are wider than would be expected from discrimination tests. Quite clearly the wide field units are used but it is difficult to understand how; presumably they function in groups. This generalization applies to vision, hearing, touch, smell, taste, and temperature senses.

V. CONVERGENCE AND COMPLEX FIELDS

Where groups of neurons converge upon a next higher-order level, sums and differences of the receptive fields of the lower order units necessarily make up the fields of the higher order unit. At present this convergence is not an observation but a theory which agrees with observations on single units at different levels. The complexity that is soon reached baffles the experimenter's ability to map higher order receptive fields.

New principles concerning the anatomic relations of units of known function are beginning to appear. One is that in both visual and touch systems, columns of neurons at right angles to the surface of the cerebral cortex contain neurons with consistently related functions at different depths (Whitsel, Petrucelli, & Werner, 1969). This is probably one example of a more general statement, indicated only for vertebrates so far, that neurons which are located near each other are those most likely to be integrated together by higher-order neurons.

We would expect that the receptive fields of neurons would agree in outline with the commonest kinds of categories to be found in the environment. Sometimes this is true, e.g., visual motion and edge detectors, but a baffling problem is how units with wide fields and especially those of mixed modality, e.g., hearing, touch, and vision, are relevant to normal perception.

VI. SUMMATION VERSUS DISCRIMINATION

In 1968 I wrote "the great problem in the sensory systems is that although behavior leads us to expect evidence of *discriminations* by central cells, the records from units show mostly *summations*" (Horridge, 1968; p. 217). That remains true but the comparison is not quite fair because the units that are so far well described have been recorded in the typical experimental situations that give immediate electrophysiological responses.

Complex behavior, however, in lower animals always takes a long time, and in higher mammals difficult discriminations always involve exploration either by eye movements, sniffing, or tactile manipulation. During the time so occupied something must be going on. "If we can translate the term 'appraisal' into terms of neurons perhaps it would be best rendered as the requirement of a long series of impulses in a particular pattern of higher sensory interneurons before an easily inhibited command interneuron will fire. The patience of an angler would be necessary to demonstrate that command fiber electrophysiologically" (Horridge, 1968; p. 284).

Within the framework of looking at behavior in terms of component neurons a major advance in outlook is to be found in a recent reconsideration of the function of the dorsal columns of the spinal cord (Wall, 1970). The dorsal columns carry detailed sensory information to the brain, but are ineffective as sensory channels when other tracts are cut, and apparently they are without additional functional value when other tracts are present. Wall's new idea is that the lack of additional functional value is only true for stimuli that are presented in standard discrimination tests, and that the speed and detailed projection in the dorsal columns improve and perhaps control the exploratory behavior which leads to improved discrimination.

VII. PHYSIOLOGICAL PATHWAYS AND ANATOMIC CONNECTIONS

We are now ready to enunciate the generalization that underlies much of the modern work—that the pattern of anatomic connections leading into a neuron, and the way in which the functionally effective synapses are arranged upon it, decides the pattern abstraction which it performs. So the analysis of the nervous system was tackled first in terms of what the units are (Ramón y Cajal, 1888), then how the units function (Adrian, 1928; Eccles, 1953), and is now being attacked in terms of how they are connected together. There is even a possibility (or is it a hope?) that plastic changes, such as learning and innate change of behavior with age, also have their basis in changes in the pattern of connections.

VIII. THE PROBLEM IN HISTORICAL PERSPECTIVE

The problem is to find out *how* the nervous system works. But what do we mean by this? We know that it is (say) a highly ordered collection of chemicals but this only tells us what it is made of. We know that behavior is highly organized, as ethology and experimental psychology describe, but that only tells us what the nervous system is capable of (see Fig. 1).

In fact there are two ways of satisfying our thirst for mechanism: one is to study a whole system, produce a set of relationships between hypothetical components, arrange them to fit the performance that we can observe, and

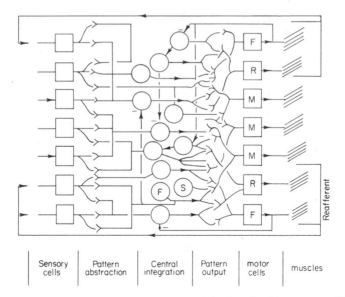

| Sensory cells | Pattern abstraction | Central integration | Pattern output | motor cells | muscles |

FIG. 1. The electrophysiologist's dream animal displayed, with sensory cells, pattern abstraction by arborization of interneurons, central neurons wth spontaneity (S) and others with feedback (F), motor output patterns and motoneurons (M) with neural feedback (F) or reafferent feedback (R) (including proprioceptors) via the movement they cause. Such a system of pathways, with time constants, hormonal and other influences added, is the sum or outcome of the electrophysiological method of analysis.

then go on devising experiments which test the properties of the whole system. This method is possible only with simple combinations of few components. Sherrington's analysis of reflexes, summarized below, provide an ideal example of this approach because his results provided the basis for subsequent explanation of a more fundamental kind. The other way is to record from individual neurons while the behavior is in progress and then try to see their activity as the cause of the behavior and vice versa, just as we would work out the mechanism of a man-made machine or electronic circuit. The second method, which involves the first, and inevitably depends on recording the receptive fields of numerous single neurons, produces an enormous volume of data which, in vertebrates, is far too detailed and diverse to be useful in explaining any apparently simple behavioral act. More of this anon; meanwhile let us consider reflexes, for perspective can come from a study of their history.

IX. REFLEXES

If we start with Sherrington's elucidation of the interaction of reflexes as components of behavior, we find a series of definitions that have been learned by generations of neurophysiologists. Formulated in 1906, systematized in 1932 (Creed, Denny-Brown, Eccles, Liddel, & Sherrington, 1932), their characteristics are listed as follows:

1. The reflex has a *localized* pathway.
2. Several muscles acting in one reflex are smoothly coordinated.
3. Contrary reflexes and antagonistic muscle groups are *reciprocally inhibited* by each other.
4. There is a central *delay* of 2–6 msec (the more complicated the reflex, the longer this is).
5. Successive stimulation of one nerve, or simultaneous stimulation of several nerves produces *summation*.
6. The motor response outlives the sensory one (*after-discharge*).
7. A *refractory period* is attributed to central synapses.
8. The contraction in a reflex is a *fractionation* of the maximum possible of the same muscles.
9. When a reflex is caused by stimulation of two nerves simultaneously the tension is less than the sum of the effect of stimulating the nerves separately. This *occlusion* was seen as a consequence of central overlap of areas of innervation.
10. A reflex that would otherwise be maintained can be definitely switched off by central *inhibition*.

11. Following inhibition there is a *rebound* of greater than normal sensitivity.
12. A subsiding reflex may be followed by the opposing reflex, and this can lead to a sequence which is considered as a chain reflex (*negative successive induction*).
13. Muscles are brought into action by gradual *recruitment,* not thrown in all at once. One explanation was that proprioceptors bring in more muscle fibers.
14. *Fatigue* is self-explanatory.
15. Strychnine reveals a state in which any sensory nerve will excite most of the motor nerves. Therefore synapses exist in many directions but are *normally blocked.*

X. ECCLES' EXPLANATORY CONTRIBUTION

With our modern knowledge of neurons it is instructive to interpret in turn each concept in this list. But in fact almost all are covered by the great simplification that was demonstrated experimentally as soon as microelectrodes were used to explore the spinal motoneuron (Eccles, 1953). This is that the response at a synapse takes the form of either an excitation which takes the cell toward generating a nerve impulse, or an inhibition which takes the membrane away from impulse initiation, and that these phenomena are summed algebraically.

The point is that the membrane of every neuron acts as a capacitor (*a*) upon which changes in charge can be stored or algebraically summed over a period of a few milliseconds and (*b*) along which charge flows so that the excitatory or inhibitory effects are spatially summed with those on neighboring parts of the membrane. The neuron is the only known entity in the nervous system which can integrate inputs and generate outputs from them. This, together with a few simple time-dependent properties of synapses, explains all the above fifteen properties of reflexes (Fig. 2).

XI. BACK TO ANATOMY

The central role occupied by this synaptic interaction in the explanation of integration is usually extended to the view that all the rapid integrative action of the nervous system follows from the spatial and temporal summation of synaptic potentials *set in their actual anatomic framework.* If this is true it leads to the conclusion that the only analysis of any lasting value is

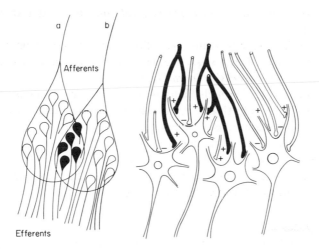

FIG. 2. The development of explanation illustrated by the spinal reflex. Left: Principles of convergence and occlusion explained geometrically as overlap (black) in the areas of motor pools that are influenced by inputs a and b, which are also expressed geometrically. Right: The same results translated into the summation of excitatory and inhibitory postsynaptic effects on motoneurons, some of which are influenced by common inputs (black).

the physiological and then the anatomic identification of pathways of excitation.

When the facts of reflex interaction were first set out there were two main sets of data known about the nervous system: the reflex effects of stimulation and the complex anatomy of neurons. In those days the regions of the nervous system were given functions as if they were organs. Then the electrode brought together the neuron as a structural and functional unit. It happened that the spinal reflexes were simple enough for the properties of reflexes to be interpreted in terms of the synaptic phenomena which became observable as real events. So, for reflexes, the microelectrode studies became explanations of the higher level of behavior. More complicated behavior is much more difficult to analyze but at present we believe that the methodology described here is the main line of advance.

XII. OTHER DEVELOPMENTS

After this the developments have been too rapid for my historical perspective to bring them into one scheme, and the topic of integration in the nervous system fragments. The following themes are significant:

1. The continuing effort to discover the normal functions of the electrophysiological units and to identify them with the anatomic neuron types. In higher invertebrates this leads toward (we do not know how far toward) the conclusion that every neuron is unique in its anatomy and activity, and therefore in its place in behavior.

2. The effort to discover the function of the neurons in systems where the part played by individual cells is not obvious. The best examples are where many neurons are excited unequally in parallel pathways, but a more demanding analysis is needed where there are feedback loops within the nervous system.

3. The analysis of systems which work quite differently from reflexes. The most important of these are systems of centrally generated sequences which require little or no feedback from the periphery. Almost all invertebrate movement seems to be controlled in this way, so far as analyzed at neuron level. Sometimes activity of a single cell causes a whole pattern of activity, such as swimming. The trend is toward accepting central control as the primary cause of patterned movements, and therefore seeing reflexes as triggered central commands, even in vertebrates.

4. Efforts to exploit the high resolution of the electron microscope to reveal physiologically significant details, e.g., the distinction between chemical and electrical synapses, and between inhibitory and excitatory synapses (Bodian, 1970).

5. Progressive analysis of neurosecreted substances, of their effects on other cells, and of the mechanisms controlling their synthesis and release.

6. Numerous attempts to pinpoint the change which constitutes memory in at least twenty different preparations that appear promising.

7. Progressive definition of what we mean by specificity whereby neurons recognize each other during development and regeneration, or in morphogenetic changes during adult life. Particularly in invertebrates, the results suggest that every neuron in an animal is unique and that it has an inbuilt mechanism by which it recognizes every other neuron that it has to encounter in its normal growth. For vertebrates, the general pattern seems to be an overproduction of embryonic neurons, many of which die when they fail to make connections that are either genetically correct or functionally appropriate.

8. A search for ways in which the responsiveness and activity of the neuron membrane is controlled by organized systems within the neuron itself, and also the way in which the events at the membrane influence the contents of the neuron.

9. Progressive discovery of a remarkable order and rigidity brought about by processes of growth, right down to the location of every synapse in some systems, and of corresponding fixed functional properties of iden-

tified units. At the same time neurons thought to be nonspecific are progressively shown to be specific but with complex fields.

In addition to these obvious and prosaic lines of advance it is certain that surprises await discovery just around the corner. Even new types of sensitivity and novel sense organs still turn up from time to time. Possibly there exists interaction between nerve cells that is not accompanied by depolarizations or hyperpolarizations. Possibly there are interactions between nerve cells which are not in synaptic contact; and conversely there may be structural synapses which are not concerned with rapid transmission. Most of the explanations of all kinds in neurobiology are only possibly correct; sometimes they are sufficient explanations, but rarely are they necessary explanations.

XIII. THE SPLINTERING FIELD

To one who had his eye on the field over the last two decades, the most obvious trend is disruptive. The accumulation of knowledge has not led to new major explanatory concepts in old areas although work has gone on there. However, many new topics have been shown to be relevant. The effect is like filling in a map most of which is still blank. Examples of all kinds come to mind: work on microtubules shows that they may be relevant to axonal transport because they may transport subcellular particules (Rudzinska, 1965). Some poisons which affect enzymes concerned with RNA appear to have an effect on learning. The rate and sometimes the direction of learning really seems to be influenced by chemicals taken from brains of trained animals and injected into naïve subjects (Ungar, Ho & Galvan, 1970).

The trophic effect of experimentally crossed neurons upon muscle that is abnormal to them is readily extrapolated to a possible effect of neurons upon other neurons (Guth, 1968). Quite a different development is the recognition of numerous types of impulse timing, which are presumptive codes, exemplified best by electric sense organs (Perkel & Bullock, 1968). Possibly pattern recognition in sensory systems is not entirely dependent on sensory fields, but impulse temporal patterns may be recognizable by a single cell. Immunological studies and responses of isolated cells to each other in tissue culture (Abercrombie, 1960) are thought to be relevant to the control of interaction between nerve cells in real nervous systems, but no observations are available to support this. Low resistance electrical pathways and their uncoupling (Lowenstein, 1968) during development are known to be relevant, but the unravelling of this topic for neurons in ganglia will be a long hard road.

Other topics, long struggling for a place in a general theory, limp on. Glia seems even more uninteresting as an essential component of coordination now that microelectrode studies (Baylor & Nicholls, 1969) and ionic phenomena (Cohen, Gerschenfeld, & Kuffler, 1968), have been well explored. Slow potentials still oscillate between being important causes and inconsequential side effects (Adey & LeBlanc, 1969).

One of the notable developments of recent years is the questioning of several tenets that have long been accepted. In each case alternative explanations, which had not previously been ruled out, have now been found to fit the facts better. Of minor importance is the demonstration that the stepping reflex in the deafferented cat spinal cord is probably an artifact of the beats caused by use of two stimulators simultaneously (Egger & Wyman, 1969). Also, it was disconcerting to find that the giant fibers of the cockroach cord, long used in demonstrations to electrophysiology classes, do not cause the legs to jump, as has been supposed since 1938 (Dagan & Parnas, 1970).

Of greater general importance is the suspicion cast upon the whole concept of presynaptic inhibition by anatomists and some physiologists. Some of the anatomic circuits predicted by presynaptic inhibition do not seem to be present (Szentágothai, 1968). Even at the terminals of sensory axons in the dorsal horn of the spinal cord it has been suggested that "the dense packing of elements within each microbundle . . . may provide the substrate for elaborate axo-axonal interactions including . . . depolarization," so that, although the phenomenon is still valid, depolarization of primary afferents need not depend on presynaptic inhibition (Scheibel & Scheibel, 1969b). Recently D. Curtis (personal communication, 1971) has concluded that accumulation of extracellular potassium must be seriously considered as an alternative explanation for the symptoms of presynaptic inhibition. So, in view of the temporary nature of some of our main tackle it would be folly to try to elaborate extensive theories of neuronal integration before the basic mechanisms are clear.

XIV. CENTRALLY DETERMINED SEQUENCES

Already in the 1930's there were objections to the view that the reflex is the element of behavior. A few preparations, such as earthworm nerve cord and fish fin movements, favored the view that a coordinated sequence of movements can be independent of sensory initiation or sensory feedback. But about 1960 it was realized in three different laboratories independently that a simple technique provides proof. The method is to compare the motor impulse sequence recorded *en passant* during a complex movement with the sequence recorded when the motor nerves have all been cut so that the movement is never performed. The movement may be spontaneous or may be one which requires sensory initiation. This analysis is possible in many invertebrates which have few large motor axons to whole muscle blocks.

As a result of this work in numerous molluskan and arthropod examples we now expect that the general form of the efferent pattern is independent of many parameters of the sensory stimulus even if such is required at all. There are several examples where stimulation of single interneurons (called "command fibers") causes a complex sequence involving many motor neurons. All the regularly repeated movements of insects such as ventilation, flight, song, walking, and optomotor responses are now considered to be coordinated mainly by central interaction of neurons. This of course, does not rule out the established facts of reflex modulation, especially of muscle tone.

The same techniques are not applicable as yet to vertebrate preparations, but the interesting point is that evidence to date does not rule out a large element of central control in the initiation and probably also in the continued coordination of vertebrate movements, as already indicated for extraocular muscles and for the swallowing action. Certainly the newt spinal cord is capable of producing an accurately timed and coordinated activity of limb muscles without sensory information from the moving limbs. This is old work recently confirmed (Székély, Czeh, & Voros, 1969). It is easier to build up a coherent picture if we start with the assumption that sensory stimuli (and central spontaneity of some kind) serve as triggers which set off centrally determined patterns that have persisted over long periods of evolution. Reflexes are then only special cases where a change in the output pattern is causally related to a change in the input *line* or of excitation in a new line, in such a way that a predictable response appears.

This thinking can be tied in with the concept of learning, especially where the repertoire is limited. To illustrate, let me cite my old informant, the crab eye preparation. The response to a moving visual field is a repeated slow following of the stimulus by a movement of the eye, interspersed with rapid flick-backs which return the eye to the start of its traverse. The whole output to the nine eye muscles is centrally coordinated irrespective of whether the eye is there or not. But in its normal traverse the eye moves in a limited space available for it in the socket. If the eye or the socket is stimulated with a shock or a touch, the traverse is curtailed and remains shorter for some hours. In context this adaptive response is adequate to ensure that the extent of the traverse is suited to the width of the socket, although the whole output is centrally determined (Horridge & Burrows, 1968).

This is an example of *preprogrammed plasticity* which is limited to a particular demand. No doubt other examples will come to be thought of in the same way. All learning is within a repertoire and is to that extent preprogrammed. The interest lies not in the matter of definition, however, but rather in the starting point for experiment. We can start with the idea of plasticity as a property of reflexes, or we can start with central programs and look for their biologically relevant plastic properties.

XV. COMPUTERS AS MODELS OF BRAINS

Computers have now been assigned their proper place: it is in the servant's quarters, not in the design department.

XVI. CIRCUITS OF RESTRICTED LOCALITY

Not long ago the regions of the nervous system were delineated and ascribed functions. This is contrary to the function of the nervous system by interactions of neurons. Over the past decade it has been found that restricted circuits, which each involve a few neurons of different types, are repeated many times in parallel. These "integrated components" may cut across the old anatomic divisions. The most important of them are:

1. *The cerebellar unit circuit.* Ito's startling finding that the Purkinje cell has a general inhibitory function is the highlight of a splendid unravelling by microelectrode, Golgi studies, and electron microscopy of the circuit linking the main cerebellar neuron types (Eccles, Ito, & Szentágothai, 1967). The unit circuit of the cerebellum is reduplicated many times in a regular array and is remarkably constant throughout the vertebrates (Llinas, 1969). This is an example where the synaptic interaction within the unit circuit has been analyzed before the interaction between unit circuits, and hence function, can be approached (Fig. 3).

2. *The vertebrate retina.* Again, combination of electron microscopy (Dowling & Werblin, 1969) with microelectrode studies (Werblin & Dowling, 1969), and confirmation in goldfish by Procion injection (Kaneko, 1970) has elucidated the basic circuit from photoreceptors to ganglion cells. The center-surround pattern is already present in bipolar cells, and amacrine cells can carry spikes (Fig. 4).

3. *The dorsal horn of the spinal cord.* A combination of Golgi studies (Réthelyi & Szentágothai, 1968) and extracellular recording (Seltzer &

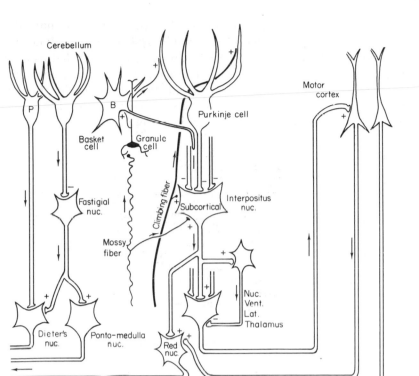

FIG. 3. Summary of the efferent unit circuit of the cerebellum, showing the types of connection, the direction of excitation, and the excitatory or inhibitory nature of the neurons. (Assembled from Eccles *et al.*, 1967.)

Spencer, 1969) has led to a circuit with presynaptic inhibition acting on primary sensory endings. This has been extended to a local circuit which explains many properties of pain perception (Melzack & Wall, 1968), and which is thought to be repeated many times over along the cord (Fig. 5).

4. *The Renshaw cell circuit.* A misunderstanding about the reality of the Renshaw cell feedback circuit from motoneuron collaterals back to other motoneurons has arisen. There are no short-axon neurons in the neighborhood of motoneurons in lamina VIII (Scheibel & Scheibel, 1969a). Marked Renshaw neurons lie in lamina VII where the motor axons emerge from the gray matter and therefore they must have long axons (Willis, 1969) (Fig. 6).

5. *Invertebrate examples.* Crab brain (Sandeman, 1969), *Aplysia* (Kandel, 1969), insect flight motor (Wyman, 1969), and insect optic lobes (Collett, 1970; Horridge, 1968) illustrate the convenience of invertebrate

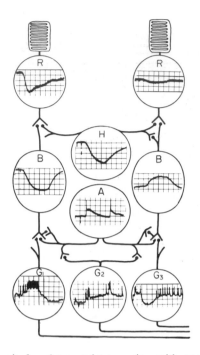

Fig. 4. The type circuit for the vertebrate retina with representative waveforms of responses to illumination of the receptor on the left. Note the hyperpolarizing response of the receptor (on center), which is carried through by the horizontal and bipolar cells (H and B). The two bipolar cells, on and off center, show opposite responses, and the field of the bipolar cells, with center and surround generated by the horizontal cell, is carried through to the ganglion cells. Note the spikes in the amacrine cell (A) and the on-off ganglion cell G_2, which is excited only by the amacrine cell. (From Dowling, 1970.)

preparations, where records can be made from neurons that are constant from preparation to preparation and where possibilities can be narrowed down by repeating experiments on identified neurons.

Any student or specialist in the field should be familiar with the main features of these circuits of restricted locality, that are repeated over and over again in parallel, for it is here that the advances will come. As yet in the vertebrates these circuits are highly abstract type circuits because the same cells are not found in each microelectrode penetration. In many invertebrates, large cells are individually identifiable and the relations between them can be analyzed. This has powerful consequences for the next stage of analysis, because when unit circuits can be individually identified a great advance can be made in understanding their differences and their relations

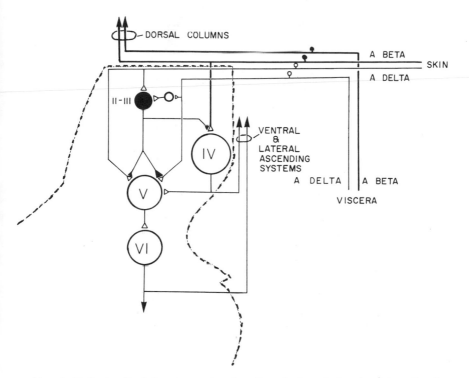

FIG. 5. Unit circuit of the sensory input to the spinal cord showing interaction between visceral and cutaneous sensory fibers. Presynaptic interactions between different sensory groups and visceral facilitation of cutaneous senses have been omitted. Inhibitory synapses are illustrated as solid triangles, excitatory ones as open. The lamina of the dorsal horn in which the cells lie are shown in roman numerals. (From Seltzer & Spencer, 1969.)

with each other. Possibly individual unit circuits have particular functions, as have identified neurons wherever they have been distinguished.

XVII. TOWARD MORE IDENTIFIED CELLS

Most of the giant fiber systems, typical of most invertebrate groups, have so few neurons that each can be recognized and given the same name in every individual of a species. These few identified neurons long foreshadowed the current view that every large neuron of an arthropod or mollusk can be so identified in every individual of a species. It has long been known from the work of Retzius and Zawarzin that the position of the cell body,

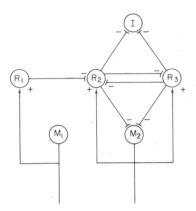

FIG. 6. Unit circuit of Renshaw cell interaction with motoneurons in the output of the spinal cord. The mutual inhibitory action between Renshaw cells is greatest among those most strongly excited by the same motoneuron, so providing spatially organized negative feedback of a negative feedback system. (From Ryall, 1970.)

the dendritic pattern and the axon connections are recognizably constant for many individual neurons in these animals. It is also common knowledge that the sensory systems of arthropods are remarkably constant from animal to animal. However, because there are numerous small cells of the so-called association areas, no one has suggested that every cell in the nervous system of a crayfish or cockroach can be numbered off in this way.

Recently new techniques have brought renewed interest. At about the time when recordings from identified *Aplysia* neurons became popular, it was discovered (Cohen & Jacklett, 1967) that cutting the axons of motor neurons in the cockroach causes a change in the RNA staining properties of the cell body. This study required the identification of individual neurons and was soon followed by the identification of many individual motor neurons with the muscles that they innervate. This opens the way to exact analysis of a much greater number of individual neurons. At the same time, methods of marking neurons intracellularly with dye steadily improved. The latest dyes (Procion yellow) diffuse into the branches of the neuron and also fluoresce in UV, so they are particularly visible (Stretton & Kravitz, 1968). Use of cobalt ions allows electron microscopy and fills fine branches. Intracellular marking means that the cell can be identified when its electrophysiology has been explored. The method is adequate to identify the penetrated cell as one of a known type of Golgi cell, and will certainly lead to progressive identification with known anatomic types of more and more physiological units found by blind probing. A method of working on individual cell constancy from animal to animal in the vertebrates has not yet been found.

XVIII. CONSTANCY OF SYNAPTIC CONNECTIONS

At this level of analysis, the action of the nervous system is the result of a pattern of (functionally effective) synaptic connections. Especially among invertebrates it is tempting to explain genetic constancy of behavior as residing in constancy of connections, and differences in behavior by differences in connections. So the actual pattern of synaptic connections (*the wiring diagram*) becomes a very important feature, whereas the details of dendritic shape or cell body position of individual neurons is of little importance.

The lack of information concerning the variability of patterns of connections (both within and between individuals) stems from the fundamental characteristics of vertebrate and invertebrate nervous systems. In the vertebrates the individual neurons are not recognizable anatomically in such a way that every one can be numbered and recognized again in a different animal. In invertebrates where the neurons are often recognizable, they are usually unique and their synapses are notoriously difficult to identify anatomically. On account of dendritic entwining the synapses themselves are almost always impossible to identify individually or with their neurons. Also, in a system of few neurons with no redundancy, a fault that is large enough to be noticed is likely to be lethal.

The interweaving of the retinula cell axons immediately behind the retina of the fly provides a situation that is favorable for an analysis of the accuracy of anatomic connections. Behind each facet there are six receptor cells with visual axes looking in six different directions and with short axons ending only 50 μm below the retina in synaptic connections upon the second-order neurons.

The pattern of connections is such that these six axons of receptor cells which look in the same direction out of six different facets converge together at the second-order level. The convergence has been demonstrated physiologically: the synaptic structures have been described at EM level. Other convenient details are that the axon terminals are blunt unbranched clubs large enough to be followed; there are thousands of them in parallel pathways so that an error of growth is of little consequence. Furthermore, a peculiarity of the symmetry about the equatorial line of the eye means that extra axons have to be correctly fitted in along this line (Fig. 7).

Of 650 of these axons, followed to their terminations, none made connection with the wrong group of second-order neurons. Moreover, the terminals lie in a particular order upon the second-order cells. Only ten errors in the order of location of terminals were found; most of these were on the equatorial line where extra axons have to be fitted in; the errors were only

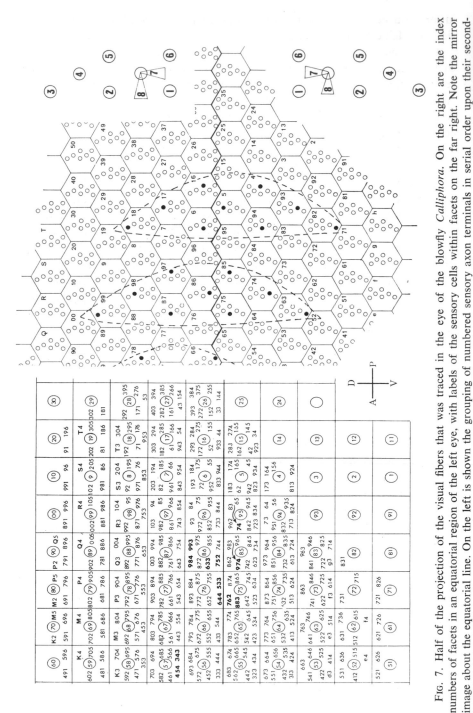

FIG. 7. Half of the projection of the visual fibers that was traced in the eye of the blowfly *Calliphora*. On the right are the index numbers of facets in an equatorial region of the left eye, with labels of the sensory cells within facets on the far right. Note the mirror image about the equatorial line. On the left is shown the grouping of numbered sensory axon terminals in serial order upon their second-

in the sequence of synapse neighborliness upon the second-order cell (Horridge & Meinertzhagen, 1970).

This demonstration of the incredible accuracy of the anatomic connectivity pattern, in a situation where it is not really critical on account of the reduplication of neurons, implies a much greater accuracy than has previously been supposed. Each of these neurons, in its growth, has correctly connected with the appropriate target cells. The question is how far can this accuracy in growth be extrapolated, to all fly large neurons, to all insect optic lobes, to all insects, to all invertebrates or even possibly to all nervous systems: Where do we stop?

This concept of genetically determined and totally fixed anatomy, beyond cell level down to synapse level, is quite at variance with the apparently random nerve nets of jellyfish and sea anemones, where the neurons have no labels that indicate their individuality or define their choice of other neurons with which they make synapses. As we ascend from the lowest worms to the arthropods (and from fish to man) there is a progressive increase in the number of classes of neurons that we can recognize as different from one another. We can only infer that these neuron types prove that they recognize their own individuality by making constant physiological pathways or anatomic patterns that are recognizable to us. The progressive evolution of more complex functions as the result of evolution of differences between neurons is one theme of a recent monograph (Horridge, 1968).

XIX. PROSPECT

Looking toward the future, the problem which troubles me most is the increasing complexity that has to be faced by anyone who attempts to cross from one aspect of the explanation of behavior to another. Consider yourself as a philosopher dealing with the mind–brain relation. How would you comment upon the results of the electrophysiologists as limited by their techniques. How can a molecular biologist, attracted by the challenge of the chemical basis of memory, do justice to the shelves of theoretical psychology? As a psychologist of human motives, how would you face up to the volumes of work on the rat? The physiological psychologist dealing with perception can possibly dip into the vast literature on the neurophysiology of the sensory systems, but how does a physiologist feel as he thumbs through the pages of illustrations of the innumerable neuron shapes drawn from Golgi preparations by neuroanatomists? Today the neurophysiologist engaged in the analysis of the function of units is already far separated from his namesake who studies properties of neurons at the membrane level. Few of the above read any neurochemistry, developmental studies, or accounts of regeneration. Any *current* explanation of neural function has to assume that there are no new principles beyond what is known already, and that the enormously complicated and possibly unique pattern of connections is subtle enough to carry out every operation. On account of the number of known functional differences which carry no morphological label, we cannot even hope that perfect anatomic knowledge will explain much at all. The safest conclusion is that advances are likely to be made by workers who straddle several disciplines and who work on the normal activity of the excitation pathways in their complete anatomic and chemical setting.

References

Abercrombie, M. Contact inhibition. The phenomenon and its biological implication. *National Cancer Institute, Monograph,* 1960, **26**, 249–373.
Adey, W. R., & LeBlanc, C. M. Slow electrical phenomena in the central nervous system. *Neurosciences Research Program, Bulletin,* 1969, **7**, 65–180.
Adrian, E. D. *The basis of sensation.* New York: Cambridge Univ. Press, 1928.
Auerbach, A. A., & Bennett, M. V. L. A rectifying electrotonic synapse in the central nervous system of a vertebrate. *Journal of General Physiology,* 1969, **53**, 211–237.
Baylor, J. G., & Nicholls, J. G. Changes in extracellular potassium concentration produced by neuronal activity in the central nervous system of the leech. *Journal of Physiology (London),* 1969, **203**, 555–569.
Bodian, D. An electron microscopic characterization of classes of synaptic vesicles by means of controlled aldehyde fixation. *Journal of Cell Biology,* 1970, **44**, 115–124.
Cohen, M. J., & Jacklett, J. W. The functional organisation of motor neurons in an insect ganglion. *Philosophical Transactions of The Royal Society of London, Series B,* 1967, **252**, 561–572.
Cohen, M. W., Gerschenfeld, H. M., & Kuffler, S. W. Ionic environment of neurones and glial cells in the brain of an amphibian. *Journal of Physiology (London),* 1968, **197**, 363–380.
Collett, T. S. Centripetal and centrifugal visual cells in the medulla of the insect optic lobe. *Journal of Neurophysiology,* 1970, **33**, 239–256.
Creed, R. S., Denny-Brown, D., Eccles, J. C., Liddel, E. G. T., & Sherrington, C. S. *Reflex activity of the spinal cord.* London and New York: Oxford Univ. Press, 1932.
Dagan, D., & Parnas, I. Giant fibre and small fibre pathways involved in the evasive response of the cockroach, *Periplaneta americana. Journal of Experimental Biology,* 1970, **52**, 313–324.
Dowling, J. E. Organization of vertebrate retinas. *Investigative Ophthalmology,* 1970, **9**, 655–680.
Dowling, J. E., & Werblin, F. S. Organization of the retina of the mudpuppy *Necturus maculosus.* 1. Synaptic structure. *Journal of Neurophysiology,* 1969, **32**, 315–338.
Eccles, J. C. *The neurophysiological basis of mind.* London and New York: Oxford Univ. Press, 1953.

Eccles, J. C., Ito, M., & Szentágothai, J. *The cerebellum as a neuronal machine.* Berlin and New York: Springer-Verlag, 1967.

Egger, M. D., & Wyman, R. J. A reappraisal of reflex stepping in the cat. *Journal of Physiology (London)*, 1969, **202**, 501–516.

Guth, L. "Trophic" influences of nerve on muscle. *Annual Review of Physiology,* 1968, **48**, 645–687.

Horridge, G. A. *Interneurons.* San Francisco, California: Freeman, 1968.

Horridge, G. A., & Burrows, M. The onset of the fast phase in the crab's optokinetic response. *Journal of Experimental Biology,* 1968, **49**, 315–324.

Horridge, G. A., & Meinertzhagen, I. A. The accuracy of patterns of connexions of the first- and second-order neurons of the visual system of *Calliphora. Proceedings of The Royal Society of London, Series B,* 1970, **175**, 69–82.

Kandel, E. R. The organization of subpopulations in the abdominal ganglion of *Aplysia.* In M. A. B. Brazier (Ed.), *The interneuron.* Berkeley: Univ. of California Press, 1969. Pp. 71–112.

Kaneko, A. Physiological and morphological identification of horizontal, bipolar and amacrine cells in goldfish retina. *Journal of Physiology (London)*, 1970, **207**, 623–633.

Kuffler, S. W. Discharge patterns and functional organization of mammalian retina. *Journal of Neurophysiology,* 1953, **16**, 37–68.

Llinas, R. R. (Ed.) *Neurobiology of cerebellar evolution and development.* Chicago, Illinois: Amer. Med. Ass., 1969.

Lowenstein, W. R. Communication through cell junctions. Implications in growth control and differentiation. *Developmental Biology, Supplement,* 1968, **2**, 151–183.

Melzack, R., & Wall, P. D. Interaction of fast and slow conducting fiber systems involved in pain and analgesia. *Proceedings of The International Pharmacological Meeting, 3rd, 1966,* 1968, Vol. 9.

Nelson, P. G. Interaction between spinal motoneurons of the cat. *Journal of Neurophysiology,* 1966, **29**, 275–287.

Perkel, D. H., & Bullock, T. H. Neural coding. *Neurosciences Research Program, Bulletin,* 1968, **6**, 221–348.

Ramón y Cajal, S. Estructura de los centros nerviosos de las aves. *Revista Trimensal Hist Norm Path* Barcelona 1st May 1888.

Réthelyi, M., & Szentágothai, J. The large synaptic complexes of the *substantia gelatinosa. Experimental Brain Research (Berlin),* 1968, **7**, 258–274.

Rudzinska, M. A. The fine structure and function of the tentacle in *Tokophrya infusionum. Journal of Cell Biology,* 1965, **25**, 459–477.

Ryall, R. W. Renshaw cell mediated inhibition of renshaw cells: Patterns of excitation and inhibition from impulses in motor axon collaterals. *Journal of Neurophysiology,* 1970, **33**, 257–270.

Sandeman, D. C. Integrative properties of a reflex motoneuron in the brain of the crab *Carcinus maenas. Zeitschrift für vergleichende Physiologie,* 1969, **64**, 450–464.

Scheibel, M. E., & Scheibel, A. B. A structural analysis of spinal interneurons and Renshaw cells. In M. A. B. Brazier (Ed.), *The interneuron.* Berkeley: Univ. of California Press, 1969. Pp. 159–208. (a)

Scheibel, M. E., & Scheibel, A. B. Terminal patterns in cat spinal cord. III. Primary afferent collaterals. *Brain Research,* 1969, **13**, 417–443. (b)

Seltzer, M., & Spencer, W. A. Interactions between visceral and cutaneous afferents in the spinal cord: Reciprocal primary afferent fiber depolarization. *Brain Research*, 1969, **14**, 349–366.

Sherrington, C. S. *The integrative action of the nervous system*. London: Constable, 1906.

Stretton, A. O. W., & Kravitz, E. A. Neuronal geometry: Determination with a technique of intracellular dye injection. *Science*, 1968, **162**, 132–134.

Strumwasser, F. Types of information stores in single neurons. In C. A. G. Wiersma (Ed.), *Invertebrate nervous systems*. Chicago, Illinois: Univ. of Chicago Press, 1967. Pp. 291–319.

Székély, G., Czeh, G., & Voros, G. Y. The activity pattern of limb muscles in freely moving deafferented newts. *Experimental Brain Research (Berlin)*, 1969, **9**, 53–62.

Szentágothai, J. 1968. Synaptic structure and the concept of presynaptic inhibition. In C. von Euler, S. Skoglund, & U. Soderberg (Eds.), *Structure and function of inhibitory neuronal mechanisms*. Oxford: Pergamon, 1968. Pp. 15–31.

Tauc, L. Excitatory and inhibitory processes. In M. A. B. Brazier (Ed.), *The interneuron*. Berkeley: Univ. of California Press, 1969. Pp. 37–70.

Ungar, G., Ho, I. K., & Galvan, L. Isolation of a behavior-inducing peptide from brain. *Proceedings of The American Society of Neurochemistry*, 1970, **1**, 73.

Wall, P. D. The sensory and motor role of impulses travelling in the dorsal columns towards cerebral cortex. *Brain*, 1970, **93**, 505–524.

Waziri, R., & Kandel, E. R. Organization of inhibition in abdominal ganglion of *Aplysia*. III. Interneurons mediating inhibition. *Journal of Neurophysiology*, 1969, **32**, 520–539.

Werblin, F. S., & Dowling, J. E. Organization of the retina of the mudpuppy, *Necturus maculosus*. II. Intracellular recording. *Journal of Neurophysiology*, 1969, **32**, 339–355.

Whitsel, B. L., Petrucelli, L. M., & Werner, G. Symmetry and connectivity in the map of the body surface in somatosensory area II of primates. *Journal of Neurophysiology*, 1969, **32**, 170–183.

Willis, W. D. The localization of functional groups of interneurons. In M. A. B. Brazier (Ed.), *The interneuron*. Berkeley: Univ. of California Press, 1969. Pp. 267–288.

Wyman, R. J. Lateral inhibition in a motor output system. *Journal of Neurophysiology*, 1969, **32**, 297–314.

Chapter 4

PRIMORDIAL SENSE ORGANS AND THE EVOLUTION OF SENSORY SYSTEMS

LAWRENCE KRUGER AND BARRY E. STEIN

I. INTRODUCTION

A description of the extensive variety of existing sensory systems and their involvement in behavior and evolutionary development constitutes a task beyond any single scholarly enterprise. Rather than pursue an impossible task, the present chapter represents an attempt, in a limited account, to document some examples of natural diversity and evolutionary divergence, with particular reference to the visual system. In some respects the present approach conflicts with the popular belief that atavism is common and that it may shed light on modern sensory specializations. The concept of atavism, or a "throwback," may be defined as a "recurrence in an organism or in any of its parts of a form typical of ancestors more remote than the parents, usually due to recombination of ancestral genes" (Merriam-Webster, 1965). Since only rarely can a true reversion be documented, the study of sensation and perception would best remain unencumbered by such notions. Instead, one usually finds a series of functional and structural modifications for the solution of a particular problem based on shifts in a diversified genetic pool, and mutations for which the genetic links are generally unknown. We shall not try to trace a sequence of events that must have led to the development of complex perception, but rather we will offer a few striking examples of sense organ and neural specialization in the belief that comparative biology may provide the most fruitful approach to the understanding of how these solutions can be reached. A wealth of relevant material may be found in standard modern reference works and symposia (Ariëns-Kappers, Huber, & Crosby, 1936; Bullock & Horridge, 1965; Carthy & Newell, 1968; Cold Spring Harbor Symposium on Quantitative Biology, 1965; Kuhlenbeck, 1967; Milne & Milne, 1959).

The Problem of Evolutionary Status

Advancement in an evolutionary sense is a somewhat arbitrary concept employed to place species in a hierarchical framework. By choosing among ambiguous criteria such as complexity and specialization in a specific organ system it is sometimes possible to impose higher and lower status to different animals, but the underlying assumptions may often be weak. The impressive "specialization" in man is expansion in the size and "complexity" of the microstructure of his brain, but can one satisfactorily place this "higher" than the small brain of the honeybee which is capable of enormous behavioral complexity with far fewer neurons? In essence, the concept of advanced species is based upon value judgements that are generally accepted as reasonable, and to which we shall reluctantly adhere in assuming, for example, that cats are "higher" than rats, and that some monkeys are "higher" than cats (although we recognize that such usage evades rigorous definition).

In a less sophisticated era of the recent past, the study of "lower" organisms was often initiated in the belief that insight might be provided into the development and evolution of complex "higher" organisms, particularly man. The concept of a primitive sensory system is, however, often misleading even in an etymological sense since many of the less elaborate forms displayed by invertebrates can hardly be conceived as prime or original (in the sense of leading to vertebrate patterns). This is particularly evident in those instances in which evolution has provided original solutions to the problem of detecting changes in environmental conditions. The description of an invertebrate system as "primitive" may often lead to the misunderstanding that it is a "step" in the development of a more "advanced" system, rather than being an example of unique sensory specialization. Thus, while a study of sense organ specialization proves particularly useful in understanding the various solutions to environmental demands, it usually cannot provide a satisfactory account of the sequence of events leading to the development of any given sensory system. In general, there is no homology between receptors activated by a given stimulus mode in different phyla. It has been appropriately emphasized by Bullock and Horridge (1965) that "eyes, statocysts, and other sense organs appear again and again, with contrasting structures in quite different parts of the body, even within a given phylum."

II. THE VARIETY OF SENSE ORGANS

The description of sensory receptors in terms of morphological and functional changes has accordingly displaced older terms such as exteroceptors, interoceptors, and proprioceptors, replacing them with designations defined in terms of the stimulus. However, even currently employed terminology is inadequate and is undergoing revision because terms such as "chemoreceptors" and "mechanoreceptors" fail to describe adequately what aspects of the stimulus are detected. There are over a dozen "mechanoreceptor" types in mammals alone, signalling different stimulus characteristics such as amplitude, velocity, acceleration, tension, position, and movement across the receptive field. For example, sense organs responsive to velocity of skin displacement might have quite different ranges of frequency sensitivity or velocity threshold. The preoccupation of modern sensory physiology has been the determination of the form of energy required for transduction and the nature of the afferent message or code. Despite rapid progress in recent years, our knowledge of sense organs (in terms of data accessible within the range of experimental methods in use) is strikingly incomplete.

A. Coding

The analysis of coded afferent messages derived from sense organs is the subject of intensive work on many organisms but, for the present, there is a paucity of investigations dealing with the interpretation of "sensory" events. Of particular interest are those neurons excited in a relatively

deterministic manner by a given range of stimuli, but capable of modification or even a form of simple "decision making" (to respond or not to)
when another afferent input is provided. This neuronal plasticity is often
overlooked in the search for invariance, and when neuronal variance is
encountered it is often attributed to lack of stimulus control. The search for
stimulus control is often in the direction of the *applied* stimulus rather than
the interaction of these stimuli and those provided by ongoing neuronal
processes. However, since the appropriate interpretation of external conditions should be dependent upon some neuronal code determined by the applied stimulus, most modern studies deal with the relatively consistent
responses of "sensory" neurons displaying an afferent message with low
variance for a given stimulus condition.

Variation of a given stimulus continuum, such as the intensity or the
wavelength of light, the frequency or sound pressure of tones, or the
velocity and amplitude of mechanoreceptor displacement can elicit a graded
series of impulses that are clearly stimulus dependent. An example of
reptilian mechanoreceptor fiber discharge, illustrated in Fig. 1, shows a

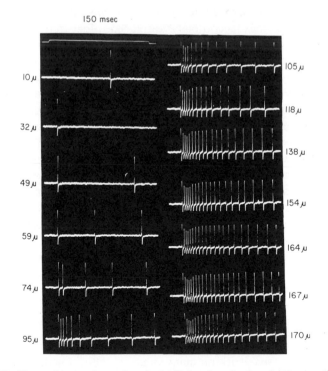

Fig. 1. Oscillographic tracings of a single first-order slowly-adapting reptilian cutaneous mechanoreceptor fiber activated by graded rectangular displacement of the skin
(upper trace). The pattern and number of impulses is a function of the amplitude of
skin displacement. (After Kenton, Kruger, & Woo, 1971; Siminoff & Kruger, 1968.)

typical series of responses for rectangular skin displacements of different amplitude. Interpretation of such afferent impulse messages is difficult because successive neurons, or the whole organism, may extract only specific aspects of the response that constitute the coded message. Thus, the number of impulses or the interspike intervals for only a portion of the spike train could provide information suitable for distinguishing between two different stimuli if response variability or "noise" in the system is measured. However, it should be obvious that many hypothetical "codes" can logically be invoked (Bullock, 1970), and there is evidence that different codes must be employed for sense organs incapable of responding with a train of impulses (Hagiwara & Morita, 1963). Modern stochastic techniques, including some applications of information theory (Kenton & Kruger, 1971; Stein, 1967; Werner & Mountcastle, 1965), have been employed to determine the transmission capacity of afferent channels, but with the exception of simple "one-bit" systems (in which a transient either elicits an impulse or fails to do so; Hagiwara & Morita, 1963), a secure choice among the possible codes that might be employed has yet to be established for most sensory systems.

B. Specialization

The complexity of response parameters, or behavior in general, cannot be related in any direct fashion to the variety of sensory input. There are examples where a whole complex response can be initiated by a single sensory neuron, but these involve elaborate rather than simple structures, such as the complex tympanal organ of notodontid moths and the tarsal contact chemoreceptors of *Diptera*. Even relatively simple organs possessing a paucity of neurons, such as the three large photoreceptor neurons in the "eye" of the barnacle, can display sufficient specialization of its membrane ionic mechanisms (an increased sodium conductance during illumination; Brown, Hagiwara, Koike, & Meech, 1970), to preclude generalization or invoking principles suggestive of evolution of vertebrate sensory systems from the rich variety of invertebrate specializations.

The extraordinary diversity and range of complexity of responses to illumination developed by various organisms probably best illustrates the numerous solutions to similar problems provided by divergent evolution in unrelated taxonomic groups. The light sense in various forms shares a common denominator in the possession of a photosensitive pigment, but the nature of the pigment differs for different types of receptors.

C. Photosensitivity

Perhaps the simplest form of photic sense is the action of light directly on an effector. An intracellular rearrangement of melanin granules within dermal and epidermal melanocytes (or melanophores) when exposed to light accounts for the well-known rapid alteration of skin color in teleosts, amphibians, and many reptiles. A true dermal or "dermatoptic" light sense involving nervous interactions has been studied in a wide variety of forms capable of displaying integrated reactions, such as the withdrawal reaction of coelenterates, kinesis of cyclostomes and blind fish, or the localized covering reaction of sea urchins. Defensive shadow reactions are widely distributed and may be elicited by uniform or directional illumination and by steady or changing intensity.

The diffuseness and lack of elaborate photoreceptor structural specialization for the dermal light sense has been widely regarded as primitive, but this view has been challenged (cf. Millott, 1968). One must consider that the sensitivity of the dermal light sense may exceed that of some specialized photoreceptors, and the fact that it may possess complex receptive surfaces as well as complex nervous organization. On the other hand, persuasive arguments can be adduced to suggest some evolutionary trends, and Gregory (1967) has presented an hypothesis supporting the view that the "first light-sensitive regions could have fed the original touch neural systems." Some support for such a view may be found in the central nervous system of *Cambarus*, in which Kennedy (1963) has shown that photosensitive neurons are also secondary integrating units for tactile stimulation. Gregory also argues that the optic chiasm decussation "probably served to relate the reversed retinal patterns to touch information from the body," but of course crossing of the tactile pathways in vertebrates must also be taken into account. Our purpose here is not to dispute or defend Gregory's thesis but rather to present a viewpoint that remains typical of the best attempts to discover broad evolutionary principles.

Gregory argues that "what is true for development of perception in the individual should be essentially true for the development of vision in evolution, for touch must have preceded vision if touch information is required to make retinal images effective symbols of the non-optical world of objects." There is no *a priori* reason why perceptual development must be paralleled by some evolutionary developmental principle, but students of perception may be tempted to look for earlier analogies to the sensory interactions that have been explored in detail in mammals.

Dermal photosensitivity often accompanies the distribution and extent of superficial nerve elements accessible to light and there have been numerous indications that neurons as well as sense organs are light sensitive; such neurons are found in the caudal abdominal ganglion of crayfish (Prosser, 1934; Welsh, 1934), in lampreys (Young, 1935), and in teleosts (de la Motte, 1964). The sensitivity may be high; in blinded minnows the threshold is only three orders of magnitude higher than human scotopic vision. Direct electrophysiological evidence of neuronal sensitivity to light was demonstrated in neurons of the visceral ganglion of the sea slug *Aplysia* by Arvanitaki and Chalazonitis (1961). These neurons contain heme-protein and carotenoid pigments and display excitatory and inhibitory reactions to light, but they are placed so deeply in the body that it is doubtful that they normally function as photoreceptors. The two types of pigment mediate changes of the cell membrane potential that are opposite in sign; heme-protein pigments are generally responsible for depolarization and the carotenoids for hyperpolarization.

D. Excitation and Inhibition

The effect of external energy (light in this case) on a sense cell is usually to cause excitation which usually takes the form of a depolarizing receptor potential, which in turn initiates impulses in the sense cell itself or by appropriate synaptic interactions in a secondary neuron. However, it is now well established that there are sense cells in mollusks and some bivalves whose photic receptors are considered to be "primitive" because light actually causes inhibition of any on-going response and vigorous activity is elicited at the cessation of illumination (Hartline, 1938; Kennedy, 1960; Land, 1968). Such receptors are found in forms in which the significant stimulus is the removal of light, as in shadow responses. In mollusks one also finds other receptors that are excited by light, but these are separate, and apparently serve to inform the animal about the intensity of light. Thus, as Land (1968) has shown in scallops, there are separate receptor systems for different aspects of the environmental stimulus; one for the overall pattern of light and dark, and the other for detection of shadows and movement that would result in small changes in total or local illumination. The cells responding to sustained illumination, the "on" response cells, display a distinctive microvillous surface. The "off" response system contains cells with modified cilia and is highly directionally selective (by virtue of a reflected image; Land, 1965) for the detection of movement.

As noted above for *Aplysia*, excitatory and inhibitory components can be found in the same cell. This has also been demonstrated in true photo-receptors in which different photoreceptive pigments can mediate excitatory and inhibitory components, as in *Spisula* (Kennedy, 1963). The opposite effects of each pigment can be shown by the marked wavelength dependence of the response. The inhibitory response has a lower threshold (6×10^{-2} erg/sec cm^2) and dominates during illumination; when the light is off, the more vigorous off-discharge is revealed as a long course excitatory event. Such a system is clearly suited for detection of sudden change in illumination and partial shading—events which signal danger or, alternatively, the presence of food or a potential host. In a sense, the invertebrate "off" systems presage the dominant "off" responses of vertebrate photoreceptor systems, all with modified cilia, but evolutionary links are lacking.

III. PRIMITIVE "EYES"

The variety of special adaptation in the sense cell and neural apparatus is paralleled by numerous evolutionary solutions to the problem of image formation. In the simplest conditions the sense cells can be seen distributed in a small depression, covered by secretion which protects the "eye pit" and may serve to increase intensity rather than to operate as an image forming lens as in the visual pit of limpets (Fig. 2a), which increases the contrast of shadows by reducing ambient light. In the "eye" of *Nautilus,* the opening is reduced to a pinhole for image formation as well as protection of the photoreceptor cells (Fig. 2b). In more advanced optical systems, a lens system is introduced in various ways, such as the external lens of the

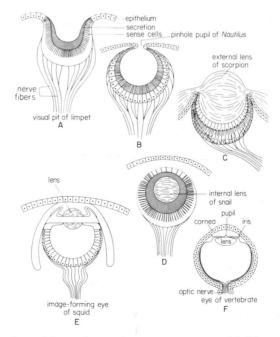

FIG. 2. A variety of invertebrate photoreceptor organs (A–E) and the vertebrate eye (F). In each the light falls upon a layer of photoreceptors through different media and image-forming mechanisms. (After Gregory, 1966.)

scorpion (Fig. 2c), the internal lens of snails (Fig. 2d), the true image-forming lens of the squid (Fig. 2e). In the general vertebrate pattern (Fig. 2f), corneal refraction (in nonaquatic forms) is added to the variable lens curvature and variable aperture provided by a pupilary mechanism, resulting in exquisite image resolution on the retinal photo-receptors. In some respects greater complexity can be found in the com-pound eyes of arthropods containing thousands of lens facets with a single receptor element for each lens. The compound eye is composed of separate units, *ommatidia,* consisting of a radial arrangement of sense cells each with an outer facet (or "corneal lens") and a second "lens cylinder." Each ommatidium is activated by light immediately in front of it and the combined signals might represent an effective single image; in some instances (as in the horseshoe crab, *Limulus*), lateral interactions have been demonstrated (Hartline, Ratliff, & Miller, 1961). In insect eyes, ommatidia are isolated from one another by cones of pigment which can migrate back to enable light to pass through the side of each ommatidium to neighboring receptors in conditions of reduced light. The problem of light and dark adaptation is solved in vertebrates by different photoreceptor cells (rods and cones) with different photopigments.

The visual system of vertebrates has been most intensively studied and the enormous literature has been summarized in several standard reference works (Duke-Elder, 1958; Polyak, 1941; Rochon-Duvigneaud, 1943; Walls, 1963; and numerous others); a detailed account may be found in Chapter 16 of this work. Although its evolutionary history is somewhat obscure (Walls, 1963), the vertebrate eye represents a distinct change in receptor structure and possesses a complex retina sufficient for the refined visual discriminations required for survival by most vertebrates. The human eye is neither the most complex or highly developed, but as we shall see, there is a distinct trend toward expansion of the neural apparatus for vision in the more "advanced" recent mammals, reaching what may be a peak evolutionary achievement in the human visual system.

Evolution is, nevertheless, frugal and conservative, and a fairly standard vertebrate eye subserves all species, although different anatomic and bio-chemical adaptations can often be related to environmental demands. Thus, nocturnal animals possess a predominantly rod retina, whereas cones, which function optimally in photopic light conditions, can be found in varying ratios in diurnal forms. A preponderance of cones is always associated with an increase in visual activity, usually with increased resolving power and color vision properties essential for the environmental requirements of diurnal forms. Sensitivity can be altered by a variety of solutions that have appeared in the course of evolution. These include pigment migration, addition of a reflective surface behind the retina in nocturnal forms (the *tapetum lucidum*) and a dynamic pupil whose shape and size range is related to environmental demands.

IV. SPECIALIZATION IN VERTEBRATES

Although the basic pattern of the vertebrate eye is stable, striking evolutionary modifications are evident as exemplified by the unusual specializations in the remarkable eye of the "four-eyed fish" *Anableps,* a species capable of simultaneous aerial and aquatic vision (Fig. 3). Each eye of this species appears to be bisected by horizontal flaps in the light-adapted condition, thus providing one pupillary aperture in air and one in water. The horizontal flaps also reduce the glare of the interface between air and water when the fish is feeding on the water surface, but a single aperture is formed by the flaps being pulled back when it is submerged. In air, the cornea serves as the principal refractive surface, requiring minimal lens curvature in the upper portion, but because corneal refraction is minimal below water, the lower portion of the lens has a markedly greater curvature. In order to adapt to either amphibious or aquatic vision it possesses a

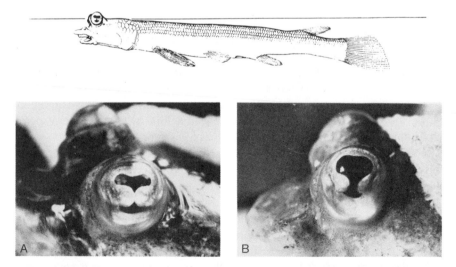

FIG. 3. The "four-eyed" fish *Anableps microlepis.* The horizontal line bisecting the pupil represents the water line. In the light adapted condition (A) the pupillary aperture is separated by iris flaps. After dark adaptation (B) the pupil is dilated and the upper and lower pupillary aperture are continuous. (From Schwassmann & Kruger, 1965.)

powerful retractor lentis muscle capable of shifting the lens position with respect to the pupillary aperture. The capture of insects swimming on the water surface requires an area of high visual acuity and the retina, correspondingly, possesses a horizontally elongated "area centralis" which receives light from the horizontal meridians immediately above the equatorial visual axis. As in most vertebrates, this portion of the retina, specialized for acuity, contains a larger ratio of cones (of differing types in teleosts) than rods, a higher proportion of ganglion cells to sense cells, and smaller "receptive fields" than elsewhere in the retina.

The neural organization of the vertebrate retina is exceedingly complex and specialized, but a basic pattern can be found throughout the class. A "receptive field," the zone of retina from which a neuron (bipolar, ganglion, horizontal, or amacrine cell) can be influenced, consists of excitatory and inhibitory zones with different spectral sensitivities. Responses of these retinal elements may consist of membrane changes of either direction, and impulse discharge patterns may appear when the light is on, off, sustained, or at both on and off. Space limitations preclude an extensive description of these interesting variants but from the viewpoint of this narrative it is noteworthy that the basic receptive field properties are similar in many respects in elasmobranchs, teleosts, and mammals (Kaneko, 1970, 1971; Kuffler, 1953; Naka, 1971; Werblin & Dowling, 1969).

Stimulus Feature Detection

Electrophysiological analyses of responses to more complex visual stimuli are difficult to summarize, partly because only a few species have been examined, but primarily because experimental approaches differ markedly and genuine species differences may be obscured by the nature of the description. The issue here is of critical importance in understanding the neural mechanisms of perception because of some recent reports concerning neuronal responses to moving and complex stimuli. The designation of response properties of retinal neurons with respect to some abstraction of the physical stimulus but without reference to receptive field organization, has led to the recognition of something resembling "perceptual" neurons. Lettvin and his co-workers (Lettvin, Maturana, McCulloch, & Pitts, 1959; Lettvin, Maturana, Pitts, & McCulloch, 1962) reported the responses from retinal ganglion cells of the frog in terms of analytic operations on the visual image, interpreting each cell as a specific "detector." These include several classes such as boundary detectors, moving dark convex edge detectors, moving or changing contrast detectors and dimming detectors, whose responses are said to be "invariant" over a wide range of conditions in other parameters (e.g., illumination level). Designating boundary detectors the "on" fibers and dimming detectors the "off" fibers of Hartline's early description (1938), as they suggest, does not satisfactorily resolve the issue because of current information that each receptive field possesses internal organization such that "on," "off" and "on–off" responses can be obtained from different loci in the receptive field with stationary stimuli and that responses can be graded by altering various parameters of the stimulus (Kuffler, 1953). The more complex "feature extraction" attributed to neurons in the brain of the frog such as "sameness" or "newness" detectors (Lettvin *et al.,* 1959) is equally difficult to interpret and incorporate into the context of experimental findings described in terms of details of receptive field organization. Species differences should prove to be of great interest judging by the scant data already available on the retinal responses to moving stimuli. Specific movement detection in the retina independent of brightness variables has been demonstrated in some forms, including mammals (Barlow, Hill, & Levick, 1964; Michael, 1968 a, b), but is apparently rare in others such as the cat (Rodieck & Stone, 1965), without revealing any firm phyletic trend. Spectral sensitivity with opponent color relationships has been demonstrated in the cone retina of several vertebrate classes (Daw, 1967; Gouras, 1968; Kaneko, 1970; MacNichol, Wolbarsht, & Wagner, 1961; Michael, 1968; Naka, 1971) but not all species.

V. THE VERTEBRATE CENTRAL NERVOUS SYSTEM

Central nervous pathways subserving vision provide the most striking examples of evolutionary trends. The basic pattern is for axons emanating from retinal ganglion cells and forming the optic nerve to completely cross to the opposite side of the brain, at the optic chiasm, and then to terminate in the forebrain (thalamus) and upper portion of the midbrain. Some additional and "accessory" optic pathways have been identified, and available comparative information has been reviewed by Giolli and Tigges (1970) and Ebbesson (1970). The basic and main vertebrate pattern is the orderly projection of the entire contralateral retina upon the optic tectum. The geometric arrangement may be approximately linear in some forms, but retinal specialization for higher acuity through a higher proportion of ganglion cells to sense cells can be related to a "magnified" central representation (Jacobson, 1962). Magnification or a greater volume of central representation per se, does not signify advanced evolutionary status, and both linear and magnified projections have been documented in a variety of species from teleosts to mammals (Kruger, 1970; Fig. 4).

Superimposed upon the basic genetically determined crossed projection pattern, an uncrossed, indirect connection, develops with visual experience

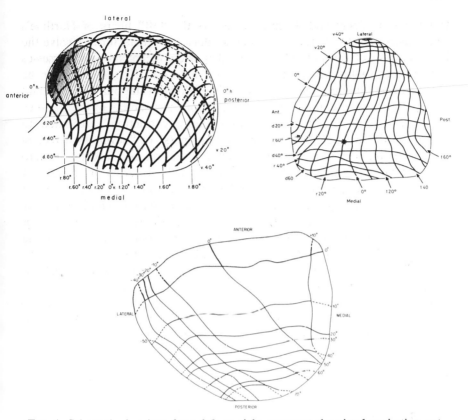

FIG. 4. Schematic drawings from left to right represent the visual projection patterns upon the optic tectum of sea bass (*Paralabrax*) and the superior colliculus of rat and cat. The vertical and horizontal meridians are marked by 0 degree and alternate 10 degree parallels are indicated and labeled in sea bass by their rostral (r), temporal (t), dorsal (d), and temporal visual field (v) location. In the sea bass, the underlying ventral portion of the tectum is represented by dashed lines and the shaded anteroventral area represents the expanded foveal projection. (From Schwassmann, 1968.) In the rat, the asterisk indicates the location of the optic disk and there is an approximately linear retinal projection pattern with no central magnification. (From Siminoff, Schwassmann & Kruger, 1966.) In the cat, the representation is binocular and, as in the sea bass, the area of central representation (near the horizontal and vertical meridian) is expanded. A second monocular representation of the contralateral temporal retina (shaded area) appears beyond the vertical meridian. (From Feldon, Feldon, & Kruger, 1970.)

in the frog (Keating & Gaze, 1970). In forms that possess binocular vision the images from each eye are projected in a superimposed manner to homotopic loci. In mammals, an uncrossed path originating in the temporal portion of the retina is added, reaching its peak in primates in which approximately half of the axons cross (those derived from the nasal retina) and the other half (from the temporal retina) remain uncrossed. Although some segregation is maintained in the central pathways, the corresponding points in the visual field for each eye are ultimately brought into "register" for binocular vision and stereopsis.

A. Midbrain Mechanisms

The optic projection to the midbrain is similar in pattern for all vertebrates examined to date (except for variation in the accessory optic pathways and the presence of centrifugal fibers to the retina from the isthmo-optic nucleus in some forms; Cowan, Adamson, & Powell, 1961). However, there are striking differences in the structure of the midbrain roof or tectum in different species of the submammalian vertebrates reaching the greatest degree of morphological specialization (in the sense of laminar differentiation) in the optic tectum of birds. The homologous mammalian structure, the superior colliculus, lacks an underlying ventricle (and thus is not a roof or tectum) and has a less elaborate laminar organization. Furthermore, the complex stimulus abstraction described for tectal neurons in the frog discussed above, has not yet been observed in any studies of the superior colliculus. Within mammals the laminar differentiation of the superior colliculus displays an evolutionary trend toward maximum development in the more advanced primates, but there is pronounced structural variation within a given order that is probably related to retinal specialization.

Interpreting the functional role of the midbrain optic projection poses a problem because experiments in different species have not always been performed in comparable fashion, especially with respect to analysis of responses to moving stimuli. Selective responses to the direction and/or the velocity of a stimulus traversing the receptive field have been reported for retinal ganglion cells in several vertebrate classes and in some, but not all, mammalian orders. Control of stimulus parameters has led to clear demonstrations of directional sensitivity to moving stimuli in the retina of amphibians (Grüsser, Finkelstein & Grüsser-Cornehls, 1968; Grüsser, Grüsser-Cornehls, Finkelstein, Henn, Patulschnik, & Butenandt, 1967), birds (Maturana & Frenk, 1963), rabbit (Barlow & Levick, 1965), and ground squirrel (Michael, 1970), but these are apparently absent in the rat (Brown & Rojas, 1965) and cat (Rodieck & Stone, 1965). Neurons in the optic tectum and superior colliculus selectively responsive to direction of movement (Fig. 5) have been described in most species, including the cat (McIlwain & Buser, 1968; Sprague, Marchiafava & Rizzolatti, 1968; Stein & Arigbede, 1972; Sterling & Wickelgren, 1969); but are reportedly absent in the rat (Humphrey, 1968) and rare in the macaque

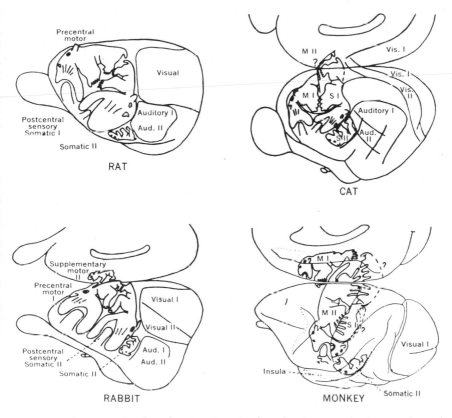

FIG. 5. An example of a directionally selective visual neuron in the superior colliculus of the cat. Dark rectangular bars were moved through the receptive field (represented by the rectangle to the left) in various directions, as indicated by arrows. Oscillographic tracings (retouched) to the right illustrate that movement was optimally effective in eliciting discharges in the horizontal axis from left to right (nasaltemporal) and of decreasing effectiveness as the stimulus was moved in other directions. (From unpublished experiments of Stein & Watanabe, 1972.)

monkey (Cynader & Berman, 1972). An evolutionary trend of "centralization" has been suggested, but the apparent discrepancies preclude such simple generalizations. The role of the midbrain in visual behavior will be discussed below in the context of a comparison with forebrain functional specialization.

The forebrain pattern of visual projection for submammalian forms also differs from that of all mammals. In general, homologous structures can be identified on the basis of form and relations in elasmobranchs, teleosts, amphibians, reptiles, and birds, but not in mammals. Transitions between the basic pattern for all mammals cannot be recognized in any extant reptile, and available evidence suggests that an abrupt evolutionary change occurred in the development of the mammalian brain. Although we have restricted this discussion to the visual system, a similar argument can be advanced for the somatosensory and auditory afferent pathways and perhaps to other sensory systems. The notable exception is the olfactory system, which remains remarkably similar throughout the entire vertebrate line. In this connection, it should be noted that in addition to the main afferent *projection* systems of the forebrain, there is a central core neural organization in the brain stem and medulla that receives connections from several afferent sources, the "reticular formation." Comparative neurologists have offered the thesis that the central reticular core nuclei represent the primitive sensory system of vertebrates and a consistent morphological plan in all classes (Herrick, 1924). Physiological evidence has been adduced to show that structures within the reticular system alter the activity of other afferent systems and the excitability of the forebrain, playing a crucial role in maintaining states of attention, wakefulness, and sleep (Magoun, 1963) by modality nonspecific effects.

B. Forebrain Organization

Those optic tract axons destined for the forebrain rather than the midbrain, enter a neuronal grouping in the lateral portion of the thalamus designated the lateral geniculate nucleus in most descriptions of the vertebrate diencephalon. The homology is based on its being the recipient of optic axons, but the organization and connections in mammals follows a distinctive evolutionary course that will be discussed below. In submammalian forms, a large thalamic nucleus rotundus, for which a mammalian homolog is not apparent, receives a massive projection from the optic tectum (Karten, 1969). Thus there are two major thalamic nuclei serving the visual system in at least teleosts, reptiles, and birds—a nucleus rotundus and a lateral geniculate body. Experimental anatomic findings in most vertebrate classes have been scanty and the connections of these structures have not yet been agreed upon, but there is some evidence to suggest that the nucleus rotundus projects upon the striatum of reptiles and birds (Powell & Cowan, 1961; Powell & Kruger, 1960) and that the lateral geniculate body sends axons to the "general sensory cortex" of reptiles (Hall & Ebner, 1970).

The forebrain development of vertebrates displays the most profound and significant evolutionary expansion. In elasmobranchs, teleosts and amphibians, the cerebral hemispheres are rudimentary and contain zones of neurons overlying the ependymal lining of the cerebral ventricles and a migratory zone which constitutes the striatum. Striatal (basal ganglia) expansion and differentiation becomes pronounced in reptiles and reaches its peak in birds. A true cerebral "cortex" is first found in reptiles, although homologous unmigrated "pallial" zones can be recognized in amphibians. The divergence between birds and reptiles is denoted by the formation of an elaborate striatum and a very small cortical zone in birds, as opposed to a somewhat less elaborate striatum with differentiated cortical zones in reptiles. The relation between reptilian and mammalian cortex remains obscure and available criteria are inadequate for imposition of homology status (Goldby & Gamble, 1957), but electrophysiological evidence suggests that the "general" cortex receives visual and somatic afferents (Kruger & Berkowitz, 1960). A six-layered "neocortex" appears abruptly in mammals and represents the most striking evolutionary advance of the mammalian line, reaching a peak of expansion and laminar differentiation in man.

VI. MAMMALIAN EVOLUTIONARY TRENDS

Several distinct anatomical trends are evident in mammalian evolution. The principal visual thalamic nucleus, the lateral geniculate body, displays a laminated pattern concomitant with the appearance of a significant uncrossed optic pathway and reaches its peak differentiation in the six-layered structure of primates. This nucleus projects upon a cortical field which becomes progressively expanded and more distinctly laminated or "striate" in more advanced mammals. Paralleling the developments of a "geniculo-striate" thalamocortical system, there is marked expansion of adjacent structures often subsumed under an "associational" designation. The trend in thalamic evolution is clearly an expansion of "intrinsic" nuclei that do not receive a major afferent supply from sensory pathways. The most prominent expansion in volume is in those nuclei near the lateral geniculate body, the pulvinar-lateral-posterior group (Kruger, 1959). This thalamic expansion is paralleled by the expansion of the "association cortex" upon which these nuclei project. Electrophysiological and anatomical experiments have shown that as mammals become more specialized the *proportion* of cortex devoted to a patterned sense organ projection (Fig. 6) becomes smaller (Rose & Woolsey, 1949; Woolsey, 1958) and cortex receiving afferents from intrinsic thalamic nuclei (or perhaps no thalamic projection) expands in more advanced mammals, especially anthropoids. The enormous expansion and folding of cerebral cortex seen in some primates is paralleled in other apparently unrelated mammalian orders (proboscideans and cetaceans), with large-brained representative species. Although quantitative

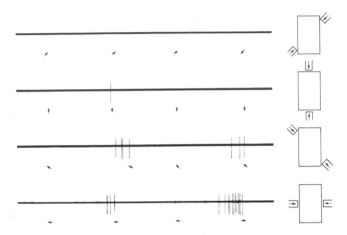

FIG. 6. Sensory projection areas on lateral and medial surfaces of the cerebral cortex in rat, rabbit, cat and monkey. The location of dual representation of motor (M I and II) and somatosensory (S I and S II) visual and auditory systems. The auditory cortex of monkey is not indicated and is hidden within the sylvian fissure. (After Woolsey, 1958.)

data and appropriate referents for comparison are lacking, the behavioral repertory of animals with an especially large cerebral cortex (e.g., man, apes, elephants, whales, and dolphins) suggests a marked advance.

The acquisition of a cerebral cortex with zones specialized for specific aspects of sensory analysis for each sense organ system constitutes the most extraordinary evolutionary advance. This evolutionary process of "encephalization" or "corticalization," also implies that basic functions are moved cephalad in the neuraxis and that advancement in sensory systems occurs at the cortical "level." Such hierarchical views of the nervous system can be supported by comparing the functional role of midbrain and cortical structures in different species. For example, removal of a zone of the optic tectum results in a "scotoma" (a zone of "blindness" in the visual field) in a fish (Schwassmann & Krag, 1970), but a comparable defect has not been found after destruction of the mammalian superior colliculus. In mammals, scotomata result from removal of the "primary" visual cortex; at least this is the case in man. In this respect, the primate cerebral cortex seems to perform a role analogous in some respects to that of the optic tectum of submammalian vertebrates. The mammalian colliculus appears to be assigned a quite different and poorly understood sensory role and its destruction produces deficits in the realm of orienting and following reflexes (Schneider 1969, Sprague & Meikle, 1965).

VII. CEREBRAL CORTEX

The kinds of complex visual stimuli to which neurons of the frog's retina and optic tectum appear to respond specifically (Lettvin *et al.*, 1959; Maturana, Lettvin, McCulloch, & Pitts, 1960) have been reported only at the cortical level in mammals. In a brilliant series of experiments, Hubel and Wiesel (1962, 1965, 1967) have shown that the concentric excitatory and inhibitory zones of receptive fields of neurons in the retina and thalamus are not mimicked at the cortical level. "Simple" cortical neurons are optimally excited by visual stimuli with a specific orientation in the visual field and others (designated as complex and hypercomplex) respond to highly specific shapes or patterns of light distribution. Unfortunately, the data for frog tectum and mammalian cortex cannot be compared easily because of differences in experimental approach and because the detailed description of "stimulus abstraction" by cortical neurons is almost certainly incomplete at a qualitative level, and quite obscure in terms of interpreting the code of impulse trains exhibited by responding neurons.

Sensory representation in the cerebral cortex also involves a replication of the peripheral sense organ topography such that each locus in the retina, on the skin, or along the cochlea is represented *at least* twice, as indicated by the maps delineating a somatic I and II, visual I and II and auditory I and II areas (Fig. 6). The signficance of dual or multiple representation of sense organs is puzzling because numerous ablation experiments in a variety of species have shown that although sensory discriminations are altered, total deficits are rarely produced, and the behavioral tasks employed here usually failed to reveal the exact nature of the defect. Observations based upon human cerebral pathology suggest that quite complex perceptual or operational deficits can be produced without loss in any specific sensory continuum such as color, brightness, etc. The multiplicity of representation at the cortical level also displays a trend toward greater complexity in the areas surrounding the "primary" projection thalamo-cortical system receiving the major supply of afferent fibers derived from specific sense organ pathways. This generalization is not easily supported for each sensory system, but for the visual system at least, neurons responding to "simple" stimuli are restricted to the "primary" geniculo-cortical (striate) projection or visual area I. Visual areas II and III are related to visual I and possess retinotopic patterns, but primarily "complex" and "hypercomplex" neuronal properties are found in these areas (Hubel & Wiesel, 1965). It is also evident that the size, and perhaps the number of cortical fields concerned with vision in a functional sense is expanded in the more advanced primates (as compared with other mammals). A note of caution that should be added here is that many of the complex tasks performed at the cortical level in mammals can be performed by animals without cortex. Size invariance for visual objects, for example, can be demonstrated in numerous species, including a variety of invertebrates.

VIII. NEURAL ORGANIZATION AND PERCEPTION

The difficulties in identifying evolutionary links do not preclude recognition of a phyletic trend in the process of encephalization and neuronal specialization. However, this might be an appropriate place to return to the hypothesis that light sensitivity is related to primitive touch systems in relatively simple invertebrates (Gregory, 1967). Visual perception appears to be dependent upon early tactual experience for the learning of visual form, as evidenced by the recovery of patients from congenital and early blindness (von Senden, 1932) and animals reared in the dark (Riesen, 1958). Held and Hein (1963) have clearly shown that "active" tactual exploration with the limbs is crucial for visual learning in mammals. Rather than relate tactual experience to visual learning as a primitive retention, a more parsimonious explanation might be found in the development of active exploratory systems as opposed to passive receptors guiding complex behavior. Neural pathways concerned with those aspects of scanning or manipulation of environmental stimuli have proven most difficult to comprehend in a functional sense. Visual perception, for example, is rapidly diminished by rendering the elaborate visual scanning mechanisms of man inactive by stabilized retinal images (Ditchburn & Ginsborg, 1952; Pritchard, Heron, & Hebb, 1960). In the tactile system there is a clear trend in mammals toward relative expansion of the dorsal column pathway of the spinal cord, the most massive tract in the human spinal cord. Yet, the deficit following its interruption in primates does not appear to be a profound loss of a specific modality, but rather a failure to orient and successfully explore extrapersonal space. It has been suggested by Wall (1970) that impulses in this pathway do not result in sensations, but instead act to initiate and control the search of messages arriving via other pathways.

The most striking examples of morphological expansion of neural systems in more advanced organisms have proven most elusive in terms of behavioral analysis. In addition to the striking example of the dorsal columns of the spinal cord, other major tracts of the central nervous system that attain their greatest relative size in man appear to be functionally unessential on superficial examination. The corpus callosum and pyramidal tract of primates are but the most prominent examples of expanding neural systems (in the phyletic sense) that may perform some role distinct from that performed by the major sensory and motor systems of less advanced animals. It is likely that these "newer" and expanding systems are involved in the active processes of manipulation and programming of exploratory mechanisms. The ability to change programs, initiate external searches, or to operate "comparator" systems, may constitute the most advanced accomplishments of nervous system evolution. Only by searching beyond simple behavioral tasks will the functional role of newer expanding structures of vertebrate nervous systems yield an understanding of the "systems" acquisitions developed to perform the more complex aspects of perception achieved in the most advanced mammals, including our own species.

We are indebted for research support from the United States Public Health Service, Grants EY-571, NS-5685 and LM 26401, which made preparation of this chapter possible.

References

Ariëns-Kappers, C. U., Huber, G. C., & Crosby, E. C. *The comparative anatomy of the nervous system in vertebrates, including man. Vol. II.* New York: Macmillan, 1936.

Arvanitaki, A., & Chalazonitis, N. Excitatory and inhibitory processes initiated by light and infra-red radiations in single identifiable nerve cells (giant ganglion cells of *Aplysia*). *In* E. Florey (Ed.), *Nervous inhibition.* Oxford: Pergamon, 1961. Pp. 194–231.

Barlow, H. B., Hill, R. M., & Levick, W. R. Retinal ganglion cells responding selectively to direction and speed of image motion in the rabbit. *Journal of Physiology (London),* 1964, **173**, 377–407.

Barlow, H. B., & Levick, W. R. The mechanisms of directionally selective units in rabbit's retina. *Journal of Physiology* (London), 1965, **178**, 477–504.

Brown, H. M., Hagiwara, S., Koike, K., & Meech, R. M. Membrane properties of a barnacle photoreceptor examined by the voltage clamp technique. *Journal of Physiology,* 1970, **208**, 385–413.

Brown, J. E., & Rojas, J. A. Rat retinal ganglion cells: Receptive field organization and maintained activity. *Journal of Neurophysiology,* 1965, **28**, 1073–1090.

Bullock, T. H. The reliability of neurons. *Journal of General Physiology,* 1970, **55**, 565–584.

Bullock, T. H., & Horridge, G. A. *Structure and function in the nervous systems of invertebrates.* Vols. 1 and 2. San Francisco, California: Freeman, 1965.

Carthy, J. D., & Newell, G. E. (Eds.) *Invertebrate receptors.* New York: Academic Press, 1968.

Cold Spring Harbor Symposium on Quantitative Biology. *Sensory receptors.* Vol. 30. Long Island, New York: Cold Spring Harbor, 1965.

Cowan, W. M., Adamson, L., & Powell, T. P. S. An experimental study of the avian visual system. *Journal of Anatomy,* 1961, **95**, 545–563.

Cynader, M., & Berman, N. Receptive field organization of monkey superior colliculus. *Journal of Neurophysiology,* 1972, **35**, 187–201.

Daw, N. W. Goldfish retina: Organization for simultaneous color contrast. *Science,* 1967, **158**, 942–944.

de la Motte, I. Untersuchungen zur vergleichenden physiologie der lichtemfindlichkeit geblendeter fische. *Zeitschrift fuer Vergleichende Physiologie,* 1964, **49**, 58–90.

Ditchburn, R. W., & Ginsborg, B. L. Vision with a stabilized retinal image. *Nature (London),* 1952, **170**, 36–37.

Duke-Elder, Sir W. S. *System of ophthalmology.* Vol. 1. *The eye in evolution.* London: Kimpton, 1958.

Ebbesson, S. O. E. On the organization of central visual pathways in vertebrates. *Brain, Behavior, & Evolution,* 1970, **3**, 178–194.

Feldon, S., Feldon, P., & Kruger, L. Topography of the retinal projection upon the superior colliculus of the cat. *Vision Research,* 1970, **10**, 135–143.

Giolli, R. A., & Tigges, J. The primary optic pathways and nuclei of primates. *In* C. R. Noback & W. Montagna (Eds.), *Advances in primatology.* Vol. 1 New York: Appleton, 1970. Pp. 29–54.

Goldby, F., & Gamble, H. J. The reptilian cerebral hemispheres. *Biological Reviews of The Cambridge Philosophical Society,* 1957, **32**, 383.

Gouras, P. Identification of cone mechanisms in monkey ganglion cells. *Journal of Physiology (London),* 1968, **199**, 533–547.

Gregory, R. L. *Eye and brain: The psychology of seeing.* New York: McGraw-Hill, 1966.

Gregory, R. L. Origin of eyes and brains. *Nature (London),* 1967, **213**, 369–372.

Grüsser, O.-J., Finkelstein, D., & Grüsser-Cornehls, U. The effect of stimulus velocity on the response of movement sensitive neurons in the frog's retina. *Pfluegers Archiv fuer die Gesamte Physiologie des Menschen und der Tiere,* 1968, **300**, 49–66.

Grüsser, O.-J., Grüsser-Cornehls, U., Finkelstein, D., Henn, V., Patulschnik, M., & Butenandt, E. A quantitative analysis of movement detecting neurons in the frog's retina. *Pfluegers Archiv fuer die Gesamte Physiologie des Menschen und der Tiere,* 1967, **293**, 100–106.

Hagiwara, S., & Morita, H. Coding mechanisms of electroreceptor fibers in some electric fish. *Journal of Neurophysiology,* 1963, **26**, 551–567.

Hall, W. C., & Ebner, F. F. Parallels in the visual afferent projections of the thalamus in the hedgehog and the turtle. *Brain, Behavior, & Evolution,* 1970, **3**, 135–154.

Hartline, H. K. The response of single optic nerve fibers of the vertebrate eye to illumination of the retina. *American Journal of Physiology,* 1938, **121**, 400–445.

Hartline, H. K., Ratliff, F., & Miller, W. H. Inhibitory interaction in the retina and its significance in vision. *In* E. Florey (Ed.), *Nervous inhibition.* Oxford: Pergamon, 1961. Pp. 241–284.

Held, R., & Hein, A. Movement-produced stimulation in the development of visually guided behavior. *Journal of Comparative and Physiological Psychology,* 1963, **56**, 872–876.

Herrick, C. J. *Neurological foundations of animal behavior.* New York: Holt, 1924.

Hubel, D. H., & Wiesel, T. N. Receptive fields, binocular interaction and functional architecture in the cat's visual cortex. *Journal of Physiology (London),* 1962, **160**, 106–154.

Hubel, D. H., & Wiesel, T. N. Receptive fields and functional architecture in two nonstriate visual areas (18 and 19) of the cat. *Journal of Neurophysiology,* 1965, **28**, 229.

Hubel, D. H., & Wiesel, T. N. Receptive fields and functional architecture of monkey striate cortex. *Journal of Physiology (London)*, 1967, **195**, 215.

Humphrey, N. K. Responses to visual stimuli of units in the superior colliculus of rats and monkeys. *Experimental Neurology*, 1968, **20**, 312–340.

Jacobson, M. The representation of the retina on the optic tectum of the frog. Correlation between retino-tectal magnification and retinal ganglion cell count. *Quarterly Journal of Experimental Physiology and Cognate Medical Sciences*, 1962, **47**, 170–178.

Kaneko, A. Physiological and morphological identification of horizontal, bipolar and amacrine cells in goldfish retina. *Journal of Physiology (London)*, 1970, **207**, 623–633.

Kaneko, A. Electrical connections between horizontal cells in the dogfish retina. *Journal of Physiology (London)*, 1971, **213**, 95–106.

Karten, H. J. The organization of the avian telencephalon and some speculations on the phylogeny of the amniote telencephalon. *Annals of the New York Academy of Sciences*, 1969, **167**, 164–179.

Keating, M. J., & Gaze, R. M. Rigidity and plasticity in the amphibian visual system. *Brain, Behavior, & Evolution*, 1970, **3**, 102–120.

Kennedy, D. Neural photoreception in a lamellibranch mollusc. *Journal of General Physiology*, 1960, **44**, 277–299.

Kennedy, D. Inhibition in visual systems. *Scientific American*, 1963, **209**, 122–130.

Kenton, B., & Kruger, L. Information transmission in slowly adapting mechanoreceptor fibers. *Experimental Neurology*, 1971, **31**, 114–139.

Kenton, B., Kruger, L., & Woo, M. Two classes of slowly adapting mechanoreceptor fibres in reptile cutaneous nerve. *Journal of Physiology (London)*, 1971, **212**, 21–44.

Kruger, L. The thalamus of the dolphin (*Tursiops truncatus*) and comparison with other mammals. *Journal of Comparative Neurology*, 1959, **111**, 133–194.

Kruger, L. The topography of the visual projection to the mesencephalon: A comparative survey. *Brain, Behavior, & Evolution*, 1970, **3**, 169–177.

Kruger, L., & Berkowitz, E. C. The main afferent connections of the reptilian telencephalon as determined by degeneration and electrophysiological methods. *Journal of Comparative Neurology*, 1960, **115**, 125–142.

Kuffler, S. W. Discharge patterns and functional organization of mammalian retina. *Journal of Neurophysiology*, 1953, **16**, 37–68.

Kuhlenbeck, H. *The central nervous system of vertebrates.* Vols. 1 & 2. New York: Academic Press, 1967.

Land, M. F. Image formation by a concave reflector in the eye of the scallop, *Pecten maximus*. *Journal of Physiology (London)*, 1965, **179**, 138–153.

Land, M. F. Functional aspects of the optical and retinal organization of the mollusc eye. *Zoological Society*, 1968, **23**, 75–96.

Lettvin, J. Y., Maturana, H. R., McCulloch, W. S., & Pitts, W. H. What the frog's eye tells the frog's brain. *Proceedings of the IRE*, 1959, **47**, 1940–1951.

Lettvin, J. Y., Maturana, H. R., Pitts, W. H., & McCulloch, W. S. Two remarks on the visual system of the frog. In W. A. Rosenblith (Ed.), *Sensory communications*. Cambridge, Massachusetts: MIT Press, 1962. Pp. 757–776.

McIlwain, J. T., & Buser, P. Receptive fields of single cells in the cat's superior colliculus. *Experimental Brain Research (Berlin)*, 1968, **5**, 314–325.

MacNichol, E. F., Wolbarsht, M. L., & Wagner, H. G. Electrophysiological evidence for a mechanism of color vision in the goldfish. In W. D. McElroy & B. Glass

(Eds.), *Light and life.* Baltimore, Maryland: Johns Hopkins Press, 1961. Pp. 795–813.

Magoun, H. W. *The waking brain.* Springfield, Illinois: Thomas, 1963.

Maturana, H. R., & Frenk, S. Directional movement and horizontal edge detectors in the pigeon retina. *Science,* 1963, **142**, 977–979.

Maturana, H. R., Lettvin, J. Y., McCulloch, W. S., & Pitts, W. H. Anatomy and physiology of vision in the frog. *Journal of General Physiology,* 1960, **43**, 129–171.

Merriam-Webster. *Webster's seventh new collegiate dictionary.* Springfield, Massachusetts: G. & C. Merriam Co., 1965.

Michael, C. R. Receptive fields of single optic nerve fibers in a mammal with an all-cone retina. II. Directional selective units. *Journal of Neurophysiology,* 1968a, **31**, 257–267.

Michael, C. R. Receptive fields of single optic nerve fibers in a mammal with an all-cone retina. III. Opponent color units. *Journal of Neurophysiology,* 1968b, **31**, 268–282.

Michael, C. R. Integration of retinal and cortical information in the superior colliculus of the ground squirrel. *Brain, Behavior, & Evolution,* 1970, **3**, 205–209.

Millott, N. The dermal light sense. In J. D. Carthy & G. E. Newell (Eds.), *Invertebrate receptors.* New York: Academic Press, New York, 1968. Pp. 1–36.

Milne, L. J., & Milne, M. Photosensitivity in invertebrate. *In* Amer. Physiol. Soc., J. Field (Ed.), *Handbook of physiology.* Sect. 1. *Neurophysiology.* Vol. I. Baltimore, Maryland: Williams & Wilkins, 1959. Pp. 621–645.

Naka, K.-I. Receptive field mechanism in the vertebrate retina. *Science,* 1971, **171**, 691–693.

Polyak, S. L. *The retina.* Chicago, Illinois: Univ. of Chicago Press, 1941.

Powell, T. P. S., & Cowan, W. M. The thalamic projection upon the telencephalon in the pigeon. *Journal of Anatomy,* 1961, **95**, 78–109.

Powell, T. P. S., & Kruger, L. The thalamic projection upon the telencephalon in *Lacerta Viridis. Journal of Anatomy,* 1960, **94**, 528–542.

Pritchard, R. M., Heron, W., & Hebb, D. O. Visual perception approached by the method of stabilized images. *Canadian Journal of Psychology,* 1960, **14**, 67–77.

Prosser, G. L. Action potentials in the nervous system of crayfish. 2. Responses to illumination of the eye and caudal ganglion. *Journal of Cellular and Comparative Physiology,* 1934, **4**, 363–377.

Riesen, A. H. Plasticity of behavior: Psychological aspects. *In* H. F. Harlow & C. Woolsey (Eds.), *Biological and biochemical bases of behavior.* Madison, Wisconsin: Univ. of Wisconsin Press, 1958. Pp. 425–450.

Rochon-Duvigneaud, A. *Les yeux et la vision des vertébrés.* Paris: Masson, 1943.

Rodieck, T. W., & Stone, J. Response of cat retinal ganglion cells to moving visual patterns. *Journal of Neurophysiology,* 1965, **28**, 819–832.

Rose, J. E., & Woolsey, C. N. Organization of the mammalian thalamus and its relationships to the cerebral cortex. *Electroencephalography and Clinical Neurophysiology,* 1949, **1**, 391–404.

Schneider, G. E. Two visual systems. *Science,* 1969, **163**, 895–902.

Schwassmann, H. O. Visual projection upon the optic tectum in foveate marine teleosts. *Vision Research,* 1968, **8**, 1337–1348.

Schwassmann, H. O., & Krag, M. H. The relation of visual field defects to retinotectal topography. *Vision Research,* 1970, **10**, 1301–1303.

Schwassmann, H. O., & Kruger, L. Experimental analysis of the visual system in the four-eyed fish *anableps microlepis*. *Vision Research* 1965, **5**, 269–281.

Siminoff, R., & Kruger, L. Properties of reptilian cutaneous mechanoreceptors. *Experimental Neurology*, 1968, **20**, 403–414.

Siminoff, R., Schwassman, H. O., & Kruger, L. An electrophysiological study of the visual projection to the superior colliculus of the rat. *Journal of Comparative Neurology*, 1966, **127**, 435–444.

Sprague, J. M., Marchiafava, P. L., & Rizzolatti, G. Unit responses to visual stimuli in the superior colliculus of the unanesthetized, midpontine cat. *Archives Italiennes de Biologie*, 1968, **106**, 169–193.

Sprague, J. M., & Meikle, T. H., Jr. The role of the superior colliculus in visually guided behavior. *Experimental Neurology*, 1965, **11**, 115–146.

Stein, R. B. The informational capacity of nerve action potentials using a frequency code. *Biophysical Journal*, 1967, **7**, 797–826.

Stein, B. E., & Arigbede, M. O. A parametric study of movement detection properties of neurons in the cat's superior colliculus. *Brain Research*, 1972, **45**, 437–454.

Sterling, P., & Wickelgren, B. G. Visual receptive fields in the superior colliculus of the cat. *Journal of Neurophysiology*, 1969, **32**, 1–13.

von Senden, M. *In* J. Barth (Ed.), *Raum- und gestaltauflassung bei operierten blindgeborenen von und nach der operation.* Leipzig, 1932. (English translation under the title *Space and light*, Glencoe, Illinois: Free Press, 1960.)

Wall, P. D. The sensory and motor role of impulses travelling in the dorsal columns towards cerebral cortex. *Brain*, 1970, **93**, 505–524.

Walls, G. L. *The vertebrate eye and its adaptive radiation.* New York: Hafner, 1963.

Welsh, J. H. Caudal photoreceptor and responses of the crayfish to light. *Journal of Cellular and Comparative Physiology*, 1934, **1**, 379–388.

Werblin, F. S., & Dowling, J. E. Organization of retina of the mudpuppy *Necturus maculosus*. II. Intracellular recording. *Journal of Neurophysiology*, 1969, **32**, 339–355.

Werner, G., & Mountcastle, V. B. Neural activity in mechanoreceptive cutaneous afferents: Stimulus-response relations, Weber functions and information transmission. *Journal of Neurophysiology*, 1965, **28**, 359–397.

Woolsey, C. N. Organization of somatic sensory and motor areas of the cerebral cortex. *In* H. F. Harlow & C. Woolsey (Eds.), *Biological and biochemical bases of behavior.* Madison, Wisconsin: Univ. of Wisconsin Press, 1958. Pp. 63–81.

Young, J. Z. The photoreceptors of lampreys. Light sensitive fibers in the lateral line nerves. *Journal of Experimental Biology*, 1935, **12**, 229–238.

Chapter 5

BEHAVIORAL EMBRYOLOGY

COLWYN B. TREVARTHEN

I. INTRODUCTION

Psychological structures may be shown to grow and differentiate through-out life. Correspondingly, the brain has a much more lengthy and involved development than any other mechanism of the body. We know little yet of how this uniquely complex process is determined, but it is certain that the principles of embryogenesis apply in all growth, including psychological growth, and not just to the morphogenesis of the body of the embryo.

Experiments with embryos show that the making of an organism is the result of two kinds of organizing process. One is intrinsic to an evolving, self-regulating genetic program transmitted from cell to cell. The other depends on interactions between parts of a multicellular body in which cells are aggregated or deployed by their own changing powers of adhesion or motility to create highly specific anatomic patterns (Gustafson & Wolpert, 1967). Integrative messenger substances (called inductors, evokators, hormones, transmitters, etc., in different contexts), which are passed between cells of different lines, help guide the various developments into the unified plan of an individual organism (Needham, 1942; Saxén & Toivonen, 1962; Waddington, 1957, 1966). However, these agents must act by their effects on mechanical mechanisms of cell interaction which create the patterning of the whole directly, and which subordinate molecular or biochemical events inside the separate cells (Wolpert, 1969).

Biological development is thus the result of equilibrations of gene products in dynamic "epigenetic" systems of each cell and within populations of many cells (Waddington, 1962). What is inherited is not gene information in any strict sense, but a highly specific instability of prefabricated building blocks: a strategy or program of how to assimilate components from the environment and how to develop further and thereby automatically gain structure. Not even the simplest protein molecule is a direct gene product, like a coin stamped from a die. The lengths of polypeptide chain read off the gene code undergo self-regulations or development to assume the complex and unique three-dimensional shape which has the specific properties of, say, an enzyme (Lehninger, 1967). The growing system of an embryo is so constituted that relatively simple instructions in the program for development lead to exceedingly intricate design when the process translating gene information into pattern is completed (Wolpert, 1969).

Development always involves competitive interaction and selection between growth products. This shapes cells and organs to specialized roles in mutual balance. The competition is essentially closed within the embryonic organism, but the more developed free-living stages, especially of the more complex forms and above all in man, actively seek by growth and behavior to obtain specific "education" from the environment, to gain "instructions" and to make feedback needed to carry the development further.

All of these developmental functions are seen in wonderful richness within the growing nervous system. Immature nerve cells in the embryo show exceptional mobility and they group and interact in complex ways (Jacobson, 1970). Subsequently, in the fetus, they grow intricate networks of extensions which selectively link up to build the fundamental circuits of behavior. At birth the human brain has achieved a particular unstable design which confers upon a neonate the drive to begin psychological differentiation.

Birth is the beginning of a process which may be called *psychogenesis*—the maturation of a system prefabricated to become an intelligent, conscious

individual who will assimilate knowledge of objects and beings in the outside world according to inherent rules. Seen in this light, even learning is a
part of the embryogenesis of a psychological mechanism, depending upon
the formulations of growing brain circuits and upon selection of prepared
alternatives of structure in them. Every aspect of psychological development is conditioned by the growth and differentiations of nerve cells.

II. THE EMBRYONIC NERVOUS SYSTEM

A. The Brain–Body Correspondence (Fig. 1.)

In the first steps of vertebrate embryogenesis, body and nervous system
grow in close association. Both soon show bilateral symmetry, anteroposterior differentiation and aspects directed out to the external milieu, and in
to the internal metabolic milieu (Arey, 1965; Barth, 1953; Hamilton, Boyd,
& Mossman, 1962; Willier, Weiss, & Hamburger, 1955).

From the start, the central nervous system is developmentally coupled

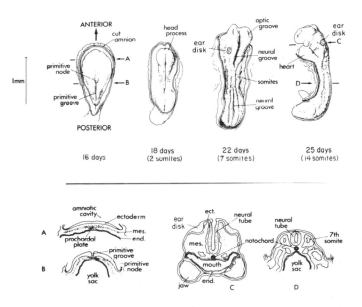

FIG. 1. Above: Human embryos from the stage of a pear-shaped embryonic disk
with no somites, through the early steps in the formation of the central nervous system, body segments (somites) and special sense organ primordia. Below: Sections
through the 16-day stage (A and B) and the 25-day stage (C and D) to show the
nerve tube formation by rolling up the dorsal neurectoderm over the notochord.

in inductive relations with the primordia of the skeletal axis and the paraxial locomotor muscles (Saxén & Toivonen, 1962). Segmentation of the body into somites (i.e., segments, which start as paired blocks of mesoderm) also divides the nerve tube into a longitudinal series of units, establishing the serial and hierarchical organization of circuits which remains fundamental to the integrative machinery of the mature nervous system.

Cell-mixing experiments with early embryos show that differentiation of fore-, mid- and hindbrain, and of brain from spinal cord, as well as dorsoventral differentiation of sensory and motor columns of cells throughout the neuraxis, depend on response of immature nerve cells to the local proportions of ectoderm and mesoderm (Toivonen & Saxén, 1968). If, as at the anterior pole of the body, there is no mesoderm, neurectoderm produces forebrain which lacks primary motor nerve cells. At the other end of the body, high proportions of mesoderm transform neurectoderm into spinal cord in which the primary neuromotor mechanisms will predominate.

From this point a correspondence is kept up between the central nervous system (CNS) and the body as a motor structure, and hence between the form of the CNS and the presumptive "field of behavior" of the organism (i.e., the totality of acts it will make). The body machinery of the embryo defines how space outside the adult body will be polarized by acts and how, because of these acts, reafferent information from the environment will impinge upon the body as a result of those acts. The neural tissues are branded so that they will continue to represent this field (the *behavioral field*) anatomically in a systematic and congruent way through development into functional stages.

Likewise, the visceral primordia and circulatory system, representing internal vital processes, appear to induce formulation of the cells of a presumptive autonomic nervous system. Autonomic neurones differentiate in the midventral core of the neural tube with integrative centers in the midventral brain (hypothalamus and medulla).

B. Differentiation of Special Organs and Reintegration

Special integrated receptor-motor organs appear in the late somite embryo: a moveable head with nose, ears, mouth, and tongue; the eyes; and the limbs with highly receptive distal parts (hands and feet) (Fig. 2A). The primordium of each of these arises at a particular place in the body, but then gains a largely autonomous ability to grow its elaborate structure. This is shown by experiments involving transplantation and grafting of primordia within the embryo body (Harrison, 1921; Stone, 1960).

Local sensory and motor fields are "reintegrated" within the whole-body scheme by growth of nerve connections according to inductive influences

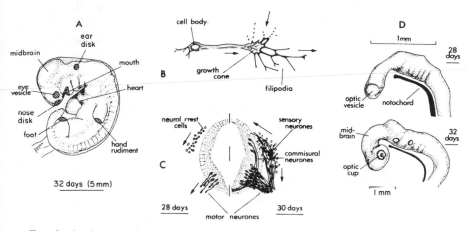

Fig. 2. A: Late-somite human embryo showing rudimentary sensory and motor organs. B: Neurone in process of growing an axon (After Ramón y Cajal; approximately ×1000). C: Human spinal cord at time of first growth of nerve fibers. D: Human brain showing flexion with rotation of forebrain and optic vesicle.

from the body. Surgical experiments with embryos of amphibia, reptiles, and chicks indicate that each rudimentary organ is excited at a specific stage to form an invisible map of cell differences which governs the growth of nerve connections to or from brain fields later. In this way each receptor location is identified with respect to its place in the scheme imprinted on the central circuits as a whole, and through this it is also mapped onto all the individual effector fields (reviews; Gaze, 1970; Jacobson, 1970; Sperry, 1951b, 1965).

For example, mapping of the visual field onto behavior is laid down in the embryo by specification of retina and midbrain roof neuroblasts so these two structures have a patterned connective affinity (Fig. 3 and above reviews). Likewise spinal sensory and motor neuroblasts become specified with respect to the way their dendrites or axons will connect to receptors and muscles labeled within the developing body segment or limb (Fig. 4). The limb-lobe has pathways which invading nerve fibers follow even before muscles are differentiated (Piatt, 1942; Taylor, 1943).

In a critical period of a few hours, first the anteroposterior axis then the dorsoventral axis of the visual field of a newt or a frog embryo is set in the eye in relation to the body (Jacobson, 1968; Stone, 1960). After this the retinal field is self-maintaining. The eyes subsequently grow around the rim and increase many times in size (Gaze, 1970; Gaze & Watson, 1968; Straznicky & Gaze, 1971). Therefore, the labeling of the axes must be kept intact during the dispersion of new generations of cells and, furthermore,

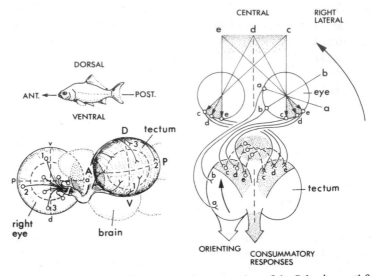

Fig. 3. Left: Mapping of retina onto optic tectum in a fish. Selective pathfinding by individual neurones. (After Attardi & Sperry, 1963.) Right: The map of the visual field onto motor functions (behavioral field). (After Trevarthen, 1968.)

the grain of specification must automatically become finer as the loci to be specified increase.

All known vertebrate retina-brain maps are "body-centered," plotting radial directions in outside space onto the brain with reference to the body, and they take account of the various angles that optic axes of different animals make in the body when the eyes are at the rest position (Trevarthen, 1968). The visual brain maps of egocentric space in different vertebrates with different eye axes are essentially the same. This shows that eye morphogenesis and retinotopic specification are separate processes.

Immediately before the retina is imprinted with the visuomotor axes, the optic vesicle inverts with respect to the inductive tissues of axial and paraxial mesoderm (Fig. 2D). This appears to be the morphogenetic solution to the rotation of the retinal image of the outside world in relation to the motor system of the body and to other receptor fields (Trevarthen, 1973).

C. Regenerated Nerve Connections; Chemo-Specificity Theory

Nerves of adult fish, urodeles, and tadpoles regenerate functional connections after they have been cut. Surgical rearrangement tests prove that embryonic specification of certain sensory, central, and motor connections determines the coordination of locomotion and orienting and feeding behaviors (Gaze, 1970; Jacobson, 1970; Jacobson & Baker, 1969; Mark, 1965; Miner, 1956; Sperry, 1943, 1944, 1945a,b, 1951a, 1958; Sperry & Arora, 1965; Weiss, 1936, 1941). These tests rule out acquisition of the basic networks through exercise, i.e., reinforcement of patterns which work, or elimination of those which fail. Even local feature-detecting circuits required for perceptual recognition of forms and colors are reestablished by regeneration in fish or frog, and visual discriminations learned before surgery and regeneration are retained afterwards (Arora & Sperry, 1963; Sperry, 1944; Weiler, 1966). Electrophysiological mapping experiments with microelectrodes have strongly confirmed the behavioral studies (Gaze, 1960, 1970; Jacobson, 1970; Maturana, Lettvin, McCulloch, & Pitts, 1959).

Sperry (1943, 1944, 1945b, 1951b, 1963, 1965) has proposed that this directed regrowth requires chemical or molecular tagging of locations along intercellular routes which the filopodia of growing axons are specified to recognize and attach to preferentially, as well as more refined labeling of different cells at the target site to determine elaborate circuits with differing functions. The chemico-specificities are established in embryological differentiation. Histological preparations showing selectively routed connections after regeneration of nerve axons cannot be reconciled with alternative "electrical-field" or "contact-guidance" theories (Attardi & Sperry, 1963).

This chemo-specificity theory, though it explains observed growth patterns and has been vindicated in a wide variety of critical experimental tests, has, as yet, no direct proof at the subcellular level. It supports one theory Cajal put forward to explain what he saw in histological preparations

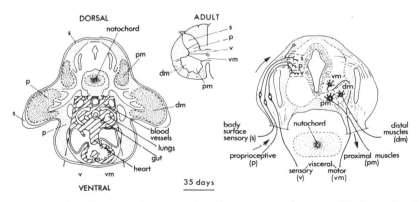

FIG. 4. Left: Diagram of the trunk of a human embryo at 35 days, showing primordia of organs and sensory and motor structures. Right: Arrangement of nerve cells and nerve fibers in spinal cord at 35 days, mapping the body onto the central nervous system. Center: Histological territories in adult human spinal cord.

of growing nerve networks (Ramón y Cajal, 1909–1911, 1929). It does not exclude plastic adjustment in growth of nerve circuits, or their refinement (differentiation) by competitive selection of optimal arrangements within mixed populations of endings (Mark, 1970; Székeley, 1966). It does assert that the determination of the synaptic patterns studied is intrinsic or phylogenetic; it is a cause not a consequence of individual behavior.

D. Production of Nerve Cells

Neurones develop (along with supporting glial cells) from cells which divide in the inner *ependymal* or *germinal zone* of the embryonic neural tube. They move outwards into the middle *mantle zone* before they become differentiated and send nerve fibers to fill the outer or *marginal zone*. Later neurone cell bodies may migrate out into the marginal zone, as in the formation of the cerebral cortex. Throughout the embryonic brain and spinal cord, cells are produced at rates which differ from region to region, and orderly accumulation of cells, modified by cell migrations, leads to the formation of nuclear masses, layered cortical regions and external lobes giving the brain its characteristic structure. Recent studies with radioactive nucleotides have demonstrated the precise timing of cell division in different parts, and the changing positions of labeled cells have been followed in a number of parts of the brain (see Jacobson, 1970, for a review of histogenesis in the nervous system).

In general, production of nerve cells in mammals is restricted to the embryonic and early fetal periods. Only small microneurones are produced in the cerebral hemispheres and cerebellum after birth (Altman, 1967).

E. Selection of Nerve Cells and Nerve Connections

Nerve connections may be determined by choice in a chemical or molecular terrain among the many fine exploratory filopodia which are produced continuously from the advancing tips of growing axons or dendrites (Fig. 2B; Harrison, 1910; Nakai, 1964). Selective amoeboid movement, with resorbtion or cutting off of fine branches must also govern the intricately patterned whole-cell migrations seen in growth of nerve systems (Levi-Montalcini, 1964).

However, selection operates at a variety of levels of structure in building the nervous system. The tips of regenerating fish optic axons appear to be guided at choice-points along the route so that each reaches a specified tectal locus without error (Attardi & Sperry, 1963), and pieces of retina implanted on the tectum of a chick embryo appear to grow axons directly to the appropriate location (De Long & Coulombre, 1967). Fibers reinnervating skin (Jacobson & Baker, 1969) or tectum (Cronly-Dillon, 1968) of amphibians show a narrowing of the large receptor fields first produced, indicating a selective pruning of branches after an initial somewhat diffuse growth of functioning connections.

Roughly specified nerve connections to a particular muscle become refined by competition which may, in some cases, involve an invisible selective inactivation of some synapses by inhibitory products from nerve endings which have more potent affinities for that muscle (Mark, 1970). Deliberate misrouting of motor nerves into wrong muscles shows that inappropriate contacts can be established as long as the nerve and muscle cells are not too incompatible according to the primary somatic fields in which they originated (Székeley, 1963), but these wrong connections are ousted if subsequently the somatotopically correct inputs are permitted to enter and form connections (Mark, 1965; Mark, von Campenhausen, & Lischinsky, 1966; Marotte & Mark, 1970; Sperry & Arora, 1965).

Selective death of whole cells is important in refinement and organization of neural mechanisms. It is conspicuous in amphibia at the time of metamorphosis when new sensory and motor structures (such as an enlarged dorsal binocular visual field, or limbs) are being incorporated to replace the larval equipment under thyroid-hormone control (Glücksmann, 1951; Hughes, 1969; Kollros, 1968; Prestige, 1967). In chick embryos visceral neurones are selected in competition with somatic cells in the spinal motor columns where massive reorganization by programmed cell death occurs (Levi-Montalcini, 1950). Programmed cell death refers to the elimination of cells of inappropriate kind by some criterion related to their specific biochemical constitution. A visceral factor (Nerve Growth Factor, a protein) has been isolated which in minute concentrations sustains chick sympathetic ganglia (Levi-Montalcini, 1966; Levi-Montalcini & Angeletti, 1968).

Experimental neuroembryology shows that the great complexity of functional nerve networks, as well as the refined shapes of different neurone types, arise from a process of cell self-differentiation, and from selective growth of cell branches and synaptic linkages according to invisible chemical or molecular affinities set up in a field that also patterns the whole body. The uniform appearance of nerve-cell substance and the confusing tangle of unanalyzed nerve networks obscure the myriad delicate specifications involved. Bioelectrical field forces and mechanical contact-guidance have been held to explain developmental patterning of neurone circuits, but such extraneural sources of structure are quite insufficient to explain the selectivity that growing neurones show in establishing their connections.

Theories attempting to explain unravelling of diffuse nerve connections by modulation of cells with information injected from sensory or motor end organs, or by selective reception of messages coded in a language of nerve impulse patterns that are broadcast mixed in the random net, have not received support (for critical review, see Gaze, 1970; Sperry, 1965).

III. THE FETUS

A. Growth of the First Nerve Circuits; Early Fetal Behavior

At 8 weeks after fertilization* the human embryo is called a fetus (Fig. 5). Then internal and external organs are characteristically human in outline. In the remaining 32 weeks before birth refinement of tissue and organ structure proceeds steadily in all parts, but the most striking growth is in the nervous system which, with its special receptors and neuromotor mechanisms, undergoes revolutionary elaborations (Arey, 1965; Coulombre, 1961; Hamilton, Boyd, & Mossman, 1962; Humphrey, 1964; Mann, 1964). At the same time behavior remains extremely limited and the fetus is usually quiescent as if in a sleep or coma.

The first nerve fibers grow in the late embryo of 4–5 weeks (Windle,

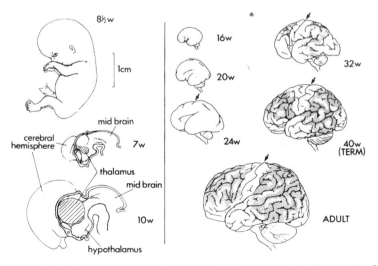

Fig. 5. Left: Early human fetus in characteristic posture. Rapid growth of cerebral hemisphere and thalamus in early fetus. Right: Growth of human brain through fetal period and after birth. All brains at same scale. Arrow indicates position of central sulcus. Stippled region is association cortex with rich commissural connections to the opposite hemisphere, indicating its relatively late appearance and maturation.

---

* Fetal ages are given in estimated time since fertilization (conceptual age). Conceptual or coital age is approximately equal to menstrual age less 14 days. Unless otherwise stated the account is restricted to *human* fetal development.

1970), and these soon establish the first synaptic connections (Bodian, 1966; Hamburger, 1969; Humphrey, 1954; 1964).

The first reflexive and spontaneous movements occur at about 5½–6 weeks while the circuits are still very immature. As in all vertebrates, sensitivity to touch first appears in the region of the mouth, and the first response is a bending of the head to one side. Mobility spreads from the neck muscles caudally, reflecting the cephalocaudal growth of neuromuscular connections (Carmichael, 1954; Hooker, 1952; Humphrey, 1964, 1969; Windle, 1940). Early autonomous development of synaptic patterns and electrical activity at this stage have been followed in tissue culture of rat fetal spinal cord (Bunge, Bunge, & Peterson, 1967; Crain, 1966; Crain & Peterson, 1967). By 8 weeks more connections are established to form a network which is close to that in lower vertebrates which governs locomotor coordination, orientation by whole-body flexion, and feeding by aiming the mouth and biting (Coghill, 1929; Herrick, 1948).

The precocious development of touch reflexes and primary vestibular circuits (Gottlieb, 1971b), as well as the relatively early appearance of postural reflexes and compensatory eye movements suggest that among the first organized efferent–afferent feedback loops are those concerned with supporting and coordinating parts of a moving body in a unified mechanical system.

However, finely individuated local face and hand movements are seen as early as 12–16 weeks (Humphrey, 1964, 1969). They appear to represent a neuromotor organization in brain stem and spinal cord that is preadapted to manual and oral prehension, but they may be parts of innate motor patterns for communication by grimace or gesture. In this same period heartbeat and some respiratory reflexes appear for the first time.

The cerebral and cerebellar cortices and associated brain-stem nuclei and tracts are rudimentary in the early fetus. They begin to grow rapidly at about 20 weeks (Fig. 5). The most detailed information on early hemispheric differentiation comes from studies of fetal sheep (Aström, 1967).

The behavior of a 20-week human fetus, spontaneous or reflexogenic, includes, (1) acts adapted to fetal maintenance, such as swallowing amniotic fluid, heartbeat, adjustment of body position and (2) erratic fragments of movement or weak coordinated patterns anticipating postnatal behaviors. Some fetal movements may have immediate morphogenetic significance, e.g., thumb sucking in the formation of the palate, or limb exercising in the shaping of bones and joints (Drachman & Sokoloff, 1966). Fetal behavior also influences the development of the nervous system itself, through stimulation of those receptors which are already functioning. Thus Gottlieb (1971a) has shown that prehatching vocalizations of ducklings are one factor in the normal development of their posthatching perception of the maternal assembly call. Vestibular, tactile, and proprioceptive systems may all receive stimulation before birth or hatching as a result of fetal acts or acts of the mother, and this may aid normal differentiation of their structure.

B. Maturation of Central Regulatory Mechanisms

From their earliest appearance, spontaneous patterns of movement in embryos show activity cycles and the bursts of movement are rhythmic or pulsating (Hamburger, 1969; Hamburger, Wenger, & Oppenheim, 1966). Rhythmic pacemaker systems may be an autogenous component of growing central networks. It appears that though sensory feedback may later control their expression and development, it does not determine their origin. Their importance in both normal and pathological behavior of infants is shown by Wolff (1966; 1968).

In man, there is a loss of responsivity and of spontaneous motor integration in the period from 24 to 37 weeks of gestation and for this time the fetus is comparatively weak and flaccid (Bergström, 1969; Humphrey, 1969; Saint-Anne Dargassies, 1966). This is often attributed to growth of reticular circuits of brain stem and cord and net inhibition of the primary mechanisms of sensory-motor coordination which were laid down in the early fetal period.

The reticular formation of the brain stem, which will regulate the modes of sleep, spontaneous activity and consciousness after birth, exhibits patterned electrical activity first at the base of the brain (pons) at about 10 weeks (Bergström, 1969). Its anatomic and physiological differentiation then advances toward anterior levels of the brain. By 24 weeks spontaneous rhythmic brain waves appear in the cortex (Dreyfus-Brisac, 1967).

Maturation of the electroencephalogram (EEG) and developmental changes in sleep cycles begin in the fetus and continue through childhood (Petre-Quadens, Hardy & De Lee, 1969) as does growth of certain parts of the hemisphere and brain stem (Yakovlev & Lecours, 1967). A marked change in the electrical activity (Dreyfus-Brisac, 1967) and in the tonus and reflexes (Saint-Anne Dargassies, 1966) of the fetus at about 37 weeks suggest a phase of accelerated development precisely at the close of the normal gestational period which prepares the way for postnatal life.

C. Autonomy of Fetal Brain Growth and Functional Regulation

Neurological examinations of premature infants and neonates show that maturation of the nervous system is closely tied to gestational age and many neural mechanisms are remarkably indifferent to the environmental effects of premature birth or to nutritional or other factors causing wide variations in body size and weight (Larroche, 1967; Schulte, Linke, Michaelis, & Nolte, 1969).

Nevertheless, embryogenesis of nerve nets may be regulated by selective transmission of neurotrophic or growth-inhibiting substances between connected cells, or via hormones transmitted in the blood stream (Jacobson, 1970). Excitation of impulse activity in immature circuits favors their development and may regulate their differentiation selectively. It has been speculated that early formed reflex arcs of embryo or fetus would permit acquisition of specific integrative connections by some kind of self-conditioning (Gottlieb & Kuo, 1965; Kuo, 1967; Lehrman, 1953; Schneirla, 1966). Recently Gottlieb (1971a) has put this hitherto unsupported hypothesis to careful test. His experiments, already cited, show that calls produced by unhatched birds aid the normal development of a species-specific response (the accurate perception of and attraction to the maternal assembly call) which becomes mature some time after hatching. Gottlieb also obtained evidence that the specification of the young bird's response was primarily intrinsic to the species, or determined genetically to be the most-favored outcome. Without normal circumstances, including prehatching auditory self-stimulation, this "expected" outcome was delayed or rendered less efficient, but it could not be redirected into the adaptive channel proper to another species. Such a system of development Gottlieb calls "probabilistic epigenesis." It is difficult to envisage how higher integrative mechanisms of behavior could originate through conditioning in development.

Experments tend to confirm that basic motor mechanisms may still undergo primary differentiation when sensory afference has been eliminated (Carmichael, 1926; Crain, Bornstein, & Peterson, 1968; Hamburger, Wenger, & Oppenheim, 1966). In general the first motor structures are formed and may begin spontaneous functioning and exhibit cycles of activity before afferent channels grow into them (Hamburger, 1969; Windle, 1970).

Hamburger (1963, 1969; Hamburger & Oppenheim, 1967) has demonstrated that a distinction should be made between erratic fragmentary discharges of movement, and smoothly coordinated patterns which show progressive integration or differentiation of form and increase of strength. The growth of coordination for the hatching behavior of a chick proceeds autonomously, without relation to the erratic kind of movement of body parts. The latter mode of activity may represent a disorganized first stage in the development of coordinations which mature after birth into acts directed to objects at a distance and requiring specialized perception functions. It may be compared to movements of extremities made by mammals in "paradoxical" or "rapid-eye-movement" sleep (Pompeiano, 1967). It is probably essential to normal morphogenesis of joints and muscles (Drachman & Sokoloff, 1966; Sullivan, 1967).

Central sensory mechanisms, likewise, self-differentiate when there is no adequate input of stimulus information for shaping of circuits. Electrical potentials evoked in the cortex of neonatal mammals by nerve stimulation, before natural receptor stimulation has had any effect, show up complex cortical circuits (Marty & Scherrer, 1964). The differentiation of electrical responses in the cortex parallels growth of dendrites and establishment of synapses there (Bernhard, Kolmodin, & Meyerson, 1967; Purpura, Shofer, Housepian, & Noback, 1964). Highly structured visual analyzer circuits have been found in the striate cortices of newborn kittens before their eyes are open (Hubel & Wiesel, 1963).

Sensory-motor coordination requires not only sensory receptors, neuro-motor structures and reflex integration, but also resetting of links between receptor fields and motor mechanisms to compensate for changes of the relative position of body parts. Also, perceptual analysis must take account of the feedback of sensory signals caused by displacement of the body relative to the external world. Anticipatory central adjustment to reafference is the essence of both perception of a stable world and motor intention (Bernstein, 1967; von Holst, 1954).

Matching "corollary discharge from efference" (Sperry, 1950) or "effer-ence copy" (von Holst, 1954) to reafference has been demonstrated in the behavior of fish and insects following inversion or interchange of the eyes with respect to the locomotor mechanism. The perverted function persists in conflict with other sense data, and this suggests that it is fundamentally innate and implastic in these animals. It may, however, be susceptible to modification or even complete rearrangement at an early embryonic stage. The efficiency of the first locomotor and orienting performance of many young birds and mammals which have matured without opportunity for practice of control by reafference also shows that the central mechanism may be laid down by intrinsic morphogenesis (Lorenz, 1965).

It is highly probable, as we shall see, that the fundamental circuits for integrating perception of the external world as a field for voluntary activity are also "inbuilt" in man within the fetus, though they are clearly incom-pletely formed and part-functional at birth, with specific dependency upon stimuli from the environment for their full expression.

IV. THE NEONATE: POSTNATAL BEHAVIOR GROWTH

A. Psychological Functions at Birth and their Early Growth

There has never been reason for regarding the brain of a human newborn as an unformed substrate for learning of sensory-motor coordinations, even by combination of elementary reflexes. Nevertheless, modern psychologists have, until recently, paid little attention to or denied the biological evidence that strategies underlying consciousness of permanent objects in space, language, thought, and, indeed, all cognitive processes are founded on genetically regulated growth of nerve circuits, the rudiments of which already have highly organized structure at birth.

Like the fetus, the newborn is helpless and with restricted motor capacity. Coordinated voluntary action is slowly acquired. However, this does not mean that it is acquired by learning alone. Observation of the process shows that the pace of development is regulated by an intrinsic program of elaboration of nerve mechanisms by growth (Lenneberg, 1967; McGraw, 1943; Peiper, 1963). Infants are born with intrinsic neural pacemaker systems that regulate the rhythms of all their spontaneous movements (Wolff, 1966; 1967; 1968). These mechanisms show progressive maturation.

Experiments with infants show that orientation of the two eyes (Dayton, Jones, Steele, & Rose, 1964; Fantz, 1961; Hershenson, 1964; Salapatek & Kessen, 1966), eye–hand coordination for reaching, coordination of auditory and visual localization, anticipation of touch feedback from grasping a seen object (Bower, Broughton, & Moore, 1970), perception of objects in three-dimensional space with size constancy corrections, and accounting for temporary occlusion in visual space (Bower, 1964, 1965, 1966a,b, 1967, 1969), all have their foundations in mechanisms which develop according to an internally controlled plan. Human communication behavior depends upon strong innate predispositions of which the much studied infant smile is only one component (Ambrose, 1961; Freedman, 1965; Wolff, 1963). The auditory mechanism of human neonates already shows properties adapted to perception of the human voice and other natural sounds (Eimas, Siqueland, Jusczyk, and Vigorito, 1971; Eisenberg, 1969; Freidlander, 1970; Trehub, and Robinovitch, 1972). Both laughter and crying are integrated with developing psychological functions from birth, they are not merely concerned with physiological regulations (Papoušek, 1969; Wolff, 1963, 1965, 1969). Speech development and acquisition of language show that an inherent structure is provided, and that it grows in an orderly way (Lenneberg, 1967). Gross deficiency of sensory feedback occasioned by blindness, deafness, or limblessness from birth does not prevent early development of complex perceptual and motor coordinations which are ultimately useless because there is no information for them to regulate.

B. The Role of Conditioning in Early Psychological Development

It has been demonstrated that conditioning aids differentiation of behavior from birth (Lipsitt, 1969) or even *in utero* (Prechtl & Knol, 1958).

Nevertheless, the character of what is learned is limited by inborn constraints on the attentive, perceptual, and intentional or volitional activity, as well as on the shape of receptors, sensory detector circuits, motor patterns, behavioral organs, and homeostatic "drive" mechanisms. These processes have a prescribed plasticity. Neonates are more readily conditioned than older infants because they are not yet equipped to select and reject stimuli according to psychological rules.

Human psychological maturation is orderly, and while dependent upon assimilation of effects of environmental stimuli, is not wholly determined by these effects (Piaget, 1950, 1967).

C. Postnatal Growth of Brain and Sense Organs

Correlation of brain growth with psychological development is only at a beginning. The human brain increases in length about 2½ times from birth to adulthood (Fig. 5). This change hides a complexity of internal regional differentiation, especially in infancy and early childhood.

As in fetal stages, the main increase in brain bulk after birth, apart from that due to glia increase, is caused by the extension of dendrites and the proliferation of connecting axons most apparent in the first two years (Conel, 1939–1963; Rabinowicz, 1964, 1967; Schadé & Van Groenigen 1961). Cortical cells of many different kinds develop elaborate branching dendrites covered with small dendritic spines to which a high proportion of synaptic connections are made (Shkol'nik-Yarros, 1971). Postnatal production of nerve cells by division of neuroblasts is restricted to certain areas, particularly in the cerebral hemispheres and cerebellum, and this results in the appearance of interstitial microneurones (stellate cells) which may have a role in modification of circuits in later stages of development (Altman, 1967). The larger nerve fibers gain a myelin sheath as they, along with the attached nerve cell body and dendritic tree, attain maturity.

Myelination indicates growth of neurones and studies of its patterning reveal that many human brain structures change greatly after birth. There is little myelin in the human cerebral cortex at birth (Rabinowicz, 1967). The hemispheres and brain stem exhibit three zones which mature postnatally at contrasting rates (Yakovlev & Lecours, 1967). The central core or median zone (hypothalamus and midline reticular nuclei of the thalamus) is concerned with visceral activity and behavior patterns regulating metabolic and reproductive functions and it shows maturation over 2–3 decades, i.e., through the years of reproductive life. Outside this, the *paramedian zone* (cingulum, limbic cortex, basal ganglia) has a short cycle which is completed at puberty. This is the mechanism governing more complex "instinctive" motricity in signalling of internal states, gestures and mimicry, postural mannerisms, and expressive vocalization. Finally, the commissural and association systems of the *outermost or supralimbic cerebral cortex zone* has the longest cycle of maturation extending through maturity to old age (Fig. 5). This development corresponds with the continuation of cognitive learning from individual experience and with the acquisition of skills important in human society, including symbolized thought, language and manufacture.

Postnatal differentiation of "association" areas is slower than in "motor," "sensory," or "limbic" cortex, and at each cortical location different cells, or different cell layers mature at different rates (Rabinowicz, 1967; Shkol'nik-Yarros, 1971).

Goldman has demonstrated that lateral and orbital areas of the frontal lobe of rhesus monkeys attain maturity at different times after birth (Goldman, 1971, 1972). Orbital cortex appears to be functionally committed in the first year, whereas lateral frontal cortex does not show functional maturity until toward the end of the second year. These areas are known to have distinct psychological functions, although while it is still growing the lateral cortex can take over the functions of ablated orbital cortex. The caudate nucleus of rhesus monkeys appears to gain its functional capacity before the cortical areas of the frontal lobe related to it (Goldman & Rosvold, 1972). A process of postnatal encorticalization of function is inferred. Such research offers an important way to elucidate the genesis of structures for higher intelligence, and hence their basic functional relations.

Human postnatal brain growth indicies show remarkable correlations with body growth and, more importantly, with psychological development. Lenneberg (1967, 1968) has reviewed these, particularly as they relate to the growth of language skills. Much remains uncharted in the most complex process of neural system formation which takes many years to complete.

Studies of commissurotomy patients support the view that cerebral maturation continuing beyond the first two decades is responsible for a progressive lateralization of functions of visual perception, thought, and language (Levy, 1969; Levy, Trevarthen, & Sperry, 1972; Sperry, 1968, 1969). It is probable that the slow-maturing association cortex-commissure system is responsible for a selective consolidation of experience differently in the two sides of the brain, a process which evidently requires the connections of the corpus callosum (Sperry, 1969).

Changes in the structure and complexity of receptor and motor structures after birth attest the regulated transformations of the whole mechanism of behavior through growth. At birth, skin and proprioceptive mechanisms are immature, and retinal rod mechanisms are well developed while the cone system, associated with the cortical circuits of focal vision, is immature (Coulombre, 1961; Humphrey, 1964; Mann, 1964).

D. Plasticity of Young Cerebral Circuits

It has been shown, in numerous studies, that the immature mammalian brain is capable of plastic adjustment of function to compensate for loss of tissue (Doty, 1961; Isaacson, 1968; Kennard, 1942; Lashley, 1938; Tucker & Kling, 1967; Wetzel, Thompson, Horel, & Meyer, 1965). In man functional recovery is more complete if brain injury occurs in the first decade of life rather than later when the brain is more mature, and hemispherectomy is less crippling in the adult if the brain half removed was already damaged, atrophied, or dysfunctional from infancy or early childhood (Basser, 1962; Teuber, 1970; Teuber & Rudel, 1962; Ueki, 1966). Congenital absence of the corpus callosum appears to result in a most remarkable compensatory organization of cerebral functions (Sperry, 1969).

Ablation experiments by Schneider (1970) reveal regenerative capacity in the newborn hamster brain comparable to that previously known, in postembryonic stages, only for lower vertebrates. He has apparently demonstrated that embryological specification of the basic somatotopic visuomotor orienting field is in the same chemical code in the optic tectum and thalamus. Recovery of visual orienting after removal of the superior colliculi (which normally transmit input from the eye to the thalamus) is achieved by a neural short-circuiting of optic nerve inputs direct to thalamic nuclei, thus replacing the lost collicular input to these nuclei. Recovery of pattern vision after (striate) cortex lesions is due to a more subtle unidentified change, possibly involving change of synaptic loci as shown in adult rat septal nucleus by Raisman (1969). Schneider's experiments show that even the primary orienting and discriminating circuits are incompletely developed in hamsters at birth. Presumably they remain, for a time, open to environmental activation and possibly even to selective reinforcement of connections. Further evidence for compensatory structural changes in the growing brain has been found after hemispherectomy in newborn rats (Hicks & D'Amato, 1970).

Recovery of fine motor coordination after removal of motor cortex in neonate monkeys (Kennard, 1938, 1942) has been related to the postnatal establishment of direct corticomotoneurone links via the pyramidal tract (Kuypers, 1962).

While the consolidation of experience within brain circuits in infancy and early childhood may be traceable to visible selective growth of nerve cells and their connections, the vast part of experience may be stored in submicroscopic cell-structure or at a macromolecular level of organization (Mark, 1970).

E. Destructive Effects of Deprivation and Abnormal Sensory Feedback

Postnatal psychological development, like all biological growth, requires active assimilation from a sufficiently rich environment. Deprivation of stimuli leads to atrophy of nerve tissues (Jacobson, 1970; Riesen, 1966). Deprivation of patterned stimuli or disorganization of the motor functions of exploratory and orienting activity results in deformed perceptomotor mechanisms (Hein & Held, 1967; Held & Hein, 1963).

In the neonatal period elaborate neuronal circuits laid down by growth are selectively reinforced or broken down in further development according to how they are used. Form-analyzers already at least partly developed in the cerebral visual cortex of neonatal kittens require input of patterned stimulation for their further postnatal growth. Connections from the two eyes to individual cortical cells (Hubel & Wiesel, 1965, 1970; Wiesel & Hubel, 1963, 1965), and groups of unit analyzers sensitive to different orientations of contours in the visual field (Blakemore & Cooper, 1970; Hirsch & Spinelli, 1970), both appear to grow in competition, and to be subject to selective influence from sensory feedback. Blakemore and Cooper (1970) have demonstrated blindness for horizontal contours in kittens which had been reared for the first few months of their visual experience with only vertical lines to look at, and these authors also recorded corresponding loss of horizontal "analyzers" in the visual cortex as detected with microelectrodes. Similarly, the visual imprinting mechanism of chicks is selectively degenerate (compared to the auditory component) when the birds are kept out of light after hatching (Bateson & Wainwright, 1972).

A possible neural model for such plasticity has been found in the central binocular visual mechanism of the frog *Xenopus* (Gaze, Keating, Székeley, & Beazley, 1970; Keating & Gaze, 1970). In this animal the primary visuo-motor orienting function is determined embryologically, as described, in a completely crossed visual input from each eye. However, growth of binocular circuits, involving a commissural projection from each tectum to a binocular map on the other side, may be open to selective growth change. Coincidence of the projections from the two eyes may be acquired after surgical distortion or inversion of the retina on one side. The process appears to depend on temporo-spatial coincidence of inputs from the two eyes. If so, it is a kind of associative learning dependent upon exposing the two eyes to patterned visual stimuli together.

The later stages of the growth of psychological mechanisms, especially those concerned with social and reproductive behavior, may depend upon highly specific environmental conditions for their normal development (Harlow, 1961; Harlow & Harlow, 1962; Lehrman, 1964). Deprivation in these conditions results, for example, in profound derangement of mating behavior or parental care, the latter transmitting effects to a subsequent generation.

V. CONCLUSION

Human intelligence, like animal intelligence, is the outcome of maturation of a neural network that organizes itself and differentiates its psychological functions by assimilation of experience. It is not possible at present to put this process on a sure foundation of biological knowledge and attempts at synthesizing theoretical approaches have produced sharp controversy.

The importance of inherent patterning of motor functions and of sensory analysis for assimilation of experience in learning has been insisted on by ethologists (Eibl-Eibesfeldt, 1970); Lorenz, 1965). Regulation by contingencies of experience has been emphasized by psychologists, some of whom have been inclined to argue that psychological functions may be fully patterned by experience. A judicious balance between the two extreme points of view is impossible to achieve without considering the nature of biological development which always counts on both gene control and adjustment of developmental products with themselves and with the environment.

Recently Jean Piaget, the psychologist who has done more than anyone else to explain human intelligence as a regulated development, has made a remarkable synthesis of embryological and psychological theory in a book that expresses his conception of the biological foundations of human cognition (Piaget, 1967). He has demonstrated that cognitive development throughout childhood depends upon the exercise of activity which is patterned internally by an inherent growth process that accommodates itself progressively to assimilated information.

Piaget's book, which makes no reference to neural structures, sets a formidable task for students of postnatal differentiation of the brain. We must conclude that human psychological development is the result of a neuronal growth process, the force and complexity of which we are only beginning to comprehend.

Addendum

A number of important review papers on the development of the nervous system and its significance for the embryology of behavior have appeared in "The Neurosciences: Second Study Program," edited by F. O. Schmitt, and published by the Rockefeller University Press, New York, 1970. The reader is particularly recommended to consult the sections in this volume on "Development of the Nervous System" and "Determinants of Neural and Behavioral Plasticity."

References

Altman, J. Postnatal growth and differentiation of the mammalian brain with implications for a morphological theory of memory. In G. Quarton, T. Melnechuk, & F. O. Schmitt (Eds.), *The neurosciences. A study program.* New York: Rockefeller Univ. Press, 1967. Pp. 723–743.

Ambrose, J. A. The development of the smiling response in early infancy. In B. M. Foss (Ed.), *Determinants of infant behavior.* Vol. I. London: Methuen, 1961. Pp. 179–201.

Arey, L. B. *Developmental anatomy.* (7th ed.) Philadelphia, Pennsylvania: Saunders, 1965.

Arora, H. L., & Sperry, R. W. Color discrimination after optic nerve regeneration in the fish *Astronotus ocellatus.* Developmental Biology, 1963, **7**, 234–243.

Aström, K.-E. On the early development of the isocortex in fetal sheep. *Progress in Brain Research,* 1967, **26**, 1–59.

Attardi, D. G., & Sperry, R. W. Preferential selection of central pathways by regenerating optic fibers. *Experimental Neurology,* 1963, **7**, 46–64.

Barth, L. G. *Embryology.* New York: Dryden Press, 1953.

Basser, L. S. Hemiplegia of early onset and the faculty of speech with special reference to the effects of hemispherectomy. *Brain,* 1962, **85**, 427–460.

Bateson, B. P. G. & Wainwright, A. A. P. The effects of prior exposure to light on the imprinting process in domestic chicks. *Behaviour,* 1972, **42**, 279–290.

Bergström, R. M. Electrical parameters of the brain during ontogeny. In R. J. Robinson (Ed.), *Brain and early behavior: Development in the fetus and infant.* New York: Academic Press, 1969. Pp. 15–41.

Bernhard, C. G., Kolmodin, G. M., & Meyerson, B. A. On the prenatal development of function and structure in the somesthetic cortex of the sheep. *Progress in Brain Research,* 1967, **26**, 60–77.

Bernstein, N. *The coordination and regulation of movements.* Oxford: Pergamon, 1967.

Blakemore, C. B., & Cooper, G. F. Development of the brain depends on the visual environment. *Nature (London),* 1970, **228**, 477–478.

Bodian, D. Development of fine structure of spinal cord in monkey foetuses. I. Motoneurone neuropil at time of onset of reflex activity. *Bulletin of the Johns Hopkins Hospital,* 1966, **119**, 129–149.

Bower, T. G. R. Discrimination of depth in premotor infants. *Psychonomic Science,* 1964, **1**, 368.

Bower, T. G. R. Stimulus variables determining space perception in infants. *Science,* 1965, **149**, 88–89.

Bower, T. G. R. Heterogeneous summation in infants. *Animal Behavior,* 1966, **14**, 395–398. (a)

Bower, T. G. R. Slant perception and space constancy in infants. *Science,* 1966, **151**, 832–834. (b)

110 COLWYN B. TREVARTHEN

Bower, T. G. R. The development of object-permanence: Some studies of existence constancy. *Perception and Psychophysics,* 1967, **2**, 411–418.
Bower, T. G. R. Perceptual functioning in early infancy. In R. J. Robinson (Ed.), *Brain and early behavior: Development in the fetus and infant.* New York: Academic Press, 1969. Pp. 211–223.
Bower, T. G. R., Broughton, J. M., & Moore, M. K. The coordination of visual and tactual input in infants. *Perception and Psychophysics,* 1970, **8**, 51–53.
Bunge, M. B., Bunge, R. P., & Peterson, E. R. The onset of synapse formation in spinal cord cultures as studied by electron microscopy. *Brain Research,* 1967, **6**, 728–749.
Carmichael, L. The development of behavior in vertebrates experimentally removed from the influence of external stimulation. *Psychological Reviews,* 1926, **33**, 51–58.
Carmichael, L. The onset and early development of behavior. In L. Carmichael (Ed.), *Manual of child psychology.* New York: Wiley, 1954. Pp. 60–185.
Coghill, E. G. *Anatomy and the problem of behavior.* London and New York: Cambridge Univ. Press, 1929.
Conel, J. LeRoy. *The postnatal development of the human cerebral cortex.* Vols. I–VI. Cambridge, Massachusetts: Harvard Univ. Press, 1939–1963.
Coulombre, A. J. Cytology of the developing eye. *International Review of Cytology,* 1961, **11**, 161–194.
Crain, S. M. Development of "organotypic" bioelectrical activities in central nervous tissues during maturation in culture. *International Review of Neurobiology,* 1966, **9**, 1–43.
Crain, S. M., Bornstein, M. B., & Peterson, E. R. Maturation of cultured embryonic C.N.S. tissue during chronic exposure to agents which prevent bioelectrical activity. *Brain Research,* 1968, **8**, 363–372.
Crain, S. M., & Peterson, E. R. Onset and development of functional interneuronal connections in explants of rat spinal cord ganglia during maturation in culture. *Brain Research,* 1967, **6**, 750–762.
Cronly-Dillon, J. Pattern of retinotectal connections after retinal regeneration. *Journal of Neurophysiology,* 1968, **31**, 410–418.
Dayton, G. O., Jones, M. H., Steele, B., & Rose, M. Developmental study of coordinated eye movements in the human infant. II. An electro-oculographic study of the *fixation reflex* in the newborn. *Archives of Ophthalmology,* 1964, **71**, 871–875.
De Long, G. R., & Coulombre, A. J. The specificity of retino-tectal connections studied by retinal grafts onto the optic tectum in chick embryos. *Developmental Biology,* 1967, **16**, 513–531.
Doty, R. W. Functional significance of the topographical aspects of the retino-cortical projection. In R. Jung & H. Kornhuber (Eds.), *Neurophysiologie und Psychophysik des visuellen Systems.* Berlin and New York: Springer-Verlag, 1961. Pp. 228–247.
Drachman, D. B., & Sokoloff, L. The role of movement in embryonic joint development. *Developmental Biology,* 1966, **14**, 401–420.
Dreyfus-Brisac, C. Ontogénèse du sommeil chez le prémature humain: Étude polygraphique. In A. Minkowski (Ed.), *Regional development of the brain in early life.* Oxford: Blackwell, 1967. Pp. 437–457.
Eibl-Eibesfeldt, I. *Ethology: The biology of behavior.* New York: Holt, 1970.

Eimas, P. D., Siqueland, E. R., Jusczyk, P., & Vigorito, J. Speech perception in infants. *Science,* 1971, 171, 303–306.

Eisenberg, R. B. Auditory behaviour in the human neonate: Functional properties of sound and their ontogenetic implications. *International Audiology,* 1969, **8**, 34–45.

Fantz, R. L. The origin of form perception. *Scientific American,* 1961, **204**, 66–72.

Freedman, D. G. Hereditary control of early social behavior. In B. M. Foss (Ed.), *Determinants of infant behavior.* Vol. III. London: Methuen, 1965. Pp. 149–159.

Freidlander, B. Z. Receptive language development in infancy: issues and problems. *Merrill-Palmer Quarterly,* 1970, 16, 7–51.

Gaze, R. M. Regeneration of the optic nerve in *Amphibia. International Review of Neurobiology,* 1960, **2**, 1–40.

Gaze, R. M. (Ed.), *Formation of nerve connections.* New York: Academic Press, 1970.

Gaze, R. M., Keating, M. J., Székely, G., & Beazley, L. Binocular interaction in the formation of specific intertectal neuronal connections. *Proceedings of the Royal Society, Series B,* 1970, **175**, 107–147.

Gaze, R. M., & Watson, W. E. Cell division and migration in the brain after optic nerve lesions. In G. E. W. Wolstenholme & M. O'Connor (Eds.), *Growth of the nervous system.* London: Churchill, 1968. Pp. 53–67.

Glücksmann, A. Cell deaths in normal vertebrate ontogeny. *Biological Reviews of The Cambridge Philosophical Society,* 1951, **26**, 59–86.

Goldman, P. S. Functional development of the prefrontal cortex in early life and the problem of neuronal plasticity. *Experimental Neurology,* 1971, **32**, 366–387.

Goldman, P. S. Developmental determinants of cortical plasticity. *Acta Neurobiologiae Experimentalis,* 1972, **32**, 495–511.

Goldman, P. S., & Rosvold, H. E. The effects of selective caudate lesions in infant and juvenile Rhesus monkeys. *Brain Research,* 1972, **43**, 53–66.

Gottlieb, G. *Development of species identification in birds: An inquiry into the prenatal determinants of perception.* Chicago, Illinois: Univ. of Chicago Press, 1971. (a)

Gottlieb, G. Ontogenesis of sensory function in birds and mammals. In E. Tobach, L. R. Aronson, & E. Shaw (Eds.), *Biopsychology of development.* New York: Academic Press, 1971. Pp. 67–128 (b)

Gottlieb, G., & Kuo, Z. Y. Development of behavior in the duck embryo. *Journal of Comparative and Physiological Psychology,* 1965, **59**, 183–188.

Gustafson, T., & Wolpert, L. Cellular movement and contact in sea urchin morphogenesis. *Biological Reviews of The Cambridge Philosophical Society,* 1967, **42**, 442–498.

Hamburger, V. Some aspects of the embryology of behavior. *Quarterly Review of Biology,* 1963, **38**, 342–365.

Hamburger, V. Origins of integrated behavior. In M. Locke (Ed.), *The emergence of order in developing systems.* New York: Academic Press, 1969. Pp. 251–271.

Hamburger, V., & Oppenheim, R. Prehatching motility and hatching behavior in the chick. *Journal of Experimental Zoology,* 1967, **166**, 171–204.

Hamburger, V., Wenger, E., & Oppenheim, R. Motility in the chick embryo in absence of sensory input. *Journal of Experimental Zoology,* 1966, **162**, 133–160.

Hamilton, W. J., Boyd, J. D., & Mossman, H. W. *Human embryology.* (3rd ed.) Cambridge, Heffer, 1962.

Harlow, H. F. The development of affectional patterns in infant monkeys. In B. M.

Foss (Ed.) *Determinants of infant behavior.* Vol. I. London: Methuen, 1961. Pp. 75–97.

Harlow, H. F., & Harlow, M. K. Social deprivation in monkeys. *Scientific American,* 1962, **207,** 137–146.

Harrison, R. G. The outgrowth of the nerve fiber as a mode of protoplasmic movement. *Journal of Experimental Zoology,* 1910, **9,** 787–848.

Harrison, R. G. On relations of symmetry in transplanted limbs. *Journal of Experimental Zoology,* 1921, **32,** 1–136.

Hein, A., & Held, R. Dissociation of the visual placing response into elicited and guided components. *Science,* 1967, **158,** 390–392.

Held, R., & Hein, A. Movement-produced stimulation in the development of visually guided behavior. *Journal of Comparative and Physiological Psychology,* 1963, **56,** 872–876.

Herrick, C. J. *The brain of the tiger salamander.* Chicago, Illinois: Univ. of Chicago Press, 1948.

Hershenson, M. Visual discrimination in the human newborn. *Journal of Comparative and Physiological Psychology,* 1964, **58,** 270–276.

Hicks, S. P., & D'Amato, C. J. Motor-sensory and visual behaviour after hemispherectomy in newborn and mature rats. *Experimental Neurology,* 1970, **29,** 416–438.

Hirsch, H. V. B., & Spinelli, D. N. Visual experience modifies distribution of horizontally and vertically oriented receptive fields in cats. *Science,* 1970, **168,** 869–871.

Hooker, D. *The prenatal origin of behavior.* Lawrence, Kansas: Univ. of Kansas Press, 1952.

Hubel, D. H., & Wiesel, T. N. Receptive fields of cells in striate cortex of very young, visually inexperienced kittens. *Journal of Neurophysiology,* 1963, **26,** 994–1002.

Hubel, D. H., & Wiesel, T. N. Binocular interaction in the striate cortex of kittens reared with artificial squint. *Journal of Neurophysiology,* 1965, **28,** 1041–1059.

Hubel, D. H., & Wiesel, T. N. The period of susceptibility to the physiological effects of unilateral eye closure in kittens. *Journal of Physiology (London),* 1970, **206,** 419–436.

Hughes, A. F. W. *Aspects of neural ontogeny.* New York: Academic Press, 1969.

Humphrey, T. The trigeminal nerve in relation to early human fetal activity. *Research Publications, Association for Research in Nervous and Mental Disease,* 1954, **33,** 127–154.

Humphrey, T. Some correlations between the appearance of human fetal reflexes and the development of the nervous system. *Progress in Brain Research,* 1964, **4,** 93–135.

Humphrey, T. Postnatal repetition of human prenatal activity sequences with some suggestions of their neuroanatomical basis. In R. J. Robinson (Ed.), *Brain and early behavior: Development in the fetus and infant.* New York: Academic Press, 1969. Pp. 43–84.

Isaacson, R. L. (Ed.), *The neuropsychology of development.* New York: Wiley, 1968.

Jacobson, M. Development of neuronal specificity in retinal ganglion cells of *Xenopus. Developmental Biology,* 1968, **17,** 202–218.

Jacobson, M. *Developmental neurobiology.* New York: Holt, 1970.

Jacobson, M., & Baker, R. E. Development of neuronal connections with skin grafts in frogs: Behavioral and electrophysiological studies. *Journal of Comparative Neurology,* 1969, **137,** 121–142.

Keating, M. J., & Gaze, R. M. Rigidity and plasticity in the amphibian visual system. *Brain, Behavior, & Evolution*, 1970, **3**, 102–120.

Kennard, M. A. Reorganization of motor function in the cerebral cortex of monkeys deprived of motor and premotor areas in infancy. *Journal of Neurophysiology*, 1938, **1**, 477–496.

Kennard, M. A. Cortical reorganization of motor function: Studies on series of monkeys of various ages from infancy to maturity. *Archives of Neurology and Psychiatry*, 1942, **47**, 227–240.

Kollros, J. J. Endocrine influences in neural development. In G. E. W. Wolstenholms & M. O'Connor (Eds.), *Growth of the nervous system*. London: Churchill, 1968. Pp. 179–192.

Kuo, Z. Y. *The dynamics of behavior development*. New York: Random House, 1967.

Kuypers, H. G. J. M. Cortico-spinal connections: Postnatal development in the Rhesus monkey. *Science*, 1962, **138**, 678–680.

Larroche, J.-C. Maturation morphologique du système nerveux central: Ses rapports avec le développement pondéral du foetus et son age gestationnel. In A. Minkowski (Ed.), *Regional development of the brain in early life*. Oxford: Blackwell, 1967. Pp. 247–256.

Lashley, K. S. Factors limiting recovery after central nervous lesions. *Journal of Nervous and Mental Disease*, 1938, **88**, 733–755.

Lehninger, A. L. The theme of conformation. In G. C. Quarton, T. Melnechuk, & F.O. Schmitt (Eds.), *The neurosciences: A study program*. New York: Rockefeller Univ. Press, 1967. Pp. 35–45.

Lehrman, D. S. A critique of Konrad Lorenz's theory of instinctive behavior. *Quarterly Review of Biology*, 1953, 28, 337–363.

Lehrman, D. S. The reproductive behavior of ring doves. *Scientific American*, 1964, **211**, 48–54.

Lenneberg, E. H. *Biological foundations of language*. New York: Wiley, 1967.

Lenneberg, E. H. The effect of age on the outcome of central nervous system disease in children. In R. Isaacson (Ed.), *The neuropsychology of development*. New York: Wiley, 1968. Pp. 147–170.

Levi-Montalcini, R. The origin and development of the visceral system in the spinal cord of the chick embryo. *Journal of Morphology*, 1950, **86**, 253–283.

Levi-Montalcini, R. Events in the developing nervous system. *Progress in Brain Research*, 1964, **4**, 1–29.

Levi-Montalcini, R. The nerve growth factor: Its mode of action on sensory and sympathetic nerve cells. *Harvey Lectures*, 1966, **60**, 217–259.

Levi-Montalcini, R., & Angeletti, P. U. Nerve growth factor. *Pharmacological Reviews*, 1968, **18**, 619–628.

Levy, J. Possible basis for the evolution of lateral specialization of the human brain. *Nature (London)*, 1969, **224**, 614–615.

Levy, J., Trevarthen, C., & Sperry, R. W. Perception of bilateral chimeric figures following hemispheric deconnexion. *Brain*, 1972, **95**, 61–78.

Lipsitt, L. P. Learning capacities of the human infant. In R. J. Robinson (Ed.), *Brain and early behavior: Development in the fetus and infant*. New York: Academic Press, 1969. Pp. 227–249.

Lorenz, K. *Evolution and the modification of behavior*. Chicago, Illinois: Univ. of Chicago Press, 1965.

McGraw, M. B. *The neuromuscular maturation of the human newborn*. New York: Columbia Univ. Press, 1943.

Mann, I. *The development of the human eye.* New York: Grune & Stratton, 1964.

Mark, R. F. Fin movements after regeneration of neuromuscular connections: An investigation of myotypic specificity. *Experimental Neurology,* 1965, **12,** 292–302.

Mark, R. F. Chemospecific synaptic repression as a possible memory store. *Nature (London),* 1970, **225,** 178–179.

Mark, R. F., von Campenhausen, G., & Lischinsky, D. J. Nerve-muscle relations in salamander: Possible relevance to nerve regeneration and muscle specificity. *Experimental Neurology,* 1966, **16,** 438–499.

Marotte, L. R., & Mark, R. F. The mechanism of selective reinnervation of fish eye muscle. II. Evidence from electronmicroscopy of nerve endings. *Brain Research,* 1970, **19,** 53–62.

Marty, R., & Scherrer, J. Critères de maturation des systèmes afférents corticaux. *Progress in Brain Research,* 1964, **4,** 222–234.

Maturana, H. R., Lettvin, J. Y., McCulloch, W. S., & Pitts, W. H. Evidence that cut optic nerve fibers in a frog regenerate to their proper places in the tectum. *Science,* 1959, **130,** 1709–1710.

Miner, N. Integumental specification of sensory fibers in the development of cutaneous local sign. *Journal of Comparative Neurology,* 1956, **105,** 161–170.

Nakai, J. The movement of neurones in tissue culture. In R. D. Allen & N. Kamiya (Eds.), *Primitive motile systems in cell biology.* New York: Academic Press, 1964. Pp. 377–385.

Needham, J. *Biochemistry and morphogenesis.* London and New York: Cambridge Univ. Press, 1942.

Papoušek, H. Individual variability in learned responses in human infants. In R. J. Robinson (Ed.), *Brain and early behavior: Development in the fetus and infant.* New York: Academic Press, 1969. Pp. 251–266.

Peiper, A. *Cerebral function in infancy and childhood.* New York: Consultants Bureau, 1963.

Petre-Quadens, O., Hardy, J. L., & De Lee, C. Comparative study of sleep in pregnancy and in the newborn. In R. J. Robinson (Ed.), *Brain and early behavior: Development in the fetus and infant.* New York: Academic Press, 1969. Pp. 177–192.

Piaget, J. *The psychology of intelligence.* M. Piercy & D. E. Berlyne (transl.) London: Routledge & Kegan Paul, 1950.

Piaget, J. *Biologie et Connaissance: Essai sur les relations entre les régulations organiques et les processus cognitifs.* Paris: Gallimard, 1967. Translated by B. Walsh, Edinburgh: Edinburgh University Press and Chicago: The University of Chicago Press, 1971.

Piatt, J. Transplantation of aneurogenic forelimbs in *Amblystoma punctatum. Journal of Experimental Zoology,* 1942, **91,** 79–101.

Pompeiano, O. The neurophysiological mechanisms of the postural and motor events during desynchronized sleep. In S. S. Kety, E. V. Evarts, & H. L. Williams (Eds.), *Sleep and altered states of consciousness.* Baltimore, Maryland: Williams & Wilkins, 1967. Pp. 351–423.

Prechtl, H. F. R., & Knol, A. R. Fuss-sohlenreflexe beim neugeborenen Kind. *Archiv fuer Psychiatrie und Nervenkrankheiten,* 1958, **196,** 542–553.

Prestige, M. C. The control of cell number in the lumbar ventral horns during the development of *Xenopus laevis* tadpoles. *Journal of Embryology and Experimental Morphology,* 1967, **18,** 359–387.

Purpura, D. P., Shofer, R. J., Housepian, E. M., & Noback, C. R. Comparative ontogenesis of structure–function relations in cerebral and cerebellar cortex. *Progress in Brain Research*, 1964, **4**, 187–221.

Rabinowicz, T. The cerebral cortex of the premature infant of the 8th month. *Progress in Brain Research*, 1964, **4**, 39–86.

Rabinowicz, T. Quantitative appraisal of the cerebral cortex of the premature infant of 8 months. In A. Minkowski (Ed.), *Regional development of the brain in early life*. Oxford: Blackwell, 1967. Pp. 91–124.

Raisman, G. Neuronal plasticity in the septal nuclei of the adult rat. *Brain Research*, 1969, **14**, 25–48.

Ramón y Cajal, S. *Histologie du système nerveux de l'homme et des vertébrés*. L. Azoulay (transl.), 2 vols. Paris: A. Maloine, 1909 & 1911. (Reprinted: Consejo Superior de Investigaciones Cientificas, Madrid. 1952 & 1955.)

Ramón y Cajal, S. *Etude sur la neurogenèse de quelques vertébrés*. Madrid 1929. (Reprinted: *Studies on vertebrate neurogenesis*. L. Guth (transl.) Springfield, Illinois: Thomas, 1960.)

Riesen, A. H. Sensory deprivation In E. Stellar & J. M. Sprague (Eds.), *Progress in physiological psychology*, Vol. I, 1966, Pp. 117–147.

Saint-Anne Dargassies, S. Neurological maturation of the premature infant of 28–41 weeks gestational age. In F. Falkner (Ed.), *Human development*. Philadelphia, Pennsylvania, Saunders, 1966. Pp. 306–325.

Salapatek, P., & Kessen, W. Visual scanning of triangles by the human newborn. *Journal of Experimental Child Psychology*, 1966, **3**, 155–167.

Saxén, L., & Toivonen, S. *Primary embryonic induction*. New York: Academic Press, 1962.

Schadé, J. P., & Van Groenigen, W. B. Structural organization of the human cerebral cortex-I. Maturation of the middle frontal gyrus. *Acta Anatomica*, 1961, **47**, 74–111.

Schneider, G. E. Mechanisms of functional recovery following lesions of visual cortex or superior colliculus in neonate and adult hamsters. *Brain, Behavior, & Evolution*, 1970, **3**, 295–323.

Schneirla, T. C. Behavioral development and comparative psychology. *Quarterly Review of Biology*, 1966, **41**, 283–302.

Schulte, F. J., Linke, I., Michaelis, R., & Nolte, R. Excitation, inhibition, and impulse conduction in spinal motoneurones of preterm, term and small-for-dates newborn infants. In R. J. Robinson (Ed.), *Brain and early behavior: Development in the fetus and infant*. New York: Academic Press, 1969, Pp. 87–114.

Shkol'nik-Yarros, E. G. *Neurones and interneuronal connections of the central visual system*. B. Haigh (transl.) New York: Plenum, 1971.

Sperry, R. W. Visuomotor coordination in the newt (*Triturus viridescens*) after regeneration of the optic nerves. *Journal of Comparative Neurology*, 1943, **79**, 33–55.

Sperry, R. W. Optic nerve regeneration with return of vision in anurans. *Journal of Neurophysiology*, 1944, **7**, 57–69.

Sperry, R. W. The problem of central nervous reorganization after nerve regeneration and muscle transposition. *Quarterly Review of Biology*, 1945, **20**, 311–369. (a)

Sperry, R. W. Restoration of vision after crossing of optic nerves and after contralateral transposition of the eye. *Journal of Neurophysiology*, 1945, **8**, 15–28. (b)

Sperry, R. W. Neural basis of the spontaneous optokinetic response produced by visual inversion. *Journal of Comparative and Physiological Psychology,* 1950, **43**, 482–489.

Sperry, R. W. Mechanisms of neural maturation. In S. S. Stevens (Ed.), *Handbook of experimental psychology.* New York: Wiley, 1951. Pp. 236–280. (a)

Sperry, R. W. Regulative factors in orderly growth of neural circuits. *Growth Symposia,* 1951, **10**, 63–87. (b)

Sperry, R. W. Developmental basis of behavior. In A. Roe & G. G. Simpson (Eds.), *Behavior and evolution.* New Haven, Connecticut: Yale Univ. Press, 1958. Pp. 128–139.

Sperry, R. W. Chemoaffinity in the orderly growth of nerve fiber patterns and connections. *Proceedings of the National Academy of Sciences of the United States,* 1963, **50**, 703–710.

Sperry, R. W. Embryogenesis of behavioral nerve nets. In R. L. De Haan & H. Ursprung (Eds.), *Organogenesis.* New York: Holt, 1965. Pp. 161–186.

Sperry, R. W. Hemisphere deconnection and unity in conscious awareness. *American Psychologist,* 1968, **23**, 723–733.

Sperry, R. W. Plasticity of neural maturation. In M. Locke (Ed.), *The emergence of order in developing systems.* New York: Academic Press, 1969. Pp. 306–327.

Sperry, R. W., & Arora, H. L. Selectivity in regeneration of the oculomotor nerve in the cichlid fish *Astronotus ocellatus. Journal of Embryology and Experimental Morphology,* 1965, **14**, 307–317.

Stone, L. S. Polarization of the retina and development of vision. *Journal of Experimental Zoology,* 1960, **145**, 85–93.

Straznicky, K., & Gaze, R. M. The growth of the retina in *Xenopus laevis:* An autoradiographic study. *Journal of Embryology and Experimental Morphology,* 1971, **26**, 67–79.

Sullivan, G. E. Abnormalities of the muscular anatomy in the shoulder region of paralysed chick embryos. *Australian Journal of Zoology,* 1967, **15**, 911–940.

Székely, G. Functional specificity of spinal cord segments in the control of limb movements. *Journal of Embryology and Experimental Morphology,* 1963, **11**, 431–444.

Székely, G. Embryonic determination of neural connections. *Advances in Morphogenesis,* 1966, **5**, 181–219.

Taylor, A. C. Development of the innervation pattern in the limb bud of the frog. *Anatomical Record,* 1943, **87**, 379–413.

Teuber, H.-L. Mental retardation after early trauma to the brain: Some issues in search of facts. In C. R. Angle & E. A. Baring (Eds.), *Psychical trauma as an etiological agent in mental retardation.* Washington, D.C.: Department of Health, Education and Welfare, N.I.N.D.S. Publication, 1970. Pp. 7–28.

Teuber, H.-L., & Rudel, R. G. Behaviour after cerebral lesions in children and adults. *Developmental Medicine and Child Neurology (London),* 1962, **4**, 3–20.

Toivonen, S., & Saxén, L. Morphogenetic interaction of presumptive neural and mesodermal cells mixed in different ratios. *Science,* 1968, **159**, 539–540.

Trehub, S. E., & Robinovitch, M. S. Audiolinguistic sensitivity in early infancy. *Developmental Psychology,* 1972, **6**, 74–77.

Trevarthen, C. B. Two mechanisms of vision in primates. *Psychologische Forschung,* 1968, **31**, 299–337.

Trevarthen, C. Cerebral embryology and the split brain. In W. L. Smith & M. Kinsbourne (Eds.), *The disconnected cerebral hemisphere and behavior.* Springfield, Illinois: Thomas, 1973, in press.

Tucker, T. J., & Kling, A. Differential effects of early and late lesions of frontal granular cortex in the monkey. *Brain Research,* 1967, **5,** 377–389.

Ueki, K. Hemispherectomy in the human with special reference to the preservation of function. *Progress in Brain Research,* 1966, **21B,** 285–338.

von Holst, E. Relations between the central nervous system and the peripheral organs. *British Journal of Animal Behaviour,* 1954, **2,** 89–94.

Waddington, C. H. *The strategy of the genes.* London: Allen & Unwin, 1957.

Waddington, C. H. *New patterns in genetics and development.* New York: Columbia Univ. Press, 1962.

Waddington, C. H. *Principles of development and differentiation.* New York: Macmillan, 1966.

Weiler, I .J. Restoration of visual acuity after optic nerve section and regeneration, in *Astronotus ocellatus. Experimental Neurology,* 1966, **15,** 377–386.

Weiss, P. Selectivity controlling the central-peripheral relations in the nervous system. *Biological Reviews of The Cambridge Philosophical Society,* 1936, **11,** 494–531.

Weiss, P. Self-differentiation of the basic patterns of coordination. *Comparative Psychological Monographs,* 1941, **17,** 1–96.

Wetzel, A. B., Thompson, V. E., Horel, J. A., & Meyer, P. M. Some consequences of perinatal lesions of the visual cortex in the cat. *Psychonmic Science,* 1965, **3,** 381–382.

Wiesel, T. N., & Hubel, D. H. Single-cell responses in striate cortex of kittens deprived of vision in one eye. *Journal of Neurophysiology,* 1963, **26,** 1003–1017.

Wiesel, T. N., & Hubel, D. H. Comparison of the effects of unilateral and bilateral eye closure on cortical unit response in kittens. *Journal of Neurophysiology,* 1965, **28,** 1029–1040.

Willier, B. H., Weiss, P., & Hamburger, V. *Analysis of development.* Philadelphia, Pennsylvania: Saunders, 1955.

Windle, W. F. *Physiology of the fetus.* Philadelphia, Pennsylvania: Saunders, 1940.

Windle, W. F. Development of neural elements in human embryos of four to seven weeks gestation. *Experimental Neurology, Supplement,* 1970, **5,** 44–83.

Wolff, P. H. The early development of smiling. In B. M. Foss (Ed.), *Determinants of infant behavior.* Vol. II. London: Methuen, 1963. Pp. 113–138.

Wolff, P. H. The development of attention in young infants. *Annals of the New York Academy of Sciences,* 1965, **118,** 815–830.

Wolff, P. H. The causes, controls and organization of behavior in the Neonate. *Psychological Issues, Monograph Series.* Vol. 5, No. 1, Monogr. 17. New York: International Universities Press, 1966.

Wolff, P. H. The role of biological rhythms in early development. *Bulletin of the Menninger Clinic,* 1967, **31,** 197–218.

Wolff, P. H. Stereotypic behavior and development. *The Canadian Psychologist,* 1968, **9,** 474–484.

Wolff, P. H. The natural history of crying and other vocalizations in early infancy. In B. M. Foss (Ed.), *Determinants of infant behavior.* Vol. IV. London: Methuen, 1969. Pp. 81–109.

Wolpert, L. Positional information and the spatial pattern of cellular differentiation. *Journal of Theoretical Biology,* 1969, **25,** 1–47.

Yakovlev, P. I., & Lecours, A.-R. The myelogenetic cycles of regional maturation of the brain. In A. Minkowski (Ed.), *Regional development of the brain in early life.* Oxford: Blackwell, 1967. Pp. 3–70.

Chapter 6

ETHOLOGY

WOLFGANG M. SCHLEIDT

I. INTRODUCTION

Ethology, as a distinct field within the hierarchy of science, can be characterized as "the study of the behavior of organisms." The same field is claimed by the comparative psychologists, but the essential difference lies in the point of view: the ethologist looks at behavior as a biological phenomenon, as the product of evolution, and as a characteristic of a species or other taxon, while the psychologist is most interested in abstract principles of behavior which are either of ultimate generality or of relevance to human behavior: "Through a certain anthropocentricity of interest we are likely to choose an organism as similar to man as is consistent with experimental convenience and control" (Skinner, 1938).

In addition to their generally biological viewpoint, ethologists share certain attitudes, certain methods, and a rather young history.

A. Basic Attitudes of Ethologists

1. EVOLUTIONARY CONSIDERATIONS

As any other scientist, the ethologist claims a certain degree of generality of the principles he chooses to extract and abstract from the study of a multitude of special cases. The special case, observed on one individual is assumed to apply to all individuals of the same *species,* with qualifications in reference to age, sex, and statistical variation within the population, and in reference to the taxonomic level. For example, the crowing of a rooster, "cock-a-doodle-doo," is assumed to be a characteristic of all mature, male, and healthy representatives of the species *Gallus domesticus;* it might also occur in such individuals of other species of the genus *Gallus,* or it might be absent in a smaller taxonomic group, e.g., in a certain subspecies, or in a specific strain. The rationale behind this concern about the taxonomic ties is that it is the population of all members of one species for which *natural selection* becomes effective (Mayr, 1963). An individual animal might appear to the observer optimally adapted to its environment. But since we find within a population of conspecifics a certain range of variability of behavior, only the population as a whole can reach an optimal state of adaptation, and even there only if the environment to which this adaptation has occurred is stable, e.g., if evolution has come to a standstill. Whenever properties of different species are compared, it is important to realize that all species are equally well adapted to their specific environment, independent of how primitive or sophisticated the behavior might be, except their populations show a persistent trend toward an increase or decrease in their number. In summary, the ethologist looks at behavior with the process of evolution and speciation in the back of his mind.

2. NATURE–NURTURE

Another striking trait in the attitude of ethologists is their concern with the problem of how adaptation of the population or the individual to the environment is achieved. The adaptation reflects the environment to which the population or the individual had responded earlier, and in this sense "information" about this environment is stored within the adapted organisms. In the specific case it can be asked whether such information is stored in the genome of this individual (and of all the conspecifics), or whether it constitutes a modification acquired by the individual; there is no other alternative form or way to store information (Lorenz, 1965). In this sense, a specific behavioral trait can be termed "environment-resistant" or "environment-dependent" in the ontogeny of an individual, a distinction which corresponds roughly to the older and less sophisticated concept of "innate" and "acquired" or "learned". This clear, dualistic principle hinges upon what we consider as a "behavioral trait": It applies only to relatively small, elementary units of behavior (e.g., to individual parameters of a fixed action pattern, such as duration). The more complex a piece of behavior is, the more likely it will be a composite of environment-resistant and environment-dependent subtraits.

3. SPONTANEITY

Most scientists, when exploring the properties of a system do this by establishing a set of reliable relations between input and output. In behavioral studies, this research strategy leads to an emphasis of stimulus and response, and distracts attention from the fact that the organism also behaves in the absence of stimulation, i.e., the organism generates spontaneous behavior. In comparison with other contemporary schools of behavior, ethologists give most attention to the phenomenon of spontaneity. Some scientists reject this concept because it can be difficult to distinguish between a case in which a still unknown environmental input triggers behavior and a case of spontaneous behavior. With some sophistication in the control of input and in the statistical treatment of the output these difficulties can be overcome (Schleidt, 1964a). I must point out that the spontaneity of the behavior of an organism in proper isolation is much easier to establish than the spontaneity of a single neuron within the brain, recorded by means of a microelectrode. This single neuron, as a system, is linked to many other similar units, and is spontaneous only in respect to a plexus, nucleus, or other supersystem, if (and only if) all inputs of said system are under control or cut off. However, in most cases the single unit is spontaneous only in respect to the supersystem "organism," i.e., the experimenter does not apply any controlled stimulation to the animal he records from.

B. Methodology

For some the most unique characteristic of ethology is the method of studying the organism in its natural environment. The saying has been attributed to Niko Tinbergen that the psychologist cages an animal in his laboratory to watch it, while the ethologist cages himself in the field to watch the animal. Along the same line one can compare a psychologist in a white laboratory coat feeding bananas to a chimpanzee with Jane Goodall in khaki being fed bananas by a chimpanzee. Considering his method from a general-systems analysis viewpoint, the ethologist attempts to minimize the change of behavior of the animal inflicted by the process of investigation. In contrast the psychologist's method is to restrict the animal to the point where it has left but only a few or one parameter to express its response. By serendipity psychologists found some highly specialized situations in the life of certain animals where even under natural conditions the set of essentials is limited (e.g., maze learning in rats, learning to peck for food in pigeons), but fail to realize why other animal species, subjected to the same experimental treatment perform poorly in comparison. In their frustration, they turn their back on the comparative approach. The ethologist, on the other hand, is faced with the problem of keeping track of a multitude of behavioral parameters not only of the individual under study but also of its environment and conspecifics. Faced with the permanent dilemma of having piles of data which too often are still not plentiful enough to yield statistically significant results, the ethologist then resorts to anecdotal descriptions. The *Gestaltwahrnehmung* used as a scientific tool (Lorenz, 1959) can effectively help the investigator from drowning in irrelevant data, but inherently brings the danger of amplifying preconceptions and biases. The ability to assess one's own *Gestaltwahrnehmung* becomes essential to the ethologist.

2. WILD ANIMALS IN CAPTIVITY

Keeping wild research animals under seminatural conditions in outdoor pens or in "luxury apartment"-type cages is a method of great importance in ethology (Hediger, 1950). It is consistent with the method of minimizing disturbances of the animal in the process of investigation (Section I,B,1), and complements it in the sense that the extent of disturbance in the more artificial situation can be estimated by comparison with the natural situation. Furthermore, the behavior of many animals is adapted so perfectly to the normal natural environment of the species, that it is hard for the observer *not* to interpret the behavior as controlled by insight. Yet under seminatural conditions the automatic nature of an action or of a response can become apparent. For example, the dusting or bathing of a bird in its natural environment looks well adapted, but when the identical sequences occur in naive, hand-reared individuals in the absence of sand or water, the first thought of the equally naive observer is that the poor animal is having an epileptic seizure. If the observer now introduces a pan with fine sand or water, depending on the requirements of the particular species, the adaptedness of this "seizure" becomes apparent. A maximum of insight into the causation and control of behavior can be gained by studying a species in both the natural environment and captivity in a concurrent or alternating research program. This is especially true if the investigator is able to extract the essential environmental conditions and substitute them in the artificial setting to a degree that the differences in behavior between wild and captive disappear. Keeping a species in captivity also has the advantage that the investigator can familiarize himself with the behavioral repertoire and observe details at close range which in the field, viewed through binoculars, might escape his attention.

Additional insight can be gained when a few individuals of the species under investigation are raised from an early age by the experimenter. An extremely time-consuming endeavour, when conscientiously done, it yields a wealth of information unobtainable in any other way. The young of some species, if separated from the mother early enough, accept the human as a parent substitute ("imprinting," Section II,B,2), and in some cases maintain this fixation for the rest of their life. Young, when raised in groups of equal age usually become "imprinted" on each other. These animals are more independent of the human guardian, and more likely to grow to be completely normal adults, while singles may later be indifferent to conspecifics, direct all sexual desires toward humans and so be unable to reproduce. Rearing individuals in seminatural conditions, which in fact is nearly always a "deprivation experiment" can be used to find out to what degree a particular behavior or a specific "releasing mechanism" (Section II,B,1) is "environment-resistant" (SectionI,A,2). It is essential for interpretable results to deprive the animal of only one or a few environmental parameters. Massive deprivation as of all visual input, of all tactile input, or all social contact usually leads to massive behavioral deficiencies and often gross morphological changes (for a more detailed discussion of the use of deprivation experiments, see Lorenz, 1965; Schleidt, 1964b).

3. THE ETHOGRAM

Behavior of one particular species is not indefinitely variable, but is characterized by the more or less frequent recurrence of certain behavioral elements, especially in the realm of locomotion, feeding, and communication. It is customary to start the study of a new species with an attempt to list and describe the basic behavioral elements in an "ethogram." In addition, the appropriate stimulus for elicitation is listed, and sometimes even the transitional probabilities from one element to others are given in tables or diagrams. The main advantages of listing the ethogram is that ambiguities in nomenclature are reduced within the record, and if the individual acts are named in accordance with established precedences in closely related species, it facilitates the comparison of different taxonomic groups. The classical case of an ethogram is Lorenz' list of the behavior patterns of ducks (1941, 1971), as part of such a comparative study. Ethograms of many other species have been compiled and published since; a few examples must suffice: fish (Morris, 1958; Myrberg, 1973; Wiepkema, 1961), chicken (Baeumer, 1955, 1959, 1962) and other domesticated animals (Hafez, 1969), rodents (Eibl-Eibesfeldt, 1951, 1953, 1955, 1958; Eisenberg, 1962, 1963), and rhesus monkey (Altmann, 1962, 1965, 1968; Hinde & Rowell, 1962). Table I and Fig.1 illustrate the basic principles of compiling such data.

C. History

Ethology developed as a natural science, in essence exploiting the implications of Darwin's concept of *natural selection* for the study of the behavior

124

WOLFGANG M. SCHLEIDT

TABLE I.

BEHAVIOR PATTERNS OF THE RHESUS MONKEY[a, b]

k	Behavior pattern	p(k)	Rank
41	Walks toward	0.1553	1
43	Walks away from	0.1128	2
51	Grooms	0.0937	3
50	Presents for grooming	0.0814	4
3	Grasps waist of	0.0478	5
4	Grips legs of	0.0387	6
9	Dismounts	0.0370	7
2	Presents sexually to	0.0369	8
5	Gives pelvic thrust to	0.0330	9
25	Plays with	0.0300	10
19	Suckles from	0.0207	11
45	Follows	0.0191	12
99	Stops doing preceeding action	0.0178	13
54	Ignores	0.0173	14
44	Runs away from	0.0167	15
38	Grimaces toward	0.0143	16
27	Hits	0.0140	17
18	Suckles	0.0125	18
24	"Ik,ik,ik. . ." + spasm	0.0107	19
42	Runs toward; chases	0.0105	20
33	Looks at	0.0104	21
26	Bites	0.0084	22
46	Walks past	0.0084	23
13	Clings to	0.0078	24
73	Open-jawed gesture + stares at	0.0076	25
29	"!Ho!"	0.0073	26
36	"Eee"	0.0073	27
53	Eats or drinks	0.0073	28
32	Stares at	0.0058	29
12	Gives ventral embrace gesture to	0.0054	30

[a] After Altmann (1962, 1965).

[b] For the thirty most frequent behavior patterns the code number (k), the relative frequency [p(k)], and the rank, based on the relative frequency in a sample of 5507 events, are given. Note that this repertoire, because it was designed for a study of communication processes, some acts were subdivided on the basis of their orientation, e.g., "walking," in walks toward, walks away from, and walks past, while others could have been split further, e.g., "eats or drinks," and "runs toward; chases." See also Fig. 1.

of animals and men. The term ethology ($\bar{e}thos$ = custom, habit) was in use as a synonym for the study of animal behavior since the beginning of this century (e.g., as subject heading in the Zoological Record 1907–1940, or in the title of papers by Heinroth, 1911). In the 1950's it became a synonym

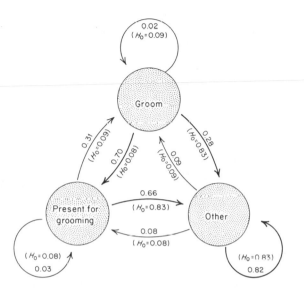

FIG. 1. Transition probabilities for grooming, presentation for grooming, and the sum of all other behavior patterns of rhesus monkeys, from a sample of 5507 events, each consisting of an interaction between two individuals. The thickness of the arrows is proportional to the probabilities that they represent (from Altmann, 1965); compare with Table I.

for Lorenz–Tinbergen-type studies, with emphasis on environmental-resistant behavior. K. Lorenz, who is considered to be the founder of modern ethology was, in his early publication (1932, 1935) quite parsimonious with explanatory principles. Indeed, he gave a broad consideration to the role of learning. The subsequent attacks from vitalists, behaviorists, and purposively and epigenetically oriented psychologists forced Lorenz to defend and clarify his view especially on the concept of innate behavior characteristics (1937, 1965; Section I,A,2). Because of this clarification some of his critics considered Lorenz as a proponent of *instinct,* although he himself has taken a decisive step to abolish the concept, and has put forth instead a set of testable working hypotheses (1937; Section II). N. Tinbergen and his school played an important role in the further development of ethological concepts such as displacement activity and hierarchical organization of behaviors and in the design of new research strategies. Tinbergen's book "The Study of Instinct" (1951) was the first attempt to review the field of ethology and was at the same time an influential introduction of ethology to the English-speaking world. Though now outdated in some respects it has become a classic. Several textbooks with different emphasis provide up-to-date reviews of the extensive literature (Eibl-Eibesfeldt, 1970; Hinde, 1966; Klopfer & Hailman, 1967; Marler & Hamilton, 1966; all available in new, updated and expanded editions; the most important papers of Lorenz are available in an authorized translation [1970, 1971]).

II. BASIC CONCEPTS OF ETHOLOGY

In earlier attempts to describe the behavioral output of an animal in an analytic way, the concept of the reflex has played a central role as the elementary unit with the monosynaptic spinal reflex as prototype and the patellar reflex as textbook example. The obvious shortcoming of this attempt is that the reflex (*reflectare* = to flex back), by implication requires a stimulus for its elicitation. However, as it has been shown in many cases, behavior often occurs spontaneously (Section I,A,3) and, furthermore, its elementary units are usually more complex than reflexes. Lorenz (1937) therefore suggested calling such behavior units "fixed action pattern" (in German originally *Triebhandlung, Instinkthandlung,* and since the 1940's *Erbkoordination*). He hypothesized that each fixed action pattern (FAP) is represented within the central nervous system as some kind of "motor coordination center" (*motorische Koordinationsinstanz,* Schleidt, 1962) with the basic properties of a relaxation oscillator ("flush-toilet model," Lorenz, 1950). According to this hypotheses the occurrence of a particular behavioral act depends upon the internal state of this oscillator, and in addition on its excitatory and inhibitory inputs from the afferent system and from the interconnected motor coordination centers of other FAP's (Fig. 2). In terms of general systems theory, the reflexologist treats the animal as a *passive* system, while Lorenz requires that it must be treated as an *active*

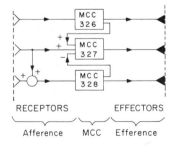

Fig. 2. Schematic representation of several motor coordination centers (MCC; numbering arbitrary), as central elements of integration of afference and efference; open triangle: receptor; filled triangle: effector; black dot: branching point; circle: junction point; +: excitatory influence; —: inhibitory influence; arrow points in direction of flow of information or control (see also Figs. 3 and 4).

system. In the analysis of the circuitry of the "black box" (the animal) the action specific motor coordination center is the most important junction of the whole system. Here at this center all controlling influxes converge and from there excitation radiates out to all the effectors which take part in the specific act (Fig. 3). I hasten to say that the term "center" refers only to the circuit diagram and does not imply that within the animal it can be traced to a specific morphological structure or location such as nucleus, cluster of neurons, or single cell. The correspondence between functional and morphological entities can be worked out only by detailed behavioral, neurophysiological, and neuroanatomic studies of the individual case.

For the purpose of discussion the system can be divided into an afferent and efferent branch with the motor coordination center as nodal point having additional influxes from within the same level. We shall not be too concerned about a certain degree of artificiality in this schema, which becomes apparent when we have to consider feedback loops within the branches, or cross connections which might by-pass the nodal point.

A. Efference: What Animals Do

1. The Fixed Action Pattern

According to the definition which was agreed upon in the only conference on ethological nomenclature and was reported by Thorpe (1951), a fixed action pattern is "an inherited relatively complex movement pattern within instinctive behavior, which is a characteristic of the species or group as are

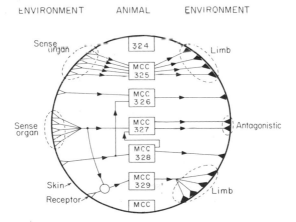

Fig. 3. Schematic representation of various forms of internal connections between inputs and outputs of an animal. For the explanation of symbols see Fig. 2 caption.

structural features. The intensity of the discharge may vary, but its form is little, if at all, modifiable by external stimuli." This wording is awkward, lacks precision, and has some antiquated concepts. However, here is not the place to change definitions but to report them, and it must suffice to point out some of their weaknesses: "an inherited . . . movement pattern" is an outmoded definition referring to the fact that the phenotypic expression of the behavioral parameters of the act is environment-resistant. The stereotypy of such acts, the "fixedness" of the fixed action pattern, is not considered in the definition, but has become an important diagnostic characteristic (Schleidt, 1971). Also, the role of the stimulus in the elicitation and orientation of the performance of the act is inadequately expressed.

Lorenz and Tinbergen (1938) and Tinbergen and Kuenen (1939) have investigated the stimulus control of fixed action patterns and succeeded in experimentally separating the effects of triggering and orienting stimuli (*auslösende und steuernde Reize*). In some cases it is possible to trigger an act with a brief stimulus, but then deprive the animal of further stimulation so that the act's continuation depends solely on the endogenous coordination. The resulting act is a "pure" fixed action pattern, whereas under natural conditions the continued stimulation controls the orientation of the act (its "taxis-component,"). The natural setting provides for flexibility of the act by means of a feedback loop, but also adds to the statistical variability. Thus, the taxis-component makes the behavior more adaptable to the specific situation and decreases its stereotypy. The classical example for the separation of a fixed action pattern and its taxis component is the egg-rolling act of the greylag goose. Egg-rolling is triggered by the visual cues of an egg outside the nest. Once the act has been started, tactile stimulation from contact with the egg, received by receptors on the lower beak, controls the proper orientation as the egg is pushed into the nest. If the movement has started and then the egg is suddenly removed, the goose continues to pull its beak back toward the nest in nearly identical fashion, but without the sideways balancing movement.

I must point out that egg-rolling has to my knowledge never been seen to occur spontaneously, i.e., in the absence of a triggering stimulus. This is not surprising however since spontaneity is found mostly in behavior acts which occur relatively often under normal conditions in the natural environment. Rarely observed acts will obviously have a very low absolute rate of spontaneous occurrence. The case in point, egg-rolling, may be done by the female goose normally less than once a year. However, the greylag goose frequently pulls grass which is its particular way of feeding. If a bird is deprived of a lawn it goes through the act of pulling grass on an inadequate object, such as a carpet or even a bare floor. The empirical finding that often performed acts are more likely to occur spontaneously than rare ones can be interpreted as result of the time constant of the action specific relaxation oscillator, i.e., the speed with which the "action specific potential" is restored (Section II,B,1).

2. APPETITES AND AVERSIONS

A mobile animal does not have to lie in wait for stimulation, but usually seeks actively for the object which provides the adequate stimulus and quiets the urge. Even a predator specialized to ambush its prey seeks a hiding place first. Human observers have long been puzzled by this and have offered an array of explanatory concepts. These concepts range widely. Bierens de Haan (1940) proposed "the" instinct as a universal vitalistic principle, one with a rather magical aspect. Others have set forth a family of instincts or drives with one for each vital function such as hunger, thirst, sexual desire and aggression (see, e.g., McDougall, 1923), or for assumed "goals" (Tolman, 1932). There have also been proposed very specific "appetites," for example a hunger for salt, controlled by internal homeostasis (Richter, 1927, 1954).

The concept which has been most influential in ethology is that of "appetitive behavior," introduced by Craig (1918), and supported by Lorenz (1935, 1937). The idea is that behavior is organized in sequences of acts, each sequence leading through a variable set of elements, the "appetitive behavior," toward a terminal and highly stereotyped "consummatory action." The latter is now usually called the consummatory act. What "makes the animal run" is an endogenous urge to seek the stimulus situation in which it can perform the consummatory act. On its way toward this goal the animal can freely use as vehicle or as tool whatever behavior might be suitable to reach it. This behavior might be an act of locomotion, of aggression, of courtship, and the like. In terms of the relaxation oscillator hypothesis, this implies that the action specific potential of the consummatory act, as it is raised by some internal pacemaker or by a deficiency or superabundance of a chemical (blood sugar, hormone, etc.) in the internal milieu, activates various other acts. If these other acts are performed, they raise the probability that the adequate stimulus situation for the elicitation of the consummatory act is found. When the animal finally reaches this situation, the doing of the consummatory act discharges its action specific potential and the appetitive behavior ceases. If, however, the action specific potential of the consummatory act reaches threshold *before* the adequate stimulus situation is attained, the consummatory act occurs spontaneously, *in vaccuo,* and the appetitive behavior is terminated as well.

The extent to which consummatory acts dominate appetitive acts apparently varies from case to case. I mentioned above that commonly performed acts apparently are more likely to occur spontaneously, and this applies to acts which are under normal conditions, elements of an appetitive sequence as well. This is well illustrated by the case of predatory mammals of the plains, who pace endlessly when closely restrained, and in extreme cases develop "cage stereotypies" (Holzapfel, 1938). In the cat, various elements of the prey-catching behavior sequence of clearly appetitive character have been shown to be individually extinguishable and relatively independent of the consummatory act of eating the prey (Leyhausen, 1965).

Craig's original concept included the supplementary term of "aversive" behavior, in the sense of an active avoidance of certain stimulus situations. Since under normal circumstances and in a natural environment a stimulus–free situation is unlikely to occur, it is difficult and most likely futile to decide whether an animal is seeking one type of stimulus situation or actually only tries to avoid all the others. This becomes evident in the cases where the animal shows appetitive behavior leading to resting or sleeping (Meyer-Holzapfel, 1940). Similarly, Schneirla's concept of approach and avoidance as depending on the strength of the stimulus (1959) offers a framework to systematize behavior, but lacks explanatory power.

B. Afference: What Animals Respond To

1. RELEASING MECHANISM AND SOCIAL RELEASER

The matching pair of terms "releasing mechanism" and "social releaser" (Lorenz, 1935), has often confused an outsider because of their similarity. Therefore, I shall sketch their meaning first, and postpone their detailed discussion. The process of communication between two organisms can be described in terms of a message emitted by a transmitter in the form of a signal. This signal is detected by a receiver, who decodes the signal and reconstructs the message (Lorenz, 1943; Shannon & Weaver, 1949). The *social releaser* is the transmitting structure, e.g., a spot of color which is made conspicuous by means of a particular movement, or the conspicuous movement itself. The *releasing mechanism* is the decoding device of the receiving animal, often represented as a filter which selects the relevant signal from a variety of stimuli, rejects irrelevant noise, and conducts the message to its destination, e.g., a specific motor coordination center. There it can trigger a fixed action pattern, which itself in turn might constitute a social releaser as well as a reply to the received message (Fig. 4).

Any communication link in which a message is encoded by the transmitter into a signal and decoded by the receiver requires that both share the same code. Applied to our ethological concepts, this means that social releasers of the transmitter and the releasing mechanisms of the receiver must be adapted to each other for each individual signal type, so as to obtain a

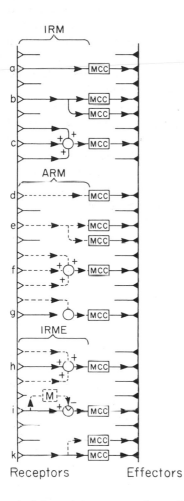

a) simple connection between stimulus and response is environment resistant;

b) connection between one stimulus type and two response types is environment resistant;

c) connection between three stimulus types and one response type is environment resistant;

d) simple connection between stimulus and response is established by a learning process;

e) connection between one stimulus type and two response types is established by a learning process;

f) connection between three stimulus types and one response type is established by a learning process; in case of gestalt perception, a multiplicative (rather than additive) computation of stimuli is likely;

g) connection between stimulus and response was originally established by means of an IRM, but was substituted by another connection on the basis of a learning process; in the final state, the IRM has ceased to function (e.g., in the case of imprinting);

h) extension of an IRM by a learning process; connection with additional stimuli (e.g., in the case of conditioning);

i) restriction of the range of an IRM by a habituation process; a stimulus, originally effective, has ceased to elicit a response;

k) extension of an IRM by a learning process; connection with additional response (e.g., in the case of shaping an operant response).

FIG. 4. Schematic representation of various examples of "innate" releasing mechanisms (IRM), "acquired" releasing mechanisms (ARM), and IRM's modified by experience (IRME). M: memory unit; solid lines: environment resistant connections; dotted lines: environment dependant connections; for the explanation of other symbols see Fig. 2 caption (after Schleidt, 1962).

sufficiently high signal-to-noise ratio and a low probablity of confusing different signal types. This requirement explains the high degree of sterotypy in displays, which serve as social releasers, and the high degree of selectivity of certain releasing mechanisms found empirically. However, one must keep in mind that natural selection works not only on such communication links, but on all the other vital properties of the species, and must lead to a theoretically perfect optimization of all requirements, but not necessarily to a perfect technical solution in the individual case. Releasers which are striking and highly efficient signals are also conspicuous for the predator. Releasing mechanisms which function in analogy to a wave filter need not work as band pass filters but can act as a high pass filter, if in the effective range other signals do not occur and ambient noise is negligible under natural conditions. This suggests the possibility of "super-normal" stimuli in the experimental situation. Indeed one can find artificial stimuli more effective than the stimuli emitted by "the real thing," the natural releaser (Lorenz, 1943). A comprehensive and well illustrated review of examples for social releasers is contained in Eible-Eibesfeldt's textbook (1970).

Releasing mechanisms are not restricted to communication links between conspecifics, but can be abstracted in any behavioral system in which a set of stimulus parameters elicite a certain response or set of responses. Environment-resistant releasing mechanisms also called Innate Releasing Mechanisms or "IRM's" (Lorenz, 1935, 1943; Schleidt, 1962) are found especially in cases in which the individual animal is required to give a prompt response, before it has had time to learn anything about the stimuli which elicit it. Thus a neonate mammal already knows, so to speak, what stimuli to follow in order to obtain milk, or a newly hatched bird with no experience of deadly predators does not have to learn what stimuli to avoid.

Cases in which an environment-resistant releasing mechanism acts on an environment-resistant fixed action pattern are especially suitable objects for experimentation and quantitative studies. Here a brief review of results most relevant for problems of perception will be given. Signals of different types of modality that can elicit the same response are usually called "key stimuli" by ethologists. When such signals are received simultaneously, their effects combine in approximately additive fashion in what has been termed "heterogeneous summation," (Seitz, 1940). The strength of the observable response depends not only on the type and strength of the signal, but on a gamut of internal parameters. The state of the action specific potential at the time the signal arrives is of importance, in the sense that immediately after a specific act has occurred the animal is refractory to further stimulation for a short time span. Recovery then follows and is proportional to the time allowed for recovery. The degree of recovery can be expressed by an increased readiness to respond or by a measure of response strength. This has led to the necessity for controlling stimulus strength *and* internal readiness to respond in order to obtain a predictable response strength. Since there are two degrees of freedom, the necessity therefore consists in "dual quantification" (Lorenz, 1950). In addition, habituation (and sensitization?) specific to individual signal types or to their stimulus parameters was found to influence the responsiveness of the animal ("threefold quantification," Hinde, 1954; Prechtl, 1953; M. Schleidt, 1954), as well as the general motivational state of the animal (Baerends, Brower, & Waterbolk, 1955). Sensory adaptation also can influence the results (W. M. Schleidt, unpublished).

In the introduction to Section II, I have emphasized that the term motor coordination center designates a part of a system, but not a specific morphological structure, and the same applies to the term "releasing mechanism." The properties of a specific releasing mechanism are the composite result of all structures involved. These structures include all afferent structures, beginning with appendices to the sense organs (e.g., eye lid, ear pinna) and up to the input of the motor coordination centers. In some cases, the essential filter properties of a releasing mechanism are built into the sense organ (e.g., Lettvin, Maturana, Pitts, & McCulloch, 1961, and the subsequent literature on visual fields; Capranica, 1965). However, in general we must expect that the sense organs are designed to handle a relatively wide range of intensity and spectral and temporal parameters, and that the essential filter properties are the result of special circuits within the central nervous system (Schleidt, 1962, 1964b).

2. IMPRINTING

Learning processes can supplement environment-resistant behavior in various ways. A very special type of learning is imprinting. It has captured the attention of ethologists since it was described by Lorenz (1931, 1935). The most essential features of imprinting are: (a) during the "critical period," a relatively short time span that is apparently programmed into the life of the individual animal; (b) without any apparent reinforcement the animal learns a response to a set of general features of a certain object; and (c) later in life responds with some specific behavior only to objects that have the same general features as the original object to which it was "imprinted."

The classical case is sexual imprinting in ducks and geese, where male animals choose at sexual maturity a mate of the same kind (species) as that with which they were raised as young. The phenomenon of imprinting is apparently found in many species. There is a large literature on experimental investigations and reports of new examples (e.g., Hess, 1959; Immelmann, 1965; Schutz, 1965; Sluckin, 1965).

C. The Internal Organization

From the viewpoint of general systems analysis, an animal is an open system with many inputs and outputs. The study of the relations between inputs and outputs should reveal the internal organization of the system, and allow us to represent it as a flow diagram of information or control. The major difficulty is the multitude of internal connections, because "everything is connected to everything" (Goldschmidt, 1954). The standard method to overcome it is to keep all but one input constant and then trace a signal through the hypothetical flow diagram to some output. In tedious permutations of this method the flow-diagram is gradually improved.

One of the general principles of internal organization, that a sequence of appetitive behavioral acts leads to the occurrence of a consummatory act, had been discussed already in Section II,A,2. Tinbergen (1951) elaborated on this principle and tried to cast it into an overall hierarchically organized system.

Another principle which has been rejected and then reintroduced many times postulates the existence of a few basic drives, motivations, or moods (for an excellent, critical discussion of these concepts, see Hinde, 1959). By means of factor analysis the existence of a few governing factors which correspond well to the basic drives of sex, aggression, and fear can be shown (Wiepkema, 1961), but it remains unclear how these factors act on individual behavior patterns. As a working hypothesis, I propose equating them with hormonal control.

One interesting phenomenon which might prove useful in elucidating some details of the internal organization is the occurrence of "displacement activities." The concept was introduced by Lorenz and Tinbergen (1938), and reviewed by Tinbergen (1940). Displacement activity refers to the phenomenon that within a sequence of behavior there is suddenly substituted a fixed action pattern from another sequence or appropriate in another context. This can happen especially if the original sequence is interrupted by interference either external or internal. Which behavior is substituted varies from species to species and with the behavioral context, but in general it is an act which (1) occurs relatively frequently in a species, and (2) involves often the same organs, the same "common final pathway" of the inhibited behavior. As an example, two rooster facing each other in an even fight, tail up and head down, eye to eye, ready to attack, can start vigorously to peck at nonexisting grain on the floor. Pecking at food is substituted for aggressive pecking at the opponent.

III. AN ETHOLOGICAL APPROACH TO THE STUDY OF PERCEPTION

There is a wide range of overlap between ethology and the psychological system-oriented study of perception, and each field can profit from the techniques, concepts, and mistakes of the other. Two aspects of ethology that might advance the understanding of perceptual mechanisms considerably deserve a brief discussion. These are the comparative study of closely related species, and the concept of releasing mechanisms.

In studies of perceptual systems and their mechanisms, emphasis is placed on discovering the basic principles, with relatively little concern for species differences, except on a rather coarse taxonomic scale. Thus the avian eye is contrasted with the mammalian eye or, more accurately, the pigeon's eye with the cat's eye. One of the few examples in which a variety of more or less closely related species were systematically investigated is Winter's (1963) study of the auditory pathways, revealing highly significant differences in cell counts of certain nuclei within this group, with extremely high values in owls. Since natural selection has no inherent purpose of creating the best of all eyes, ears, etc., but apparently works in a way in which each species has the eye, ear, etc., it needs to survive, we might discover striking differences in design or function of sense organs and sensory mechanisms, even between closely related species, if we look for them.

The concept of releasing mechanism might help not only to explain such differences, but could lead to a better understanding of the sensory mechanisms of our standard laboratory animals, and help to design more sensible experiments or to ask deeper questions. There is no reason to be apologetic about using clicks as auditory test stimuli in research on cats or rats, because such stimuli play a vital role in their natural environment to detect prey or escape from a predator. But to a bird's ear they might sound artificial indeed. Yet trains of extremely fast frequency sweeps over a range of one octave in 10 msec, might be just right as a powerful natural stimulus for a bird, because in bird songs we can find frequency modulations at that rate.

References

Altmann, S. A. A field study of the sociobiology of rhesus monkeys, *Macaca mulatta. Annals New York Academy of Sciences,* 1962, **102**, Art. 2, 338–435.

Altmann, S. A. Sociobiology of rhesus monkeys. II. Stochastics of social communication. *Journal of Theoretical Biology,* 1965, **8**, 490–522.

Altmann, S. A. Sociobiology of rhesus monkeys. III. Basic communication networks. *Behaviour,* 1968, **32**, 17–32.

Baerends, G. P., Brower, R., & Waterbolk, H. T. Ethological studies on *Lebistes reticulatus* Peter. I. Analysis of the male courtship pattern. *Behaviour,* 1955, **8**, 249–334.

Baeumer, E. Lebensart des Haushuhns. *Zeitschrift für Tierpsychologie,* 1955, **12**, 387–401.

Baeumer, E. Verhaltensstudie über das Haushuhn, -dessen Lebensart. 2. Teil. *Zeitschrift für Tierpsychologie,* 1959, **16**, 284–296.

Baeumer, E. Lebensart des Haushuhns. 3. Teil. Über seine Laute und allgemeine Ergänzungen. *Zeitschrift für Tierpsychologie,* 1962, **19**, 394–416.

Bierens de Haan, J. A. *Die tierischen Instinkte und ihr Umbau durch Erfahrung.* Leiden: Brill, 1940.

Capranica, R. R. The evoked vocal response of the bull frog. *Massachusetts Institute of Technology Research Monographs,* 1965, **33**.

Craig, W. Appetites and aversions as constituents of instincts. *Biological Bulletin,* 1918, **34**, 91–107.

Eibl-Eibesfeldt, L. Gefangenschaftsbeobachtungen an der persischen Wüstenmaus (*Meriones persicus persicus* Blanford): Ein Beitrag zur vergleichenden Ethologie der Nager. *Zeitschrift für Tierpsychologie,* 1951, **8**, 400–423.

Eibl-Eibesfeldt, I. Zur Ethologie des Hamsters (*Cricetus cricetus* L.) *Zeitschrift für Tierpsychologie,* 1953, **10**, 204–254.

Eibl-Eibesfeldt, I. Angeborenes und Erworbenes im Nestbauverhalten der Wanderratte. *Naturwissenschaften,* 1955, **42**, 633–634.

Eibl-Eibesfeldt, I. Das Verhalten der Nagetiere. *Handbuch der Zoologie,* 1958, **8** (10/13), 1–88.

Eibl-Eibesfeldt, I. *Ethology, biology of behavior.* New York: Holt, 1970.

Eisenberg, J. Studies on the behavior of *Peromyscus maniculatus gambelii* and *Peromyscus californicus parasiticus. Behaviour,* 1962, **19**, 177–207.

Eisenberg, J. The behavior of heteromyid rodents. *University of California, Berkeley, Publications in Zoology,* 1963, **69**, 1–114.

Goldschmidt, R. Einführung in die Wissenschaft vom Leben-Ascaris. (3rd ed.) *Verständliche Wissenschaft,* 1954, **3–4**.

Hafez, E. S. *The behavior of domestic animals.* (2nd. Ed.) London: Baillière, 1969.

Hediger, H. *Wild animals in captivity.* London: Butterworth, 1950.

Heinroth, O. Beiträge zur Biologie, namentlich Ethologie und Psychologie der Anatiden. *Proceedings of the International Ornithological Congress, 5th, 1911,* 1911, pp. 589–702.

Hess, E. H. Imprinting, an effect of early experience. *Science,* 1959, **130**, 133–141.

Hinde, R. A. Factors governing the changes in strength of a partially inborn response, as shown by the mobbing behavior of the chaffinch (*Fringilla coelebs*). II. The waning of the response. *Proceedings of the Royal Society, Series B,* 1954, **142**, 331–358.

Hinde, R. A. Unitary drives. *Animal Behaviour,* 1959, **7**, 130–141.

Hinde, R. A. *Animal behaviour.* New York: McGraw-Hill, 1966.

Hinde, R. A., & Rowell, T. E. Communication by postures and facial expressions in the rhesus monkey (*Macaca mulatta*). *Proceedings of the Zoological Society of London,* 1962, **138**, 1–21.

Holzapfel, M. Über Bewegungsstereotypien bei gehaltenen Säugern. I and II. *Zeitschrift für Tierpsychologie,* 1938, **2**, 46–72.

Immelmann, K. Prägungserscheinungen in der Gesangentwicklung junger Zebrafinken. *Naturwissenschaften,* 1965, **52**, 169–170.

Klopfer, P., & Hailman J. P. *An introduction to animal behavior.* Englewood Cliffs, New Jersey: Prentice Hall, 1967.

Lettvin, J. Y., Maturana, H. R., Pitts, W. H., & McCulloch, W. S. Two remarks on the visual system of the frog. In W. W. Rosenblith (Ed.), *Sensory communication.* New York: Wiley, 1961. pp. 757–776.

Leyhausen, P. Über die Funktion der relativen Stimmungshierarchie. *Zeitschrift für Tierpsychologie,* 1965, **22**, 412–494.

*Lorenz, K. Z. Beiträge zur Ethologie sozialer Corviden. *Journal für Ornithologie,* 1931, **79**, 67–127.

*Lorenz, K. Z. Betrachtungen über das Erkennen arteigener Triebhandlungen bei Vögeln. *Journal für Ornithologie,* 1932, **80**, 50–98.

*Lorenz, K. Z. Der Kumpan in der Umwelt des Vogels. *Journal für Ornithologie,* 1935, **83**, 137–413.

*Lorenz, K. Z. Über die Bildung des Instinktbegriffes. *Naturwissenschaften,* 1937, **25**, 289–300, 307–318, 325–331.

*Lorenz, K. Z. Vergleichende Bewegungsstudien an Anatinen. *Journal für Ornithologie,* 1941, **89**, 194–293.

*Lorenz, K. Z. Die angeborenen Formen möglicher Erfahrung. *Zeitschrift für Tierpsychologie,* 1943, **5**, 235–409.

*Lorenz, K. Z. The comparative method in studying innate behaviour patterns. *Symposia of the Society for Experimental Biology,* 1950, **4**, 221–268.

*Lorenz, K. Z. Gestaltwahrnehmung als Quelle wissenschaftlicher Erkenntnis. *Zeitschrift für experimentelle und angewandte Psychologie,* 1959, **6**, 118–165.

Lorenz, K. Z. *Evolution and modification of behavior.* Chicago, Illinois: Univ. of Chicago Press, 1965.

Lorenz, K. Z. *Studies in animal and human behavior.* Vol. I. Cambridge, Massachusetts: Harvard Univ. Press, 1970.

Lorenz, K. Z. *Studies in animal and human behavior.* Vol. II. Cambridge, Massachusetts: Harvard Univ. Press, 1971.

*Lorenz, K. Z., & Tinbergen, N. Taxis und Instinkthandlungen in der Eirollbewegung der Graugans. *Zeitschrift für Tierpsychologie,* 1938, **2**, 1–29.

McDougall, W. *An outline of psychology.* London: Methuen, 1923.

Marler, P. R., & Hamilton, W. J. *Mechanisms of animal behavior.* New York: Wiley, 1966.

Mayr, E. *Animal species and evolution.* Cambridge, Massachusetts: Harvard Univ. Press, 1963.

Meyer-Holzapfel, M. Triebbedingte Ruhezustände als Ziel von Appetenzverhalten. *Naturwissenschaften,* 1940, **28**, 273–280.

Morris, D. The reproductive behavior of the ten-spined stickleback (*Pygosteus pungitius* L.). *Behaviour, Supplement,* 1958, **6**, 1–154.

Myrberg, A. A., Jr. Ethology of the bicolor damselfish, *Eupomacentrus partitus* (Pisces, Pomacentridae). A comparative analysis of laboratory and field behavior. *Animal Behaviour Monographs,* 1973, in press.

Prechtl, H. F. R. Zur Physiologie der angeborenen auslösenden Mechanismen. I. Quantitative Untersuchungen über die Sperrbewegung junger Singvögel. *Behaviour,* 1953, **5**, 32–50.

Richter, C. P. Animal behavior and internal drives. *Quarterly Review of Biology,* 1927, **2**, 307–343.

Richter, C. P. Behavioral regulators of carbohydrate homeostasis. *Acta Neurovegetativa,* 1954, **9**, 247–259.

Schleidt, M. Untersuchungen über die Auslösung des Kollerns beim Truthahn. *Zeitschrift für Tierpsychologie,* 1954, **11**, 417–435.

Schleidt, W. M. Die historische Entwicklung der Begriffe "Angeborenes auslösendes Schema" und "Angeborener Auslösemechanismus." *Zeitschrift für Tierpsychologie,* 1962, **19**, 697–722.

* This paper was translated into English and is contained in Lorenz (1970, 1971).

Schleidt, W. M. Über die Spontanëität von Erbkoordinationen. *Zeitschrift für Tierpsychologie*, 1964, **21**, 235–256. (a)

Schleidt, W. M. Wirkungen äusserer Faktoren auf das Verhalten. *Fortschritte der Zoologie*, 1964, **16**, 469–499. (b)

Schleidt, W. M. How "fixed" is a fixed action pattern? *American Zoologist*, 1971, **11**, 620.

Schneirla, T. C. An evolutionary and developmental theory of diphasic processes underlying approach and withdrawal. In M. R. Dones (Ed.), *Nebraska symposium on motivation*. Lincoln: Univ. of Nebraska Press, 1959, pp. 1–41.

Schutz, F. Sexuelle Prägung bei Anatiden. *Zeitschrift für Tierpsychologie*, 1965, **22**, 50–103.

Seitz, A. Die Paarbildung bei einigen Zichliden. *Zeitschrift für Tierpsychologie*, 1940, **4**, 40–84.

Shannon, C. E., & Weaver, W. *The mathematical theory of communication*. Urbana: Univ. of Illinois Press, 1949.

Skinner, B. F. *The behavior of organisms*. New York: Appleton, 1938.

Sluckin, W. *Imprinting and early learning*. Chicago, Illinois: Aldine, 1965.

Thorpe, W. H. The definition of some terms used in animal behavior studies. *Animal Behaviour Bulletin*, 1951, **9**, 34–49.

Tinbergen, N. Die Übersprungbewegung. *Zeitschrift für Tierpsychologie*, 1940, **4**, 1–40.

Tinbergen, N. *The study of instinct*. London and New York: Oxford Univ. Press, 1951.

Tinbergen, N., & Kuenen, D. J. Über die auslösenden und richtung-gebenden Reizsituationen der Sperrbewegung von jungen Drosseln (*Turdus m. merula L.* und *T. e. ericetorum* TURTON), *Zeitschrift für Tierpsychologie*, 1939, **3**, 37–60.

Tolman, E. C. *Purposive behavior in animals and men*. New York: Appleton, 1932.

Wiepkema, P. R. An ethological analysis of the reproductive behavior of the bitterling (*Rhodeus amarus* Bloch). *Archives Neerlandaises de Zoologie*, 1961, **14**, 103–199.

Winter, P. Vergleichende qualitative und quantitative Untersuchungen an der Hörbahn von Vögel. *Zeitschrift für Morphologie und Oekologie der Tiere*, 1963, **52**, 365–400.

Chapter 7

GENETIC CONTROL

KARLA BUTLER THOMAS

I. OBJECTIVES AND METHODS OF BEHAVIOR-GENETIC ANALYSIS

In 1951, Hall described four objectives of an area which he termed *psychogenetics* or the genetics of behavior. These objectives were, "(1) to discover whether a given behavior pattern is transmitted from generation to generation, (2) to determine the number and nature of the genetic factors involved in the trait, (3) to locate the gene or genes on the chromosomes, and (4) to determine the manner in which the genes act to produce the trait" (Hall, 1951, p. 304).

Twenty years later, Hall's science of psychogenetics has been renamed *behavior(al) genetics* (Fuller & Thompson, 1960; Manosevitz, Lindzey, & Thiessen, 1969) or *behavior-genetic analysis* (Hirsch, 1967a). A growing number of investigators have made attempts to describe various behaviors according to Hall's objectives. This chapter summarizes the progress which has been made in the area of the genetics of variation in sensory and perceptual responses.

A. Dual Control of Behavior by Genes and Environment

Sensory and perceptual responses, like other observable characteristics (*phenotypes*), are controlled by both genetic and environmental factors. Therefore, Hall's first objective had to be revised because it implied that some behavior patterns might be genetically controlled while others might not. The difficulties inherent in such an "either-or" dichotomy have been spelled out by Lehrman (1970). Hall's first objective can be rephrased: to discover, within populations, the extent to which differences in behavior patterns can be accounted for by differences in genetic factors. In other words, we can ask what proportion of the total observed (phenotypic) variance is accounted for by the variance due to genetic differences in the population (Roberts, 1967).

With the possible exception of cytoplasmic or extranuclear inheritance (Jinks, 1964), the nuclear material (chromosomes, carrying the genes) is all that is transmitted genetically from one generation to the next. The term *genotype* refers to the hypothetical set of genes which distinguishes one animal from another within a population. If variation in only one gene produces the phenotypic difference, the system is *single-unit* or *Mendelian*. If several genes contribute to the phenotypic variation, the system is *polygenic*. In a broad sense, the ratio of the variance attributable to genotypes to the total phenotypic variance is a measure of *heritability* or, more precisely, *degree of genetic determination* of the differences observed within the population (Falconer, 1963).

Although phenotypic variation within a population can be described in terms of genetic and environmental components, there is no way to separate genetic and environmental influences during individual development. Within each cell the genetic material interacts with its environment. Environmental agents may, in fact, regulate gene action in conjunction with "regulator" genes (Moore, 1963, Chap. 22; Ptashne & Gilbert, 1970). The continuous interplay of environmental and genetic factors precludes identification of an "environmental zero point" in development. Therefore, the genetic control of sensory and perceptual capacities cannot be assessed by means of the classical deprivation experiment, in which newborn animals are deprived of certain stimuli and are tested at a later stage of development to determine whether or not the relevant sensory system functions as well as that of nondeprived animals. To the extent that such experiments are useful, they provide information about some of the stimulus requirements for a specific behavior. The best of these experiments

define the characteristics and timing of such stimulation; some of them
have been collected and discussed by McCleary (1970).

B. Genotypes as Variables in Animal Experiments

In most deprivation experiments, genes or genotypes are not manipu-
lated or controlled; genotype is rarely a *variable* of consideration. Just as
it is true that very little can be said about stimulus control of a response
in the absence of variation of the stimulus, little can be said about genetic
control in the absence of variation of the genotype. For this reason, experimental methods in behavior genetics involve the manipulation of
genotypes as well as manipulation or control of the environment.

Species, strain, and even individual comparisons all involve variation
in genotype. However, such comparisons are of limited value unless it
can be assumed that the environment affects all genotypes equally. If so,
then the main effects of strain, species, and individual differences may be
considered as due to genetic differences. But the assumption of equality
of environmental influence is hazardous (DeFries, 1967; Hirsch, 1967c)
and requires empirical justification for each comparison. Moreover, the
finding of unspecified genetic differences is relatively uninformative.

Breeding experiments are commonly employed in animal experimentation because they can provide information about genetic mechanisms. Inbred strains may be crossed in the classical Mendelian manner (described
in most introductory textbooks of genetics) and the distributions of the
phenotypes observed in various derived generations can be compared to
values predicted from classical or neoclassical single-gene or multiple-gene
models. Selective breeding experiments have also been employed with success in the study of sensory and perceptual capacities (Dobzhansky,
1967). For detailed descriptions of systems of mating and methods of
analysis of the results obtained from breeding experiments, see Mather
(1949), Falconer (1960), Burdette (1963), and Hirsch (1967a).

C. Human Behavior Genetics

Methods of analysis appropriate to human behavior genetics are discussed by Burdette (1962), Haseman and Elston (1970), Jinks and
Fulker (1970), and Vandenberg (1965). Human matings cannot be pre-
arranged for scientific purposes, so investigators must rely on analysis of
pedigrees and data obtained through studies of related and unrelated individuals. Especially useful are comparisons between monozygotic (genetically identical) and dizygotic (fraternal) twins. Bulmer (1970) has
summarized information about types of twins, the biology of twinning,
and research methods involving twins as subjects. McClearn (1963) and
Scarr (1968) have discussed environmental bias in twin studies.

D. Population Specificity of Genetic Statements

Statements about the genetic factors underlying phenotypic differences are relative to specific human and animal populations (Hirsch, 1967c), and since the gene pools of populations change over time,* statements about the mode of inheritance of behavioral differences are time-specific. Within these limits, it is sometimes possible to estimate the following characteristics: heritability, number of independently assorting genetic factors, dominance relationships among alleles (genes) at a single locus, and linkage relationships (Falconer, 1960, 1963; Hirsch, 1967b; Mather, 1949; Roberts, 1967).

E. Single-Gene Methods

A gross sensory or sensory-motor defect can often be traced to a single mutant allele which can be identified as being carried on a specific chromosome. (*Alleles* are alternate genes that can substitute for each other at the same chromosome locus.) Known mutant animals can be produced (Green, 1966), and their neural and morphological development, physiology, and biochemistry can be compared with that of non-mutant animals of the same species. Merrell (1965) has advocated that behavioral geneticists shift from the study of strain differences and strain crosses to the study of the effects of single genes on behavior. Such an approach would avoid the difficulties frequently encountered when quantitative methods are used. Merrell argues for the study of systematic substitutions of known single mutant alleles onto genetic backgrounds which can be randomized or held constant. Merrell's approach is probably most useful where more traditional behavior-genetic and physiological methods have provided information to guide the selection of appropriate single-gene substitutions (Collins, 1970, p. 108).

II. RESEARCH FINDINGS

A. Responses to Light and Visual Patterns

1. COLOR VISION*

Several types of color defect occur in humans who carry a mutant allele as a substitute for a normal gene. The two most common types of color

* For treatment of the statistical properties of populations undergoing change, see Malecót (1969) and Wright (1968, 1969).
* This discussion of human color deficiency depends heavily on reviews by Hsia and Graham (1965), Kalmus (1965), and Pickford (1964).

deficiency are the *protan* and *deutan* groups. Protans are sometimes described as red-blind and deutans as green-blind. The alleles associated with these two classes of color deficiency are carried on the X chromosome in humans; they are sex-linked, recessive genes. Males, who carry one X and one Y chromosome, are many times more likely to be affected than are females, who carry two X chromosomes. The possession of a defective X chromosome by a male is sufficient for expression of the color defect because the short Y chromosome lacks the site which could carry a normal allele. Affected women must possess two defective X chromosomes. Women who are heterozygotes, that is, who possess one normal and one defective X chromosome, may show slight deficiencies in making precise color matches, especially if the defective chromosome carries an allele of the protan type.

In both the protan and deutan defects, either of two mutant alleles can substitute for the normal gene. The alleles which produce the less severe forms of the defects (protanomaly and deuteranomaly) show dominance over those connected with the more severe forms (protanopia and deuteranopia). For example, a woman with one allele for protanopia and another for protanomaly ordinarily will be protanomalous in phenotype.

The genes associated with protan and deutan deficiencies probably reside at two separate loci on the X chromosome, although some geneticists believe that only one locus is involved. The two-locus hypothesis can be tested through identification of women who are double heterozygotes (who carry a protan allele on one X chromosome and a deutan allele on the other). Such women can produce protan or deutan sons. If the two-locus hypothesis is correct, these women also can produce normal sons through crossing-over of pieces of the X chromosomes. To date, only two families of this type have been located; Thuline, Hodgkin, Fraser, and Motulsky (1969) have reviewed the evidence for the two-locus hypothesis.

With respect to the biochemistry of color vision, Rushton (1962) concluded that protanopes lack the photopigment *erythrolabe* (red-grabber) and that deuteranopes lack the photopigment *chlorolabe* (green-grabber). Since genes control protein synthesis (Watson, 1965), it is probable that in each of these color defects the mutant allele fails to code for some protein, perhaps an enzyme, needed for normal functioning of the photopigment. The less severe defects, protanomaly and deuteranomaly, may be due to the presence of alleles which only partially fail to code for the relevant chemical substance, or which code for a different form of it.

Other varieties of color deficiency (e.g., tritanopia, rod monochromatism, cone monochromatism) occur even less frequently in human populations, and the genetic mechanisms relevant to them are less clearly formulated than are those pertaining to protan and deutan defects.

Within no species other than man has color vision been systematically studied with respect to genotype. Primate color vision has been reviewed by DeValois and Jacobs (1968). Carthy (1958, Chaps. 2 and 3) and Duke-Elder (1958) have provided extensive coverage of the structure and functions of invertebrate and vertebrate visual systems.

2. SENSITIVITY TO LIGHT

Except for some cave-dwelling and deep-sea animals, most animals respond to light. Marriott (1960) compared the light sensitivities of five phylogenetically distinct species and concluded that all have evolved quite efficient, though structurally different, systems for light detection.

But in certain individuals the system fails, and in some populations the incidence of individual failures is closely related to the incidence of mutant genes. In some human families, congenital stationary night-blindness, a reduced ability to see in dim illumination, may be transmitted as an autosomal (non–sex-linked) dominant or a sex-linked recessive factor (Kalmus, 1959). More severe forms of night-blindness and retinal dystrophy have been traced to genetic factors in dogs (Burns & Fraser, 1966), humans (François, 1961; Waardenburg, Franceschetti, & Klein, 1961), and rodents. The following two cases of retinal rod degeneration in rodents exemplify research directed toward discovery of the physiological pathway between the gene and the development of blindness.

In several strains of mice a single autosomal (non–sex-linked) recessive gene, *rd,* is associated with retinal degeneration. Adult *rd/rd* animals are almost if not completely blind. The rods begin to develop normally, but at about 10 days after birth, when the outer segments of the rods are just forming, degeneration begins. By 20 days of age, there is no photoreceptor layer on the retina (Sidman, Green, & Appel, 1965, p. 45).

In the RCS strain of rats, rod degeneration also is inherited as an autosomal recessive factor. In this case, however, the rods develop completely, as do the epithelial pigment cells. These epithelial pigment cells in normal animals function as scavengers of old photopigment disks which have been pushed to the ends of the rods by newly formed disks (Young, 1970). The epithelial cells of RCS rats fail to perform their function as scavengers, but the exact nature of this failure is unknown (Bok & Hall, 1971; Herron, Riegel, Myers, & Rubin, 1969). The behavioral phenotypes of *rd/rd* mice and RCS rats are similar to the syndromes observed in human cases of retinal degeneration, but just as the mechanisms leading to blindness differ in these two groups of animals, the human syndromes vary in etiology (François, 1961; Waardenburg *et al.,* 1961).

3. PHOTOTAXIS IN INSECTS

Populations of *Drosophila melanogaster* show variability in response to light. Individuals approach or withdraw from a light source (positive or negative phototaxis, respectively) or may show a neutral response. Using mechanical screening devices, Hirsch and Boudreau (1958) and Hadler (1964) selectively bred flies for positive and negative phototaxis; both concluded that more than half the phenotypic variance in their populations could be attributed to genetic variability. Single-gene analyses indicate that phototaxis in *Drosophila* is a complex behavior which may be interrupted by mutations at any of several genetic loci, each of which may specify a separate component of the total behavior. For example, the mutant alleles *tan* and *ebony* are associated with abnormal electroretinograms and nonphototactic or poor phototactic responses. Other mutant flies may, however, show normal electroretinograms yet behave nonphototactically (Hotta & Benzer, 1969).

4. RESPONSES TO STIMULUS PATTERNS AND COMPLEX VISUAL STIMULI

Only a few studies of responses to complex and patterned stimuli have employed genetic controls or comparisons among genotypes. A few workers have compared the responses of human twins to certain visual illusions such as the Müller-Lyer figure (Vandenberg, 1967). Vandenberg (1962) tested monozygotic (identical) twins and dizygotic (fraternal) twins on various cognitive-perceptual tasks, such as imbedded figures, gestalt completion, and perception of upright position. The scores were more similar for monozygotic than for dizygotic pairs. Osborne and Gregor (1966) found similar results on six tests of visual-spatial perception and reported that much of the total variance on a task of this type could be accounted for by genetic variation. If we can accept the assumption that environmental conditions are equivalent for different types of twins, the results obtained in the twin studies suggest that variation in human response to complex perceptual tasks is highly heritable in some populations.

B. Responses to Sound

1. SENSITIVITY TO DIFFERENT AUDITORY FREQUENCIES

Species differences in the capacity to respond to tones are well known. Dogs, cats, rats, and chimpanzees can hear tones above 20,000 Hz, which are ultrasonic for humans (Denny & Ratner, 1970, Ch. 3). Within species, individual differences also may be pronounced, but much of this variability could be developed following differential exposure to high-intensity sounds (Davis, 1951). However, Vandenberg's (1962) monozygotic twins showed closer similarity in audiograms than did dizygotic twins, a finding which suggests a relationship between genotype and auditory response in humans. Since monozygotic twins are more likely than dizygotic twins to share similar environments (Scarr, 1968), they may be more equally subject to the permanent or temporary deafening effects of intense sounds.

Intense high frequency sound also can induce fatal convulsions in young mice of the DBA strains. The genetics and physiological bases of such seizures have received much experimental attention (e.g., Collins, 1970; Fuller & Sjursen, 1967; MacInnes, Boggan, & Schlesinger, 1970).

2. CONGENITAL DEAFNESSES

Certain gross auditory defects are known to be linked with recessive genes in several mammals. For example, several breeds of dog carry a factor which produces "merled" or spotted coat color when present in single dose and white coat color in double dose; the white animals are usually deaf and blind (Burns & Fraser, 1966). A dominant mutant allele may produce the deafness which is usually observed in blue-eyed white cats (Bosher & Hallpike, 1965).

In mice, several different mutant alleles produce deafness, often in association with other neurological aberrations (Sidman et al., 1965). In two cases, the mutant animals show malformation of the embryonic neural tube; and the otic vesicle subsequently develops without normal inductive effects from the neural tube (Deol, 1964a, 1964b). Thus, a gene which acts early in development can indirectly affect structures which develop at later stages.

Another mutant gene, v^{df}, produces uncomplicated deafness in the mouse. Much of the basilar membrane of the cochlea degenerates post-natally. Although v^{df} is an allele of *waltzer* (the "dancing mouse" of Yerkes, 1907), animals of the v^{df}/v^{df} genotype show no disturbance of equilibrium and no vestibular degeneration (Sidman et al., 1965, p. 65).

Congenital deafness has also been described in humans, and a variety of genetic defects are associated with the syndrome; in other words, just as is the case in mice, several different defective alleles capable of affecting hearing may exist in human populations. For reviews of the role of genetic factors in human deafness, see Fraser (1964) and Brown (1969).

3. COMPLEX AUDITORY ABILITIES

The concepts of tone-deafness and absolute pitch are controversial on two counts: (*a*) do these extremes exist? (*b*) are they heritable within human populations? Neu (1947) presented the point of view that absolute pitch is a highly trained ability to discriminate among tones varying in frequency; according to this point of view, anyone should be able to develop absolute pitch. Even if this is true, some people apparently develop fine pitch discrimination more easily than others; and degrees of ability to learn to discriminate among pitches may well vary according to genotype (Vandenberg, 1962). On the other hand, some individuals seem to have great difficulty in mastering even simple pitch discriminations. Kalmus (1949) has suggested that this "tune deafness" may be related to a single dominant factor.

Development of complex auditory abilities is pronounced not only in humans but also in other species. Several studies point out the influence of differential auditory experience in the development and modification of the songs of various songbirds (Marler & Hamilton, 1966, pp. 684–702). Other vertebrates, notably the bats, have evolved systems of echolocation by which orientation to the environment and prey is facilitated by an ability to analyze the echoes of their own cries. Different families of bats have developed quite distinct types of echolocation (Moehres, 1960).

C. Responses to Chemical Stimuli

1. Sensitivity to the Taste of PTC

Phenylthiocarbamide (PTC) is a synthetic compound which tastes bitter to most people but has practically no taste at all to others. It is chemically related to naturally occurring substances which inhibit thyroid activity (Boyd, 1950). The frequency of insensitivity to PTC varies widely in human populations (Spuhler & Lindzey, 1967), but the precise estimation of incidence depends on the method of testing. Insensitivity to PTC is probably inherited as a single unit recessive character (Blakeslee, 1932; Snyder, 1932), but much variation still exists within groups classified as "tasters" and "nontasters" (Hoyme, 1955). Nonhuman primates also vary in PTC sensitivity: Fisher, Ford, and Huxley (1939) found that 26% of the chimpanzees they tested did not reject a sugar solution which contained 400 ppm PTC (a concentration which "tasters" reject). Fisher *et al.*, suggested that natural selection may have favored individuals who were heterozygotic for the PTC factor. If sensitivity to PTC is related to adaptive behavior in mammals, it may be related to avoidance of natural substances which have an antithyroid effect (Kalmus, 1959) or to general systemic reactivity (Kaplan, 1968).

2. Responses to other Gustatory Stimuli

Differences in sensitivity to and acceptance of other gustatory stimuli are also related to genetic differences within certain groups. In a short-term experiment, Nachman (1959) selectively bred rats for high and low saccharin preference. Strains of mice differ in preference thresholds for saccharin, acetic acid, sodium chloride, PTC (Hoshishima, Yokoyama, & Seto, 1962), and ethyl alcohol (Thomas, 1969). Preference for 10% ethyl alcohol solution varies with genotype in mice and rats, but recent estimates of heritability are relatively low (Whitney, McClearn, & DeFries, 1970). Fuller (1964) noted that estimates of dominance relationships among genes relevant to alcohol preference vary depending on the specific crosses which are tested. In the case of alcohol selection, the question arises as to whether or not acceptance of alcohol solutions is mediated by gustatory, olfactory, or common chemical sensitivity or by some combination of these, and whether or not mice of different genotypes employ the same sensory mechanisms for selecting or avoiding alcohol.

3. OLFACTION

Genetic determinants of differences in olfactory capacity essentially remain unstudied, mainly because of the difficulty of controlling olfactory stimuli. The olfactory capacity of some species, such as dogs, exceeds that of humans, but within the species some breeds develop more sensitivity than others (Neuhaus, 1957; Schnitzer, Fuller, & Schnitzer, 1962).

Genetic differences may determine some of the differences in olfactory sensitivity among humans. Some people may be insensitive to specific odors in a manner analogous to PTC insensitivity (Mainland, 1945). Moncrieff (1966) has demonstrated age and sex differences in human preferences for many odors; an unknown proportion of these differences is due to cultural and environmental differences.

D. Responses to Gravity

1. GEOTAXIS

The genetic determinants of individual differences in geotaxis (moving upward or downward in a multiple-choice chamber) have been studied in detail in *Drosophila melanogaster*. Hirsch and Erlenmeyer-Kimling (1962) assayed the influence on geotaxis of three of the four chromosomes of this species. Using a classical genetic technique, the use of "marker" genes on chromosomes (Hirsch, 1967b), these workers produced eight groups whose genotypes were known from the pattern of occurrence of the "markers" in the phenotypes. The genetically-defined groups were then tested for geotactic responses. The results indicated that variations in all three chromosomes were related to differences in geotaxis in these animals.

Beginning with a neutrally geotactic population of *Drosophila pseudoobscura,* Dobzhansky and Spassky (1962) also selected populations which differed in response to gravity and noted that positive and negative response to selection favored different chromosomal backgrounds. When selection pressure was relaxed, both selected groups reverted back to a nearly neutral response. Hostetter and Hirsch (1967) practiced reverse selection on animals drawn from *D. melanogaster* populations which had been previously selected for positive and negative geotaxis. Instead of simply relaxing selection pressure, they selected for the *opposite* geotactic response in each group. When they compared the reverse-selected animals with animals from the original (forward-selected) populations, Hostetter & Hirsch found that the groups were not genetically identical. Thus, similar phenotypes were found in animals which were genetically dissimilar.

The genetic determination of differences in geotaxis (orientation to an inclined plane) in rodents was studied by Crozier and Pincus (1929, 1931a, 1931b, 1932, 1936) and has been followed up by Lindzey and Thiessen (1970), who reported that their results best fit a two-factor model of genetic transmission.

2. Sense of Equilibrium

Many of the neurological mutants of mice (Sidman *et al.*, 1965) affect the vestibular system; the affected animals exhibit a variety of circling and head-shaking movements and may be unable to right themselves. For example, the otoliths are unilaterally or bilaterally absent in *muted* and *pallid* mice. Lindzey and Thiessen (1970) studied the role of the otoliths in geotaxis by testing mice possessing the *pallid* gene. This mutant allele modified but did not abolish the geotactic response to the inclined plane.

A possible interaction between the *pallid* gene and manganese metabolism is suggested by Erway, Hurley, and Fraser (1966), who were able to prevent the expression of postural defects in *pallid* mice by feeding their mothers a diet rich in manganese during pregnancy.

E. Other Sensory and Sensory-Motor Responses

A variety of other sensory and sensory-motor responses has been studied from a behavior-genetic point of view, but in most of these cases research has not been extensive. In humans, congenital insensitivity to pain is puzzling (Sternbach, 1963). In lower animals, the following behaviors require further investigation: differences in thermal sensitivity and positive thigmotaxis (wall-hugging) in rodents (Fuller & Thompson, 1960); differences in approach to imprinting stimuli in chicks (Graves & Siegel, 1968); and the general problems of differential stimulus determination of mate, food, and habitat selection (e.g., Connolly, Burnet, & Sewell, 1969; Haskins & Haskins, 1958; Waddington, Woolf, & Perry, 1954).

III. GENERAL CONCLUSIONS

The four objectives proposed by Hall (1951) were modeled after the traditional transmission genetics of Mendel, and much of the work in the genetics of sensory and perceptual differences has followed this pattern during the last 20 years.

Transmission from generation to generation. It is now recognized that there is no clear way to separate genetic and environmental influences within an individual, since the genes and the environment continually interact. But within specific populations significant genetic components have been reported for differences in such diverse behaviors as phototaxis in *Drosophila* species and responses to visual-spatial tests in humans.

Number and nature of genetic factors. The modes of inheritance of the protan and deutan color defects and of PTC insensitivity were already well researched before 1951. The number of factors and their dominance relationships are fairly well known today. Advances have been slower for responses which show continuous rather than discrete distributions of scores within populations. Most workers have been unable to determine the number and nature of relevant genes, even with the aid of quantitative genetic methods.

Mapping of the genes on the chromosomes. In mice, many mutant alleles producing sensory defects have been identified as being carried on specific chromosomes. In flies, it has been shown that a continuously distributed response, geotaxis, is mediated by factors on several chromosomes, and that phototaxis, also continuously distributed, can be interrupted by mutations at many different loci. Many complex behaviors gradually will yield to this type of single-gene analysis.

Manner in which the genes act to produce behavior. Identification of mutant alleles with behavioral changes facilitates the investigation of the fourth and most basic goal of behavior genetics, the description of the pathway between genes and behavior. Since this pathway involves biochemical reactions which in turn influence anatomic and physiological differences among organisms, it is clear that advances in the genetics of sensation and perception depend heavily on advances in biochemistry and allied disciplines. Many behaviorally oriented scientists today study the sensory systems from a neurophysiological point of view. To the extent that these investigators employ experimental animals whose genotypes are known or standardized, they will hasten the day when the pathway between genes and perceptual responses will be more completely understood.

References

Blakeslee, A. F. Genetics of sensory thresholds: Taste for phenyl thio carbamide. *Proceedings of the National Academy of Sciences of The United States,* 1932, **18,** 120–130.

Bok, D., & Hall, M. O. The role of the pigment epithelium in the etiology of inherited retinal dystrophy in the rat. *Journal of Cell Biology,* 1971, **49,** 664–682.

Bosher, S. K., & Hallpike, C. S. Observations on the histological features, development and pathogenesis of the inner ear degeneration of the deaf white cat. *Proceedings of the Royal Society, Series B,* 1965, **162,** 147–170.

Boyd, W. C. Taste reactions to antithyroid substances. *Science,* 1950, **112,** 153.

Brown, K. S. Genetic and environmental factors in profound prelingual deafness. *Medical Clinics of North America,* 1969, **53,** 741–772.

Bulmer, M. G. *The biology of twinning in man.* London and New York: Oxford Univ. Press (Clarendon), 1970.

Burdette, W. J. (Ed.) *Methodology in human genetics.* San Francisco, California: Holden Day, 1962.

Burdette, W. J. (Ed.) *Methodology in mammalian genetics.* San Francisco, California: Holden-Day, 1963.

Burns, M., & Fraser, M. N. *Genetics of the dog.* Edinburgh: Oliver & Boyd, 1966.

Carthy, J. D. *An introduction to the behaviour of invertebrates.* London: Allen & Unwin, 1958.

Collins, R. L. A new genetic locus mapped from behavioral variation in mice: Audiogenic seizure prone *(ASP). Behavior Genetics,* 1970, **1,** 99–109.

Connolly, K., Burnet, B., & Sewell, D. Selective mating and eye pigmentation: An analysis of the visual component in the courtship behavior of *Drosophila melanogaster. Evolution,* 1969, **23,** 548–559.

Crozier, W. J., & Pincus, G. Analysis of the geotropic orientation of young rats. I & II. *Journal of General Physiology,* 1929, **13,** 57–119.

Crozier, W. J., & Pincus, G. Analysis of the geotropic orientation of young rats. III. *Journal of General Physiology,* 1931, **15,** 201–242. (a).

Crozier, W. J., & Pincus, G. Analysis of the geotropic orientation of young rats. IV. *Journal of General Physiology,* 1931, **15,** 243–256. (b).

Crozier, W. J., & Pincus, G. Analysis of the geotropic orientation of young rats. VI. *Journal of General Physiology,* 1932, **15,** 437–462.

Crozier, W. J., & Pincus, G. Analysis of the geotropic orientation of young rats. X. *Journal of General Physiology,* 1936, **20,** 111–144.

Davis H. Psychophysiology of hearing and deafness. In S. S. Stevens (Ed.), *Handbook of experimental psychology.* New York: Wiley, 1951. Pp. 1116–1142.

DeFries, J. C. Quantitative genetics and behavior: Overview and perspective. In J. Hirsch (Ed.), *Behavior-genetic analysis.* New York: McGraw-Hill, 1967. Pp. 416–435.

Denny, M. R., & Ratner, S. C. *Comparative psychology: Research in animal behavior.* Homewood, Illinois: Dorsey Press, 1970.

Deol, M. S. The abnormalities of the inner ear in *kreisler* mice. *Journal of Embryology and Experimental Morphology,* 1964, **12**, 475–490. (a)

Deol, M. S. The origin of the abnormalities of the inner ear in dreher mice. *Journal of Embryology and Experimental Morphology,* 1964, **12**, 727–733. (b)

DeValois, R. L., & Jacobs, G. H. Primate color vision. *Science,* 1968, **162**, 533–540.

Dobzhansky, T. Of flies and men. *American Psychologist,* 1967, **22**, 41–48.

Dobzhansky, T., & Spassky, B. Selection for geotaxis in monomorphic and polymorphic populations of *Drosophila pseudoobscura. Proceedings of the National Academy of Sciences of the United States,* 1962, **48**, 1704–1712.

Duke-Elder, S. *System of ophthalmology.* Vol. I. *The eye in evolution.* London: Kimpton, 1958.

Erway, L., Hurley, L. S., & Fraser, A. Neurological defect: Manganese in phenocopy and prevention of a genetic abnormality of the inner ear. *Science,* 1966, **152**, 1766–1768.

Falconer, D. S. *Introduction to quantitative genetics.* New York: Ronald Press, 1960.

Falconer, D. S. Quantitative inheritance. In W. J. Burdette (Ed.), *Methodology in mammalian genetics.* San Francisco, California: Holden-Day, 1963. Pp. 193–216.

Fisher, R. A., Ford, E. B., & Huxley, J. Taste-testing the anthropoid apes. *Nature (London),* 1939, **144**, 750.

François, J. *Heredity in ophthalmology.* St. Louis, Missouri: Mosby, 1961.

Fraser, G. R. Profound childhood deafness. *Journal of Medical Genetics,* 1964, **1**, 118–151.

Fuller, J. L. Measurement of alcohol preference in genetic experiments. *Journal of Comparative and Physiological Psychology,* 1964, **57**, 85–88.

Fuller, J. L., & Sjursen, F. H. Audiogenic seizures in eleven mouse strains. *Journal of Heredity,* 1967, **58**, 135–140.

Fuller, J. L., & Thompson, W. R. *Behavior genetics.* New York: Wiley, 1960.

Graves, H. B., & Siegel, P. B. Chick's response to an imprinting stimulus: Heterosis and evolution. *Science,* 1968, **160**, 329–330.

Green, E. L. Breeding systems. In E. L. Green (Ed.), *Biology of the laboratory mouse.* (2nd ed.) New York: McGraw-Hill, 1966. Pp. 11–22.

Hadler, N. Heritability and phototaxis in *Drosophila melanogaster. Genetics,* 1964, **50**, 1269–1277.

Hall, C. S. The genetics of behavior. In S. S. Stevens (Ed.), *Handbook of experimental psychology.* New York: Wiley, 1951. Pp. 304–329.

Haseman, J. K., & Elston, R. C. The estimation of genetic variance from twin data. *Behavior Genetics,* 1970, **1**, 11–19.

Haskins, C. P., & Haskins, E. F. Note on the inheritance of behavior patterns for food selection and cocoon spinning in F_1 hybrids of *Callosamia promethea* X *C. angulifera. Behaviour,* 1958, **13**, 89–95.

Herron, W. L., Riegel, B. W., Myers, O. E., & Rubin, M. L. Retinal dystrophy in the rat—a pigment epithelial disease. *Investigative Ophthalmology,* 1969, **8**, 595–604.

Hirsch, J. (Ed.). *Behavior-genetic analysis.* New York: McGraw-Hill, 1967. (a)

Hirsch, J. Behavior-genetic analysis at the chromosome level of organization. In J. Hirsch (Ed.), *Behavior-genetic analysis.* New York: McGraw-Hill, 1967. Pp. 258–269. (b)

Hirsch, J. Behavior-genetic analysis. In J. Hirsch (Ed.), *Behavior-genetic analysis.* New York: McGraw-Hill, 1967. Pp. 416–435. (c)

Hirsch, J., & Boudreau, J. C. Studies in experimental behavior genetics. I. The heritability of phototaxis in a population of *Drosophila melanogaster*. *Journal of Comparative and Physiological Psychology*, 1958, **51**, 647–651.

Hirsch, J., & Erlenmeyer-Kimling, L. Studies in experimental behavior genetics. IV. Chromosome analyses for geotaxis. *Journal of Comparative and Physiological Psychology*, 1962, **55**, 732–739.

Hoshishima, K., Yokoyama, S., & Seto, K. Taste sensitivity in various strains of mice. *American Journal of Physiology*, 1962, **202**, 1200–1204.

Hostetter, R. C., & Hirsch, J. Genetic analysis of geotaxis in *Drosophila melanogaster:* Complementation between forward and reverse selection lines. *Journal of Comparative and Physiological Psychology*, 1967, **63**, 66–70.

Hotta, Y., & Benzer, S. Abnormal electroretinograms in visual mutants of *Drosophila*. *Nature (London)*, 1969, **222**, 354–356.

Hoyme, L. E. Genetics, physiology, and phenylthiocarbamide. *Journal of Heredity*, 1955, **46**, 167–175.

Hsia, Y., & Graham, C. H. Color blindness. In C. H. Graham (Ed.), *Vision and visual perception*. New York: Wiley, 1965. Pp. 395–413.

Jinks, J. L. *Extrachromosomal inheritance.* Englewood Cliffs, New Jersey: Prentice-Hall, 1964.

Jinks, J. L., & Fulker, D. W. Comparison of the biometrical genetical, MAVA, and classical approaches to the analysis of human behavior. *Psychological Bulletin*, 1970, **73**, 311–349.

Kalmus, H. Tune deafness and its inheritance. *Proceedings of the 8th International Congress of Genetics, 1948*, 1949. P. 605.

Kalmus, H. Genetical variation and sense perception. In G. E. W. Wolstenholme & C. M. O'Connor (Eds.), *Biochemistry of human genetics*. London: Churchill, 1959. Pp. 60–72.

Kalmus, H. *Diagnosis and genetics of defective colour vision*. Oxford: Pergamon, 1965.

Kaplan, A. R. Physiological and pathological correlates of differences in taste acuity. In S. G. Vandenberg (Ed.), *Progress in human behavior genetics*. Baltimore, Maryland: Johns Hopkins Press, 1968. Pp. 31–66.

Lehrman, D. S. Semantic and conceptual issues in the nature–nurture problem. In L. R. Aronson et al. (Eds.), *Development and evolution of behavior: Essays in memory of T. C. Schneirla*. San Francisco, California: Freeman, 1970. Pp. 17–52.

Lindzey, G., & Thiessen, D. D. Genetic aspects of negative geotaxis in mice. *Behavior Genetics*, 1970, **1**, 21–34.

McClearn, G. E. The inheritance of behavior. In L. Postman (Ed.), *Psychology in the making*. New York: Knopf, 1963. Pp. 144–252.

McCleary, R. A. *Genetic and experiential factors in perception. Research and commentary*. Glenview, Illinois: Scott, Foresman, 1970.

MacInnes, J. W., Boggan, W. O., & Schlesinger, K. Seizure susceptibility in mice: Differences in brain ATP production *in vitro*. *Behavior Genetics*, 1970, **1**, 35–42.

Mainland, R. C. Absence of olfactory sensation. *Journal of Heredity*, 1945, **36**, 143–144.

Malecót, G. *The mathematics of heredity*. San Francisco, California: Freeman, 1969.

Manosevitz, M., Lindzey, G., & Thiessen, D. D. (Eds.) *Behavioral genetics: Method and research*. New York: Appleton, 1969.

154   KARLA BUTLER THOMAS

Marler, P. R., & Hamilton, W. J. *Mechanisms of animal behavior.* New York: Wiley, 1966.

Marriott, F. H. C. The sensitivity limits of photoreceptors. *Symposia of the Zoological Society of London,* 1960, No. 3, 67–83.

Mather, K. *Biometrical genetics. The study of continuous variation.* New York: Dover, 1949.

Merrell, D. J. Methodology in behavior genetics. *Journal of Heredity,* 1965, **56**, 263–266.

Moehres, F. P. Sonic orientation of bats and other animals. *Symposia of the Zoological Society of London,* 1960, No. 3, 57–66.

Moncrieff, R. W. *Odour preferences.* New York: Wiley, 1966.

Moore, J. A. *Heredity and development.* London and New York: Oxford Univ. Press, 1963.

Nachman, M. The inheritance of saccharin preference. *Journal of Comparative and Physiological Psychology,* 1959, **52**, 451–457.

Neu, D. M. A critical review of the literature on "absolute pitch." *Psychological Bulletin,* 1947, **44**, 249–266.

Neuhaus, W. Unterschiede in der Riechschärfe bei Hunden. (Differences in keenness of scent in dogs.) *Zeitschrift fuer Vergleichende Physiologie,* 1957, **40**, 65–72. (Cited by Burns & Fraser, 1966.)

Osborne, R. T., & Gregor, A. J. The heritability of visualization, perceptual speed, and spatial orientation. *Perceptual and Motor Skills,* 1966, **23**, 379–390.

Pickford, R. W. The genetics of colour blindness. *British Journal of Physiological Optics,* 1964, **21**, 39–47.

Ptashne, M., & Gilbert, W. Genetic repressors. *Scientific American,* 1970, **222**, 36–44.

Roberts, R. C. Some concepts and methods in quantitative genetics. In J. Hirsch (Ed.), *Behavior-genetic analysis.* New York: McGraw-Hill, 1967. Pp. 214–257.

Rushton, W. A. H. *Visual pigments in man.* Liverpool: Liverpool Univ. Press, 1962.

Scarr, S. Environmental bias in twin studies. In S. G. Vandenberg (Ed.), *Progress in human behavior genetics.* Baltimore, Maryland: Johns Hopkins Press, 1968. Pp. 205–213.

Schnitzer, S. B., Fuller, J. L., & Schnitzer, M. E. Breed differences in locating hidden persons and animals. *American Zoologist,* 1962, **2**, 446. (Abstract) (Cited by Burns & Fraser, 1966.)

Sidman, R. L., Green, M. C., & Appel, S. H. *Catalog of the neurological mutants of the mouse.* (2nd ed.) Cambridge, Massachusetts: Harvard Univ. Press, 1965.

Snyder, L. H. Studies in human inheritance. IX. The inheritance of taste deficiency in man. *Ohio Journal of Science,* 1932, **32**, 436–440.

Spuhler, J. N., & Lindzey, G. Racial differences in behavior. In J. Hirsch (Ed.), *Behavior-genetic analysis.* New York: McGraw-Hill, 1967. Pp. 366–414.

Sternbach, R. A. Congenital insensitivity to pain: A critique. *Psychological Bulletin,* 1963, **60**, 252–264.

Thomas, K. Selection and avoidance of alcohol solutions by two strains of inbred mice and derived generations. *Quarterly Journal of Studies on Alcohol,* 1969, **30**, 849–861.

Thuline, M. C., Hodgkin, W. E., Fraser, G. R., & Motulsky, A. G. Genetics of protan and deutan color vision anomalies: An instructive family. *American Journal of Human Genetics,* 1969, **21**, 581–592.

Vandenberg, S. G. The hereditary abilities study: Hereditary components in a psychological test battery. *American Journal of Human Genetics,* 1962, **14**, 220–237.

Vandenberg, S. G. (Ed.) *Methods and goals in human behavior genetics.* New York: Academic Press, 1965.

Vandenberg, S. G. Hereditary factors in psychological variables in man, with a special emphasis on cognition. In J. N. Spuhler (Ed.), *Genetic diversity and human behavior.* Chicago, Illinois: Aldine, 1967. Pp. 99–133.

Waardenburg, P. J., Franceschetti, A., & Klein, D. *Genetics and ophthalmology.* 2 vols. Springfield, Illinois: Thomas, 1961.

Waddington, C. H., Woolf, B., & Perry, M. M. Environment selection by *Drosophila* mutants. *Evolution,* 1954, **8**, 89–96.

Watson, J. D. *The molecular biology of the gene.* New York: Benjamin, 1965.

Whitney, G., McClearn, G. E., & DeFries, J. C. Heritability of alcohol preference in laboratory mice and rats. *Journal of Heredity,* 1970, **61**, 165–169.

Wright, S. *Evolution and the genetics of population.* Vol. I. *Genetic and biometric foundations.* Chicago, Illinois: Univ. of Chicago Press, 1968.

Wright, S. *Evolution and the genetics of populations.* Vol. II. *The theory of gene frequencies.* Chicago, Illinois: Univ. of Chicago Press, 1969.

Yerkes, R. M. *The dancing mouse.* New York: Macmillan, 1907.

Young, R. W. Visual cells. *Scientific American,* 1970, **223**, 80–91.

Chapter 8

OBJECT RECOGNITION

N. S. SUTHERLAND

I. INTRODUCTION

Patterns are of importance to animals and man only in so far as they signify objects. It is the recognition of objects that is vital for survival and as a guide to action, and the patterned stimulation of our receptors is of use only because it is possible to construct from it the nature of the object from which it emanated. The Gestalt psychologists were well aware of this: they insisted on the distinction between the proximal and the distant stimulus and believed that the nervous system transformed the proximal stimulus into a structure that was isomorphic with experience; the resulting structure corresponded more closely to the distant stimulus than to the proximal stimulus (regression to the real object). The brain interprets patterns not only in the identification of three-dimensional objects but in recognizing such diverse things as spoken words, written letters, the mating call of the great crested grebe, the perpendicular style of window tracery and so on. Although it seems a truism that the analysis of pattern is only undertaken by organisms in order to arrive at the structure of objects, it is a truism that most theories of pattern recognition ignore.

In order to provide some guidance to the interpretation of the findings that will be reviewed, it will be useful to give some theoretical orientation at the outset. Sutherland (1968) has argued that pattern recognition involves the formation, storage and retrieval of structural descriptions. A description comprises a list of entities, the properties of those entities and the relationships obtaining between them. There are many different descriptive domains. For example, on the input side a picture can be described as a set of picture points having specified x and y coordinates where each point takes a particular brightness value (ignoring the complications introduced by differences in wavelength). The same picture can be redescribed in the object domain as representing an object consisting of a set of surfaces having certain albedos and shapes and related to one another in various ways, for example by being joined at a convex (or concave) edge (compare Clowes, 1971). Two examples may help to make this clearer.

The structure of an upper case letter "L" might be described as ⟨a vertical bar joined at its bottom end to the left end of a horizontal bar where the horizontal bar is about half the length of the vertical⟩. If the description of an L is held by the brain in a form such as this, then the description fits the first three shapes in Fig. 1, provided that the three different types of bar shown are all assigned the description ⟨bar⟩. In the case of Fig. 1(b) this would involve a routine that identifies closed regions demarcated by lines and which then proceeds to label any such closed region whose edges are parallel and long in relation to their width apart as a ⟨bar⟩. In Fig. 1(c) it would require a routine that first described the individual circles in the

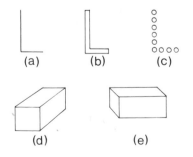

(a)   (b)   (c)

(d)   (e)

FIG. 1. Different representations of the same object.

picture and then relabeled any collinear and neighboring series of similar entities as a bar.

Again, consider the pattern shown in Fig. 1(d). It could be fully described by giving the brightness values produced at each point on the retina; to store such a description would be useless since it is unlikely that the retina is ever stimulated twice in exactly the same way. It could also be described as eight straight lines of certain relative lengths, running in particular directions, and joined at certain points. Alternatively, it could be said to comprise three regions—a square and two parallelograms joined together in certain ways. Finally, it could be described as a two-dimensional representation of a cuboid with two square surfaces and four rectangular surfaces. Only if a description of the last kind is stored will the pattern subsequently be identified as representing the same object as the pattern shown in Fig. 1(e). Each of these descriptions belongs to a different domain. Each domain contains entities appropriate to it and, depending upon the type of entity, certain relationships between the entities may obtain. The four domains instanced above contain, respectively, black and white picture points, lines, regions, and surfaces. A given domain will contain more than one type of entity; for example, the relationship between lines can only be described by using the entity ⟨end⟩, while ⟨edge⟩ belongs to the same domain as ⟨surface⟩. It should be clear that a description in one domain may be mapped in many different ways onto another domain. Depending upon angle of regard, lighting conditions and so on, the descriptions a face gives rise to at the level of the picture domain will be very different, but if we are to recognize a face as the same when seen at different times, these different pictures must all be mapped onto the same descriptive structure in the object domain. Similarly, it may happen (as in the Boring, 1930, wife mother-in-law figure) that the same picture can be mapped into different structural descriptions at the level of objects.

If object recognition is to be achieved in this manner, there must exist a set of rules that makes it possible to map from one domain onto another. An example of such rules are those loosely formulated above for arriving at a description in term of bars. In addition, as Clowes (1971) has stressed, a knowledge of what structures are permissible in a given domain is necessary in order to carry out such mappings. For example, in the case of solid objects composed of plane surfaces, each surface must be joined at its edges to other surfaces and at a corner at least three surfaces must meet.

A similar type of process underlies the recognition of speech. The input sound wave may be described (omitting phase information) in terms of the distribution of energies present at each frequency extended over time. This domain can be mapped into such entities as formants (frequency bands containing relatively high energies) which have different relative energies, frequencies and onset times, etc. From a mapping of the input signal onto this domain, it is possible to map onto the domain of phonemes: further domains contain syllables, words, and sentences. There are rules governing what structures may appear in each domain, and the mapping of a speech signal onto higher domains involves a knowledge of these rules together with a knowledge of the mapping rules.

Because speech (particularly at the level of sentences) clearly involves conventions invented by man, it is more commonly accepted that the analysis of speech involves the formation of structural descriptions than in the case of visual pattern analysis. Moreover, considerable attention has been directed to the problem of specifying the permissible speech structures, particularly at the level of the sentence, and the rules for mapping between different domains.

The above informal introduction to the notion of structural description is very inadequate, but it is hoped that it will help in the interpretation of some of the phenomena that will be reviewed below.

There is a vast literature on pattern recognition and it will only be possible to summarize a few selected findings here. Most of the work has been done in the field of vision. We know almost nothing about the recognition of auditory patterns except speech sounds, and most of the experiments undertaken on tactile recognition have been attempts to discover whether there is transfer between touch and vision. So little is known about taste that we cannot even specify what physical properties sugar and saccharine molecules have in common that result in their both tasting sweet, and the recognition of osmic patterns is practically a virgin field. Until we can define the physical properties of the molecules that are responsible for the differential stimulation of chemoreceptors, it is hard to see how much progress can be achieved on pattern recognition in this field. In what follows, then, most of the discussion will necessarily center upon vision. An attempt will be made to review some of the known facts, and several theories will then be discussed.

II. FACTS

A. Absolute versus Relative Properties

The nervous system is remarkably bad at storing the absolute value of a physical stimulus on a dimension. If a human subject is asked to assign stimuli varying on a single dimension to different categories, he can only make accurate use of between four to seven categories. This applies to judgments of frequency of pure tones (Pollack, 1952), judgments of visual size (Eriksen & Hake, 1955), and judgments of loudness (Schipper,

1953). Increasing the range over which the stimulus varies leads to little or no increase in the number of categories that can be accurately used; nor does allowing the use of more than about seven categories result in any more information being transmitted.

Variations of a stimulus along a single dimension are seldom of importance for object recognition. The intensity of light reflected to the eye varies with the lighting conditions; the intensity of a sound and the size an object subtends on the retina both vary with distance. What remains constant when the same object is presented is the relationship between the elements making up the pattern.

Similarly in speech recognition, it is the relational properties of the signal rather than its absolute properties that are of importance. It seems likely that the peripheral vocal apparatus can more readily keep such relational properties constant than any absolute properties such as frequency or volume. If absolute properties were important, the common cold would render the sufferer unintelligible. Since few inanimate objects produce characteristic sound patterns, sound is of little use for object identification except in the special case of echolocation.

If an animal is trained to respond differentially to two objects using one part of the retina, it will continue to respond correctly when the objects are presented to another part of the retina [Cronly-Dillon, Sutherland, & Wolfe, 1966 (goldfish); Muntz, 1963 (octopuses); Muntz & Sutherland, 1964 (rats)]. All these experiments show transfer between different parts of the visual field; the same point is made by experiments on interocular transfer (e.g., Myers & Sperry, 1958) but here the transfer could be mediated either by convergence of fibers from the two retinas in the cortex or by point-to-point connections through the corpus collosum. Intermanual transfer of tactile discrimination occurs (e.g., Stamm & Sperry, 1957); although no one has examined transfer from one finger to another, such transfer would almost certainly be found. At least in the case of simple patterns (horizontal and vertical bars) transfer from one part of the retina to another is innate (Ganz & Wilson, 1967).

Animals trained to make differential responses to two shapes usually show good transfer when the brightness or size of the shapes is changed. Transfer to new sizes appears to be innate (Ganz & Wilson, 1967). The reversal of all brightness values (as in a photographic negative of a face) makes recognition difficult. Man can recognize melodies and speech patterns despite changes in intensity and absolute frequency: curiously enough, few experiments appear to have been undertaken on the recognition of auditory patterns by animals after changes in absolute intensity or frequency.

Animals are known to transfer visual discriminations when an outline shape is substituted for a filled-in one at least in some circumstances

(Sutherland, 1961). In all modalities, animals have a remarkable capacity to disregard minor perturbations of the original input. We can identify a drawn letter "A" even when none of the strokes are straight and none of them are properly joined up. The spectrogram of a word produced by different speakers and even by the same speaker on different occasions of utterance varies so much that it is extremely difficult by examination of the spectrogram to decide what properties of it have remained constant and are used in recognition.

The above phenomena suggest that organisms store information about relational properties of the elements in a pattern rather than about absolute properties such as brightness, frequency or retinal position. Transfer from outline to filled-in shapes can be achieved by descriptions cast in terms of regions where the boundaries of a region may be formed either by a line or an edge.

B. Discriminability and Confusions

One technique for investigating pattern recognition is to discover which pairs of patterned stimuli organisms can readily learn to discriminate and which are difficult (or impossible) to discriminate. A second technique is to train an organism to make a response to a patterned object and then see what further objects elicit the same response. Where a response is already attached to an object either innately or through previous learning, it is possible to study the range of patterns that will elicit the response without giving specific training and hence establish what patterns are readily confused. Any adequate theory of pattern recognition must explain why it is that some pairs of patterns are less readily discriminable than others and must account for the confusions found between different patterns.

Using these techniques to investigate visual pattern recognition, it has been established that many species have more difficulty in discriminating between mirror-image shapes than between shapes of comparable complexity that are not mirror-images of one another [Mackintosh & Sutherland, 1963 (goldfish); Rudel & Teuber, 1963 (children); Sutherland, 1957 (octopuses); Zeigler & Schmerla, 1965 (pigeons)]. Similarly, in transfer tests a mirror-image of one of the original training shapes is usually treated in the way the animal has learned to respond to the training shape itself. The difficulty in discriminating is particularly acute when the mirror-image shapes are oblique rectangles at 45 and 135 degrees to horizontal, though for some unexplained reason cats do not find this discrimination any more difficult than that between horizontal and vertical rectangles (Sutherland, 1963b; Warren, 1969). Since many real objects give rise to mirror-image patterns depending upon the angle from which they are seen (for example, a human face in profile), it would normally be of biological utility to respond to mirror-image patterns of stimulation as though they represented the same object. It is not known whether the tendency to confuse mirror-images is innate though it would be simple enough to conduct the experiment on an animal reared in conditions of visual deprivation, and it is high time someone did so.

It is likely that the explanation of this confusion lies in the way in which information about a shape is stored (Sutherland, 1968): if the stored representation of a shape does not include information about the absolute left–right direction, then confusion between mirror-images will result. The confusion does not arise in the initial analysis of the pattern: different cells respond to differently orientated oblique bars (Hubel & Wiesel, 1962). Moreover, despite the difficulty children have in recognizing a lower case "b" as different from a "d," it is almost certain that they could point accurately to the position of the vertical bar and closed loop in each case. It is likely that different mechanisms subserve orienting behavior (such as moving around the environment without bumping into things) and recognition, and Schneider (1967) has obtained evidence that in hamsters the former mechanisms involve the tectal system whereas the latter involve the geniculocortical system.

Sutherland has investigated the confusions made by rats, goldfish, and octopuses between different shapes (for a review, see Sutherland [1963a] and for general reviews of the literature, see Dodwell [1970a], Sutherland [1961], and Zusne [1970]). In learning to discriminate between different shapes, animals often rely on the presence or absence of a local feature. In the jumping stand rats tend to respond in terms of differences in the lower parts of the shapes (Lashley, 1938), whereas in at least two different training situations goldfish rely on differences at the top (Bowman & Sutherland, 1969; Hemmings, 1965). Recent experiments suggest that animals make use of very abstract descriptions in classifying shapes. For example, after training on shapes (a) and (b) in Fig. 2, goldfish treat shape (c) as equivalent to shape (a); again (Sutherland & Williams, 1969) after being trained to discriminate a regular checkerboard pattern from one containing an irregularity, rats treat a variety of new irregular checkerboard patterns as equivalent to the original irregular one (Fig. 3).

Sutherland (1963a) found that when rats or octopuses are trained on shapes differing in the ratio of contour to square root of area, their responses to transfer shapes are rather well predicted by the position the shape occupies on this dimension.

Although no consistent interpretation of all the results gathered by this type of experiment is available, there is one feature of the findings that deserves further comment. The similarity of the findings for species as

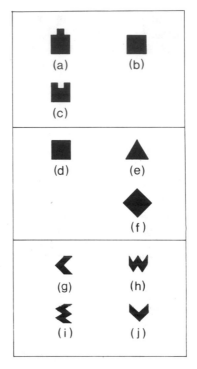

Fig. 2. Some training and transfer shapes. The first pair of shapes in each cell was used in training; transfer shapes are shown in the second line of each cell and each was treated as equivalent to the training shape immediately above it.

different as the octopus, the goldfish, and the rat is very much more striking than are the differences (see, for example, Sutherland, 1969). This strongly suggests that there is some optimal way to process visual information and that this method has been discovered in the course of evolution independently by cephalopods and vertebrates.

Attempts have been made to establish confusion matrices in the investigation of auditory pattern recognition but they have mainly been limited to the study of human speech. Jakobson and Halle (1956) proposed that phonemes could be identified in terms of the value each has on a set of twelve binary distinctive features. For identification, only the values on some of these features are important for each phoneme. For example, one distinctive feature takes the values grave or acute: a phoneme having the value grave has a concentration of energy in the lower frequencies of the sound spectrum, whereas a phoneme having the value acute has more relative energy in the upper frequencies. The phonemes /e/ (as in "let") and /i/ (as in "lit") are differentiated in terms of this one distinctive feature, the

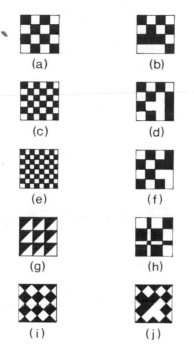

FIG. 3. Regular and irregular checkerboard patterns. (After Sutherland and Williams, 1969.) Rats were trained to discriminate between patterns (a) and (b); the remaining patterns were presented in transfer tests: those shown in the left hand column were equivalent to pattern (a) and those in the right hand column to pattern (b).

former having the value grave, the latter the value acute. It is possible to test this account of how phonemes are identified by presenting phonemes in noise and constructing a confusion matrix. Phonemes differing by only one (or a small number) of distinctive features should be more readily confused with one another than those differing in several distinctive features. Brown and Hildum (1956) performed essentially this experiment and found that over half the confusions made by subjects were confusions involving a change in only one distinctive feature. Similar findings were obtained by Tikofsky and McInish (1968) using a different technique: two syllables were successively presented and the subject had to respond "same" or "different." Errors again tended to occur when the syllables differed by only a single distinctive feature, though changes in some distinctive features produced many more errors than changes in others. The use of artificially synthesized speech has been of great value in increasing our understanding of speech recognition. It has been shown that the identification of English vowel sounds depends largely upon the relative positions of the first three formants (i.e., the three formants of lowest frequency). A formant is produced by the resonant frequencies of the vocal tract, and the values of these frequencies alter with changes in the shape of the tract.

Particularly in the case of consonants, the features of the sound signal used for mapping onto phonemes change with the phonemic context in which the phoneme is uttered. The plosives (/p/, /t/, /k/) can be separately identified by two characteristics of the sound wave, either of which may be sufficient for identification in some circumstances. First, they normally give rise to a short burst of energy concentrated at a particular frequency which varies between the three plosives. However, a plosive burst at a particular frequency may cause a subject consistently to hear /k/ if followed by one vowel and /p/ if followed by another. Secondly, the plosives may be identified by the shape of the second formant transition— they produce a brief initial rise or fall in the frequency of the second formant. Whether a rise or fall is produced by a given plosive depends upon the frequency of the second formant. Thus the shape of the formant transition is not enough to identify a given plosive since the shape itself depends upon the second formant frequency of the following vowel.

This illustrates the following points. Changes in a single distinctive feature of the sort proposed by Jakobson and Halle may result in several changes in the form of the speech wave, and in some circumstances the presence of any one of these changes may be enough for identification of the phoneme. Secondly, the pattern produced by a given phoneme depends upon the phonemic context and the actual phoneme can only be identified if the listener takes phonemic context into account.

C. Rotation and Symmetry

The extent to which a visually presented shape can be recognized as the same when it is rotated is the subject of considerable controversy. In experiments with animals, it has often been found that when transfer tests are given with rotated shapes, the transfer shape is not responded to as equivalent to the original unrotated shape. Indeed it is often treated as equivalent to the other training shape. For example, after being trained to discriminate between a square and a triangle, rats and octopuses (Sutherland, 1961) respond to a rotated square (i.e., a diamond) in the way they have learned to respond to the triangle [see Fig. 2(d)–(f)]: presumably the animals have learned to discriminate between the two shapes by detecting the presence versus absence either of oblique contours or of a point at the top. Another example of the failure of octopuses to transfer between rotated shapes (Sutherland, 1959a) is given in Fig. 2(g)–(j). However, transfer does sometimes occur to rotated shapes, for example, when the training shapes differ widely in the ratio of periphery to square root of area, the rotated shape is usually treated as equivalent to the original training shape (Sutherland, 1963a). Again, the presence of a special feature may mediate transfer to a rotated shape. For example, goldfish show no transfer to a diamond after training on square versus circle, but if a knob is added to the square, good transfer occurs to the square with knob rotated through 45 degrees (Sutherland & Bowman, 1969). Whether or not transfer occurs depends upon the description assigned to the shapes by the animal. Moreover, the fact that after training on a pair of shapes shown in a single orientation, transfer fails to occur to new rotations does not prove that animals *cannot* (if given a set to do so) detect the similarity between rotated versions of the same shape.

Men can identify letters in unusual orientations correctly (Kolers & Perkins, 1969) but it is not known whether this ability depends on having had previous experience with letters in unusual orientations. One has the feeling that it is possible to rotate the image of an object mentally, but this ability is almost certainly far from perfect, as witness the difficulty of identifying a photograph of a familiar face upside down. Shepard and Metzler (1971) performed an experiment on man's ability to recognize pictures of three-dimensional shapes rotated about a vertical axis. Subjects were shown pictures of shapes made from square blocks joined together and tilted so that the surfaces were not aligned with the horizontal and vertical axes. The time taken to judge whether two shapes were identical increased linearly with the angle through which they were rotated relative to each other: this suggests that mental rotation can occur and that it takes a constant time per unit angle of rotation.

Symmetrical shapes are more accurately recalled by man than nonsymmetrical shapes of equivalent complexity, particularly if they are symmetrical about their vertical axis (Attneave, 1955; Fitts, Weinstein, Rappaport, Anderson, & Leonard, 1956). This suggests that the stored description of a symmetrical shape is shorter than that of a nonsymmetrical shape. Instead of storing independently a description of both halves of the shape, it may be possible to store a description of one half only together with the information that this half is reflected to produce the whole shape. Except in the case of radial symmetry, it appears to be difficult to see symmetry around more than one axis at a time. Attneave (1968) demonstrated this for the case of equilateral triangles. When the triangle has no line which is horizontal, it is seen as pointing in a particular direction and with the opposite line as a base line: it appears that in such cases the description of the shape is referred to an axis other than the horizontal in order to simplify the ensuing description. Attneave presents another nice demonstration of this point. In Fig. 2(f) the diamond is clearly seen as a diamond and not

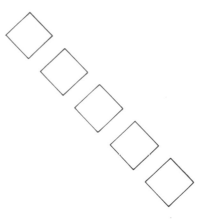

Fɪɢ. 4. An oblique row of squares. (After Attneave, 1968.)

as a square. However, if an oblique line of diamonds is presented the picture tends to be seen as an oblique row of squares (Fig. 4). The diamonds are referred to a new orientation (that of the whole row) in order to simplify the resulting description.

D. Segmentation and Grouping

The same pattern can be segmented in different ways: for example, the capital letter "H" can be seen as two vertical lines joined by a horizontal line, as a vertical line on the left joined to a "T" on its side, as a rectilinear upright "U" sharing a common base line with an upside down "U," and so on. Similarly any sequence of sounds can be grouped in different ways. Although patterns can be segmented in many ways, there are certain principles that determine how we tend to segment them. These were enunciated by Wertheimer (1923) and since their importance has largely been overlooked by subsequent theorists, it may be worth repeating them here.

1. The nearer elements are together the more likely it is that they will be grouped together. Figure 5(a) tends to be seen as four rows of circles rather than as four columns. If a sequence of taps is given with short and long pauses alternating between them, the taps will be grouped into the pairs that have a short pause between their members.

2. Similar elements tend to be grouped together. Figure 5(b) is seen as four columns not as four rows. Similarly if taps are made at regular intervals with alternating pairs loud and soft, the sequence tends to be heard in pairs of the same volume.

3. Elements moving together tend to be grouped together. If the

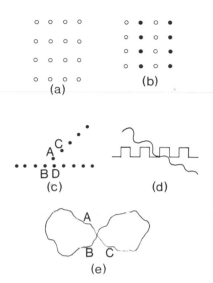

FIG. 5. Grouping of perceptual elements. (After Wertheimer, 1923.)

circles in Figure 5(a) are set in motion in such a way that all the circles in a given column undergo the same movement but different movements are imposed on each column, then this pattern will segment into *columns* of circles instead of into rows.

4. Elements having good continuity are taken together. In the case of vision, straight lines have good continuity: for example in Fig. 5(c) dot A is grouped with dots B and C although it is nearer to dot D. Elements forming simple curves also have good continuity, and are grouped together; in addition we tend to group repeating structures together (Fig. 5d). An auditory equivalent of good continuation is the tendency to group together a series of tones that regularly increase in frequency and to break the series at a point where a descent in frequency occurs.

5. Contours tend to be grouped into the boundaries of closed regions. In Fig. 5(e) line A tends to be grouped with line B although good continuation of the line (ignoring closure) would dictate that it should be grouped with line C.

6. Elements tend to be grouped in such a way as to produce a symmetrical outcome.

7. Once a pattern has been organized in a particular way, that organization may persist when the pattern is changed. For example having seen Fig. 5(a) as rows, we usually continue to see rows if the horizontal and vertical spacing between dots is made equal.

8. Past experience may influence the ways in which we group. Cursive

script is grouped into individual letters; spoken speech does not contain pauses between most word pairs yet it is grouped into words and we "hear" nonexistent pauses between the words.

Little experimental work has been undertaken on the problem of grouping: those experiments that have been performed have confirmed Wertheimer's insights (e.g., Hochberg & Silverstein, 1956). Krechevsky (1938) and Dodwell (1970b) have demonstrated perceptual grouping in rats and squirrels. There may be other principles of grouping waiting to be discovered: it is likely for example that, other things being equal, we tend to impose a vertical or horizontal organization on the elements of a figure rather than organizing them into oblique lines.

There are several reasons why grouping should occur in conformance to the above principles if we are efficiently to recognize objects in the world around us. Similar and neighboring visual structures are likely to belong to the same object: consider the appearance of the branch of a tree interrupted by leaves. Similarly, structures that move in synchrony with one another are likely to be parts of the same object. Similar sounds are again likely to emanate from the same source and in using the sound sequence to recognize the object producing it, it is necessary to analyze trains of similar sounds together and to disregard background sounds.

E. Perceptual Learning

The question of how far we have to learn to see and hear has been extensively discussed over the last 100 years. The Gestalt psychologists argued that most of the principles of grouping were innate, while Hebb (1949) took an extreme empiricist position. Recent evidence suggests that many of the mechanisms involved in the processing of patterns are innate. Some of the evidence may be summarized (inadequately) as follows: (1) Neurophysiological studies have revealed intricate and specific mechanisms existing at birth in the visual cortex (e.g., Hubel & Wiesel, 1963). (2) Although animals brought up under conditions of visual deprivation are impaired on difficult pattern discriminations, they learn simple discriminations almost as readily as normal animals (Ganz, 1969), particularly if trained under conditions where they do not have to move around their environment (Myers & McCleary, 1964). Studies with visually deprived animals are difficult to interpret since there are many factors that might produce a deficit in pattern recognition other than the lack of previous perceptual learning (Sutherland, 1959b). (3) A recent case study of a human patient who had a congenital cataract removed as an adult (Gregory & Wallace, 1963) again suggests the operation of many innate factors in perception;

however, the patient was probably not blind from birth. Wertheimer (1951) pointed out that von Senden's (1960) interpretation of the case studies he reports involves considerable special pleading, and Hebb (1949) distorted the evidence even further. (4) Several species are known to make innate responses to patterned stimuli [e.g., Arctic tern chicks (Quine & Cullen, 1964); domestic chicks (Fantz, 1957); sepia (Wells, 1958)]. Moreover, recognition of a sudden drop and avoidance of it appears to be innate as demonstrated in the ingenious visual cliff apparatus devised by E. J. Gibson (Walk & Gibson, 1961). (5) The visual constancies are probably present in 6-week-old children (Bower, 1966). (6) As already mentioned, intra-retinal transfer and size transfer have been shown to be present in infant monkeys without previous visual experience (Ganz & Wilson, 1967). More experiments of this type are needed.

Although complicated and specific innate mechanisms are involved in pattern processing, perceptual learning plays an important role particularly with complex patterns. It is obvious that experience with a given type of object (e.g., aeroplanes, Chinese faces, Gothic cathedrals) greatly facilitates our ability to remember accurately new instances of objects of the same type and to identify them subsequently, though there are few experimental demonstrations of this phenomenon. One of the most convincing is reported by Gibson (1963). She presented subjects with a squiggle that resembled the profile of a face if vertically presented, and appeared like cursive script of a totally new kind when presented horizontally. Subjects were required to identify the original squiggle when subsequently shown among eleven similar squiggles. Subjects performed better when the squiggles were vertical than when they were horizontal, presumably because they could fit the vertical squiggle into previously learned structures for describing faces.

The problem of perceptual learning is carefully reviewed by Gibson (1969) in a recent book. She takes the view that object recognition is based on feature recognition and that in perceptual learning we both learn what features differentiate the members of a class of object and we also improve our ability to differentiate these features. She presents convincing evidence to show that the detection of small differences along a dimension may improve with experience (and without knowledge of results). One of the most interesting examples of this is our ability to make very fine auditory distinctions across a phoneme boundary. For example, /d/ and /t/ contain the same formants but differ from one another in the relative onset time of the first and second formant. If the onset of the first formant occurs less than 20 msec after the onset of the second formant, we almost invariably hear /d/; if it occurs more than 30 msec after the second formant we hear /t/. Using synthesized speech, Liberman, Harris, Kinney, and Lane (1961) obtained the following findings. First, discrimination between two sounds in which the onset times of the two formants differ by 10 msec is very much more accurate when the first formant occurs at 20 msec and at 30 msec after the second than at any other 10-msec interval of difference (e.g., when the first formant occurs 0 msec and 10 msec after the second formant). This means that discrimination of the same physical difference is more accurate when the difference is across a phonemic boundary than when it is within a single phoneme. Secondly, if the relative frequencies of the formants are changed so that the sounds are no longer heard as speech, then discrimination between onset times differing by 10 msec is unaffected by where the interval occurs (e.g., it makes no difference whether one formant precedes another by 0 msec and 10 msec or by 20 msec and 30 msec). Moreover, the discriminability of the non-speech signals was the same as the discriminability of speech signals when the difference occurred at a position that was not critical for phoneme differentiation (within a phoneme boundary).

Although, therefore, learning to discriminate a critical feature of the input with greater accuracy is one aspect of perceptual learning, there are almost certainly other kinds of learning going on. For example, learning what structures are possible within a given domain will greatly facilitate our ability to map from another domain onto that one by eliminating impossible structures. This is obvious in the case of words where only certain sequences are permissible, but it may well apply to such problems as facial recognition. Moreover, we almost certainly learn what properties and relationships are important for individuating a member of a particular class of objects. Albedo is normally of no importance for the recognition of symbols such as letters and digits, but may be critical for facial recognition (compare the difficulty of recognizing a face in a photographic negative).

There is another reason why perceptual learning is of importance and this has to do with overcoming a limitation on the way the nervous system itself functions. It is likely that we can only form and store comparatively few new relationships at any one time. Compare the limitations on immediate memory and the magic of the "magic number seven" (Miller, 1956): there is no reason to suppose that there is not a similar limit to the number of chunks that can be dealt with at one time in visual perception. When first confronted with a face, the human infant simply could not store the detailed relationships obtaining between the entities that compose it (eyes, ears, nose, mouth, cheeks, etc.), together with an adequate description of each of these entities. With more experience of faces, the general structure of the face will already be stored as a description of the shape of each of the parts and the relationships obtaining between them. If this description can be accessed when a new face is seen, the whole structure will not have to be built up from scratch but merely modified in certain ways that characterize the new face as different from other faces.

De Groot (1965) gives a nice example of the operation of such chunking in vision. Whereas a master chess player, after spending 5 seconds inspecting a board position containing twenty-six pieces, can replace the pieces exactly as they were, a novice will replace about seven pieces correctly and the rest at random. However, the master chess player does no better than the novice if the pieces are initially placed randomly on the board rather than in positions that can occur during an actual game. The master chess player has existing structural descriptions in his head which correspond to certain recurrent groupings (e.g., castling on queen's side) and to obtain a complete description of the position he needs only to set up a few pointers to such existing structures. The novice lacking such existing structures would have to set up a separate pointer to the position of each piece and this proves to be impossible. The existence of previous structural descriptions for a type of object thus serves two purposes. It ensures that we have already learned how to describe this sort of object in a way that will be useful for future recognition and it cuts down the amount of information that it is necessary to store in order correctly to identify a new member of a class of objects. This sort of idea is of course very similar to the notion of the schema proposed by Bartlett (1932).

F. Cross Modality Transfer

When chimpanzees (Davenport & Rogers, 1970) and 3-year-old children (Rudel & Teuber, 1964) are presented visually with an object, they can pick out that object by touch from an array of objects. Experiments testing for cross-modal transfer by training an animal to discriminate between two visually presented shapes and then testing transfer to the learning of a touch discrimination between the same objects (or vice versa) have often produced negative results. This is scarcely surprising in view of the fact that after a visual discrimination has been established in an animal in one situation, the animal may fail to show any savings to relearn a discrimination between the same objects if a different experimental situation is used. Ettlinger (1960) found that monkeys trained on a tactile discrimination in the dark showed no transfer to the same discrimination in the light even though they were given the opportunity to continue to use touch.

Our ability to perform cross modality matching suggests that we store a description in terms of highly abstract structures and that we possess mapping rules that enable us to form the same description at this level from both a visual and a tactile input.

III. THEORY

Several types of theories of pattern processing may be distinguished.
Most are wholly inadequate.

A. Random Neural Networks

Hebb (1949) proposed that beyond the striate cortex there was random
connectivity. When two patterns appear successively on different parts of
the retina, as a result of increments in the probability of firing across
synapses having common inputs from both patterns, the two patterns will
come to fire consistently the same sets of cells. Since successive patterns
on the retina often represent the same object seen from different points of
view, any object will eventually come to fire the same set of cells regardless
of the point from which it is viewed. This theory does not begin to account
for the evidence reviewed above: for example it cannot account for "grouping," or innate reactions to specific patterns and it is inconsistent with
recent neurophysiological findings. More sophisticated versions of the attempt to account for pattern recognition on the basis of random connectivity
have also proved unsuccessful (Rosenblatt, 1959; Uttley, 1956; see Minsky
& Papert, 1969, for some of the theoretical reasons for their lack of
success).

B. Template Matching

In its extreme form this theory holds that a template of the input is made
and when a new input matches the original input it is recognized as the
same; where an exact match cannot be found the template which matches
the input most closely is selected. Such a theory fails completely to account
for the known facts of transfer: for example if a template of shapes (a)
and (b) in Fig. 3 were made, shape (d) would match all squares in shape
(a) except two, whereas it would fail to match (b) at four points; nevertheless rats after training on shapes (a) and (b), respond to shape (d) in
the way they have learned to respond to (b) [compare also Fig. 2, shapes
(a), (b), and (c)].

Template matching will also not account readily for such phenomena as
size invariance. It can be made to do so if it is assumed that certain transformations can be carried out on the input shape before the matching operation takes place. For example, the size of the shape could be rescaled and
the shape could be rotated to discover whether a really good fit could be
obtained with one of the stored templates. Although there is some evidence

that such transforms may occur (e.g., Shepard & Metzler, 1971, described above), there are no known transforms that could explain the type of transfer shown in Fig. 3; moreover, it would be difficult for template matching to account for our ability to disregard "jitter." Finally, to account for object recognition, it is necessary to assume that the structure of objects is stored in a much more abstract form than is conceived of in theories based on template matching.

Although template matching does not carry us very far as an account of the detailed mechanisms of pattern recognition, something like it undoubtedly occurs at an early stage of the system. Local features (bars and edges in different orientations) are extracted by a set of innate templates multiplied across the whole retinal surface.

C. Recognition by Features

We have seen that a theory of speech recognition in terms of distinctive features has been proposed: many of these features are structurally complex. Gibson (1969) has proposed a similar theory for visual recognition particularly of letters. Capital letters can be classified correctly merely on the basis of whether or not they possess each of a set of about a dozen features such as a horizontal line ("A" but not "V"), a closed curve ("B" but not "I"), an intersection ("X" but not "U"), and so on. Although feature analysis and recognition may play an important part in object recognition much more must be involved. Given any finite set of features defining the letters of the alphabet, it would always be possible to construct a pattern that possessed all the features appropriate to a particular letter, but if the pattern differed from that letter in other ways, there would be no tendency to see it as that letter.

The word "feature" is itself rather vague and we should distinguish features of at least three different kinds. First, there are local features such as the presence of a curved line, the presence of a T junction and so on: such features could be extracted (at least in some instances) by templates. Secondly, there are global features such as symmetry, or the position occupied on the dimension length of periphery divided by the square root of area. Such features cannot in principle be extracted by any form of template analysis. Finally, there are concatenations of local features: for example a P possesses the feature of having a vertical line with a closed loop at the top and to the right of the vertical line. If we allow concatenations of features to be a type of feature then recognition by features becomes almost indistinguishable from recognition by structural descriptions. Many local features are in themselves complex: for example an apex is the junction of two boundaries with an internal angle of less than 180 degrees.

In summary, it is likely that all object recognition involves the abstraction of features but recognition can rarely be achieved merely by listing the features found. Rather, it is necessary to describe the relationships between features and in many cases to map from a description in one domain onto a description in some other domain; this idea is not captured by the notion of feature analysis.

D. Encoding Theories

Several theories (e.g., Deutsch, 1955; Dodwell, 1970a; Sutherland, 1957) have been put forward to explain transfer test results in terms of encoding operations that result in the loss of certain types of information and hence in confusions between different patterns. Sutherland, for example, suggested that octopuses compute the total vertical extent of a shape at all points on the horizontal axis and the total horizontal extent at each point along the vertical axis. The resulting transformation of the input shape can be shown to result in identical outputs for mirror image oblique rectangles and for such shapes as (g) and (i), and (h) and (j) in Fig. 2. Further elaboration of the theory made it possible to account for a considerable quantity of empirical data. However, such theories fail to give any account of segmentation, grouping, and perceptual learning; nor do they capture the idea that in storing a description of a three-dimensional object we map the input into structures that correspond to the structure of the real object. Moreover, no coding theory has ever been completely specified insofar as the output from the encoding mechanisms is still a pattern (albeit transformed from the input pattern) and some mechanism is required to classify the output patterns: for a further discussion of some examples of such theories, see Dodwell (1970a).

E. Analysis by Synthesis

Several workers, particularly in speech recognition, have proposed models based on analysis by synthesis. In its purest form, this theory holds that in recognition a knowledge of the possible structures in a higher domain is used to generate corresponding structures in a lower domain. For example, the same phoneme may have many different spectrographic representations: such representations could be generated until one is found that matches the current input and recognition is then achieved. Nobody has ever held the theory in such an extreme form: it is supposed that some preliminary analysis of the input is undertaken from which it is possible to eliminate some structures in the higher domain: representations in the lower domain may then be generated from the remaining structures that it is necessary to choose between. The theory is superficially attractive in speech recognition since it is likely that at some point in the control of speech there is a representation of phonemes in the motor command system, and the actual structure of the speech wave depends upon the rules that translate an instruction to issue a series of phonemes into a particular set of commands to the peripheral musculature. The rules governing the translation between a phoneme sequence and a set of muscular contractions must be known to the native speaker and it would seem economical to use the same set of rules to help in decoding the incoming speech signal onto phonemes (compare Stevens & Halle, 1967).

To match an auditory signal with a generated signal it would be necessary to generate a representation of an acoustic signal and since we do not make audible manipulations of our vocal tract in listening to speech, it is not clear how involvement of the motor system would help in speech recognition. Moreover, the congenitally dumb can learn to recognize speech and Denes (1967) has shown that practice in producing spoken copies of speech subjected to systematic distortions does not necessarily help in recognizing such distorted speech. Theories of this kind have remained rather vague and many workers in speech recognition think there is no necessity for analysis by synthesis (Fant, 1967). Until much more detailed work has been undertaken both on the recognition of speech by computer and on the human listener, we will not know how far analysis by synthesis is implicated in speech recognition. Insofar as it is impossible to run generative rules in reverse, some element of analysis by synthesis must enter into recognition. It has already been pointed out that a knowledge of the possible structures in the domain onto which we are mapping the input stimulus is of crucial importance for recognition. The production of an impossible structure in a higher level domain must lead to reinterpretation of the input stimulus, and at least to this extent our knowledge of higher level domains must influence parsing at lower levels. The extent to which such parsing in a lower domain can only be achieved by generating representations from a higher level domain is, however, still not known.

F. Structural Descriptions

At the beginning of this chapter an approach to object recognition in terms of structural descriptions was advanced, and an attempt has been made to interpret some of the data in the light of this approach. Although this approach seems to be the only one that is wide enough to encompass all the phenomena of pattern recognition, it is of course very far from giving an adequate account of most of these phenomena at the present time since it has not been worked out in sufficient detail. Indeed there are many totally unsolved problems in the area. For example, our knowledge of what structures are permissible in a higher level domain must often be induced from instances; compare the difficulty of learning from the speech input what a phoneme is. Neither in the case of vision nor in speech recognition have we any idea of the mechanisms that underlie this type of perceptual learning; nor has any attempt been made to specify what innate biases must be present if we are to make the right inferences about deep structures from the perceptual input we receive.

Moreover, a theory based on structural descriptions incorporates many aspects of other theories and recognition can almost certainly be achieved in more than one way. Animals are known often to base responses on some feature of the object to which they are responding rather than on any description of the whole object, and in the case where a human subject is searching for a particular object it is likely that he can screen out other objects by using feature detection without forming elaborate structural descriptions of these objects (Neisser, 1967; Rabbitt, 1967).

G. Picture Processing by Machine

It should be pointed out that the notion of structural descriptions and the idea that the input is mapped onto more abstract domains containing different objects and relationships from the input domain owes much to recent work in artificial intelligence. In particular Clowes (1971) has shown how a two-dimensional picture of a three-dimensional scene can be mapped into a description that explicitly represents the different three-dimensional objects present, and their structure in terms of surfaces joined at convex and concave edges. The program also recovers the existence of hidden surfaces (i.e., surfaces having edges not directly represented in the two-dimensional picture because they are obscured by other surfaces). For an earlier program that achieves the same goal for a limited set of objects, see Roberts (1965). Clowes (1970) describes a program for character recognition which again is based on redescribing the input in terms of certain higher level objects (such as strokes and vertices) and describing the way these objects are articulated. The program goes some way to dealing with the problem that in the input picture a stroke may have many different representations (compare the three L's drawn in Fig. 1).

Several workers in artificial intelligence (e.g., Clowes, 1970; Narasimhan, 1964), have called attention to the possibility that there may be some formal similarities between the types of system best fitted to handle the processing of pictures and the phrase structure and transformational grammars developed for describing the structure of language. It is, however, doubtful whether such grammars will turn out to be powerful enough to handle pictures (or even natural language, Winograd, 1971).

Much work has been undertaken on specific problems in picture processing—for example the automatic interpretation of pictures of chromosomes (Rutovitz, 1969) or of bubble chambers (Watts, 1968). Again the idea of articulating pictorial objects into their component parts appears, but the generality of such programs is often too narrow for them to be of much interest to those concerned with the way in which organisms process patterned visual stimuli.

The problem of pattern processing is currently receiving much attention by workers in the field of artificial intelligence partly as a result of the attempt to build robots capable of intelligent interaction with a real environment. Such work has produced more problems than solutions. One such problem (largely ignored by psychologists) is that the pictures received by the retina (or T.V. camera) from the real world are invariably extremely "dirty." In particular an edge between two surfaces may often be present in the real world but not represented by any difference in brightness in the input picture. Again brightness differences may be present between different regions of the picture where the regions are contained within the same surface and the brightness differences are due to the way the picture is lit or even to defects in the lens. Decomposing the input picture into regions that correspond to surfaces or to objects and getting rid of the "noise" is a major problem. Many heuristics have been proposed in an attempt to tackle problems of this general kind (compare, e.g., Brice & Fennema, 1970; Rosenfeld, 1969) but none are wholly successful. It is likely that this problem can only be solved by providing the program with "knowledge" of what possible three-dimensional structures may appear in a picture and using this knowledge to decompose the picture into appropriate entities.

Another approach to picture recognition by machine has been the attempt to define property spaces which can then be partitioned in such a way that all members of a given class of objects give rise to pictures that lie within one region of the property space (see, e.g., Cooper, 1969). This approach has much in common with the feature detection theories discussed above. It has proved singularly fruitless since it ignores the problem of segmentation and of what structures are represented in pictures; moreover, in any complex case it is impossible to partition a space in a way that corresponds to different types of object.

In the writer's opinion the concepts developed by workers in artificial intelligence for attempting to make machines process pictures are likely to be increasingly fruitful in suggesting mechanisms that may be used by organisms. Problems that seem superficially easy often turn out to be very intractable and to require new methods of information processing; when a serious attempt is made to program computers to solve such problems, it often emerges that processes we thought we understood are really very poorly understood. Understanding the visual system—or any other part of the brain—cannot be achieved simply by having a wiring diagram of the system: we need to develop much higher level concepts in order to understand how the wiring diagram mediates the relationships between input and output actually obtained. Readers interested in following up recent developments in picture processing by machine are referred to Grasselli (1969) and Kaneff (1970).

H. Conclusion

For reasons of space many problems have been glossed over. For example although phonemes in some sense have a real existence (as proved by trained phoneticians' ability to agree on the phonemic interpretation of a speech sound wave), understanding speech does not necessarily involve decomposition into units at this level. Indeed if the speech wave is divided into segments of equal length and alternated from one ear to the other, or if the sound in every other interval is replaced with silence, the rate of clipping that has the most deleterious effect on intelligibility corresponds to the length of the syllable rather than to the length of the phoneme (Huggins, 1964). Liberman (e.g., Liberman, Cooper, Shankwiller, & Studdert-Kennedy, 1967—an excellent review of work on speech perception) has repeatedly emphasized that the unit of analysis in speech must be bigger than the phoneme since it is impossible to chop speech into distinct segments corresponding to phonemes; he has suggested that if phonemes were discrete units in time we could not recognize speech at the rate we do (up to about 30 phonemes a second) since it is not possible to identify anything like as many as 30 discrete sounds a second. Similarly, although written language is made up of discrete spatial units (letters) it is likely that after practice in reading, it may be possible to identify words without explicit parsing into letters or syllables.

The reader is also warned that in an area as vast as that of pattern processing it has been possible to review only a tiny fragment of the literature. Since, in the present state of knowledge, it is impossible to know which experiments and observations will ultimately have most theoretical significance, the fragments reviewed have of necessity been selected in a highly arbitrary way.

ACKNOWLEDGMENT

This chapter was prepared while I held a visiting appointment at Rockefeller University and I am grateful for the peace afforded there. I am also grateful to S.R.C. for a grant in support of some of the experimental work described and to Dr. Clowes and Dr. Oatley for helpful comments on the manuscript.

References

Attneave, F. Symmetry, information and memory for patterns. *American Journal of Psychology,* 1955, **68**, 209–222.

Attneave, F. Triangles as ambiguous figures. *American Journal of Psychology,* 1968, **81**, 447–453.

Bartlett, F. C. *Remembering: A study in experimental and social psychology.* London and New York: Cambridge Univ. Press, 1932.

Boring, E. G. A new ambiguous figure. *American Journal of Psychology,* 1930, **42**, 444–445.

Bower, T. G. R. Slant perception and shape constancy in infants. *Science,* 1966, **151**, 832–834.

Bowman, R., & Sutherland, N. S. Discrimination of "W" and "V" shapes by goldfish. *Quarterly Journal of Experimental Psychology,* 1969, **21**, 69–76.

Brice, C. R., & Fennema, C. L. Scene analysis using regions. *Artificial Intelligence,* 1970, **1**, 205–226.

Brown, R., & Hildum, D. C. Expectancy and the perception of symbols. *Language,* 1956, **32**, 411–419.

Clowes, M. B. Picture syntax. In S. Kaneff (Ed.), *Picture language machines.* New York: Academic Press, 1970. Pp. 119–229.

Clowes, M. B. On seeing things. *Artificial Intelligence,* 1971, **2**, 76–119.

Cooper, P. W. Fundamentals of statistical decisions and learning. In A. Grasselli (Ed.), *Automatic interpretation and classification of images.* New York: Academic Press, 1969. Pp. 97–129.

Cronly-Dillon, J. R., Sutherland, N. S., & Wolfe, J. B. Intraretinal transfer of a learned visual shape discrimination in goldfish after section and regeneration of the optic nerve bracchia. *Experimental Neurology,* 1966, **15**, 455–462.

Davenport, R. K., & Rogers, C. M. Intermodal equivalence of stimuli in apes. *Science,* 1970, **168**, 279–280.

de Groot, A. D. *Thought and choice in chess.* The Hague: Mouton, 1965.

Denes, P. B. On the motor theory of speech perception. In W. Wathen-Dunn (Ed.), *Models for the perception of speech and visual form.* Cambridge, Massachusetts: MIT Press, 1967. Pp. 309–314.

Deutsch, J. A. A theory of shape recognition. *British Journal of Psychology,* 1955, **185**, 443–446.

Dodwell, P. C. *Visual pattern recognition.* New York: Holt, 1970. (a)

Dodwell, P. C. Anomalous transfer effects after pattern discrimination training in rats and squirrels. *Journal of Comparative and Physiological Psychology,* 1970, **71**, 42–51. (b)

Eriksen, C. W., & Hake, H. W. Absolute judgements as a function of the stimulus

182   N. S. SUTHERLAND

range and the number of stimulus and response categories. *Journal of Experimental Psychology,* 1955, **49**, 323-332.

Ettlinger, G. Cross-modal transfer of training in monkeys. *Behaviour,* 1960, **16**, 56-65.

Fant, G. Auditory patterns of speech. In W. Wathen-Dunn (Ed.), *Models for the perception of speech and visual form.* Cambridge, Massachusetts: MIT Press, 1967. Pp. 111-126.

Fantz, R. L. Form preferences in newly hatched chicks. *Journal of Comparative and Physiological Psychology,* 1957, **50**, 422-430.

Fitts, P. M., Weinstein, M., Rappaport, M., Anderson, N. S., & Leonard, J. A. Stimulus correlates of visual pattern recognition: A probability approach. *Journal of Experimental Psychology,* 1956, **51**, 1-11.

Ganz, L. Analysis of pattern perception through visual deprivation. Talk given at AAAS meeting, Boston, 1969.

Ganz, L., & Wilson, P. D. Innate generalization of a form discrimination without contouring eye movements. *Journal of Comparative and Physiological Psychology,* 1967, **63**, 258-269.

Gibson, E. J. Perceptual development. In H. W. Stevenson, J. Kagan, & C. Spiker (Eds.), *Child psychology: Sixty-second yearbook of the National Society for the Study of Education.* 1963. Pp. 144-195.

Gibson, E. J. *Principles of perceptual learning and development.* New York: Appleton, 1969.

Grasselli, A. (Ed.) *Automatic interpretation and classification of images.* New York: Academic Press, 1969.

Gregory, R. L., & Wallace, J. G. Recovery from early blindness. *Experimental Psychology Society Monograph,* 1963, No. 2.

Hebb, D. O. *The organization of behavior.* New York: Wiley, 1949.

Hemmings, G. *Pretraining and transfer in shape.* Unpublished Ph.D. thesis, University of Hull, 1965.

Hochberg, J., & Silverstein, A. A quantitative index of stimulus similarity proximity versus differences in brightness. *American Journal of Psychology,* 1956, **69**, 456-458.

Hubel, D. H., & Wiesel, T. N. Receptive fields, binocular interaction and functional architecture in the cat's visual cortex. *Journal of Physiology (London),* 1962, **160**, 106-154.

Hubel, D. H., & Wiesel, T. N. Receptive fields of cells in striate cortex of very young, visually inexperienced kittens. *Journal of Neurophysiology,* 1963, **26**, 994-1002.

Huggins, A. W. F. Distortion of the temporal pattern of speech: Interruption and alteration. *Journal of the Acoustical Society of America,* 1964, **36**, 1055-1064.

Jakobson, R., & Halle, M. *Fundamentals of language.* The Hague: Mouton, 1956.

Kaneff, S. (Ed.) *Picture language machines.* New York: Academic Press, 1970.

Kolers, P. A., & Perkins, D. N. Orientation of letters and their speed of recognition. *Perception and Psychophysics,* 1969, **5**, 275-280.

Krechevsky, I. A note on the perception of linear gestalten in the rat. *Journal of Genetic Psychology,* 1938, **52**, 241-246.

Lashley, K. S. The mechanism of vision. XV. Preliminary studies of the rat's capacity for detail vision. *Journal of General Psychology,* 1938, **18**, 123-193.

Liberman, A. M., Cooper, F. S., Shankweiler, D. P., & Studdert-Kennedy, M. Perception of the speech code. *Psychological Review,* 1967, **74**, 431-461.

Liberman, A. M., Harris, S., Kinney, J. A., & Lane, H. The discrimination of relative onset-time of the components of certain speech and nonspeech patterns. *Journal of Experimental Psychology*, 1961, **61**, 379–388.

Mackintosh, J., & Sutherland, N. S. Visual discrimination by goldfish: The orientation of rectangles. *Animal Behaviour*, 1963, **11**, 135–141.

Miller, G. A. The magical number seven, plus or minus two: Some limits on our capacity for processing information. *Psychological Review*, 1956, **63**, 81–97.

Minsky, M., & Papert, S. *Perceptrons: An introduction to computational geometry.* Cambridge, Massachusetts: MIT Press, 1969.

Muntz, W. R. A. Intraretinal transfer and the function of the optic lobes in octopus. *Quarterly Journal of Experimental Psychology*, 1963, **15**, 116–124.

Muntz, W. R. A., & Sutherland, N. S. The role of crossed and uncrossed optic nerve fibres in the visual discrimination of shape by rats. *Journal of Comparative Neurology*, 1964, **122**, 69–78.

Myers, B., & McCleary, R. A. Interocular transfer of a pattern discrimination in pattern-deprived cats. *Journal of Comparative and Physiological Psychology*, 1964, **57**, 16–21.

Myers, R. E., & Sperry, R. W. Interhemispheric communication through the corpus callosum. *Archives of Neurology and Psychiatry*, 1958, **80**, 298–303.

Narasimhan, R. Labelling schematic and syntactic descriptions of pictures. *Information and Control*, 1964, **7**, 151–179.

Neisser, V. *Cognitive psychology.* New York: Appleton, 1967.

Pollack, I. The information of elementary auditory displays. *Journal of the Acoustical Society of America*, 1952, **24**, 745–749.

Quine, D. A., & Cullen, J. M. The pecking response of young arctic terns *Sterna macrura* and the adaptiveness of the "releasing mechanism." *Ibis*, 1964, **106**, 145–173.

Rabbitt, P. M. Learning to ignore irrelevant information. *American Journal of Psychology*, 1967, **80**, 1–13.

Roberts, L. G. Machine perception of three-dimensional solids. In J. T. Tippett *et al.* (Eds.), *Optical and electro-optical information processing.* Cambridge, Massachusetts: MIT Press, 1965. Pp. 159–197.

Rosenblatt, F. Two theorems of statistical separability in the perceptron. In *Proceedings of a symposium on the mechanisation of thought processes.* London: HM Stationery Office, 1959, Pp 419 450.

Rosenfeld, A. *Picture processing by computer.* New York: Academic Press, 1969.

Rudel, R. G., & Teuber, H-L. Discrimination of direction of line in children. *Journal of Comparative and Physiological Psychology*, 1963, **56**, 892–898.

Rudel, R. G., & Teuber, H-L. Crossmodal transfer of shape discrimination by children. *Neuropsychologia*, 1964, **2**, 1–8.

Rutovitz, D. Centromere finding: Some shape description for small chromosome outlines. In B. Meltzer & D. Michie (Eds.), *Machine intelligence.* Vol. 5. Edinburgh: Edinburgh Univ. Press, 1969. Pp. 435–462.

Schipper, L. An analysis of information transmitted to human observers with auditory signals as a function of number of stimuli and stimulus intensity interval size. Unpublished doctoral dissertation; University of Wisconsin, 1953.

Schneider, G. E. Contrasting visuomotor function of tectum and cortex. *Psychologische Forschung*, 1967, **31**, 52–62.

Shepard, R. N., & Metzler, R. J. Mental rotation of three-dimensional objects. *Science*, 1971, **171**, 701–703.

Stamm, J. S., & Sperry, R. W. Function of corpus callosum in contralateral transfer of somesthetic discrimination in cats. *Journal of Comparative and Physiological Psychology*, 1957, **50**, 138–143.

Stevens, K. N., & Halle, M. Remarks on analysis by synthesis and distinctive features. In W. Wathen-Dunn (Ed.), *Models for the perception of speech and visual form*. Cambridge, Massachusetts: MIT Press, 1967. Pp. 88–102.

Sutherland, N. S. Visual discrimination of orientation and shape by the octopus. *Nature (London)*, 1957, **179**, 11–13.

Sutherland, N. S. A test of a theory of shape discrimination in *Octopus vulgaris* Lamarck. *Journal of Comparative and Physiological Psychology*, 1959, **52**, 135–141. (a)

Sutherland, N. S. Stimulus analysing mechanisms. In *Proceedings of a symposium on the mechanisation of thought processes*. Vol. 2. London: HM Stationery Office, 1959. Pp. 575–609. (b)

Sutherland, N. S. The methods and findings of experiments on the visual discrimination of shape by animals. *Quarterly Journal of Experimental Psychology Monographs*, 1961, **1**, 1–68.

Sutherland, N. S. Shape discrimination and receptive fields. *Nature (London)*, 1963, **197**, 118–122. (a)

Sutherland, N. S. Cat's ability to discriminate oblique rectangles. *Science*, 1963, **139**, 209–210. (b)

Sutherland, N. S. Outlines of a theory of pattern recognition in animals and man. *Proceedings of the Royal Society, Series B*, 1968, **171**, 297–317.

Sutherland, N. S. Shape discrimination in rat, octopus and goldfish: A comparative study. *Journal of Comparative and Physiological Psychology*, 1969, **67**, 160–176.

Sutherland, N. S., & Bowman, R. Discrimination of circles and squares with and without knobs by goldfish. *Quarterly Journal of Experimental Psychology*, 1969, **21**, 330–338.

Sutherland, N. S., & Williams, C. Discrimination of checkerboard patterns by rats. *Quarterly Journal of Experimental Psychology*, 1969, **21**, 77–84.

Tikofsky, R. S., & McInish, J. R. Consonant discrimination by seven year olds: A pilot study. *Psychonomic Science*, 1968, **10**, 61–62.

Uttley, A. M. Temporal and spatial patterns in a conditioned probability machine. In C. E. Shannon & J. McCarthy (Eds.), *Automata studies*. Princeton, New Jersey: Princeton Univ. Press, 1956. Pp. 277–285.

von Senden, M. *Space and sight*. London: Methuen, 1960.

Walk, R. D., & Gibson, E. J. A comparative and analytical study of visual depth perception. *Psychological Monographs*, 1961, **75**, 1–44.

Warren, J. M. Discrimination of mirror-images by cats. *Journal of Comparative and Physiological Psychology*, 1969, **69**, 9–11.

Watts, T. L. Scanning and measuring photographs of bubble chamber tracks using a computer controlled line segment ("PEPR"). In G. C. Cheng *et al.* (Eds.), *Pictorial pattern recognition*. Washington, D.C.: Thompson, 1968. Pp. 175–198.

Wells, M. J. Factors affecting reactions to mysis by newly hatched sepia. *Behaviour*, 1958, **8**, 96–111.

Wertheimer, M. Untersuchung zur Lehre von der Gestalt. II. *Psychologische Forschung*, 1923, **4**, 301–350.

Wertheimer, M. Hebb and Senden on the role of learning in perception. *American Journal of Psychology*, 1951, **64**, 133–137.

Winograd, T. Procedures as a representation for data in a computer program for understanding natural language. Doctoral thesis, Massachusetts Institute of Technology, 1971.

Zeigler, H. P., & Schmerla, S. Visual discrimination by pigeons. *Animal Behaviour,* 1965, **13**, 475–477.

Zusne, L. *Visual perception of form.* New York: Academic Press, 1970.

Chapter 9

CHEMORECEPTION

BERNICE M. WENZEL

I. INTRODUCTION

The term "chemoreception" implies transduction of any type of chemical stimulating energy into nervous impulses. It does not by itself specify particular receptors, ranges of stimulus energy, or types of stimuli. It seems likely that the earliest animal forms received messages from their environments by means of chemical signals alone. As a means of communication, it is undoubtedly as venerable as any, if not the most venerable of all. Consequently, every form of modern animal probably possesses some sort of chemoreceptor but relatively few of these organs have ever been studied in detail.

This discussion is restricted to the conventional categories of taste and smell, those chemoreceptive routes that are characterized by specialized receptors in specific receptor sites, the mouth and nose. Chemical stimulation is also effective in many other places on both the inside and outside of the body through free nerve endings. Such endings occur in the mouth and nose as well, and contribute in ways not yet fully appreciated to the total experiences of odor and flavor.

For more extensive information on chemoreception, a number of books are available that contain research reports on a wide variety of topics (Hayashi, 1967; Kuehner, 1964; Pfaffmann, 1969; Schneider, 1972; Tanyolaç,

1968; Wolstenholme & Knight, 1970; Zotterman, 1963). In large part, the references given for the material in this chapter are in these volumes; further detailed bibliographies can be found there. A few other review articles are also available (Moulton & Beidler, 1967; Tucker & Smith, 1969; Wenzel & Sieck, 1966). In addition, an important reference volume is now available (Beidler, 1971) which should be consulted on all of the topics summarized here, and a new series on chemoreception has been initiated (Johnston, Moulton, & Turk, 1970). An older reference work (Moncrieff, 1967) is still of interest for its breadth of coverage.

II. MORPHOLOGY OF CHEMORECEPTORS

None of man's chemoreceptors appear to be notably unique, either structurally or functionally, compared to those of his mammalian relatives. Indeed, similarities are apparent throughout the vertebrates and to some extent among insects as well. Brief descriptions are included here for all of these groups, therefore, to stress the general continuity.

A. Taste

1. INSECTS

Gustatory sense organs, called taste hairs, have been described on the labellae of various flies. These sensilla are specialized to respond to sugar or salt solutions or to water although no corresponding structural differences have been found. In general, they consist of a projecting cuticular hair and socket. The chemoreceptive cells are bipolar with the cell bodies in the base of the socket and the dendrites extending into the hair and terminating at the base of a pore opening at the tip of the hair. The receptor axons exit through the base of the socket (cf. Slifer, 1970; Stürckow, 1967).

2. VERTEBRATES

In all except fish, taste buds are restricted to the oral cavity, primarily on the tongue and palate, although in man they also occur on the pharynx and, paradoxically, even on the larynx. On the tongue, they are located in the fungiform, foliate, and circumvallate papillae (Fig. 1). In fish, however, they are found on the body surface, often in profuse distribution, as well on the lips and in the mouth (Hara, 1971).

The general structure of all vertebrate taste buds appears to be similar, although some specific differences do occur (Graziadei, 1969; Murray, 1969). They are unique among chemoreceptors in containing specialized sensory cells distinct from the afferent sensory neurons. Forty to sixty taste cells, about 10 μm in diameter, are enclosed in a rounded structure approximately 50 μm in diameter (Fig. 2). A pore opens to the outside, through which the sapid solution can penetrate to reach the taste cells. Unmyelinated nerve fibers, ranging from 0.05 to 1.0 μm, penetrate the base of the bud and make contact with the taste cells in different ways according to species. In mammals, the fibers are invaginated in taste cell pockets close to the pore. In lower vertebrates, the contacts occur farther away at the base of the taste cells. Typical synaptic contacts have been observed in some forms (e.g., human, rabbit, frog, fish) but have not been seen in others (e.g., most mammals). Several taste cells are contacted by branches of one nerve fiber and one cell is contacted by branches of several fibers (Beidler, 1969). How cell and nerve fiber find each other during the continual replacement process is still to be explained.

The taste cells in a single bud have different appearances, which have not yet been satisfactorily identified as different types of mature cells or as cells in different stages of development. The latter possibility is indicated by the facts that (1) a normal turnover rate of 10–11 days has been found for taste cells in the fungiform papillae, (2) taste cells are capable of regeneration following the degenerative effect of nerve section, and (3) both of these phenomena depend on mitosis of surrounding epithelial cells. In lower vertebrates, definite supporting cells are present. At the ultrastructural level, taste cells are supplied with microvilli, about 2.5 μm wide and 0.5–2 μm long, which communicate with the taste pore. Tight junctions in the apical region prevent leakage into the bud by other routes.

The sense of taste is served almost entirely by two cranial nerves (VII and IX) rather than a single one as is the case with the other special senses. The chorda tympani branch of the VIIth (facial) nerve innervates the taste buds of the anterior mammalian tongue; the taste buds of the posterior third are supplied by the IXth (glossopharyngeal) nerve. The relative contributions of the two cranial nerves vary among the different orders. Because of the wider distribution of taste buds in fish, spinal nerves are sometimes involved in the taste pathway. All of the taste fibers join in the medulla to form the tractus solitarius and terminate primarily in the rostral part of the nucleus tractus solitarius. Secondary fibers then ascend in the medial lemniscus to the thalamus where taste representation is distinct from but adjacent to such other qualities of lingual stimulation as touch and temperature. The exact thalamic taste area varies somewhat from species to species; in man, the posteromedial ventral nucleus or accessory semilunar nucleus are generally credited with this function. The

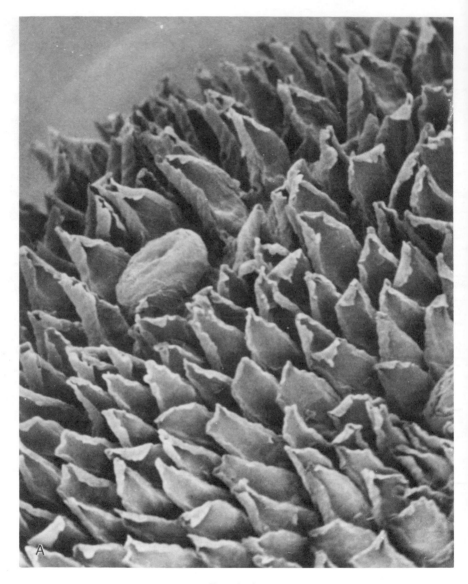

FIG. 1. A.

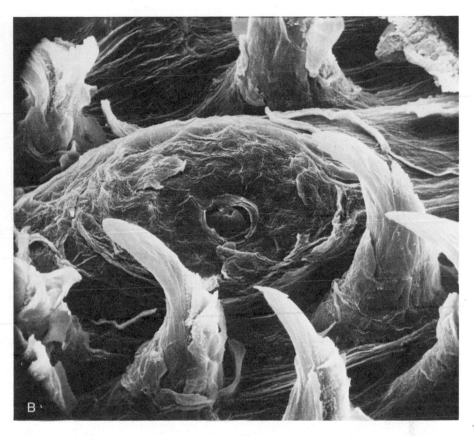

FIG. 1. B.

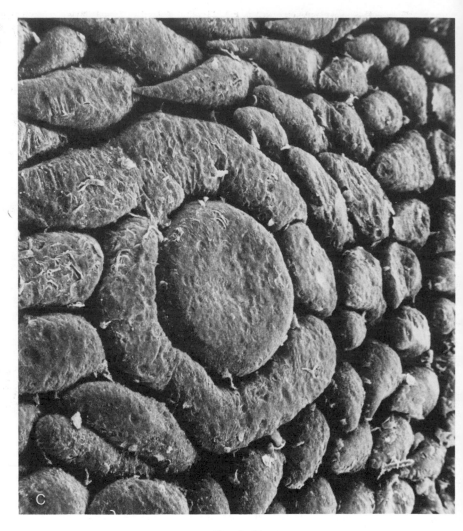

FIG. 1. C.

FIG. 1. D.

FIG. 1. A: Surface of rabbit tongue with filiform papillae and one fungiform papilla. Magnification, ×238. B: Rat fungiform papilla surrounded by filiform papillae. Magnification, ×1200. C: Circumvallate papilla from three-week old puppy. Taste buds are in trenches. Magnification, ×152. D: Foliate papillae of rabbit. Taste buds are in grooves. Magnification, ×212. (From Beidler, 1969.)

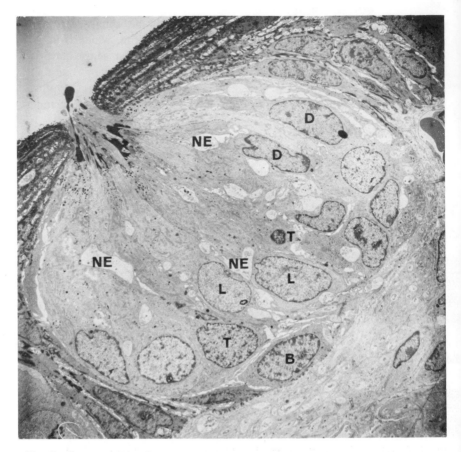

FIG. 2. Cross section of taste bud from rabbit foliate papilla. Various cell types (L: light; D: dark; T: type III; B: basal) are present as well as nerve endings (NE). Magnification: ×2200. (From Murray, 1969.)

thalamocortical pathway terminates in general near the somatosensory oral representation, again with specific differences in different forms. In man, it is in area 43 at the base of the postcentral gyrus.

B. Smell

1. INSECTS

Chemoreceptors for airborne stimuli are situated in sensilla on insects' antennae, sometimes along with sense cells for other modalities such as humidity (Boeckh, Kaissling, & Schneider, 1965). The olfactory cells are bipolar with dendrites directed outward into a sense hair and the axons passing directly to the central nervous system without synapse. Stimulus material reaches the ciliary distal portion of the dendrite, which is in contact with sensillum liquor, through pores in the cuticular sense hair. The number of olfactory cells in one sensillum typically varies from one to six although much larger numbers have been found. Axon diameter is approximately 0.1–0.3 μm and the fibers are unmyelinated. The general arrangement of a sensillum is shown diagrammatically in Fig. 3.

2. VERTEBRATES

In all vertebrates, the olfactory receptors are situated in the nose. In terrestrial forms, this placement puts them in potential contact with inspired air. In fish, the nose is separate from the respiratory channel and various mechanisms have been developed for bringing the water into contact with the sense cells. In aquatic mammals, the olfactory system is apparently vestigial or even absent, as in porpoises.

Within the nasal cavity, the receptor cells lie in the olfactory mucosa, which occupies the posterior region. The extent of its distribution varies. Sometimes it is spread over the upper septum and the superior concha so that its area is increased considerably. It rests on a basement membrane and consists of the sustentacular, supporting cells, and sensory cells. It is covered by a mucous layer in terrestrial forms that is secreted by Bowman's glands. Secretory organs have also been described in some fish but their frequency and function are unknown.

The chemosensitive cells in the mucosa (Steinbrecht, 1969) are essentially the same as those found in insects' sensilla, i.e., bipolar cells with dendrites (1 μm in diameter) extending peripherally, and axons (averaging 0.2 μm in diameter) passing directly into the olfactory bulb of the forebrain. The dendrites commonly terminate in a knob just above the mucosal limit, from which extend cilia of varying length (3–200 μm) and frequency (averaging 6–12). Occasionally, the terminations are in microvilli in addition to or instead of cilia. Supporting cells usually have microvilli. These terminations are in contact with the mucous covering of the epithelium. If the olfactory nerve is cut, the cells degenerate, possibly permanently, although the likelihood of regeneration has not been ruled out. The sustentacular cells typically lie between olfactory cells and prevent their direct contact but some sense cells do touch each other even at the level of the distal processes (de Lorenzo, 1970; Reese & Brightman, 1970). The total number of olfactory cells is a function of the amount of epithelium and the cell density. Estimates have varied from 10,000,000 in man to 224,000,000 in one dog, a German shepherd (Moulton & Beidler, 1967).

The axons (0.2 μm in diameter) of the receptor cells constitute the

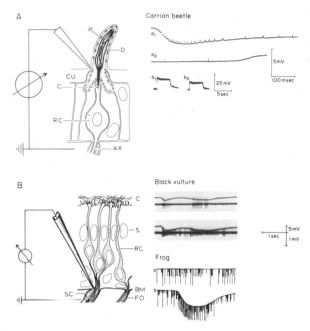

FIG. 3. Olfactory receptor cells and recordings of their electrical activity. A: Insect. At left, an antennal olfactory hair (sensillum basiconicum) of a carrion beetle (*Necrophorus*) with the recording electrode. AX = axon; RC = receptor cell; C = ciliar structure; CU = cuticle; D = dendrite; P = pore in the hair wall. At right, recordings of electrical activity: a_1, start of excitation, stimulus carrion odor; negative downward. The slow potential goes in negative direction; the nerve impulses with their first phase go in positive direction. After several hundred milliseconds, the slow potential and the impulse frequency have reached their plateau. End of the reaction, a_2; after offset of the stimulation the slow potential immediately drops, and the impulses disappear. Slow potentials are shown in b_1 and b_2. Stimulus is carrion odor, four times stronger at b_1 than at b_2. B: Vertebrate. At left is dog olfactory epithelium with the recording electrode. BM = basement membrane; FO = filum olfactorium; SC = Schwann cell; RC = receptor cell; S = supporting cell with microvilli; C = cilium. Right side, electrical activity. Black vulture (*Coragyps atratus*) recording from a single unit in the olfactory epithelium. Slow potentials (upper trace) indicate inspiration (first deflection) and expiration (second deflection). Stimulus in the upper record is 1%, in the lower record 10% saturated atmosphere (20°C) of hexylacetate. Frog (*Rana pipiens*) action potentials recorded with metal-filled micropipettes. Several units are active. Upper record, "resting" activity; lower record, reaction to tetraethyl tin. The superimposed EOG is recorded with an extra electrode. The largest amplitude is about 200 μV; the sweep duration is 10 sec. (From Boeckh, 1969.)

olfactory nerve and pass without synapse into the olfactory bulb at the anterior pole of the brain. The fibers are characteristically ensheathed as groups, rather than individually as is customary elsewhere, an arrangement

that has important implications for patterns of conduction. They may be
collected into two discrete bundles on the left and right as in man, or, if
the distance from mucosa to bulb is very short, the fibers may remain
spread out as fila olfactoria and never become nerve bundles.

The olfactory bulb is a layered structure (Fig. 4) with the unmyelinated
axon terminals of the olfactory nerve fibers outermost. Just under this fiber
layer is the glomerular layer, the zone of contact between the primary and
secondary neurons. Both sets of processes form dense, bushy terminal complexes called glomeruli, in which the synaptic contacts take place at a ratio
of about 1000 axons to one dendrite where estimates have been made.
One axon also contacts several secondary neurons. A variety of other types
of contact have also been seen, including dendrodendritic, dendroaxonic,
and somatodendritic (Andres, 1970; Reese & Brightman, 1970). The cell
bodies of the tufted and mitral cells lie in interior layers. Finally, there is
a deep layer of granule cells and the myelinated axons of the mitral and

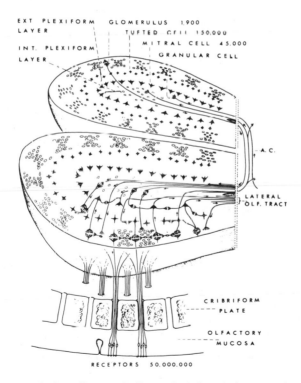

FIG. 4. Structure of the olfactory bulbs and their relations to the nerves and
mucosa. A.C. = anterior commissure. The figures are estimates of the numbers of
each type of cell in an olfactory bulb and in the olfactory mucosa lining one nasal
cavity of the rabbit. (From Moulton & Tucker, 1964.)

tufted cells, which form the olfactory tract. The tract is subdivided into lateral and medial portions, each with a different destination. The medial tract crosses to the opposite side of the brain by way of the anterior commissure and the lateral tract continues to the prepyriform and periamygdaloid areas, part of the cortical amygdaloid nucleus, the olfactory tubercle and olfactory peduncle, and the ventrolateral entorhinal area (Heimer, 1968). In submammalian forms, the distribution of secondary olfactory fibers may be somewhat different but it has not been widely studied. Existing evidence suggests that the olfactory outflow reaches generally analogous regions to those above but in some forms may be even more extensively distributed. A unique feature of this modality is its lack of precortical representation in the thalamus. Further downstream pathways have been shown to reach the anterior hypothalamus and the dorsomedial and lateral habenular nuclei of the thalamus (Powell, Cowan, & Raisman, 1965). Centrifugal fibers reach the bulb from the horizontal limb of the diagonal band by way of the lateral olfactory tract (Price & Powell, 1970).

The nasal cavity of all forms is supplied with free nerve endings of the Vth (trigeminal) nerve, which are sensitive to chemical stimuli. These endings are apparently widely distributed throughout the nasal epithelium. Another very important receptive region for chemical stimuli is the vomeronasal organ. This is found in the majority of vertebrates, with birds and higher primates being the notable exceptions. The epithelium generally resembles the olfactory epithelium except for the absence of basal cells and possible absence of cilia. The nerve fibers project to the accessory olfactory bulb, which projects in turn to the medial and cortical amygdaloid nuclei (Winans & Scalia, 1970).

III. ELECTROPHYSIOLOGY

A. Taste

The basic mechanism for taste is not known and may well be different for different qualities. A recent summary of current hypotheses has been given by Beidler (1970).

The electrical characteristics of the taste pathway have been extensively studied from the individual taste cell in the taste bud to the aggregate response at central sites but as yet there is no complete explanation for the discreteness of separate taste qualities. The convention is widely known that there are four basic taste qualities for man—salt, sweet, sour, and bitter—each with a somewhat different distribution of sensitivity on the tongue so that the thresholds for sweet are lowest at the tip, for sour on the sides, for salt at the tip and sides, and for bitter at the base. No simple morphological or electrical correlates for quality are known in vertebrates. Intracellular recordings from taste cells show that the same cell responds with a positive-going shift in potential to sodium chloride, sucrose, hydrochloric acid, and quinine. In addition, the magnitude of these receptor potentials is closely correlated with the size of the integrated chorda tympani responses (Kimura & Beidler, 1961). Response frequency in individual fibers of the chorda tympani nerve typically increases with concentration of the stimulus, at least up to a point; the relationship appears to be U-shaped in some cases. In a population of neurons, the number of units firing also increases with stimulus concentration. Response magnitude decreases with continuous stimulation.

As soon as research was begun on the responses of single taste fibers, it became apparent that individual vertebrate taste neurons respond to more than one taste quality in the majority of cases, in contrast to insect taste receptors. As information accumulated, it was further realized that the responses of successive neurons in the central pathway become less sharp in this respect, unlike those mediating other sense modalities. The alternative for neuron specificity in stimulus coding is pattern specificity in group responses (Fig. 5) and the available evidence supports this mechanism from the taste neuron to the thalamic relay (Erickson, 1963; Pfaffmann, 1970). At the first synapse in the medulla, there is both a reduction in the distinctiveness of the response patterns in chorda tympani neurons and an increase in response amplitude, a combination that promotes not only the preservation but possibly the improvement of discriminability among patterns (Hal-

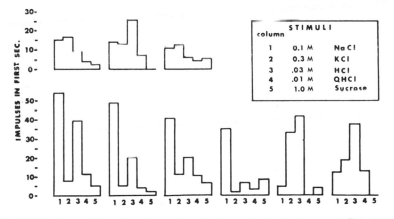

FIG. 5. Number of impulses in each of nine rat chorda tympani fibers during first second of activity evoked by five different stimuli. (From Erickson, 1963.)

pern, 1967). Few data have been collected from the thalamic neurons. The general picture, however, is similar to that of the medulla (Frommer, 1961). Curiously, although a cortical area has been defined on the basis of lesion studies (Benjamin, 1963; Bornstein, 1940), it is sometimes difficult to find responsive cells there. The characteristics of the cortical response have not been determined but recent work indicates modality specificity in some cells and a general spatial organization according to modality, which may vary from species to species (Funakoshi, Kasahara, Yamamoto, & Kawamura, 1972).

Thanks to the fact that the human chorda tympani nerve is exposed during middle ear surgery, valuable data have been obtained on the relation between the intensity of taste perception and the magnitude of the total neural response. The very high correspondence between the two functions (Fig. 6) has led to the suggestion that intensity coding is complete in the afferent neuron and no central mechanisms other than transmission are required to effect perception (Diamant & Zotterman, 1969).

B. Smell

The continuing absence of an accepted theory about what constitutes the adequate olfactory stimulus promotes some inexactness in experimentation. This situation is not the result of lack of interest or efforts; the question simply has not yet yielded its answer. Current hypotheses cannot be discussed here but can be found readily in other sources (Amoore, 1970; Davies, 1970; Wright & Burgess, 1970). A characteristic of olfactory perception is the lack of primary odors and the difficulty of establishing distinct qualitative categories by which the large array of recognizably separate odors can be summarized.

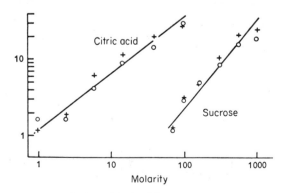

FIG. 6. Nerve responses (◯) and judged intensities (+) for two patients to citric acid and sucrose solutions. (Diamant & Zotterman, 1969.)

A recording electrode placed in contact with the olfactory membrane detects a negative-going potential starting approximately 200 msec after presentation of an odorous stimulus and graded in amplitude with both stimulus intensity and magnitude of the olfactory nerve response. (See Fig. 7 for illustrations of the different electrical responses discussed throughout this section). This potential is called the electro-olfactogram (EOG) (Ottoson, 1970). A small positive potential also occurs, which has been interpreted as the composite of positive potentials originating in both olfactory and supporting cells (Takagi, Aoki, Iino, & Yajima, 1969). Whether or not the EOG is the generator potential for the receptor cell discharge is still unsettled, as is the precise point of its origin. The total trace has been described as the product of negative and positive potentials (Takagi *et al.,* 1969). The proposal has been made that the transducing sites are located on the olfactory cilia when these are present or else on whatever extensions of the sense cell occur, such as microvilli. A disturbing observation that

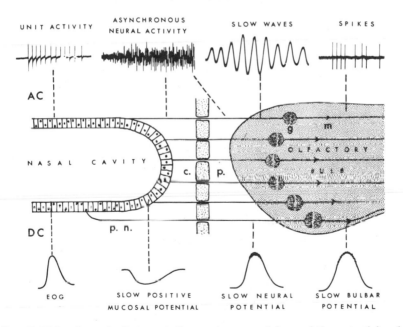

FIG. 7. This schematic diagram indicates the general form of the potentials which can be recorded from various sites in the olfactory mucosa, nerve, and bulb in response to odor stimulation of the mucosa. The distance between the bulb and the mucosa is greatly exaggerated. They are separated only by the cribriform plate. The potentials on the top row are those obtained with A.C. recording; those on the bottom row, D.C. Abbreviations: c.p., cribriform plate; m., mitral cells; p.n., primary olfactory neurones; g., glomerulus; EOG, electro-olfactogram (slow negative mucosal potential). (From Moulton & Tucker, 1964.)

has not yet been accounted for is that the neural response is propagated in preparations in which the EOG has disappeared following removal of the cilia.

No intracellular unit recordings have been made because of the extremely small size of the olfactory cell. Extracellular records, obtained from cell bodies in the epithelium or from individual fibers in the olfactory nerve, have shown that a single unit responds to most, if not all, odors presented but with some differences in pattern (Gesteland, 1967; Shibuya & Tucker, 1967). There is not necessarily a consistent relationship between stimulus intensity and number of spikes recorded from a single fiber (cf. Moulton & Beidler, 1967; Moulton & Tucker, 1964). Some insect receptors differ markedly from mammalian olfactory cells in that they respond maximally to only one natural odorant associated with food or prey, or a sex pheromone.

The striking feature of the bulbar electrical activity is the induced waves, sinusoidal envelopes of varying frequency (as high as 85 Hz) and large amplitude (as high as 200 μV). On the basis of frequency analysis of these bursts in rabbit, monkey, and man, it has been suggested that olfactory quality is coded in burst frequency and that there is a relationship between burst amplitude and both detection and recognition of the stimulus (Hughes, Hendrix, Wetzel, & Johnston, 1969). This matter is far from settled, however, and at the present time neither the significance nor the origin of the induced waves is understood. Spike discharges are also recorded from the bulb as a consequence of odorous stimulation and various types of fibers have been found, such as on, on–off, and off units (Mancia, von Baumgarten, & Green, 1962). Although it appears that the relative amounts of activity at different bulbar sites change with stimulus quality, no meaningful relation of this information to bulbar structure has yet been provided (Higashino, Takeuchi, & Amoore, 1969; Moulton, 1967). Different odorants excite different glomeruli, with a majority of those studied responding to unique sets of stimuli (Leveteau & MacLeod, 1969). Slowly but steadily, data are accumulating about many features of bulbar electrical activity. Much of the information still describes relatively isolated events which cannot yet be expressed as summary generalizations and are too detailed for presentation here. Important generalities that can be mentioned include the significance of centrifugal influences on the bulb from other brain structures, interbulbar inhibitory and facilitatory effects, intrabulbar inhibitory circuits, and a developing impression that the bulb is functioning in a manner very similar to that of the retina, as would be suggested by their structural similarities.

Just as the paths of the olfactory higher-order neurons are only partially known, so their electrical activity is also in need of study (cf. Adey, 1970).

Wave bursts resembling the induced waves recorded from the olfactory bulb occur at a number of downstream locations including the prepyriform cortex and the amygdala. Their significance at these sites appears to involve more than odor reception and is thought to be related to motivational variables. Unit activity in prepyriform cortex is inhibited in the majority of cases by odor presentation, in contrast to the pattern observed in units of the olfactory nerve (Haberly, 1969).

On the basis of the present electrophysiological evidence, it is not possible to say how odor quality or intensity is discriminated. Døving has introduced sophisticated statistical analytic methods "in an attempt to make kosmos out of seeming chaos" (1970, p. 199), an approach that may be especially useful for identifying basic mechanisms. The accelerating pace of research on all aspects of chemoreception should provide very cogent information in the near future.

Acknowledgments

Bibliographic assistance from the Brain Information Service under Contract NIH 70-2063 is gratefully acknowledged.

References

Adey, W. R. Higher olfactory centres. In G. E. W. Wolstenholme & J. Knight. (Eds.), *Taste and smell in vertebrates.* London: Churchill, 1970. Pp. 357–378.

Amoore, J. E. *Molecular basis of odor.* Springfield, Illinois: Thomas, 1970.

Andres, K. H. Anatomy and ultrastructure of the olfactory bulb in fish, amphibia, reptiles, birds, and mammals. In G. E. W. Wolstenholme & J. Knight (Eds.), *Taste and smell in vertebrates.* London: Churchill, 1970. Pp. 177–196.

Beidler, L. M. Innervation of rat fungiform papilla. In C. Pfaffmann (Ed.), *Olfaction and taste III.* New York: Rockefeller Univ. Press, 1969. Pp. 352–369,

Beidler, L. M. Physiological properties of mammalian taste receptors. In G. E. W. Wolstenholme & J. Knight (Eds.), *Taste and smell in vertebrates.* London: Churchill, 1970. Pp. 51–70.

Beidler, L. M. (Ed.) *The chemical senses.* Vol. 4, Part 1. *Handbook of sensory physiology.* Berlin and New York: Springer-Verlag, 1971.

Benjamin, R. M. Some thalamic and cortical mechanisms of taste. In Y. Zotterman (Ed.), *Olfaction and taste.* Oxford: Pergamon, 1963. Pp. 309–329.

Boeckh, J. Electrical activity in olfactory receptor cells. In C. Pfaffmann (Ed.), *Olfaction and taste III.* New York: Rockefeller Univ. Press, 1969. Pp. 34–51.

Boeckh, J., Kaissling, K. E., & Schneider, D. Insect olfactory receptors. *Cold Spring Harbor Symposia on Quantitative Biology,* 1965, **30,** 263–280.

Bornstein, W. S. Cortical representation of taste in man and monkey. II. The localization of the cortical taste area in man and a method of measuring impairment of taste in man. *Yale Journal of Biology and Medicine,* 1940, **13,** 133–156.

Davies, J. T. Recent developments in the "penetration and puncturing" theory of odour. In G. E. W. Wolstenholme & J. Knight (Eds), *Taste and smell in verte-brates.* London: Churchill, 1970. Pp. 265–291.

de Lorenzo, A. J. D. The olfactory neuron and the blood-brain barrier. In G. E. W. Wolstenholme & J. Knight (Eds.), *Taste and smell in vertebrates.* London: Churchill, 1970. Pp. 151–176.

Diamant, H., & Zotterman, Y. A comparative study on the neural and psycho-physical response to taste stimuli. In C. Pfaffmann (Ed.), *Olfaction and taste III.* New York: Rockefeller Univ. Press, 1969. Pp. 428–435.

Døving, K. B. Experiments in olfaction. In G. E. W. Wolstenholme & J. Knight (Eds.), *Taste and smell in vertebrates.* London: Churchill, 1970. Pp. 197–225.

Erickson, R. P. Sensory neural patterns and gustation. In Y. Zotterman (Ed.), *Ol-faction and taste.* Oxford: Pergamon, 1963. Pp. 205–213.

Frommer, G. P. Gustatory afferent response in the thalamus. In M. R. Kare & B. O. Halpern (Eds.), *Physiological and behavioral aspects of taste.* Chicago, Illinois: Univ. of Chicago Press, 1961. Pp. 50–65.

Funakoshi, M., Kasahara, Y., Yamamoto, T., & Kawamura, Y. Taste coding and central perception. In D. Schneider (Ed.), *Olfaction and taste IV.* Stuttgart: Wissenschaftliche Verlagsgesellschaft MBH, 1972. Pp. 336–342.

Gesteland, R. C. Differential impedance changes of the olfactory mucosa with odorous stimulation. In T. Hayashi (Ed.), *Olfaction and taste II.* Oxford: Pergamon, 1967. Pp. 821–831.

Graziadei, P. P. C. The ultrastructure of vertebrate taste buds. In C. Pfaffmann (Ed.), *Olfaction and taste III.* New York: Rockefeller Univ. Press, 1969. Pp. 315–330.

Haberly, L. B. Single unit responses to odor in the prepyriform cortex of the rat. *Brain Research,* 1969, **12**, 481–484.

Halpern, B. P. Chemotopic coding for sucrose and quinine hydrochloride in the nucleus of the fasciculus solitarius. In T. Hayashi (Ed.), *Olfaction and taste II.* Oxford: Pergamon, 1967. Pp. 549–562.

Hara, T. J. Chemoreception. In W. S. Hoar & D. J. Randall (Eds.), *Fish Physiology.* Vol. 5. New York: Academic Press, 1971. Pp. 79–120.

Hayashi, T. (Ed.) *Olfaction and taste II.* Oxford: Pergamon, 1967.

Heimer, L. Synaptic distribution of centripetal and centrifugal nerve fibres in the olfactory system of the rat. An experimental anatomical study. *Journal of Anatomy,* 1968, **103**, 413–432.

Higashino, S., Takeuchi, H., & Amoore, J. E. Mechanism of olfactory discrimination in the olfactory bulb of the bullfrog. In C. Pfaffmann (Ed.), *Olfaction and taste III.* Rockefeller Univ. Press, 1969. Pp. 192–211.

Hughes, J. R., Hendrix, D. E., Wetzel, N., & Johnston, J. W., Jr. Correlations between electrophysiological activity from the human olfactory bulb and the subjective response to odoriferous stimuli. In C. Pfaffmann (Ed.), *Olfaction and taste III.* New York: Rockefeller Univ. Press, 1969. Pp. 172–191.

Johnston, J. W., Jr., Moulton, D. G., & Turk, A. (Eds.) *Advances in chemoreception.* Vol. 1. *Communication by chemical signals.* New York: Appleton, 1970.

Kimura, K., & Beidler, L. M. Microelectrode study of taste receptors of rat and hamster. *Journal of Cellular and Comparative Physiology,* 1961, **58**, 131–139.

Kuehner, R. L. (Ed.) Recent advances in odor: Theory, measurement, and control. *Annals of the New York Academy of Sciences,* 1964, **116**, Art. 2, 357–746.

Leveteau, J., & MacLeod, P. La discrimination des odeurs par les glomérules olfactifs du lapin: Influence de la concentration du stimulus. *Journal de Physiologie (Paris)*, 1969, **61**, 5–16.

Mancia, M., von Baumgarten, R., & Green, J. D. Response patterns of olfactory bulb neurons. *Archives Italiennes de Biologie*, 1962, **100**, 449–462.

Moncrieff, R. W. *The chemical senses*, 3rd ed. London: Hill, 1967.

Moulton, D. G. Spatio-temporal patterning of response in the olfactory system. In T. Hayashi (Ed.), *Olfaction and taste II*. Oxford: Pergamon, 1967. Pp. 109–116.

Moulton, D. G., & Beidler, L. M. Structure and function in the peripheral olfactory system. *Physiological Reviews*, 1967, **47**, 1–52.

Moulton, D. G., & Tucker, D. Electrophysiology of the olfactory system. *Annals of the New York Academy of Sciences*, 1964, **116**, Art. 2, 380–428.

Murray, R. G. Cell types in rabbit taste buds. In C. Pfaffmann (Ed.), *Olfaction and taste III*. New York: Rockefeller Univ. Press, 1969. Pp. 331–344.

Ottoson, D. Electrical signs of olfactory transducer action. In G. E. W. Wolstenholme & J. Knight (Eds.), *Taste and smell in vertebrates*. London: Churchill, 1970. Pp. 343–356.

Pfaffmann, C. (Ed.) *Olfaction and taste III*. New York: Rockefeller Univ. Press, 1969.

Pfaffmann, C. Physiological and behavioural processes of the sense of taste. In G. E. W. Wolstenholme & J. Knight (Eds.), *Taste and smell in vertebrates*. London: Churchill, 1970. Pp. 31–50.

Pfaffmann, C., Fisher, G. L., & Frank, M. K. The sensory and behavioral factors in taste preferences. In T. Hayashi (Ed.), *Olfaction and taste II*. Oxford: Pergamon, 1967. Pp. 361–381.

Powell, T. P. S., Cowan, W. M., & Raisman, G. The central olfactory connexions. *Journal of Anatomy*, 1965, **99**, 791–813.

Price, J. L., & Powell, T. P. S. An experimental study of the origin and the course of the centrifugal fibres to the olfactory bulb in the rat. *Journal of Anatomy*, 1970, **107**, 215–237.

Reese, T. S., & Brightman, M. W. Olfactory surface and central olfactory connexions in some vertebrates. In G. E. W. Wolstenholme & J. Knight (Eds.), *Taste and smell in vertebrates*. London: Churchill, 1970. Pp. 115–149.

Schneider, D. (Ed.) *Olfaction and taste IV*. Stuttgart: Wissenschaftliche Verlagsgesellschaft MBH, 1972.

Shibuya, T., & Tucker, D. Single unit responses of olfactory receptors in vultures. In T. Hayashi (Ed.), *Olfaction and taste II*. Oxford: Pergamon, 1967. Pp. 219–233.

Slifer, E. H. The structure of arthropod chemoreceptors. *Annual Review of Entomology*, 1970, **15**, 121–142.

Steinbrecht, R. A. Comparative morphology of olfactory receptors. In C. Pfaffmann (Ed.), *Olfaction and taste III*. New York: Rockefeller Univ. Press, 1969. Pp. 3–21.

Stürckow, B. Occurrence of a viscous substance at the tip of the labellar taste hair of the blowfly. In T. Hayashi (Ed.), *Olfaction and taste II*. Oxford: Pergamon, 1967. Pp. 707–720.

Takagi, S. F., Aoki, K., Iino, M., & Yajima, T. The electropositive potential in the normal and degenerating olfactory epithelium. In C. Pfaffmann (Ed.), *Olfaction and taste III*. New York: Rockefeller Univ. Press, 1969. Pp. 92–108.

Tanyolaç, N. (Ed.) *Theories of odors and odor measurement*. Bebek, Istanbul, Turkey: Robert College Research Center, 1968.

Tucker, D., & Smith, J. C. The chemical senses. *Annual Review of Psychology,* 1969, **20,** 129–158.

Wenzel, B. M., & Sieck, M. H. Olfaction. *Annual Review of Physiology,* 1966, **28,** 381–434.

Winans, S. S., & Scalia, F. Amygdaloid nucleus: New afferent input from the vomeronasal organ. *Science,* 1970, **170,** 330–332.

Wolstenholme, G. E. W., & Knight, J. (Eds.) *Taste and smell in vertebrates.* London: Churchill, 1970.

Wright, R. H., & Burgess, R. E. Specific physicochemical mechanism of olfactory stimulation. In G. E. W. Wolstenholme & J. Knight (Eds.), *Taste and smell in vertebrates.* London: Churchill, 1970. Pp. 325–342.

Yamada, K. The glossopharyngeal nerve response to taste and thermal stimuli in the rat, rabbit, and cat. In T. Hayashi (Ed.), *Olfaction and taste II.* Oxford: Pergamon, 1967. Pp. 459–464.

Zotterman, Y. (Ed.) *Olfaction and taste.* Oxford: Pergamon, 1963.

Chapter 10

TASTING AND SMELLING

BERNICE M. WENZEL

I. INTRODUCTION

The extent to which chemical stimuli regulate animals' lives must vary from almost not at all to almost completely. Such an assertion is admittedly difficult to quantify, and there has been no serious attempt to construct a continuum. Convention would place man close to the lowest point. Nonetheless, it seems fair to say that taste stimuli influence human beings considerably even to the point of assisting survival by preventing ingestion of noxious food and drink, and it can be argued that olfactory stimuli also are more effective than often realized. Not only do they warn of possible danger but they improve many aspects of our less vital activities such as grooming and housekeeping and their contribution to flavor is widely recognized. While it is true that human beings do not identify their acquaintances in terms of their odors, it seems equally true that they prefer not to do so even when they can. Indeed, it has often been suggested that the great age of exploration was much encouraged by the desire for spices and scents to disguise the disagreeable tastes and malodors that abounded at the time. Such influences can hardly be said to be insignificant. The loss of ability to smell is usually tolerable, though often unhappily so, but ageusia frequently is accompanied by profound dissatisfaction due to the loss of familiar and appealing tastes, and can lead to malnutrition and even anorexia.

This chapter is concerned with gustatory and olfactory influences on several aspects of vertebrate behavior. It should be considered as only a minimal introduction to the subject, which has many ramifications and raises implications that have been little appreciated in the past.

II. SENSITIVITY

Any threshold value is dependent upon many variables in the experimental situation, from the psychophysical method used and the condition of the subjects to the physical characteristics of the environment during stimulation. The goal of such research, aside from the practical one of establishing norms for diagnosis or environmental control, is to establish a general order of magnitude of both absolute and differential sensitivity, which is essential information for the development of theories about receptor function.

Table I shows some thresholds for man to give an idea of the values ob-

TABLE I

EXAMPLES OF HUMAN OLFACTORY AND GUSTATORY THRESHOLDS[a]

Stimulus	Concentration	Source
Odors		
n-Butyric acid	2.4×10^{-11}	Neuhaus & Goldenberg (1966, p. 26)
Ethyl caprinate	4.0×10^{-11}	Neuhaus & Goldenberg (1966, p. 26)
Ethyl undecylate	7.2×10^{-12}	Neuhaus & Goldenberg (1966, p. 26)
α-Ionone	8.9×10^{-13}	Neuhaus & Goldenberg (1966, p. 26)
Propionic acid	2.2×10^{-10}	Neuhaus & Goldenberg (1966, p. 26)
Benzene	4.7×10^{-7}	Köster (1971, pp. 71–72)
Cyclopentanone	5.6×10^{-6}	Köster (1971, pp. 71–72)
β-Ionone	6.0×10^{-7}	Köster (1971, pp. 71–72)
Methyl salicylate	7.3×10^{-7}	Köster (1971, pp. 71–72)
Isopropanol	8.0×10^{-5}	Köster (1971, pp. 71–72)
m-Xylene	5.1×10^{-8}	Köster (1971, pp. 71–72)
Tastes		
Citric acid	$0.0023\ N$	Pfaffmann (1959, pp. 514–521)
Hydrochloric acid	$0.009\ N$	Pfaffmann (1959, pp. 514–521)
Sodium chloride	$0.01\ M$	Pfaffmann (1959, pp. 514–521)
Sodium iodide	$0.028\ M$	Pfaffmann (1959, pp. 514–521)
Saccharin	$0.000023\ M$	Pfaffmann (1959, pp. 514–521)
Sucrose	$0.01\ M$	Pfaffmann (1959, pp. 514–521)
Quinine hydrochloride	$0.00003\ M$	Pfaffmann (1959, pp. 514–521)
Quinine sulfate	$0.00008\ M$	Pfaffmann (1959, pp. 514–521)

[a]Odor concentrations are expressed as moles/liter of air. Detection level is 50% for the first five and 70% for the last six. Taste thresholds are based on various experiments and are typically 50% detection values.

tained. Some interesting effects on detection thresholds for both taste and smell stimuli (Henkin, 1969) show the contribution of hormonal and metabolic factors to the operation of chemoreceptors (see Section IV). Limited work on infants (Reese & Lipsitt, 1970, pp. 56–62) has indicated that both tastes and smells are adequate stimuli on the first days after birth but no reliable estimates of sensitivity are available. Acuity appears to decline with smoking and age (Amoore, 1970; Kimbrell & Furchtgott, 1963). With the multiplicity of odors man perceives, it is possible to have normal acuity for almost all of them and very limited acuity for a small group. This condition in its clearest form is called specific anosmia and has been used to help identify separate odor classes (Amoore, 1970).

The importance of the method used to determine threshold is impressively documented by an experiment in which the technique of conditioned suppression, with aversive brain stimulation as reinforcement, was used to measure absolute taste thresholds in rats. The values obtained for saccharin, sodium chloride, hydrochloric acid, and quinine hydrochloride were three to six times lower than those previously reported from behavioral experiments (Shaber, Brent, & Rumsey, 1970). The same technique, with shock applied peripherally rather than centrally, has been used to measure both absolute and differential olfactory thresholds in rats (Davis, 1971) and pigeons (Henton, Smith, & Tucker, 1966; Shumake, Smith, & Tucker, 1969). From these studies, Davis concluded that man's threshold for detection is between that of the rat and of the pigeon but appears to be lower than theirs for intensity discrimination.

As with other modalities, the stimuli for both taste and smell represent a variety of qualities. Although the categories of sweet, sour, salt, and bitter have not been seriously challenged for human taste, the addition of a water taste has been receiving increasingly serious attention (McBurney & Bartoshuk, 1972; McBurney & Shick, 1971). An analogous list of odor qualities has never been agreed upon. Discrimination is said to be comparable to that for visual and auditory stimuli (Engen, 1970). Absolute odor identification is rather limited, contrary to impressions gained from descriptions of perfumers' prowess, and also appears consistent with this ability in other modalities (Jones, 1968). The parameters of olfactory stimuli are still debatable and may remain so until the transduction mechanism is understood (cf. Amoore, 1970; Harper, Bate Smith, & Land, 1968).

A common observation about odors is the rapidity and severity of adaptation. Research on this phenomenon has shown that recovery, after a controlled sniff of odor at low intensity, occurs at different rates for different stimuli and in some cases is biphasic, fast initially and then slower (Köster, 1971). The hope that cross adaptation effects, the influence of one stimulus on sensitivity to another, would contribute to understanding of basic odor qualities and receptor action has not been realized. Such effects occur but take a variety of forms. Two generalizations of interest are (*1*) that no odorous stimulus increases sensitivity to another, and (*2*) the greatest reduction in sensitivity is always created by prior exposure to the same odor rather than any other (Köster, 1971).

Adaptation to taste stimuli is less marked under ordinary conditions of stimulation than it is to odors. Experiments on cross adaptation (McBurney, 1969) indicate that the qualities other than salt may not be unitary in terms of sense organ or neural functioning. An interesting, rarely recognized, example is the effect of saliva on sensitivity to salt. Sodium chloride thresholds in human subjects are lower if the tongue is rinsed with distilled water between stimuli, and are raised to levels just above those of rinses of different NaCl concentrations (McBurney & Pfaffmann, 1963). Such a relationship can explain lower thresholds for salt reported in connection with conditions of sodium depletion (cf. Section IV).

The intensity of taste sensations can also be influenced by substances called taste modifiers. Two of these have been of special recent interest (Kurihara, Kurihara, & Beidler, 1969) because of their implications for understanding basic mechanisms of taste. A protein from the fruit of an African shrub (*Synsephalum dulcificum*) has the property of inducing a sweet taste from an acid stimulus that normally produces only sourness. Because of this property, the berry is called miracle fruit. It does not affect thresholds and its effect is specific to acids, as well as directly proportional to the sourness of the acid. Conversely, gymnemic acid, extracted from the leaves of an Indian plant (*Gymnema sylvestre*), suppresses sweetness including that produced by miracle fruit (Bartoshuk, Dateo, Vanderbelt, Buttrick, & Long, 1969). These compounds, and others that may not yet be known, have potential practical importance in addition to their scientific value.

III. PREFERENCES

The complex results obtained in studies on this topic suggest that two categories can be considered, one for basic long-term preferences and aversions that are probably based on a combination of genetic and profound experiential influences, and a second that expresses temporary special conditions such as metabolic imbalances. Chemical stimuli are somewhat different from those for the other special senses in that there is usually an hedonic quality as well as the cognitive aspect. Such stimuli, therefore, have both positive and negative reinforcing properties. Pfaffmann (1960) has discussed interesting ramifications and implications of this aspect of chemical stimulation.

Reactions to taste stimuli have been widely studied in both man and other animals and innate preference-aversion tendencies have been consistently found. The sweet taste is almost universally appealing as bitter is almost universally rejected. Within the category of sweetness, some compounds are more highly preferred than others. These relationships cannot yet be accounted for in terms of chemical characteristics or neural response patterns. The innate tendencies can be modified by such factors as rate of ingestion, amount ingested, nutritional status, preceding stimuli, etc. Experiments with animals have demonstrated the reality of the familiar human experience that sudden aversions may develop for foods that are followed by gastrointestinal illness shortly after ingestion. Rats that are poisoned with a single intragastric injection of lithium chloride shortly after eating or drinking specific substances show a subsequent aversion to that substance (Nachman, 1963). Even a 12-hour delay between ingestion and illness can be effective (Smith & Roll, 1967). An important result of this work has been to show the crucial nature of taste stimulation. If the ingested substances are placed directly into the stomach rather than passing through the mouth in the usual way, no aversion occurs subsequent to the illness (Smith, 1970).

As with taste, there appear to be widespread similarities among human subjects with respect to preferences and aversions for odors. The accumulating evidence on nonhuman animals, however, suggests that cross-species similarities are less uniform than for gustatory stimuli. This question has not been attacked directly, but indirect evidence comes from research discussed below (Section V).

A wealth of material on human preference behavior regarding odors has been presented by Moncrieff (1966). It is too extensive even to summarize here, other than to indicate that he found unanimous agreement about "really bad smells," considerable agreement about "really good smells," greater influence of age than sex on preferences, and higher preference for natural odors than for synthetics. The latter result was less true for children and may represent the increased familiarity of contemporary children with synthetic materials rather than a true age effect in this case.

IV. DIETARY AND METABOLIC FACTORS

The development of specific appetites can be considered as an extension of the topic of preferences discussed above. Inasmuch as metabolism is affected to some extent by the chemical mixture ingested, taste preferences can have an indirect metabolic effect through their control over food selection. The additional fact that taste preferences can be modified by metabolic conditions sets the stage for a regulatory feedback loop (Tepperman, 1961). Little research in this area has been conducted with human subjects but it is clear from experiments on rats, for example, that specific conditions of feeding can affect subsequent dietary habits. LeMagnen (1963) demonstrated that rats can be made to regulate food intake on the basis of olfactory cues. Intake of their standard diet, flavored with either citral or eucalyptol, was reduced as a result of daily postprandial injections of glucose amounting to an additional 25% of the caloric intake. Normal amounts were consumed of the dietary mixture that had not been associated with subsequent glucose injections. Further studies showed that olfactory differences between the two food mixtures were more potent for later choice than were tactile, visual, or spatial differences.

It is well known that specific deficiencies can lead to compensatory intake. This type of adjustment has never been clearly demonstrated for man nor has the rat's mechanism been identified by which taste acceptability is altered. Rats maintained on a sodium-deficient diet increase their intake of sodium chloride solutions but no differences have been found in chorda tympani activity (Nachman & Pfaffmann, 1963). The effect of salivary sodium levels on salt thresholds is discussed above (Section II).

The changes in taste acuity that accompany certain diseases and altered metabolic states may help to explain specific appetites. Persons with adrenal cortical insufficiency experience a craving for salt presumably analogous to the condition of rats maintained on sodium deficient diets. Tests of their taste sensitivity show that their detection thresholds are lower than normal for all taste qualities and not for salt alone (Henkin, 1969). Threshold levels returned to normal during treatment with prednisolone, a carbohydrate-active steroid, but not with deoxycorticosterone acetate although the latter compound does affect preference thresholds for salt in rats (Fregly, 1969). On the basis of Henkin's finding that olfactory, auditory, and proprioceptive acuities are all improved with adrenal cortical insufficiency, he has proposed that the effect is a direct one on neural transmission. A decline in taste acuity is associated with either increased levels of thiols or a reduction in serum copper concentration. If these levels are returned to normal, the hypogeusia is also corrected. In such cases, Henkin feels that the effect occurs at the level of the taste buds and reflects a change in protein conformation (Henkin & Bradley, 1969).

It is not clear to what extent special conditions may affect taste and smell sensitivity separately nor is it clear whether olfactory sensitivity is critically important in regulating intake. The role of olfactory sensitivity is most likely to be a modifying, rather than a determining, one. The direct involvement of the olfactory bulbs in control of water intake, at least after sodium loading, has been indicated by experiments with rats (Vance, 1967). There is some evidence that human olfactory acuity is lower after eating (Berg, Pangborn, Roessler, & Webb, 1963) although nothing is known of the mechanism for such a change if it is actually genuine.

Although olfactory sensations, as well as gustatory ones, can be useful in regulating intake, they are not essential for a normal rat whose food is provided, as in a laboratory situation. If rats are maintained in such a way that all food and water enter the stomach directly and completely bypass oropharyngeal receptors, normal levels of fluid and caloric intake are maintained over long periods. The importance of gustatory stimulation appears dramatically in an animal with bilateral lesions in the lateral hypothalamus and resultant aphagia and adipsia. If highly palatable food is provided, such an animal will begin to eat after the initial stage in which it must be tube-fed. Conversely, an animal with ventral hypothalamic lesions, who becomes hyperphagic, shows a greater than normal reluctance to eat food with quinine added (Teitelbaum & Epstein, 1963). Exactly how much control such stimulation exerts when caloric intake is not naturally maintained at a constant level, as in human beings, is largely unknown. The presumption is that it becomes progressively more important as other regulating factors decline.

V. CHEMICAL COMMUNICATION AND PHEROMONES

It is when humans contemplate the dog, or even the ant, tracking an odorous trail that they probably feel at their most inadequate in terms of olfactory ability. Although there are isolated instances, largely anecdotal, of human beings following scent trails, this is an activity at which human beings are simply not generally adept. McCartney (1968) briefly summarizes data on acuity of groups of island natives and of blind subjects. Not surprisingly, the results are too inconsistent to permit conclusions about the possible benefits for olfactory acuity of remoteness from civilization or of deprivation in other sensory modalities.

The ubiquitous character of olfactory signals in the lives of animals in general is being increasingly demonstrated by research in the very rapidly growing field of olfactory communication. Not only is the range of communication impressive but the delicacy of interaction between the endocrine and olfactory systems, which is beginning to emerge, is also noteworthy. Only a few examples can be discussed here to give notice of a topic that should not be overlooked. Its possible implications for human perception are still in the future although at least one author (Kloek, 1961) has already considered some of them in detail. A valuable summary of research on organisms from insects to man has recently been published (Johnston, Moulton & Turk, 1970).

As Wilson (1965) has made clear, much of insect society may well be under the influence of chemical signals, which have been termed pheromones and defined as "substances which are secreted to the outside of an individual and received by a second individual of the same species, in which they release a specific action, for example, a definite behavioural or developmental process" (Kalmus, 1965, p. 188). Interest in sex pheromones has been prominent in the work on insects, and the compounds have been identified in many instances and even synthesized in some. It appears that the sexes find each other primarily by this means. The same compound is produced in some instances by several members of a subfamily; segregation of species then depends on the influence of other characteristics such as diurnal cycles and territorial distribution. In addition to sex attractants, other insect pheromones are involved in actual mating, in marking of both aerial and terrestrial trails, food sources, nest entrances, etc., in alerting, in both temporary and long-term aggregations, and in sexual maturation.

Among vertebrates and especially mammals, the only other group studied at all extensively in this connection, the participation of odors in behavioral control has been demonstrated in a variety of situations and the story is only beginning to unfold (Cowley & Wise, 1970; Johnston, Moulton, & Turk, 1970). The same categories of behavior mentioned above are affected by the pheromones of vertebrates. The presumed general significance of such communication is stressed by the following statement (Bardach & Todd, 1970, pp. 236–237): "Many fish probably have evolved pheromones as a means whereby individuality and status can be communicated irrespective of water transparency or time of day and, thus, they have taken a step to the subsequent evolution of complex social behavior." Primate behavior as well has been shown to be influenced in some of these ways and it would be surprising if this sort of behavioral control has become completely ineffective for human beings (Michael, Keverne, & Bonsall, 1971). Some of the types of relationships discovered are illustrated in the following examples, which include both primer and releaser effects, the former developing slowly through endocrine mediation and the latter occurring promptly, presumably through neural mediation.

A frightened fish emits a pheromone that releases escape behavior in adjacent fish of the same species (Kleerekoper, 1969). Infant rats, separated from their mothers, reduce their motor activity in response to maternal odor (Schapiro & Salas, 1970) and this effect can be related to changes in the electrical activity of the olfactory bulbs during development (Salas, Schapiro, & Guzman-Flores, 1970). Wild deermice of one species

(*Peromyscus maniculatus*) show regular orienting responses to odors of male and female mice of their own species but not to those of a different species (*P. polionotus*), who in turn show no such discrete response pattern. This type of behavioral specialization has been suggested as important in maintaining independence of species (Moore, 1965). Laboratory rats can be trained to respond differentially in a lever pressing task to odors of stressed and unstressed rats, a discrimination shown to be independent of possible recognition of odors of individual rats (Valenta & Rigby, 1968). Removal of the olfactory bulbs from male golden hamsters eliminates all mating behavior and this effect is not seen after blinding, unilateral bulbectomy, or sham operation (Murphy & Schneider, 1970). A very well-known effect is the pregnancy block in female mice caused by the odor of strange male mice (Bruce, 1959). Recent work has shown that neurons in the olfactory bulb, preoptic area, and lateral hypothalamus of female mice respond to the odor of male urine but responding is not limited to urine odors nor is it typically differentiated between odors from normal and castrated males (Scott & Pfaff, 1970). The latter point is important because females of the strain used show both estrous and behavioral sensitivity to the distinction in male sexual condition. How the nervous system produces the response differentiations is not yet understood.

The varied behavioral evidence that is steadily accumulating for many types of chemical communication, especially intraspecific, accentuates the current lack of information about the chemical identity, source, mode of reception, and central neural processing for most of the suspected compounds involved. This work lies ahead and will undoubtedly reveal many different mechanisms and chemical compounds. What it will reveal about human perception is impossible to predict. The argument has been made (LeMagnen, 1970, p. 400) that chemical communicating is favored by animals that flourish in dark or silent habitats, and that man, conversely, "is diurnal, has discovered artificial illumination, and is also a very noisy and chattering animal." He may, therefore, have sacrificed a rich olfactory heritage.

Acknowledgments

Bibliographic assistance from the Brain Information Service under contract NIH 70-2063 is gratefully acknowledged.

References

Amoore, J. E. *Molecular basis of odor.* Springfield, Illinois: Thomas, 1970.
Bardach, J. E., & Todd, J. H. Chemical communication in fish. In J. W. Johnston,

Jr., D. G. Moulton, & A. Turk (Eds.), *Advances in chemoreception*. Vol. I. *Communication by chemical signals*. New York: Appleton, 1970. Pp. 205–240.

Bartoshuk, L. M., Dateo, G. P., Vanderbelt, D. J., Buttrick, R. L., & Long, L. J. Effects of *Gymnema sylvestre* and *Synsephalum dulcificum* on taste in man. In C. Pfaffmann (Ed.), *Olfaction and taste III*. New York: Rockefeller Univ. Press, 1969. Pp. 436–444.

Berg, H. W., Pangborn, R. M., Roessler, E. B., & Webb, A. D. Influence of hunger on olfactory acuity. *Nature (London)*, 1963, **197**, 108.

Bruce, H. M. An exteroceptive block to pregnancy in the mouse. *Nature (London)*, 1959, **184**, 105.

Cowley, J. J., & Wise, D. R. Pheromones, growth and behaviour. In R. Porter & J. Birch (Eds.), *Chemical influences on behaviour*. London: Churchill, 1970. Pp. 144–170.

Davis, R. G. Olfactory psychophysical measurements in the rat with a conditioned suppression behavior. University Microfilms, Ann Arbor, Mich. No. 71-29, 296-1971.

Engen, T. Man's ability to perceive odors. In J. W. Johnston, Jr., D. G. Moulton, & A. Turk (Eds.), *Advances in chemoreception*. Vol. I. *Communication by chemical signals*. New York: Appleton, 1970. Pp. 361–383.

Fregly, M. J. Preference threshold and appetite for NaCl solution as affected by propylthiouracil and desoxycorticosterone acetate in rats. In C. Pfaffmann (Ed.), *Olfaction and taste III*. New York: Rockefeller Univ. Press, 1969. Pp. 554–561.

Harper, R., Bate Smith, E. C., & Land, D. G. *Odour description and odour classification*. London: Churchill, 1968.

Henkin, R. I. The metabolic regulation of taste acuity. In C. Pfaffmann (Ed.), *Olfaction and taste III*. New York: Rockefeller Univ. Press, 1969. Pp. 574–585.

Henkin, R. I., & Bradley, D. F. Regulation of taste acuity by thiols and metal ions. *Proceedings of the National Academy of Sciences of the United States*, 1969, **62**, 30–37.

Henton, W. W., Smith, J. C., & Tucker, D. Odor discrimination in pigeons. *Science*, 1966, **153**, 1138–1139.

Jones, F. N. The informational content of olfactory quality. In N. Tanyolaç (Ed.), *Theories of odor and odor measurement*. Bebek, Istanbul, Turkey: Robert College Research Center, 1968. Pp. 133–141.

Johnston, J. W., Jr., Moulton, D. G., & Turk, A. (Eds.) *Advances in chemoreception*. Vol. I. *Communication by chemical signals*. New York: Appleton, 1970.

Kalmus, H. Possibilities and constraints of chemical telecommunication. In S. Taylor (Ed.) Amsterdam and New York: Excerpta Medica Foundation, 1965. *Proceedings of the 2nd international congress on endocrinology*. Part 1. Pp. 188–192.

Kimbrell, G. McA., & Furchtgott, E. The effect of aging on olfactory threshold. *Journal of Gerontology*, 1963, **18**, 364–365.

Kleerekoper, H. *Olfaction in fishes*. Bloomington, Indiana: Indiana Univ. Press, 1969.

Kloek, J. The smell of some steroid sex-hormones and their metabolites. Reflections and experiments concerning the significance of smell for the mutual relation of the sexes. *Psychiatria, Neurologia, Neurochirurgia*, 1961, **64**, 309–344.

Köster, E. P. *Adaptation and cross-adaptation in olfaction*. Rotterdam: Bronder-Offset, 1971.

Kurihara, K., Kurihara, Y., & Beidler, L. M. Isolation and mechanism of taste modifiers; taste-modifying protein and gymnemic acids. In C. Pfaffmann (Ed.), *Olfaction and taste III.* New York: Rockefeller Univ. Press, 1969. Pp. 450–469.

LeMagnen, J. Olfactory identification of chemical units and mixtures and its role in behavior. In Y. Zotterman (Ed.), *Olfaction and taste.* Oxford: Pergamon, 1963. Pp. 337–345.

LeMagnen, J. Communication by chemical signals: Conclusion. In J. W. Johnston, Jr., D. G. Moulton, & A. Turk (Eds.), *Advances in chemoreception.* Vol. I. *Communication by chemical signals.* New York: Appleton, 1970. Pp. 393 404.

McBurney, D. H. Effects of adaptation on human taste function. In C. Pfaffmann (Ed.), *Olfaction and taste III.* New York: Rockefeller Univ. Press, 1969. Pp. 407–419.

McBurney, D. H., & Bartoshuk, L. M. Water taste in mammals. In D. Schneider (Ed.), *Olfaction and taste IV.* Stuttgart: Wissenschaftliche Verlagsgesellschaft MBH, 1972. Pp. 329–335.

McBurney, D. H., & Pfaffmann, C. Gustatory adaptation to saliva and sodium chloride. *Journal of Experimental Psychology,* 1963, **65,** 523–529.

McBurney, D. H., & Shick, T. R. Taste and water taste of 26 compounds for man. *Perception & Psychophysics,* 1971, **10,** 249–252.

McCartney, W. *Olfaction and odours.* Berlin and New York: Springer-Verlag, 1968. Pp. 103–107.

Michael, R. P., Keverne, E. B., & Bonsall, R. W. Pheromones: Isolation of male sex attractants from a female primate. *Science,* 1971, **172,** 964–966.

Moncrieff, R. W. *Odour preferences.* London: Hill, 1966.

Moore, R. E. Olfactory discrimination as an isolating mechanism between *Peromyscus maniculatus* and *Peromyscus polionotus. American Midland Naturalist,* 1965, **73,** 85–100.

Murphy, M. R., & Schneider, G. E. Olfactory bulb removal eliminates mating behavior in the male golden hamster. *Science,* 1970, **167,** 302–304.

Nachman, M. Learned aversion to the taste of lithium chloride and generalization to other salts. *Journal of Comparative and Physiological Psychology,* 1963, **56,** 343–349.

Nachman, M., & Pfaffmann, C. Gustatory nerve discharge in normal and sodium-deficient rats. *Journal of Comparative and Physiological Psychology,* 1963, **56,** 1007–1011.

Neuhaus, W., & Goldenberg, D, M Perception of single and mixed odors in man Final Technical Report, European Research Office. United States Army, Contract No. DA-91-591-EUC-3630, February 1966. University of Erlangen-Nurenberg, Erlangen, Federal Republic of Germany.

Pfaffmann, C. The sense of taste. In Amer. Physiol. Soc., J. Field (Ed.), *Handbook of physiology.* Sect. 1. *Neurophysiology.* Vol. I. Baltimore, Maryland: Williams & Wilkins, 1959. Pp. 507–533.

Pfaffmann, C. The pleasures of sensation. *Psychological Review,* 1960, **67,** 253–268.

Reese, H. W., & Lipsitt, L. P. *Experimental child psychology.* New York: Academic Press, 1970.

Salas, M., Schapiro, S., & Guzman-Flores, C. Development of olfactory bulb discrimination between maternal and food odors. *Physiology & Behavior,* 1970, **5,** 1261–1264.

Schapiro, S., & Salas, M. Behavioral response of infant rats to maternal odor. *Physiology & Behavior,* 1970, **5,** 815–818.

Scott, J. W., & Pfaff, D. W. Behavioral and electrophysiological responses of female mice to male urine odors. *Physiology & Behavior*, 1970, **5**, 407–411.

Shaber, G. S., Brent, R. L., & Rumsey, J. A. Conditioned suppression taste thresholds in the rat. *Journal of Comparative and Physiological Psychology*, 1970, **73**, 193–201.

Shumake, S. A., Smith, J. C., & Tucker, D. Olfactory intensity-difference thresholds in the pigeon. *Journal of Comparative and Physiological Psychology*, 1969, **67**, 64–69.

Smith, J. C., & Roll, D. L. Trace conditioning with X-rays as an aversive stimulus. *Psychonomic Science*, 1967, **9**, 11–12.

Smith, R. G. The role of alimentary chemoreceptors in the development of taste aversion. *Communications in Behavioral Biology, Part A*, 1970, **5**, 199–204.

Teitelbaum, P., & Epstein, A. N. The role of taste and smell in the regulation of food and water intake. In Y. Zotterman (Ed.), *Olfaction and taste*. Oxford: Pergamon, 1963. Pp. 347–360.

Tepperman, J. Metabolic and taste interactions. In M. R. Kare & B. O. Halpern (Eds.), *Physiological and behavioral aspects of taste*. Chicago, Illinois: Univ. of Chicago Press, 1961. Pp. 92–103.

Valenta, J. G., & Rigby, M. K. Discrimination of the odor of stressed rats. *Science*, 1968, **161**, 599–601.

Vance, W. B. Olfactory bulb resection and water intake in the white rat. *Psychonomic Science*, 1967, **8**, 131.

Wilson, E. O. Chemical communication in the social insects. *Science*, 1965, **149**, 1064–1071.

Chapter 11

CUTANEOUS MECHANORECEPTORS

PAUL R. BURGESS

Primary sensory neurons (also called primary afferent neurons) extend from the various tissues of the body, such as skin, muscle, periosteum, gut, etc., to the central nervous system. The terminal portions of the neuron which lie in the peripheral tissue constitute the receptive part of the cell. Here the stimulus is received and translated into nerve impulses. These "all or nothing" impulses propogate along the transmissive (axonal) portion of the neuron and convey whatever sensory information reaches the central nervous system about the stimulus.

This chapter is concerned with mammalian cutaneous mechanoreceptors, i.e., receptors that respond to non-noxious deformation of the skin. Certain terms are used in describing receptor properties. These terms are listed and some are illustrated in Fig. 1. It will be useful to define these terms before discussing cutaneous mechanoreceptors specifically since they reflect the criteria used for classifying mechanoreceptors.

I. CRITERIA FOR CLASSIFICATION OF CUTANEOUS MECHANORECEPTIVE NEURONS

1. TRANSMISSIVE PORTION OF NEURON

a. DIAMETER OF AFFERENT AXON. Primary sensory axons are not all of the same size. Most of those supplying the skin of the cat fall into three

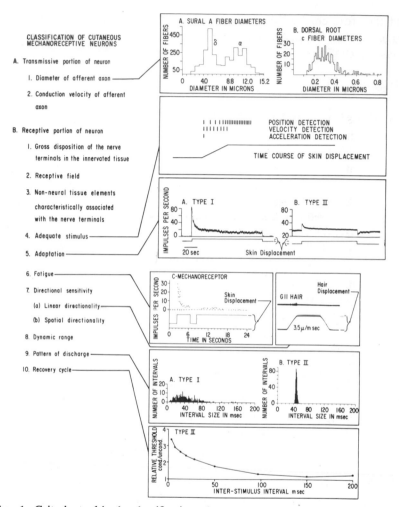

FIG. 1. Criteria used in the classification of cutaneous mechanoreceptive neurons.

major categories: alpha myelinated fibers (diameter 7–13 μm including myelin), delta myelinated fibers (diameter 1–6 μm including myelin) and unmyelinated or C fibers (diameter 0.4–1.1 μm). Similar groupings of fibers are found in the cutaneous nerves of other mammals. Mechanoreceptors are associated with fibers in all three categories.

b. CONDUCTION VELOCITY OF AFFERENT AXON. The conduction velocity of an axon is related to its diameter. If alpha fiber diameter in μm is multiplied by a factor of six, the approximate conduction velocity can be obtained (Hursh, 1939). A conversion factor near four seems more appropriate for delta fibers (see Burgess, Petit, & Warren, 1968). C Fibers lack myelin and therefore conduct disproportionately slowly. A factor of 1.7 has been suggested for the conversion of C fiber diameter to conduction velocity (Gasser, 1955).

2. RECEPTIVE PORTION OF NEURON

a. GROSS DISPOSITION OF THE NERVE TERMINALS IN THE INNERVATED TISSUE. The disposition of the nerve terminals in the skin varies from one receptor type to another and is a function of the amount of branching which the afferent fiber undergoes as well as the length and relative position of the branches.

b. RECEPTIVE FIELD. The "receptive field" of a sensory neuron is defined as the peripheral area from which it can be excited by a stimulus that exceeds threshold by some stated amount. In many cases, this area appears to be roughly coextensive with the region where the neuron terminals are located. In other cases, the receptor can be readily excited by stimuli propagating from remote sites.

c. NON-NEURAL TISSUE ELEMENTS CHARACTERISTICALLY ASSOCIATED WITH THE NERVE TERMINALS. Non-neural elements associated with nerve terminals, such as encapsulating cells or hair follicles, are of interest because they are the structures which must be deformed to excite the endings and thus may select the type of stimulus that is effective. A distinctive type of non-neural specialization is the "receptor" cell. In the skin, specialized epithelial cells (Merkel cells) are found in association with certain sensory nerve terminals. The relationship has some features suggestive of a synapse, the epithelial cell being presynaptic (Andres, 1966). There is evidence that such cells are important in the transduction of the stimulus and sometimes they have been called receptors. In the present usage the sensory nerve terminals proper are considered the receptor since non-neural receptor cells are not found in association with most mechanoreceptive endings.

The mechanical properties of the non-neural tissues interposed between the external stimulus and the receptive neural membrane should also be considered. In the case of a receptor responding to hair movement, for example, the hair shaft provides a link between the stimulator and the follicle where the nerve terminals are located, and the mechanical properties of the hair shaft will be important in determining how the stimulus is transmitted.

d. ADEQUATE STIMULUS. The adequate stimulus of a receptor will be defined as the stimulus to which it responds with greatest sensitivity. A description of the mechanical status of a structure at any moment in time can be made in terms of (1) the position of the structure, (2) the rate at which the position is changing (velocity), (3) the rate at which the velocity is changing (acceleration), (4) the rate at which the acceleration is changing (jerk), etc. Each of these terms will be considered a "mode" of mechanical stimulation and a potential adequate stimulus for a mechanoreceptor. When cutaneous mechanoreceptors are examined in terms of the nature of the adequate stimulus, three main classes of behavior can be distinguished: (*1*) position detection, (*2*) velocity detection, and (*3*) detection of "rapid transients."

The meaning of the rest of the physiological criteria to be used in receptor classification can perhaps best be illustrated with an example. For simplicity, let us consider a receptor which provides information only about the position of some body part. Imagine that the innervated structure (a hair follicle, for example) can move back and forth in more than one direction. When external forces are minimal, the structure will assume a certain "rest" position. Ongoing mechanoreceptor activity is generally at its lowest level when the innervated structure is at rest, suggesting that nerve terminal deformation is least under these conditions. The rest position of an innervated structure thus defines a physiological zero point from which to measure receptor output as a function of displacement. Let us assign the number zero to the position of the structure at rest and the number 100 to maximum deviation from the rest position in a particular direction. One way in which position information could be signalled is for the frequency of occurrence of the impulses produced by the fiber to be proportional to position.

Various factors influence the precision with which the position of a structure can be specified by receptor activity.

e. ADAPTATION. Precision is increased if the discharge frequency is independent of the time that a particular position is held or the speed with which it is reached. A decline in the discharge of a receptor while the stimulus to which it responds is unchanging is called adaptation (Adrian & Zotterman, 1926). An accurate position response is favored by the absence of adaptation or any source of sensitivity to the rate of stimulus application.

f. FATIGUE. Greater precision is possible when the response is reproducible. One source of systematic variability is fatigue. Fatigue is present when a receptor responds less vigorously to repeated applications of the same stimulus. An ideal position detector should not fatigue or be subjected to variability from other sources.

g. LINEAR AND SPATIAL DIRECTIONALITY. Precision is increased if the frequency is independent of the direction that the structure moves to arrive at a particular position. Directional sensitivity would be present if the discharge at position 20 were different when that position was reached by moving, for example, from 0 to 20 as compared with moving from 50 to 20. Directional sensitivity of this sort (which might be called "linear directionality") should be distinguished from the responsiveness of a receptor to movements in different directions. A receptor that responds when a structure is moved in certain directions but not others is said to show "spatial directionality."

h. DYNAMIC RANGE. A large dynamic range adds to the precision with which the position of an innervated structure can be specified. In defining the dynamic range of a receptor, it is necessary to make some specific assumption about how the information is "coded." The nature of the physiologically meaningful code is dictated by how central neurons respond to the sensory discharge. There is some evidence that central neurons are influenced in proportion to the frequency of receptor nerve impulses, at least in the case of mechanoreceptors signalling position (Jansen, Nicolaysen, & Rudjord, 1966; see also Harrington & Merzenich, 1970; Hartline & Ratliff, 1957; Mountcastle, Talbot, & Kornhuber, 1966; Werner & Mountcastle, 1965). Assuming that the "physiological" code is a frequency code, the dynamic range of a position receptor is defined as the frequency when deformation is greatest minus the frequency when deformation is least. The change in frequency for a given change in position ("sensitivity") need not be linear over the entire range through which the structure can be displaced. In most receptors sensitivity decreases as stimulus intensity increases.

i. PATTERN OF DISCHARGE. The accuracy with which the position of the structure is specified as a function of time is related to the pattern of discharge. If the receptor produces nerve impulses in a regular train so that the intervals between successive impulses do not differ much from one another, less time is required to establish what the frequency is than if the discharge is more irregular.

j. RECOVERY CYCLE. An important factor influencing the dynamic range and pattern of discharge of a receptor is its recovery cycle. The recovery cycle refers to a decrease in receptor excitability that follows the generation of an impulse. It is readily measured by exciting the receptor with two short duration mechanical pulses which are separated by varying intervals. At a particular interstimulus interval, the threshold is determined for the second of the two stimuli (which is called the conditioned stimulus) and this threshold is compared with that obtained when the first stimulus of the pair is not given. (In this case, the stimulus is unconditioned.) Another interval is chosen and the process repeated until the range of intervals for which the conditioned and unconditioned stimuli differ in threshold has been explored. The results are expressed as the ratio of the conditioned to the unconditioned stimuli at various interstimulus intervals.

The above discussion defines some of the criteria used in receptor classification and indicates in a general way factors which influence information transmission from a single receptor which signals position. Strict position receptors are rare in nature and are not found in the skin. However, the principles which govern information transmission are of general significance and apply whether a receptor signals position, velocity, or rapid transients. In the subsequent discussion, receptor types that appear designed to detect similar stimuli will be considered together for comparison. Receptors in hairy skin will be presented first, followed by a discussion of receptors associated with certain specialized structures such as teeth, vibrissae, and glabrous skin.

II. MECHANORECEPTORS IN HAIRY SKIN

Mechanoreceptors in hairy skin have been most thoroughly studied in the cat, but rabbits and monkeys have been used also. There is remarkable similarity in the mechanoreceptor populations of these different animals and the receptors described below have been found in all three groups.

A. Receptors Detecting Position and Velocity

One way to assess the adequate stimulus of a mechanoreceptor is to determine the response to stimuli of constant position, constant velocity, constant acceleration, etc. A constant position stimulus can be obtained by abruptly displacing the skin to a new location and holding it there. Any receptor which discharges when a stimulator is stationary will be defined as a "position detector." Cutaneous position detectors differ in the degree to which the position response is developed. In all cases the position response adapts, i.e., the rate of firing reaches a peak at the time the indentation is applied and then declines while the stimulator remains steady (see Fig. 1, Adaptation). The discharge of many receptors adapts to zero within a few seconds, and neurons of this type will be treated in the next section since they appear to be primarily concerned with velocity detection. What will be discussed in this section are two receptors in mammalian hairy skin (Type I and Type II) that have a position response which, after a period of initial adaptation, becomes time independent (Fig. 1, Adaptation). Receptors like these which generate a nonadapting position response will be considered to have "static displacement detection".

When a receptor with position detection is subjected to constant velocity indentation, the frequency of discharge will increase as a function of displacement without being influenced by ramp velocity, if the receptor does not adapt (Fig. 1, Position Detection). The response of the receptor will depend on the velocity of the ramp if adaptation occurs. Let us consider a receptor which first adapts rapidly and then ceases to adapt such that a static displacement discharge is produced. Low velocity ramps will plot the frequency of this static response as a function of displacement, since slow ramps will allow time for adaptation to occur. When ramps of increasing velocity exceed the rate of decay of adaptation, the frequency-versus-displacement curves will steepen, increasing the dynamic range of the response (Figs. 2 and 3). Thus adaptation may impart rate sensitivity to a position receptor. The rate sensitivity of the receptor is enhanced still further if the receptor also has "velocity detection" as such. Both Type I and Type II cutaneous receptors possess this property.

If a receptor lacks position detection but produces a nonadapting response

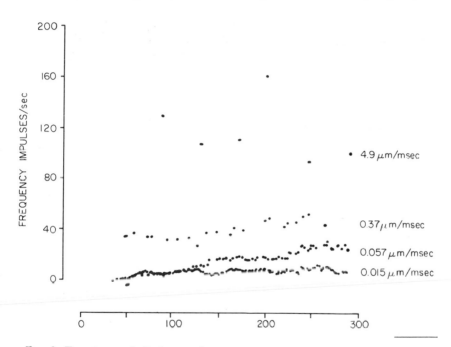

FIG. 2. Frequency of discharge of a Type I cutaneous receptor plotted against skin displacement at the indicated velocities of skin displacement. A single stimulus repetition is plotted at each velocity. The lowest velocity was not slow enough to give a steady-state response. At the highest velocity each point represents the reciprocal of the interval between two successive impulses plotted at the displacement of the second impulse, giving an "instantaneous" frequency. At the lower velocities a sliding average frequency has been plotted to smooth irregularities in the discharge. A sliding average is computed by averaging the instantaneous frequencies of an odd number of intervals and plotting the averaged value at the displacement of the second impulse of the central interval. The process is then repeated after shifting one impulse along the discharge. The frequencies of seven intervals were averaged at 0.37 μm/msec, eleven intervals at 0.057 μm/msec, and eleven intervals at 0.015 μm/msec.

which is proportional to stimulus velocity (see Fig. 1, Velocity Detection), a plot of frequency versus displacement yields a horizontal line when a constant velocity stimulus is used (Brown & Iggo, 1967; Lindblom, 1962). (Whenever frequency-versus-displacement plots are referred to it is assumed that frequency is represented on the ordinate and displacement on the abscissa, as in Figs. 2 and 3.) If the velocity response adapts, a downward sloping curve is obtained. As stimulus velocity increases, the curves, whatever their shape, are displaced upward to progressively higher frequencies. A receptor with these properties will be called a "velocity detector". When a receptor possesses both an adapting position response and velocity detection, plots of frequency versus displacement will both steepen with increasing ramp velocity and be displaced upward (Figs. 2 and 3) (Chambers, Andres, v. Duering, & Iggo, 1972; Iggo & Muir, 1969). The relative magnitude of these effects will depend upon the rate and extent of the adaptation of the position response and the degree to which the receptor detects velocity. In general, only steepening of the curves is seen with low velocity ramps since the velocity term is small under these conditions (Figs. 2 and 3). As would be expected, velocity signalling becomes more prominent with higher velocity

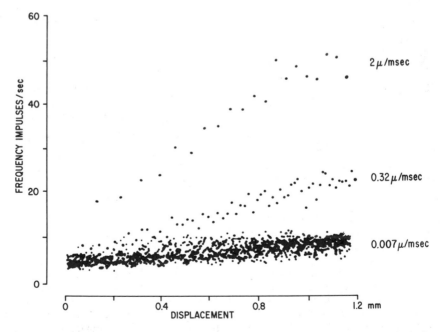

FIG. 3. Frequency of discharge of a Type II cutaneous receptor plotted against skin displacement. Each set of points represents the instantaneous frequency produced by a single stimulus repetition at the indicated velocity. The lowest velocity produced a near steady-state response.

ramps and receptors may fail to signal position during high velocity stimuli (Fig. 2). Similar arguments can be made to distinguish between an adapting velocity response and "true" acceleration detection.

When Type I and Type II cutaneous receptors are studied with constant velocity displacements of varying rate certain differences are observed. Although both Type I and Type II endings detect position and velocity, Type II receptors are more responsive to position and less to velocity than Type I receptors. Low velocity ramps, 500–1000 μm in amplitude, reveal that the dynamic range of the Type I static displacement response is only about 10 impulses/sec. The static Type II response has a dynamic range of 20–25 impulses/sec in those receptors where it is well developed (Burgess et al., 1968). It may be concluded that Type I receptors do not provide much information about skin position under steady-state conditions. Individual Type II receptors provide more steady-state information, but still are not comparable to certain other receptors like secondary muscle spindle endings which appear to be more specialized for position detection.

As ramp velocity increases, the frequency-versus-displacement curves of Type I and Type II endings both steepen and are displaced upward (Chambers et al, 1972; Iggo & Muir, 1969). In the case of Type II receptors, the upward displacement is less on the average, indicating lower velocity sensitivity (compare Figs. 2 and 3). With further increases in stimulus velocity, the position response of Type I receptors decreases (Fig. 2) and the frequency versus displacement curves may assume a horizontal orientation or, at very high velocities, a downward slope (P. R. Burgess & K. W. Horch, unpublished; Nilsson, 1969; Tapper, 1965, Fig. 3). It is not known why this loss of position response occurs, but it is clear that receptors in which the ratio of velocity sensitivity to static sensitivity is high are more readily converted to "pure" velocity receptors during rapid stimulator movement than those in which this ratio is lower (Lindblom, 1963; Matthews, 1963; Stuart, Ott, Ishikawa, & Eldred, 1965). Thus Type II receptors typically shift toward velocity detection at higher ramp velocities than Type I receptors, as illustrated by Figs. 2 and 3.

During high velocity stimulation Type I receptors may discharge briefly at frequencies as high as 1000/sec. Type II receptors respond to comparable stimuli at frequencies up to 800/sec (Chambers et al., 1972). If a stimulus is abruptly applied and maintained, the high velocity of the initial displacement causes a high frequency discharge which eventually adapts to the static levels described above. Thus, the dynamic range of the response will be greater as the discharge is sampled progressively earlier after stimulus application. If an appreciable fraction of the full frequency range of either of these receptors is to be utilized, the stimulator must be moving or have recently stopped.

1. MORPHOLOGY

A single Type I fiber characteristically supplies two or three small dome-like elevations on the skin, each 200–500 μm across (Iggo, 1963; Tapper, 1964). As Iggo (1963) and Iggo and Muir (1969) have shown, the nerve fiber in each dome branches to supply a number of specialized epithelial cells (Merkel cells) located at the base of the thickened epithelium which invests the structure. Further studies by Iggo (1966) and Chambers et al. (1972) have shown that individual Type II fibers are not associated with domes but end at a single low threshold point where a Ruffini ending is located.

2. DISCHARGE PATTERN AND RECOVERY CYCLE

Type II receptors generate a more regular pattern of discharge under constant stimulus conditions than Type I receptors (see Fig. 1, Pattern of Discharge) (Burgess et al., 1968; Chambers et al., 1972; Iggo, 1966; Iggo & Muir, 1969). For example, a Type II receptor discharging at a mean frequency of 20 impulses/sec may produce no intervals shorter than 40 msec or longer than 69 msec. A Type I receptor discharging at the same mean frequency commonly produces intervals as short as 5 msec and as long as 100 msec.

Type I and Type II receptors also have recovery cycles that differ in magnitude and duration. The significance of the recovery cycle of a receptor for its pattern of discharge and the dynamic range of its response can be appreciated by examining the way in which receptors generate nerve impulses. Studies of various mechanoreceptors have indicated the following steps: (1) The stimulus deforms the sensory nerve terminals, causing them to depolarize. This depolarization (called the generator potential) increases with increasing stimulus strength. (2) The generator potential spreads electrotonically to a low threshold portion of the sensory neuron (the impulse generating zone) where nerve impulses are set up, if the depolarization is suprathreshold. The rate at which nerve impulses recur will be influenced by the magnitude and duration of the depression of receptor excitability that follows each impulse. If the excitability depression following an impulse lasts only a few msec the effective dynamic range of the receptor will be reduced, should there be no other means for the generation of a low frequency discharge. A receptor with a short recovery cycle can produce a low frequency discharge which is graded as a function of stimulus intensity if the stimulus increases the frequency and/or amplitude of generator potential oscillations which are sometimes above and sometimes below threshold.

Type I receptors have substantially shorter recovery cycles than Type II receptors. After a Type I receptor discharges an orthodromic impulse, clear excitability depression cannot be detected for longer than 40–50 msec (Lindblom & Tapper, 1967). Excitability may be depressed in Type II receptors for over 100 msec after an impulse has occurred (Fig. 1, Recovery Cycle) (P. R. Burgess & K. W. Horch, unpublished). However, the difference in recovery cycles is insufficient to explain the different firing patterns of these receptors and Type I receptors also seem to have larger "effective" generator potential fluctuations than Type II receptors.

Thus, the irregularity of Type I discharge as compared with Type II activity appears to be due both to a shorter recovery cycle and a more variable generator potential. The overall consequence is a receptor that increases its frequency of discharge as a function of increasing stimulus intensity by increasing the frequency and/or amplitude of the fluctuations on the generator potential. The origin of these fluctuations is uncertain, but the relationship between Type I nerve terminals and Merkel cells has some features suggestive of a synapse (Andres, 1966; Iggo & Muir, 1969). In particular, the Merkel cell cytoplasm near the nerve terminal has dense core vesicles which might be liberated onto the terminal and produce a transient depolarization. This notion must be considered hypothetical until more direct evidence is obtained for such a "synapse" in the skin, especially since the actual size of the generator potential fluctuations is unknown.

Whether the difference in discharge pattern between Type I and Type II receptors is important in the subsequent transmission of sensory information is not known. Less information per unit time is transmitted by irregular interspike intervals than by a regular impulse train. On the other hand, the irregular Type I discharge favors the occurrence of closely spaced impulses onto any second order system where Type I fibers converge. If closely spaced impulses have important summative properties at central synapses, a Type I discharge pattern might have functional significance.

3. INPUT–OUTPUT FUNCTIONS AND DYNAMIC RANGE

In order to know the dynamic range of a receptor, an input–output function must be defined. This is an expression which relates the frequency of discharge of the receptor to the position, velocity or acceleration, etc, of the stimulus. In general, a receptor will not discharge until a certain threshold has been exceeded. The discharge then increases in some fashion as the stimulus is further increased until a saturation value is reached beyond which no appreciable increase in discharge occurs. Different receptor types have shown different input–output functions. In some cases, a linear function has been found to provide a good description ($y = a + bx$, where y = frequency of discharge, x = suprathreshold stimulus, and a and b are constants). Other receptors are best described by a log function ($y = a +$

$b \log x$), a power function ($y = ax^b$), or an exponential function ($\log y = a + bx$).

In determining input–output relationships for receptors which signal both position and velocity, it is important to distinguish the aspect of the receptors' behavior being measured. Most studies have been concerned with some aspect of the position response, evaluating frequency of discharge as a function of indentation. Abrupt indentations have generally been used, and the frequency of discharge measured for the first 500–1000 msec of the response. The dynamic range for these times varied from 100 to 300 impulses/sec with displacements of 500–1000 μm. The earlier the frequency was sampled after indentation the larger was the dynamic range.

The sensitivity of a receptor decreases with increasing indentation when the input–output relationship is described by a power function with an exponent less than one. The sensitivity is uniform with indentation when the relationship is linear and the sensitivity increases with indentation when the input–output function is exponential. The first and second of these relationships have been suggested for Type I receptors (Harrington & Merzenich, 1970; Kenton, Kruger & Woo, 1971; Tapper, 1964; Werner & Mountcastle, 1965), and the first and third for Type II receptors (Harrington & Merzenich, 1970; Kenton, Kruger, & Woo, 1971; Werner & Mountcastle, 1965). The reasons for the different results obtained by different investigators is not clear although species differences may be responsible in part.

The position response of Type II receptors has also been studied 15–20 sec after the beginning of an abrupt indentation (Werner & Mountcastle, 1965). Since considerable adaptation has occurred by this time, the dynamic range of the receptor is limited (less than 30 impulses/sec for indentations of 1000 μm). The sensitivity was generally uniform at different levels of indentation and the input–output function tended toward linearity. A similar trend was observed by Jänig, Schmidt, and Zimmermann (1968) when input–output functions were assessed at progressively longer times after the onset of a stimulus. A number of receptors from a variety of sources have been shown to produce linear input–output functions when the position response is tested sometime after the onset of an abrupt stimulus and this may be a general property of adapted position responses.

An input–output function has been obtained for the velocity response of Type I receptors (Tapper, 1965). Stimuli of constant amplitude were used and the velocity systematically varied. The stimuli were rapid for the most part so that the receptor functioned largely as a velocity detector (Tapper, 1965, Fig. 3). The dynamic range of the response exceeded 600 impulses/sec with stimulus velocities up to 50 μm/msec and the input–output relationship was well described by power functions with exponents ranging from 0.3 to 0.55. Therefore, the sensitivity of the velocity response decreased at higher stimulus velocities. As will be discussed in greater detail below, relationships of this sort commonly have been found when testing the velocity responses of mechanoreceptors.

4. Linear Directionality

Type I and Type II cutaneous receptors resemble other receptors with both position and velocity sensitivity in that the velocity discharge occurs only during movement away from the rest position (P. R. Burgess & K. W. Horch, unpublished). Thus directionality of the velocity response is pronounced. Linear directionality of the position responses of Type I and Type II receptors might be expected to differ in magnitude. Since Type II receptors are more specialized for position detection than Type I receptors they would be expected to show less directionality. Detailed studies of mammalian receptors have not been made, but in reptilian skin, Kenton et al. (1971) have found that Type II receptors fatigue less readily than Type I receptors. If a receptor fatigues, its threshold increases during a maintained response and this will clearly contribute to linear directionality.

5. Spatial Directionality and Sensitivity to Skin Stretch

Type I receptors are not readily excited unless the stimulator contacts the dome directly; stretching the dome by remote stimulation produces little discharge. Type II receptors are effectively excited by a stimulator that encounters the focus of the receptor, but they can also be activated when the focus is stretched by stimulation at a distance. Type II receptors show spatial directionality when stimulated by skin stretch. If the receptor is most easily excited by stretch in one direction, stretch applied at an angle of 90 degrees usually causes a decrease in activity (Chambers et al. 1972; Knibestöl & Vallbo, 1970). Type II receptors commonly have a resting discharge, sometimes as high as 20 impulses/sec, in the absence of deliberate stimulation. This is presumably caused by some persistent stretch of the focal region. Type I receptors rarely have a resting discharge in excess of 1–2 impulses/sec, which is consistent with their lack of stretch sensitivity.

6. Conduction Velocity of Afferent Fibers

Both Type I and Type II fibers have diameters in the alpha range and are among the rapidly conducting fibers in cutaneous nerves. Type II fibers conduct slower than Type I fibers on the average.

7. SUMMARY

Type I and Type II cutaneous mechanoreceptors are *similar* in several respects (Fig. 4): (*1*) Both detect position and velocity. (*2*) The nerve terminals are localized to a small area such that the receptive fields are focused or punctate. (*3*) Displacements of the order of 5–15 μm are sufficient to elicit activity when applied to the focus. (*4*) Linear directionality is present.

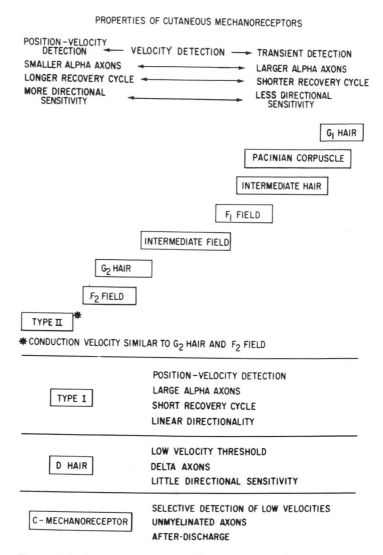

FIG. 4. Distribution of properties among cutaneous mechanoreceptors.

There are also *differences* between these receptors: (*1*) Type I endings have less capacity for static displacement detection and a more vigorous velocity response than Type II endings. (*2*) Type I fibers usually form two or three sensitive foci, Type II fibers only one, and the terminal morphology differs. (*3*) Type II endings are excited by skin stretch and show spatial directionality when so stimulated. (*4*) Type II receptors have longer recovery cycles and a more regular pattern of discharge than Type I receptors.

Type II endings have properties that are comparable in many respects to static displacement detectors in the deeper tissues of mammals. Such receptors in muscles, tendons, ligaments, etc., have confined terminations often of the Ruffini-type, static responses that are typically well developed, patterns of discharge which are regular, long duration recovery cycles and are activated when the tissue that contains them is stretched. Type I and other Merkel cell receptors emerge, therefore, as distinctive; no other mammalian mechanoreceptors are known which, when subjected to a near threshold stationary stimulus, produce an irregular discharge containing short intervals (Fig. 4).

B. Receptors Detecting Velocity

The receptors included in this section have little or no position response and alter their discharge primarily as a function of stimulus velocity. Their neurons have axons that span the entire diameter range present in cutaneous nerves; there are velocity receptors which are the terminations of alpha fibers, delta fibers and C fibers.

1. VELOCITY DETECTORS WITH ALPHA FIBERS

Two classes of velocity detectors are derived from alpha fibers, "hair" receptors and "field" receptors. Hair receptors are distinguished by the fact that they respond vigorously to hair movement. Axons giving rise to hair receptors branch to supply several follicles and only a single isolated hair shaft need be displaced to produce an appreciable response. Field receptor fibers also branch before terminating and each fiber supplies an area (field) of skin.

2. PHYSIOLOGICAL PROPERTIES OF HAIR RECEPTORS

Although there is a continuous distribution of certain physiological properties across the alpha hair receptor population, these receptors have been arbitrarily divided into three categories so that receptors with different features can be identified. Hair receptors that respond to slow hair movement have been called guard$_2$ or G$_2$ receptors; those that require a more rapid displacement are called intermediate hair receptors; and those that respond only if high velocity stimuli are used are called G_1 receptors (see Brown & Iggo, 1967; Burgess *et al.*, 1968; Cremers, 1971; Hunt & McIntyre, 1960b; Merzenich & Harrington, 1969; Perl, 1968). (Guard hairs are long outer coat hairs movement of which excites G_2, intermediate and G_1 hair receptors.) G_2, intermediate and G_1 receptors are derived from alpha fibers that increase in average conduction velocity in that order (Fig. 4). G_1 receptors have been classified as transient detectors because of their high velocity requirement and brief response and will be discussed in the next section.

The distinction between G_2 and intermediate hair receptors can best be appreciated when a G_2 and intermediate fiber supply the same follicle. If the hair is moved slowly away from the rest position and then released, the G_2 ending responds during deviation from the rest position and the intermediate ending during the rapid movement as the hair springs back. Using rapid movements both away from and back to the rest position it can be shown that the intermediate ending has little linear directionality. Directionality of this type is well developed in the case of G_2 endings as would be expected from the absence of a flyback response (see Fig. 1, Linear Directionality). When the hair is moved rapidly and held displaced, G_2 receptors typically show a rapidly declining discharge for 1–2 sec after the hair becomes stationary. Little or no persistent discharge is recorded from intermediate receptors when stimulated in this fashion. If the hair is moved in different directions, some poorly developed spatial directionality may be observed in the G_2 population (see Cremers, 1971). Little spatial directionality is evident among intermediate hair receptors.

When the pattern of discharge produced by these two receptor types is examined, it is seen that the impulses from the G_2 receptor are evenly spaced during a constant velocity stimulus. This suggests that the receptors have a well-developed recovery cycle and a detectable depression of excitability could be observed at test intervals of 100 msec (P. R. Burgess & K. W. Horch, unpublished). Intermediate hair receptors, on the other hand, discharge in a less regular fashion and closely spaced impulses may occur when the rate of a constant velocity displacement exceeds threshold. This suggests a shorter recovery cycle and, in fact, it was difficult to detect any decrease in excitability with test intervals longer than 30–50 msec.

Brown and Iggo (1967) have shown that hair receptors with a range of velocity thresholds increase their frequency of discharge with increasing stimulus velocity in a way that is well described by power functions with exponents less than one.

3. PHYSIOLOGICAL PROPERTIES OF FIELD RECEPTORS

Field receptors show a continuum of properties not unlike hair receptors. All field fibers conduct at alpha velocities but the more rapidly conducting field fibers terminate as receptors (called F_1 field receptors) that have little position response or linear directionality. Such receptors do not respond unless a stimulator moves the skin at a moderate rate and they resemble intermediate hair receptors in velocity threshold as well as in the duration of the recovery cycle.

Field receptors derived from more slowly conducting fibers (called F_2 field receptors) have some position response and obvious linear directionality. The latter serves, as in other receptors, to signal deviations from the rest position; discharge occurs when the skin is indented but not when it returns to the rest position. The position response of F_2 receptors is somewhat better developed than in the case of G_2 endings and a low frequency discharge may persist of 10–15 sec after a displacement which is applied abruptly. F_2 receptors have long and well developed recovery cycles which are reflected in a tendency for the receptor to discharge in a regular fashion.

4. SUMMARY OF PHYSIOLOGICAL CHARACTERISTICS

The population of alpha receptors classed as velocity detectors includes, at one end of the continuum, receptors (the G_2 and F_2 types) with a weak position response, marked linear directionality of both position and velocity responses, well-developed recovery cycles and a regular discharge during constant velocity stimulation. It may be argued that Type II receptor behavior (see previous section) exemplifies a further development of this series of properties (Fig. 4) with the possible exception that the Type II position response may show less linear directionality. At the other end of the continuum of properties attributed to alpha velocity detectors are receptors with no clear position response, short recovery cycles, closely spaced impulses and a velocity response with little linear or spatial directionality. These properties link velocity detectors with receptors that signal transients, since these characteristics are still more strikingly developed in transient detectors (Fig. 4).

5. MORPHOLOGICAL CHARACTERISTICS

There is no obvious difference in the receptive field organization of F_1 and F_2 field receptors. Differences have been noted, however, in the way different hair follicles are innervated by particular hair receptor fibers. The general body hair of the cat can be divided into three major types (Danforth, 1925): (1) numerous down hairs, which form the undercoat, and are thin and flexible throughout their length; (2) awn hairs, which are nearly as thin at the base as down hairs but thicken near the tip; and (3) guard hairs, which are thicker than awn and down hairs at the base and expand still more toward the end of the shaft. These three types do not form distinctly separate classes and many intermediate hairs can be found (Danforth, 1925). Guard hairs differ somewhat in length and thickness but generally extend above the rest of the hair. A class of guard hairs, called tylotrich hairs, has been distinguished from other hairs of the guard type on the basis of their proximity to Type I domes and certain morphological features of the follicle (Mann & Straile, 1965; Straile, 1960). The tylotrich hair shaft itself does not appear to be particularly distinctive. If the posterior thigh of the cat is examined, guard hairs emerging near domes are usually found not to be the longest of the guard type although they are typically among the thickest. However, they, or other similar hairs on the posterior thigh, do not form a distinct group on the basis of diameter measurements made at a number of points along their length from base to tip (J. L. Burgess, K. W. Horch, & P. R. Burgess, unpublished). Tylotrich follicles in rodents are more distinctive than in the cat and rodent tylotrich hairs are clearly longer than other guard hairs (Straile, 1960). There are no obvious tylotrich hairs in primates.

Brown and Iggo (1967) have described alpha hair receptors in the cat and rabbit associated exclusively with tylotrich follicles (T hair receptors) and others that are activated predominantly by movement of guard hairs other than tylotrichs (G hair receptors). Movement of down hairs is not effective in exciting alpha hair receptors nor is an appreciable response obtained from awn hairs (Brown & Iggo, 1967; Burgess et al., 1968; Merzenich & Harrington, 1969). It is not clear what relationship, if any, exists between the type of hair innervated and the physiological properties of the receptor. Receptors classed as G or T on morphological grounds seem to have a range of physiological properties (Brown & Iggo, 1967). However, both Brown and Iggo (1967) and Burgess et al. (1968) noted a tendency for receptors with higher velocity thresholds to be associated with longer and stiffer hairs. Some "matching" between the mechanical properties of the innervated hairs and the type of information signalled by the receptors might be expected but more study will be necessary to establish whether such a correlation exists.

6. VELOCITY DETECTORS WITH DELTA FIBERS

The velocity detectors that are derived from delta fibers are hair receptors in the sense that they respond readily to movements of individual hairs. These receptors are easily excited by movements of down hairs or isolated guard hairs. Effective activation from down hairs generally requires that a small group of these hairs be moved. The receptors have been called D hair receptors because of their response to down hair movement (Brown & Iggo, 1967) but it should not be forgotten that they readily respond to guard hair movement as well. This term is also appropriate for these receptors because of the conduction velocities of their fibers.

The properties of D hair fibers are quite uniform. Slow hair displacement is effective and they are more sensitive to movements of this type than G_2 endings. Like other hair receptors, the frequency of discharge increases with increasing velocity of hair displacement. This input–output relationship is described by a power function with exponents less than one (Brown & Iggo, 1967). Some position response can be demonstrated, as would be anticipated from the low velocity threshold of these receptors; in the cat a discharge persists for a second or two after a rapid hair movement. The position response is better developed in primates (Merzenich, 1968; Perl, 1968). In addition to differences in threshold, axon conduction velocity and effective hair type, these receptors differ from G_2 hair receptors in one other respect: they lack appreciable linear directionality (Merzenich, 1968). Spatial directionality is also not well developed. Thus the information they provide is less "discriminative" than that from G_2 receptors. It is perhaps not surprising that D hair receptors show no linear directionality. Down hairs are sufficiently thin and flexible that they do not assume a repeatable rest position. In order to signal a deviation from any prevailing down hair position, D hair receptors must respond to down hair movement in any direction. This lack of directionality also extends to D hair terminals associated with guard hairs even though these hairs are stiffer and generally return to approximately the same position after a displacement.

Recovery cycles have not been determined for D hair endings. In most receptors some information about recovery cycles can be obtained by examining the discharge for periodicity. D hair receptors have such low thresholds that slight vibrations in a stimulator that appears to be smoothly advancing are detected, with the result that variably spaced intervals are produced. It is unlikely that any natural stimulus would do otherwise, and these receptors seem adapted to detect movement of any hair type in any direction with great sensitivity.

7. VELOCITY DETECTORS WITH C FIBERS

Mechanoreceptors with unmyelinated axons (C-mechanoreceptors) have properties that contrast markedly with those of velocity detectors derived from myelinated fibers. C-mechanoreceptors lack the ability to signal rapidly changing stimuli. In fact, a stimulator must remain in contact with the skin for a surprisingly long time (150–200 msec at six times threshold) if any consistent response is to be obtained (Bessou, Burgess, Perl, & Taylor, 1971). Mechanoreceptors with myelinated fibers generally have minimal contact times of less than 3 msec. C-mechanoreceptors fatigue readily (Fig. 1, Fatigue) (Iggo, 1960) and if any appreciable activity has occurred in the preceding minute, minimal contact times for a single impulse are increased beyond 500 msec. Thus, when C-mechanoreceptors are subjected to repeated sinusoidal oscillations, frequencies in excess of 1–2 Hz evoke little activity. These receptors, therefore, are unable to signal changes in a continuously varying displacement unless the changes are slow.

As might be anticipated from the observation that C-mechanoreceptors have long minimal contact times, a stimulator that moves quickly across the receptive field evokes fewer impulses at lower frequency than one which moves more slowly, although very slow movement once again results in decreased activity. Mechanoreceptors with myelinated fibers, on the other hand, respond at progressively higher frequencies as the rate of movement across the receptive filed increases through the same range. As Zotterman (1939) has pointed out, these receptors are most effectively excited by stimuli that produce tickle sensations in man.

C-mechanoreceptors have a position response; if a displacement is abruptly applied and maintained, the discharge declines rapidly for 3–4 seconds with an occasional impulse occurring for as long as 15–20 seconds. The C-mechanoreceptor position response adapts in about the same time as the position discharge of an F_2 field receptor after a comparable stimulus. As the rate of skin indentation is decreased, C-mechanoreceptors do not show a decrease in peak discharge frequency until the rate becomes low (Bessou et al., 1971). F_2 field receptors and other velocity detecting receptors with myelinated fibers display a pronounced decrease in discharge frequency as the rate of stimulator displacement is decreased through the same range. Because C-mechanoreceptors lack static displacement detection, a sufficiently slow indentation of the skin evokes no response. These observations indicate that essentially the entire frequency range of a C-mechanoreceptor is employed for signalling slow displacements. Although myelinated velocity detectors with low velocity thresholds also signal differences in the velocities of slowly moving stimulators, they devote a relatively small fraction of their potential frequency range to detecting such changes.

Iggo and Kornhuber (1968) and Sassen and Zimmermann (1971) have examined the input–output functions of C-mechanoreceptors, measuring the first 1–2 seconds of activity produced by an abrupt stimulus. Since any velocity response of the receptor would be saturated under these conditions, changes in discharge frequency as a function of changes in stimulus amplitude would presumably represent an alteration in the position response. The frequency of discharge was found to be linearly related to indentation. C-mechanoreceptors, however, transmit less information than mechanoreceptors with myelinated fibers. This is due in part to a smaller dynamic range. There is a relationship between the diameter of an afferent fiber and the maximum frequency at which it can conduct impulses. The larger alpha myelinated fibers can transmit impulses which are separated by as little as

1 msec. Delta myelinated fibers can carry impulses 2 msec apart. C-mechanoreceptor fibers rarely convey impulses closer together than 6–7 msec. Another factor limiting the information transmission of C-mechanoreceptors is the variability of the response (Zimmermann, 1972). Even if stimuli are spaced so that fatigue effects are minimized (intervals of 3 min or more are required between tests), there is still considerable variability with a corresponding reduction in the precision of the response.

C-mechanoreceptors show typical linear directionality. The response occurs during skin indentation but weakly or not at all during retraction of the stimulator. However, if the stimulator is abruptly withdrawn, activity may occur after the stimulator is no longer in contact with the skin (after-discharge) (Douglas & Ritchie, 1957; Iggo, 1960; Zotterman, 1939). Such behavior is not shown by mechanoreceptors with myelinated fibers. C-mechanoreceptor after-discharge is especially prominent when a stimulator moves *across* the receptive field.

The conduction velocities of C-mechanoreceptor fibers in a particular animal have been found to range from 0.8–1.0 m/sec. Assuming a conduction velocity range of 0.8–0.9 m/sec, activity from a population of C-mechanoreceptors synchronously activated from the hindfoot would arrive at the spinal cord over a period of about 35 msec in an average sized cat. Since summation is likely to be required for transmission across synapses in the spinal cord, temporal dispersion of this sort would significantly decrease the signal to noise ratio for information about rapidly changing stimuli that was to be transmitted with high temporal resolution. As indicated above, C-mechanoreceptors do not respond to rapidly changing stimuli and so have properties that match the transmissive characteristics of the axons from which they are derived.

C-mechanoreceptor recovery cycles cannot be measured in the usual way because of long minimal contact times, but the impulses tend to occur periodically suggesting the presence of an effective recovery cycle.

C-mechanoreceptor fibers branch before terminating. The terminals, however, are confined to a small area which is comparatively uniform in sensitivity (Iggo, 1960). The receptive field organization of C-mechanoreceptors thus resembles that of field fibers with myelinated fibers, except the fields are smaller.

In summary, C-mechanoreceptors are designed to detect lingering mechanical stimuli. Best activation is produced by a moving stimulator, but one that moves slowly across the skin. Rapidly changing stimuli are not sensed and the precise time of onset and cessation of a brief stimulus is obscured by a long minimal contact time and the frequent presence of after-discharge. The unmyelinated fibers that convey impulses from C-mechanoreceptors to the central nervous system conduct so slowly that the input is greatly dispersed in time when it reaches central synapses where summation is presumably required for transmission. All these factors contribute to making this a system with slow response characteristics.

C. Receptors Detecting Transients

Two receptor types are included in this category, Pacinian corpuscle receptors and G_1 hair receptors. G_1 receptors are found in the skin whereas Pacinian corpuscle (PC) endings are typically located in deeper tissues where, nevertheless, they are easily excited from the skin surface (Hunt & McIntyre, 1960a; Lindblom & Lund, 1966; Merzenich & Harrington, 1969; Skoglund, 1960).

1. PACINIAN CORPUSCLE RECEPTORS

Morphologically, Pacinian corpuscles are distinctive. The receptor (nerve terminal) is surrounded by a multilamellated accessory structure of non-neural tissue. This structure has mechanical filtering properties that effectively prevent a slow displacement of the outer lamellae from deforming the nerve ending (Hubbard, 1958). On the other hand, the structure readily transmits an abrupt displacement of the outer lamellae. Thus, PC receptors display no position response even with rapidly applied stimuli, although at one time it was thought that they did (Adrian & Umrath, 1929).

PC receptors respond readily to vibrations transmitted from remote stimulus locations (Hunt & McIntyre, 1960a; Lindblom & Lund, 1966; Lynn, 1971; Merzenich & Harrington, 1969; Skoglund, 1960), and PC endings have sometimes been referred to as vibration receptors. They are "tuned" to frequencies in the range of 150–300 Hz in the sense that at these frequencies sinusoidal displacements of the smallest amplitude (in some cases less than 1 μm) are effective in exciting the receptors (Hunt, 1961; Jänig et al., 1968; Lindblom & Lund, 1966; Merzenich & Harrington, 1969; Nilsson, 1969; Sato, 1961; Talbot, Darian-Smith, Kornhuber, & Mountcastle, 1968). If the displacement required for some threshold response (e.g., one impulse per stimulus cycle) is determined as a function of stimulus frequency (plotting a so-called tuning curve) the shape of the relationship suggests that above 100 Hz these receptors respond to acceleration or jerk (M. Zimmermann, personal communication). This idea is supported by the observation that Pacinian corpuscle endings discharge preferentially at the onset or termination of the constant velocity portions of a ramp stimulus; i.e., at those points where the velocity is changing (Fig. 1, Acceleration Detection). Acceleration detection promotes high frequency tuning since acceleration is appreciable when the position of a stimulator changes rapidly even though the amplitude of the displacement is small.

Pacinian corpuscle receptors lack appreciable linear directionality. If a stimulator is positioned to move at right angles to the skin, discharge occurs on indentation and retraction under similar stimulus conditions (Armett & Hunsperger, 1961; Lynn, 1971). Thus, these receptors can provide little information about the direction of movement. Also, fatigue is not prominent (Lindblom & Lund, 1966; Talbot *et al.*, 1968). Recovery cycles are short; it is often difficult to detect any decrease in excitability at interstimulus intervals longer than 5–6 msec (Gray & Malcolm, 1950) and it is common for short interspike intervals to be produced when suprathreshold stimuli are applied to these receptors.

Pacinian corpuscle receptors have a certain cluster of properties: high frequency tuning apparently achieved by acceleration detection, a lack of linear or spatial directionality, short recovery cycles, and little fatigue (Fig. 4). In terms of threshold, these receptors are designed to respond to rapid changes in displacement. Because of a short recovery cycle and the absence of fatigue, corpuscles are unhindered in responding repeatedly and at short intervals to the higher frequency components of a continuously varying displacement.

Pacinian corpuscle fibers are rapidly conducting, falling within the upper half of the alpha range. Most of the Pacinian fibers innervating the hindlimb have a central branch that extends the length of the spinal cord without interruption, ending in the caudal part of the brain where a synapse occurs with cells of the nucleus gracilis (Perl, Whitlock, & Gentry, 1962). Although other cutaneous mechanoreceptor fibers reach the nucleus gracilis (see Brown, 1968; Petit & Burgess, 1968), Pacinian fibers have a distinctive property which they share with no other mechanoreceptor class: there is usually no decrease in the conduction velocity of these fibers after they enter the fasciculus gracilis (D. Whitehorn, M. C. Cornwall, & P. R. Burgess, unpublished). For this reason, activity synchronously evoked from the hindfoot in a population of Pacinian fibers will show little temporal dispersion when it arrives at the nucleus gracilis (0.3–2.5 msec for small populations of fibers in different experiments). If any summation is required for transmission through the nucleus gracilis, and information with high temporal resolution is to be transmitted directly, the absence of appreciable temporal dispersion in the input will increase the signal to noise ratio.

2. G_1 Hair Receptors

Like PC receptors, G_1 hair receptors are tuned to high frequencies. Rapid hair displacement is required to evoke G_1 activity. Even large amplitude sinusoidal displacements do not produce a discharge at frequencies below 60–80 Hz. These receptors show a declining threshold as stimulus frequency increases from 80 to 200 Hz, but do not respond to small amplitude (less than 50 μm) sinusoidal oscillations applied to either skin or hair at any frequency up to 500 Hz. In this respect they differ markedly from PC receptors and the shape of the G_1 tuning curve does not suggest acceleration detection. The curves are more consistent with a response to velocity and G_1 endings are apparently related to velocity detecting hair receptors of the intermediate and G_2 type, except that they have higher velocity thresholds. Thus, G_1 receptors do not respond to vibrations propagating from distant regions and are effectively activated only by the larger amplitude movements that hair shafts typically undergo.

G_1 hair receptors resemble PC receptors in showing little linear or spatial directionality (Fig. 4). Recovery cycles are also short; it is difficult to detect any decrease in G_1 excitability with test intervals longer than 10 msec. As would be expected from this finding, these receptors typically respond with short intervals once a stimulus exceeds threshold. It can be argued, as in the case of PC receptors, that short recovery cycles are appropriate if these receptors are to respond with multiple discharge to a single stimulus since the rapidity of a suprathreshold displacement makes the stimulus duration short. It is rare for these receptors to produce more than two to three impulses per stimulus even when hair deflection is near maximal in extent.

G_1 hair receptor fibers are typically the most rapidly conducting in cutaneous nerves (Burgess et al., 1968; Hunt & McIntyre, 1960b). Like PC fibers, hindlimb G_1 fibers extend the length of the spinal cord to the nucleus gracilis (Petit & Burgess, 1968). However, they differ from corpuscle fibers by showing a decrement in conduction velocity shortly after entering the spinal cord and also just below the cervical enlargement. Nevertheless, synchronously initiated activity on a population of G_1 fibers will reach the spinal cord and nucleus gracilis with little temporal dispersion because of the high conduction velocity of the pathway.

It may be suggested that G_1 receptors are well adapted to signal rapid displacements with high temporal resolution. In fact, a rapid displacement is required to excite these receptors. G_1 endings resemble PC receptors in several ways: high frequency tuning, little directional sensitivity, a short recovery cycle, and rapidly conducting axons. They differ from PC receptors by responding to velocity rather than acceleration, by not detecting low amplitude displacements, and by showing fatigue when subjected to repeated stimulation. Thus, G_1 endings are not as well designed to detect rapidly repeated stimuli as are PC receptors.

III. MECHANORECEPTORS IN GLABROUS SKIN

It is convenient to first consider receptors in the cat since they have been the most thoroughly studied. Receptors in primate palm and sole skin will then be discussed.

A. Cat

Receptors with F_1 and F_2 properties are common in the glabrous skin of the cat's toe pads and foot (Jänig, 1971; Jänig et al., 1968; Lynn, 1969). Low threshold receptors derived from delta fibers are present but are relatively less common than D hair receptors in the adjacent hairy skin. C-mechanoreceptors appear to be entirely absent from the glabrous skin of the cat's foot (Bessou et al., 1971; M. Zimmermann, personal communication). Type II receptors are rarely found and pad position is signalled almost exclusively by receptors which discharge with an irregular pattern like that from Type I receptors in hairy skin. No domes are visible on the pad but collections of Merkel cells are present at the junction of the epithelium and dermis and Jänig (1971) has provided evidence that the irregular slowly adapting position discharge originates from endings associated with these cells. In addition to discharge pattern, receptors of this type in pad skin resemble Type I receptors from hairy skin in the magnitude and duration of the recovery cycle, the adaptation rate and the dynamic range of the position response, linear directionality of position and velocity responses and the conduction velocity of the fibers. The central projection pattern from the hindlimb is also distinctive (an ascending collateral extends in the fasciculus gracilis to upper lumbar or lower thoracic levels but not to C_1) and is identical to that of Type I fibers from hairy skin (Whitehorn, Cornwall, & Burgess, 1971). Thus it would seem appropriate to refer to these receptors as Type I pad receptors.

B. Primates

The receptors in the glabrous skin of the primate hand and foot are similar to those in the foot and toe pads of cats. Receptors with F_1 and F_2 field properties are present in monkeys (Lindblom, 1965; Talbot et al., 1968) and in man (Hagbarth, Hongell, Hallin, & Torebjörk, 1970; Knibestöl & Vallbo, 1970). Merkel cells are common in primate glabrous skin and by analogy with the cat might be expected to contribute to a static displacement response with irregular discharge. Such activity has been recorded from the monkey palm (A. Iggo, personal communication) and from the human hand (Knibestöl & Vallbo, 1970). Receptors with Type II properties have also been observed (Talbot et al., 1968), although they are apparently less common than receptors with Type I properties (A. Iggo, personal communication; Knibestöl & Vallbo, 1970). It would be expected that an ending of the Ruffini type would be responsible for Type II activity. Meissner corpuscles are plentiful in primate glabrous skin and might give rise to F_1 and F_2 type discharge. Encapsulated endings similar to Meissner corpuscles are found in comparable locations in cat glabrous skin and Jänig (1971) has associated these with F_1–F_2 type activity.

IV. MECHANORECEPTORS ASSOCIATED WITH SINUS HAIRS, TEETH, AND CLAWS

Many mammals have specialized tactile hairs such as vibrissae. They are generally the longest and thickest hairs on the body and originate from follicles that have a number of distinctive morphological features including a blood sinus that envelops the external root sheath. For this reason, they are referred to as sinus hairs. Sinus hairs differ from the general body hair in having a population of receptors with static displacement detection (Fitzgerald, 1940). Receptors detecting velocity and transients are also present. It seems a general rule that only body projections that are relatively sturdy like sinus hairs, claws, and teeth are associated with static displacement detectors. Claws are rigidly attached to the terminal phalangeal joint in the cat and, thus, receptors that sense claw position are in fact articular receptors. In the most general sense, the appendages of an animal may be considered projections from the axial frame and each articulation of the appendage may be considered the base of another projecting part. Certain common features are evident in the design of receptor populations that signal the static position of projecting structures. There is minimal sustained activity when the innervated structure is in the rest position. In the case of teeth and most sinus hairs, the rest position of the structure is at or near the mid-position. Most articulations also occupy an intermediate position at rest. Thus, when a joint or tooth is displaced in one direction, certain receptors begin to discharge, or increase their discharge if already active, and this discharge becomes greater with greater displacement. If the structure is returned to the mid-position and then displaced in the opposite direction, a different population of receptors shows progressively increasing activity. This is because individual static displacement receptors have well-developed spatial directionality. There are, therefore, what might be called "opponent" receptor populations, rather than a system using receptors with maximal persistent activity at one extreme position, intermediate activity at intermediate positions, and minimal activity at the opposite extreme position. Greater numbers of receptors are required to establish opponent populations than would apparently be needed if individual receptors responded over the whole range of movement, but activity at rest is minimal in the first case and would be appreciable with full range receptors. Many other factors may also have dictated the employment of opponent rather than full range receptor populations, some perhaps dependent on the way in which the stimulus can be transmitted to the nerve endings.

Another design possibility which does not seem to be employed is what might be called "spatial tuning". It is possible to imagine that a particular slowly adapting receptor might show maximal activity at some intermediate or partially offset position with a decline in discharge occurring as the projecting structure is moved to either side of this position. A population of such receptors tuned to different positions might then specify the position of the structure. Receptors of this type have not been reported from sinus hairs, teeth, or claws. A few have been described in association with the knee joint, but they must be comparatively rare (Burgess & Clark, 1969; Skoglund, 1956). Rather, the receptors display an "end position bias"; they discharge at progressively increasing frequencies as the structure they are associated with is progressively displaced from intermediate to end position.

V. CONCLUSION

The receptor classification proposed in this review assumes that mechano-receptors are specialized to detect different modes of mechanical stimulation and may be considered an extension of the concept of receptor specificity. It should be thought of as provisional and is proposed simply as one way in which the properties of these receptors might be organized. If it is accepted that mechanoreceptors encode different modes of mechanical stimulation, the significance of receptors that respond to more than one mode of stimulation must be considered. One of several possibilities is that information from position-velocity receptors is always interpreted centrally as position and the velocity term serves to compensate for delays in the system. Thus, during a rapid movement, the velocity response would in-crease the discharge so that the frequency which arrived at some central processing point after transmission delays was that which would be ap-propriate for the position of the structure by the time the information ar-rived. Regardless of the ultimate fate of the information, if the position response adapts relatively rapidly, as is the case when the skin is stimulated, discriminations must be made soon after stimulus application if an ap-preciable fraction of the receptor's frequency range is to be utilized.

One consequence of treating mechanoreceptors as specifically designed to respond to certain modes of mechanical stimulation is that the term adapta-tion takes on a new meaning. As the term was originally used (Adrian & Zotterman, 1926), slowly adapting receptors were those with static dis-placement detection and rapidly adapting receptors were those with little or no position response. In the context of the present classification, adaptation is considered to occur if the discharge of a receptor declines while the mode of mechanical stimulation it detects is held constant. Thus, a receptor which detects velocity would show no adaptation by this criterion if the discharge did not decline during constant velocity stimulation, whereas it would be considered rapidly adapting according to the original usage. As more investigators have begun to treat receptors in terms of sensitivity to different modes of mechanical stimulation, adaptation as a descriptive term has been less used. The terms "dynamic" and "static" have been applied to muscle spindles (see Matthews, 1964). The important studies of Lindblom (1962, 1963) on frog skin mechanoreceptors clearly embody the concept of velocity and position sensitivity as distinct aspects of a receptor's response to mechanical stimulation. Brown and Iggo (1967), Iggo and Muir (1969), and Chambers *et al.* (1972) have also used this approach as have Barker, Hazelton, and Welker (1970). M. Zimmermann (personal communication) has explicitly proposed that the alpha mechanoreceptors of the cat's glabrous pad skin be treated in terms of position, velocity and acceleration detection. Ultimately the usefulness of the scheme proposed here will be determined by the generality with which it can be applied. It will be of interest to determine whether the same clusters of mechanoreceptor properties identified in mammals can be found in other animals.

References

Adrian, E. D., & Umrath, K. The impulse discharge from the Pacinian corpuscle. *Journal of Physiology (London)*, 1929, **68**, 139–154.

Adrian, E. D., & Zotterman, Y. The impulses produced by sensory nerve endings. Part III. Impulses set up by touch and pressure. *Journal of Physiology (London)*, 1926, **61**, 465–483.

Andres, K. H. Über Die Feinstruktur Der Rezeptoren An Sinushaaren. *Zeitschrift für Zellforschung und Mikroskopische Anatomie*, 1966, **75**, 339–365.

Armett, C. J., & Hunsperger, R. W. Excitation of receptors in the pad of the cat by single and double mechanical pulses. *Journal of Physiology (London)*, 1961, **158**, 15–38.

Barker, D. J., Hazelton, D. W., & Welker, W. I. Neural coding of skin displacement and velocity in raccoon Rhinarium. *Federation Proceedings, Federation of American Societies for Experimental Biology*, 1970, **29**, 522. (Abstract)

Bessou, P., Burgess, P. R., Perl, E. R., & Taylor, C. B. Dynamic properties of mechanoreceptors with unmyelinated (C) fibers. *Journal of Neurophysiology*, 1971, **34**, 116–131.

Brown, A. G. Cutaneous afferent fibre collaterals in the dorsal columns of the cat. *Experimental Brain Research (Berlin)*, 1968, **5**, 293–305.

Brown, A. G., & Iggo, A. A quantitative study of cutaneous receptors and afferent fibres in the cat and rabbit. *Journal of Physiology (London)*, 1967, **193**, 707–733.

Burgess, P. R., & Clark, F. J. Characteristics of knee joint receptors in the cat. *Journal of Physiology (London)*, 1969, **203**, 317–335.

Burgess, P. R., Petit, D., & Warren, R. M. Receptor types in cat hairy skin supplied by myelinated fibers. *Journal of Neurophysiology*, 1968, **31**, 833–848.

Chambers, M. R., Andres, K. H., von Duering, M., & Iggo, A. The structure and function of the slowly adapting type II receptor in hairy skin. *Quart. J. Exp. Physiol.*, 1972, **57**, 417–445.

Cremers, P.F.L.J.M. Responses of single units in the nervus suralis and the nucleus gracilis to stimulation of a hair receptor of cat and rat. Ph.D. thesis, The Catholic University in Nijmegen, 1971.

Danforth, C. H. Studies on hair. *Archives of Dermatology and Syphilology*, 1925, **11**, 637–653.

Douglas, W. W., & Ritchie, J. M. Non-medullated fibres in the saphenous nerve which signal touch. *Journal of Physiology (London)*, 1957, **139**, 385–399.

Fitzgerald, O. Discharges from the sensory organs of the cat's vibrissae and the modification in their activity by ions. *Journal of Physiology (London)*, 1940, **98**, 163–178.

Gasser, H. S. Properties of dorsal root unmedullated fibers on the two sides of the ganglion. *Journal of General Physiology*, 1955, **38**, 709–728.

Gray, J. A. B., & Malcolm, J. L. The initiation of nerve impulses by mesenteric Pacinian corpuscles. *Proceedings of the Royal Society, Series B*, 1950, **137**, 96–114.

Hagbarth, K. -E., Hongell, A., Hallin, R. G., & Torebjörk, H. E. Afferent impulses in median nerve fascicles evoked by tactile stimuli of the human hand. *Brain Research*, 1970, **24**, 423–442.

Harrington, T., & Merzenich, M. M. Neural coding in the sense of touch: Human sensations of skin indentation compared with the responses of slowly adapting mechanoreceptive afferents innervating the hairy skin of monkeys. *Experimental Brain Research (Berlin)*, 1970, **10**, 251–264.

Hartline, H. K., & Ratliff, F. Inhibitory interaction of receptor units in the eye of limulus. *Journal of General Physiology*, 1957, **40**, 357–376.

Hubbard, S. J. A study of rapid mechanical events in a mechanoreceptor. *Journal of Physiology (London)*, 1958, **141**, 198–218.

Hunt, C. C. On the nature of vibration receptors in the hind limb of the cat. *Journal of Physiology (London)*, 1961, **155**, 175–186.

Hunt, C. C., & McIntyre, A. K. Characteristics of responses from receptors from the flexor longus digitorum muscle and the adjoining interosseous region of the cat. *Journal of Physiology (London)*, 1960, **153**, 74–87. (a)

Hunt, C. C., & McIntyre, A. K. An analysis of fibre diameter and receptor characteristics of myelinated cutaneous afferent fibres in cat. *Journal of Physiology (London)*, 1960, **153**, 99–112. (b)

Hursh, J. B. Conduction velocity and diameter of nerve fibers. *American Journal of Physiology*, 1939, **127**, 131–139.

Iggo, A. Cutaneous mechanoreceptors with afferent C fibres. *Journal of Physiology (London)*, 1960, **152**, 337–353.

Iggo, A. New specific sensory structures in hairy skin. *Acta Neurovegetativa*, 1963, **24**, 175–180.

Iggo, A. Cutaneous receptors with a high sensitivity to mechanical displacement. *Touch, Heat and Pain, Ciba Foundation Symposium, 1965*, 1966, pp. 237–256.

Iggo, A., & Kornhuber, H. H. A quantitative analysis of nonmyelinated cutaneous mechanoreceptors. *Journal of Physiology (London)*, 1968, **198**, 113P.

Iggo, A., & Muir, A. R. The structure and function of a slowly adapting touch corpuscle in hairy skin. *Journal of Physiology (London)*, 1969, **200**, 763–796.

Jänig, W. Morphology of rapidly and slowly adapting mechanoreceptors in the hairless skin the cat's hind foot. *Brain Research*, 1971, **28**, 217–232.

Jänig, W., Schmidt, R. F., & Zimmermann, M. Single unit responses and the total afferent outflow from the cat's foot pad upon mechanical stimulation. *Experimental Brain Research (Berlin)*, 1968, **6**, 100–115.

Jansen, J. K. S., Nicolaysen, K., & Rudjord, R. Discharge pattern of neurons of the dorsal spinocerebellar tract activated by static extension of primary endings of muscle spindles. *Journal of Neurophysiology*, 1966, **29**, 1061–1086.

Kenton, B., Kruger, L., & Woo, M. Two classes of slowly adapting mechanoreceptor fibres in reptile cutaneous nerve. *Journal of Physiology (London)*, 1971, **212**, 21–44.

Knibestöl, M., & Vallbo, Å. B. Single unit analysis of mechanoreceptor activity from the human glabrous skin. *Acta Physiologica Scandinavica*, 1970, **80**, 178–195.

Lindblom, U. The relation between stimulus and discharge in a rapidly adapting touch receptor. *Acta Physiologica Scandinavica*, 1962, **56**, 349–361.

Lindblom, U. Phasic and static excitability of touch receptors in toad skin. *Acta Physiologica Scandinavica*, 1963, **59**, 410–423.

Lindblom, U. Properties of touch receptors in distal glabrous skin of the monkey. *Journal of Neurophysiology*, 1965, **28**, 966–985.

Lindblom, U., & Lund, L. The discharge from vibration-sensitive receptors in the monkey foot. *Experimental Neurology*, 1966, **15**, 401–417.

Lindblom, U., & Tapper, D. N. Terminal properties of a vibro-tactile sensor. *Experimental Neurology*, 1967, **17**, 1–15.

Lynn, B. The nature and location of certain phasic mechanoreceptors in the cat's foot. *Journal of Physiology (London)*, 1969, **201**, 765–773.

Lynn, B. The form and distribution of the receptive fields of Pacinian corpuscles found in and around the cat's large foot pad. *Journal of Physiology*, 1971, **217**, 755–771.

Mann, S. J., & Straile, W. E. Tylotrich (hair) follicle: Association with a slowly adapting tactile receptor in the cat. *Science*, 1965, **147**, 1043–1045.

Matthews, P. B. C. The response of de-efferented muscle spindle receptors to stretching at different velocities. *Journal of Physiology (London)*, 1963, **168**, 660–678.

Matthews, P. B. C. Muscle spindles and their motor control. *Physiological Reviews*, 1964, **44**, 219–288.

Merzenich, M. Some observations on the encoding of somesthetic stimuli by receptor populations in the hairy skin of primates. Ph.D. thesis, Johns Hopkins University, 1968.

Merzenich, M. M., & Harrington, T. The sense of flutter-vibration evoked by stimulation of the hairy skin of primates: Comparison of human sensory capacity with the responses of mechanoreceptive afferents innervating the hairy skin of monkeys. *Experimental Brain Research (Berlin)*, 1969, **9**, 236–260.

Mountcastle, V. B., Talbot, W. H., & Kornhuber, H. H. The neural transformation of mechanical stimuli delivered to the monkey's hand. In *Touch, Heat and Pain, Ciba Foundation Symposium, 1965*, 1966, pp. 325–345.

Nilsson, B. Y. Hair discs and Pacinian corpuscles functionally associated with the carpal tactile hairs in the cat. *Acta Physiologica Scandinavica*, 1969, **77**, 417–428.

Perl, E. R. Myelinated afferent fibres innervating the primate skin and their response to noxious stimuli. *Journal of Physiology (London)*, 1968, **197**, 593–615.

Perl, E. R., Whitlock, D. G., & Gentry, J. R. Cutaneous projection to second order neurons of the dorsal column system. *Journal of Neurophysiology*, 1962, **25**, 337–358.

Petit, D., & Burgess, P. R. Dorsal column projection of receptors in cat hairy skin supplied by myelinated fibers. *Journal of Neurophysiology*, 1968, **31**, 849–855.

Sassen, M., & Zimmermann, M. Capacity of cutaneous C fibre mechanoreceptors to transmit information on stimulus intensity. *Proceedings of the International Union of Physiological Sciences*, 1971, **9**, 493.

Sato, M. Response of Pacinian corpuscles to sinusoidal vibration. *Journal of Physiology (London)*, 1961, **159**, 391–409.

Skoglund, C. R. Properties of Pacinian corpuscles of ulnar and tibial location in cat and fowl. *Acta Physiologica Scandinavica*, 1960, **50**, 385–386.

Skoglund, S. Anatomical and physiological studies of knee joint innervation in the cat. *Acta Physiologica Scandinavica*, 1956, **36**, 1–101.

Straile, W. E. Sensory hair follicles in mammalian skin: The tylotrich follicle. *American Journal of Anatomy*, 1960, **106**, 133–147.

Stuart, D., Ott, K., Ishikawa, K., & Eldred, E. Muscle receptor responses to sinusoidal stretch. *Experimental Neurology*, 1965, **13**, 82–95.

Talbot, W. H., Darian-Smith, I., Kornhuber, H. H., & Mountcastle, V. B. The sense of flutter-vibration: Comparison of the human capacity with response patterns of mechanoreceptive afferents from the monkey hand. *Journal of Neurophysiology*, 1968, **31**, 301–334.

Tapper, D. N. Cutaneous slowly adapting mechanoreceptors in the cat. *Science*, 1964, **143**, 53–54.

Tapper, D. N. Stimulus–response relationships in the cutaneous slowly-adapting mechanoreceptor in hairy skin of the cat. *Experimental Neurology*, 1965, **13**, 364–385.

Werner, G., & Mountcastle, V. B. Neural activity in mechanoreceptive cutaneous afferents: Stimulus–response relations, Weber functions and information transmission. *Journal of Neurophysiology*, 1965, **28**, 359–397.

Whitehorn, D., Cornwall, M. C., & Burgess, P. R. Central course of identified cutaneous afferents from cat hindlimb. *Federation Proceedings, Federation of American Societies for Experimental Biology*, 1971, **30**, 433. (Abstract)

Zimmermann, M. Cutaneous C-fibres; peripheral properties and central connections. *In* V. Aschoff & H. H. Kornhuber (*Eds.*), *The somatosensory system.* Stuttgart: Thieme, in press.

Zotterman, Y. Touch, pain and tickling: An electrophysiological investigation on cutaneous sensory nerves. *Journal of Physiology (London)*, 1939, **95**, 1–28.

Chapter 12

TACTUAL PERCEPTION OF TEXTURE

M. M. TAYLOR, S. J. LEDERMAN, AND R. H. GIBSON*

There is more to touch than meets the eye!

I. INTRODUCTION

Consider the richness of our tactual impressions—the exquisite smoothness of soapstone used in an Eskimo carving, the softness of a kitten's fur, the roughness of sandpaper, the warmth of a woolen blanket. Consider how a passionate kiss, a sharp slap, a gentle touch on the cheek can communicate a world of emotion. When we think of touch in this way the frequently made suggestions that vision is "more accurate than" (e.g., Cashdan, 1968; Lobb, 1965) or "dominates" (e.g., Rock & Victor, 1964) touch seems to miss the point. Suggestions of this kind derive from the notion that touch exists only to do what vision can do better. Touch is not simply an inferior form of vision, nor yet of hearing. Touch, as touch, has its own capabilities and limitations.

* DCIEM Research Paper No. 820.

Touch is old and intimate, and ill understood. Whether or not hearing evolved from a touch-like vibratory sense, the touch of which we are possessed is complex. A partial list of object properties readily determined by touch and not by vision or hearing might include temperature, hardness, roughness, elasticity, stickiness, slipperiness, rubberiness, the homogeneity of what lies under the surface, and so forth. Combinations of these properties are together perceived as texture, and texture, not form alone, is the prime province of touch. The perception of texture by touch is at least as complex as the perception of auditory qualities, and may well prove to be more so.

II. EXPERIMENTS RELATED TO TEXTURE PERCEPTION

A. Historical Direction of Touch Research

What does academic research tell us about touch as a means of determining the properties of the external world? Unfortunately, to date very little. With the two major exceptions of Katz (1925, 1930b) and Revesz (1950), most of the work before 15 years ago considered the sense of touch along with pressure, pain, and temperature under the more general rubric of cutaneous sensitivity. In most of these experiments, fine rigid hairs, the tips of hot or cold metal cylinders, mild electric shocks and sharp pins, to name a few of the popular stimulators, were used to prick, prod, poke, stroke, shock, or vibrate immobile (and sometimes heroic) observers. The tactile effects were brought about by an external agent applied, presumably, under the experimenter's control. The emphasis was upon the nature of the cutaneous sensations arising from the stimulation rather than on the observers' perceptions of the properties of the stimulus objects. Such forms of stimulation were used to determine two-point separation thresholds, and intensity thresholds for sensations such as pressure, pain, heat, cold, and chemical sensitivity over various parts of the outside and the inside (e.g., Boring, 1915) of the body. One major result of this work was finding that different spots on the body were differentially sensitive to the various stimuli. There exist warm- sensitive, cold-sensitive, pressure-sensitive spots, and so forth. Much of the work has been referenced by Boring (1942), and a more up-to-date annotated bibliography has been produced by Baker and Hall (1969). An interesting variant was the major study on tactual illusions conducted by Reiber (1903) which compared illusions produced tactually by patterns of skin stimulation with illusions produced visually, and found that in many cases the same illusions appeared.

More relevant to the consideration of texture perception are studies on the tactual vibration sense. The vibration sense has been compared to hearing (Katz, 1930b; von Békésy, 1959), which is a refreshing change from the usual comparison with vision. Moreover, the comparison with hearing can yield some insights into the functioning of the vibration sense through consideration of the more comprehensively studied hearing sense. Just as can hearing, the vibration sense can detect differences in frequency, or, more properly, in power spectrum, as well as in timing differences between two vibration sources. The capability of detecting timing differences apparently gives one the ability to externalize sources of vibration, as can be done routinely with sound sources. Katz (1930b), for example, claimed that if the two hands are placed on the edge of a table which is then tapped, the observer can usually tell where the table was tapped. Since the observers in Katz' study were deaf and blindfolded, the direction sensing was almost certainly performed by touch. In the same paper, Katz reported another experiment in which timed impulses were delivered to the two hands. His observers were able to discriminate intervals of as little as 140 μsec between pulses, a remarkably small interval. Although his methods were ingenious, his apparatus was crude, and the exact figure would probably not stand the test of more modern experimental verification.

Katz (1930b) further discussed several cases of deaf persons for whom the vibration sense had come to serve as a substitute for many of the functions of hearing. For example, he mentioned some who could understand speech by placing the hand on the speaker's body, and others who were able to appreciate music through vibrations felt in the chest or through the feet. Although for these people the vibration sense could serve as a form of surrogate hearing, the fact that it is not more widely used in this way suggests that the sonic world perceived through vibration must be far less rich than when it is processed through the normal hearing channels. However it has been suggested (e.g., Gibson, 1968) that a rich vibratory substitute for hearing might be provided by frequency division and time compression of the sound signal, to bring the auditory information down into a frequency range more suited to the vibratory sense without unduly slowing the sequence of auditory events.

The work on the vibration sense by Katz and von Békésy was, like the more psychophysical studies, based on stimuli applied to an observer who had no control over them. On the other hand, the perceptions studied, such as directionality, refer to external objects, not to skin sensations, and in this respect are more like studies of texture perception.

Some more recent studies have considered the experiences of an observer who brings about the contact under his own control. Most such experiments have used objects as stimuli, and have thus involved relatively large skin areas, in contrast to the small regions or points stimulated by the classical hairs, prods, and shocking coils. However, they have concentrated mainly on qualities of form such as size, shape, and orientation. Since these are primarily suited to vision, it is not surprising that many of the experiments compared the development and relative accuracy of visual and tactual form perception. Similarly neither is the general result surprising that the visual modality proves superior in these tasks (e.g., Cashdan, 1968; Lobb, 1965; Rock & Victor, 1964).

B. Active and Passive Touch

We have followed a train of thought which develops the expansion of the touching experience from brief punctate stimuli of well-specified kinds, through the involvement of larger skin areas for greater lengths of time, to the point where touching requires the active participation of the observer using his muscles and whatever features of his skin senses he cares to bring to bear. This increasing involvement of the observer seems to increase the "object nature" of the percept. We must pause here to give greater consideration to what seems a central feature of the touching process as it is used in everyday life.

There are two very different modes of "touching" in the cited experiments. In one situation, the immobile observer is stimulated by an external agent over which he has no control, while in the other he can actively explore the stimulus object as he chooses. Few writers before Gibson (1962), other than Katz (1925) and Revesz (1950), even distinguished the existence of these two modes. In spite of this history of neglect, Gibson observed very great differences in percept depending on whether a given stimulation was brought about by the observer or by the experimenter. The former leads to concentration on the properties of the object, while the latter gives rise to labile skin sensations. These skin sensations do not seem to exist if the object-perception occurs. Gibson refers to the classical technique as "passive touch": "being touched by a moving object," which he contrasts with "active (haptic) touch": "the touching of a stationary object." He provides several examples of the differences between active and passive touch. Active touch exhibits object-constancy, but passive touch does not. By active touch one feels stable corners and edges, solid surfaces, and so forth, while similar patterns of skin deformation caused by the experimenter give rise to rapidly changing sensations with no stable referent. An object felt actively with two fingers feels like one object, while felt passively it feels like two touches. With active touch, an increase in the amount of skin deformation with increased force is felt as object rigidity, whereas with passive touch it is felt as increasing pressure on the skin.

In a related experiment, Katori and Natori (1967) compared the reproductions of simple geometric forms seen by subjects with the reproductions they made after touching the form with various amounts of experimenter control. If the experimenter moved the original form under a finger held stationary, or if the subject moved a finger along the lines of the form in a continuous manner, the reproduction tended to be made with a single line. The active condition was more accurate than the passive. If, however, the touching was done freely by the subject, using as many fingers as he liked in any manner at all, then the reproductions tended to be done with several individual strokes, as was the case when the originals were seen. Free active touch appeared to provide percepts much more akin to those of vision than did the controlled active or the passive touch conditions.

It is possible that the extreme nature of the differences reported by J. J. Gibson between active and passive touch was due in part to the instructions given to his subjects. They were simply asked to describe what they felt, and if there were a bias toward the sort of descriptions given, this bias would be self-reinforcing. It would also be subject to the sort of unconscious experimenter biases noted by Rosenthal and Rosnow (1969). Judging from experiments as informal as Gibson's, we believe that both active and passive touch can lead to either skin-centered or object-centered perception, although the tendency is definitely to feel in the manner described by Gibson. All the same, the results of Katori and Natori (1967) also indicate real differences in perception between active and passive touch. We discuss the perceptual qualities of active and passive touch from a different point of view in Section III of this chapter.

C. Texture Perception

Texture is as much the essence of touching as form is of seeing. However, few studies have dealt with the nature of texture perception as such. Katz (1925) seems to have been one of the first to discuss the question in any detail; he considered the effects of different manners of touching and of different components of the touching process, such as hand rate and finger force. His classic monograph has yet to be translated into English, although highlights have been reviewed by Zigler (1926) and Krueger (1970).

Passive touch was used at about the same time in two other studies following the introspective tradition. Meenes and Zigler (1923) investigated the perceived roughness of objects, and Sullivan (1927) studied the perception of hardness and softness. Meenes and Zigler, in particular, provided some interesting results on the perception of cutaneous stimulation by surfaces of different roughness, on the value of relative motion between hand

and object, and on the effect of varying the force of the object against the skin. In addition, they suggested that there might be a physiological difference between processes responsible for "roughness" and those giving "smoothness." Sullivan discussed the differences in the perceptions of hardness and softness and the effects on these percepts of varying the object temperature. A strong perception of hardness required a cool object.

Binns (e.g., 1937) conducted a series of experiments in the textile industry. Using both trained and naive judges, he examined visual and tactual judgments of the fineness, softness, and value of wools. His finding was that experience improved visual judgments, but had little effect on tactual skill. Gliner (1967), on the other hand, determined discrimination thresholds for shape and texture using kindergarten and third-grade children, and found the older children to be better at texture discrimination. Texture discrimination seems to improve with age but not with training.

Using magnitude estimation techniques, Stevens and Harris (1962) found that perceived roughness and smoothness were power functions of the grit number of sandpaper; the two exponents were equal and opposite. They concluded that smoothness and roughness were opposite poles of the same continuum, in apparent disagreement with Meenes and Zigler (1923). Ekman, Hosman, and Lindstrom (1965) found perceived roughness to be a power function of the coefficient of friction between the fingers and various paper and sandpaper surfaces. They found great individual differences in the values of the exponent.

Yoshida (1968a,b) conducted an ambitious series of experiments designed to discover the principal dimensions of tactual impression. He used stimulus samples differing in size, shape, and texture. His factor analysis showed that 70% of the variance could be accounted for by three factors, which he designated (1) heaviness-coldness, (2) wetness-smoothness, and (3) hardness.

D. Roughness and the Vibration Sense

We have recently been interested in surface roughness as one important aspect of texture. The vibration sense is closely related, since roughness is perceived in a surface only when the interaction between skin and surface sets up a vibration in the skin. Passively sensed fingertip vibration is indistinguishable from the vibration induced by stroking a rough surface except that it occurs in the absence of relative motion between skin and surface, and without sideways deformation of the fingertip.

Surface roughness is explored by moving the fingers across the surface, and sensing the various interactions that then occur. This process is considered in more detail in Section III. One of the more prominent interactions is the varying skin deformation which sets up the physical vibration. Depending on the speed and force of hand movement and on the spacing and size of surface prominences, the vibration will vary in dominant frequency and in overall energy. Variations in the perception of roughness may depend on the overall energy of the vibration modulated by the sensitivity characteristic of the sensors (as loudness depends on the energy of the sound and on the spectral sensitivity of the ear) or it may depend on the vibratory frequency. Since this reflects on the studies performed and on their interpretation, a disagreement should be stated here. MMT and SJL feel that the primary component of the roughness percept is the vibratory energy transmitted to the fingertip at frequencies to which the finger is sensitive. Frequency has the effect of changing the quality of the roughness, but otherwise has no effect except insofar as the receptors are not equally sensitive to all frequencies. RHG feels that frequency is the primary contributor to the roughness sensation and that variations in frequency should be matched by concomitant variations in perceived roughness; overall energy also modulates the perceived roughness. With the data currently available, either view is tenable.

If vibratory frequency is important in the perception of roughness, studies of vibratory frequency discrimination are important, even those done using passive touch, since they should indicate the limits bounding the degree to which tactile vibration could serve as a cue to surface texture. One may presume that frequency sensitivity is at least as good in passive studies as in active, since in the active condition many information sources are competing for the observer's attention whereas in the passive situation the frequency to be discriminated can be given his whole attention.

Gott (1967) studied vibratory frequency discrimination at the fingertip, using bands of vibrotactile stimuli matched beforehand in apparent intensity. The frequency JND (just noticeable difference) ratio $\Delta f/f$ was about 0.2 for frequencies below about 100 Hz at 35 dB SL (Sensation Level). Above 100 Hz, the value of the JND rose sharply, until it was nearly doubled at 200 Hz, showing a markedly reduced sensitivity to frequency differences. At a lower vibratory intensity, 20 dB SL, the JND was larger. If judgments of roughness depend on sensory factors which determine vibratory frequency discrimination, then when frequencies produced by rapid hand motions (coupled with finely spaced surface crests) are in a region showing poor frequency discrimination, the related roughness judgments might show a sharp increase in variability or might display a shift in the shape of the function relating roughness to surface character.

In an experiment to determine the ability to recognize letters presented by a moving band of small air jets striking the palm, accuracies of above 50% were found after about 900 trials for strings of letters moving at 30 five-letter groups per minute (Rogers, 1970). These rates were obtained with three relatively inexperienced subjects, and they held true only for high stimulator frequencies of 160 Hz; when the pulse repetition rates were reduced to 20 or 40 Hz, reading rates fell by one-third. This reduction seems at first puzzling, when one considers recent neurophysiological evidence that there are at least two separate touch receptor systems in the hairless skin of man (cf. Lindblom, 1970); there is a low (below 40 Hz) frequency system with small receptive fields and relatively low sensitivity, and a high frequency (peaking around 250 Hz) system with wide receptive fields. On this basis, one might expect that the lower frequency pulses would stimulate the system with the small receptive fields, thus giving higher acuity and better ability to read the letters. But there are at least two possible reasons why this reasoning might be false. One is that as in the retinal periphery, the large high-frequency receptive fields might be suited to perception of moving stimuli, and thus be well adapted to the determination of the letter patterns being pulsed at high rates while moving across the skin. The second argument is that the letters moved appreciably between pulses at the 40 Hz pulse rate, thus giving an impression akin to stroboscopic lighting. Writing is notoriously hard to read if it moves in a stroboscopic manner, and a similar effect might be occurring with the letters. In any event, the vibration sensitivity of the fingertip is shown by this experiment to be more complex than might have been supposed from simple frequency discrimination studies (e.g., Goff, 1967).

Vibrotactile stimulation studies lead naturally to a consideration of Braille reading rates as a possible index of the information carrying capacity of the vibration sense. Braille patterns consist of rectangular arrays of raised dots which characteristically represent one letter. Braille transmission rates therefore refer not to a single skin region, but to sets of independently stimulated regions, and should be more directly relevant to texture perception than are the frequency discrimination data. However, this seems not to be the case, since studies of Braille capacity (e.g., Nolan & Kederis, 1969) report upper limits for symbol transmission speed of the same order of magnitude as those found for visual reception of letters presented serially (Taenzer, 1970) and for auditory "spelled speech" (Metfessel, 1963). Using either modality, an appropriately trained observer can receive at a rate of about 10 characters/second. Just as Sperling, Budiansky, Spivak, and Johnson (1971) have shown that this is not a visual transmission channel limit, so it seems likely not to represent a tactual transmission channel limit. Rather, it probably is a limit in the more central processing to do with identification of letters as such.

Taenzer (1970) compared visual reading in a "moving window" study with a similar tactile study by Bliss and Linville (1966). Letters were displayed moving across an array of neon lights (Taenzer) or (Bliss and Linville) an array of tactual vibrators. In each condition comprehension was excellent at up to 50 words/minute, provided that the size of the window was sufficient to permit each point of the moving display to be available for at least 150 msec in its transit across the aperture. This result again suggests that the limit is not in the sensory channel but in the more central processing. It does, however, place a lower bound of about 25 bit/sec on the capacity of the vibration channel. Although this situation gives a lower bound which is probably an order of magnitude or more below the full capacity of the channel, it does show that the vibration channel has a respectable capacity, and is capable of playing its postulated role (see Section III) in the perception of texture.

E. Current Research on Roughness Perception

Lederman and Taylor (1972) controlled the finger force applied to the surface, and showed that the perceived roughness of metal plates with parallel grooves increased with groove width and with the fingertip force applied, but decreased slightly with increases in the width of the flat top (the "land") between the grooves. The slope of the magnitude estimation function also increased with increasing finger force, implying that roughness contrast is greater with greater finger force. In a subsequent experiment, the observer was free to use whatever force he wished, and the perceived roughness was found to be appropriate for the force chosen. Perceived roughness depends strongly on the width of the grooves in these plates, and weakly in the other direction on the width of the lands. It therefore does not depend directly on the frequency of the vibrations induced in the fingertips by the successive grooves. On the other hand, the vibration energy might well increase with increases in the applied fingertip force.

Continuing this series of experiments, Lederman (1973) found that rate of hand motion had a consistent effect on perceived roughness which was negligible relative to the groove width and finger force effects. As groove width was held constant while rate varied, the experiment provided additional support for the idea that vibratory frequency does not directly affect perceived roughness.

In another study, the coefficient of friction between skin and surface material was found to have no influence whatsoever on perceived roughness. The seeming contradiction between this result and that of Ekman, Hosman and Lindstrom (1965) may be explained by the distinction between apparent friction due to gross features of the surface, and friction due to the quality of the material. Ekman, Hosman, and Lindstrom (1965) probably measured the former, while Lederman (1973) measured the latter. This problem is discussed further in Lederman (1973).

R. H. Gibson (unpublished study) has found that observers who freely stroke a grooved surface rapidly press considerably harder than do those who stroke more slowly. Those subjects who press harder show lower slopes of the magnitude estimation function, in apparent contradiction with Lederman and Taylor's result. RHG suggests that the contradiction may be explained by the fact that vibrotactile frequency discrimination gets worse with increasing vibration frequency above 50 Hz, but is improved with greater stimulus intensity (Goff, 1967). Therefore, an observer moving his fingers rapidly over a rippled surface (thus producing higher frequencies) may, by pressing harder, improve his vibrotactile frequency discrimination. On the other hand, SJL and MMT suggest that possibly those of Gibson's subjects who were less sensitive to texture variation might have pressed harder to provide some compensation for their deficiency. They would then tend to move their hands faster, to prevent their fingers sticking on the surface, which tends to happen when large force and low speed are combined.

R. H. Gibson and M. Cinanni, in a study still in progress, used a signal detection procedure with category ratings to determine the ability to discriminate ruled tactile grids, and calculated the resulting vibration frequencies produced at the fingertip. Preliminary findings were that the implied frequency JND values fell close to those reported by Goff (1967) for passive fingertip vibration frequencies, suggesting that there may be a common mode of operation or vibrotactile frequency discrimination and for this aspect of texture discrimination.

Finally, R. H. Gibson and A. Sztepa (unpublished study) have found that the exponent of a perceived roughness function is not influenced by the temperature (within $10°C$ of room temperature) of the textured surface. With a warm hand on a warm textured surface, the whole function was the same as that found with stimuli and hands at normal room temperatures. However, when the stimuli and hands were cooled $10°C$, the function was substantially lowered with no change in exponent. Cold textured surfaces feel smoother than neutral or warm ones. These parametric and rather psychophysical studies of roughness are a far cry from the studies of texture perception that need to be done. But they are a necessary prologue. It is remarkable how little is known about perception by touch after more than a century of experimental sensory psychology. The reason may lie partly in the extreme difficulty of stimulus construction, but hopefully, modern technology may put control of complex stimuli within our reach. We still disagree over a matter as fundamental as roughness. Perhaps more progress will be made when touch is viewed as a sense with its own qualities. The model sketched in Section III is intended as a frame-work for such a viewpoint.

III. TOWARD A CONCEPTUAL MODEL OF TEXTURE PERCEPTION

A. Introduction

Among the means by which perception achieves its goal of permitting one to act effectively is the construction in memory of a model of the world. The structure of the world attained through perception provides a basis for projecting the possibilities of future action. For one's current purposes some facts about the world are important, some irrelevant. A well-adapted perceiving mechanism must take this into account, and husband its resources by working only on the parts of the world that are probably relevant. The different senses give rise to one world, rather than several, because any action may cause changes in any of the world's varied aspects. There is not a "World of Colour" and a "World of Touch" as the titles of Katz' monographs would have it (Katz, 1925, 1930a); there is a World of Perception.

Usual perceptual experience does not come from the stimulation of single receptors, or from the simple stimulus patterns so much used by those of us who call ourselves psychophysicists. It comes from rich and complex patterns of stimulation of various senses, from coordinated variation in the outputs of logically independent receptors, from information deliberately sought and from information fortuitously acquired, from patterns of motion kinesthetically sensed combined with patterns of motion visually, auditorily, and tactually sensed. Information arising from a single receptor, unsupported by a relevant pattern of information from other receptors, is usually and properly discarded as noise. It leads to no perceptual experience. Only coordination among receptors in the retina permits us to sense the movement of shapes in the visual field. Only coordination among taste, smell, touch, vision, and kinesthesis permits us to savour a fine wine or reject a poor steak.

Although it is perhaps not obvious, the tactual perception of texture provides a prime example of the coordinated action of independent sensory systems. We shall contend not only that several disparate skin senses are involved, but also that the kinesthetic and proprioceptive systems which yield information about body motion and static bodily states, as well as hearing and vision, are deeply involved in the perception of texture obtained by touching a surface. The single "tactile" percept does not depend on the unaided operation of any one sensory system, but results from a widespread pattern of coordinated activities. We shall further contend that it is this "multimodal" nature of touching which gives touch the feeling of providing substance and reality to the perceived world.

We do not know of any experimental work relevant to this view of texture perception; we must therefore present the following "cybernetic" model unsupported except by its own plausibility and internal coherence.

B. The Sensations and Modes of Touching

Introspect, modern psychologist though you may be. Try a small experiment and feel the texture of a surface near you. What did you do? Probably you first moved your hand until your fingertips made a light contact with the surface. Most likely, you were guided by vision until you sensed tactually the fact that your fingertips had arrived at the surface. Next, using only a light force on the surface, you probably began a smooth and fairly slow back-and-forth motion over the surface, looking at your fingers and listening, perhaps without being aware of it, to the noises your fingers made on the surface. This initial motion taught you a lot about the surface, perhaps enough to satisfy you. But if you wanted to learn more about the object, you would have had to change how you were touching it. What you did next depended on what you had already learned and what you wanted to find out.

Touch can tell you about temperature, and thus about thermal conductivity. If you are feeling a bright silvery surface and it feels cold for a while after you start to touch it, you probably feel "metal" rather than "hard, cold." But if a visually identical surface feels cold and warms up rapidly under your touch, you feel "plastic." To tell the difference, you must let your finger rest on one spot long enough to let you judge the rate of temperature change. On the other hand, Katz (1930b) has shown that one can tell differences among a great variety of materials with a single tap lasting no more than 10 msec. Since the experiments were conducted with sound cues excluded, this ability probably depends, as Katz suggested, on the ability to sense the vibrations set up in the material by the tap. Another mode of touching is needed if you want to determine the substructure under a deformable surface. Experiencing "furry" or "leather," for example, depends on surfaces and on depths; you will probably use a variety of pressures, gliding rates and other manipulations to determine the quality of a leather coat.

What sensations are available to you as you glide your fingers over the surface? You can see where your hand is in relation to visual patterns on the surface, even if the object is itself moving. You can feel through kinesthesis how your hand moves and what forces you are applying to the object. The forces include the lateral force due to friction between fingertip and surface. As you press and move, your fingertip is grossly squashed inwards and sideways, and deep sensors can detect those deformations, which depend on the forces and on the resilience of the object. In addition to the gross deformations, your skin partially conforms to minor irregularities of the surface, and changes in these minor deformations of the skin as you move over the surface can be sensed as vibration. Sharper irregularities passing under the fingerprint patterns may snag the skin, causing sharp impulse sensations. Not only can you feel the vibrations and snags, but also you can often hear them and the resonances they induce in the object you are feeling. The sound may be an important constituent of the total percept, especially the resonance which may help in determining the mechanical qualities of the whole object. Another important sensation arises from the heat flow between the fingers and the object, from which you learn something about the temperature and the physical properties of the object.

There is also an additional important but often ignored "sensation." This is the feeling that you have the freedom to choose where on the surface you want to touch. This exploratory freedom permits you to generalize the sensations derived from one part of the surface to any other part that you might as well have sampled. If you have no reason to suppose that the untouched parts of the surface are characteristically different from the part that you actually touched, you can and probably will generalize, thereby attaining the perception of a complete object existing independently of yourself. If you do not have this freedom of choice as to where you can touch, you have no rational grounds for assuming the object to exist beyond the points actually touched or beyond the region within which you do have apparent freedom to explore. You may perceive a complete object, if you have other grounds to support generalization, but you will be more likely to refer the sensations to your own skin rather than to an external object. Gibson (1962) made this point very clearly, although without using the sampling rationale, when comparing the sensations induced by passive and active touching of the same object. He indicated for several different "sensory" experiences that, "In all cases the sensory impression can be aroused by an experimenter (bringing an object into contact with the observer's hand), but when the observer himself brings them about they seem to disappear." With the active participation of the observer, stable objects in the real world are perceived, but when the experimenter controls the touching process, the perception is of labile sensations referred to the skin. The difference may well be attributed to the observer's impression of freedom of choice about where to touch.

Although it does not lead to a "sensation," the purposive nature of the active touching process is important when the observer is free to choose what and how to touch. It permits the observer to use information gathered at an early stage to direct his search for further relevant information. What you feel in the early stages modifies the manner of later touching. Formally the touch process in the real world is a feedback process. This formal statement is fundamentally important to an understanding of touch.

C. A Model of Texture Perception

1. THE IDEA OF THE TRANSDUCER FUNCTION

A transducer is a device which changes energy in one form to energy in another form. A loudspeaker is a transducer which takes electrical energy as its input and changes it into sound and heat. We usually ignore the heat, but it is as much a part of the loudspeaker's output as is the sound. A transducer in general can be described as a black box with inputs and outputs, which are connected by a transducer function as in Fig. 1(a). The transducer function in the figure is labeled "X". X is more correctly called an "operator" than a "function," since it operates on the inputs to provide the outputs. The term "operator," however, is easily confused with the human operator of a machine, so that we will continue to use the term "transducer function" to describe the input–output relationships of the transducer.

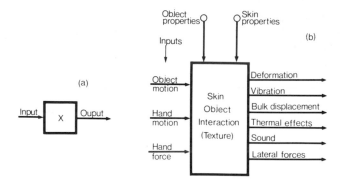

FIG. 1. Transducers. (a) A general block diagram of a transducer; the transducer operator (function) "X" transforms input energy into output energy, which may be of an entirely different form. (b) The transducer describing the interaction between the fingertip and an object being touched. The transducer function is determined by the properties of the object and of the skin, which may be thought of as controlling the transducer. The inputs are the relative motions of object and skin and the force between the hand and the object; the outputs are of several different kinds: skin deformation, variation in which leads to vibration, lateral (friction) and vertical (resistance) forces, bulk deformation of the fingertip, thermal effects, and sound.

Consider the interaction between an object surface and the skin as a transducer. The transducer has the large low bandwidth movements of the hand as input, while its outputs are the various vibrations, sounds, and heat flows which can be sensed [Fig. 1(b)]. The transducer function that relates the input to the output is determined by the surface texture coupled with the mechanical state of the skin. Providing that the skin state is known, it would not be far wrong to say that the transducer function *is* the texture. The *perception* of texture is the *analysis* of the transducer function. The function contains all the information which can be derived from the mobile contact between hand and surface.

Given the input to a transducer, the properties of the transducer function determine the output. Hence, if the input and the output are known, the tranducer function can, in principle, be found. However, with a transducer as complex as texture, defined by the skin–surface interaction, there are many different simple transducer functions, which correspond to the different components of texture, such as roughness, hardness, and so forth. No single type of input can tap all components of such a complex transducer function, no matter how precisely it and its corresponding output are known. No one manner of touching permits the simultaneous determination of thermal conductivity and surface roughness, for example. Only by varying the input over its entire useful range can the complete transducer function be determined. Only by using all different modes of touching can the full richness of the feel of an object be found.

Notice that the transducer function is determined by the properties of the skin as well as those of the object, and that unexpected properties of the skin will thus affect the perceived texture of the object. If your skin is dry, objects feel different. If they are unfamiliar, you may not even notice that your skin is dry. But if the object is familiar, the difference is immediately attributed to the skin condition, not to the object's texture. More formally stated, the transducer function is a joint function of object and skin properties. Only if one is known can the other be uniquely recovered by the analysis of the transducer function.

2. INFORMATION AND CONTROL FLOW

The simple transducer function of Fig. 1(b) represents only a small part of the texture perception system. As we pointed out above, feedback is an important characteristic of the total system, both in the small scale of controlling the motions and in the larger sense implied by the purposive nature of active touch.

At least three basic behavioral feedback loops are probably important (Fig. 2). The major one is an overall control loop (i) whose function is to carry out the policy decision to look for a certain feature of the texture, such

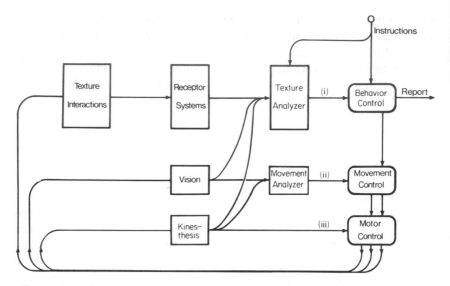

Fig. 2. The three feedback loops involved in the control and information flow. Control flows from the instructions to the Behavior Control element down to the Movement Control element and to the Motor Control element which controls the individual muscles. Information about the actual movements accomplished is fed back through kinesthesis to the Motor Control element. Information about the relative movement patterns of hand and object is fed via vision and kinesthesis to a Movement Analyzer which combines their information and feeds back to the Movement Control the results of its commands. The relative motions and forces between hand and object cause the various interactions which can be sensed, analyzed as texture, and so passed to the Behavior Control element to complete the major feedback loop. If the texture percept satisfies the requirements of the original instructions, a response is output.

as roughness or elasticity. The original intention to touch something, to investigate an aspect of texture such as roughness, is taken to be a command to the major loop control element, labeled Behavior Control. The function of this module is to select a touching strategy adequate for the job. In the case of roughness, the appropriate mode of touching involves a light sweeping motion of the fingertips back and forth over the surface. Probing for subsurface objects in an elastic medium, such as a pea under a foam mattress, requires an entirely different mode of touching.

The secondary loop (ii) has the function of executing the individual motions required to implement the desired touching mode. Its commands are produced by the element labeled Movement Control. This element breaks down the general command from the Behavior Control into a sequence of specific motion commands, which go to the control element of the innermost loop (iii) labeled Motor Control. This is the familiar kinesthetic control loop, which breaks down the individual movement commands into muscle commands and monitors the effects to ensure that the movement command is properly executed.

It is interesting to note that Leo and Vitelli (1971) found that "On the basis of literature review and the experience of our group. . . [a] hierarchical structure seems to be the best for control purposes: in this structure three levels are distinguished: dynamic control [our iii] . . . algorithmic control [our ii] . . . strategic control [our i] . . . ." Leo and Vitelli's system, developed for an entirely different purpose (the construction of a six-legged walking machine) seems to be almost identical to the one we propose for the control of touch activities.

At this point the fingers are moving across the surface, and all the interactions that form the transducer function of Fig. 1(b) are happening. We now consider the flow of information rather than control. The transducer outputs are available as inputs to the skin senses, to the ear, and to the kinesthetic sense. Analysis of the transducer function requires information about the transducer's input as well as its output. The relative motions between hand and object can be sensed visually and perhaps kinesthetically, the hand forces kinesthetically. All the sensory inputs from the transducer input and output are available to the large and largely unknown module labeled Texture Analyzer. This module also has as input the information from the Behavior Control module concerning the intent of the motion. It would be pointless for the Texture Analyzer to look for structures in depth if the Behavior Control wants roughness information. We cannot suggest any reasonable structure for the Texture Analyzer at this point, other than to suggest that the problems it faces are very like those facing other pattern recognition devices in the perceptual system and that its solutions to those problems are probably "ordinary" pattern recognition solutions.

As its output, the Texture Analyzer provides a "texture evaluation" (for lack of a better term). If this evaluation satisfies the requirements of the command to the Behavior Control module, then the touching process has been completed. But if the information so far gained is insufficient to satisfy the command, then the movement strategy must be continued or modified. Hence the informational link between the Texture Analyzer and the Behavior Control element completes the major strategic feedback loop. The entire pattern of control and information flow is shown in Fig. 3.

3. DISCUSSION OF THE MODEL

Apart from the interrelations postulated for the various control elements in the feedback loops, which depend more on a theory of motor control than on texture theory, the other paths of information and control flow in

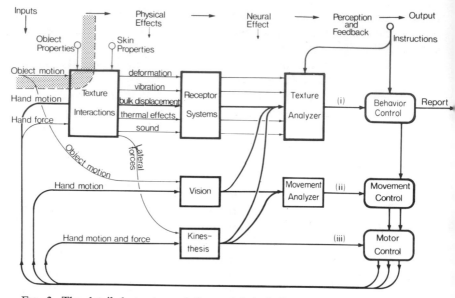

Fɪɢ. 3. The detailed structure of the model, including the various different physical effects produced by the skin–surface interaction transducer. The main feedback paths from Fig. 2 are shown with heavy lines. As in Fig. 2, information from efferent systems is ignored for the sake of simplicity.

Fig. 3 seem to be a necessary part of any model of texture perception. The benefits to be obtained from this attempt to systematize the patterns of information flow probably derive largely from the questions that arise from considerations of the importance of the different pathways. The model currently has as its main function the direction of experiments toward functional aspects of the touching process rather than toward the commonly studied psychophysical parameters. Parametric studies are clearly required in the definition of what happens when we touch, but, for the most part, they are not the studies that have been done as yet.

To determine the importance of the various pathways postulated among the different modules of the texture perception system, experiments should be performed in which the different pathways are blocked or provided with irrelevant information. If the logically independent sources of information about the transducer function, for example, are made to give incompatible results, the relative weightings applied to the channels in different circumstances might be derived. It is perhaps possible, for example, to mask the vibration channel by introducing an extraneous vibration into the hand or into the object being touched. As another example, the sounds of touching may be unimportant as a general rule or may perhaps be used to determine features different from those obtained from the vibration sense. The implications of this question can be tested by masking or falsifying the auditory channel. Sounds appropriate to touching some other object could be deliberately introduced along with vibration to mask the vibration channel, to determine whether the feel of the false object could be induced by its sound. So far as we know, there has been no formal research along these lines.

Another indicator of the relative importance of the different pathways is their capacity as information channels. Channel capacity depends on both the speed and the precision with which a channel responds. Again we know little about the capacities of the channels implicated in texture perception. The studies cited in Section II on discrimination of vibratory frequency and on Braille reading rates give a little information about the vibration channel, but the other tactual channel capacities remain unstudied.

The rate at which information can be obtained about the texture transducer function depends not only on the channel capacities of the output channels, but also on the precision with which the input is known. This means that the positions, rates, and forces of hand motion must be well specified by kinesthetic or visual information. The analysis of the transducer function can be only as precise as input and output allow. Timing precision is an important aspect of the stability of the percept, as, for example, in the discrimination of the difference between a rolling grain of sand and a fixed piece of grit on a surface. The required timing precision may possibly be more readily attained with fast hand motions, but these same fast motions induce faster sequences of sensory events in the output of the transducer function, thus more nearly overloading the output channels. The mating of hand motion to channel load for different surfaces and different purposes is one function of the feedback systems, expecially the Movement Control.

We are conducting a series of experiments interfering with the motor control aspect of the touching process. The attempt is to do for the control processes what the experiments suggested above would do for the information channels. In the Lederman and Taylor study (1972), the subject was not permitted to vary his touching force. In other experiments, touching speed has been controlled (e.g., R. H. Gibson, unpublished study; Lederman, 1973), and in yet others, the subject's hand has been directly moved by the experimenter. While these experiments do not change the information flow, they do have effects, not all yet fully analyzed, on the perception of roughness. Other components of texture have not yet been considered in these studies.

Studies using interference with the control flow to manipulate the texture percept attack the active–passive dichotomy in a way which clarifies the meanings of the two terms. Active and passive are not simply two opposed possibilities. Rather, they refer to two extremes of a continuum. At one end of the continuum, the observer has complete control over all aspects of how he touches. This is pure active touch. At the other end, the experimenter controls the whole touching procedure, and the observer is passive. But in between these two poles, there lies a wide range of possibilities. Any aspect of the touching process may be controlled by the experimenter, while the observer is free to do as he wishes with the other aspects. The experimenter may even limit the range of freedom that a subject is allowed to exercise over an aspect he otherwise controls, as, for example when the experimenter trains the observer to move his fingers across a surface at a given rate. Studies of the effects of such partial control show promise of being able to determine what is important about the control processes in active touch.

As experiments provide more information about the nature of the feedback systems involved in the control of touching behavior, and about the information processing performed by different elements, so the model may be revised or refined, and become a true model rather than the sketchy outline that we have here presented.

IV. GENERAL DISCUSSION AND CONCLUSION

Touch is the "reality sense." When one kicks a stone to refute the idea of a solipsist universe, he is appealing to a general impression that things touched are more "real" than things seen. Certainly in this day of full color holographic reproduction one cannot be assured that seen objects have any necessary reality to the other senses. One can pass one's hands through what seems to be a perfectly real object. Indeed, the same thing can be done with real images created in more old-fashioned ways, and very good stage illusions have been created in this way. But one would not be inclined to say that these images were real objects in the same sense that an invisible pane of glass on which one has just cracked one's head is real.

The "reality" of the touch sensation may possibly be related to the multimodal nature of touch. A thing seen and heard is more "real" than is the disembodied voice of a singer heard on a stereo system. A thing touched may be at once sensed as a vibrating object, a warm one, and a hard one. The touch may also be heard. Correlative information from three or four senses yields a much more stable perceptual experience than does information from a single sense unsupported by independent corroboration. Vision only yields a single pattern of information. Touch always gives two or three, possibly four independent proofs of the existence of the touched object.

A second, but related aspect of the "reality" of actively touched objects derives from the exploratory nature of active touch. By exploring freely, one obtains a succession of independent chunks of information about the object, such as could only in very unlikely circumstances have been produced by anything other than a real object. The same freedom of choice that permits generalization across the surface from the small sample of points actually touched also permits the inference that a real object does exist. The requisite data independence derived from the presumption that, being randomly selected, the place touched has no special qualities. Similarly improved appearances of reality occur for purely visual phenomena if free exploration is allowed on all sides of the object. The unreal visual effects, like holographic or classical images, lose their appearance of reality on being examined from all sides, and images on a screen have even less tolerance for changes of viewpoint. In spite of this, the reality of the object is usually given the final test by touch.

Returning from the wider problems of the touch sense to texture perception, we must observe that very little work has been done since the early introspective studies. What work has been reported has not been done within any coherent conceptual framework. The model presented in this chapter is a first attempt to provide such a framework. It suggests experiments of many different kinds, and although we do not yet know its predictive value, the quantitative results of relevant experiments might well make it useful.

References

Baker, C. H., & Hall, R. J. Cutaneous sensitivity: A review of some literature, problems and approaches. U.S. Army Human Engineering Laboratories, AMCMS problems and approaches. U.S. Army Human Engineering Laboratories, AM Code 5016.11.84400 Technical Memorandum 21–69, 1969.

Binns, H. Visual and tactual 'judgement' as illustrated in a practical experiment. *British Journal of Psychology,* 1937, **27**, 404.

Bliss, J. C. and Linville, J. G. Reading alphabetic shapes tactually. In *Sensory devices for the blind.* London, England: Arrowsmith, 1966 P 389.

Boring, E. G. The sensations of the alimentary canal. *American Journal of Psychology,* 1915, **26**, 1.

Boring, E. G. *Sensation and perception in the history of experimental psychology.* New York: Appleton, 1942.

Cashdan, S. Visual and haptic form discrimination under conditions of successive stimulation. *Journal of Experimental Psychology,* 1968, **76**, 215.

Ekman, G., Hosman, J., & Lindstrom, B. Roughness, smoothness, and preference; a study of quantitative relations in individual subjects. *Journal of Experimental Psychology,* 1965, **70**, 18.

Gibson, J. J. Observations on active touch. *Psychological Review,* 1962, **69**, 477.

Gibson, R. H. Electrical stimulation of pain and touch. In D. R. Kenshalo (Ed.), *The skin senses.* Springfield, Illinois: Thomas, 1968. P. 223.

Gliner, C. R. Tactual discrimination thresholds for shape and texture in young children. *Journal of Experimental Psychology,* 1967, **5**, 536.

Goff, G. D. Differential discrimination of frequency of cutaneous mechanical vibration. *Journal of Experimental Psychology,* 1967, **74**, 294.

Katori, H. and Natori, N. The immediate reproduction of tactually perceived figures and the drawing process in reproducing the figures. *Japanese Journal of Psychology,* 1967, **38**, 121.

Katz, D. *Der Aufbau der Tastwelt.* Leipzig: Barth, 1925.

Katz, D. *Der Aufbau der Farbwelt.* Leipzig: Barth, 1930. (Translated as *The world of colour.* London; Kegan Paul, Trench, Trubner, 1935.) (a)

Katz, D. The vibratory sense. *University of Maine Bulletin,* 1930, **32**, 90. (b)

Krueger, L. David Katz' Der Aufbau Der Tastwelt (The World of Touch): A synopsis. *Perception and Psychophysics,* 1970, **7**, 337.

Lederman, S. J. The perception of surface roughness by touch. Unpublished Ph.D. dissertation, University of Toronto, 1973.

Lederman, S. J., & Taylor, M. M. Fingertip force, surface, geometry, and the perception of roughness by active touch. *Perception and Psychophysics,* 1972, **12**, 401.

Leo, T., & Vitelli, R. Kynematic aspects of project of unconventional locomotion vehicles. Paper read at the AGARD 21st Avionics Technical Symposium on "Artificial Intelligence," Rome, 1971.

Lindblom, U. The afferent discharge elicited by vibrotactile stimulation. *IEEE Transactions on Man-Machine Systems,* 1970, **11**, 2.

Lobb, H. Vision versus touch in form discrimination. *Canadian Journal of Psychology,* 1965, **19**, 175.

Meenes, M., & Zigler, M. J. An experimental study of the perceptions roughness and smoothness. *American Journal of Psychology,* 1923, **34**, 542.

Metfessel, M. Experimental studies of human factors in perception and learning of spelled speech. In *Proceedings of the international congress of technology and blindness,* Vol. 1. New York: American Foundation for the Blind, 1963. P. 305.

Nolan, C. Y., & Kederis, C. J. *Perceptual factors in Braille word recognition.* New York: American Foundation for the Blind, 1969.

Reiber, C. H. Tactual illusions. *Psychological Review,* 1903 (Monogr. Suppl. 4), also known as *Harvard Psychological Studies,* **1**.

Revesz, G. *Psychology and art of the blind.* New York: Longmans, Green, 1950.

Rock, I., & Victor, J. Vision and touch: An experimentally created conflict between the two senses. *Science,* 1964, **143**, 594.

Rogers, C. H. Choice of stimulator frequency for tactile arrays. *IEEE Transactions on Man-Machine Systems,* 1970, **11**, 5.

Rosenthal, R., & Rosnow, R. L. *Artifact in behavioral research.* New York: Academic Press, 1969.

Sperling, G., Budiansky, J., Spivak, J. G., & Johnson, M. C. Extremely rapid visual search: The maximum rate of scanning letters for the presence of a numeral. *Science,* 1971, **175**, 307.

Stevens, S. S., & Harris, J. R. The scaling of subjective roughness and smoothness. *Journal of Experimental Psychology,* 1962, **64**, 489.

Sullivan, A. The cutaneous perceptions of softness and hardness. *Journal of Experimental Psychology,* 1927, **10**, 447.

Taenzer, J. C. Visual word reading. *IEEE Transaction on Man-Machine Systems,* 1970, **11**, 44.

von Békésy, G. Similarities between hearing and skin sensations. *Psychological Review,* 1959, **66**, 1.

Yoshida, M. Dimensions of tactual impressions (1). *Japanese Psychological Research,* 1968, **10**, 123. (a)

Yoshida, M. Dimensions of tactual impressions (2). *Japanese Psychological Research,* 1968, **10**, 157. (b)

Zigler, M. J. Review of Katz "Der Aufbau der Tastwelt." *Psychological Bulletin,* 1926, **23**, 326.

Chapter 13

THE SPATIAL SENSES

I. P. HOWARD

The senses concerned with spatial orientation are listed in Table I. For the sake of completeness the table includes the corollary discharge which is postulated to accompany motor outflow, although this is not a sense in the ordinary meaning of the word. Vision, touch, and the chemical sense are described in other chapters and will therefore not be discussed here. The chemical sense is included in the table as a spatial sense because certain animals, such as ants and moths, use scent for finding their way. Interested readers should refer to Fraenkel and Gunn (1961).

Certain fish, such as *Gymnarchus*, emit a continuous weak electric discharge and are able to locate obstacles by the distortion which the obstacles cause in the electric field around the fishes' body. The details of this mechanism will not be discussed here, interested readers may refer to Machin (1962). The remaining spatial senses in the table will now be discussed.

I. AUDITORY LOCALIZATION

A variety of mechanisms has evolved to enable animals to localize distant sources of vibration, especially when these are members of their own

TABLE I

THE SPATIAL SENSES

Energy	Organ	End-organ	Sensory Function
Radiant (light)	Eye	Retina, rods, and cones	Visual space ⎫ Distance receptors
Mechanical	Ear (and skin)	Basilar membrane, organ of Corti, lateral line	Auditory space ⎭
	Utricle	Macula Cristae	Linear acceleration ⎱ Vestibular
	Vestibular canals	Ampulla cristae	Rotary acceleration ⎰
	Joint capsule	Spray-type	Position and movement, ⎱ Kinesthesis
	Muscle spindles	Muscle spindles	Uncertain
	Tendons	Golgi organs	Tension ⎰
	Skin	Meissner, Workel, and Krause endings	Touch Somesthesis
Chemical	Nose	Olfactory epithelium	Olfaction
Electrical	Skin of certain fish	Pit organs	Electrical field detection
Motor outflow	Corollary discharge	—	Sense of effort

Proprioceptive (bracket over Vestibular and Kinesthesis)

species, their predators or their prey. Some of these mechanisms do not depend on an auditory cochlea and these will be discussed first.

A. Sound Localization by the Skin

Sound energy in water is much greater than in air and aquatic animals are therefore particularly adept at localizing distant sources of vibration. The duck leech, for instance, is attracted to its moving host. Blindfolded fish, such as the pike, eel and minnow, and amphibia, such as the axalotl and toad (*Xenopus*) are able to localize sources of low-frequency vibration, and the ability has been shown to depend upon the integrity of the lateral-line system (Fraenkel & Gunn, 1961).

The lateral-line system is a series of ciliated sensory cells in fluid-filled canals distributed over the head and sides of the body. The afferent nerve fibers feed into a common center in the medulla. The directional localization of a source presumably depends upon the relative intensity of stimulation over the body surface. Pumphrey (1950) has argued that the lateral-line system is capable of localizing the distance as well as the direction of a source. The compression waves from a source near the body are more convex than those from more distant sources, and recurring patterns of asynchrony in the firing of the line of receptors therefore could code distance. Such a system works only for low-frequency sources (below 10 Hz) such as small moving creatures. At higher frequencies the successive waves interfere with each other (Enger, 1968).

Many land-living invertebrates can also localize sources of vibration by special "tactile" organs. For instance, the spider waits in the center of its web, or goes there as soon as a signal is received, and detects the location of its prey by sensing which radius of its web vibrates by means of sensory hairs (trichobothia) on its legs.

It has even been found possible to train human beings to localize sound sources when acoustic stimuli are delivered "stereophonically" through loudspeakers to two skin areas (von Békésy, 1955). This ability probably depends on the comparison of intensity differences at the two areas of skin (Gescheider, 1968).

B. Sound Localization by the Ear

In vertebrates the evolution of the cochlea extended the frequency range of their vibratory sense. Human beings are able to locate the source of a sound in the median plane to an accuracy of about 1 degree, and of a sound in the lateral position to within about 17 degrees. They can also separately localize each of several simultaneous sounds, and these things can be done with only one ear, although not so well as with two.

1. BINAURAL CUES

Consider a sound source to the left of the listener. The left ear will be stimulated at a greater intensity than the right ear because it is nearer the source and because the right ear is in the "shadow" of the head. If the sound is a brief click, it will arrive at the left ear before the right. If it is a continuous tone, it will arrive at one ear out of phase with its arrival at the other ear. These differences of intensity, time and phase are the basis of binaural sound localization.

Interaural intensity differences may be as great as ±20 decibels, for a high-frequency sound in the lateral position. However, intensity differences are not related in any regular way to the azimuth (lateral) position of the sound because of the complex shape of the head and pinna, and because high-frequency sounds cast a sharper "shadow" than low frequency sounds.

It takes sound about 650 μsec to traverse the human head, so that this is the largest time difference normally produced when the sound is in the lateral position. However, sounds arriving up to 2 msec remain subjectively fused as one. As a source moves towards the median plane, physical measurements at the ear have shown that the time difference diminishes fairly regularly. The smallest time difference which gives rise to a discriminable lateralization effect is about 10 μsec (ten-millionths of a second!). The phase shift that a given time difference produces obviously depends upon the frequency of the tone. When the wavelength of the tone becomes small relative to the size of the head, the phase cue becomes ambiguous. The time and phase cues are less effective for a listener under water because sound travels over four times as fast under water than it does in air and time differences are correspondingly diminished (Bauer & Torick, 1966).

Intensity differences are therefore more effective at high frequencies (above about 1500 Hz), and phase differences are more effective for tones below that frequency.

Everyday sounds are not pure tones but have complex wave forms and transient peaks, and the time and phase differences between these sound features may be used even though the component tones are above the frequency at which phase differences could be expected to serve localization. (For a fuller discussion of binaural cues, see Deatherage, 1966.)

2. THE COCKTAIL PARTY EFFECT

In effect, the auditory system runs a continuous cross-correlation on the two complex wave forms arriving at the two ears. If there are several complex sounds emitting at once (as at a cocktail party) the system must know which patterns in one ear to correlate with what patterns in the other. To do this it must be able to recognize the various sources or in some way discriminate them as separate coherent inputs. It is quite impossible to discriminate or localize simultaneous white-noise sources. The listener must either discriminate the sources he is listening to before localizing them or try coupling difference sound patterns at the two ears until he finds pairs which resolve into meaningful signals. Either way, localization and recognition are intimately connected functions. The task is rather like that of finding visual patterns among many overlaying patterns.

3. THE PRECEDENCE EFFECT

When we are listening indoors, sounds echo, and each ear receives the same signal several times over from apparently different places. This would make localization impossible, were it not for the fact that under such circumstances the auditory system only accepts the first pair of signals as its basis for localization; subsequently received sounds of the same kind are referred to this same position in space. This is known as the precedence effect (see Gardner, 1968).

4. MONAURAL CUES

The position of a complex sound within the median plane of the head may also be discriminated. Furthermore, sounds may be localized to some extent by monaural subjects. These abilities cannot depend upon binaural cues. Slight movements of the head would provide one means by which this could be done, and indeed it has been demonstrated that movements of the head enable even a monaural subject to localize pure tones (Wallach, 1940). Monaural and median-plane discriminations may also be made on the basis of the fact that different tones are diffracted and reflected differentially by surfaces of the pinna. If the sound is delivered to the ear through stethoscope ear pieces, or if the pinnae are filled with wax, the ability to make median-plane discriminations is lost. If artificial pinnae are built onto the ends of the stethoscope tubes the ability is restored (Batteau, 1968; Fisher & Freedman, 1968). Frequency-dependent reflections over the convoluted surface of the pinna produce a pattern of delays in the complex sound. This pattern of delays varies with the position of the source and is thought to serve as a basis for monaural and median-plane discriminations. Even animals which at first glance do not have pinnae, such as the dolphin and the owl, do have structures of differential acoustic density round their external auditory canals which serve the same purpose. Some animals, such as the dog, use their pinnae to focus sounds into the external ear and no doubt base their localization responses upon the sense of the position of the pinnae. The outer part of such pinnae is smooth and collects the sound; it is only at the root that the pinnae are convoluted to produce complex reflections.

5. THE NEUROLOGY OF AUDITORY LOCALIZATION

Our knowledge of the neurological processes underlying auditory localization is sketchy. Both cochlea are represented in each auditory cortex, although the contralateral representation is stronger than the ipsilateral. The relative strengths of cortical potentials in the two hemispheres has been found to vary with dichotic time differences of the same magnitude as those produced by changes in the azimuth position of a sound (Rosenzweig, 1954). However, interactions of a similar kind have also been recorded at subcortical nuclei, particularly at the inferior colliculus and superior olivary nucleus (see Neff, 1968, and Harrison and Feldman, 1970, for a review of this area).

6. ECHOLOCATION

It is well known that bats are able to locate even very small objects by echolocation (sonar), that is, by timing the echoes of high-pitched sounds which the bat emits (for a review of this work, see Griffin, 1958). Dolphins have the same ability and are able to detect an object the size of a pea at several yards (see Kellogg, 1961). It is less well known that human beings can also localize stationary objects by the echolocation of breathing or other sounds (see Rice, 1967, for a recent review).

II. JOINT RECEPTORS

The articular surfaces and ligaments of mammalian skeletal joints are well provided with sensory endings. The commonest types are the Ruffini "spray-type." There are also Golgi-type endings similar to those found in tendons. Electrophysiological recordings from single afferent fibers have shown that the frequency of discharge of ligament receptors is related to tension in the ligament. Certain receptors fire only at the onset of tension, others maintain a steady discharge over long periods (Andrew, 1954). In the natural state, the degree of tension in a ligament is a function of the angular position of the joint, and is not affected by the tension in the muscles attached across that joint. Joint receptors therefore register the position and changes in position of the joint whether produced by active muscular contraction or by some outside force.

The afferents from joint receptors project via the dorsal spinal root into the lemniscal system, up to the thalamus, and finally to the sensory cortex.

Less is known about the joint receptors in most non-mammalian species and invertebrates. Insects possess hair sensilla which are sensitive to position and tension and which are distributed in the membranes between the cuticular plates of the exoskeleton (Pringle, 1938).

III. MUSCLE SPINDLES AND TENDON ORGANS

No muscle can work efficiently unless the neural centers which control it are informed about its state of tension and length. This is so because the degree of motor innervation required to bring a limb to a given position varies according to the load against which it is acting. Furthermore, vertical posture depends upon a constant correction for changes in muscle tension imposed by movements over uneven ground. Such corrections are brought about by *stretch reflexes* in response to sensed changes in muscle length. Muscle "sense" is also required to warn the system to relax when tension in a muscle has reached a dangerous level (jackknife reflex). Deafferented muscles will function, but movements are maladaptive except under the simplest of conditions (Taub & Berman, 1968).

Although muscle spindles are required for efficient muscle control, they are probably not involved in the conscious sense of limb position and movement. It is difficult to see how they could be in limbs which move under varying conditions of load and in which tension is therefore not uniquely related to limb position or velocity. Before this question can be pursued further the structure and mode of action in muscle receptors must be discussed in more detail.

In vertebrates, sensory end organs in muscles are known as *muscle spindles* and end organs in tendons are known as *tendon organs*. Muscle spindles in mammals are structurally complex (see Fig. 1). Each muscle contains many thousands of these sensory muscle spindles interspersed among, and parallel with, ordinary (extrafusal) muscle fibers, which they resemble. Each spindle consists of two elongated poles, and a central swelling or equatorial region which contains the sensory structures and which is protected by an outer capsule. Most spindles have two types of sensory ending, *annulo-spiral* endings which signal the momentary small changes in the length of the muscle and its rate of stretching (i.e., differentiated signals), and *flower-spray* endings which signal slower changes in length. Muscle spindles which are attached "in parallel" with muscle fibers are well placed to indicate changes in the length of the muscle, whereas

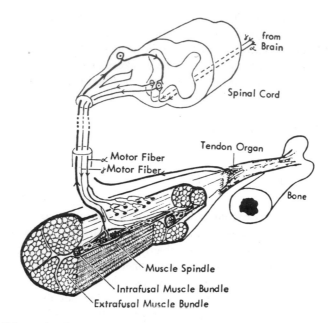

FIG 1. Schematic diagram of the structure and innervation of skeletal muscle (From Barker, D. Zoology and Medical Science, Durham: University of Durham Press, 1963, p. 7).

spindles, or receptors in tendons "in series" with muscle fibers are well placed to signal changes in muscle tension.

The afferent neurons from muscle spindles and tendon organs feed into the spinal cord and ascend to the cerebellum. It has generally been believed that these afferents do not reach the cerebral cortex. However, Oscarsson (1966) has recently found that some of them do, at least in the cat.

The Gamma System

Each muscle spindle contains several contractile muscle fibers (intrafusal fibers) innervated by special motor neurons known as gamma (γ) efferents to distinguish them from ordinary motor neurons or alpha (α) efferents. The γ efferents are controlled from the cerebellum. These intrafusal muscle fibers do not contribute significantly to the tension in the main muscle; their function is to prevent the spindle from becoming flaccid as the muscle contracts.

It is generally believed that the γ system sometimes fires before the α system. When this happens the spindles contract and induce a sensory discharge from the spindle end organs which in turn triggers off a reflex response of the main α system, and hence a muscular contraction. This contraction continues until the extrafusal muscles "catch up" with the contracted spindles, at which point the tension in the spindles is relieved and further contraction ceases. In this way the γ system "instructs" the muscle how much it is required to contract. The process is called "gamma leading." Not that all voluntary movements involve γ-leading, the direct route is also available and is presumably used in fast, well-learned movements. The muscle-spindle system also helps to smooth muscle contractions and to regulate reciprocal inhibition in agonist–antagonist muscle groups.

IV. THE VESTIBULAR SYSTEM

Organs sensitive to inertial forces (acceleration and gravity) are represented in all groups of animals, and even in plants. In the protozoa we find a fully elaborated statocyst organ sensitive to gravity, and there is a great variety of statocysts among other invertebrates. The function of these organs was established by the classical experiment of Kreidl in 1893 in which he replaced the statoliths of the crayfish (*Palaemon*) by iron particles and was able to control its posture with a magnet. Many invertebrate statocysts are also probably responsive to low-frequency sound, which is after all a form of inertial stimulus.

The vestibular apparatus of mammals consists of sense organs in the bony labyrinths of the inner ear. These sense organs evolved in primitive vertebrates from simple, ciliated sense organs which were probably tactile organs at first, sensitive to touch and vibrations produced by moving objects not in contact with the skin. They eventually lost their tactile function and became enclosed in pits in the skin where they were unaffected by cruder mechanical disturbances. They became specialized as receptors for very low-frequency inertial stimulation (acceleration) and higher-frequency inertial stimulation (sound). A fish is more or less homogeneously dense, and sound waves produce no differential vibrations in such an object. A fish is, in effect, "transparent" to sound and other low-frequency mechanical vibrations. Particles of dense material (otoconia) on the free ends of the sensory cilia therefore developed. The lateral line of a fish is a series of such organs arranged along each side of the body and over the head.

One group of such sensory structures evolved into the cochlea of the ear, sensitive to high-frequency stimulation, and another group into the vestibular system, sensitive to low-frequency stimulation down to zero frequency (i.e., acceleration and gravity). The selective response of each system to its own waveband is as much the result of the mechanical resonant properties of the associated structural components, as it is of the sensory cells and neural structures (Tumarkin, 1968). Eventually, the role of the otoconia in hearing was taken over by the bony cochlea; the mass of the sensory cilia was accordingly reduced and the system could respond to higher frequencies.

The vestibular system evolved into two main subdivisions, the *utricle,* sensitive to linear acceleration (including gravity) and the *semicircular canals,* sensitive to rotary acceleration. The otoconia are retained in the utricle, because it is only by having high-density objects attached to the distal end of the sensory cilia that the system can respond to very low- and zero-frequency (D.C.) linear accelerations. The otoconia are absent in the semicircular canals so that they are not affected by linear acceleration or gravity. Their annular shape allows for the inertial lag of the fluid contents relative to the walls without any need for a substance of higher density attached to the distal end of the cilia.

A false distinction is commonly made between gravitational and inertial forces. Einstein showed that these two forces are identical in their effects on any instrument (or sense organ). Indeed, he showed that they are best regarded as one force. It just so happens that we live in a gravitational field, that is we are subjected to a linear accelerative force of constant strength and direction. It is as if we are living in an elevator in outer space forever accelerating; our utricles are constantly stimulated. We do not live in a rotating world (the actual rotation of the world is too slow to be sensed—at least by man), hence we must rotate our bodies to stimulate the semicircular canals. In spite of this difference in stimulation, the utricles and semicircular canals are basically analogous in function; the utricles respond to the extent and direction of linear acceleration (including gravity) and the canals as a triplet, to the extent and direction of rotary acceleration. There is a difference however: the canals are a three-dimensional organ designed to respond to rotation about any axis in space, whereas the utricular sensory epithelium is approximately a horizontal plane and therefore responds mainly to those components of linear motion in that plane. This difference is presumably due to the fact that whereas the head may rotate about any axis, its linear movements are normally in a horizontal plane. Another reason is probably that the utricles are concerned to detect the tilt of the head in relation to gravity rather than acceleration due to head movements. For this purpose a "two-dimensional" receptor is all that is required. The more detailed structure and mode of action of the vestibular organs will now be discussed.

A. The Vestibular Canals

The vestibular canals are known as semicircular canals, but the prefix "semi" is misleading, for each canal is functionally a complete and independent fluid circuit even though the three canals share a common cavity at certain points. In any case, for the sake of brevity, I shall use the word "canal."

The general anatomic arrangement of the canals and associated structures is shown in Fig. 2. The canals, sacs, and cochlea are suspended in perilymph fluid in the bony cavity of the inner ear. Inside the organs there is one continuous cavity filled with endolymph fluid. The three canals on each side are roughly at right angles to each other and each canal has a parallel contralateral partner or synergist. The synergistic pairs are: the two horizontal canals, the left posterior and the right superior, and the right superior and left posterior (see Fig. 3).

At one point in each canal is a swelling or *ampulla,* which contains the sensory epithelium or *crista ampullaris.* It can be seen from Fig. 4 that each crista consists of a ridge of ciliated epithelium. All the cilia are embedded in a single gelatinous mass or *cupula* which projects into the *lumen* of the canal so as to form a complete fluid seal. The cupula is free to swing against the canal wall which is arched at this point. In effect, the cupula is a pendulum which is damped by the endolymph and its own viscosity, and which has a tendency to spring back to a central position. Such a pendulum is known to engineers as a damped, torsion pendulum. The cupula is difficult to see because it is the same color as the endolymph, and its presence and function did not become known until 1931 when Steinhausen injected India ink into the canal of the ray and observed how the cupula responded

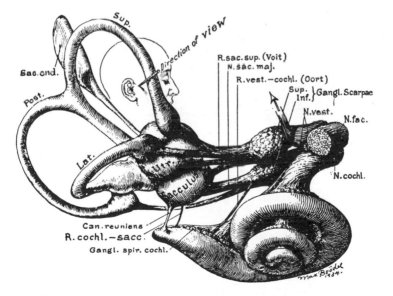

FIG. 2. Diagram of the inner ear, showing the semicircular canals, utricle, saccule, and cochlea, together with the nerves innervating them. (From Hardy, 1934.)

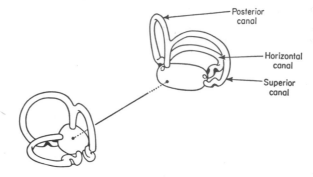

FIG. 3. The arrangement of the vestibular canals on each side of the head. (Adapted from Groen, 1961.)

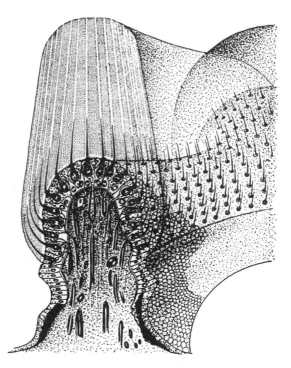

FIG. 4. Schematic drawing of one-half of a crista ampullaris, showing innervation of its epithelium. Thick nerve fibers forming nerve calyces round type I hair cells at the summit of the crista; medium caliber fibers innervating type I hair cells on the slope of the crista; medium caliber and fine nerve fibers forming a nerve plexus innervating hair cells of type II. The sensory hairs pass from the hair cells into fine canals in the cupula, which is separated from the epithelium by a narrow subcupular space. (From Wersäll, 1956.)

as the canal was rotated. Its behavior was found to conform reasonably well to the formula which engineers use to describe the behavior of a simple damped, torsion pendulum, namely:

$$\text{H}\,\ddot{\xi} + \pi\,\dot{\xi} + \Delta\,\xi = \alpha\,\text{H}$$

where H = moment of inertia (mass), π = moment of friction (damping), Δ = directional momentum at unit angle (springyness), ξ = angular displacement of the cupula, $\dot{\xi}$ = angular velocity, $\ddot{\xi}$ = angular acceleration, and α = angular acceleration of the skull in the plane of the canal.

Although this formula describes the performance of the mechanical components of the system, nonlinearities (departures from the above formula) come in when one tries to predict the behavior which the stimulation induces (Young, 1969).

From this description of its structure it should be clear how a canal works. When the canal is rotated in its own plane the endolymph lags behind the canal wall and exerts pressure against the cupula which is deflected in a direction opposite to the rotation. The amount of its deflection is a function of the degree of rotary acceleration imposed upon it. The deflection of the cupula induces shearing forces in the cilia which in turn initiate nerve impulses. However, if the rotation continues at a steady angular velocity, the fluid catches up with the canal walls, the cupula returns to its resting position and stimulation ceases. If the canal is now decelerated and brought to rest, the cupula will be displaced in the reverse direction and, because of its own inertia, will take some time to regain its neutral position. During this recovery period the person will feel, and behave, as if he is still rotating. He will fall to one side, feel dizzy and his eyes will show the characteristic to and fro nystagmic motion which vestibular stimulation induces (see p. 302). However, a voluntary turning of the head or body is usually quickly followed by a deceleration, and under these circumstances the two opposed deflections of the cupula cancel out, leaving no residual deflection and no after effect. Provided the movement does not last longer than about 3 sec, a person is able to judge accurately the angle of turning and hence velocity. Thus, although the stimulus is rotary acceleration, the input can be integrated over short periods to allow the system to detect the amplitude and velocity of ordinary body rotations.

The histological structure of the sensory epithelium of the crista is shown in Fig. 4. Some of the sensory cells are flask-shaped and are enclosed in a goblet-shaped nerve calyx with large diameter axons. Other sensory cells are cylindrical and innervated by knob-shaped nerve endings. Each cell has about seventy fine *stereocilia* and one large *kinocilium*. Microelectrode studies have revealed that a resting potential of about 160 mV exists across the membrane of the cilia, so that the whole structure is, in effect, a "charge condenser." When the cilia are deflected one way, the membrane becomes depolarized and the afferent discharge increases. When the cilia are deflected the other way the membrane becomes hyperpolarized, and the afferent discharge decreases. The membrane as a whole is thus bidirectional. Such an asymmetrical bidirectional process implies an asymmetrical structure; this is the significance of the single kinocilium whch is always on that side of the stereocilia in the direction of depolarization (increased excitation).

A deflection of the cupula away from the utricle (ampullofugal) in the horizontal canals is accompanied by hyperpolarization and decreased afferent firing. In the vertical canals, ampullofugal deflection is accompanied by depolarization and increasing firing. These relationships between the direction of cupula deflection and polarization are probably a fortuitous consequence of embryological growth and have no behavioral significance. However, it is behaviorally significant that for each synergic pair of canals (left and right horizontal, left posterior–right superior, and left superior–right posterior) rotation of the head in a given direction induces hyperpolarization in one member of the pair and depolarization in its partner in the other side. Inspection of Fig. 3 should make these relationships clear. Each pair acts in balanced opposition; hyperpolarization on one side being balanced by depolarization on the other. At least this is so in higher vertebrates; in lower vertebrates, such as the frog, there is no response to depolarization which means that each canal only responds to rotation in one direction and is said to show complete *directional preponderance*. In each synergic pair the canal on one side responds to turns in one direction, and the canal on the other side responds to turns in the opposite direction. Such an animal would not be able to compensate for the loss of one ear. The canals of birds have some responsiveness to a decrease in polarization but still show a relative directional preponderance. In man, there is little if any directional preponderance, at least for mild stimuli (Dohlman, 1960). The bidirectionality of the cupular mechanism in man allows him to compensate for the loss of one vestibular organ, although an individual does not achieve this compensation until he has gone through a disturbing period of adjustment.

B. The Utricles

The mammalian utricle or statolith is a sac at the junction of the three vestibular canals (see Fig. 2). Inside is a ciliated sensory epithelium or *macula*. When the head is erect, the macula surface is approximately horizontal with the cilia protruding upwards into a gelatinous mass containing calcareous particles—the otoliths or otoconia. The otoliths are three times as dense as the endolymph fluid in which they are submerged. Records of the potential changes in the sensory cells have revealed that only bending or shearing forces are effective; pressure at right angles to the epithelium has no effect (Trincker, 1962).

This structure is ideally suited for the detection of sideways or fro-and-aft tilt of the head and linear acceleration. Linear acceleration at right angles to the macula should have no effect, and furthermore, such a system should not be able to distinguish between head tilt and linear, horizontal acceleration in the same direction—both would produce the same shearing of the cilia. It is well known that aircraft pilots flying in clouds do in fact interpret velocity changes as a banking of the aircraft, and fatal accidents have been caused by this confusion. Furthermore, when a person is rotated in a centrifuge, the change in the resultant direction of "gravity" is interpreted as a tilting of the revolving cabin. The fact that such ambiguous stimulation is interpreted as tilt rather than as a change of speed suggests that the utricle is primarily an organ for registering changes of attitude of the head to gravity rather than nongravitational acceleration. Its essentially two-dimensional structure is well suited to this function. It may not be entirely two dimensional however; one end of the macula is set at a slight angle to the rest, but the functional significance of this is not known.

The utricle can detect the attitude of the head, for certain receptors fire steadily at a given position of the head. Others, however, fire only during head movement. Some receptor cells are bidirectional, that is they have a resting discharge which increases with tilt in one direction and decreases with tilt in the opposite direction. Others respond to any deviation from the normal position with the same change in their activity, and might be called "out-of-position receptors" (Lowenstein, 1956).

The utricles exert a general tonic effect in the musculature of the body and their stimulation triggers off postural righting reflexes and reflex torsional eye movements. Their absence in man is not disabling, for other proprioceptive stimuli, as well as touch and vision, are adequate for the maintenance of posture. However, a person without utricles is at a disadvantage when walking over an uneven or unsteady surface with eyes closed.

C. The Vestibular Pathways

All nerve fibers from the mammalian vestibular system gather in the vestibular part of the eighth cranial nerve. The cell bodies of these bipolar cells lie in two vestibular ganglia in the internal acoustic meatus. The axons terminate in the four vestibular nuclei which lie in the floor of the fourth ventricle. These nuclei are: the superior or nucleus of Bechterew, the lateral or Deiter's nucleus, the medial, and the inferior or descending nucleus. Some vestibular fibers also terminate in the cerebellum.

These nuclei give off fibers to various parts of the central nervous system. The lateral nucleus gives rise to the lateral vestibulospinal tract, which mediates vestibular-spinal reflexes, the medial nucleus gives rise to the descending branch of the *medial longitudinal fasciculus* which descends with both crossed and uncrossed fibers into the spinal cord as the ventral vestibulospinal tract. Other fibers of the medial longitudinal fasciculus ascend the brain stem and terminate in the oculomotor nuclei, i.e., the nuclei of cranial nerves III, IV, and VI which control the eye muscles. These connections mediate the reflex eye movements known as vestibular nystagmus (see p. 302). By recording from particular eye muscles while deflecting particular cupulae, Szentágothai (1950) found that each crista has a predominant connection with a pair of ocular muscles as follows:

> Horizontal canal: ipsilateral medial rectus and contralateral lateral rectus
> Superior canal: ipsilateral superior rectus and contralateral inferior oblique
> Posterior canal: ipsilateral superior oblique and contralateral inferior rectus.

Other fibers in the medial longitudinal fasciculus pass to levels rostral to the oculumotor nuclei, probably to the thalamus. These fibers may mediate the vague sensations which vestibular stimulation produces.

The inferior vestibular nucleus sends fibers to the flocculonodular lobe of the cerebellum. This system is a very primitive one concerned with body-balance reflexes. A small number of fibers has been identified in the cat traveling out centrifugally from vestibular nuclei along the vestibular nerve to the receptor organs. Their function is as yet unknown, but it seems to be a general principle that receptors receive an efferent innervation, making possible some central control of their activity.

All the sites to which fibers are sent from the vestibular nuclei send return fibers to those nuclei, thus providing the neural substratum for complex feedback control systems (see Brodal, Pompeiano, & Walbert, 1962; Rasmussen and Windle, 1965, for further details of these pathways). The further behavioral significance of these various connections will be discussed in the next chapter.

References

Andrew, B. L. The sensory innervation of the medial ligament of the knee joint. *Journal of Physiology* (*London*), 1954, **123**, 241–250.

Barker, D. (Ed.). *Symposium on muscle receptors.* Hong Kong: Hong Kong University Press, 1962.

Batteau, D. W. Listening with the naked ear. In S. J. Freedman (Ed.), *The neurophysiology of spatially oriented behaviour.* Homewood, Illinois: Dorsey Press, 1968. Pp. 109–133.

Bauer, B. B., & Torick, E. L. Experimental studies in underwater directional communication. *Journal of the Acoustical Society of America,* 1966, **38**, 25–34.

Brodal, A., Pompeiano, O., & Walberg, F. *The vestibular nuclei and their connections, anatomy and functional correlations,* Edinburgh: Oliver & Boyd, 1962.

Deatherage, B. H. Examination of binaural interaction. *Journal of the Acoustical Society of America,* 1966, **39**, 232–249.

Dohlman, G. On the case for repeal of Ewald's second law. *Acta Oto-Laryngologica, Supplementum,* 1960, **159**, 15–24.

Enger, P. S. Hearing in fish. In A. V. S. de Reuck & J. Knight (Eds.), *Ciba Foundation symposiums on hearing mechanisms in vertebrates.* London: Churchill, 1968. Pp. 4–11.

Fisher, H. G., & Freedman, S. J. The role of the pinna in auditory localization. *Journal of Auditory Research,* 1968, **8**, 15–26.

Fraenkel, G. S., & Gunn, D. L. *The orientation of animals.* New York: Dover, 1961.

Gardner, M. B. Historical background of the Haas and/or precedence effect. *Journal of the Acoustical Society of America,* 1968, **43**, 1243–1248.

Gescheider, G. A. Role of phase-difference cues in the cutaneous analog of auditory sound localization. *Journal of the Acoustical Society of America,* 1968, **43**, 1249–1254.

Griffin, D. R. *Listening in the dark.* New Haven, Connecticut: Yale Univ. Press, 1958.

Groen, J. J. The problems of the spinning top applied to the semi-circular canals. *Confinia Neurologica,* Basel, 1961, **21**, 454–455.

Hardy, M. Observations on the innervation of the macula sacculi in man. *Anatomical Record,* 1934, **59**, 403–418.

Harrison, J. M., & Feldman, M. L. Anatomical aspects of the cochlear nucleus and superior olivary complex. In W. D. Neff (Ed.), *Contributions to sensory physiology.* New York: Academic Press, 1970, Pp. 95–142.

Kellogg, W. N. *Porpoises and sonar.* Chicago, Illinois: Univ. of Chicago Press, 1961.

Kreidl, A. Weitere Beitrage zur Physiologie des Ohrlabyrinths. *Sitzungsberich der Oestlichen Akademie fur Philosophie-Historisch,* 1893, **102**, 149.

Lowenstein, O. Comparative physiology of the otolith organs. *British Medical Bulletin,* 1956, **12**, 110–113.

Machin, K. E. 1962. Electric receptors. *Symposia of the Society for Experimental Biology,* 1962, **16**, 227–244.

Neff, W. D. Localization and lateralization of sound in space. In A. V. S. de Reuck & J. Knight (Eds.), *Ciba Foundation symposium on hearing mechanisms in vertebrates.* London: Churchill, 1968. Pp. 207–230.

Oscarsson, O. The projection of Group I muscle afferents to the cat cerebral cortex. In R. Granit (Ed.), *Muscular afferents and motor control.* New York: Wiley, 1966. Pp. 167–178.

Pringle, J. W. S. Proprioception in insects. *Journal of Experimental Biology,* 1938, **15**, 101–131 and 467–473.

I. P. HOWARD

Pumphrey, R. J. Hearing. *Symposia of The Society for Experimental Biology*, 1950, **4**, 3–18.

Rasmussen, G. L., & Windle, W. F. *Neural mechanisms of the auditory and vestibular systems.* Springfield, Illinois: Thomas, 1965.

Rice, C. E. Human echo perception. *Science*, 1967, **155**, 656–664.

Rosenzweig, M. R. Cortical correlates of auditory localization and of related perceptual phenomena. *Journal of Comparative and Physiological Psychology*, 1954, **47**, 269–276.

Steinhausen, W. Über den Nachweis der Bewegung der Cupola in der intakten Bogengansampulle des Labyrinths bei der nätürlichen rotatorischen und calorischen Reizung. *Pflüger's Archives gesempt Physiologie*, 1931, **228**, 322–328.

Szentágothai, J. The elementary vestibulo-ocular reflex arc. *Journal of Neurophysiology*, 1950, **13**, 395–407.

Taub, E., & Berman, A. J. Movement and learning in the absence of sensory feedback. In S. J. Freedman (Ed.), *The neuropsychology of spatially oriented behavior.* Homewood, Illinois: Dorsey Press, 1968. Pp. 173–192.

Trincker, D. E. W. The transformation of mechanical stimulus into nervous excitation by the labyrinthine receptors. *Symposia of the Society for Experimental Biology*, 1962, **16**, 289–316.

Tumarkin, A. Evolution of the auditory conducting apparatus in terrestrial vertebrates. In A. V. S. de Reuck & J. Knight (Eds.), *Ciba Foundation symposium on hearing mechanisms of vertebrates.* London: Churchill, 1968. Pp. 18–36.

von Békésy, G. Human skin perception of traveling waves similar to those of the cochlea. *Journal of the Acoustical Society of America*, 1955, **27**, 830–841.

Wallach, H. The role of head movements and vestibular and visual cues in sound localisation. *Journal of Experimental Psychology*, 1940, **27**, 339–368.

Wersäll, J. Studies on the structure and innervation of the sensory epithelium of the cristae ampullaris in the guinea pig. *Acta Oto-Laryngologica, Supplementum*, 1956, 126.

Young, L. R. The current status of vestibular system models. *Automatica*, 1969, **5**, 369–383.

Chapter 14

ORIENTATION AND MOTION IN SPACE

I. P. HOWARD

Overt behavior is spatially organized within a matrix of constraints imposed upon it by the structure and functions of the body and the structure of the world. The organization of spatially coordinated behavior occurs at several levels. The first and most basic level is that of *sensorimotor topology* or the basic ground plan of the sensorimotor system laid down during embryological development. The next level is that of *kinesthesis and the body schema* which denote the sense of position and of movement of the body and the sense of familiarity of the body. The next level is that of the repertoire of *orientation mechanisms* of the body and its parts in relation to features of external space such as gravity, the ground, and objects. All the levels of organization mentioned so far provide a necessary substratum for purposive behavior, which usually involves locomotion toward an object or a locality in three-dimensional space by means of a repertoire of *navigation* skills. Orientation and navigation are so intimately related that they will be considered together. Finally, the end-point of behavior usually involves the manipulation of objects, which requires fine sensorimotor coordination. Each of these levels of spatial behavior will now be discussed in more detail.

I. THE TOPOLOGY OF THE SENSORIMOTOR SYSTEM

The pioneer work on the way in which the spatial topology of the nervous system develops was done on the neuromuscular system by Weiss, and is summarized in his 1941 and 1950 papers. His basic method was to transplant limbs in the salamander and toad and allow the motor nerves to reinnervate the muscles. He found that a limb transplanted to the opposite side of the body responded in the same manner and at the same time as the neighboring normal limb on that side. Weiss called this the *myotypic response*. He concluded that the motor fibers reinnervate the transplanted muscles in an essentially random manner and become "modulated" by the muscle fibers which they reach, in such a way that they are induced to set up appropriate central connections in the spinal cord. It is as if each muscle informed the neural centers what kind of muscle it is, by a process which Weiss called *myoneural modulation*.

Recently this conception has been seriously challenged by Sperry and Arora (1965) who have shown that normal responses occur in the extrinsic eye muscles of a fish only when reinnervation brings nerve fibers back to their normal muscles. Other evidence against the phenomenon of myoneural modulation is summarized by Gaze (1970), who concludes that the existence of the phenomenon is unproven, and that restoration of myotypic responses is probably due to the selective reinnervation of muscles by appropriate neurons which are somehow guided to their proper place. According to this view, the basic spinal neuronal networks for limb control are fixed. Székely (1968) has devised models of these spinal networks, although some of his physiological assumptions are speculative.

Weiss extended his concept of neuronal modulation to sensory neurons. He suggested that during embryological development sensory nerve fibers of a given sensory nerve grow out to innervate a particular sense organ more or less randomly, and have their specificity biochemically imprinted on them by contact with the particular sensory cells they happen to reach. This imprinted specificity, he suggested, induces the development of appropriate central connections. Evidence for this view came from an experiment in which Weiss found that touching an eye transplanted to the region of the ear in the larval toad (*Triturus torosus*) produced a normal blink reflex of the normal eye on the same side. However, Székely (1959) was able to invoke the same blink reflex by transplanting and stimulating noncorneal tissue, which demonstrates that the concept of specific sensory modulation of nerves is unnecessary to explain Weiss's original result. It seems that stimulation of any newly innervated sensory tissue in that region induces blinking.

Gaze (1970) reviews other evidence which seems to support Weiss's idea of sensory modulation of central connections, and argues that in each case it is possible to reinterpret the results to fit the alternative theory of selective reinnervation originally suggested by Sperry. According to this theory, regrowing sensory roots send out "pioneer" fibers, some of which find the right end organ by some *cytochemical recognition* process and guide the subsequent growth of other fibers. Those fibers that do not "make it," degenerate. Some form of feedback from periphery to center is required on either theory, the difference is whether this feedback induces an alteration in preformed central connections, as Weiss suggested, or merely the outgrowth of new fibers along the "pioneer" route and the cytochemical matching to their appropriate target region (Sperry, 1965).

Electrophysiological evidence which would help to finally decide between these two theories for the somatic sensory system is lacking. However, such evidence is available for the visual systems of fish and amphibia, in which it has been found that the electrophysiological map of retinal-central projections after section and regeneration of the optic nerve are essentially normal (Gaze, 1970). This finding dramatically confirms Sperry's theory of selective reinnervation, which his earlier experiments on the regeneration of the optic nerve had supported. In these experiments Sperry (1944, 1945) found that normal visually controlled behavior was restored after regeneration of the optic nerve in urodeles. However, if the cut optic nerves were directed back to the wrong side of the brain the animal made permanently reversed responses to objects in its visual field, showing that no modulation of the central connections had occurred, as Weiss' theory would have predicted.

The evidence strongly suggests therefore that the topology of neuromuscular and sensory systems is determined both centrally and peripherally, and that the two predetermined systems become coordinated by the selective growth of nerve fibers which are somehow guided to their proper destination and coupled to their proper partners by some form of cytochemical matching.

II. KINESTHESIS

Kinesthesis is the ability to discriminate the position of body parts and their direction, amplitude, and speed of movement, whether actively or passively produced, and the pressure exerted by body parts. The term is normally reserved for discriminations based upon sense receptors in joints, muscles, tendons, and the vestibular system, or upon the motor discharge (sense of effort) associated with muscular contractions. Gibson's (1966) recent extension of the term kinesthesis to include visual and other sensory channels has the virtue of stressing the integrative properties of sensory systems, but conflicts with common usage.

The sensitivity of joints to passive movement varies from joint to joint but is in the region of 1 degree at a speed of 1 degree/second (see Cleghorn & Darcus, 1952).

There are two basic procedures for measuring the active position sensitivity of a limb. The first is to ask the subject to place his unseen finger on a reference point and then regain the same position. Cohen (1958) found a mean error of about 2 degrees at the finger tip of the extended arm with this procedure. The problem is that this performance reflects the sensitivity of initial registration, of storage and recall, and of subsequent reaiming. Merton (1961) measured the steadiness with which the position of the extended arm could be held and relocated, and found a mean drift of 0.1–0.2 degree after 1 second; this figure may be nearer to reflecting the basic sensitivity of the system.

The second procedure for studying active position sense is to ask the blindfolded subject to bring his fingers together (with a plate of glass between them to prevent knowledge of results). This test has been used clinically rather than experimentally.

Loading a limb has remarkably little effect on its position sense (Bahrick, Fitts, & Schneider, 1955; Cohen, 1958). Furthermore, pulling on the exposed tendons at the wrist and ankle has been found not to affect the sense of position of the limb if the limb did not move (Gelfan & Carter, 1967). These two facts, together with the fact that paralysis of joint receptors destroys position sense in a finger even though muscle and tendon receptors are intact (Provins, 1958), strongly suggest that position sense depends upon joint receptors and not upon tendon organs, muscle receptors, or motor outflow. Whether forms of kinesthetic judgment, other than position sense, depend only upon joint receptors is not known. The position sense of the eye does not depend upon joint receptors, but the eye is a special case (see Section V, A, 3).

III. THE BODY SCHEMA

The concept of the body schema was first introduced by Sir Henry Head in 1911 to account for certain neurological disorders. He conceived it as being an acquired, neural organization which underlies the sense of familiarity of the body. The need to assume some such mnemonic neural organization is evident when one is confronted with two phenomena, namely, the phantom limb and neglect. Most amputees, for some time after losing a limb, vividly experience the presence of the missing limb. This phantom is experienced as moving to command and may even "wear" a wedding ring if the real limb did. Phantoms eventually disappear as the amputee learns to live without his limb, and they do not occur at all in children with early or congenital loss of a limb.

The second phenomenon, neglect, is a symptom which is generally thought to result from damage to the nondominant parietal lobe. The patient feels that a limb, the whole of one side of the body, or even the whole body is not his own. Stimuli applied to the affected part are still felt but as if they were applied to something outside the body. The affected limb may be moved voluntarily but the patient prefers not to use the affected part, and tends not to wash or dress it. He may have difficulty in finding that part of the body when asked to locate it, and will tend to deny that it is his when it is pointed out to him.

It is evident from these facts that the body schema is not merely the sum total of contemporaneous stimulation or voluntary commands to movement. It is most probably learned, because the phenomenon of the phantom limb is absent in child amputees, and it must be capable of modification as the body grows or as one gets used to the absence of a limb. It is not the same thing as the mental image one has of one's body, nor is it the conceptual knowledge one has of one's anatomy. For further information see Schilder, (1935), Critchley (1953), and Shontz (1969).

So far we have discussed the mechanisms which underlie what may be called the internal spatial reference system of the body. A distinction between internal and external spatial systems is arbitrary and is used for expository convenience—in the last analysis the two develop and function as one system. All animals possess a variety of mechanisms by which they maintain a particular angular position relative to external landmarks or directions, or by which they make judgments about the location of things. These mechanisms fall roughly into three categories: gravitational, egocentric, and geographical, which will be discussed in turn. Egocentric and geographical orientation are the bases for navigation or directed movement toward a goal.

IV. GRAVITATIONAL ORIENTATION

The sensory systems concerned with gravitational orientations are the utricle, vision, kinesthesis, and touch; and in this context their primary concern is with the initiation of complex patterns of righting reflexes. The discussion of righting reflexes is beyond the scope of this chapter; for a review see Magnus (1926), Peiper (1963), and Hess (1957).

A. The Body Vertical

The perception of the vertical position of the body has usually been studied by seating a blindfolded subject in a tilting chair and asking him to indicate when it has been restored to the vertical. Under these conditions a person is able to restore his body to the vertical with a precision of about 1 degree, and precision seems to be greater in the lateral than in the sagittal plane. A constant error of up to 2 degrees tends to occur in the direction of initial tilt. Performance on this task has been found to be little affected by the absence of the vestibular system or by anesthetizing the skin areas in contact with the chair. That is not to say that neither of these cues is ever used, it probably means that one cue can fully substitute for another.

In real-life situations, posture is maintained while the person is standing or moving about, and the important questions can be studied only under such dynamic conditions. The usual method for studying postural stability is the sway test, in which the sway of a standing person is recorded in any desired plane. The degree of sway is generally greater in men than women, and has been found to be increased by alcohol, muscle tension, fatigue, and suggestion. The influence of suggestion has led to the use of the sway test as a measure of hypnotizability.

Sway increases a little when a normal person is blindfolded, although normally blind people have no difficulty in standing steadily. However, swaying visual surroundings can cause people to lose their balance completely. A person with bilateral labyrinthectomy is little affected, even when blindfolded, unless the ground upon which he is standing is unstable, in which case he is less able than a normal person to maintain his balance. Tabetic patients, who lose proprioceptive sense from their lower body as a result of spinal infection, are very unstable when blindfolded, which suggests that the single most important sensory system in the maintenance of upright posture in man is comprised of the muscle and joint receptors associated with the hip joint and spine. These receptors feed impulses into the cerebellum, vestibular nuclei, and basal ganglia-centers which control the bilateral balance of body tonus. The body is always swaying slightly, invoking small corrective muscle contractions. For detailed references on the subject of postural orientation, see Howard and Templeton (1966) and Begbie (1967).

B. The Visual Vertical

Visual objects which are oriented vertically or horizontally are salient stimuli in many ways. For instance, human beings are able to set a luminous line in dark surroundings consistently to within about 1 degree of the vertical or horizontal but less accurately and precisely to other angles. Young children and animals have difficulty in learning to discriminate a left oblique line from a right oblique line, but are easily able to discriminate a vertical line from a horizontal line. Furthermore, visual acuity is better for stimuli in line with the normally vertical or horizontal meridians of the retina than for retinally oblique stimuli, a fact known as *retinal astigmatism*. Maffei and Campbell (1970) have recently produced evidence of an electrophysiological correlate of this effect at the level of the occipital cortex. The basic reason for the saliency of verticals and horizontals is that the visual world contains a predominance of lines in these directions, and these lines form the framework in relation to which other things are judged.

When the head is tilted to one side a vertical line no longer stimulates the normally vertical meridian of the eye, and yet, for tilts up to about 60 degrees, judgments of the vertical remain accurate to within a few degrees. Some people experience an apparent tilt of a luminous line in the opposite direction to the tilt of the head (Aubert effect); other people experience an apparent tilt of the line in the same direction as the head (Muller effect). At large angles of head tilt these illusory effects may be very large, but the reason for them remains obscure.

The apparent vertical position of a visible object may also be affected by the visual surroundings. This point is illustrated by Koffka's report of an experience he had when traveling in a mountain train; trees growing on a steep hillside seemed to be growing at an angle when viewed through the tilted window of the train (Koffka, 1935, p. 216). Many people are now familiar with similar effects seen from banking aircraft. Many experiments have been done on the extent to which such visual-frame effects override postural cues to the vertical. Werner, Wapner, and others worked within the so-called *sensory-tonic* theoretical framework which stressed the interaction between sensory factors (vision, audition, and touch) and tonic factors (proprioception and movement) in judgments of direction (see Wapner & Werner, 1957, for a general statement). Witkin and others, working within a similar framework, did an extensive series of experiments on the relative strengths of the postural and visual cues to the apparent vertical position of a luminous rod. In these experiments, subjects were asked to set a rod to the vertical in the presence of a visual surround, consisting of a simple square frame or a room, which could be tilted to any angle. In some conditions, the subject could also be tilted in the same direction as the frame or in the opposite direction. The investigations revealed that the tilted visual frame influenced the judgments of some people more than others. The extent of this influence was said to measure "frame dependence," and this factor was reported to be correlated with sex and other variables, such as introversion–extraversion (see Witkin, Lewis, Hertzman, Machover, Meissner, & Wapner, 1954).

C. The Tilt Aftereffect

If an isolated line, tilted in the frontal plane, is viewed for some time, a vertical line seen subsequently appears to be tilted 1 or 2 degrees in the opposite direction. Gibson explained such effects in the following words, "If a sensory process which has an opposite, is made to persist by a constant application of its stimulus-conditions, the quality will diminish in the direction of becoming neutral, and therewith the quality evoked by any stimulus for the dimension in question will be shifted temporarily towards the opposite or complementary quality" (Gibson, 1937, p. 223). Gibson thus saw the aftereffect as being an incidental byproduct of the primary fact of adaptation to a norm.

The normalization theory cannot account for the fact that inspection of a vertical line causes an apparent repulsion of a tilted test line. This effect is smaller than the Gibson effect and it would seem that there are two processes operating in the tilt aftereffect; a normalization effect and a figural aftereffect—a general tendency for figures to be apparently repelled from the position of previously inspected figures (Templeton, Howard, & Easting, 1965). If the whole problem is reformulated, however, it is possible to account for all the facts in terms of a single-factor theory. Hubel and Wiesel (1962) have shown that there are orientation-specific contour detectors in the cortex of the cat, each of which responds maximally to one orientation of the stimulus and with decreasing intensity as the stimulus is rotated from this preferred orientation up to about ±10 degrees. These units become less sensitive when stimulated. Such detectors will clearly account for the figural aftereffect of an inspected line on a test line in a slightly different orientation. The test line will fall into an asymmetrically fatigued zone and the distribution of its effect on the detector units will be correspondingly skewed away from the inspection line (Coltheart, 1971; Over, 1971). In a similar way one can account for the normalization effect, if one assumes that the vertical and horizontal cortical detectors are in a permanent state of fatigue because of the predominance of vertically and horizontally oriented lines in the world. According to this view, the initial effect of looking at a tilted inspection line is for it to appear more tilted than it is, and as the vertical detectors recover their sensitivity, the distribution of excitation among detectors about the tilted inspection line gradually becomes more symmetrical. If the vertical line is now exposed it will fall into an asymmetrical excitation field and appear tilted the other way. Normalization may therefore be due not to a tilting line coming gradually to look more vertical, as Gibson suggested, but rather to the recovery of sensitivity in vertical detectors and the gradual restoration of a symmetrical field about the tilted line (see Coren & Festinger, 1967 for a similar statement).

D. Visual Polarity

Most objects and features of the world have a top and a bottom, and quite commonly an axis of symmetry which is usually vertical. There seem to be certain general characteristics of objects, such as taper, shading gradients, and the distribution of visual mass, which people use to make consistent judgments as to whether an object is upright (Ghent, 1961). The basis for these discriminations may depend to some extent upon innate tendencies. There is evidence that such tendencies exist in animals; fish swim with their backs to the light, even in the absence of the utricles, and vertebrates have a reflex tendency to adopt a normal posture with respect to a visual surface. However, the perceived uprightness of most objects for humans must surely depend on learning, for the upright position of many objects is purely conventional. In any case, one way or the other, the perceptual behavior of people is heavily conditioned by the ecological polarity of the visual world. An object which is normally seen in one orientation (mono-oriented) is more easily recognized when upright than when upside down and is more easily discriminated from another object when both are upright than when both are upside down or in different orientations.

A question which has received considerable attention is whether the discrimination of shapes is more affected by a relative difference in orientation with respect to the retina, to gravity, or to the visual framework. The details of the studies are complex and the results are equivocal (see Ghent & Bernstein, 1961; Howard & Templeton, 1966, Chs. 12 and 13; Kolers & Perkins, 1969; Rock & Heimer, 1957). For meaningful, mono-oriented shapes, especially when disoriented by more than 90°, retinal disorientation seems to be more disruptive than gravitational disorientation. This is certainly true of printed words, which are hard to read when upside down on the retina, even though upright in respect to gravity (that is, when an upright book is viewed with upside-down head). On the other hand, when a subject is asked to select from among several abstract shapes one that he has been shown before, the absence of an easily recognizable "top" causes his performance to be more affected by gravitational disorientation than by retinal disorientation or disorientation with respect to a visual frame. This is probably because people habitually tend to look to the gravitational "top" of the visual field to find the top of an object, and base their judgments about the similarity of shapes upon the "top" which they find there. When the shapes are very familiar, such as printed words, the true location of the top of the picture is easy to find whether it is in the expected place or not and, once that part of the task is accomplished, consistent retinal orientation is the dominant factor determining recognizability or discriminability.

There has been a history of interest in the effects of inverting the visual world. Ever since Stratton's studies of this question in the 1890's, the usual procedure has been to study the behavior of a subject wearing optical devices which invert the optical array (see especially, Kohler, 1951; Kottenhoff, 1961; Taylor, 1962). The problem with this technique is that it confounds the effects of three types of disturbance: the pictorial inversion of the scene, disturbed visual-motor coordination, and the disturbed intersensory relationships. Under these circumstances it has proved impossible to get clear answers to particular questions. The question which is usually asked is whether the world comes to appear "upright." However, unless it is specified in what sense the word "upright" is used, the question has no meaning. Certainly subjects eventually come to adjust their movements to the visual world, and in that sense behave as if the world were upright. Furthermore, the unfamiliar upside-down appearance of the world diminishes; but this does not mean, as has often been assumed, that the visual scene experientially swings round to come to look as it does normally. No subject has reported *that* experience, and there is no reason to expect that to happen. A simple illustration of how silly such an expectation is, consists of imagining what would happen if one were allowed to view only upside-down reading material. Reading would at first be difficult, and the material would look strange. After a week or so, reading speed would probably be back to normal and the material would no longer look strange. However, it would not have "righted" itself in experience—it would not have come to look pictorially like normal printing. It is merely that one would have learned to recognize the material. One could imagine being presented with normal printing at the end of such an experiment and having some initial difficulty reading it. Furthermore, it would occasion no surprise to discover after such training, when normal and inverted printing are viewed at the same time, that they both look equally "upright" in the sense of being familiar and readable and yet differently oriented in a gravitational or pictorial sense. It is hoped that this illustration will reduce the misunderstanding associated with this question, and explain how two things can appear to be in the same orientation and in different orientations at the same time.

V. EGOCENTRIC ORIENTATION

The eyes, head, and trunk each have three principal planes and three axes of rotation. Egocentric orientation refers to the ability to judge or behave with respect to the position of an object in relation to one or other of these planes and axes.

A. Visual Egocentric Orientation

1. THE STATIONARY EYE

Stimulation of any one point in the retina is normally associated with a unique subjective visual direction relative to the eyes' position at the time. The fovea is unique, and defines the principal visual direction. The relative oculocentric directional values of retinal locations are topologically maintained through the optic nerve, geniculate body, and primary visual cortex. All objects which stimulate a given retinal location for a given position of the eye are judged to be in the same direction. This is the fundamental law of visual direction which Hering first proposed, and is true except in rare cases of monocular double vision. The capacity of the visual system to distinguish visual directions is limited by visual acuity which, under favorable circumstances, may be as little as a few seconds of arc. For every retinal point in one eye there is a corresponding point in the retina of the other eye which has an identical oculocentric space value, and identical egocentric space values as long as there is no squint. The common center to which the egocentric directions of binocularly observed objects is subjectively referred is known as the *cyclopian eye* and is commonly said to be located midway between the two eyes. A simple way to demonstrate this communality of binocular space values is to view along a horizontal card upon which is drawn two lines, each running from an eye to a common fixation point. When this is done, a single line will be seen running out from the "cyclopian" eye. This type of demonstration reveals that the egocentric direction of all objects outside the plane of fixation (horopter) is misjudged. This has little behavioral significance however, because animals normally attend to and behave toward only those objects which are fixated. An implication of this cyclopian system is that single objects outside the horopter stimulate disparate points of the two retinas, and this is of course the basis of binocular stereopsis.

If one views an isolated point of light in a dark room, it appears to wander about; this phenomenon is known as *autokinesis*. Involuntary movements of the eyes, which are produced after rotation of the head for instance, can certainly induce a strong autokinesis, although eye movements are not necessary for its occurrence. The direction of the apparent movement is influenced by many factors including vestibular stimulation, the direction of gaze, suggestion, and the presence of other visible objects. See Royce, Carran, Aftinas, Lehman, and Blumenthal (1966) for a recent review. An analogous effect in audition has been reported (Anderson & Moss, 1964).

2. THE MOBILE EYE

If an animal is to decode visual information, the retinal image must be kept reasonably still for some time in spite of movements of the animal's head or movements of the visual target. Furthermore, the decoding process is simplified if the image of the scene always occurs in the same orientation. The most primitive eye-movement reflex serving these purposes is *optokinetic nystagmus,* which consists of the involuntary pursuit of the moving scene interspersed with quick return sweeps. This optokinetic response occurs horizontally, vertically, and also about the optic axis (torsion) and may be readily observed in the eyes of a person viewing a pattern of moving stripes. Von Holst and Mittelstaedt have studied the consequences of reversing the direction of the image motion produced by a given eye motion. They did this in the fly (*Eristalis*) for instance by rotating the fly's head through 180 degrees. Under these circumstances, a negative feedback loop has become an unstable positive feedback loop, and the fly's head movements become unstable (see Mittelstaedt, 1964). The author produced the same effect in a human subject by mounting dove prisms on contact lenses (Howard, 1970). The eyes and the visual world appeared to swing nystagmically to and fro with a slow component sometimes in one direction sometimes in the other, and sometimes a slow phase in both directions. Any small slow drift of the eyes normally induces a corrective eye movement, but under conditions of image-motion reversal the corrective eye movement induces increased image motion which in turn induces further drift of the eyes. *Vestibular nystagmus* is also a to-and-fro eye movement, induced by vestibular stimulation, which may be demonstrated by feeling the eyeballs under the closed eyelids as the body is rotated (see Bender, 1964; Davson, 1962; Reinecke, 1961).

These compensatory eye movements occur even in animals whose eyes have no fovea. Foveate animals possess, in addition, the *foveal pursuit reflex* which serves to maintain the image of the object, to which the animal is attending, on the fovea. Without a moving target, animals cannot voluntarily move their eyes slowly and steadily over a stationary field of view, because such movements immediately cause a movement of the retinal image which induces involuntary optokinetic eye movements in the opposite direction. This fact may be easily verified by observing the eyes of a person who attempts to move his eyes steadily. Whenever a foveate animal wishes to change its direction of gaze it does so by a *saccadic* movement which is so rapid (up to 400 degrees/sec) that the stabilizing reflexes are not triggered.

One final type of eye movement occurs in animals with binocular stereoscopic vision; these are the *vergence movements* which keep the principal lines of sight directed to whatever object is being inspected.

3. Eye Movements and the Sense of Direction

The object of attention is normally imaged on the fovea, and the task of judging the visual direction of an object in relation to the head therefore boils down to "knowing" the position of the eyes in the head. All the evidence suggests that there are no proprioceptors which indicate eye position (Merton, 1964). Eye position is apparently coded as follows. By virtue of the springiness of the extraocular muscles, the eyes have a tendency to return to a central position. The degree of tension in an extraocular muscle is a linear function of the length of that muscle (Robinson, O'Meara, Scott, & Collins, 1969), and thus, for every position of the eye, each agonist must match the tension in its antagonist. This tension is always the same for any one eye position because the eye is not subjected to external loads. The unique pattern of innervation, or its corollary discharge, associated with each eye position is thus ideally suited to serve the sense of eye position.

It is presumably this dead-reckoning system which provides the information necessary for stable egocentric (at least head-centric) directional judgments. It has been proposed that it also provides for the stability of the visual world *during* changes of fixation. According to the *cancellation theory,* the motor outflow "cancels" the resultant retinal-image motion to produce experienced stability (Gregory, 1958). It is most unlikely that any such mechanism could work except in a gross fashion, because the velocity-time features of a saccade are complex, and the "computations" for proper cancellation would have to be extremely rapid and involved. In any case, visual stability during such rapid movements would not serve any behavioral purpose. What evidence there is suggests that continuous compensation is indeed not achieved (Matin, Matin, & Pola, 1970). Vision seems to be somewhat suppressed during saccades (Starr, Angel, & Yeates, 1969) and we normally pay no attention to what we see at such times.

What *is* important is that, as soon as possible after a saccadic eye movement, the egocentric direction values of oculocentric space be shifted to coincide with the new position of the eyes in the head. It is also important that animals maintain the correct egocentric location of an object which their eyes slowly pursue; an animal's ability to catch moving prey, or a human being's ability to catch a ball attest to the presence of this ability. To what extent the directional stability of the stationary background during slow pursuit movements is maintained is not known. It would seem that experimenters in this field have been concerned to find evidence for visual stability *during* saccades, which is a behaviorally trivial matter, and have ignored the biologically more significant questions concerning (*a*) the egocentric accuracy of visual location for different eye positions and image positions, and (*b*) stability of target and background during slow-pursuit eye movements.

There are circumstances under which the visual world apparently loses its stability. For instance, immediately after a period of rotation the world appears to spin; this phenomenon is known as the *oculogyral illusion.* This is due in part to postrotational nystagmus (see p. 285). When the head is turning, the slow pursuit phase of vestibular nystagmus is appropriately adjusted to the consequent motion of the retinal image, and this combination of vestibular stimulation, eye movement, and lack of image movement indicates a non-moving world. However, in postrotational nystagmus the body is not rotating, and the slow phase of the nystagmus is accompanied by image motion, which is therefore interpreted as motion of the world. The oculogyral illusion outlasts the postrotational nystagmus which cannot therefore be the only cause of the illusion (Lester & Morant, 1969). Postrotational nystagmus does not occur in people like figure skaters who learn to overcome it by concentrating on a stationary point in the visual scene, and such people do not suffer from illusory aftereffects to the same extent as unpracticed people, as long as they have their eyes open (Collins, 1968).

B. Intersensory Localization

Normally the visual egocentric position of an object coincides with its position as felt or heard (if the object makes a noise). If the visual direction of an object is artificially dissociated from its felt position or the direction of an associated sound, what usually happens is that vision dominates; that is, the object feels or sounds as if it were situated where it is seen to be. This is the basis of the well-known ventriloquism effect and is referred to as *visual dominance* or *visual capture*. If the discrepancy is too great the experienced cohesion of the separate sensations breaks down (see Howard & Templeton, 1966, Ch. 14; Pick, Warren, & Hay, 1969; Singer & Day, 1969).

Up to now we have viewed the different modalities as alternative, in-parallel channels of information about direction. Certain spatial tasks involve the in-series integration of information from different modalities. Cases of this type are discussed in Section VII of this chapter.

VI. GEOGRAPHIC ORIENTATION AND NAVIGATION

Geographical orientation refers to the ability of an animal to set its body axis at some angle with respect to an external landmark. If the animal locomotes while maintaining an orientation, it may be said to be navigating. But animals may reach a given location without orienting, by a process known as kinesis.

A. Kinesis

Woodlice (*Forcellio scaber*) aggregate in moist places because their rate of random *movement* is reduced as they enter a moist zone. Thus, once they have entered a moist zone, they are unlikely to leave it. This mechanism is known as *orthokinesis*. A similar aggregation mechanism is known as *klinokinesis*. In this case the rate of random *turning* is said to be reduced as the target zone is entered. Ullyott suggested that this is the way that the planarian (*Dendrocoelum lacteum*) aggregates in the dark. However, it has been questioned whether such a mechanism really operates (Hinde, 1966).

B. Taxes

A taxis is a directed movement in relation to an external object or location—a true navigation. The simplest navigation process is known as *klinotaxis*. It is exemplified by the movement of a maggot away from light. The maggot does this by alternately sampling the light intensity on each side of the body and appropriately adjusting the symmetry of its side-to-side body movements so as to keep heading away from the light—rather like a blind man feeling his way down a passage with a stick.

Tropotaxis is a similar process, but instead of alternately sampling stimulus intensity, the animal simultaneously compares intensity by means of a pair of symmetrically placed sense organs. If there are two sources of stimulation, for instance two lights, the animal navigates down the locus of symmetrical stimulation, which is along the bisector of the angle which the lights subtend at the animal. Unilaterally removing one sense organ results in circular movements (the circus reaction).

Telotaxis describes the navigation of an animal which has the ability to move directly toward one of several targets even when one sense organ is destroyed. Such an ability implies the presence of an image-forming sense organ. For further details of these simple navigation processes, see Fraenkel and Gunn (1961).

The subject of animal navigation by means of landmarks, geophysical forces, or astronomic features is too vast to be treated here. Interested readers should consult Adler (1970).

C. Human Geographic Orientation

Human beings have no difficulty in moving toward particular objects which are seen or heard. However, they are easily deceived when external guides are absent, and tend gradually to veer one way or the other, as anyone who has been lost in a mist or the desert will know. Consistent veering tendencies are probably due to asymmetries in body structure or of vestibular function. There is no evidence of a magnetic, or other terrestrial orientation sense in man except that which depends upon the visual or auditory recognition of landmarks. Anecdotal accounts of remarkable abilities of primitive peoples to navigate in the absence of landmarks probably reflect the stupidity of the observers rather than any extraordinary abilities of the primitive people, and probably also a general reluctance to credit "primitive" people with common sense (See Gladwin, 1970).

Geographic disorientation is a commonly reported symptom of brain damage, particularly of damage to the parietal lobes. The patient may "forget" familiar landmarks or be unable to relate the position of one part of his environment to another. He may even have difficulty getting about his own home (see Howard & Templeton, 1966, Ch. 10 for a review of human geographic orientation).

VII. SENSORI-MOTOR COORDINATION

The task of aiming with unseen hand at a visual target at eye level will be taken as a paradigm or visual-motor coordination. The physical components involved are the target, the retina, the eyes, the head, the body, and the arm. Each component is linked to the next at what may be called an articulation (skeletal joints in the case of the arm and head, a non-skeletal joint in the case of the eyeball, and a sensory surface in the retina). The whole system is therefore an open-loop, in-series control system. It becomes a closed-loop system as soon as the person is allowed to see the error of his aiming response.

A person is normally able to point with unseen hand to within approximately 1 degree of a visible target at arm's length, although accuracy varies with the position of the hand and of the target (Edgington, 1953; Sandström, 1951).

In order to study the function of any control system it is necessary to have some means of systematically disturbing it. Introducing a displacement of the optical array is a convenient means of achieving this end in the visual-motor system. In the typical experiment, the subject wears prisms which displace the field of view to one side by about 15 degrees. He is then exposed to a training condition in which he is allowed to view his moving arm (Held technique) or in which he is asked to aim at visual targets with a seen hand (continuous exposure), or with a hand which remains covered until the finger reaches the target (terminal exposure). Tests are then applied, in which the subject is not allowed to see his hand, in order to discover what the effects of training have been. In so far as the subject has learned to compensate for the prisms during training, the information from one or more of the articulations must have become "recalibrated," that is, there must have been some remapping of sensory inflow or motor command in terms of the internal schema which underlie directed movement.

There are two basic questions that may be investigated about the visual-motor system using this experimental paradigm. These will be dealt with under separate headings.

A. The Lability of Elements of the Visual-motor System

The first basic question concerns the relative lability of parts of the visual-motor system. The lability of an articulation in the visual-motor system is the extent to which sensory or motor events associated with that articulation are recalibrated in terms of the rest of the system during a specified training procedure. Several attempts have been made to locate the site or sites of the recalibration involved in adjusting to visual displacement.

At first glance, the alternatives are (1) the retinal space values, (2) the sense of the position of the eye in the socket, or (3) of the head on the shoulders, or (4) of the arm on the body. These may be further subdivided according to whether the change involves the interpretation of afferent signals or of the motor command (or its corollary discharge). All these possibilities are listed in Table I. The table also lists some of the various tests which have been used to decide where the lability is. For instance, if the effects of training one arm with one eye open transfer to a test situation in which the other eye is open (as they do), it would seem that the effect is not related to the sense of position of the trained eye. If the effect transfers from one arm to the other (by and large it does not) the lability is is not connected with the trained arm. It is hoped that the other tests in the table are self-explanatory. In each case there is entered in the table a statement of whether the test should reveal the effects of training given that the articulation in question is the site of the lability, and, coupled with each prediction at the bottom of the table, is a statement of whether or not the prediction has been borne out, although the evidence is sometimes conflicting.

All recent investigators are agreed that there is no change in retinal local sign (oculocentric space values). However, this may merely be due to the procedural "accident" that they all used foveally fixated visual targets. It is also agreed that the change is not merely in particular motor command signals. This would seem to leave only changes in proprioception (felt-position) of one or other articulation (in the case of the eye, this depends on motor corollary discharges). Harris (1965) has championed such a view, and most of the evidence reviewed in Table I supports it. However, Hardt, Held, and Steinbach (1971) have produced evidence that the adaptive shift is not associated with any single proprioceptive component but involves what they call a "sensorimotor" change or change in "matching orientations" of one part of the system with respect to another. I have proposed (Howard, 1971a) a schematic representation of the visual-motor system which attempts to make these distinctions clear (see Fig. 1).

In this scheme spatial coding proceeds at several levels in hierarchical order. The primary level consists of muscles and joint receptors which receive neural discharges at "motor end plates" or trigger neural discharges in "sensory end-organs." At the next level, the "spatial coders" on the motor side transform the internal spatial motor code into the activation of specific motor end-plates, and the sensory "spatial coders" transform the arbitrary neural input from the retina and the joint receptors into whatever internal spatial code is being used at the time. At a higher level the motor "integrators" enable limb segments in a multijointed limb to act as a team, so as to achieve a given task in several ways. For instance, one can point to a given location with the arm in various postures, as long as the algebraic sum of the positions of the limb components is the correct value.

TABLE I

THE SPATIALLY CODED SUBSYSTEMS OF THE VISUAL-MOTOR SYSTEM AND THE CONSEQUENCES (PREDICTED AND ACTUAL) OF ASSUMING THAT EACH IN TURN IS THE SITE OF RECALIBRATION IN RESPONSE TO EXPOSURE TO VISUAL DISPLACEMENT, WITH THE ARM AS THE AIMING ORGAN

Spatially coded subsystems as possible sites for recalibration		Transfer-of-training expectations for different tests given after exposure						
Articulation	Source of information	Interocular transfer	Intermanual transfer	Pointing at auditory target	Pointing at other unseen hand	Relocation of hand to remembered position	Looking at unseen trained hand	Directing the head to the trained arm
Position of image on retina	Foveal local sign (i.e., foveal target)	Not predicted	Predicted	Not predicted	Not predicted	Not predicted	Not predicted	Not predicted
	Peripheral, local sign (i.e., peripheral target)	Not predicted	Predicted	Not predicted	Not predicted	Not predicted	Not predicted	Not predicted
Position of eye-in-socket	Motor outflow (corollary discharge) There are no afferent signals for eye position	Predicted (because the two eyes always move together)	Predicted	Not predicted	Not predicted	Not predicted	Predicted	Not predicted
Position of head on shoulders	No distinctions made	Predicted	Predicted	Predicted	Not predicted	Not predicted	Predicted	Predicted
Position of arm-on-body	Proprioception (joint receptors)	Predicted	Not predicted	Predicted	Predicted	Predicted	Predicted	Predicted
	Motor outflow (corollary discharge)	Predicted[a]	Not predicted	Predicted[a]	Predicted[a]	Predicted[a]	Not predicted (for stationary arm)	Not predicted (for stationary arm)
Actual Consequences								
		Found	Sometimes found but not in full	Found, at least early in training	Found	Not found by some, found by others	Found	Found

[a] Assuming that proprioceptive information is ignored.

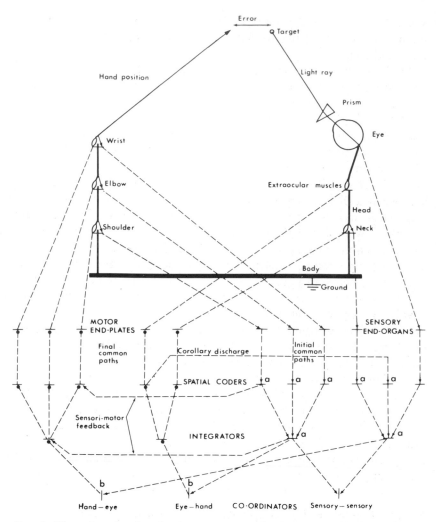

Fig. 1. Flow chart for the visual-motor system. In the upper half of the diagram, basic structural components of the eye-hand coordination system are drawn in lines of medium thickness (the instantaneous position of the hand and the light ray from target to eye and retina are also considered to be structural components—lighter lines). The body (extra thick line) is considered to be fixed to the ground. Components are linked by articulations; the following symbols are used:

                                   position-sensitive receptors
                                   muscular elements

In the central and lower parts of the figure, neural elements are drawn in interrupted lines; junctions represent neural coding processes; arrows depict inputs to sensory elements; and filled circles depict inputs to motor elements. Sites of lability according to Harris are marked 'a'; those according to Held are marked 'b.' (From Howard, 1971b, p. 249.)

Similarly, on the sensory side, the integrators enable one to judge the position of an object relative to the body for different positions of the image, eye, and head.

At the level of the coordinators, the integrated sensory information is mapped on to the motor spatial system so that, for instance, the arm may be aimed at a visual target (hand-eye) or the eye moved to look at the hand (eye-hand). Sensory-sensory, or even motor-motor coordinators are also possible, and there is also the possibility of sensorimotor (local feedback) or motor-sensory (corollary discharge) connections at lower levels of the system. The "higher-order-control" is any nonspecific input from or to higher cognitive centers. Each coding element is potentially modifiable when a discrepancy (discordance) in its functioning is detected, indeed such modifications must occur to accommodate changes during growth. Lower parts of the system—the initial and final common pathways —are probably immune to the effects of short-term experience. Changes in the separate coding elements are presumably possible, and when they occur, they necessarily affect inputs to all higher parts of the system because the higher centers receive inputs from the lower elements. However, changes in higher control centers do not necessarily affect skills which depend only on the output of lower stages. Held argues for the importance of changes in coordinators which may not affect tasks at lower levels. Harris's theory, insofar as it differs from Held's theory, denies the existence of recalibration in coordinators, and argues that the total visual-motor shift is the sum of shifts at individual subsystems. There is some evidence for such an additivity hypothesis (Wilkinson, 1971). However, such evidence is not easy to interpret because the selection of proper subtasks is somewhat arbitrary. It would seem wisest at the moment to assume that any part of the system, at any level except the most peripheral, is modifiable if the training is appropriate.

B. The Conditions for Adjustment of Visual-motor Control

The second basic question concerns the conditions under which the visual-motor system develops or adapts to novel inputs. Held proposed the first precise model to account to the adaptability of visual-motor behavior (Held, 1961). It is a reafference model similar to the earlier von Holt model except that it adds a memory store to allow for the modification of the system during training to unusual efferent-reafferent relationships. The essential point of Held's model is that adaptation of the system to displaced vision requires self-produced movements to be associated with the new sensory consequences of that movement (reafference). The mere association of passive limb movements (imposed from outside) with the sensory consequences (kinesthesis and sight of the limb) is not sufficient (see, for example, Held & Hein, 1958). It has been argued that Held's original prism experiments in support of this theory were not a proper test of the theory (Howard, 1971a), and in any case, evidence has been produced that passive movement may lead to adaptation under certain circumstances (Pick & Hay, 1965). Held may be right, however, in that self-produced movement, although not necessary, is a particularly effective form of training, and it may have some priority as a mechanism in young animals. The experiments which have come out of Held's laboratory on the effects of restricted opportunities for reafferent stimulation in young cats and monkeys would seem to support such a view (Hein, Gower, & Diamond, 1970; Hein, Held, & Gower, 1970). However, deprivation studies are always open to the criticism that the procedures cause the degeneration of structures and functions, rather than merely remove the conditions necessary for their growth.

The view of the author is that sensorimotor behavior will develop and change in response to properly displayed *discordance* including (*a*) intersensory discordance, or an unusual spatial association of stimuli in different modalities, (*b*) sensory-motor discordance, or unusual association between motor innervation and consequent sensory inputs (reafference) (Howard, 1966). Held's theory is a special case of this broader theory.

This concludes this brief outline of spatial behavior. The human being has sense organs mounted on mobile parts of the body which "view" the changing world from ever changing vantage points. Things are rarely chaotic, however; the body moves in certain ways in response to commands, the world is polarized, and has landmarks, and the stimulus array is predictably changed by changes in vantage point. These consistencies or invariants may be complex, as Gibson (1966) has pointed out, but if they have important consequences for the person, they are eventually mastered and determine spatial behavior.

References

Adler, H. E. Ontogeny and phylogeny of orientation. *In* L. R. Aronson *et al.* (Eds.), *Development and evolution of behavior*. San Francisco, California: Freeman, 1970. Pp. 303–336.

Anderson, D. C., & Moss, C. A. The auditory autokinetic effect. *American Journal of Psychology*, 1964, **77**, 502.

Bahrick, H. P., Fitts, P. M., & Schneider, R. The reproduction of simple movements as a function of proprioceptive feedback. *Journal of Experimental Psychology*, 1955, **49**, 445–454.

Begbie, G. H. Some problems of postural sway. In A. V. S. de Reuck & J. Knight (Eds.), *Myotatic, kinesthetic and vestibular mechanisms*. London: Churchill, 1967. Pp. 80–91.

Bender, M. B. (Ed.) *The oculomotor system.* New York: Harper, 1964.

Cleghorn, T. E., & Darcus, H. D. The sensibility to passive movement of the human elbow joint. *Quarterly Journal of Experimental Psychology,* 1952, **4,** 66–77.

Cohen, H. B. Some critical factors in prism adaptation. *American Journal of Psychology,* 1966, **79,** 285–290.

Cohen, L. A. Analysis of position sense in human shoulder. *Journal of Neurophysiology,* 1958, **21,** 550–562.

Collins, W. E. Modification of vestibular nystagmus and "vertigo" by means of visual stimulation. *American Academy of Ophthalmology and Otolaryngology,* 1968, **72,** 962–979.

Coltheart, M. Visual feature-analysers and aftereffects of tilt and curvature. *Psychological Review,* 1971, **78,** 114–121.

Coren, S., & Festinger, L. An alternative view of the "Gibson normalization effect." *Perception and Psychophysics,* 1967, **2,** 621–626.

Critchley, M. 1953. *The parietal lobes.* London: Arnold.

Davson, H. (Ed.) *The eye.* (1st ed.) Vol. 3. *Muscular mechanisms.* New York: Academic Press, 1962.

Edgington, E. S. Kinesthetically guided movements of head and arm. *Journal of Psychology,* 1953, **36,** 51–57.

Fraenkel, G. S., & Gunn, D. L. *The orientation of animals.* New York: Dover, 1961.

Gaze, R. M. *Formation of nerve connections.* New York: Academic Press, 1970.

Gelfan, S., & Carter, S. Muscle sense in man. *Experimental Neurology,* 1967, **18,** 469–473.

Ghent, L. Form and its orientation: A child's-eye view. *American Journal of Psychology,* 1961, **74,** 177–190.

Ghent, L., & Bernstein, L. Influence of the orientation of geometric forms on their recognition by children. *Perceptual and Motor Skills,* 1961, **12,** 95–101.

Gibson, J. J. Adaptation with negative after-effects. *Psychological Review,* 1937, **44,** 222–244.

Gibson, J. J. *The senses considered as perceptual systems.* Boston, Massachusetts: Houghton, 1966.

Gladwin, T, *East is a big bird.* Camb, Mass.: Harvard Univ. Press, 1970.

Gregory, R. L. Eye movements and the stability of the visual world. *Nature (London),* 1958, **182,** 1214–1216.

Hardt, M. E., Held, R., and Steinbach, M. J. Adaptation to displaced vision: A change in the central control of sensorimotor coordination. 1971, *J. Exp. Psychol.* **89,** 229–239.

Harris, C. Perceptual adaptation to inverted, reversed and displaced vision. *Psychological Review,* 1965, **72,** 419–444.

Hein, A., Gower, E. C., & Diamond, R. M. Exposure requirements for developing the triggered component of the visual-placing response. *Journal of Comparative and Physiological Psychology,* 1970, **73,** 188–192.

Hein, A., Held, R., & Gower, E. C. 1970. Development and segmentation of visually controlled movement by selective exposure during rearing. *Journal of Comparative and Physiological Psychology,* 1970, **73,** 181–187.

Held, R. Exposure history as a factor in maintaining stability of perception and coordination. *Journal of Nervous and Mental Disease,* 1961, **132,** 26–32.

Held, R., & Hein, A. Adaptation of disarranged hand-eye coordination contingent upon re-afferent stimulation. *Perceptual and Motor Skills,* 1958, **8,** 87–90.

Hess, W. R. *The functional organization of the diencephalon.* New York: Grune & Stratton, 1957.

Hinde, R. A. *Animal behaviour: A synthesis of ethology and comparative psychology.* New York: McGraw-Hill, 1966.

Howard, I. P. Displacing the optical array. In S. J. Freedman (Ed.), *Psychophysiology of spatially oriented behavior.* Homewood, Illinois: Dorsey, 1966 Pp. 19–36.

Howard, I. P. Vergence, eye signature and stereopsis. *Psychonomic Monographs, Supplement,* 1970, **3** (Whole No. 45), 201–219.

Howard, I. P. The adaptability of the visual-motor system. In K. Konnelley (Ed.), *Motor development.* London: Churchill, 1971. Pp. 337–352. (a)

Howard, I. P. Perceptual learning and adaptation. *British Medical Bulletin,* 1971, **27**, 248–252. (b)

Howard, I. P., & Templeton, W.B. *Human spatial orientation.* New York: Wiley, 1966.

Hubel, D. H., and Wiesel, T. N. Receptive fields, binocular interaction and functional architecture in the cat's visual cortex. *Journal of Physiology,* 1962, **160**, 106–154.

Koffka, K. *Principles of Gestalt psychology.* London: Routledge & Kegan Paul, 1935.

Kohler, I. *Über Aufbau und Wandlungen der Wahrnehmungswelt, insbesondere über 'bedingte' Empfindungen.* Vienna: Rohrer, 1951.

Kolers, P. A., & Perkins, D. N. Orientation of letters and errors in their recognition. *Perception and Psychophysics,* 1969, **5**, 265–269.

Kottenhoff, H. *Was ist Richtiges Sehen mit Umkehrbrillen und in Welchem Sinne Stellt Sich Das Sehen um?* Meisenheim am Glan, Germany: Anton Hain, 1961.

Lester, G., & Morant, R. B. The role of the felt position of the head in the audiogyral illusion. *Acta Psychologica,* 1969, **31**, 375–384.

Maffei, L., & Campbell, F. W. Neurophysical localization of the vertical and horizontal visual coordinates in man. *Science,* 1970, **167**, 386–387.

Magnus, R. Some results of studies in the physiology of posture. The Cameron Prize Lectures. *Lancet,* 1926, **2**, 531–536, 583–588.

Matin, L., Matin, E., & Pola, J. Visual perception of direction when voluntary saccades occur. II. Relation of visual direction of a fixation target extinguished before a saccade to a subsequent test flash presented before the saccade. *Perception and Psychophysics,* 1970, **8**, 9–14.

Merton, P. A. The accuracy of directing the eyes and the hand in the dark. *Journal of Physiology (London),* 1961, **156**, 555–577.

Merton, P. A. Absence of conscious position sense in the human eyes. In M. B. Bender (Ed.), *The oculomotor system.* New York: Harper, 1964. Pp. 314–320.

Mittelstaedt, H. Basic control patterns of orientational homeostasis. *Symposia of The Society for Experimental Biology,* 1964, **18**, 365–385.

Over, R. Comparison of normaliztaion theory, and neural enhancement explanation of negative aftereffects. *Psychological Bulletin,* 1971, **75**, 225–243.

Peiper, A. *Cerebral function in infancy and childhood.* London: Pitman, 1963.

Pick, H. L., & Hay, J. C. A passive test of the Held reafference hypothesis. *Perceptual and Motor Skills,* 1965, **20**, 1070–1072.

Pick, H. L., Warren, D. H., & Hay, J. C. Sensory conflicts in judgments of spatial direction. *Perception and Psychophysics,* 1969, **6**, 203–205.

Provins, K. A. The effect of peripheral nerve block on the appreciation and execution of finger movements. *Journal of Physiology (London),* 1958, **143**, 55–67.

Reinecke, R. D. Review of optokinetic nystagmus from 1954–1960. *Archives of Ophthalmology,* 1961, **65**, 609–615.

Robinson, D. A., O'Meara, D. M., Scott, A. B., & Collins, C. C. Mechanical components of human eye movements. *Journal of Applied Physiology,* 1969, **26**, 548–553.

Rock, L., & Heimer, W. The effect of retinal and phenomenal orientation on the perception of form. *American Journal of Psychology,* 1957, **70**, 493–511.

Royce, J. R., Carran, A. B., Aftinas, M., Lehman, R. S., & Blumenthal, A. The autokinetic phenomenon—a critical review. *Psychological Bulletin,* 1966, **65**, 243–260.

Sandström, C. L. *Orientation in the present space.* Stockholm: Almqvist & Wiksell, 1951.

Schilder, P. *The image and appearance of the human body.* London: Kegan Paul, 1935.

Shontz, F. C. *Perceptual and cognitive aspects of body experience.* New York: Academic Press, 1969.

Singer, G., & Day, R. H. Visual capture of haptically judged depth. *Perception and Psychophysics,* 1969, **5**, 315–316.

Sperry, R. W. Optic nerve regeneration with return of vision in anurans. *Journal of Neurophysiology,* 1944, **7**, 57–70.

Sperry, R. W. Restoration of vision after crossing of optic nerves and after contralateral transplantation of eye. *Journal of Neurophysiology,* 1945, **8**, 15–28.

Sperry, R. W. Embryogenesis of behavioral nerve nets. In R. L. DeHaan and H. Ursprung (Eds.), *Organogenesis.* New York: Holt, 1965. Pp. 161–186.

Sperry, R. W., & Arora, H. L. Selectivity in regeneration of the oculomotor nerve in the cichlid fish, Astronotus ocellatus. *Journal of Embryology and Experimental Morphology,* 1965, **14**, 307–317.

Starr, A., Angel, R., & Yeates, H. Visual suppression during smooth following and saccadic eye movements. *Vision Research,* 1969, **9**, 195–198.

Székely, G. The apparent "corneal specificity" of sensory neurons. *Journal of Embryology and Experimental Morphology,* 1959, **7**, 375–379.

Székely, G. Development of limb movements: embryological, physiological and model studies. In A. V. S. de Reuck & J. Knight (Eds.), *Growth of the nervous system.* London: Churchill, 1968. Pp. 77–92.

Taylor, J. G. *The behavioural basis of perception.* New Haven, Connecticut: Yale Univ. Press, 1962.

Templeton, W. B., Howard, I. P., & Easting, G. Satiation and the tilt after-effect. *American Journal of Psychology,* 1965, **78**, 656–659.

Wapner, S., & Werner, H. *Perceptual development: An investigation within the framework of sensory-tonic field theory.* Worcester, Massachusetts: Clark Univ. Press, 1957.

Weiss, P. Self-differentiation of the basic patterns of coordination. *Comparative Psychology Monographs,* 1941, **17**, 1–96.

Weiss, P. Experimental analysis of co-ordination by the disarrangement of central-peripheral relations. *Symposia of The Society for Experimental Biology,* 1950, **4**, 92–111.

Wilkinson, D. A. The visual-motor control loop: A linear system? *Journal of Experimental Psychology,* 1971, **89**, 250–257.

Witkin, H. A., Lewis, H. B., Hertzman, M., Machover, K., Meissner, P. B., and Wapner, S. *Personality through perception.* New York: Harper, 1954.

Chapter 15

TEMPERATURE RECEPTION

HERBERT HENSEL

I. THERMAL SENSATIONS

A. Structure of Temperature Sensation

From the manifold of cutaneous sensations we can discriminate the phenomenal qualities of "warm" and "cold." Both qualities form a sensory continuum of various intensities: indifferent → lukewarm → warm → hot → heat pain, and indifferent → cool → cold → cold pain. In addition, certain qualitative differences may be ascribed to these steps, in particular in the extreme range. Whether the sensation of heat is only a more intense warm sensation or a mixture of various qualities is not quite clear (see Hensel, 1952). Perhaps heat might be a quality of its own, its neurophysiological correlate being the activity of particular heat fibers (Iggo, 1959).

The experience of thermal comfort and discomfort is not only a matter of temperature sensations but reflects the integrated state of the thermoregulatory system.

B. Cold and Warm Spots

With small thermal stimulators a discrete pattern of cold and warm spots in the skin can be demonstrated. Although these spots have no practical significance for thermal sensation, they are important in connection with the problem of sensory specificity and the localization of receptive structures. As shown by adequate or inadequate (electrical) stimulation, cold spots give rise to a specific cold sensation, whereas specific warm sensations are confined only to the warm spots (topography of temperature spots; see Hensel, 1952; von Skramlik, 1937).

C. The Adequate Stimulus

Because of their intracutaneous site, thermoreceptors have neither the temperature of the skin surface nor that of the blood. Any reliable metrics of thermal stimuli has thus to account for the temperatures in different layers of the skin (Hensel, 1952).

The adequate stimulus for thermal sensations can be described as a function of (1) the temperature (T) of the skin, (2) the rate of change (dT/dt), and (3) the stimulus area, whereas slope or direction of a spatial intracutaneous temperature gradient (dT/dx) per se has no significance (Hensel, 1952, 1966).

When linear temperature changes are applied to the skin from a thermally indifferent starting point (33°C), the threshold ΔT deviates the more from this point, the slower the temperature is changed. By plotting dT/dt versus ΔT (Fig. 1), a hyperbolic function is obtained (Hensel, 1952, 1966; Kenshalo, Holmes, & Wood, 1968). At high or low temperatures, the threshold rate becomes zero which means that steady sensations occur at constant skin temperatures.

Starting from various adapting temperatures, the threshold (ΔT) for warm sensations increases with decreasing adapting temperature (Fig. 6), whereas the highest cold thresholds are found at high adapting temperatures (Kenshalo, 1970; Thauer & Ebaugh, 1952).

The stimulus area has considerable influence on the thresholds and intensities of temperature sensation (Hardy & Oppel, 1938; Hensel, 1952). With stimulus areas between 1 and 1000 cm² the threshold (ΔT) can vary by several degrees (Fig. 2). The limits of complete adaptation to constant temperatures are 20°C on the cold side and 40°C on the warm side for stimulus areas of 20 cm². Exposure of the whole body narrows these limits to about 31° and 35°C (Maréchaux & Schäfer, 1949).

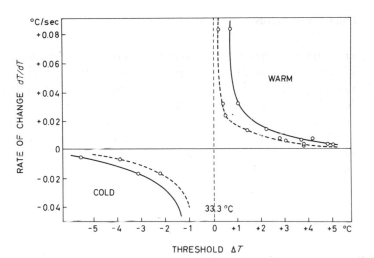

FIG. 1. Average thresholds (ΔT) of warm and cold sensations on the forearm (20 cm²) as a function of rate of temperature change (dT/dt). Initial temperature 33.3°C. Dashed lines: thresholds; solid lines: distinct sensations. (From Hensel, 1952.)

D. Inadequate Stimulation

A "paradoxical" cold sensation can be elicited by skin temperatures above 45°C. It is not certain whether a "paradoxical" warm sensation exists.

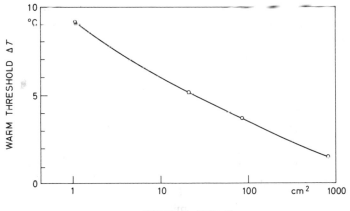

FIG. 2. Average thresholds (ΔT) of warm sensations on the forearm for linear temperature rises of 0.017°C/sec as a function of stimulus area (F). Initial temperature 30°C. (From Hensel, 1952.)

Menthol leads to a cold sensation at otherwise indifferent skin temperatures. Warm sensations can be elicited by intravenous injections of calcium
and by local application of carbon dioxide. Certain substances extracted
from spices, such as capsaicine, cinnamonylacrylic acid piperidide and
undecylenic acid vanillyl amide elicit strong warm sensations but also pain
(see Hensel, 1952).

II. NEUROPHYSIOLOGY OF THERMORECEPTION

A. Receptive Fields and Afferent Innervation

The morphological substrates of cutaneous cold and warm receptors are
unmyelinated nerve endings. Cold receptors have a tree-like structure whose
branches are in close contact with the basal cells of the epidermis (Hensel,
1973; Kenshalo, Hensel, Graziadei, & Fruhstorfer, 1971). Warm receptors
are not identified yet but we can assume that they are situated in a deeper
layer of the skin.

In primates the warm receptors are innervated by unmyelinated fibers,
whereas the cold receptors are served either by thin myelinated or by unmyelinated fibers (Hensel & Iggo, 1971). In most cases single thermosensitive fibers innervate one peripheral spot in the skin (Hensel & Kenshalo,
1969; Iggo, 1969).

B. Function of Thermoreceptors

Specific cutaneous thermoreceptors have been identified by electrophysiological methods in various mammals and in human subjects (see Hensel,
1973; Zotterman, 1959). The general properties of these receptors can be
described as follows: (1) they have a static discharge at constant temperatures (T), (2) they show a dynamic response to temperature changes
(dT/dt), with either a positive temperature coefficient (warm receptors)
or a negative coefficient (cold receptors), (3) they are not excited by
mechanical stimuli within reasonable limits of intensity.

The slope or direction of the intracutaneous spatial temperature gradient
(dT/dx) per se has no influence on the thermoreceptor excitation (Hensel
& Witt, 1959).

By the criterion of their dynamic sensitivity, the variety of thermoreceptors can be divided into the well-defined classes of warm and cold receptors
(Fig. 3). Irrespective of the initial temperature, a warm receptor will always
show an overshoot of its discharge on sudden warming and a transient in-

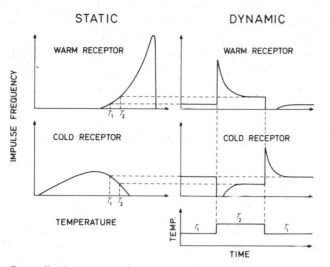

FIG. 3. Generalized response of cutaneous single warm and cold receptors to constant temperatures (static response) and to rapid temperature changes (dynamic response).

hibition on sudden cooling, whereas a warm receptor will respond in the opposite way. There are also typical differences in the static frequency curves, in that the temperature of the maximum discharge is much lower for cold receptors than it is for warm receptors.

At constant skin temperatures in the normal range all cold receptors are firing continuously (Fig. 4). The average maximum of this static discharge is at 27°C (Fig. 5), and the extreme limits of static activity are 5° and 43°C. On sudden cooling, the dynamic overshoot (Fig. 3 and 4) can be 30 times higher than the static maximum frequency (Hensel, 1973).

Cutaneous warm receptors have been studied mainly in the cat's nose

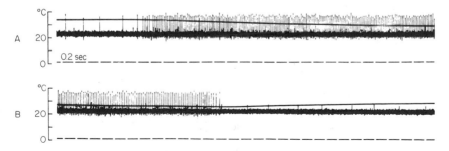

FIG. 4. Afferent impulses of single cold fiber from the superficial branch of the radial nerve in man and skin temperature when applying thermal stimuli to the hand. A: Cooling; B: rewarming. (From Hensel & Boman, 1960.)

(Hensel & Kenshalo, 1969) and in the skin of monkeys (Hensel, 1969; Hensel & Iggo, 1971). Their static activity begins at 30°C, reaches a maximum at temperatures between 41° and 46°C and then steeply falls off (Fig. 5). On sudden warming, the dynamic overshoot may be several times higher than the static frequency (Hensel & Huopaniemi, 1969).

When applying identical temperature changes (ΔT), the amount of the dynamic overshoot of cold and warm fibers varies with adapting temperature. In first approximation the curve of the dynamic maxima as a function of temperature goes parallel with the static frequency curve.

C. Inadequate Stimulation of Thermoreceptors

At temperatures above 45°C cold receptors exhibit a "paradoxical" discharge (Dodt & Zotterman, 1952). Menthol causes a shift in the activity range of cold receptors towards higher temperatures. Increased CO_2 concentrations inhibit the discharge of cold receptors and enhance that of warm receptors (see Hensel, 1973).

D. Central Information Processing

Little is known about the processing of thermal information within the central nervous system. Unimodal responses to peripheral cold stimuli have been recorded in single neurons at the thalamic level (Poulos & Benjamin,

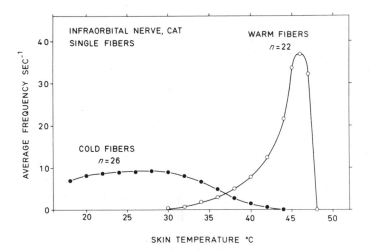

Fig. 5. Average frequency of the static discharge as a function of temperature for populations of single warm and cold fibers from the cat's infraorbital nerve supplying the nose. (From Hensel & Kenshalo, 1969.)

1968), the discharge frequency reflecting the static temperature characteristics of peripheral cold receptors. Even in the somatosensory cortex specific thermosensitive cells have been found (Landgren, 1957) but there is also considerable convergence of thermal and other cutaneous afferents.

III. COMPARISON OF VARIOUS APPROACHES TO TEMPERATURE RECEPTION

A. Thermal Afferents and Sensation

The present state of research allows only a limited synopsis of sensory, neurophysiological, behavioral, and thermoregulatory approaches to thermoreception. Since only a few direct measurements of afferent impulses from cutaneous thermoreceptors in human subjects are available (Hensel & Boman, 1960), one has to rely largely on conclusions from animal experiments.

At skin temperatures near 33°C cold and warm receptors are continuously active (Fig. 4 and 5) but no conscious temperature sensation occurs. The latter begins only when a higher number of impulses per unit of time reaches the central nervous system. This "central" threshold may be expressed as the magnitude of a slow cortical potential which, in turn, is dependent (1) on the average impulse frequency, and (2) on the number of simultaneously active receptors. The frequency is a function of temperature (T) and rate of change (dT/dt), whereas the number of active receptors is a function of stimulus area.

The presence of separate cold and warm spots in human skin and the electrophysiological findings of specific cutaneous cold and warm receptors strongly suggest that the sensory qualities of "cold" and "warmth" can be ascribed to a dual set of receptors. The assumption of only one receptor system accounting for all facts of human temperature sensation would be incompatible with several experimental facts.

B. Behavior and Thermoregulation

Behavioral measurements of the threshold (ΔT) for thermal stimulation as a function of adapting temperature (T) in the face of cats have revealed a temperature sensitivity comparable with that of the human forearm, provided that the surface areas are accounted for (Fig. 6). By using equal magnitudes of the integrated response as a criterion, electrophysiological "threshold" curves as a function of adapting temperature were obtained (Kenshalo & Brearley, 1970). In this case the criterion on the warm side

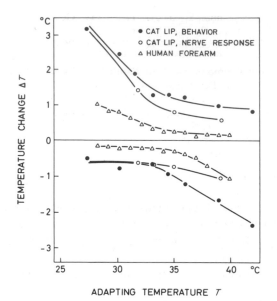

ADAPTING TEMPERATURE T

FIG. 6. Behaviorally measured warm and cool thresholds ($\Delta\ T$) of the cat's upper lip (1.7 cm^2) and electrophysiologically measured "thresholds" (equal magnitudes of integrated nerve potential) as a function of adapting temperature (T). Thermal thresholds on human forearm (14.4 cm^2) are also shown for comparison. (From Kenshalo & Brearley, 1970; human threshold data from Kenshalo, 1970.)

was inhibition of the integrated cold fiber discharge. The question remains open whether this means "warm" or "less cool" for the cat. Further, the possibility cannot be excluded that small impulses from warm fibers are masked by larger spikes in the integrated discharge.

Afferents from cutaneous thermoreceptors are also a very important input for the system of temperature regulation. They signal thermal disturbances from the skin before the central temperature of the body has been influenced. This function of cutaneous receptors is favored by their high dynamic sensitivity to rapid temperature changes. Thermoregulatory reflexes from cutaneous cold and warm receptors may be elicited even when no conscious sensations or behavioral responses are present, e.g., during sleep.

References

Dodt, E., & Zotterman, Y. The discharge of specific cold fibres at high temperatures. (The paradoxical cold.) *Acta Physiologica Scandinavica*, 1952, **26**, 358–365.

Hardy, J. D., & Oppel, T. W. Studies in temperature sensation. IV. *Journal of Clinical Investigation*, 1938, **17**, 771–778.

Hensel, H. Physiologie der Thermoreception. *Ergebnisse der Physiologie, Biologischen Chemie und Experimentellen Pharmakologie*, 1952, **47**, 166–368.

Hensel, H. Allgemeine Sinnesphysiologie. Hautsinne, Geschmack, Geruch. Berlin, Heidelberg, New York: Springer-Verlag, 1966.

Hensel, H. Cutane Wärmereceptoren bei Primaten. *Pflügers Archiv*, 1969, **313**, 150–152.

Hensel, H. Cutaneous thermoreceptors. In *Handbook of sensory physiology*. Vol. II. *Somatosensory system*. Berlin and New York: Springer-Verlag, 1973. Pp. 75–106.

Hensel, H., & Boman, K. Afferent impulses in cutaneous sensory nerves in human subjects. *Journal of Neurophysiology*, 1960, **23**, 564–578.

Hensel, H., & Huopaniemi, T. Static and dynamic properties of warm fibres in the infraorbital nerve. *Pflügers Archiv*, 1969, **309**, 1–10.

Hensel, H., & Iggo, A. Analysis of cutaneous warm and cold fibres in primates. *Pflügers Archiv*, 1971, **329**, 1–8.

Hensel, H., & Kenshalo, D. R. Warm receptors in the nasal region of cats. *Journal of Physiology (London)*, 1969, **204**, 99–112.

Hensel, H., & Witt, I. Spatial temperature gradient and thermoreceptor stimulation. *Journal of Physiology (London)*, 1959, **148**, 180–189.

Iggo, A. Cutaneous heat and cold receptors with slowly-conducting (C) afferent fibres. *Quarterly Journal of Experimental Physiology and Cognate Medical Sciences*, 1959, **44**, 362–370.

Iggo, A. Cutaneous thermoreceptors in primates and sub-primates. *Journal of Physiology (London)*, 1969, **200**, 403–430.

Kenshalo, D. R. Psychophysical studies of temperature sensitivity. In W. D. Neff (Ed.), *Contributions to sensory physiology*. Vol. 4. New York: Academic Press, 1970. Pp. 19–74.

Kenshalo, D. R., & Brearley, E. A. Electrophysiological measurements of the sensitivity of cat's upper lip to warm and cool stimuli. *Journal of Comparative and Physiological Psychology*, 1970, **70**, 5–14.

Kenshalo, D. R., Hensel, H., Graziadei, P. P. C., & Fruhstorfer, H. On the anatomy, physiology and psychophysics of the cat's temperature sensing system. In R. Dubner and Y. Kawamura (Eds.), *Oral-facial sensory and motor mechanisms*, New York: Appleton-Century-Crofts, Meredith Corp. 1971. Pp. 23–45.

Kenshalo, D. R., Holmes, C. E., & Wood, P. B. Warm and cool thresholds as a function of rate of stimulus temperature change. *Perception and Psychophysics*, 1968, **3**, 81–84.

Landgren, S. Convergence of tactile, thermal, and gustatory impulses on single cortical cells. *Acta Physiologica Scandinavica*, 1957, **40**, 210–221.

Maréchaux, E. W., & Schäfer, K. E. Über Temperaturempfindungen bei Einwirkung von Temperaturreizen verschiedener Steilheit auf den ganzen Körper. *Pflügers Archiv für die gesamte Physiologie des Menschen und der Tiere*, 1949, **251**, 765–784.

Poulos, D. A., & Benjamin, R. M. Response of thalamic neurons to thermal stimulation of the tongue. *Journal of Neurophysiology*, 1968, **31**, 28–43.

Thauer, R., & Ebaugh, F. G. Die Unterschiedsschwelle der Kalt- und Warmempfindung in Abhängigkeit von der absoluten Luft- bzw. Hauttemperatur. *Pflügers Archiv für die gesamte Physiologie des Menschen und der Tiere*, 1952, **225**, 27–45.

von Skramlik, E. Psychophysiologie der Tastsinne. *Archiv für Psychologie*. Vol. 4, Parts 1 and 2. Leipzig: Akad. Verlagsges., 1937.

Zotterman, Y. Thermal sensations. In Amer. Physiol. Soc., J. Field (Ed.), *Handbook of physiology*. Sect. 1, *Neurophysiology*. Vol. I. Baltimore, Maryland: Williams & Wilkins, 1959. Pp. 431–458.

Chapter 16

VISION*

ISRAEL ABRAMOV AND JAMES GORDON

The eye has often been likened to a camera, and it is true that the eye's optics focus an image of the world onto a light sensitive layer, the retina, at the rear of the eye. But here the analogy breaks down. The pattern of light energy on the retina is not transferred in some direct and mysterious fashion to the sensorium which then "views" the image. Rather, the light energy is absorbed by photopigments which transduce the radiant energy, and the information about the retinal image is recorded and processed into neural messages which pass along the optic nerve to the brain. In this chapter we will consider how the light energy is transduced and what sort of code is used to transmit visual information.

I. LIGHT

Light can be described as a form of wave motion whose wavelengths, ranging approximately from 400 to 700 nm, occupy a narrow region in the radiant energy (electromagnetic) spectrum. (One nanometer, abbreviated nm, is 10^{-9} meters; one millimicron, abbreviated mμ, is the same quantity.)

---

* References cited in this chapter and the next are by no means exhaustive; nor are references given for historical importance but for their comprehensive coverage of a topic, and they should be treated as starting points for further study.

If, as Newton observed, the different wavelengths of white light are viewed separately they appear colored. Figure 1 shows the colors usually associated with the different wavelengths (or frequencies—which are inversely proportional to wavelength—and are termed wavenumbers); it should be emphasized that the colors indicated are by no means the only ones perceived—they shade smoothly into one another—and are only given here to help the reader in understanding the stimuli which will be described by wavelength or frequency.

Light "energy" can be measured in various ways: one way (radiometry) measures light in the familiar physical manner, that is in terms of its ability to do work; this is the form which will generally be used in this chapter. Another way (photometry) measures light in terms of its ability to affect the visual system and will be dealt with in the next chapter. Light can also be considered as energy radiated by a source in the form of individual quanta whose energy is proportional to their frequency (wavenumber). Thus, another measure, related to the radiometric measurement of energy, is the number of quanta; the total energy radiated by a source is the sum of the separate energies of all the quanta emitted. (See Riggs [1965] and Walsh [1965] for additional information.)

II. PHOTOPIGMENTS

The first stage in the transduction of light to neural messages is the absorption of light by the photopigments in the retina's receptors. (See Dart-

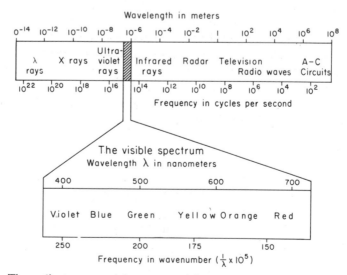

FIG. 1. The radiant energy (electromagnetic) spectrum.

nall, 1962, for a comprehensive treatment of photopigments.) Most retinas contain two types of receptors, rods and cones, which will be described in detail later. The pigments are photolabile; that is, the events initiated by light absorption result eventually in the breakdown, or "bleaching," of the pigments. One of the pigments, rhodopsin (the rod pigment), has been known for over a century and has been studied extensively (Wald, 1959). Since all visual photopigments seem to have very similar structures and properties, a brief description will be given of rhodopsin.

Rhodopsin is a complex molecule consisting of a protein (opsin) and a chromophore (retinal—a derivative of vitamin A). This molecule normally exists in a specific configuration, the 11-*cis* isomer. A quantum of light absorbed by the molecule changes, or isomerizes it, from the 11-*cis* to the all-*trans* configuration. Following this change in configuration the molecules become successively a series of intermediate products which are stages in the thermal degradation of the molecule; light initiates the process while the later changes can take place either in light or dark (Fig. 2). The molecule is said to be "bleached" when it finally splits into free opsin and all-*trans* retinal. Given that a molecule has absorbed a quantum, the probability of bleaching is about 0.5. Light not only initiates the breakdown of rhodopsin but can also reverse it; if one of the intermediate pigments

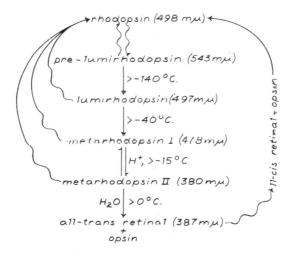

FIG. 2. The bleaching of rhodopsin. Wavy lines indicate reactions initiated by absorption of light; straight lines indicate thermal reactions. Cooling below any of the given temperatures halts the process at that stage. Rhodopsin absorbs light maximally at about 500 nm. The intermediate stages are also light absorbing pigments; they absorb light maximally at the indicated wavelengths. Note: this figure is based on an extract of cattle rhodopsin and the values for human rhodopsin may be slightly different. (From Matthews, Hubbard, Brown, & Wald, 1963.)

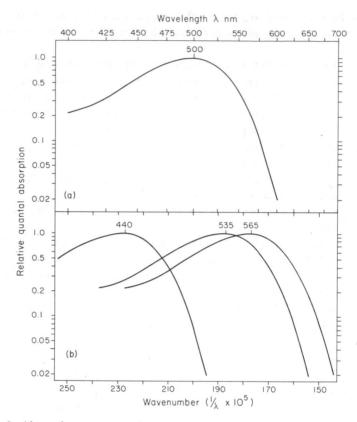

FIG. 3. Absorption spectra of human visual photopigments; wavelengths of maximal absorption are indicated. The functions obtained by various investigators differ slightly from each other, and the ones given are merely representative. a: Rhodopsin, the rod photopigment. b: Cone photopigments.

absorbs a quantum it can be re-isomerized back to rhodopsin (see Fig. 2); but because the intermediates are very short-lived the second quantum must be absorbed very soon after the first.

The probability that a pigment will absorb a given quantum depends on frequency. Fig. 3a shows the proportion (relative to maximum) of incident light quanta absorbed by rhodopsin across the spectrum; this function can be considered as the relative probability of capturing quanta of different frequencies. However, once absorbed, any quantum can start the above series of events even though the energy of a given quantum depends on its frequency. The major difference between rhodopsin and other visual pigments is in their spectral absorption functions; in general, in a given species, the pigments all appear to have the same retinal but probably have different proteins. In man there are three other pigments, which are in the cones of the retina, and any given cone contains only one of these pigments (Fig. 3b).

Cones of other species may contain pigments with different absorption functions, but the functions of all visual pigments have one important attribute in common: if the absorption curves are the proportion of incident quanta absorbed as a function of frequency, all the curves have the same shape and can be superimposed on each other (Fig. 3). Note that if the abscissa were drawn linear with wavelength, rather than frequency, the shapes would no longer be the same. This general shape can be described by a visual pigment nomogram which provides a graphic solution of a pigment's absorption function; thus, stating the wavelength of maximal absorption is sufficient to describe a pigment's spectral characteristics (Dartnall, 1962).

One must now consider how absorption functions like these in Fig. 3 were obtained. Rhodopsin can be extracted quite readily from the eye and studied *in vitro*. However, it has proven very difficult to extract cone pigments. So far only avian cone pigments have been extracted: iodopsin from the chicken (Wald, Brown, & Smith, 1955) and another from the pigeon (Bridges, 1962). Thus, the spectral characteristics of cone pigments have usually had to be measured *in situ*. One technique, reflection densitometry, allows measurement of pigments in the living eye (Rushton, 1963, 1965; Weale, 1965). The retina is illuminated with spectral lights and the amounts reflected back out of the eye (and hence not absorbed) are measured. Since various elements other than the photopigments could be contributing to the absorption, an additional step is needed. After measuring the spectral reflection from the eye, intense light is used to bleach all photolabile pigments and spectral reflection is remeasured; the ratio of incident light absorbed before bleaching to that absorbed after bleaching is termed the difference spectrum. The change in spectral reflection is due only to pigments which have been bleached, since absorption by non-photolabile elements is unaffected by bleaching. Thus the difference spectrum defines the spectral absorption of the photolabile pigments existing prior to bleaching. (See Dartnall, 1962, for more on the properties of difference spectra.)

If the reflection measurements are restricted to the very center of the retina, which is largely rod-free, the results will be due only to cone pigments. But since there is more than one cone pigment the absorption spectrum obtained will be some function of all the pigments. This problem can be avoided by bleaching with long-wavelength light which affects primarily the pigment absorbing best at that wavelength and does not bleach the other pigments to any great extent; the difference spectrum following such a partial chromatic bleach would describe the pigment most sensitive to long wavelengths; successive bleachings at shorter wavelengths would define the remaining pigments.

However from the above experiments we still cannot tell which structures contain the photopigments, nor if they are segregated in separate receptors. Several laboratories have developed sophisticated techniques for measuring light absorption by single receptors in excised retinas. The approach is closely related to that used in reflection densitometry, but with the prime difference that now the light is confined to a single photoreceptor identified under a microscope. The spectral transmission of the receptor is measured before and after bleaching and the ratio of the two transmission measures (difference spectrum) specifies the spectral absorption of the photolabile pigment. Single receptors have now been examined in excised retinas of both macaque monkeys and humans (Brown & Wald, 1964; Marks, Dobelle, & MacNichol, 1964). The cone pigments in both these species appear virtually identical; their spectral functions are shown in Fig. 3b.

III. ANATOMY

A. Retina

The vertebrate retina contains five types of neurons which are directly involved in the visual pathway (Boycott & Dowling, 1969; Polyak, 1957; Walls, 1942). Figure 4 shows a typical section of a primate retina viewed through the light microscope; the drawings of the cells are derived from special staining methods which stain individual cells in their entirety and show their distinctive shapes. The cell bodies of the neurons are confined to three distinct layers (outer nuclear layer, inner nuclear layer, ganglion cells) while the synaptic connections are confined to the plexiform layers between the layers of cell bodies. The outer nuclear layer (i.e., farthest from the cornea) consists of the cell bodies of the receptors. Many retinas contain two types of receptors, rods and cones; their respective photopigments have already been described and differences in their functions will become clearer later. The receptors are connected through bipolar cells (inner nuclear layer) to the ganglion cells whose axons course across the surface of the retina until they exit from the eye to form the optic nerve. Wide-spreading lateral interconnections are provided by two cell types in the inner nuclear layer, horizontal and amacrine cells. Horizontal cells send long branching processes through the outer plexiform layer toward the bases of the receptors; note that horizontal cell processes spread over

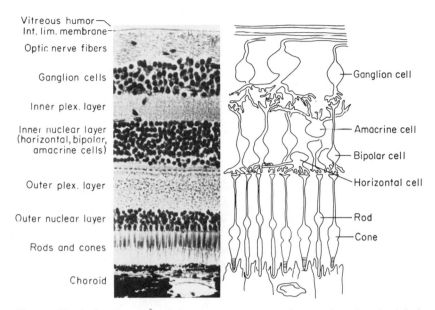

Vitreous humor
Int. lim. membrane
Optic nerve fibers
Ganglion cells
Inner plex. layer
Inner nuclear layer
(horizontal, bipolar,
amacrine cells)
Outer plex. layer
Outer nuclear layer
Rods and cones
Choroid

Ganglion cell
Amacrine cell
Bipolar cell
Horizontal cell
Rod
Cone

Fig. 1. Vertical section of a primate (macaque monkey) retina. On the left is a photograph of a microscope section stained to emphasize the cell bodies. On the right is a stylized drawing of the various cell types; this is based on sections treated so that individual cells are stained in their entirety. In this figure light would enter the retina from the top. See text for description of cells and layers. (Photomicrograph from Brown *et al.*, 1965.)

much wider areas than do those of bipolar cells. In the inner plexiform layer, very long processes from amacrine cells provide lateral connections in the region of the junctions between bipolar and ganglion cells.

Many species have in the center of the retina a more or less obvious depression, the fovea, on which is imaged any object being fixated. Since the vertebrate retina is inverted (receptors are the farthest structure from the light), light tends to be scattered before reaching the receptors, thus degrading the optical quality; to ensure the clarity at least of objects directly fixated, the retinal blood vessels and neurons other than receptors are pushed aside at the center of the retina to form the fovea.

The various types of neurons are not distributed evenly across the retina, as shown for the primate retina in Fig. 5. The receptors in the fovea are almost exclusively cones, whereas the rods are most numerous some 15–20 degrees from the fovea. The fovea has virtually no inner nuclear or ganglion cell layer but this does not imply a functional lack of these units; they have merely been moved to the sides of the foveal pit. In peripheral regions of the retina there are fewer bipolar and ganglion cells relative to receptors; thus, away from the fovea, there must be a greater degree of

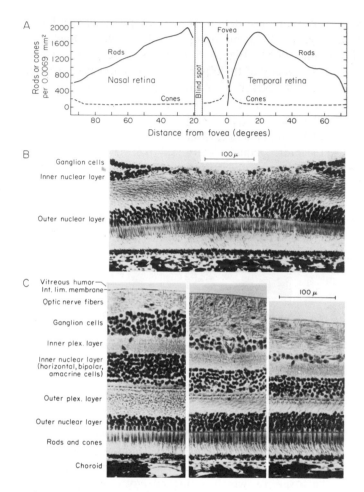

FIG. 5. Distribution of cell types across the retina. A: Density of rods and cones as a function of horizontal location across a human retina. The blindspot is formed by the optic nerve leaving the eye; there are no receptors in this area. (After Øster- berg, 1935.) B: Vertical section through the fovea of a macaque monkey. C: Rep- resentative retinal sections (macaque) at increasing distances from the fovea; sec- tion on left is closest to fovea, while that on right is from peripheral retina. (Photo- micrographs from Brown et al., 1965.)

convergence of receptors onto ganglion cells. In fact, the relative numbers of the cell types and their lateral ramifications make it obvious that the rule throughout the retina is considerable overlapping of pathways; in a human retina there are altogether about 6.5 million cones, 120 million rods, and only 1 million ganglion cells.

During the past decade the electron microscope has been employed extensively to examine the details of the synaptic organization of the system seen through the light microscope (Cohen, 1963; Dowling & Boycott, 1966; Sjöstrand, 1965). Figure 6 provides a schematic summary (not drawn to scale) of many of the observations on monkey and human retinas. A receptor can be divided into an outer segment, an inner segment, the cell nucleus, and a long (much longer than drawn—see Fig. 4) process ending in a synaptic terminal in the outer plexiform layer; the outer segment is divided into disks, or lamellae, which are thought to contain the photopigment. A receptor's synaptic terminal has several deep invaginations each of which contains processes from bipolar and horizontal cells; in general the central element in an invagination is from a bipolar cell while the lateral elements are from horizontal cells. Most bipolar cells have synapses with several receptors and some are quite diffuse in their contacts;

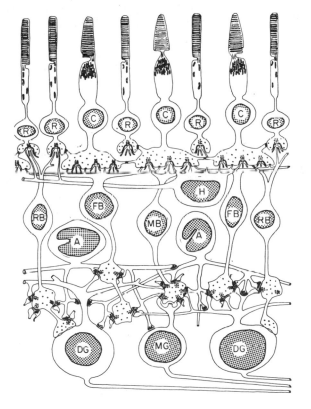

FIG. 6. A schematic summary of synaptic contacts in a typical primate retina; based on observations with the electron microscope. See text for details. R, rod; C, cone; RB, rod bipolar; FB, flat bipolar; MB, midget bipolar; H, horizontal cell; A, amacrine cell; DG, diffuse ganglion cell. (Modified from Dowling & Boycott, 1966.)

but in and about the fovea there are midget bipolars which send all of their processes to a single cone. There appear to be separate rod and cone bipolars. A horizontal cell sends processes into several receptors near its cell body, and a relatively long lateral process to a group of more distant receptors; the processes near its cell body typically end in cone terminals while its long lateral fiber ends in rods (Kolb, 1970). In the inner plexiform layer of primates each synaptic connection is between three elements: bipolar, ganglion, and amacrine cells. Midget bipolars synapse directly with only one ganglion cell but most bipolars have contacts with several ganglion cells; at each of these contacts there is a process from an amacrine cell, a cell which usually ramifies very widely.

Even from this very cursory description it is apparent that there are already very complex interconnections at the first synaptic stage. In some cases there seems to be a narrow and specific path from a single cone through a midget bipolar and ganglion cell, but even in these cases the contacts with horizontal and amacrine cells could allow lateral interactions.

The synaptic organization described above is representative of vertebrates in general with the exceptions that in some species (e.g., goldfish) there may be more than one layer of horizontal cells, and that in lower vertebrates the inner plexiform layer becomes more and more complicated. At lower levels of the phylogenetic scale direct synapses between bipolar cells and ganglion cells become rarer; interposed between these cells are amacrine cells which function as interneurons. The amacrine cells also show involved patterns of mutual interconnection as well as recurrent "feedback" processes. This presumably indicates a greater degree of distal visual processing in lower species (Dowling, 1970).

B. Central Visual Pathways

The major components of the visual pathways through the central nervous system (CNS) are shown in Fig. 7. (See Walls [1942] and Polyak [1957] for more detailed descriptions.) The ganglion cells' axons form the two optic nerves which meet just before they enter the brain. At this point, the chiasma, the fibers from each eye decussate; that is, they split so that fibers from the temporal half of a given retina pass into the brain on the same side, while fibers from the nasal half cross over into the contralateral hemisphere. Since a given temporal retina and the nasal retina of the other eye both view the same half of the visual field, the input from one optic tract to a given brain hemisphere is only from the contralateral half of the visual field. The degree of decussation at the chiasma is a function of the

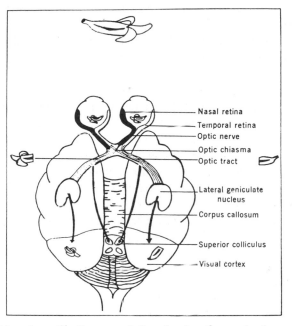

FIG. 7. Highly schematic diagram of the visual pathways in the central nervous system of a primate. The figure shows how the image of a banana is projected through the various stages of the system. The image on the retina is inverted; because of the crossing of the nasal retinal fibers, only half the image is represented in each optic tract. Only the major terminations of the optic tract are shown. (From Glickstein, 1969. Copyright 1969 by the American Association for the Advancement of Science).

amount of binocular vision possessed by a given species—that is, how much the fields of view of the two eyes overlap. In some cases (usually lower vertebrates) each optic nerve crosses *in toto* to the other hemisphere.

In lower vertebrates and birds most optic nerve fibers end on cells in the homologue of the superior colliculus, the optic tectum. However at higher levels of the phylogenetic scale neocortex increases, and a second CNS pathway to the lateral geniculate nucleus (LGN) of the thalamus increases in importance. In mammals, and especially primates, the major pathway is to the LGN. Many fibers, as well as collateral branches from those terminating in the LGN, still pass to the superior colliculus (SCL); but the role of the SCL is diminished. The SCL does not project directly to primary visual cortex; fibers from the SCL pass to various other nuclei of the thalamus, especially pulvinar, which in turn project to cortex. Optic nerve fibers also project to a variety of other structures, such as the reticular formation, but as yet neither the anatomy nor the function of these projections is very clear.

In higher animals the LGN is a laminated structure which, in some primates including man, has six distinct layers of cells; cells in a given layer receive inputs from one eye only and, because of the decussation of the optic nerve, each LGN receives information only about the contralateral half of the visual field. In spite of its highly structured appearance, there is no clear evidence for any major reprocessing of visual inputs at the LGN, nor is it clear why there are separate cell layers; however, the LGN does receive many inputs from other areas in the CNS, in particular the reticular formation and efferents returning from the cortex (Arden & Söderberg, 1961; Hull, 1968). The axons of LGN cells terminate in the visual cortex on the same side of the CNS.

Visual cortex has been divided, on anatomic grounds, into three regions labeled areas 17, 18, and 19 in the most widely used scheme. Area 17 is on the occipital cortical lobe and is the primary projection area in which fibers from the LGN terminate; it is also known as "striate cortex" because in cross section the incoming fibers from the LGN form a prominent white band. Area 17 cells receive inputs from more than one LGN layer; at least in higher primates, this is probably the first level at which inputs from both eyes converge onto individual neurons.

Area 17 of one hemisphere still has only about half the visual field represented in it. However each area 17 does receive some input from the entire foveal region; this suggests that the decussation at the chiasma is not entirely rigid (Glickstein, 1969; Stone, 1966). There is, broadly speaking, a topographic mapping of each half retina (one ipsilateral, one contralateral) onto an area 17, but the region of the retina which includes the fovea occupies a disproportionately large part of the total area; this reflects, among other things, the greater density of ganglion cells and receptors associated with the central retina. Areas 18 and 19 are usually termed "visual association areas" and appear to subserve higher visual functions. Cells in area 17 project to area 18 which in turn project to area 19. (Area 18 may also receive direct inputs from the LGN; this is clearly so in the cat [Glickstein, 1969].) Areas 18 and 19 both project to their contralateral counterparts, largely through the corpus callosum. Thus these areas are no longer restricted to information about only a half of the visual field (Hubel & Wiesel, 1965).

The above is by no means a complete description or even summary of the entire visual system. Other areas, such as the temporal lobes of the cortex, play an important role in what is usually considered visual functioning. However this is not the place to deal with these more diffuse and abstract aspects.

IV. ELECTRICAL RESPONSES—RETINA

When neural tissue is stimulated, a characteristic part of its response is some electrical event. We have the choice either of recording these electrical events from individual neural elements, or of recording gross potentials which reflect the summed activity of many neural elements. In the latter case there is the problem that the recording is simultaneously from units whose responses have different time courses, different electrical signs, and so on. However, in recording from individual units we are faced with problems of obtaining representative samples from vast populations of cells; also, the small size of the units makes it difficult to isolate their responses and increases the probability of injuring them or modifying their response patterns.

A. Gross Potentials

One gross potential has been recorded from the visual system for over a century. This is the electroretinogram (ERG) which has been studied extensively in many species, including man (Granit, 1962). The potential is developed across the retina and can be recorded between electrodes on either surface of the retina, or between an electrode on the cornea and an indifferent electrode elsewhere on the body. The main components of the ERG response are common to most vertebrates. Figure 8A provides an example of a corneally recorded ERG and shows the four most commonly identified components: a, b, c, and d waves. Figure 8B shows a human ERG in which we note that a and b waves have rod and cone related parts and the latter are faster. The a wave (negative going) has been identified with receptors, while the b wave (positive going) derives largely from the region of bipolar cells. The d wave, recorded at offset of light, is largely associated with the off responses of a and b components. The c wave is not observed in ERG's from retinas excised from the eye; it is extraretinal in origin and reflects activity of cells providing nutrition and support for the retina. More comprehensive treatments of the ERG are provided by Granit (1962) and Brown (1968).

Recently the initial parts of the ERG have been examined in detail with strikingly similar results from a variety of species (Brown, Watanabe, & Murakami, 1965). The first part of the response is the early receptor potential (ERP; see Fig. 8C). It is generated by the initial light-induced changes in the photopigment molecules and provides a most direct way of investigating these changes. The next component, with a latency of 1–5 msec, is the late receptor potential (LRP) which is maximal near the

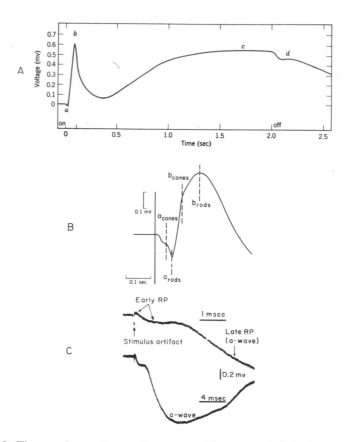

Fig. 8. The vertebrate electroretinogram (ERG); upward deflections are positive going potentials. A: ERG in response to a bright light; a, b, c, and d waves are shown. (Redrawn from Granit, 1962.) B: "On" components of the ERG in a human eye. The a and b waves contain cone and rod components. (Redrawn from Armington, Johnson, & Rigg, 1952.) C: Initial segment of cone ERG from macaque monkey. The two traces are for identical stimuli but with different time scales. The early receptor potential is biphasic. The late receptor potential forms the leading edge of the a wave. (Redrawn from Brown et al., 1965.)

receptors' synaptic endings and reflects the output of the receptors. The ERP is linear with light intensity, whereas the LRP is already markedly nonlinear, varying approximately logarithmically with intensity. It is difficult to separate completely the ERG's components in an intact eye since the various components have different sign and latencies and so mask each other. However, the ERP can be isolated by virtue of its extremely short latency; moreover it is very resistant to manipulations which block the other components even to the extent of killing the eye. The LRP, in the usual case, is the leading edge of the a wave. The b wave can be selectively eliminated by clamping the retinal artery which supplies the inner layers of the retina; the receptor layer is maintained by a separate set of blood vessels in the outer layers of the eye. In the absence of the b wave the entire time course of the LRP can be studied; the LRP is a negative going potential which is maintained at a constant amplitude throughout a light stimulus.

The other gross potential commonly recorded from the visual system— the visually evoked response (VER)—can be obtained from electrodes placed on the scalp over the visual cortex. The VER is very complex and as yet is too little understood for any simple analysis; for more information, see Granit (1962).

B. Unit Responses

Nerve cells in a quiescent state have a resting potential across their membranes; they respond to stimulation with a change in this potential (either hyperpolarization or depolarization) whose magnitude is graded in some fashion according to the strength of the stimulus. In most cells graded depolarizing potentials trigger rapid spike potentials which are then propagated along the cells' axons to their synaptic connections with the next cells in the chain. Since spikes from a given cell are all of the same shape and size, stimulus variations must be coded by changes in frequency of spike firing. Cells of this sort in sensory systems often maintain a "spontaneous rate" in the absence of specifiable stimulation, so that responses can be either increases or decreases from spontaneous rate.

In the CNS, cells generating spikes are the rule, but in the retina only ganglion cells generate spikes; other retinal cells respond with graded potentials (Fig. 9). Note that graded potentials in some retinal cells have a spike-like component (Fig. 9F) but in these spikes, as in the rest of the response, stimulus magnitude is still coded by amplitude changes and not frequency of firing. Graded hyperpolarization of a cell is generally due to an inhibitory input while depolarization signals excitation; in units such as ganglion cells depolarization of the cell body causes spikes to be fired down the axon, while hyperpolarization stops spiking (Fig. 9G). But a ganglion cell often receives antagonistic inputs, one of which tends to depolarize the cell while the other tends to hyperpolarize it; the spike rate reflects the net result of these inputs.

An important aspect of a cell's response is the area of the retina which must be stimulated by light to affect that cell's responses. This area is the cell's receptive field—a concept first put forth by Hartline (1938) to describe responses in the frog's eye. Another complexity is that the time

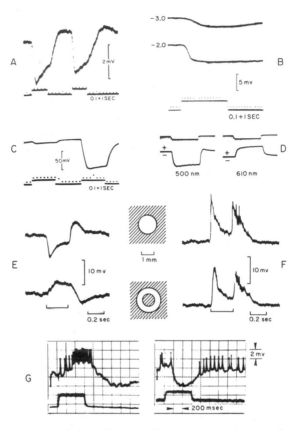

FIG. 9. The responses of the different cell types in vertebrate retinas. Recordings were intracellular and upward deflections of the response traces are positive going potentials; stimulus markers and time scales are shown under the response traces, except in D where they are the upper traces. A: Responses of a single cone in the carp. The first stimulus was a very small spot while the second was large; the amplitudes of the two responses are very similar, indicating no substantial effect of stimulus area at the receptor level. (From Tomita, 1965.) B: Responses of a single rod in the frog. Stimulus intensity was increased by one long unit between upper and lower response traces. Note the slow decay time after stimulus offset. (From Toyoda, Hashimoto, Anno, & Tomita, in Tomita, 1970.) C: S-potentials from carp. The first stimulus was much smaller in area than the second; since the larger stimulus evoked a greater response, the S-unit sums light over a large area. (From Tomita, 1965.) D: Spectrally opponent S-potentials from a marine fish. Light of 500 nm elicits hyperpolarization from this cell while 610 nm elicits depolarization. (From MacNichol & Svaetichin, 1958.) E: Responses of a bipolar cell in the goldfish. The stimuli are shown on the right. The cell is hyperpolarized for the duration of a spot (upper trace), but depolarized by a larger annulus (lower trace), indicating a spatially opponent receptive field. (From Kaneko, 1970.) F: Responses of an amacrine cell in the goldfish. Stimuli are on the left. This cell is transiently depolarized at stimulus onset and offset and does not exhibit any obvious spatial antagonisms.

course of responses varies from cell to cell, thus some cells maintain their response for the duration of the stimulus (tonic units) while others might respond only at onset and offset of light (phasic units). All these variations in response reflect in one way or another differing interplays of excitation and inhibition. With these factors in mind we can now consider the responses of the different cell types in the retina. It is technically difficult to record from many of the cells in mammals; cells other than ganglion cells have usually been investigated in lower vertebrates. However the general anatomic features and the responses of ganglion cells appear common to most vertebrates; thus the response characteristics observed in lower vertebrates are probably also applicable to higher animals.

1. GRADED POTENTIALS

Receptors in invertebrate eyes are excited by light; that is, they are depolarized by light (Hagins, 1965; Hartline, Wagner, & MacNichol, 1952). But until very recently vertebrate receptors had not been investigated directly due to their small size. However there were indications in the ERG that vertebrate receptors are hyperpolarized by light (Brown et al., 1965; Granit, 1962). This has now been confirmed by impaling with microelectrodes the inner segments of individual receptors and recording their responses to light flashes; the receptors were identified by injecting dye into them from the microelectrode and later examining the retina histologically (Tomita, 1970). Single receptors (cones or rods) have been examined in carp, frog, gekko, and mudpuppy (Figs. 9A, 9B, and 10). In all cases the receptor response is a maintained hyperpolarization, but note that at offset the rod response recovers much more slowly; the magnitude of the response increases nonlinearly with stimulus intensity. The extracellularly recorded LRP (Fig. 8C) is probably the sum of these potentials from the inner segments of the receptors.

A given receptor's response depends not only on cell type and light intensity but also on the spectral characteristics of the photopigment it contains. For example, the goldfish retina contains three types of cone pigment and records of cone potentials fall into three different classes whose spectral functions are similar to those of the cone pigments (Fig. 10). The

---

(From Kaneko, 1970.) G: Ganglion cell responses from the mudpuppy. The stimulus for the trace on the left was a small spot which elicited depolarization and a maintained discharge of spikes. The trace on the right is from the same cell; the small spot was on continuously and an annulus was added as shown by the stimulus marker. The annulus hyperpolarized the cell, thus inhibiting the maintained discharge due to the small spot; this demonstrates a spatially opponent receptive field. (From Werblin & Dowling, 1969.)

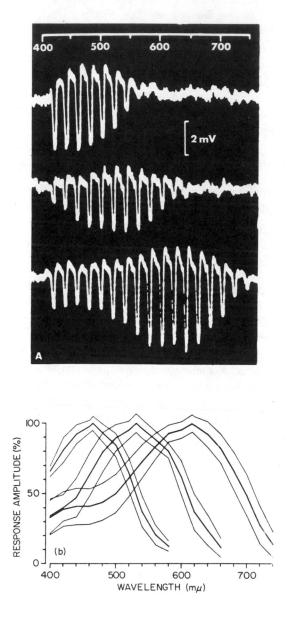

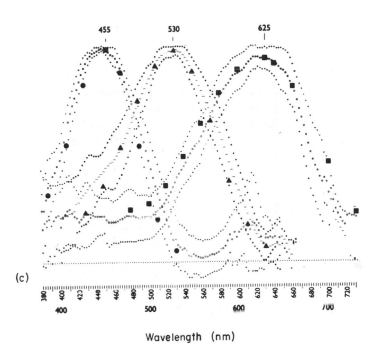

Wavelength (nm)

FIG. 10. Spectral characteristics of single cones. A: Intracellular responses of three separate carp cones. In a given trace each downward deflection (hyperpolarization) is a response to a flash of light of wavelength indicated by the scale at the top; all flashes contained the same number of quanta. Each of these cones is maximally sensitive to a different spectral region. (From Tomita, Kaneko, Murakami, & Pautler, 1967.) (b): Averaged spectral response functions and standard deviation curves of the three types of cone in carp. (From Tomita *et al.*, 1967.) (c): Spectral functions of photopigments in cones of goldfish, a relative of the carp. The small symbols are the means and standard deviations of difference spectra obtained from single cones. The large symbols show the absorption functions for three hypothetical pigments generated from a nomogram. These pigment functions agree quite nicely with the cone response functions shown above. (From Marks, 1965.)

receptive field of a receptor is very small and possibly limited to the receptor itself since increasing the size of a small stimulus spot does not increase the response of the receptor (Fig. 9A); however there is evidence that neighboring cones in the turtle retina do interact (Baylor, Fuortes, & O'Bryan, 1971).

The characteristics of other cells responding with graded potentials are more complex and varied. One kind of response has been known for some time: the S-potential (Svaetichin & MacNichol, 1958). Horizontal cells have now been identified by dye-marking as a source of the S-potential (Kaneko, 1970). The receptive fields of S-units are very large and sometimes encompass a large area of the retina; in these units increasing stimulus area increases response amplitude (Fig. 9C). S-potentials have been observed in many vertebrates ranging from mudpuppies to cats (Tomita, 1965). These potentials are particularly interesting for color vision: some S-units respond to all wavelengths in the same fashion (either maintained depolarization or hyperpolarization), but other S-units show spectrally opponent responses—that is, they hyperpolarize when the retina is stimulated by light from one part of the spectrum and depolarize in response to the rest of the spectrum (Fig. 9D). These spectrally opponent S-units illustrate nicely one of the consequences of opposed excitatory and inhibitory inputs from groups of cones of different spectral characteristics.

Responses of bipolar and amacrine cells (identified by dye marking) have been recorded from mudpuppy and goldfish retinas (Kaneko, 1970; Werblin & Dowling, 1969). As with S-units, bipolar cells have opponent responses but the antagonisms are spatial rather than spectral. Stimulating one retinal area excites a bipolar cell while stimulating another area inhibits it; generally these antagonistic zones are concentric. Responses of bipolar cells exhibit both transient and maintained components (Fig. 9E). Amacrine cells can be divided broadly into two types; the response of one is tonic while the response of the other is phasic (Fig. 9F). The responses of amacrines are complicated and include excitatory and inhibitory inputs but the antagonisms are not clear cut or simple; they have large receptive fields, though not as extensive as those of horizontal cells. It was pointed out earlier that the anatomic organization of the amacrine cell layer increases greatly in complexity at lower levels of the phylogenetic scale. As will be seen, in lower vertebrates very complex visual processing takes place in the retina, and this may well be a function of the amacrine cells. However, in higher species, as the geniculocortical system develops, complex processing is relegated more and more to the cortex.

2. GANGLION CELLS

Ganglion cells are the first level at which spike potentials are the rule and coding is in terms of variations in frequency of firing. Figures 9G, 11, and 13 show examples of intracellular and extracellular records from ganglion cells.

The commonest form of organization at the ganglion cell level (first described for the cat; Kuffler, 1953) is a concentric, antagonistic receptive field. Figure 11 shows an example in which a light flashed anywhere in the circular central area of the receptive field elicits a response at light onset ("on" response), while stimulation of the surround evokes an "off" response; stimulation of both areas together, or of the

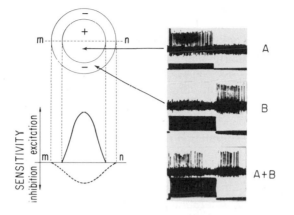

FIG. 11. Typical organization of the receptive field of a ganglion cell. The cell receives inputs from excitatory and inhibitory systems. Each of these systems varies in sensitivity across the receptive field; the graphs in the lower left show how the sensitivities of the opposed systems might be distributed across the field. A small spot on the center of the field stimulates the excitatory system more than the inhibitory, thereby eliciting an "on" response; similarly a spot near the edge of the field stimulates primarily the inhibitory system, eliciting an "off" response. On the top left is shown a map of the areas giving rise to "on" and "off" responses. On the right are shown records from a single ganglion cell in the cat. Records A and B show the responses of the cell evoked by small spots imaged respectively on the field's center and periphery. When both spots are presented together, an "on–off" response is produced which is less than the sum of the separate responses in A and B. (Records from Kuffler, 1953.)

boundary region, produces an "on–off" response which is less than the sum of the separate "on" and "off" responses. The opposite form of receptive field with an "off" center and "on" surround is also found. By itself this description of the receptive field is misleadingly simple; the center and surround of the receptive field are not necessarily purely excitatory or inhibitory, but reflect a summation of excitatory and inhibitory inputs. The spatial distributions of these antagonistic inputs often overlap and both are usually maximal in the center of the field; however, the one predominating in the center drops more rapidly in sensitivity away from the center, allowing the other to predominate in the surround thus creating the spatially opponent organization. The most effective stimulus for such cells is either a spot or an annulus appropriately centered on the field. A stimulus covering the field uniformly is less effective, but it is not completely ineffective because the total excitatory and inhibitory inputs are usually not exactly balanced; in general, whichever process predominates in the center will predominate when the entire field is stimulated. The dimensions of such receptive fields can be related quite closely to the lateral extent of processes of single ganglion cells.

The above organization is not the only one. In some species (e.g., frog) the surround is weak; stimulating the surround alone elicits no response, but its antagonistic effect is clear when it is stimulated together with the center: stimulation of the surround diminishes the responses to stimulation of the field's center (Barlow, 1953). Furthermore the apparent organization of a receptive field depends on the stimulus conditions. For example, a cell can be influenced by stimulation far outside the "boundaries" of its receptive field; the image of a moving object almost anywhere on the retina can affect a given cell's response to stimulation within its receptive field (McIlwain, 1964). The level of ambient illumination also affects the organization and function of many cells. If a retina is left in the dark for some time, a cell with a concentrically organized receptive field appears to lose its opponent surround; also the response of the center seems to spread beyond its previous boundary, but this is only because the sensitivity of the mechanism predominating in the surround decreases revealing the full extent of the center mechanism (Barlow, FitzHugh, & Kuffler, 1957).

In species whose retinas contain both rods and cones it is the cones which usually provide the inputs to cells at relatively high levels of ambient illumination, but after a period in the dark the inputs often switch to rods (Donner & Rushton, 1959; Wiesel & Hubel, 1966). Usually only one or other receptor class determines the response under a given set of illumination conditions; whichever of the rods or cones is activated most strongly monopolizes the system and blocks the responses from the other (Gouras & Link, 1966).

In species with good color vision (e.g., fish, birds, primates) the responses of ganglion cells have additional features which depend on the wavelength of the stimulus. As noted for S-units, there are cells which receive inputs from systems (cones) with different spectral sensitivities so that these cells are excited by some wavelengths and inhibited by others (Fig. 12; this is from the lateral geniculate nucleus of the macaque but can illustrate responses of ganglion cells as well). The spectrally opponent inputs are not usually distributed evenly over the cell's receptive field. Most of these cells in primates have receptive fields of simple, concentric shape (as in cats) but the excitatory and inhibitory regions are each maximally sensitive to different parts of the spectrum. Thus these cells can exhibit both spatial and chromatic antagonisms, depending on the stimuli. More will be said about wavelength dependent cells of primates in the next chapter.

As indicated earlier, the amacrine cell layer is very complex in lower vertebrates so that one might expect their ganglion cells to display the results of more complex visual analysis and processing. Responses of

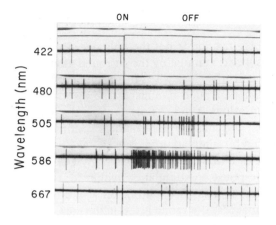

FIG. 12. A series of records of the responses of a spectrally opponent cell in the lateral geniculate nucleus of the macaque monkey to various wavelengths (equated for energy). The stimulus period (1 sec) is indicated. Note that the cell is spontaneously active in the dark before the stimulus. (From De Valois, Abramov, & Jacobs, 1966.)

spectrally opponent cells in goldfish provide a good illustration of this complexity. The receptive fields of these cells were initially mapped using small spots of light and appeared to have simple, concentric receptive fields in which the excitatory and inhibitory inputs had different spectral characteristics (Fig. 13A; Wagner, MacNichol, & Wolbarsht, 1963). However, using annular stimuli as well as spots, it was found that the entire simple field was itself only the center of a much larger receptive field (Fig. 13B; Daw, 1968). There is a very extensive surround area which is also spectrally opponent but is of opposite type to the center; if the center is excited by short wavelengths and inhibited by long, the large surround will be excited by long wavelengths and inhibited by short (Fig. 13C). This large surround is rather weak so that it is best demonstrated with an annulus which activates a large part of it. Due to this organization a goldfish's ganglion cell can show a variety of antagonisms or summations depending on the stimulus. A uniform stimulus covering the entire field is less effective than one covering the center alone. However, if the center is stimulated with short wavelength light while the surround is simultaneously illuminated by long wavelengths, both inputs will be of the same sign and will sum to maximum effect.

Another example of complex retinal processing deals with the detection of motion. Cells with simple, concentric receptive fields respond in the same manner to stimuli moving across their fields in any direction. However, in the rabbit retina there are some cells which respond selectively to direction of stimulus movement (Barlow, Hill, & Levick, 1964). Moving a stimulus in a

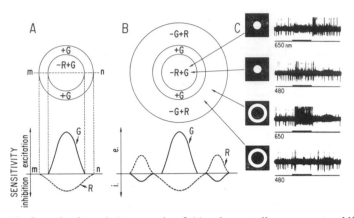

FIG. 13. Organization of the receptive fields of spectrally opponent goldfish gang-lion cells. A: The receptive field as inferred from mapping with small spots. The graphs are the same as in Fig. 11, but with the addition that the excitatory and in-hibitory systems have different spectral sensitivities; in this example the excitatory system is maximally sensitive to shorter wavelengths (green). B: The receptive field of a similar cell as inferred from mapping with spots and annular stimuli. See text for details. C: Responses of a single cell whose receptive field was of the type shown in B. The shape of the stimulus is shown next to each record and the stimulus marker and wavelength are under each record. (Unpublished records from I. Abramov and M. W. Levine.)

specific direction over the field elicits an increase in spike firing, while the reverse motion elicits a decrease. Stimuli moving perpendicular to the pre-ferred direction elicit the same response in either direction; movement in the preferred direction elicits the maximal response (Fig. 14).

V. ELECTRICAL RESPONSES—CNS

Most fibers from the optic nerve terminate on cells in the lateral geniculate nucleus (LGN); but many of these also send collaterals which, together with other optic nerve fibers, end in the superior colliculus (SCL). The main sensory pathway in higher vertebrates is through LGN to cortex and it will be dealt with first. As noted earlier, the LGN also receives inputs from areas other than the retina, which suggests that some additional processing may occur at this level. The LGN appears to act largely as a relay station to the cortex and the other inputs to the LGN might serve as a general control on level of sensitivity or "attention" (Arden & Söderberg, 1961; Granit, 1962). Nothing else will be said at this stage about the LGN because responses of its cells to light are essentially the same as those

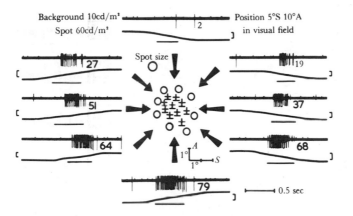

FIG. 14. Records of a rabbit ganglion cell responding selectively to direction of stimulus movement. The map of the receptive field is in the center; a stationary spot elicited "on–off" responses in positions marked O. Each record is the response to movement of the spot completely across the receptive field in the direction shown by the arrow; the upper trace shows the cell's responses with the number of spikes written underneath; the lower trace is the stimulus marker showing movement of the spot; the horizontal bar indicates when the spot was in the receptive field. Cd/m^2 are units of luminance. (From Barlow, *et al.*, 1964.)

already described for ganglion cells in cats and monkeys (Hubel & Wiesel, 1961; Wiesel & Hubel, 1966).

A. Cortex

The most obvious change between cells in cortex and LGN or retina is in their receptive field organization. In higher animals retinal and LGN cells typically have simple, concentric receptive fields for which the optimal stimulus is either a spot or an annulus appropriately centered on the field. At the cortical level this is no longer generally true. Single units in area 17 of cortex in cats and macaque monkeys have been investigated extensively (Hubel & Wiesel, 1962, 1968). Most of these cells are poorly activated by uniform stimuli covering the entire field. However cells in area 17 are readily activated by small spots of light which can be used to explore the shape and extent of their receptive fields.

As with receptive fields of cells in the LGN and retina, stimulation of specific retinal areas elicits either net excitation or net inhibition. But these areas are not concentric for cortical cells; rather, the boundaries between the excitatory and inhibitory zones tend to be straight lines. A wide variety of field shapes has been observed and some typical ones are shown in Fig. 15. These cells have been termed "simple" cortical cells. The size, shape,

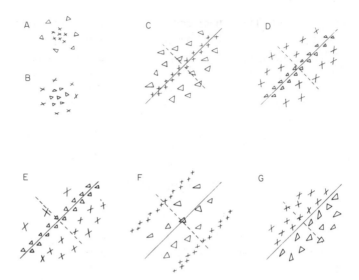

Fig. 15. Typical forms of receptive fields of cells in the cat's lateral geniculate nucleus and cortex. Areas giving "on" responses are marked x, while areas giving "off" responses are marked Δ. A and B: "On" center and "off" center geniculate fields. C–G: Various forms of simple cortical receptive fields; all are drawn oblique but each form occurs in all orientations. (From Hubel & Wiesel, 1962).

orientation, and retinal locus of the most effective stimulus can readily be predicted from the maps of a simple cell's receptive field. Extending a stimulus beyond the boundaries mapped with small spots adds nothing to the response; for example, with a cell for which a bar is the preferred stimulus, elongating it beyond the apparent receptive field does not affect the cell's response.

If the electrode is lowered into the cortex on a track perpendicular to the cortical surface, all the cells encountered will have similar receptive fields; that is, their preferred stimuli will all have the same orientation and approximately the same position in the visual field (Hubel & Wiesel, 1962). This columnar organization of the cortex is also found in the primary cortical projection areas of other sensory modalities (Mountcastle, 1957).

Cells reflecting a higher level of processing ("complex" cortical cells) predominate in area 18, although in the macaque monkey they are also widely found in area 17 (Hubel & Wiesel, 1965, 1968). As for simple cells, a bar or edge of specific orientation is the best stimulus, and elongating it beyond a certain point produces no additional effect. However, position of the stimulus in the visual field is no longer crucial; a specifically oriented bar placed anywhere in a large part of the visual field will elicit responses from a complex cell. Thus these cells do not have receptive fields with excitatory and inhibitory areas in specific retinal locations.

Cells with responses of the next order of complexity (termed "hyper-complex" cells) are usually found in area 19. As with simpler cells, a bar is the most effective stimulus, but for these cells extending one or both ends of the bar reduces the response. The bar must be of a specific length. Thus these cells have inhibitory areas but in order to observe them the excitatory areas must also be stimulated; furthermore, like the excitatory area, the inhibitory area requires a precisely shaped and oriented stimulus.

The trend from LGN through successive cortical areas is one of increasing complexity. A model has been suggested for the possible interconnections which would give rise to this (Hubel & Wiesel, 1962). A simple cortical cell receives inputs from a number of LGN cells whose receptive fields are located in line one next to the other across the retina (Fig. 16A). Complex cells can then be constructed from the outputs of many simple cortical cells responding to a bar of given orientation; the correct bar almost anywhere in

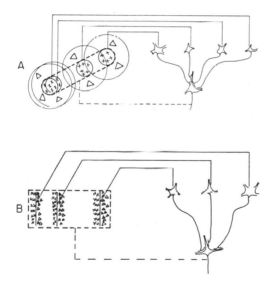

FIG. 16. Models of simple and complex cortical cells. A: A simple cortical cell (schematically drawn on the right) receives inputs from a number of lateral geniculate cells whose receptive fields (shown on the left) are located in a straight line across the retina; areas of the fields marked x are excitatory and those marked Δ are inhibitory. The receptive field of the simple cortical cell shown will have an elongated "on" center bounded by the dashed line on the left; this field is similar to that shown in Fig. 15C. B: Receptive fields of complex cortical cells can be constructed by summing the outputs of many simple cortical cells whose receptive fields all have the same orientation. (From Hubel & Wiesel, 1962).

the visual field would be imaged on the receptive field of at least one of the simple cells involved (Fig. 16B).

Other examples of complex cortical response patterns can be found if moving or colored stimuli are used. Whereas in the rabbit "movement detectors" are found in the retina, in primates they occur in the cortex. Similarly, with respect to color, cortical cells in monkeys are not obviously spectrally opponent. They show instead a greater complexity suggesting a higher summation of spectrally opponent LGN cells; for instance, some cortical cells have receptive fields whose spectral characteristics are of the complex variety described previously for the goldfish retina.

B. Superior Colliculus

We have already noted that with the evolution of the geniculocortical pathway the superior colliculus (SCL) declines in importance. In mammals its primary role seems to be related to orientation, eye movements, and similar functions (Sprague & Meikle, 1965). The SCL receives its major inputs both directly from the optic tract and indirectly via visual cortex. The response properties of SCL cells are very similar to those of complex and hypercomplex cortical cells described above (Michael, 1970; Wickelgren & Sterling, 1969). Many of the units are also sensitive to stimuli moving in specific directions and this is presumably related to the role of the SCL.

Acknowledgments

This work was partially supported by the following grants: Research Grant EY 00188 from the National Eye Institute, U. S. Public Health Service; Research Grant GB 6540 from the National Science Foundation; and Training Grant GM 01789 from the National Institute of General Medicine, U. S. Public Health Service.

The authors thank Drs. Norma Graham and Donald Hood for critically reading the manuscript and offering many helpful suggestions.

References

Arden, G. B., & Söderberg, U. The transfer of optic information through the lateral geniculate body of the rabbit. In W. A. Rosenblith (Ed.), *Sensory communication*. New York: Wiley, 1961. Pp. 521–544.

Armington, J. C., Johnson, E. P., & Riggs, L. A. The scotopic A-wave in the electrical response of the human retina. *Journal of Physiology (London)*, 1952, **118**, 289–298.

Barlow, H. B. Summation and inhibition in the frog's retina. *Journal of Physiology* (*London*), 1953, **119**, 69–88.

Barlow, H. B., FitzHugh, R., & Kuffler, S. W. Change of organization in the receptive fields of the cat's retina during dark adaptation. *Journal of Physiology* (*London*), 1957, **137**, 338–354.

Barlow, H. B., Hill, R. M., & Levick, W. R. Retinal ganglion cells responding selectively to direction and speed of image motion in the rabbit. *Journal of Physiology* (*London*), 1964, **173**, 377–407.

Baylor, D. A., Fuortes, M. G. F., & O'Bryan, P. M. Receptive fields of cones in the retina of the turtle. *Journal of Physiology* (*London*), 1971, **214**, 265–294.

Boycott, B. B., & Dowling, J. E. Organisation of the primate retina: Light microscopy. *Philosophical Transactions of The Royal Society of London, Series B,* 1969, **255**, 109–184.

Bridges, C. D. B. Visual pigment 544, a presumptive cone pigment from the retina of the pigeon. *Nature* (*London*), 1962, **195**, 40–42.

Brown, K. T. The electroretinogram: Its components and their origins. *Vision Research,* 1968, **8**, 633–677.

Brown, K. T., Watanabe, K., & Murakami, M. The early and late receptor potentials of monkey cones and rods. *Cold Spring Harbor Symposia on Quantitative Biology,* 1965, **30**, 457–482.

Brown, P. K., & Wald, G. Visual pigments in single rods and cones of the human retina. *Science,* 1964, **144**, 45–52.

Cohen, A. I. Vertebrate retinal cells and their organization. *Biological Reviews of The Cambridge Philosophical Society,* 1963, **38**, 427–459.

Dartnall, H. J. A. The photobiology of visual processes. In H. Davson (Ed.), *The eye.* (1st ed.) Vol. 2. New York: Academic Press, 1962. Pp. 321–533.

Daw, N. W. Colour-coded ganglion cells in the goldfish retina: Extensions of their receptive fields by means of new stimuli. *Journal of Physiology* (*London*), 1968, **197**, 567–592.

De Valois, R. L., Abramov, I., & Jacobs, G. H. Analysis of response patterns of LGN cells. *Journal of The Optical Society of America,* 1966, **56**, 966–977.

Donner, K. O., & Rushton, W. A. H. Rod–cone interaction in the frog's retina analysed by the Stiles-Crawford effect and by dark adaptation. *Journal of Physiology* (*London*), 1959, **149**, 303–317.

Dowling, J. E. Organization of vertebrate retinas. *Investigative Ophthalmology,* 1970, **9**, 655–680.

Dowling, J. E., & Boycott, B. B. Organization of the primate retina: Electron microscopy. *Proceedings of The Royal Society of London, Series B,* 1966, **166**, 80–111.

Glickstein, M. Organization of the visual pathways. *Science,* 1969, **164**, 917–926.

Gouras, P., & Link, K. Rod and cone interaction in dark-adapted monkey ganglion cells. *Journal of Physiology* (*London*), 1966, **184**, 499–510.

Granit, R. The visual pathway. In H. Davson (Ed.), *The eye.* (1st ed.) Vol. 2. New York: Academic Press, 1962. Pp. 537–763.

Hagins, W. A. Electrical signs of information flow in photoreceptors. *Cold Spring Harbor Symposia on Quantitative Biology,* 1965, **30**, 403–418.

Hartline, H. K. The response of single optic nerve fibers of the vertebrate eye to illumination of the retina. *American Journal of Physiology,* 1938, **121**, 400–415.

Hartline, H. K., Wagner, H. G., & MacNichol, E. F., Jr. The peripheral origin of nervous activity in the visual system. *Cold Spring Harbor Symposia on Quantitative Biology*, 1952, **17**, 125–141.

Hubel, D. H., & Wiesel, T. N. Integrative action in the cat's lateral geniculate body. *Journal of Physiology (London)*, 1961, **155**, 385–398.

Hubel, D. H., & Wiesel, T. N. Receptive fields, binocular interaction and functional architecture in the cat's visual cortex. *Journal of Physiology (London)*, 1962, **160**, 106–154.

Hubel, D. H., & Wiesel, T. N. Receptive fields and functional architecture in two non-striate visual areas (18 and 19) of the cat. *Journal of Neurophysiology*, 1965, **28**, 229–289.

Hubel, D. H., & Wiesel, T. N. Receptive fields and functional architecture of monkey striate cortex. *Journal of Physiology (London)*, 1968, **195**, 215–243.

Hull, E. M. Corticofugal influence in the macaque lateral geniculate nucleus. *Vision Research*, 1968, **8**, 1285–1298.

Kaneko, A. Physiological and morphological identification of horizontal, bipolar, and amacrine cells in goldfish retina. *Journal of Physiology (London)*, 1970, **207**, 623–633.

Kolb, H. Organization of the outer plexiform layer of the primate retina: Electron microscopy of Golgi-impregnated cells. *Philosophical Transaction of The Royal Society of London, Series B*, 1970, **258**, 261–283.

Kuffler, S. W. Discharge patterns and functional organization of mammalian retina. *Journal of Neurophysiology*, 1953, **16**, 37–68.

McIlwain, J. T. Receptive fields of optic tract axons and lateral geniculate cells: Peripheral extent and barbiturate sensitivity. *Journal of Neurophysiology*, 1964, **27**, 1154–1173.

MacNichol, E. F., Jr., & Svaetichin, G. Electric responses from the isolated retinas of fishes. *American Journal of Ophthalmology*, 1958, **46**, 26–46.

Marks, W. B. Visual pigments of single goldfish cones. *Journal of Physiology (London)*, 1965, **178**, 14–32.

Marks, W. B., Dobelle, W. H., & MacNichol, E. F., Jr. Visual pigments of single primate cones. *Science*, 1964, **143**, 1181–1183.

Matthews, R. G., Hubbard, R., Brown, P. K., & Wald, G. Tautomeric forms of metarhodopsin. *Journal of General Physiology*, 1963, **47**, 215–240.

Michael, C. R. Integration of retinal and cortical information in the superior colliculus of the ground squirrel. *Brain, Behavior & Evolution*, 1970, **3**, 205–209.

Mountcastle, V. B. Modality and topographic properties of single neurons of cat's somatic sensory cortex. *Journal of Neurophysiology*, 1957, **20**, 408–434.

Østerberg, G. Topography of the layer of rods and cones in the human retina. *Acta Ophthalmologica, Supplementum* **6**, 1935.

Polyak, S. L. *The vertebrate visual system*. Chicago, Illinois: Univ. of Chicago Press, 1957.

Riggs, L. A. Light as a stimulus for vision. In C. H. Graham (Ed.), *Vision and visual perception*. New York: Wiley, 1965, Pp. 1–38.

Rushton, W. A. H. A cone pigment in the protanope. *Journal of Physiology (London)*, 1963, **168**, 345–359.

Rushton, W. A. H. A foveal pigment in the deuteranope. *Journal of Physiology (London)*, 1965, **176**, 24–37.

Sjöstrand, F. S. The synaptology of the retina. *Colour Vision; Physiology and Experimental Psychology, Ciba Foundation Symposium, 1964*, 1965, pp. 110–151.

Sprague, J. M., & Meikle, T. H., Jr. The role of the superior colliculus in visually guided behavior. *Experimental Neurology,* 1965, **11,** 115–146.

Stone, J. The naso-temporal division of the cat's retina. *Journal of Comparative Neurology,* 1966, **126,** 585–599.

Svaetichin, G., & MacNichol, E. F., Jr. Retinal mechanisms for chromatic and achromatic vision. *Annals of The New York Academy of Sciences,* 1958, **74,** 385–404.

Tomita, T. Electrophysiological study of the mechanisms subserving color coding in the fish retina. *Cold Spring Harbor Symposia on Quantitative Biology,* 1965, **30,** 559–566.

Tomita, T. Electrical activity of vertebrate photoreceptors. *Quarterly Review of Biophysics,* 1970, **3,** 179–222.

Tomita, T., Kaneko, A., Murakami, M., & Pautler, E. L. Spectral response curves of single cones in the carp. *Vision Research,* 1967, **7,** 519–531.

Wagner, H. G., MacNichol, E. F., Jr., & Wolbarsht, M. L. Functional basis for "on"-center and "off"-center receptive fields in the retina. *Journal of The Optical Society of America,* 1963, **53,** 66–70.

Wald, G. The photoreceptor process in vision. In Amer. Physiol. Soc., J. Field (Ed.), *Handbook of physiology.* Sect. 1. *Neurophysiology.* Vol. I. Baltimore, Maryland: Williams & Wilkins, 1959. Pp. 671–692.

Wald, G., Brown, P. K., & Smith, P. H. Iodopsin. *Journal of General Physiology,* 1955, **38,** 623–681.

Walls, G. L. *The vertebrate eye and its adaptive radiation.* New York: Hafner, 1942. (Reprinted 1963.)

Walsh, J. W. T. *Photometry.* New York: Dover, 1965.

Weale, R. A. Vision and fundus reflectometry: A review. *Photochemistry and Photobiology,* 1965, **4,** 67–87.

Werblin, F. S., & Dowling, J. E. Organization of the retina of the mudpuppy, *Necturus maculosus.* II. Intracellular recording. *Journal of Neurophysiology,* 1969, **32,** 339–355.

Wickelgren, B. G., & Sterling, P. Influences of visual cortex on receptive fields in the superior colliculus of the cat. *Journal of Neurophysiology,* 1969, **32,** 16–23

Wiesel, T. N., & Hubel, D. H. Spatial and chromatic interaction in the lateral geniculate body of the rhesus monkey. *Journal of Neurophysiology,* 1966, **29,** 1115–1156.

Chapter 17

SEEING

ISRAEL ABRAMOV AND JAMES GORDON

The visual sense has probably been studied longer and more intensively than any other sensory modality; it is impossible to give in one chapter even the briefest summary of the entire field. The first part of this chapter will be restricted to some of the most basic visual phenomena; that is, the responses to very simple stimuli presented to one eye alone—binocular vision and higher perceptual functions will not be considered. The second part will deal specifically with some of the physiological mechanisms underlying the psychophysical observations. Both parts should be read with a view to relating them to the more detailed physiology given in the previous chapter.

I. PSYCHOPHYSICS

A. Sensitivity

Everyone has made the observation that when going into a darkened room one's eyes gradually become more sensitive. Dark-adaptation of this sort has been studied very extensively (Bartlett, 1965). Usually, intensity of a test light required for some threshold of detection is measured at successive

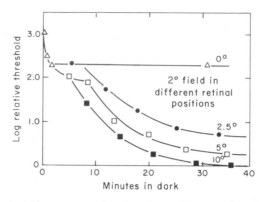

FIG. 1. Dark-adaptation curves showing threshold as a function of time after offset of an adapting light. The 2° test field was presented at different retinal locations; the locations are marked in degrees from the fovea. (From Hecht, Haig, & Wald, 1935.)

time intervals starting from the time a fixed adapting light is switched off. Figure 1 shows typical dark-adaptation curves in which energy at threshold (for convenience the scale is logarithmic) is plotted against time after offset of the adapting light; in all cases the test stimulus was the same but was viewed in different positions on the retina. Consider the curve for the test stimulus at 5 degrees from the fovea: there is a rapid initial recovery of sensitivity (less energy required for detection at threshold) and the curve quickly reaches a plateau; but after a few more minutes in the dark, threshold again starts dropping. The two parts of the curve strongly suggest two mechanisms each with a different time course for arriving at its absolute threshold. There is a wide variety of evidence that the first part of the curve reflects the recovery of the cones and the second, later portion, that of the rods (Pirenne, 1962). For example, if the test light is restricted to the rod-free fovea only the first part of the curve is obtained (0° curve in Fig. 1).

If the lower part of the functions in Fig. 1 is due to the rods, then sensitivity at those times during dark-adaptation should be related to rhodopsin, the rod photopigment. Rhodopsin does not absorb all wavelengths equally (see Fig. 3A in Chap. 16); for example, rhodopsin absorbs about ten times as much light at 500 nm as at 590 nm. Therefore, once sensitivity has fully recovered, one would expect that flashes of monochromatic lights of equal energy would not appear equally bright; to appear equally bright a 590 nm stimulus should contain ten times more energy than one at 500 nm. Using monochromatic lights, dark-adaptation curves have been measured both for humans and a variety of animal subjects; Fig. 2A shows, for the pigeon, representative curves at two stimulus wavelengths. At the plateau, the energy at threshold for each wavelength defines the relative

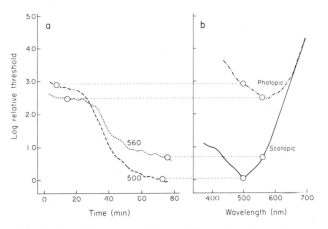

FIG. 2. a: Dark-adaptation curves obtained from the pigeon by a psychophysical technique; each curve was obtained using the wavelength indicated. The curves show two plateaus the first of which is determined by the photopic system and the second by the scotopic system. b: Relative thresholds as a function of wavelength for the photopic and scotopic systems of the pigeon. These curves were obtained from dark-adaptation curves at a series of wavelengths; examples for 500 and 560 nm are shown. (Redrawn from Blough, 1957.)

ability of each wavelength to activate the system detecting the lights. If dark-adaptation curves are obtained for each of a number of wavelengths, the functions shown in Fig. 2B can be obtained. The system (cones) determining the initial segment of the dark-adaptation curve is termed the photopic system, while the system (rods) determining the later portion is termed the scotopic system.

The scotopic function in Fig. 2B is redrawn in Fig. 3A in the more conventional way in which sensitivity is given as the reciprocal of the energy at threshold for each wavelength. Fig. 3A also shows the scotopic sensitivity function for a lensless human together with the absorption function of rhodopsin. The two sensitivity functions, peaking at about 500 nm, agree quite closely with rhodopsin indicating that the later portion of the dark-adaptation curve is due to rods. (Note that the rhodopsin function is, in this figure, plotted on an energy rather than quantal ordinate; psychophysicists generally measure energy for threshold rather than number of quanta. A lensless subject was used because the human lens, unlike the pigeon's, absorbs short wavelengths strongly and complicates comparisons with photopigment functions.) Some representative human photopic spectral sensitivities are given in Fig. 3B. The curves, peaking at about 560 nm, are broader than the spectral absorption function of any single photopigment; this is presumably because there are three cone photopigments (see Fig. 3B in Chap. 16).

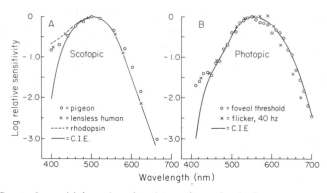

FIG. 3. Spectral sensitivity; that is, the reciprocal of the energy required for threshold detection at each wavelength. A: Scotopic spectral sensitivity functions for the pigeon (Blough, 1957) and a lensless human (Wald, 1959). Also shown are the absorption functions of rhodopsin (Wald, 1959) and the standard C.I.E. scotopic function. B: Human photopic spectral sensitivity functions obtained by different methods. One function was obtained by measuring absolute foveal thresholds at different wavelengths (Hsia & Graham, 1952). The other was obtained using monochromatic lights flickering at 40 Hz and measuring the energy required to detect the flicker (Heath, 1958). The C.I.E. photopic function is also shown.

There are various other techniques for measuring spectral sensitivity as, for example, adjusting the intensities of various spectral lights until they appear as bright as some reference standard, magnitude estimation of the brightness of different wavelengths, methods based on the eye's ability to resolve flickering lights, and so on (see Le Grand, 1957; Pirenne, 1962). Most methods give consistent results for the scotopic function, but the photopic functions, although they all tend to peak at about 560 nm, vary widely in shape of the curve; some methods favor the appearance of subsidiary peaks in the curve, reemphasizing that the photopic system is based on inputs from several cone types (Fig. 3B).

The variability in spectral sensitivity functions raises serious problems. All the methods essentially attempt to define the effectiveness of different spectral lights in eliciting the sensation of light. However the variety of curves strongly suggest that the different methods are not measuring quite the same thing; depending on the situation, the subject makes use of somewhat different parts of the inputs available to him from his visual system—the second part of this chapter deals with this in greater detail. In Chap. 16 it was mentioned that light intensity could be quantified photometrically according to its ability to activate the visual system. To avoid confusions due to different luminosity functions, the Commission Internationale de l'Éclairage (C.I.E.) published the internationally accepted scotopic and photopic luminosity (relative sensitivity) functions for the standard observer. Stimuli are often specified in terms of their luminance, where luminance is energy (radiance) scaled by the luminosity function; the photopic function is intended unless the scotopic function is specifically stated. The scotopic curve is given in Fig. 3A. The C.I.E. scotopic observer, as well as most dark-adapted human observers, is less sensitive to short wavelengths than might be expected on the basis of the rhodopsin function; the difference is due to absorption of short wavelengths by preretinal structures such as the lens. The C.I.E. photopic function is included in Fig. 3B. Note that under given conditions the luminosity function of a real observer may differ greatly from the standard.

Dark-adaptation, and adaptation in general, will be dealt with more carefully later. However one should note some consequences of the shift during dark-adaptation between systems of different spectral sensitivity. The photopic system is more sensitive to long wavelengths than the scotopic; thus if two spectral lights, e.g., 500 and 600 nm, are made equally bright when light-adapted, the 500 nm light will appear much brighter once sensitivity shifts to the scotopic system. This shift is named after the first person to describe it, Purkinje. But the change from one system to another does not occur suddenly during dark-adaptation; for times shortly after cone plateau (Fig. 1), spectral sensitivity is some intermediate function of both photopic and scotopic systems and is termed mesopic.

B. Color

1. HUE AND WAVELENGTH DISCRIMINATION

The above section dealt only with the visual system's sensitivity to various spectral lights, and the relative changes in this sensitivity during dark-adaptation. There is, however, one change which was not considered. When vision is determined by the photopic system, a monochromatic test light appears colored, but after the shift to the scotopic system it is colorless. Moreover, under photopic conditions, changing the wavelength of the light changes the color perceived. Psychophysical techniques are available for measuring the color changes. For example, subjects can be asked to use the color names "red," "yellow," "green," and "blue" (or paired names, such as "green-yellow") to describe different stimulus wavelengths which have been adjusted to equal photopic intensity (Boynton & Gordon, 1965). The responses can then be scaled to give the relative frequencies with which spectral lights are perceived to be of one or other of these four hues. Some of the results are given in Fig. 4A from which it can be seen, for example, that light of about 580 nm almost always appears yellow; however if the

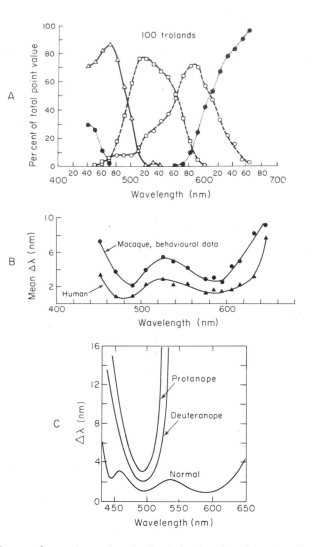

FIG. 4. Color naming and wavelength discrimination functions. A: Curves showing relative frequencies (see text) with which spectral lights are named red (filled
circles), yellow (open circles), green (squares), blue (triangles). Trolands are units
of retinal illuminance. (Replotted from data of Boynton & Gordon, 1965.) B:
Wavelength discrimination of humans and macaque monkeys. The functions show
change in wavelength needed at each point in the spectrum, to detect a difference.
(Redrawn from De Valois & Jacobs, 1968.) C: Wavelength discrimination functions
of normal (trichromat) and colorblind (dichromat) humans. ("Normal" curve
redrawn from Wright & Pitt, 1934; "protanope" and "deuteranope" curves redrawn
from Pitt, 1944.)

wavelength is changed even slightly the percept includes either red or green depending on the direction of change.

From the color-naming data one could deduce the ability to detect changes in wavelength at any given spectral region; where the proportions of the different color names change most rapidly with respect to each other, changes in wavelength should be most discriminable. However the more direct method is to measure the smallest difference in wavelength which is detectable at various points in the spectrum; this approach can also be used with animal subjects since one asks merely for a judgment of "different." In such an experiment, to ensure that the stimuli vary only in color, all the lights must be equated for photopic intensity, otherwise they will differ in brightness as well; the photopic luminosity function for the given species provides the necessary correction factors. Typical wavelength discrimination functions obtained under identical conditions from humans and macaque monkeys are shown in Fig. 4B; the macaque is included because a variety of tests demonstrate that it has color vision essentially identical to human and it has been used extensively in physiological investigations. The functions show that, except for the ends of the spectrum, wavelength discrimination is very good and is optimal in two regions—at about 490 and 590 nm.

The ability to differentiate lights of different wavelengths, even when they are equated for luminosity, is a defining characteristic of color vision. The question now is why this is possible under photopic conditions, but not under scotopic conditions once the lights are equated for scotopic intensity. In the latter case the rods are the only effective receptors; since they all have the same spectral sensitivity (determined by rhodopsin) they cannot discriminate between different lights which have been equated for ability to stimulate the rods. In order to distinguish lights differing only in wavelength one must have at least two sets of receptors of different spectral sensitivities whose outputs can be compared. Both sets of receptors will be stimulated to some degree by all wavelengths, but the ratio of their responses will vary as wavelength is changed. This ratio will change most rapidly in the spectral region where the two spectral sensitivity functions intersect; hence wavelength discrimination will be best about that region. For good wavelength discrimination across the spectrum it is probably necessary to have more than two primary spectral systems.

2. TRICHROMACY AND PRIMARY MECHANISMS

There is now a very large body of evidence showing that our color vision is based on three separate channels (Brindley, 1960; Marriott, 1962). Essentially, the evidence is that given any four lights it is possible to choose one of them as a standard and exactly match its appearance with the other three "primaries." Generally this can be done by mixing the three primaries and appropriately adjusting their intensities. But in some cases two of the primaries must be added and the third substracted; this is achieved by adding the third primary to the light being matched. Provided that the intensities of the primaries can be continuously and separately adjusted the match will be exact. Thus, three independent, continuous parameters are sufficient to specify our color discrimination. However, from psychophysical experiments it was impossible to derive unequivocally the individual spectral sensitivities of the three systems involved in color vision. This had to await the more recent work, described in the previous chapter, which demonstrated three separate cone types and measured their spectral functions (Fig. 3B in Chap. 16). However results from some types of psychophysical experiments came very close to the direct measurements of the photopigments; these experiments will be described in some detail later.

Color blindness must now be mentioned, but only the briefest summary can be given here; see Hsia and Graham (1965) and Marriott (1962) for additional information. Some observers can only discriminate between wavelengths in restricted regions of the spectrum, and color-matching functions from them show that only two parameters are needed to describe their color vision (e.g., Pitt, 1944). The simplest reason for this deficiency would be an absence of one of the three cone photopigments, and this has been supported by using reflection densitometry (see Chap. 16) to measure the cone pigments in such people (Rushton, 1964). The commonest types of dichromat cannot discriminate between wavelengths of light longer than about 540 nm (Fig. 4C). These dichromats probably lack either the 565 nm or 535 nm cone pigment; the former are termed "protanopes" and the latter, "deuteranopes." The much rarer "tritanope" apparently lacks the short-wavelength cones. Extremely rare individuals, "monochromats" ("achromats"), have only one cone pigment so that even under photopic conditions they lack any color vision; but they do show some shift in their spectral sensitivity when dark-adapted. In rare cases a subject may have no cone pigments. Finally, there are the "anomalous trichromats"; these people require three primaries in their color matches but the functions are quite unlike those of normal trichromats. At present the reason for these anomalies is unclear.

Many attempts have been made to measure, psychophysically, the spectral sensitivities of the primary cone systems. From the direct cone photopigment data now available it can be said that the most successful attempts were either those which measured the spectral sensitivities of dichromats, or those of normal subjects under conditions of chromatic adaptation. These experiments depend on the fact that the short-wavelength mechanism appears to be greatly reduced in the fovea. Thus for a protanope or deuteranope, spectral sensitivity in the fovea should be determined mostly by one cone system. Such experiments (Hsia & Graham, 1957; Willmer, 1955) showed two systems (Fig. 5A) whose spectral sensitivity functions, peaking at about 530–540 and 560–570 nm, agree reasonably well with two of the three cone pigments. The sensitivity of the short-wavelength system was obtained from monochromats who apparently had a system maximally sensitive at about 440 nm (Blackwell & Blackwell, 1961); this is similar to the sensitivity of the third type of cone. For normal subjects, foveal sensitivity is largely a function of two cone pigments; if the sensitivity of one of their cone types can be depressed selectively, the fovea will be in a state of artificial color-blindness and the experiment can proceed as before. Intense background lights of appropriate wavelength have been used to bleach preferentially a given cone pigment, and in this way systems were isolated which agreed closely with those of dichromats (Brindley, 1953; Wald, 1964; Willmer, 1955).

The above experiments isolated single cone types by bleaching most of the other pigments. However, it is possible to desensitize a receptor system without bleaching large amounts of pigment (see next section on adaptation). Chromatic backgrounds, like those referred to above but of much lower intensity, can differentially change the sensitivities of the systems so that only one will be left sufficiently sensitive at threshold to detect test flashes of various wavelengths. Using such threshold procedures a total of five separate cone-related systems (termed π mechanisms, Fig. 5B) have been isolated (Stiles, 1949, 1959; Marriott, 1962, provides a good summary). Only two of these (π_3 and π_4) can be closely related to single cone pigments. This suggests that even though the initial restriction of trichromacy is imposed at the very first stage of light transduction, the outputs of the cones may be combined in various ways to yield a multiplicity of separate systems; without bleaching away large amounts of pigment, these systems can not be broken down into more elementary units. The ways in which the outputs of the three cone types are combined to yield complex neural systems will be discussed in greater detail in the section on color vision.

C. Adaptation

1. Dark-Adaptation and Photopigments

The data in Fig. 1 show that the eye recovers its sensitivity in the dark but so far we have not considered the mechanisms involved. In the previous chapter we noted that light breaks down the photopigment. Since the pigment is also constantly being regenerated, the amount of pigment available reaches an equilibrium in the presence of any constant light; in

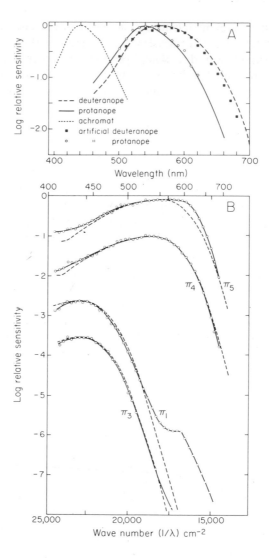

FIG. 5. A: The curves show the foveal spectral sensitivities of three types of color-blind humans. The data points are from normal subjects made temporarily color-blind by the use of intense chromatic adaptation. Each function is probably largely determined by one of the three cone systems. ("Deuteranope" and "protanope" from Willmer, 1955; "achromat" from Blackwell & Blackwell, 1961; "artificial deuteranope and protanope" from Brindley, 1953.) B: Spectral sensitivities of cone-related systems isolated by chromatic adaptation. Dashed curves show the spectral characteristics of single hypothetical photopigments. (From Stiles, 1959.)

the dark all the pigment eventually is regenerated. Amount of pigment present is probably related in some way to sensitivity; the earlier hypotheses were that sensitivity was directly proportional to amount of pigment, but this simple proportionality has since been shown to be incorrect. (Wald [1959] Bartlett [1965], and Rushton [1965a] provide summaries of this whole topic.)

The time course, measured psychophysically, of dark-adaptation from some fixed light level is known (Fig. 1); if, starting from the same light level, the time course of pigment regeneration were known, then the relationship between the functions could be examined. Three different methods have been used to follow regeneration. Rhodopsin has been extracted, bleached, and its regeneration measured *in vitro* (Wald, 1959). In other experiments, rats (predominantly rod eyes) were light-adapted, and then sacrificed at various times after the start of dark-adaptation; the retinas were removed and the amount of rhodopsin present was measured (Dowling, 1963). Finally, the technique of reflection densitometry (see Chap. 16) has been used to measure regeneration in the living eye; this method permits measurement of cone pigments as well as rhodopsin (Rushton, 1963, 1965b).

All the results agree quite closely. Rhodopsin is fully regenerated at the same time as the rod segment of the dark-adaptation curve reaches its asymptote, but prior to that point, threshold and amount of rhodopsin are nonlinearly related; at any given time, it is the logarithm of the threshold which is proportional to the amount of pigment still in the bleached state. If dark-adaptation is started after all rhodopsin has been bleached, it will take about 40 min to reach final threshold; but in normal individuals, with cones as well as rods, the first part of the rod curve is obscured by the cone system. Indeed the rods only start determining threshold after the cones have reached their absolute threshold, at which time only some 10% of the rhodopsin remains bleached—obviously small changes in amount of pigment have very large effects on threshold. Cone pigments regenerate much more rapidly, taking only 7–10 min for complete regeneration; this is one of the reasons cones are the effective receptors at higher light levels.

2. ABSOLUTE THRESHOLDS

Precisely how good are the cones and rods as light detectors? The curves in Fig. 1 suggest the rods have a much lower absolute threshold than the cones, but this is somewhat misleading. The rod system because of its greater degree of convergence, can integrate energy over a much larger area so that the larger the stimulus, the more it favors the rods. (Some caution is needed since the rods and cones are not evenly distributed across the retina—see Fig. 5, in Chap. 16.) If a sufficiently small test stimulus is used outside the fovea, the absolute threshold for the rod system is only slightly lower than for cones (Arden & Weale, 1954; Rushton & Cohen, 1954). Thus individual rods and cones are almost equal in their performance as detectors at low levels.

At very low light levels detection poses some very serious problems (Barlow, 1965; Pirenne, 1962). There are so few quanta incident on the retina at threshold that the stimulus at any given moment and place is an uncertain event; moreover some of the quanta may either pass between receptors or fail to be absorbed by the photopigment. Added to this "noise" in the stimulus is the possibility of noise inherent in the visual system, perhaps from the uneven spontaneous firing rate of the neurons. Careful experiments under conditions optimal for the rod system have shown that about 7 quanta must be absorbed within some short period of time for reliable detection of a flash at absolute threshold (Hecht, Shlaer, & Pirenne, 1942). Considering the small number of quanta and their probable distribution over the relatively large stimulus area, it was extremely unlikely that a given rod could have absorbed more than one quantum. The conclusion was that a single quantum absorbed can activate a rod, but several rods must be simultaneously activated for the detection of a light. Electrical responses related to absorption of single quanta have been found in records from individual photoreceptors, containing rhodopsin, in the eye of the horseshoe crab *Limulus* (Yeandle, 1958).

At high levels the rods saturate (that is, no longer detect any increment in light) at intensities well below those which saturate the cones. Usually the responses of the rods cannot be followed to saturation levels, since they are masked by the cones; visual thresholds are generally determined by whichever system is the most sensitive in any situation and at high light levels the cones are relatively more sensitive. Saturation of the rods has been measured in one of those rare individuals who apparently has no cones (Blakemore & Rushton, 1965); in normal individuals this was achieved by a special technique which takes advantage of some of the optical properties of the receptors to reduce the sensitivity of the cones relative to the rods (Aguilar & Stiles, 1954). Rod saturation occurs at levels well below those required to bleach all rhodopsin and well before the cones saturate; this may be related to the slower rate of regeneration of rhodopsin.

3. EQUIVALENT BACKGROUNDS AND AFTER-IMAGES

It was pointed out, in discussing the absolute sensitivities of rods and cones, that the thresholds of the rod segment of a dark-adaptation curve depend on the duration of the test flash used for measuring the threshold, and a host of other stimulus parameters. It is difficult therefore to specify state of adaptation without also specifying the precise stimulus used to measure threshold. However, there are some observations which provide a means of coping with this problem (Crawford, 1947). Figure 6A shows a series of dark-adaptation curves obtained with test stimuli of different sizes, but all starting from the same preadaptation of the eye as a whole, and therefore the same amount of bleached pigment.

Using the same test stimuli, and subject, the experiment can be reversed. The absolute threshold of a fully dark-adapted subject is measured; a weak background light is turned on and after a short while threshold is again measured for the test flash superimposed on the background; and so on, through a series of increasingly intense backgrounds. The results of this increment-threshold experiment are given in Fig. 6B; the most striking feature of these curves is that they appear to be "mirror images" of the dark-adaptation functions in Fig. 6A. The vertical line through the curves in 6A cuts all of them at some fixed time into dark-adaptation; at that time some specific amount of rhodopsin has been regenerated. The points in 6B which mark the same threshold values as in 6A fall on a vertical line

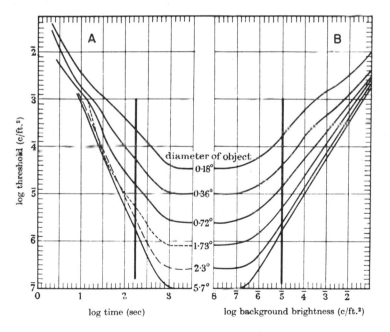

FIG. 6. Dark-adaptation and equivalent background. The ordinate shows the intensities required for detection of test flashes of various diameters. A: Dark-adaptation curves; thresholds as a function of time in the dark. B: Increment thresholds as a function of background intensity. (From Crawford, 1947.)

which specifies a background of given intensity. Thus, threshold (related to amount of pigment present) at some time after extinguishing an adapting light is equivalent to the increment-threshold measured on a given background, irrespective of diameter of test stimulus. In this way state of adaptation can generally be given in terms of the background required to raise threshold to the same level without referring to any specific parameters of the test stimulus. For any given background rhodopsin concentration reaches equilibrium at the same level as at the equivalent time into dark-adaptation. Since only a small amount of bleached pigment raises threshold greatly and bleaching is much more rapid than regeneration, sensitivity stabilizes more quickly when moving to a brighter than to a dimmer background. Because there are three cone photopigments, the concept of equivalent background must be used cautiously with regard to the photopic system; but if the wavelengths of preadapting and background lights are the same and the test flashes are of a specified wavelength, then the above description holds for cones as well (Du Croz & Rushton, 1966). Finally, note in Fig. 6B that there is a considerable range over which increment threshold is directly proportional to background intensity (Weber's law).

Thresholds measured during dark-adaptation can be equated with thresholds measured against a real background. Is there some source in the visual system for an apparent background during dark-adaptation? Attempts were made to identify this apparent background with the after-image of the adapting light. A test-field was imaged next to the after-image and the subject asked to keep adjusting its brightness to match the fading after-image; it was found that the brightness of the after-image decreased too rapidly to account for the slow course of dark-adaptation (Craik & Vernon, 1941). However, the above procedure was not entirely appropriate. As will be discussed later, an image which is stabilized on the retina soon fades and becomes invisible. An after-image is of necessity a stabilized retinal image so it is more appropriate to follow its brightness with a test-field which is also stabilized on the retina. If this is done, both images soon fade from view yet subjects are still able to adjust the "invisible" test patch to match the brightness of the after-image. When the adjusted intensities of the stabilized test field are plotted against time, the curve agrees exactly with the dark-adaptation curve obtained in the more usual manner (Barlow & Sparrock, 1964).

The above experiments suggest that rods with bleached pigment continue to signal just as if they were being illuminated, and this "bleached-rhodopsin" signal is maintained until all the pigment is regenerated. A nice demonstration of this signal was provided by observing the pupillary reflex to light (Alpern & Campbell, 1962). Both pupils function in unison and constrict when either or both eyes are illuminated. In the demonstration, one eye was dark-adapted while the photopigments in the other were bleached; with the subject in the dark, both pupils were constricted. The bleached eye was then temporarily blinded by pressing on it to raise intraocular pressure thereby occluding the retinal artery and blocking the ganglion cells from functioning. At this point both pupils dilated, but again constricted when the light-adapted eye was allowed to recover. In this situation only one eye had bleached pigment which could provide the "adaptation signal"; when that eye was blocked, the pupils responded as if there were no retinal signal.

The signals set off by bleached pigment molecules apparently decrease the sensitivity of the system so that greater intensities are required for light detection. But this change in sensitivity does not occur entirely at the receptors. The increment-threshold measured on a narrow adapting field is the same as the threshold for an area immediately adjacent to the adapting field; similarly, if a circumscribed retinal area is bleached, dark-adaptation thresholds on that area and on the area next to it will be the same (Rushton & Westheimer, 1962). Thus light-adapted receptors change the sensitivity of neighboring, dark-adapted regions as if they too were light-adapted. Much of adaptation therefore occurs at a stage beyond the receptors, a stage at which the outputs of many receptors are pooled.

Up to this point only threshold intensities have been considered. Subjects can be asked, however, to estimate the brightness of flashes whose intensity increases well beyond threshold, and these brightness functions have been obtained for a variety of adaptation levels (Stevens & Stevens, 1963). At any given adaptation level there is a narrow range of test intensities (less than ten times adapting intensity) over which brightness increases markedly—that is, over this range small changes in intensity elicit large changes in brightness; beyond this range much greater increments in intensity are needed for increases in brightness. If adaptation level is shifted, for example to a higher level, there is again a limited range over which intensity increments elicit marked increases in brightness. It seems as if the visual system operates best over some restricted range of intensities where the starting point of this range is set by the adaptation level.

4. EARLY LIGHT- AND DARK-ADAPTATION

Typically the first few seconds of dark-adaptation, or the immediate changes in increment threshold when a background is turned on, are not measured; however, some interesting events occur at these transitions (Baker, 1963; Crawford, 1947). Figure 7 shows in detail the changes in thresholds immediately following abrupt changes in adaptation conditions. As soon as a background is turned on there is a sharp rise in threshold,

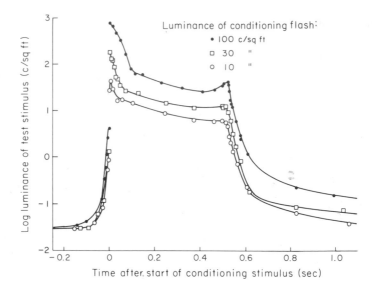

FIG. 7. Elevation of thresholds at onset and offset of a background (conditioning) field. Duration of the conditioning stimulus was 0.5 sec and started at time zero; the test flash was 10 msec long.(Redrawn from Crawford, 1947.)

but this quickly drops to a lower, steady value; light-adaptation is a rapid process. The steady-state threshold value while the adapting light is on corresponds to the one usually obtained in measures of an equivalent background and is the one which is related to pigment concentration. When the background is extinguished there is, as at onset, an initial rise in threshold, followed by a large rapid drop, tapering to the usual gradual decline to absolute threshold. In both cases, the magnitude of the transient elevation in threshold increases with the intensity of the adapting field, and for high intensities the transient can be very large. These transients are interpreted as reflecting a neural stage of adaptation, or an accentuation by the nervous system of the effects of rapid changes in a stimulus.

Although the thresholds in Fig. 7 rise before the adapting light is turned on or off, this reversal of causal relations is more apparent than real. The latency of neural responses depends in part on stimulus intensity—more intense stimuli elicit responses of shorter latency. The test flash is much less intense than the adapting light so that even though it is delivered earlier in time, the neural responses to it may occur after the responses to the adapting light. The dependence of latency on intensity is also the basis of the phenomenon of metacontrast: a bright annulus presented at some optimum interval (about 60–100 msec) after a dim flash presented in its center will mask the flash, which may then appear even dimmer or invisible (Alpern, 1953).

D. Temporal Factors

1. STIMULUS DURATION

There is a minimum amount of energy required, at any given level of adaptation, for an observer to detect reliably a light flash; if the flash duration is below some critical duration it does not matter how the energy is distributed in that time period. There is some time period over which the visual system can integrate light energy to reach threshold. Within that time, intensity (energy per unit time) and duration are reciprocally related; if the flash duration is halved, light intensity must be doubled, and so on (Bunsen-Roscoe, or Bloch's law). This critical duration varies with adaptation level; it is about 100 msec when the eye is fully dark-adapted (Graham & Margaria, 1935), and decreases with light-adaptation to some 30 msec at relatively high photopic levels of illumination (Graham & Kemp, 1938).

2. FLICKERING STIMULI

Related to the shortening of the critical duration at higher adaptation levels, is an improved ability to follow and resolve flickering lights. In the older experiments, light was interrupted by a rotating, sectored disk in order to produce a field which alternated between equal intervals of light and dark; Fig. 8A shows the change in light intensity over time for such a stimulus. At a given light intensity, the frequency of alternation was increased until the subject no longer detected flicker; that point defined the critical flicker frequency (CFF) for the particular stimulus conditions. The relationship between CFF and light intensity is shown in Fig. 9A; a small flickering light was presented at several retinal locations and CFF measured. The curves all show that CFF increases with light intensity up to some limit, the limiting frequency in this case depending on stimulus position; many other parameters, such as stimulus area, also affect CFF (Brown, 1965).

In Fig. 9A; the curves for stimuli outside the fovea exhibit two segments, which suggests that there is a shift at some level of light adaptation from one mechanism to another—presumably from rods to cones. This is confirmed by the results (Fig. 9B) of an experiment which measured CFF for a series of wavelengths whose intensities had been adjusted for equal effect on the photopic system. As expected, at high photopic adaptation levels the CFF's for all stimuli fall on the same curve; but at lower intensities, where vision is determined by the rods which are relatively more sensitive to shorter wavelengths, the CFF's follow different functions. In fact a scotopic spectral sensitivity function can be derived from the intensity at which fusion occurs for each wavelength at a given flicker rate. These results indicate that the rods cannot follow flicker beyond about 15 Hz, the limiting rate depend-

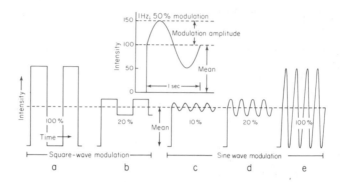

FIG. 8. Examples of stimuli whose intensity varies as a function of time. All the stimuli in a–e have the same average intensity over time, as shown by the dashed line. The curves in a and e represent the maximum possible variation (modulation) about this mean level (on each cycle the intensity falls to zero); b, c, and d show lesser degrees of modulation. In a and b the intensity varies as a square-wave while in c, d, and e it varies sinusoidally. The inset shows a stimulus modulated sinusoidally at 1 Hz; the amplitude of modulation is usually defined as half the peak-to-peak variation in intensity; a common description of such a stimulus is the ratio of modulation amplitude to the mean, which in the inset is 50%. The percentages in a–e are this ratio.

ing, as for the cones, on size and position of stimulus. The ability of the cones to follow much faster flicker provides a useful method for isolating their functions from those of rods.

3. MODULATION TRANSFER FUNCTION

The problem with the earlier measures of CFF is that they inextricably mix adaptation level and temporal resolution. At each intensity level only the limit of temporal resolution is measured but not the temporal capabilities at lower frequencies. Moreover, since the stimulus alternates between complete darkness and light (Fig. 8A), the mean level of light will increase as intensity is increased, thereby changing adaptation. A preferable method, in many ways, is to generate a flickering stimulus by superimposing equal increments and decrements in light on a steady background, as shown in Fig. 8B. In this situation the amplitude of modulation about the mean is usually reduced until the subject no longer detects flicker; this can be done using different flicker rates in order to determine temporal resolution at all frequencies. Since the mean light level does not change with frequency, adaptation remains constant; the effect of adaptation on temporal resolution can be investigated by repeating the experiment at various mean light levels. A common measure in these experiments is the ratio of half the peak-to-peak modulation to the mean, as shown in the inset to Fig. 8. For

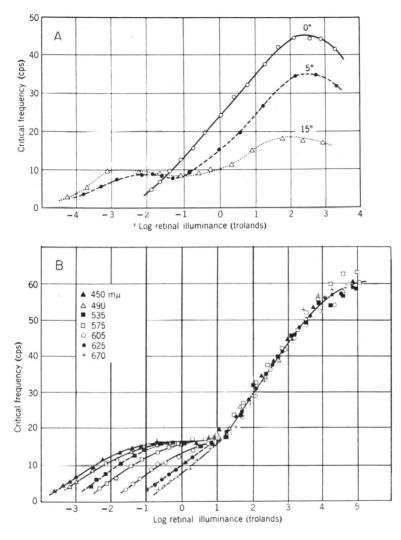

FIG. 9. Critical flicker frequency (CFF, i.e., maximum frequency at which flicker can be detected) as a function of stimulus intensity. A: Relation of CFF to retinal illuminance for a 2 degree field (white light) presented at each of the three retinal locations indicated. (From Hecht & Verrijp, 1933.) B: Relation of CFF to retinal illuminance for various monochromatic lights (19 degree field centrally fixated) equated for photopic luminosity. (From Hecht & Shlaer, 1936.)

a given mean light level, the limit of temporal resolution is reached when the required modulation equals the mean (100% modulation); the frequency at which this occurs for square-wave modulation is the same as the older CFF, provided all other conditions are the same.

In temporal modulation experiments square-wave stimuli can be used, but a more convenient approach is to use sinusoidal modulation (Fig. 8). Sine waves are a very simple form of temporal change; any repetitive stimulus can be completely constructed by summing a suitably chosen set of sine waves of different frequencies, amplitudes, and phases. The techniques for building up given distributions from sine-wave components, or, conversely, analyzing a given distribution into such components are based on Fourier's theorem (Cornsweet, 1970, provides an excellent introductory discussion).

The minimum sinusoidal modulation for detection of flicker can be measured at a series of frequencies and so define the visual system's sensitivity to each of these frequencies. The function relating sensitivity and frequency of a sinusoidally flickered stimulus is termed the modulation transfer function (MTF); apart from convenience, it has additional virtues provided the visual system can be considered "linear." For a system to be linear means, among other things, that if the input to the system is a sine wave then the output will be a sine wave of the same frequency. The output may only change in amplitude (and phase) depending on the system's sensitivity to that frequency; moreover the amplitude of the sine wave at output will always be the same even if the input is superimposed on some steady mean level. Any repetitive input (stimulus) can be analyzed into its component sine waves; if the system is linear, each of these components can be scaled according to the system's sensitivity (given by the MTF), and the scaled components summed to predict the system's output (response). If two different inputs give rise to the same output, once their components have been scaled and re-summed, these two stimuli will be indistinguishable.

But is linear system analysis applicable to the visual system? In Chap. 16 it was stated that the visual system is already nonlinear at its most peripheral stage (as seen in the late receptor potential). However, most nonlinear systems are approximately linear if we consider only small changes in response from resting level. In obtaining the MTF the subject is asked to report minimal changes in his response; provided the stimuli do not perturb the system too greatly (as is the case at threshold), it is irrelevant that the stimuli may vary greatly from the mean.

The temporal MTF has been measured for a wide variety of stimulus and adaptation conditions (De Lange, 1958; Kelly, 1961). A comprehensive set of functions, for a very large field, is plotted in two ways in Fig. 10, in which the intensities shown are the mean light levels; these range from scotopic to moderately high photopic levels. (Note that in the older work, as in Fig. 9, the intensity given is for the field during the fully illuminated portion of the cycle; this is twice the mean value.) The curves show that

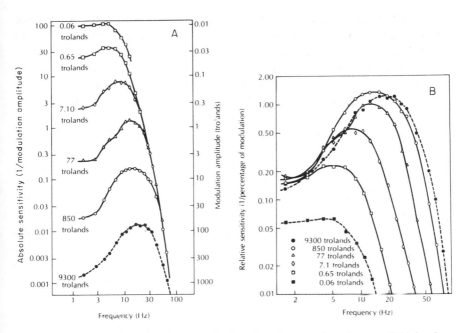

FIG. 10. Temporal modulation transfer function for a series of mean light levels. The modulation amplitude needed for perception of flicker was measured as a function of frequency at each mean level. A very large centrally fixated field was used. A: Absolute sensitivity; for each mean level the data points give the reciprocal of the modulation amplitude required for detection of flicker. B: The same data as in A replotted on a relative basis; for each mean level the points are the reciprocal of the ratio of modulation amplitude to the mean. (From Kelly, 1961.)

at any mean level the system is maximally sensitive to frequencies between 5 and 25 Hz. As mean level is increased, not only can higher frequencies be perceived (as in Fig. 9), but the region of maximal sensitivity shifts to higher frequencies. At high mean levels there is a reduction in sensitivity to low frequencies which becomes less marked at lower mean levels.

In Fig. 10A the ordinate is absolute sensitivity (reciprocal of difference between maximum and mean light levels) to a given amplitude of modulation regardless of mean level. When plotted this way, the curves all tend to coincide at high frequencies; this means that at any given high frequency some fixed amplitude of modulation (difference between maximum and mean light levels) is needed, irrespective of the mean level. This is a necessary property of linear systems; thus at high frequencies the visual system behaves linearly. However at low frequencies, changing the mean light level gives different functions. The same data are replotted in Fig. 10B as sensitivity in terms of percentage modulation; here sensitivity is the ratio of mean light level to modulation amplitude. In this case the curves coincide at low frequencies, meaning that at low frequencies the modulation must be some fixed proportion of the mean level for perception of flicker. It seems that there are two separate mechanisms which determine the visual system's temporal characteristics; the low-frequency system is nonlinear while the high-frequency mechanism is linear. These mechanisms are not to be interpreted as being the rods and cones since both temporal mechanisms operate at all adaptation levels from scotopic to photopic.

It has been observed that a field of given luminance appears brighter if it is flickered (Bartley, 1961). This brightness enhancement occurs at frequencies between 2 and 20 Hz; it is greatest between 10 and 20 Hz at high luminances but occurs at lower frequencies when stimulus luminance is decreased. These frequencies may appear brighter because the visual system is most sensitive to intermittent stimuli at some intermediate range of frequencies.

E. Spatial Factors

Up to this point we have ignored the fact that most stimuli are bounded in a specific way—they have contours. This section will consider the spatial aspects of vision implied by the existence of contours and edges. The first question is whether a structured visual field is necessary for normal visual functioning. This can be tested by looking for some time at a bright, featureless field (a "ganzfield") covering the whole of the field of view; this may be achieved by placing half a ping-pong ball over each eye and facing a well-lit blank wall. After a short while the phenomenon of "white-out" is experienced; this can best be described as a feeling that the eyes have stopped functioning and is accompanied by a sense of disorientation. It seems, then, that some structure to the visual field is necessary.

1. STABILIZED IMAGES

The eye is constantly in motion. Even when the eye is fixated on an object it has a residual oscillation (nystagmus) so that the images of contours in the field are not static on the retina. However, various optical methods are available for stabilizing an image on the retina so that the image moves with the eye and constantly stimulates the same retinal area (Ditchburn & Ginsborg, 1952; Riggs, Ratliff, Cornsweet, & Cornsweet, 1953; Yarbus, 1967). When this is done, the stabilized image very quickly fades and disappears, indicating that some small movement of the image on the retina is essential for vision to be maintained. However, even if the image is stabilized, it will not fade if it is flashed on and off repetitively; in this situation it is no longer static.

An after-image of a bright light is a common form of stabilized image and some aspects of it have been described in the section on dark-adapta-iton. Once an after-image has faded it can be restored either by blinking or by looking at a different background. This is analogous to flashing a stabilized image, except that when we blink the background is "turned off" rather than the stimulus; in either case there is a change in illumination. In general, any given area of retina needs a continuously changing stimulus in order to function.

Since the eye is constantly moving, retinal images will never be stabilized under ordinary circumstances. However, consider the situation when a large, uniform stimulus is viewed. Its edge is not stabilized but if the eye fixates, the center of the stimulus is effectively stabilized; if the stimulus is uniform, those retinal regions on which its center is imaged will always be uniformly stimulated. And yet the center of such a stimulus does not seem to fade or change its appearance. It seems as though retinal events occurring at the contour can determine the appearance of the entire en-closed area. This was elegantly demonstrated in an experiment in which the stimulus was a red circle surrounded by a broad green band; the inner contour between the red and green areas was stabilized on the retina, whereas the outer boundary was free to move over the retina when the eye moved. After a short viewing period the inner contour faded and at that point the entire stimulus was seen as a uniform green field (Krauskopf, 1963).

2. MODULATION TRANSFER FUNCTION

In discussing temporal factors it was shown that the visual system is most sensitive to intermediate temporal frequencies. Is there an analogous situation with respect to spatial resolution? As with temporal stimuli, a spatially varying stimulus can be analyzed into a set of spatial sine waves. Similarly one can obtain for a subject a spatial MTF. Sine wave gratings (i.e., light intensity varies sinusoidally across the grating, and frequency is expressed in cycles/degree of visual subtense) are the stimuli, and, as in the temporal case, the intensity is modulated about some mean level; for each spatial frequency the measure is the minimum contrast (i.e., ratio of modulation to mean, in similar fashion to the inset in Fig. 8) required for the subject to detect the presence of a grating as opposed to a uniform field.

Some spatial MTF's for a small centrally fixated test field are given in Fig. 11 and can be compared with the temporal functions in Fig. 10. As

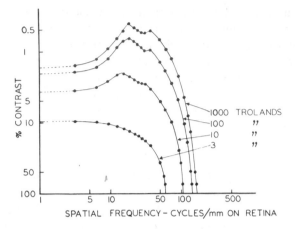

SPATIAL FREQUENCY – CYCLES/mm ON RETINA

Fig. 11. Spatial modulation transfer functions for sinusoidal gratings at different mean retinal illuminances. Test field was small and centrally fixated. Percent contrast is the ratio of half the peak-to-peak modulation to the mean. (From Patel, 1966.)

mean level of illumination is increased, finer gratings can be resolved. At higher light levels the eye is apparently less sensitive to low spatial frequencies, and operates best over an intermediate range between about 5 and 15 cycles/degree. At low light levels the low frequency "cut-off" may not be apparent; this is not necessarily related to a shift from cones to rods since the change in shape of the MTF is continuous and can be found at levels above the scotopic (Patel, 1966). Indeed the magnitude of the low frequency "cut-off" is very variable and depends, among other things, on the size of the test field; if there are fewer than four cycles of the grating across the field, thresholds are raised considerably (Campbell & Robson, 1968). Note that the finding of a low-frequency decline does not imply that large objects are less visible than somewhat smaller ones. Visibility depends on the sharpness of the contour or edge of an object and this does not usually depend on its size; all well-defined contours contain the preferred intermediate sine wave components.

At low temporal frequencies detection requires that modulation be some fixed proportion of the mean light level. But this is not true of spatial discrimination of high or low spatial frequencies, since the curves in Fig. 11 do not coincide. Nor do the curves coincide if they are replotted on the basis of absolute amplitudes; thus the mechanisms underlying spatial discrimination are not linear over any large range of mean levels.

The temporal MTF only measures the resolving capabilities of the neural network involved. However the spatial MTF depends not only on the neural mechanisms but also on the optical characteristics of the eye; the latter must ultimately limit high frequency resolution. The entire system cannot restore an image when it is too fine for the cornea and lens to project onto the retina, although, as described later, the neural system may "sharpen" contours imaged on the retina. A purely neural MTF has been obtained for sine wave gratings created directly at the retina by means of interference patterns (in which case the optics of the eye are bypassed and cannot degrade the retinal image); these MTF's differ very slightly from those already described indicating that the limit to spatial resolution is not optical (Campbell & Gubisch, 1966).

Finally, the concept of a spatial MTF should be related to the more common measures of acuity. Just as the CFF is only a measure of temporal resolution at its limit, so the traditional measures of acuity are the minimum line width, or bar size in a grating, which can be detected under given conditions. This is equivalent to the highest frequency sine wave detectable at 100% modulation under the same conditions. It is much more tedious to obtain a MTF rather than just measuring acuity, but the entire function does prescribe performance at all lower frequencies.

3. EDGE EFFECTS

The spatial MTF has been used quite successfully to analyze and predict various perceptual phenomena associated with edges, contours, and similar abrupt changes in contrast. Since any stimulus pattern can be analyzed into some set of sine wave components, the output of the visual system can be predicted by appropriately scaling the input components according to the MTF. If two different stimuli produce the same result when scaled according to the MTF, then these stimuli should be indistinguishable.

Figure 12 provides an interesting example of such a case. Two disks of black and white paper (Fig. 12A, and E) were rotated rapidly and photographed to give the stimuli in B and F, while parts C and G show the intensity distributions of these stimuli. If these intensity distributions are then appropriately analyzed and scaled by a spatial MTF similar to one of those in Fig. 11, the resulting outputs of the spatial system are given in parts D and H of Fig. 12. Both outputs are nearly the same and as predicted, the two stimuli appear very similar. The reasons for this can best be understood as follows: abrupt changes in stimulus intensity contain high frequency components while steady or slowly changing regions contain large low frequency components. The step stimulus (Fig. 12B) contains more low frequency components than the other (Fig. 12F); but the visual system attenuates low frequencies (see Fig. 11) so that the outputs of the system will be nearly the same in both cases. Thus the appearance of a stimulus depends to a large extent on its high frequency components—the

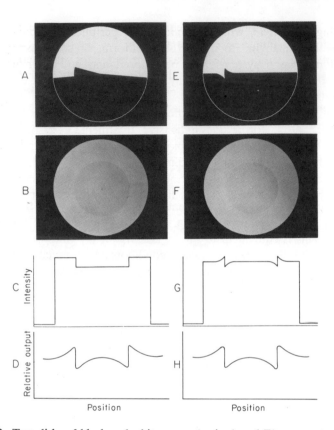

FIG. 12. Two disks of black and white paper (as in A and E) were rotated rapidly and photographed to give the stimuli in B and F. Parts C and G show the distribution of light intensity measured across B and F. If these intensity distributions are scaled according to a spatial modulation transfer function for the visual system, the outputs of the system will be as shown in D and H. (From Cornsweet, 1970.)

major effects occur at edges or boundaries and do not depend so much on steady levels. This can be demonstrated quite nicely by bending a wire or cutting out a paper ring which just covers the inner boundary in Fig. 12F; the inner circle will no longer appear darker.

Although the spatial MTF can be used to predict perceptual similarities, it cannot necessarily be used to predict the appearance of a stimulus. For example, it is tempting to assume that the output functions in Fig. 12D and H not only predict the similarity of the stimuli but also the apparent brightness across each figure. And yet this is clearly not the case, since the inner circle of each stimulus appears relatively uniform and neither has the appearance of the output functions. The reasons for this are not entirely clear. Even though the MTF may represent the basic limitations of the system which determines spatial resolution, there may be other, possibly higher centers, which reevaluate the peripheral outputs; enclosed areas may be "filled in" to make them uniform, or some aspects of the output of peripheral systems may be ignored and not contribute to appearance. In addition part of this may be due to differences in psychophysical methods (Cornsweet, 1970).

Some of the best studied edge effects are those known as Mach bands (see Ratliff, 1965, for a comprehensive treatment). A stimulus which consists of a dark field shading rapidly to a light field appears to have a band of enhanced brightness immediately at the edge of the light area and a similar dark band at the edge of the dark area. The apparent brightness of these bands can be measured by having the subject adjust the intensity of a comparison field to match the intensity at succeeding points across the stimulus. Data of this sort are shown in Fig. 13A in which the dashed

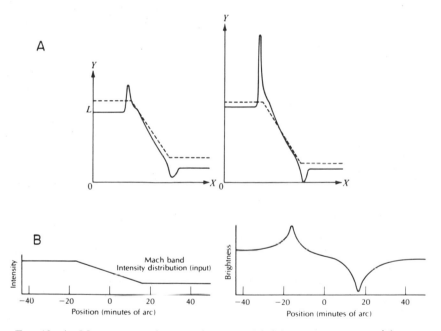

FIG. 13. A: Measurements by two observers of brightness across a spatial pattern whose luminance distribution is indicated by the dashed lines. The measurements (solid curves) were made by adjusting the luminance of a separate field to match the appearance of each point across the pattern. Luminance is plotted on the ordinate and spatial position along the abscissa. The accentuations of brightness and darkness perceived at the intensity changes in the stimulus are known as Mach bands. (From Fiorentini & Radici, 1957.) B: A luminance distribution, similar to that used in A to produce Mach bands, is shown on the left. If this distribution is appropriately scaled according to the spatial modulation transfer function its predicted appearance is shown on the right. (From Davidson, 1966, cited in Cornsweet, 1970.)

lines are the intensity across the stimulus while the solid curves are the luminances required to match the appearance of each point across the pattern. The changes in the stimulus appear greatly accentuated. The intensity distribution of the Mach band figure can be scaled by the MTF in similar fashion to the stimuli discussed earlier; the results are shown in Fig. 13B. In this case the output of the system does correspond in its qualitative features to the appearance of the stimulus. That is, the limitations imposed by the MTF do predict the appearance of Mach bands for this stimulus. But note that a step stimulus should also show Mach bands (see Fig. 12C and D); however most observers do not see them at such sharp boundaries.

Related to the above edge effects are the variations in threshold for detecting a small spot flashed in different positions across either a step or a Mach band stimulus. Even though these stimuli appear different (Mach bands are usually not seen in the former), the increment threshold functions are similar. There is a sharp elevation in threshold at the edge of the bright part of the field, but no corresponding drop in threshold on the dark edge; the magnitude of the threshold elevation increases as the change from light to dark in the stimulus pattern become sharper (Fig. 14). These changes in threshold appear analogous to the elevation of thresholds at temporal transients in a stimulus (see Fig. 7). Indeed some of the mechanisms involved may be the same; since the eye is never stationary, a sharp edge in a stimulus becomes a temporal transient on any given area of retina. There is support for this idea from an experiment (Teller, 1968) in which threshold was first measured for a small test flash on a large illuminated background and then on a narrow black bar, across the background. Threshold was elevated when measured on a narrow black bar, but this increase in threshold became less marked as the bar was widened; close to a spatial transient (the bar) threshold went up. However when the stimuli were stabilized on the retina, threshold measured on a narrow bar was no higher than on the full background and dropped as bar width increased. In the stabilized image the bar could not move across the retina creating temporal transients at the point where threshold was being measured.

4. AREA EFFECTS

In the discussion of adaptation it was noted that an adapting background affects thresholds even in retinal areas away from the background. More basically, the visual system can sum stimulus energy over a considerable area in order to reach threshold. Just as there is some critical duration within which stimulus luminance can be integrated, so there is a maximum

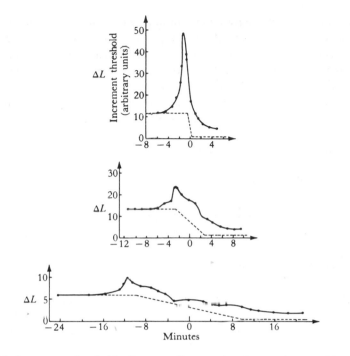

Fɪɢ. 14. Increment thresholds for a small spot placed at various positions across stimuli whose luminance distributions are given by the dashed lines. The abscissae are in minutes of visual angle. (From Fiorentini, Jeanne, & Toraldo di Francia, 1955.)

area over which complete summation can occur. This area, for which the product of area and luminance is a constant (Ricco's law), is small; as area is increased further, there is partial summation and at very large areas, where threshold luminance is independent of area, no additional summation of area takes place (Brown & Mueller, 1965). All these area measurements are complicated by the inhomogeneity of the retina; the numbers of the various neurons, especially the receptors, vary drastically across the retina (see Chap. 16).

Only the briefest mention can be made of the voluminous topics of brightness and color contrast (see Jameson and Hurvich [1964] and Hurvich and Jameson [1966] for more extensive discussions). The appearance of a stimulus depends strongly on the surrounding areas. Thus a gray circle on a black field appears brighter than the same circle on a white field. Similarly, in color contrast, a gray circle on a blue field appears slightly colored with the complementary hue, yellow. These contrast or induction phenomena are not simply the result of "interpretation" by some higher center of the retinal message. A retinal area in which a contrast color is induced responds in some circumstances as if it were illuminated by that color; for example, in color matches contrast colors sum with real light. The various inductions can also become very complicated; a neutral area, which by contrast acquires some hue, may in turn induce a complementary hue in an area adjacent to it, and so on. The Land (e.g., 1959) color demonstrations provide very striking examples of such complex interactions over highly structured fields.

Because contrast phenomena seem to result from the influence of relatively large areas and the effects extend over entire areas it might be thought that they are not closely related to edge effects; for instance, changes in thresholds or Mach bands are limited to the boundary regions. However it is clear that events at an edge can influence the appearance of areas at considerable distances from the edge. The luminance of the entire stimulus in Fig. 12F is the same except for the narrow zone delimiting the inner circle, and yet the inner circle appears uniformly darker than the surround. Similarly in the discussion of stabilized images it was pointed out that once a stabilized interior contour of a figure fades the appearance of the entire figure is determined by the unstabilized contours (Krauskopf, 1963). Contrast and edge phenomena must to some extent be due to common underlying mechanisms.

II. PHYSIOLOGICAL CORRELATES

The anatomy and physiological functioning of the various parts of the visual system are described in some detail in Chap. 16. The first part of this chapter contains a discussion of some of the basic psychophysical facts of vision, presented where possible in a way which allows the reader to relate the findings of these two approaches. The rest of this chapter is devoted to a more detailed discussion of how physiological mechanisms might determine psychophysical observations. Only a few aspects of vision will be dealt with here, more by way of example of the approach than in an attempt to cover the topic exhaustively. The discussion will be limited largely to the areas of color and edge effects; a large body of physiological data is now available from situations which can readily be related to these topics.

A. Color Vision

1. SPECTRALLY OPPONENT AND NONOPPONENT CELLS

Much of the data in this section will be from the macaque monkey, since a wide range of psychophysical tests have shown that this species has color vision essentially identical to that of man (De Valois, 1965; De Valois & Jacobs, 1968). The macaque's cone photopigments were specified in the previous chapter (Fig. 3 in Chap. 16); it was also noted that responses of retinal ganglion cells and cells in the lateral geniculate nucleus (LGN) could be classified as spectrally opponent and nonopponent (Fig. 12 in Chap. 16).

Two types of spectrally nonopponent cells (either inhibited or excited by all wavelengths) and four types of opponent cells have been identified in the macaque LGN (De Valois, Abramov, & Jacobs, 1966). Figure 15 shows the mean response functions for the four opponent types to monochromatic lights equated for energy (not luminance); the four types are

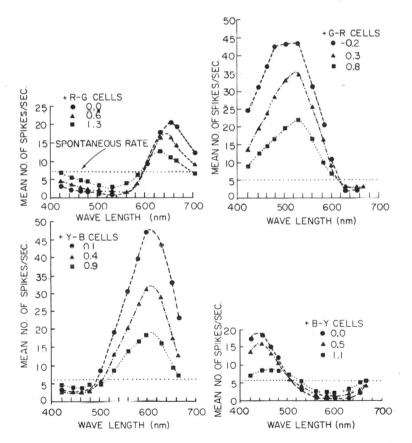

FIG. 15. Mean responses of the four types of spectrally opponent cells in the lateral geniculate nucleus of the macaque monkey. Stimuli are equated for energy. In each case the three curves are for different energy levels: the symbols indicate the log attenuation relative to maximum light available. Dotted horizontal lines show mean firing rate in the absence of stimulation. (Redrawn from De Valois *et al.*, 1966.)

+R—G (red-excitatory and green-inhibitory), +G—R, +Y—B, and +B—Y, the names referring to the spectral loci of maximal excitatory or inhibitory responses.

By the nature of their responses, opponent cells must be associated with at least two photopigments, and the different cell types presumably reflect various ways of linking the inputs from different cone types. The usual method of identifying the inputs is adaptation by chromatic backgrounds chosen to desensitize one or more of the possible inputs and then examination of the remaining spectral responses; this is in principle the same method used in photopigment measurements and in psychophysical experiments described earlier. The results, from these and similar experiments (Abramov, 1973; De Valois, 1965), are summarized in Fig. 16. All cell types

RECEPTOR   CONNECTIONS

i) Opponent Cells

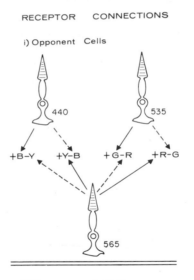

ii) Non-opponent Cells

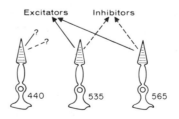

FIG. 16. The functional connections between the three cone types and the various types of spectrally opponent and nonopponent cells in the macaque monkey. The numbers next to each representation of a cone denote its spectral locus of maximal light absorption. Solid lines indicate excitatory inputs and dashed lines indicate inhibitory inputs.

receive an input (excitatory or inhibitory, depending on type) from the 565 nm cones so that, for example, the +R and +Y portions of +R—G and +Y—B cells are due to the same input; however the short wavelength input to +R—G and +G—R cells is from the 535 nm cones while the +Y—B and +B—Y cells have an input from 440 nm cones; nonopponent cells probably receive inputs from all three cone types. Thus the opponent cells are generally dichromatic, although there are indications that the scheme in Fig. 16 is over-simplified; cells with inputs from the 440 and 565 nm cones may also have an input from the remaining cone type (Abramov & Levine, 1973). The responses discussed here are to diffuse illumination, so that spatial organization of the receptive fields is ignored; for example, a nonopponent excitatory cell may also have inhibitory inputs from some regions (Wiesel & Hubel, 1966), but the net result appears purely excitatory.

Since spectrally opponent cells signal a difference between inputs of different spectral sensitivity they could form the basis for wavelength discrimination; nonopponent cells, however, could only signal color if they had different spectral sensitivities and their responses were compared at some higher stage of processing (see earlier discussion of color). It might be argued, therefore, that spectrally opponent cells constitute a color channel while nonopponent cells encode intensity or luminance.

2. Luminosity

Spectrally nonopponent cells probably do not signal color since all wavelengths can be adjusted in intensity so as to elicit the same response; nor does there seem to be a wide variety of nonopponent cells. But this by itself is not enough; if they are to constitute the luminosity channel, their spectral sensitivity function should fit the luminosity function of the given species. The psychophysical determination of photopic and scotopic luminosity functions has been described; physiologically, spectral sensitivity is usually defined as the reciprocal of the energy required for a criterion response (number of spikes) at any wavelength. Fig. 17A compares the photopic spectral sensitivity of nonopponent cells in the macaque LGN with macaque and human photopic luminosity functions; the behavioral functions were obtained using rapidly flickering monochromatic stimuli (thereby avoiding rod contributions) and measuring energy required to detect the flicker. Similar experiments with squirrel monkeys have shown that the relative spectral sensitivities of both inhibitory and excitatory nonopponent LGN cells agree very closely with the animal's psychophysical photopic functions (Fig. 17B); this species is protanomalous and less sensitive to long wavelengths than macaque or man.

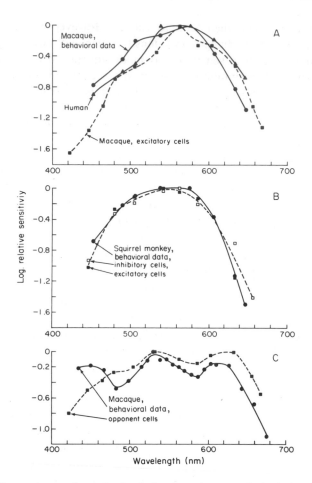

FIG. 17. Comparisons of psychophysical measurements of photopic spectral sensitivity with the spectral functions of various cells in the lateral geniculate nucleus. A: Behavioral data from humans and macaque compared with spectrally nonopponent excitatory cells in the macaque monkey. B: Similar functions obtained from squirrel monkeys. C: Psychophysical function obtained under conditions of high light adaptation. This function is compared with the sensitivity of the entire class of spectrally opponent cells in the macaque. (A and B redrawn from De Valois and Jacobs [1968] and Jacobs [1964]. Behavioral data in C are the average of data given by Sperling, Sidley, Dockens, and Jolliffe [1968], physiological data from De Valois et al. [1966]. Entire figure from Abramov [1973].)

The hypothesis that nonopponent cells subserve luminosity can be pursued further. Opponent cells respond well to changes in intensity only in some regions of the spectrum (see Fig. 15); and if the stimulus is white light they may respond only slightly since white light activates both antagonistic inputs which then tend to cancel. However nonopponent cells are highly sensitive to changes in intensity, even with white light. These cells also maintain their sensitivity to moderate intensity changes over a very large range of adaptation levels. In the section on adaptation it was stated that at any given adaptation level there is only a limited range of intensities over which brightness changes markedly. The responses of spectrally nonopponent LGN cells in the squirrel monkey have been measured for a range of intensities about various levels of adapting background (Jacobs, 1965). At each background intensity there was only a limited range over which response increased with flash intensity; beyond that range the system "saturated" and all further increments elicited similar responses. But if the retina was adapted to some higher background intensity, stimuli which previously "saturated" the system now elicited different responses according to their intensity. As the system adapts to some new level its sensitivity is apparently reset; this allows it to continue functioning over a wide range of light levels even though at any given level its dynamic range is limited.

The macaque photopic function has also been obtained from measurements of thresholds of monochromatic lights superimposed on an intense, white adapting field. This function (Fig. 17C) is markedly different from other photopic functions (see Figs. 3B and 17A) and is not at all similar to that of the nonopponent cells; thus nonopponent cells may not be the sole luminosity channel. In some circumstances opponent cells may also contribute; the function in Fig. 17C is similar to the spectral sensitivity of a system derived from all the opponent cells. This physiological system was obtained by summing arithmetically the responses of the opponent cells, weighted according to the frequency of occurrence of each type.

In the psychophysical section on sensitivity it was pointed out that individual rods and cones function over similar ranges of light intensity. However, under light-adapted conditions there is relatively little evidence of rod activity and vice versa under dark-adapted conditions. Similarly cells receiving rod and cone inputs appear to be driven only by the cones if the stimuli are intense enough, or the retina is light-adapted. The reasons for this depend on the observations that the more strongly activated system responds with the shorter latency. Responses of individual rods are in general slower than those of cones (see Fig. 9A, B in Chap. 16) but the rod system as a whole can be overwhelmingly favored by certain stimulus conditions, such as a large, dim stimulus presented to a dark-adapted eye. If the rod system is activated more strongly than the cone system its responses will reach the ganglion cells ahead of responses from the cone system, and vice versa. It appears, further, that whichever messages arrive first at the ganglion cells, preempt the channels and actively prevent the responses of the other receptors from passing along the optic nerve (Gouras & Link, 1966). Under conditions of dark-adaptation, and with very dim stimuli, many nonopponent cells have spectral sensitivities which fit the scotopic (rod) luminosity function, and some opponent cells also change from cone to rod inputs during dark-adaptation (Wiesel & Hubel, 1966).

3. HUE AND WAVELENGTH DISCRIMINATION

The relation of hue to wavelength of light was described earlier (see Fig. 4A). If the spectrally opponent cells subserve color and the four types described (Fig. 15) represent functional divisions, there should be some correspondence between their responses and hue, as indexed, for example, by color naming. Since the opponent cell types are each maximally responsive to different spectral regions, a simple approach would be to assume that hue is signalled by the response magnitudes of the various cell types. For example, a given stimulus would appear red if it elicited more spikes from +R—G cells than from any of the others.

More specifically the frequency distributions of color names can be compared with the relative contributions of each of the spectrally opponent cell types to the total activity in the opponent (color) system. This was done in the following way (De Valois *et al.,* 1966): because +R—G are associated with the same cone types and appear to be "mirror images" of each other, it was assumed that excitation in one signifies the same as inhibition in the other; similar considerations were applied to +Y—B and +B—Y cells. The changes in response rate from spontaneous were therefore summed for +R and —R, +Y and —Y, +G and —G, +B and —B components; each sum was then expressed as percentage of the total of all four sums obtained for each stimulus. The results are given in Fig. 18A, while Fig. 18B reproduces the color naming functions from Fig. 4A. The resemblance between the two parts of the figure is very marked. For example, at these low photopic intensities wavelengths greater than about 620 nm usually appear red (but occasionally somewhat yellow as well); in this region the +R and —R component contributes increasingly to the total response from the opponent cells, and so on.

Although this description of color mechanisms is derived directly from physiological data, a very similar set of mechanisms had been predicted in the last century by Hering and other psychophysicists working in his tradition (see Hering, 1964). They had postulated that color vision depends on pairs of red-green and yellow-blue opponent processes and it was the relative balance between them which determined hue. The opponent-pairs theorists were opposed by other psychophysicists (von Helmholtz, 1962) who relied more heavily on the trichromatic nature of vision and thought

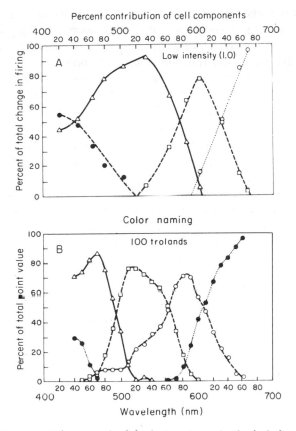

Percent contribution of cell components

Color naming

Wavelength (nm)

Fig. 18. Hue. comparison of physiological and psychophysical data. A: Relative contributions of each of the four components underlying the responses of opponent cells in the lateral geniculate nucleus of the macaque monkey. From right to left the curves are respectively for +R and −R, +Y and −Y, +G and −G, +B and −B. See text for derivation of the components and method of computation. (From De Valois et al., 1966.) B: Color naming as a function of wavelength. From right to left the curves are respectively for the categories "red," "yellow," "green," and "blue." See text for further details. (Replotted from Boynton & Gordon, 1965.)

that hue depended upon comparing the relative amounts of response of each primary system. Of course, the two approaches are not necessarily incompatible and indeed both now seem correct: there are only three cone types but these are linked to give two sets of red-green and yellow-blue opponent systems. (See Hurvich and Jameson [1957] for a good summary of a modern psychophysical opponent-processes theory.)

It is a common misconception to think of the different cone types as color receptors. The so called "red" cones (565 nm pigment) absorb light across the entire spectrum (Fig. 3B in Chap. 16), and all cell types appear to have an input from these cones. Thus it cannot be that we see red whenever the 565 nm cones are stimulated. Rather, the percept of red is determined by the relative responses of opponent cell types.

The change in hue of different spectral lights can also be studied by measuring the ability to discriminate changes in wavelength. Figure 4B gave the wavelength discrimination functions from humans and macaques. Similar procedures have been used in experiments on single cells in the macaque LGN (De Valois, Abramov, & Mead, 1967). Standard wavelengths were chosen across the spectrum; each one was then alternated with a comparison stimulus of slightly different wavelength and the magnitude of the difference for a criterion change in spike rate obtained. As in the psychophysical experiments, all the stimuli were equated for photopic luminosity; the stimuli were therefore equated for ability to stimulate the nonopponent cells so that they could not respond to the shifts in stimulus wavelength. The opponent cells, however, readily detected even small changes in wavelength, as shown in Fig. 19A. The different cell types were not equally sensitive throughout the spectrum; $+R-G$ and $+G-R$ cells discriminated best around 590 nm (which is the region where their responses changes from excitation to inhibition) while the other types were better in the shorter wavelengths. Assuming that in any situation discrimination is determined by whichever cell type is the most sensitive to the given wavelength differences, a wavelength discrimination function can be obtained by superimposing the functions from the four cell types and taking their lower bound; this function is shown in Fig. 19B, together with the macaque psychophysical function from Fig. 4B, and their similarity is evident.

The preceding comparisons dealt with situations in which spatial parameters were not specifically involved; some of these aspects, such as edges and contours, are dealt with later. As far as color is concerned there is the phenomenon of simultaneous color contrast in which a colored region of a stimulus induces the complementary hue in a neighboring region; a red circle appears redder still if it is surrounded by green, and so on.

There is good evidence that color contrast is encoded before the signals from the two eyes meet (De Valois & Walraven, 1967; Land & Daw, 1962). Since color contrast appears even in the absence of luminance differences, the cells involved are probably spectrally opponent. The receptive fields of goldfish ganglion cells (see Fig. 13B in Chap. 16) are organized in a manner consistent with the phenomena of simultaneous color contrast. The unit described in that figure had a green-"on" center but a red-"on" surround, and neither a green circle in the center nor a red annulus on the surround gave as much "on" response as the two together. However,

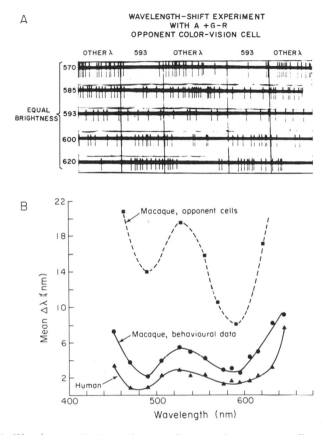

FIG. 19. Wavelength discrimination. A: Records from a spectrally opponent cell (+G−R) in the lateral geniculate nucleus of the macaque monkey. Stimulus wavelength alternates between 593 nm and the wavelength indicated at the left of each record. Stimuli are all equated on the basis of the macaque photopic luminosity curve. (From De Valois, 1965.) B: Psychophysical determinations of wavelength discrimination by humans and macaques are shown as the solid curves. (Redrawn from De Valois and Jacobs, 1968.) The dashed curve is obtained from all types of spectrally opponent cells in the lateral geniculate nucleus. (Redrawn from De Valois et al., 1967.)

the receptive fields of spectrally opponent ganglion or LGN cells in primates have simple receptive fields not unlike those in the cat retina, with the difference that the excitatory and inhibitory inputs also have different spectral sensitivities. Cells of this sort cannot by themselves encode simultaneous color contrast but units like the goldfish retinal cells are found in area 17 of the cortex of the macaque (Hubel & Wiesel, 1968).

B. Edges and Contours

1. LATERAL INHIBITION

There are reciprocal antagonisms between elements in the retina and such antagonisms are probably the basis of the psychophysical edge accentuation effects considered earlier. The first and perhaps the clearest demonstration of these interactions comes from the work on the horseshoe crab *Limulus* Hartline, 1949, 1969). The *Limulus* studies (reviewed by Hartline & Ratliff, 1972; Ratliff, 1965) will be considered in detail before the related work on the vertebrate retina is described.

Limulus has a compound eye which is divided into ommatidia, or receptors, which can be stimulated separately; each ommatidium has one optic nerve fiber leading off from it. There is also a lateral plexus of neural elements which interconnects the optic nerve fibers and enables each receptor to affect its neighbors. Stimulation by light excites a receptor, generating spikes in its optic nerve fiber; the rate of firing increases monotonically with increasing light intensity and, as with vertebrates, the relationship is nonlinear. But this is not the only effect of stimulating a receptor; each receptor can also inhibit its neighbors through the lateral plexus. The inhibitory effect is a mutual one and the degree of inhibition is linearly related to the rate of firing of the inhibiting fibers. For example, if two fibers are stimulated individually each will respond at a certain rate; but if they are stimulated simultaneously each will fire at a lower rate since they will both be inhibiting one another (Fig. 20). The amount of inhibitory interaction between any pair of ommatidia is, for the most part, a decreasing function of the distance between them—the further apart, the less the inhibitory interaction.

The output of the *Limulus* eye, when stimulated by a step change in intensity (edge), can be predicted from the above considerations. All receptors on the lighter side will be excited equally; on the darker side all receptors will also be equally excited but to a lesser degree. A receptor in the middle of the lighter side will be strongly inhibited by its neighbors on all sides. But a receptor in the lighter side near the edge will receive less total inhibition, since its neighbors on the darker side are less strongly excited and thus exert less of an inhibitory influence on it. Thus firing rate should increase as the border is approached on the lighter side of the stimulus. Similar arguments hold in reverse on the darker side. There is more inhibition from the lighter side of the stimulus on receptors close to the border but in the darker side; thus their firing rate is less than that of receptors in the middle of the darker side.

In practice it is very difficult to record simultaneously from several recep-

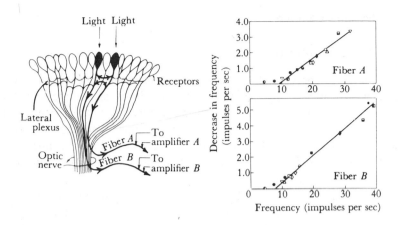

FIG. 20. Lateral inhibition in the eye of *Limulus*. Spikes were recorded simultaneously from the optic nerve fibers of two receptors, as shown on the left. Each receptor was either stimulated alone or together with the other. The graphs on the right plot the inhibitory effect of one receptor unit on the other; the ordinate gives the decrease in a given fiber's responses as a function of the rate of response in the other when both are stimulated together. For example, in the upper graph, fiber A fires about 3 spikes per second fewer when fiber B is firing at a rate of about 30 spikes per second. (From Hartline & Ratliff, 1957.)

tors spaced across the stimulus. Instead, responses from a single receptor can be recorded and the stimulus moved to different positions on the eye with respect to it. When this is done, firing rate increases as the receptor is stimulated by the areas near the edge on the lighter side of the stimulus, and decreases near the border on the darker side of the edge. The receptor's output, as a function of stimulus position, looks remarkably like the brightness distribution seen in Mach bands (Fig. 21). If all of the ommatidia, except the one being recorded, are covered up and the same stimulus moved across the eye, a different result is obtained. The firing rate increases since lateral inhibitory effects have been eliminated; more importantly, there is no longer any edge accentuation in the output of the receptor (Fig. 21).

2. EDGE EFFECTS

The above findings demonstrate that lateral inhibitory interactions can provide a mechanism for edge accentuation and related phenomena. These mechanisms in *Limulus* are very similar to those postulated in the last century by Mach (in Ratliff, 1965) and Hering (1964) to account for the appearance of Mach bands and it is probable that vertebrate eyes have similar lateral inhibitory systems.

The receptive fields of vertebrate retinal ganglion cells have concentric

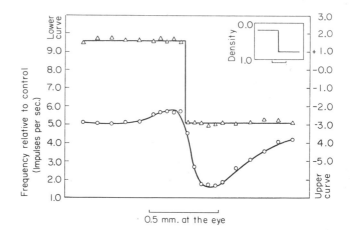

FIG. 21. Response of a single optic nerve fiber in *Limulus* to a step pattern of illumination (inset); the pattern was successively exposed so that its light-dark border fell at different positions on the eye. If all receptors were occluded, except the one whose fiber was being observed, the responses were as shown in the upper curve; the left portion of the curve shows the responses when the light side of the stimulus fell on the given receptor, and the right portion shows responses to the darker side. The lower curve shows the responses under the same conditions but with all receptors exposed. The differences between the curves are due to lateral inhibitory interactions which take place when more than one receptor is stimulated. Both ordinates have arbitrary zero points; they have been adjusted so that when a single receptor is stimulated the response rates are higher than when a group is stimulated. (From Ratliff & Hartline, 1959.)

excitatory and inhibitory areas (see Fig. 11 in Chap. 16), and it is possible to relate this antagonistic arrangement to the high sensitivity of these cells to edges (Kuffler, 1953). The first experiments which clearly demonstrated the accentuation of edges by vertebrate ganglion cells were all performed on the cat (Baumgartner, 1961; Enroth-Cugell & Robson, 1966; Rodieck & Stone, 1965). In one of these experiments, the border between a lighter and a darker area was flashed in various positions on the receptive fields of a single ganglion cell. On-center cells showed an increase in firing when the cell's receptive-field center was near the edge in the lighter side of the stimulus, and a decrease in firing when the cell's receptive field center was in the darker part of the field near the edge (Fig. 22). These findings can be explained in the same way as discussed above for *Limulus:* the excitatory center of the receptive field is analogous to just one ommatidium, and the inhibitory surround to the neighboring ommatidia. The same results have been obtained from frog ganglion cells; furthermore, if only the center of the field (similar to a single *Limulus* ommatidium) is stimulated, no edge accentuation is found (Gordon, 1973).

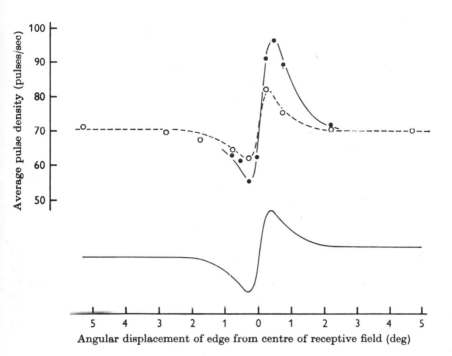

FIG. 22. Responses of a single ganglion cell in the cat to a step pattern of illumination; the border was presented at different positions on the cell's receptive field. Two different luminance steps were used; responses to the step with the larger difference are shown as filled circles while the responses to the smaller difference are the open circles; mean luminance was the same in both cases. If the step stimulus is appropriately scaled according to the spatial modulation transfer function of this cell, the predicted output of the cell is shown as the lower curve. (From Enroth-Cugell & Robson, 1966.)

In Section 1 of this chapter we described how the spatial modulation transfer function of the visual system is measured psychophysically. Similarly, it is possible to measure the spatial MTF of a retinal ganglion cell by stimulating the cell with sinusoidal gratings and measuring the contrast necessary for a criterion response (Enroth-Cugell & Robson, 1966). A luminance step can be analyzed into its sinusoidal components, scaled according to the MTF, and the result used to predict the output of the ganglion cell to stimulation by that simulus. As shown in Fig. 22, the predicted output and actual output agree very closely, both functions accentuating the edge.

The more complex aspects of edges and contours associated with form perception are probably analyzed at the cortical level. In the visual cortex cells receive inputs from several ganglion cells (via the lateral geniculate nucleus) and are most sensitive to edges or contours in specific orientations and of specific lengths and widths. These cells, together with a model of their connections, were described in detail in Chap. 16.

References

Abramov, I. Physiology of the visual system: Mechanisms of colour vision. In A. Cole (Ed.), *Theoretical and experimental biophysics*. Vol. 3. New York: Dekker, 1973.

Abramov, I., & M. W. Levine. A model of the responses of LGN cells to monochromatic stimuli. 1973, in preparation.

Aguilar, M., & Stiles, W. S. Saturation of the rod mechanism of the retina at high levels of stimulation. *Optica Acta*, 1954, **1**, 59–65.

Alpern, M. Metacontrast. *Journal of The Optical Society of America*, 1953, **43**, 648–657.

Alpern, M., & Campbell, F. W. The spectral sensitivity of the consensual light reflex. *Journal of Physiology (London)*, 1962, **164**, 478–507.

Arden, G. B., & Weale, R. A. Nervous mechanisms and dark-adaptation. *Journal of Physiology (London)*, 1954, **125**, 417–426.

Baker, H. Initial stages of dark and light adaptation. *Journal of The Optical Society of America*, 1963, **53**, 98–103.

Barlow, H. B. Optic nerve impulses and Weber's law. *Cold Spring Harbor Symposia on Quantitative Biology*, 1965, **30**, 539–546.

Barlow, H. B., & Sparrock, J. M. B. The role of after-images in dark adaptation. *Science*, 1964, **144**, 1309–1314.

Bartlett, N. R. Dark adaptation and light adaptation. In C. H. Graham (Ed.), *Vision and visual perception*. New York: Wiley, 1965, Pp. 185–207.

Bartley, S. H. A clarification of some of the procedures and concepts involved in dealing with the optic pathway. In R. Jung & H. Kornhuber (Eds.), *The visual system: Neurophysiology and psychophysics*. Berlin and New York: Springer-Verlag, 1961. Pp. 386–400.

Baumgartner, G. Kontrastlichteffekte an retinalen ganglienzellen: Ableitungen vom Tractus opticus der Katze. In R. Jung & H. Kornhuber (Eds.), *The visual system: Neurophysiology and psychophysics*. Berlin and New York: Springer-Verlag, 1961. Pp. 45–53.

Blackwell, H. R., & Blackwell, O. M. Rod and cone receptor mechanisms in typical and atypical congenital achromatopsia. *Vision Research*, 1961, **1**, 62–107.

Blakemore, C. B., & Rushton, W. A. H. Dark adaptation and increment threshold in a rod monochromat. *Journal of Physiology (London)*, 1965, **181**, 612–628.

Blough, D. S. Spectral sensitivity in the pigeon. *Journal of The Optical Society of America*, 1957, **47**, 827–833.

Boynton, R. M., & Gordon, J. Bezold-Brücke hue shift measured by color-naming technique. *Journal of The Optical Society of America*, 1965, **55**, 78–86.

Brindley, G. S. The effects on colour vision of adaptation to very bright lights. *Journal of Physiology (London)*, 1953, **122**, 332–350.

Brindley, G. S. *Physiology of the retina and the visual pathway*. London: Arnold, 1960.

Brown, J. L. Flicker and intermittent stimulation. In C. H. Graham (Ed.), *Vision and visual perception*. New York: Wiley, 1965. Pp. 251–320.

Brown, J. L., & Mueller, C. G. Brightness discrimination and brightness contrast. In C. H. Graham (Ed.), *Vision and visual perception.* New York: Wiley, 1965. Pp. 208–250.

Campbell, F. W., & Gubisch, R. W. Optical quality of the human eye. *Journal of Physiology (London)*, 1966, **186**, 558–578.

Campbell, F. W., & Robson, J. G. Application of Fourier analysis to the visibility of gratings. *Journal of Physiology (London)*, 1968, **197**, 551–566.

Cornsweet, T. N. *Visual perception.* New York: Academic Press, 1970.

Craik, K. J. W., & Vernon, M. D. The nature of dark adaptation. Part I. Evidence as to the locus of the process. *British Journal of Psychology*, 1941, **32**, 62–81.

Crawford, B. H. Visual adaptation in relation to brief conditioning stimuli. *Proceedings of The Royal Society, Series B,* 1947, **134**, 283–302.

De Lange, H. Research into the dynamic nature of the human fovea-cortex systems with intermittent and modulated light. I. Attenuation characteristics with white and colored light. *Journal of The Optical Society of America,* 1958, **48**, 777–784.

De Valois, R. L. Analysis and coding of color vision in the primate visual system. *Cold Spring Harbor Symposia on Quantitative Biology,* 1965, **30**, 567–579.

De Valois, R. L., Abramov, I., & Jacobs, G. H. Analysis of response patterns of LGN cells. *Journal of the Optical Society of America,* 1966, **56**, 966–977.

De Valois, R. L., Abramov, I., & Mead, W. R. Single cell analysis of wavelength discrimination at the lateral geniculate nucleus in the macaque. *Journal of Neurophysiology,* 1967, **30**, 415–433.

De Valois, R. L., & Jacobs, G. H. Primate color vision. *Science,* 1968, **162**, 533–540.

De Valois, R. L., & Walraven, J. Monocular and binocular aftereffects of chromatic adaptation. *Science,* 1967, **155**, 463 465.

Ditchburn, R. W., & Ginsborg, B. L. Vision with a stabilized retinal image. *Nature (London)*, 1952, **170**, 36–37.

Dowling, J. E. Neural and photochemical mechanisms of visual adaptation in the rat. *Journal of General Physiology,* 1963, **46**, 1287–1301.

Du Croz, J. J., & Rushton, W. A. H. The separation of cone mechanisms in dark adaptation. *Journal of Physiology (London)*, 1966, **183**, 481–496.

Enroth-Cugell, C., & Robson, J. G. The contrast sensitivity of the retinal ganglion cells of the cat. *Journal of Physiology (London)*, 1966, **187**, 517–552.

Fiorentini, A., Jeanne, M., & Toraldo di Francia, G. Measurements of differential threshold in the presence of a spatial illumination gradient. *Atti della Fondazione Giorgio Ronchi e Contributi dell'Istituto Nazionale di Ottica,* 1955, **10**, 371–379.

Fiorentini, A., & Radici, T. Binocular measurements of brightness on a field presenting a luminance gradient. *Atti della Fondazione Giorgio Ronchi e Contributi dell'Istituto Nazionale di Ottica,* 1957, **12**, 453–461.

Gordon, J. Edge accentuation in the frog retina. 1973, in preparation.

Gouras, P., & Link, K. Rod and cone interaction in dark-adapted monkey ganglion cells. *Journal of Physiology (London)*, 1966, **184**, 499–510.

Graham, C. H., & Kemp, E. H. Brightness discrimination as a function of the duration of the increment in intensity. *Journal of General Physiology,* 1938, **21**, 635–650.

Graham, C. H., & Margaria, R. Area and the intensity-time in the peripheral retina. *American Journal of Physiology,* 1935, **113**, 299–305.

Hartline, H. K. Inhibition of activity of visual receptors by illuminating nearby retinal elements in the *Limulus* eye. *Federation Proceedings, Federation of American Societies for Experimental Biology,* 1949, **8,** 69.

Hartline, H. K. Visual receptors and retinal interaction. *Science,* 1969, **164,** 270–278.

Hartline, H. K., & Ratliff, F. Inhibitory interaction of receptor units in the eye of *Limulus. Journal of General Physiology,* 1957, **40,** 357–376.

Hartline, H. K., & Ratliff, F. Inhibitory interaction in the retina of *Limulus.* In M.G.F. Fuortes (Ed.), *Physiology of photoreceptor organs. Handbook of sensory physiology.* Vol. 7/2. Berlin and New York: Springer-Verlag, 1972. Pp. 381–447.

Heath, G. G. Luminosity curves of normal and dichromatic observers. *Science,* 1958, **128,** 775–776.

Hecht, S., Haig, C., & Wald, G. The dark adaptation of retinal fields of different size and location. *Journal of General Physiology,* 1935, **19,** 321–337.

Hecht, S., Shlaer, S., & Pirenne, M. H. Energy, quanta, and vision. *Journal of General Physiology,* 1942, **25,** 819–840.

Hecht, S., & Shlaer, S. Intermittent stimulation by light. V. The relation between intensity and critical frequency for different parts of the spectrum. *Journal of General Physiology,* 1936, **19,** 965–979.

Hecht, S., & Verrijp, C. D. Intermittent stimulation by light. III. The relation between intensity and critical fusion frequency for different retinal locations. *Journal of General Physiology,* 1933, **17,** 251–265.

Hering, E. *Outlines of a theory of the light sense.* (Translated by L.M. Hurvich & D. Jameson.) Cambridge, Massachusetts: Harvard Univ. Press, 1964.

Hsia, Y., & Graham, C. H. Spectral sensitivity of the cones in the dark adapted human eye. *Proceedings of the National Academy of Sciences of the United States,* 1952, **38,** 80–85.

Hsia, Y., & Graham, C. H. Spectral luminosity curves of protanopic, deuteranopic, and normal subjects. *Proceedings of the National Academy of Sciences of the United States,* 1957, **43,** 1011–1019.

Hsia, Y. & Graham, C. H. Color blindness. In C. H. Graham (Ed.), *Vision and visual perception.* New York: Wiley, 1965. Pp. 395–413.

Hubel, D. H., & Wiesel, T. N. Receptive fields and functional architecture of monkey striate cortex. *Journal of Physiology (London),* 1968, **195,** 215–243.

Hurvich, L. M., & Jameson, D. An opponent-process theory of color vision. *Psychological Review,* 1957, **64,** 384–404.

Hurvich, L. M., & Jameson D. *The perception of brightness and darkness.* Boston: Allyn & Bacon, 1966.

Jacobs, G. H. Single cells in squirrel monkey lateral geniculate nucleus with broad spectral sensitivity. *Vision Research,* 1964, **4,** 221–232.

Jacobs, G. H. Effects of adaptation on the lateral geniculate response to light increment and decrement. *Journal of the Optical Society of America,* 1965, **55,** 1535–1540.

Jameson, D., & Hurvich, L. M. Theory of brightness and color contrast in human vision. *Vision Research,* 1964, **4,** 135–154.

Kelly, D. H. Visual responses to time-dependent stimuli. I. Amplitude sensitivity measurements. *Journal of the Optical Society of America,* 1961, **51,** 422–429.

Krauskopf, J. Effect of retinal image stabilization on the appearance of heterochromatic targets. *Journal of the Optical Society of America,* 1963, **53,** 741–744.

Kuffler, S. W. Discharge patterns and functional organization of mammalian retina. *Journal of Neurophysiology,* 1953, **16,** 37–68.

Land, E. H. Experiments in color vision. *Scientific American,* 1959, **200**, 84–94.

Land, E. H., & Daw, N. W. Binocular combination of projected images. *Science,* 1962, **138**, 589–590.

Le Grand, Y. *Light, colour and vision.* (Translated by R. W. G. Hunt, J. W. T. Walsh, & F. R. W. Hunt.) London: Chapman & Hall, 1957.

Marriott, F. H. C. Colour vision. In H. Davson (Ed.), *The eye.* (1st ed.) Vol. 2. New York: Academic Press, 1962. Pp. 219–320.

Patel, A. S. Spatial resolution by the human visual system. The effect of mean retinal illuminance. *Journal of the Optical Society of America,* 1966, **56**, 689–694.

Pirenne, M. H. Visual functions in man. In H. Davson (Ed.), *The eye.* (1st ed.) Vol. 2. New York: Academic Press, 1962. Pp. 3–217.

Pitt, F. H. G. The nature of normal trichromatic and dichromatic vision. *Proceedings of the Royal Society, Series B, Lond.,* 1944, **132**, 101–117.

Ratliff, F. *Mach bands: Quantitative studies on neural networks in the retina.* San Francisco, California: Holden-Day, 1965.

Ratliff, F., & Hartline, H. K. The response of *Limulus* optic nerve fibers to patterns of illumination on the receptor mosaic. *Journal of General Physiology,* 1959, **42**, 1241–1255.

Riggs, L. A., Ratliff, F., Cornsweet, J. C., & Cornsweet, T. N. The disappearance of steadily fixated visual test objects. *Journal of the Optical Society of America,* 1953, **43**, 495–501.

Rodieck, T. W., & Stone, J. Response of cat retinal ganglion cells to moving visual patterns. *Journal of Neurophysiology,* 1965, **28**, 819–832.

Rushton, W. A. H. A cone pigment in the protanope. *Journal of Physiology (London),* 1963, **168**, 345–359.

Rushton, W. A. H. Colour blindness and cone pigments. *American Journal of Optometry,* 1964, **41**, 265–282.

Rushton, W. A. H. The Ferrier Lecture, 1962. Visual adaptation. *Proceedings of the Royal Society, Series B,* 1965, **162**, 20–46. (a)

Rushton, W. A. H. A foveal pigment in the deuteranope. *Journal of Physiology (London),* 1965, **176**, 24–37. (b)

Rushton, W. A. H., & Cohen, R. D. Visual purple level and the course of dark adaptation. *Nature (London),* 1954, **173**, 301–302.

Rushton, W. A. H., & Westheimer, G. The effect upon the rod threshold of bleaching neighbouring rods. *Journal of Physiology (London),* 1962, **164**, 318–329.

Sperling, H. G., Sidley, N. A., Dockens, W. S., & Jolliffe, C. L. Increment-threshold and spectral sensitivity of the rhesus monkey as a function of the spectral composition of the background field. *Journal of The Optical Society of America,* 1968, **58**, 263–268.

Stevens, J. C., & Stevens, S. S. Brightness function: Effects of adaptation. *Journal of The Optical Society of America,* 1963, **53**, 375–385.

Stiles, W. S. Increment thresholds and the mechanisms of color vision. *Documenta Ophthalmologica,* 1949, **3**, 138–165.

Stiles, W. S. Color vision: The approach through increment-threshold sensitivity. *Proceedings of the National Academy of Sciences of the United States,* 1959, **45**, 100–114.

Teller, D. Y. Increment thresholds on black bars. *Vision Research,* 1968, **8**, 713–718.

von Helmholtz, H. In J. P. C. Southall (Ed.), *Helmholtz's treatise on physiological optics*. New York: Dover, 1962.

Wald, G. The photoreceptor process in vision. In Amer. Physiol. Soc., J. Field (Ed.), *Handbook of physiology*. Sect. 1. *Neurophysiology*. Vol. I. Baltimore, Maryland: Williams & Wilkins, 1959. Pp. 671–692.

Wald, G. The receptors of human color vision. *Science*, 1964, **145**, 1007–1017.

Wiesel, T. N., & Hubel, D. H. Spatial and chromatic interaction in the lateral geniculate body of the rhesus monkey. *Journal of Neurophysiology*, 1966, **29**, 1115–1156.

Willmer, E. N. A physiological basis for human colour vision in the central fovea. *Documenta Ophthalmologica*, 1955, **9**, 235–313.

Wright, W. D., & Pitt, F. H. G. Hue discrimination in normal colour vision. *Proceedings of The Physical Society of London*, 1934, **46**, 459–473.

Yarbus, A. L. *Eye movements and vision*. New York: Plenum, 1967.

Yeandle, S. Evidence of quantized slow potentials in the eye of *Limulus*. *American Journal of Ophthalmology*, 1958, **46**, 82–87.

Chapter 18

HEARING: CENTRAL NEURAL MECHANISMS

BRUCE MASTERTON AND IRVING T. DIAMOND

To keep the subject of hearing and its neural basis within manageable proportions, it is necessary to impose one or another restriction. This discussion will be confined to animals that possess a cochlea, that is, to land vertebrates or tetrapods. We will also emphasize the contribution of the central nervous system rather than the contribution of the ear itself. It should be recognized that these restrictions exclude from consideration many interesting questions such as "How do insects hear?" and also questions such as "How does the ear transform auditory stimulation into neural activity?"

Contributing most to the organization of the chapter and the selection of material for inclusion in it, is the principle of evolution. Accordingly, the origin and evolution of the auditory system is described first and the sources of selective pressure on hearing and the evolution of sound reception second. These two sections lead to the conclusion that detection of *brief* sounds and their localization provide a chief and continuing source for selection; the third section then reviews current ideas of the contributions of the various structures of the central auditory system to sound detection and localization. Finally, in this last section we want to point to directions research in the neurophysiology of audition may take in the future; this we hope to achieve by indicating that ablation of the auditory cortex in higher mammals results in complex perceptual changes—changes much more complicated than envisioned by analysis of the physical dimensions of the stimuli.

I. THE EVOLUTION OF THE VERTEBRATE AUDITORY SYSTEM

A. The Origin of the Cochlea and the Hindbrain Auditory System

The cochlea and the cochlear division of the eighth cranial nerve can be traced back through geological history in an almost unbroken line to the time of the origin of amphibia but not further. To be sure, the ancestors of the first land vertebrates, which of course inhabited the seas, lakes and rivers, possessed a number of organs that contributed wholly, or in part, to the origin of the tetrapod auditory system. These fish-like creatures had lateral-line organs capable of detecting local water currents, vestibular organs for detecting accelerations of the head and body, and possibly, an air bladder capable of detecting low-frequency pressure changes. It is from these preamphibian systems and their central nervous system connections that the tetrapod auditory system arose. For details of the origin of the cochlea and its relation to precursor organs which were sensitive to mechanical vibrations, the reader is referred to van Bergeijk (1967). For the present purpose it will suffice to compare the homologous structures in three genera of extant Amphibia: *Necturus, Amblystoma* and *Rana*. This comparison will provide some clues to the transformations of the ear and nervous system that probably took place during the origin of the auditory system. For example, the mudpuppy (*Necturus*), which leaves the water only under extraordinary circumstances, has neither cochlea nor auditory nerve. The salamander (*Amblystoma*), leading an adult life both on land and water, has a rudimentary cochlea and an auditory nerve which is only a small fraction of the total eighth nerve. In contrast, adult frogs (*Rana*) have a well-developed cochlea, and the auditory component of the eighth nerve subserving it is conspicuous (Herrick, 1948). It follows that the cochlea is an adaptation to life in air; and with the cochlea and the cochlear portion of the eighth nerve there arose further changes in the brainstem now to be described. In addition to differences in the cochlea, these same three amphibians show marked differences in the auditory tracts in their hindbrain and midbrain. Where the mudpuppy has few, if any, fibers which can be identified as auditory and the salamander has a small complement of such fibers, the frog has a relatively large and conspicuous tract which is clearly auditory in its connections and, further, occupies the same position as the lateral lemniscus in other vertebrates. The auditory nerve of the frog (that is, the cochlear division of the eighth nerve) ends in the hindbrain on a *cochlear nucleus* which is distinctly differentiated from the surrounding vestibular nuclei. Second order fibers arising in the cochlear nucleus course either across the medulla to the contralateral *superior olive* as a primordial trapezoid body, or towards the midbrain as a primordial *lateral lemniscus* (Ariëns-Kappers, Huber, & Crosby, 1936).

From comparisons among extant Amphibia alone, therefore, it seems likely that the tetrapod plan of the auditory hindbrain—the *cochlear nucleus and superior olivary complex,* the connections between these structures (*trapezoid body*), and the connections between them and the midbrain (*lateral lemniscus*)—was gained very early in the evolutionary history of land vertebrates.

To sum up, the early evolutionary record of the auditory apparatus is sufficiently well known through direct paleontological evidence and indirect comparative and ontogenetic evidence that its origin is relatively clear (Herrick, 1948; Larsell, 1934; Young, 1962). It can be concluded from this evidence that a cochlear auditory system, at least from ear to hindbrain and from hindbrain to midbrain, is as old as land vertebrates. Since that time, the further evolution of the auditory system in reptiles and mammals has been characterized by an enlargement and differentiation of these older parts together with a multiplication of cellular types and a progressive penetration of auditory fibers into the forebrain (Fig. 1). Once this penetration of auditory fibers into the forebrain established auditory centers in the thalamus and telencephalon, these structures also began to enlarge and differentiate.

B. The Midbrain and Forebrain Auditory System in Non-mammalian Tetrapods

Since the auditory hindbrain and midbrain is as old as the cochlea, the question arises whether or not there also exist homologs or precursors of the mammalian thalamus and neocortex in reptiles and birds. In amphibians,

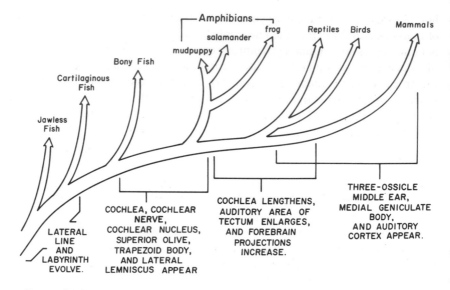

FIG. 1. Major features in the evolution of the tetrapod auditory system.

reptiles and birds the lateral lemniscus ends beneath the *optic tectum* in the *torus semicircularis,* the primordial *inferior colliculus,* and a primoridal nucleus of the lateral lemniscus (Ariëns-Kappers *et al.,* 1936; Nauta and Karten, 1970; Papez, 1936). Since there exists a projection of these auditory midbrain structures into the diencephalon (*nucleus reuniens*) and, in turn, to the *dorsal ventricular ridge* of the telencephalon, it would seem certain that some part of the ancient forebrain was also auditory. In reptiles and birds these forward projections from the auditory structures of the midbrain are much more meager than in mammals, but they are distinguishable from the surrounding neuropil in much the same fashion as they are in mammals (Nauta and Karten, 1970.) Indeed, the studies by Karten (e.g., 1967, 1968) and others have suggested that other nonolfactory sensory systems reach the forebrain of birds and reptiles, so audition is not exceptional in this respect. Thus, there may be a greater similarity between the forebrains of non-mammals and mammals than was once thought to be the case. Nevertheless, there remain several qualitative characteristics of the mammalian thalamus and telencephalon that seem to set it apart from its non-mammalian precursors.

In all mammals, the *brachium of the inferior colliculus* is a well-defined and conspicuous pathway that leads from the inferior colliculus to the *medial geniculate nucleus* and the *posterior nuclei* of the thalamus. It remains a matter of conjecture whether the thalamic target (*nucleus reuniens*) of the tract originating in the auditory tectum of reptiles is homologous to either medial geniculate or posterior nuclei in the thalamus of mammals; and whether the telencephalic target (*dorsal ventricular ridge*) is homologous to mammalian auditory cortex. However, even if the weight of evidence suggests that the auditory forebrain of modern reptiles resembles the precursor to the mammalian auditory forebrain, the similarities probably reflect a remote and extinct ancestor, and whatever the genetic affinities, it is certain that the reptile forebrain is minute in comparison to the massive thalamic structures and thalamocortical projections found even in the most primitive mammals.

C. The Origin of the Mammalian Auditory System

The evolution of mammal-like reptiles in the Jurassic brought not only an increase in the forebrain and in the number of auditory fibers which reach it, but also resulted in a significant change in the ear itself (Fig. 1). The middle-ear linkage which transmits vibrations from the tympanum to the oval window of the cochlea was transformed from one ossicle (stapes or columella) to three ossicles (malleus, incus, and stapes) (Young, 1962). This remarkable transformation was accomplished first, by a reduction and migration of two of the reptilian jaw bones (which probably increased the biting power of the jaw), and then, by their recruitment into the middle ear. Meanwhile, a third reptilian jaw bone encircled the tympanum providing it with rigid support (Young, 1962). These changes in the jaw and ear have been used by several generations of paleontologists as a hallmark for classifying a fossil as "mammal." If a fossil skull has three middle-ear bones, it is judged to be the skull of a mammal; if it has only one, it is considered the skull of a non-mammal.

The rearrangement of the middle ear provided primitive mammals with a lever-like device whose mechanical advantage matches the impedance of air with the impedance of the fluid contained in the cochlea (von Békèsy, 1960). As will be seen in a later section, this modification of the auditory apparatus resulted in an equally significant modification of hearing ability.

A second characteristic distinguishing the mammalian from the non-mammalian auditory system lies in the great difference in the size of the cochlea and the length of the basilar membrane within it. In amphibians, the basilar membrane is almost circular, in most reptiles it is oblong, and in mammals it is a long, thin, triangular strip (Manley, 1970, 1971). Because sounds of different frequencies result in stimulation at different places along the basilar membrane, this lengthening of the receptor organ almost certainly means that there existed a strong and persistent pressure on the ancestors of mammals for wider range and finer discrimination of frequency.

1. THE MAMMALIAN PLAN OF THE AUDITORY SYSTEM: HINDBRAIN

In addition to these differences in the ear, the central components of the system reveal characters that also serve to distinguish mammalian from non-mammalian auditory systems (Fig. 2). In general, the brainstem auditory nuclei in mammals are a great deal larger and more differentiated than they are in amphibians, birds, or reptiles. These differences in size and degree of differentiation parallel both the larger number of fibers present in the auditory nerve of mammals and the size and length of their cochlea. Thus, many of the quantitative differences between the central auditory structures of mammals and non-mammals may be a simple consequence of the differences in the number of auditory nerve fibers.

There are some differences in the nuclei of the auditory system in mammals, however, that would not be expected just from differences in the size

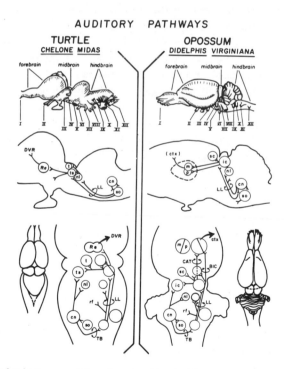

FIG. 2. Major brainstem nuclei and tracts in primitive reptile (left) and primitive mammal (right). Lateral view above, dorsal view below. Only major projections of the left ear are shown. Abbreviations: BIC, brachium of the inferior colliculus; CAT, central acoustic tract; cn, cochlear nucleus; ctx, neocortex; ic, inferior colliculus; LL, lateral lemniscus m, medial geniculate; nl, nucleus of the lateral lemniscus; p, posterior nucleus; rf, reticular formation; sc, superior colliculus; so, superior olive; t, tectum; TB, trapezoid body; ts, torus semicircularis.

of the auditory nerve alone. For example, the cochlear nucleus not only enlarged in the evolution of mammals, but it bceame divided into three major substructures (dorsal cochlear nucleus and anterior and posterior divisions of ventral cochlear nucleus), each of which contains a variety of neuronal types (Harrison & Feldman, 1970; Lorente de No, 1933; Osen, 1969). Perhaps more outstanding was the change which took place in thc superior olivary complex. Although a superior olive can be identified even in amphibians (and thus like other hindbrain structures it is as old as the cochlea itself), this structure also differentiated into various subdivisions, each of which shows differing degrees of development in the several mammalian lines of descent—a fact which, in a later section, will prove to be important (Harrison & Feldman, 1970). In all tetrapods, mammalian and non-mammalian alike, the superior olivary complex receives projections from the cochlear nuclei on both sides and, consequently, it is the first structure in the central auditory system which is in a position to integrate stimulation reaching the two ears (Fig. 9, p. 436). In a later section of this chapter, we will present evidence to show that the contribution of the superior olivary complex to hearing in mammals includes the analysis of small differences in the sounds reaching the two ears. The function which this analysis serves, namely, localizing the source of a sound, will be a major topic when we turn to the question of selective pressures which resulted in the transformation of the ear and the auditory system. Thus, where the hindbrain nuclei in non-mammals (cochlear nucleus and superior olive) are rclatively small and inconspicuous, the homologous structures in primitive mammals are large and well differentiated and this difference is undoubtedly related to the greater variety of uses of hearing by mammals.

2. AUDITORY MIDBRAIN IN MAMMALS

In general, the devclopment of the midbrain auditory structures in mammals parallels the development of the hindbrain auditory nuclei. In non-mammals, the *torus semicircularis* (the *inferior colliculus*) is imbedded beneath the optic tectum and, like the hindbrain nuclei, is relatively small and inconspicuous. In contrast, in most mammalian lines of descent the inferior colliculus has expanded to a size which is at least the equal of the *optic tectum* or *superior colliculus*. In Insectivores, Chiroptera, Carnivora, and Cetacea, for example, the inferior colliculus is much larger than the superior colliculus. Only in the few mammals which rely heavily on vision such as primates, squirrels, phalangers, etc., is the superior colliculus larger than the inferior colliculus. These differences are obviously related to the relative roles of audition and vision in the life of the various mammals (Jane, Masterton, & Diamond, 1965).

3. AUDITORY FOREBRAIN IN MAMMALS

In mammals, the forebrain receives auditory input via the brachium of the inferior colliculus and the fibers lying medial to it (called the "central acoustic tract" by Papez, 1936). These tracts project to the medial geniculate and posterior nuclei of the thalamus which project, in turn, to neocortex (Fig. 2). In primitive mammals, the fibers leaving the medial geniculate take the shortest route to the neocortex terminating in a region just dorsal to the rhinal fissure and rostral to the visual areas (Diamond & Utley, 1963; Lende, 1963, 1964).

The exact target of the cortical projections of the medial geniculate in the different mammalian lines of descent remains a matter of continuing inquiry. For the present, suffice it to say that the general locus of auditory cortex in the temporal areas of neocortex was established by its position in early mammals, while its size and complexity vary considerably among modern mammals. For example, in the cat which relies heavily on auditory cues for night hunting, auditory cortex occupies almost all of the temporal areas from the visual cortex to the rhinal fissure. In contrast, most of the temporal lobe in primates is devoted not to the auditory system but to the visual system, either by way of the thalamocortical or corticocortical pathways, while auditory cortex is restricted to the banks of the Sylvian fissure.

When compared with its form in more advanced mammals, the medial geniculate nucleus in the thalamus of primitive mammals is not sharply separated from the posterior nucleus ("m" and "p" in Fig. 2). Recent studies of the mammalian thalamus have shown that the posterior nuclei also receive auditory fibers from the midbrain and, indeed, there is even some evidence that in primitive mammals, auditory impulses also reach the ventral posterior nucleus—the nucleus chiefly concerned with somatosensory input to the forebrain (e.g., Erickson, Jane, Waite, & Diamond, 1964). If this evidence can be taken as representative of primitive mammals in general, the conclusion is suggested that auditory and somatosensory systems in the forebrain may have been incompletely differentiated in the early stages of mammalian evolution. Indeed, even in some advanced mammals (e.g., cat) the posterior nuclei still retain connections with both the somatosensory and the auditory systems (Poggio & Mountcastle, 1963).

While it is difficult to prove that the auditory projections from thalamus to cortex are diffuse in primitive mammals (this is because sustaining collaterals may be spatially organized, but such an order is not easy to establish by retrograde degeneration), they are not precisely topographic in the way the lateral geniculate projects to area 17 in higher mammals. Apparently, the medial geniculate and posterior nuclei in the opossum and hedgehog send overlapping projections to neocortex, although to different cellular layers within the neocortex (e.g., Diamond & Utley, 1963; Ravizza & Diamond, 1972). In correspondence, the tissue in these neocortical targets in primitive mammals shows no obvious cytoarchitectonic subdivisions. In contrast to this primtive mammalian condition, both the medial geniculate nucleus and its cortical target have several subdivisions in most advanced mammals and many subdivisions in some. For example, in the cat auditory cortex has at least seven distinct subdivisions (Rose, 1949; Woolsey, 1960) and in correspondence, the size and degree of differentiation in the medial geniculate and posterior nuclei is much greater than in opossum and hedgehog (Morest, 1964, 1965).

The relationship of the organization of the auditory nuclei within the thalamus and the organization of the auditory cortex have been investigated chiefly in the cat and the results contain several further points of importance. First, the thalamocortical fibers from both nuclei are reciprocated by corticothalamic fibers; that is, efferent centrifugal or "descending auditory" fibers (e.g., Desmedt & Mechelse, 1959; Diamond, Jones, & Powell, 1969). Indeed, the entire auditory pathway from the ear to the neocortex is reciprocated by an efferent pathway originating at neocortex and extending down the auditory system, structure-by-structure all the way to the cochlea (Rasmussen, 1964). Second, in the auditory thalamus of cats, the auditory receptor is represented at least twice, once in a part of the posterior nucleus and at least once again in the medial geniculate nucleus. Each of these thalamic representations projects to separate cortical areas. Finally, insofar as different parts of the auditory receptor can be related to different frequencies of sound, the relatively orderly spatial projection from ear to auditory cortex implies that different parts of the neocortex are differentially sensitive to frequency, and indeed, this point has often been demonstrated electrophysiologically (cf. Hind, 1953; Tunturi, 1944; Whitfield, 1967; Woolsey & Walzl, 1942). There still remains a difference in opinion concerning how sharply tonotopic this cortical representation is even in advanced mammals, but this question is beyond the scope of this chapter. Certainly, the functional significance of topographic projections to the neocortex remains a matter for further inquiry.

To sum up, we have distinguished two phases in the evolution of the auditory system: the first begins with the earliest land vertebrates and ends with the earliest mammals, and the second begins where the first ends and continues to present-day advanced mammals. In the second period the auditory forebrain has undergone an increase in size and in degree of differentiation which is not unlike the increase in size and differentiation of the brainstem nuclei which took place in the first period. The result is that in cats certainly, and other advanced mammals possibly, there are several anatomic subdivisions present both at the thalamic and cortical levels. With these general differences between advanced and primitive mammals in mind, it is even possible to try to reconstruct the phylogenetic development of thalamo-cortical relations beginning with ancient mammals and ending with a highly specialized auditory mammal. In ancient mammals the cortical projections of medial geniculate and posterior nuclei probably overlapped in extent, although they projected to different cortical layers within their common cortical target (Ravizza & Diamond, 1972). In advanced mammals, in contrast, the two thalamic nuclei probably project to different (though adjacent) areas of cortex, each of which has differentiated into obvious subdivisions.

It remains to be seen whether the same kind and degree of development in the auditory forebrain was attained in the several lines of mammalian descent. We can only suggest the beginning of an answer to this question. In primates, an order of mammals that relies heavily on vision, most of the temporal area of the neocortex is devoted to vision. The primate auditory area seems to be restricted to the banks of the Sylvian fissure, but even this fundamental question is not yet satisfactorily resolved. In any case, it remains possible and even likely that the degree and type of development of the auditory cortex in the highly visual primates may be different from the highly auditory cats, bats, etc. Indeed, whether the auditory cortex of cats (which has been studied most intensively) provides the rule or an exception for advanced or specialized mammals is still a matter of conjecture. While a number of questions concerning the comparison of the various lines of mammals remain unanswered, it is safe to say that some similarities, resulting from common ancestry and parallel or convergent evolution, will be found in the auditory cortex of all mammals, while some differences, resulting from divergent evolution, will also be found.

II.   THE EVOLUTION OF SOUND RECEPTION

Some of the major structural modifications accompanying the evolution of the auditory system have been described in the previous section. In the remaining sections, the topic turns first to the evolutionary modifications in hearing that paralleled the morphological changes and the probable selective pressures that brought them about, and then, to the consequences of these selective pressures as they are now seen in the function of the structures that compose the central auditory system.

A. Phylogenetic History of the Audible Field in Man's Ancestral Lineage

The range of an animal's hearing is usually portrayed in a diagram called an *audiogram*. In abstract, an audiogram divides the plane determined by a frequency dimension and an intensity dimension into two regions. One region, called the "audible field," contains all frequency and intensity combinations to which the animal responds; the other region contains all frequency and intensity combinations to which the animal does not respond. Thus, audiograms allow quantitative comparisons of the physical limits of hearing among animals.

Although rigorous behavioral audiograms have been obtained on only very few amphibians and reptiles, the broad outline of the evolution of the audible field among the four classes of tetrapods can be deduced (Fig. 3) (cf. McGill, 1960; Masterton, Heffner, & Ravizza, 1969; Schwartzkopff, 1955). The figure shows that the audible field of an amphibian (frog) is smaller in area than that of a reptile (turtle) and both are smaller in area than that of a primitive mammal (opossum). This increase in the audible field in the direction of mankind's ancestral lineage is due partly to an increase in absolute sensitivity (i.e., the vertical dimension in the audiogram) and partly to an expansion of the range of hearing (i.e., the horizontal dimension) to include higher frequencies.

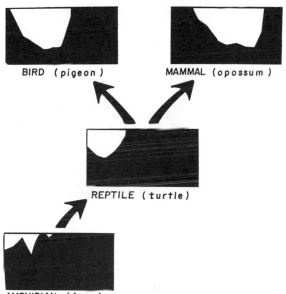

BIRD (pigeon)   MAMMAL (opossum)

REPTILE (turtle)

AMPHIBIAN (frog)

FIG. 3. Representative audiograms from the four classes of tetrapods scaled to the same units for ease of comparison. The horizontal axis of each audiogram spans the frequencies from 60 Hz to 200 kHz in an octave, or logarithmic scale. The vertical axis spans the intensity range from −20 to +100 in dB relative to 2×10^{-4} dynes/cm.^{2}. Note increase in area of the audible field (white portion) and its shift to include high frequencies. (After McGill, 1960; Ravizza and Masterton, 1972; Schwartzkopff, 1955.)

Figure 3 also shows the audiogram of a bird (pigeon) (c.f. Schwartz-kopff, 1955). A cursory comparison of the avian and mammalian audio-grams reveals that the essential differences between these two classes lies not in absolute sensitivity but, instead, in the ability of mammals to hear high frequencies (e.g., above 12–15 kHz). This gross difference in fre-quency range is almost certainly the effect of the three-ossicle middle ear of mammals. By matching the impedance of air to cochlear fluid, the middle-ear linkage in mammals allowed the reception of frequencies several octaves above that which is possible with a single ossicle.

The outline of the further evolution of the audible field in mankind's lineage can be deduced by comparing the audiograms of mammals which have successive common ancestry with mankind: opossum (Fig. 3), hedge-hog, bushbaby, monkey, and man (Fig. 4). These comparisons reveal that the audible field probably first enlarged due to an increase in absolute

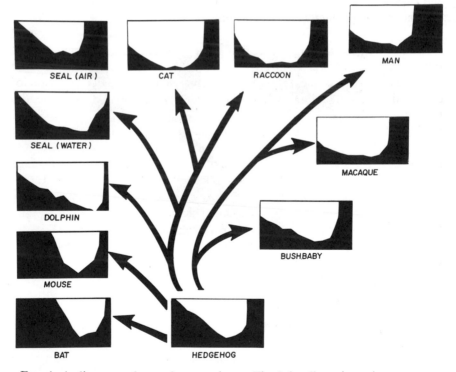

Fig. 4. Audiograms of several mammals, see Fig. 3 for dimensions. Arrows repre-sent probable lines of descent and kinship. Note similarity of audiograms in bat and mouse despite remote common ancestry; and dissimilarity of the audiograms of the seal when it is in air and when it is in water (seal data from Mohl, 1968; see Master-ton *et al.*, 1969, for references to data for other animals).

sensitivity to low frequencies, and then decreased due to a loss of sensitivity to very high frequencies (Masterton *et al.*, 1969).

SPECIALIZED AUDIBLE FIELDS

Figure 4 also illustrates an array of audiograms of mammals less closely related to man's lineage and includes some of the more bizarre types of hearing known to exist among mammals. The two extremes of hearing range are represented by dolphins, mice, and bats on one hand, and humans on the other. The ranges of bats, mice, and dolphins include very high frequencies, while the hearing range of humans (and apes) is restricted to relatively low frequencies. Among mammals whose audiograms are now known, the highly specialized nocturnal carnivores, cat and raccoon, have the widest range of hearing and the largest area of the audible field, while the primitive opossum has the smallest area (Masterton *et al.*, 1969).

B. The Biological Significance of Sounds

When a large array of mammalian audiograms is studied, a wide variation in audible fields is seen. At first glance, this variation seems so wide it is tempting to assume that it is the result of the special adaptation of each of the different animals to its unique ecological niche, and consequently, that no common characteristics exist. For example, it is difficult to avoid the idea that cats may hear high frequencies (64 kHz) because they stalk mice at night and mice squeak at high pitches; or that humans hear low frequencies because they now use their ears to receive spoken language and human voices are relatively low-pitched. Although this sort of reasoning is not improper in principle and may lead to the discovery of one or another selective advantage in a particular audiogram it is essential to note first that audiograms themselves depict the hearing of an animal in an "abstract" or "synthetic" way. By "abstract" or "synthetic" we mean that the audiograms are based on an animal's sensitivity to long-duration pure tones, and it is almost trivial to note that long-duration pure tones occur infrequently in nature. Therefore, pure-tone detection could hardly present the chief source of selective pressure on hearing.

Instead, most natural sounds and almost all natural sounds that warn an animal of a potentially dangerous intruder are very brief sounds—sounds too brief to have tonality. Consequently, the sources of selective pressure resulting in the variation in mammalian audiograms are to be found in an acoustic environment made up not of enduring pure tones or even their simple combinations, but instead, of sounds such as snaps, pops, crackles, thumps, and thuds. In the search for the sources of selective pressure on the auditory system in general, and audiograms in particular, therefore, naturalistic observation becomes necessary. As it turns out, at least three observations prove to be useful for our purpose.

Conspicuously missing from our list will be the role of intraspecies communication in evolution. Since such communication has an important part to play in mating and other species-specific traits that are necessary for survival of the species, the omission of this topic requires a few sentences of explanation. First is the mundane matter of space; there is a large body of literature on this subject and to review it even in a summary way would require a chapter at least the size of the present one (cf., Busnel, 1963, for a review). Second, the neural mechanisms for intraspecies communication are not very well known, and we chose the evolution of the nervous system as our starting point. To be sure, we could point out that the receptor itself can serve as the selective mechanism in frogs—that is to say, it is the unique character of the ear which permits the croak of a member of the same species to be a provocative stimulus and which prevents the croak of another species even from being heard (Capranica, 1966). On the other hand, in higher primates the significance of certain cries and calls must surely depend on central and possibly cortical mechanisms (P. G. Nelson and P. Winter, personal communication, 1971). But besides the very general truism that for lower vertebrates the significance of stimuli depends less on learning, there is very little to say in the way of a phylogeny of the neural mechanisms for communication. Indeed, most of the literature concerning intraspecies communication is aimed at showing the significance of the signs and how this communication serves in the species' adaptation to the specific niche occupied. With these restrictions in our subject in mind, the clues we seek in the adaptive behavior of land vertebrates must be derived from very general considerations, that is, ones that apply to a great variety of niches and indeed, perhaps to all vertebrates which hear.

First, sounds occur only as a result of movement. Therefore, in the evolution of hearing, the reception of a sound by an animal has come to *mean* the presence of a moving thing in the vicinity.

Second, an animal's reaction to an abrupt sound differs from its reaction to a steady or periodic sound. Animals tend to react to abrupt, arrythmic, or stacatto sounds as if their source were animate, whether or not it is. In contrast, they tend to react to continuous, periodic or legato sounds, or sounds with a slow onset, as if their source were inanimate or part of the background of ambient stimulation. (To illustrate this point, imagine a prey-animal's reaction to the snap of a twig). It follows from this close relationship of sound onset to biological meaning ("another animal present" versus "no other animals") that the *abruptness* and *brevity* of sounds provide cues to an animal for assessing the current condition of its environment and for determining its behavior in the immediate future.

Third, animals either orient to, approach, or avoid the source of an abrupt sound. These behavioral reactions are evidence that the animal must perceive its location. Therefore, the locus of a sound source would seem to be an important attribute.

By observations and arguments of this kind, we are led to two important conclusions. First, it is the detection, localization, and identification of other animals (and, therefore, of brief sounds) that provides a primary, source of selective pressure on animal auditory systems. Second, there must exist neural mechanisms in the central nervous system that synthesize these psychological dimensions from the ear's analysis of sound stimulation.

In the remainder of the chapter the further discussion of hearing and its neural basis is centered on this point of view. In the last part of this section, the psychophysics of sound source localization and identification are reviewed in order to see how selective pressure for localization acuity and veridicality has affected mammalian audiograms. In the next section the analytic and synthetic functions of the central auditory system for the detection, localization, and identification of animate sound sources will be described.

C. Localization of the Source of a Brief Sound

In abstract, the locus of a sound source is most naturally expressed in polar coordinates: that is, azimuth, elevation, and distance. When the auditory system analyzes the stimulation and synthesizes neural correlates of these three parameters, the sound source is localized to one and only one point in the environment.

1. DISTANCE

The intensity of a sound is by far the most direct cue for establishing the distance of its source. But because high frequencies decay faster over distance than low frequencies, the proportion of high frequency content in the spectrum of stimulation reaching the ears provides an additional cue for the distance of its source. Thus, a source that is nearby is both loud and wide in spectrum while the same source far away is less loud and its frequency spectrum is biased toward the low frequency end. Man and probably most, if not all, other mammals exploit these physical attributes of sounds in establishing the relative distance of a sound source, and they can do so with only one ear acting as a simple sound spectrograph (e.g.,

Coleman, 1963). Furthermore, they can also use these cues to establish the absolute distance of a sound source, providing that there exists a reference spectrum for comparison. Presumably, this reference spectrum (when it exists) is generated by the memory either of other sources emitting similar spectra or of the same source at a different distance. Thus, the determination of absolute distance probably requires at least short-term memory, while the determination of relative distance (that is, "source approaching" or "source receding") may not require any previous experience whatever.

2. ELEVATION

Cues for the elevation of a sound source, somewhat like the secondary cues for distance, are contained in the frequency spectrum of the sound reaching the ears. The apparent elevation of a sound source is related to the high-frequency content of a sound in such a way that high-pitched sounds are perceived as higher in elevation than low-pitched sounds (Roffler & Butler, 1968). Whether or not this is an inherent characteristic in species other than man is not yet known.

3. AZIMUTH

Information about the azimuth of a brief sound source (i.e., its direction in a horizontal plane) is provided both by monaural and binaural cues, but it is the binaural cues that are most accurate and least dependent on experience. In humans, the binaural cues for azimuth are of two different sorts: first, a cue which is provided by the difference in the time of arrival of a sound wave at the two ears (the so-called Δt cue); and second, a cue provided by the difference in the frequency spectra of the sound reaching the two ears (the Δfi cue). Both of these binaural cues result from the longer and more indirect path traveled by the sound around the head to the far ear.

D. Other Biological Characteristics of Sound Sources

Summarizing the discussion so far, since brief, abrupt, or arrhythmic sounds are almost always produced by animals, the auditory system has evolved to make use of these sounds to signify the presence of other animals. When these sounds occur, they usually evoke an immediate orienting response directed to their source. This directional orienting response allows the use of the other distance senses for further identification of the characteristics of the sound source. Thus, for identifying the presence and characteristics of other animals, hearing provides wide-range "early-warn-ing" service which is exquisitely tuned to detect an animal's presence and which serves to narrow its probable locus in the immediate environment (Pumphrey, 1950).

Beyond its primary role as a wide-range detector and localizer of animals, however, hearing serves to affirm the further analyses of the other senses and, if necessary, can itself provide a subtle analysis of the character-istics of the source. Most of these further analyses depend on the frequency-intensity spectrum of the sound received and also on its variation over short time intervals. Although the exact nature and the limits of these analyses are yet to be discovered, it is obvious that sound detection and localization do not exhaust the class of transformations of physical cues to biological attributes that are routinely achieved by the central auditory system.

E. The Effect on Mammalian Audiograms of Selective Pressure for the Detection and Localization of Animate Sounds

Having described some of the main sources of selective pressure on the auditory system, it is now possible to return to a consideration of mammalian audiograms to see what effects these pressures have produced.

1. SELECTIVE PRESSURE FOR HIGH-FREQUENCY HEARING

Beginning with an animal's need to *detect* brief sounds, it is important to note that the amount of high frequency content in a sound is a direct function of the abruptness of the sound's onset: the more abrupt the onset, the more high-frequency content; the less abrupt, the less high-frequency content. Therefore, selective pressure to detect brief sounds results in selective pressure to detect high frequencies.

Selective pressure to detect even the briefest of sounds undoubtedly has played a large role in the evolutionary extension of the tetrapod audiogram into progressively higher and higher frequency ranges (Fig. 3). It is not impossible that this single source of selective pressure may account entirely for every audiogram that reaches as high as 8–10 kHz, which now seems likely to be the upper limit of non-mammalian (i.e., one-ossicle) ears. But selective pressure on brief-sound detection does not provide a satisfactory explanation of the uniquely mammalian extension of the frequency range to still higher frequencies. Sensitivity to these very high frequencies (over 12 kHz) is not necessary for animal detection because even the briefest of natural sounds contain frequencies below 12 kHz. Therefore, the mam-malian extension of the upper limit of hearing to an average of more than

50 kHz is probably *not* the result of selective pressure for more sensitive sound detection. It is more likely the result of pressure for more accurate sound localization (Masterton *et al.*, 1969).

To see the relation between sound localization and high-frequency hearing, recall that the perception of the azimuth of a sound source depends on either or both of two binaural cues, each cue resulting from the longer distance that a sound must travel to the farther of the two ears. Of these two cues the spectrum-difference (or frequency-by-intensity difference, or Δfi) cue is available to all animals because the head and ears serve as a sound-shadow. In contrast, the time-difference (or Δt) cue is not available to all animals. It is available only to animals with relatively wide-set ears because it is only in these animals that Δt cues become large enough for the central auditory structures to analyze them accurately.

There are two conditions under which Δt cues would not be adequate for sound localization. The first and most obvious condition exists if the head is too small and the ears are too close-set. Mice, shrews, bats, etc., fall into this class. A second, less obvious condition exists if the animal has reasonably wide-set ears but inhabits water (e.g., dolphins, small whales, seals, etc.). Since sound travels three times faster in water than in air, and since in water it also travels *through* an animal's head instead of *around* it to the farther ear, the range of Δt's that an animal can experience underwater is much narrower than for the same-sized animal in air. It can be calculated that for seals and dolphins, at least, the range of available Δt cues is also too narrow for even a reasonably large population of time-sensitive neurons to analyze. Therefore, in all small-headed animals, and in all moderately-sized marine animals, sound localization based on Δt cues is certainly inadequate and, in most cases, is probably entirely absent. Consequently, the other binaural cue, $\Delta fi,$ provides the only basis for judging the azimuth of a sound source.

Since animals unable to utilize Δt cues must depend on Δfi cues for sound localization, selective pressure for accurate localization is transformed into selective pressure for widening the range of available Δfi cues. This widening of the range of Δfi cues, in turn, has been accomplished by mammals in several ways. In some, the external ears have grown large and moveable, thereby increasing the effectiveness of their sound shadow. However, in most, if not all, mammals which cannot take advantage of Δt cues, the range of Δfi cues has been widened still further by extending the range of the audible field to include very high frequencies (i.e., above 32 kHz). Because these high frequencies are much more effectively shadowed by the head and ears than are lower frequencies, the higher an animal can hear, the wider the range of Δfi cues that become available for localization.

Thus, there exists a second indirect source of selective pressure for high frequency hearing. The lack of adequate Δt cues requires a maximization of cues provided by Δfi and this requirement, in turn, is satisfied by sensitivity to high frequencies. It is this mode of adaptation that results in a close inverse relationship between the upper frequency limit of hearing and the maximum Δt that an animal can experience: mammals with functionally close-set ears and an inadequately narrow Δt range hear very high frequencies. By the same token, those with wide-set ears and a more adequate Δt range do not hear frequencies as high (Fig. 5).

In summary, the upper frequency limits of mammalian audiograms are not as randomly variable or as quixotic as might first appear. By far the largest part of the variation in high-frequency limit of hearing seems to be due to a persistent demand for accuracy in sound localization. The increasing sensitivity to high frequencies in vertebrate evolution can be accounted for by two types of accomplishment. First, there was selective pressure on sensitivity to brief or abrupt sounds. This pressure resulted in extending the range of hearing to about 10–12 kHz. The limit of this evolutionary trend is now exemplified by the audiograms of modern birds. Second, there was a further extension of the upper limit in mammals, this time to maximize Δfi cues for sound localization.

2. Selective Pressures on Low-Frequency Hearing

Turning now to the low-frequency end of the mammalian audiogram, a somewhat different set of observations prove to be pertinent. Unlike high-

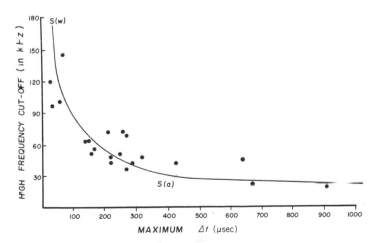

Fig. 5. The relation of high frequency hearing to the availability of binaural time cues for sound localization. Each point represents a genus of mammals, except S (a) and S (w) which represent the seal when in water (w); and when in air (a) (see Fig. 4 for references).

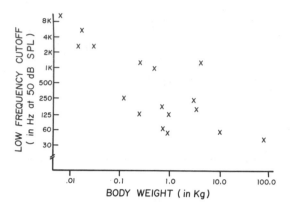

FIG. 6. The relation of low frequency hearing to body weight. Each ✕ represents a genus of mammals. Note the general trend from upper left to lower right.

frequency hearing, not all mammals are sensitive to low frequencies and, with very few exceptions, it is the smallest mammals that are least sensitive to low frequencies (e.g., less than 1 kHz; Fig. 6). In seeking a source of selective pressure to explain this relationship between body size and low-frequency hearing, it has been suggested that high-frequency sensitivity may be incompatible with low-frequency sensitivity for strictly physiological reasons (e.g., a taut tympanum and basilar membrane are better for high-frequency hearing, while relatively large and loose membranes are better for low-frequency hearing). This incompatibility would explain the poor low-frequency hearing of small mammals because it is these same animals that usually have close-set ears and are forced to hear high frequencies as a result of selective pressure on accurate sound localization. An example of the data behind this idea can be seen by comparing the human audiogram with the bat and mouse audiogram in Fig. 4. The relationship between low-frequency and high-frequency hearing for sixteen mammals is shown in Fig. 7. However, it is now known that some mammals are very sensitive *both* to high and to low frequencies (e.g., see cat, raccoon, and dolphin in Fig. 4). These audiograms indicate that at least one other source of selective pressure must be exerted on low-frequency hearing in addition, if not instead of, a physiological incompatibility between high- and low-frequency sensitivity.

In order to find what these other sources of selective pressure for low-frequency sensitivity might be, two observations mentioned in the previous section become important. First, low frequencies travel farther than high frequencies. It follows that animals which are more sensitive to low frequencies are also able to detect brief sounds from a longer distance. Second, large animals make high "volume" sounds, and volume depends on

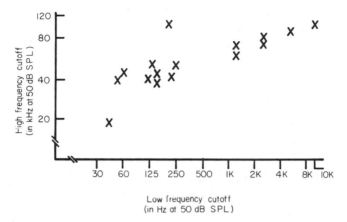

Fig. 7. Relation between high frequency hearing and low frequency hearing. Each point represents a genus of mammals. Note trend from lower left to upper right.

low-frequency content as well as on intensity. Therefore, animals that hear low frequencies are probably more accurate in their assessment of the size of other large animals in their vicinity than are animals less sensitive to low frequencies. Either of these observations suggests a reason for large animals to be sensitive to low frequencies. Because larger animals usually have larger "life-spaces" than smaller animals and therefore are more concerned with distant events and because large animals are also more interested in the activities of other large animals in the vicinity, either of these selective pressures might be expected to result in large animals being more sensitive to low frequencies than small animals.

But even these several sources of selective pressure do not entirely explain the wide variation in low-frequency hearing that now appears to exist among mammals. Certainly they do not explain the remarkable case of the kangaroo rat whose low-frequency hearing may rival man's. This peculiarity of kangaroo rats has been elegantly explained by Webster and Webster (1971) who have shown that the low-frequency sensitivity serves in the detection of owls and snakes—the kangaroo rat's chief predators. Therefore, still further selective pressures for low-frequency hearing exist in many ecological niches. Beyond ecological idosyncrasy, however, the source of these pressures is not yet known.

In summary, low-frequency hearing, unlike high-frequency hearing, is not necessary either for animal detection or for accurate sound localization. Consequently, not all mammals are sensitive to low frequencies. Since it is almost always large mammals that have good low-frequency hearing, however, it would appear that one general source of selective pressure is related to their size, at least indirectly. The two most obvious possibilities, other than unique ecological demands, seem to be the need for more distant sound detection and the need to identify the nature of other large animals in the vicinity.

III. THE CONTRIBUTION OF CENTRAL AUDITORY STRUCTURES TO HEARING

Having discussed the evolution of the vertebrate auditory system, the evolution of sound reception and some of the sources of selective pressure that caused their evolution, it remains to describe the neural mechanisms subserving the detection and localization of brief sounds. But before undertaking this detailed description, it is useful first to describe the general arrangement of the central auditory system in a way which will be helpful in understanding its functional analysis. Therefore, the three subsections within this section deal respectively with an overview of the central auditory system, the contribution of central auditory structures to the detection of brief sounds, and finally, their contribution to the localization of the source of brief sounds.

A. The Central Auditory System

It is not uncommon to describe the central auditory system as a pathway from ear to cerebral cortex. But it can be seen from Fig. 8 that each central auditory stucture, regardless of how "high" or how "low" it is stationed in the "pathway," is much more than a relay or stepping stone to cortex. Instead, each structure in the auditory system is known to act in at least four diverse ways. First, as the usual view would suggest, each structure serves as a relay in the pathway from the ear to higher structures in the system, at least in the sense that its ablation always disrupts or severs the connections between the higher structures and the ear.

Second, every structure in the auditory system transforms its neural input into an output which always differs from its input, and along at least some descriptive dimensions, the "neural code" transmitted by a center is entirely incommensurable with the "code" arriving at the center. Underlying these synaptic transformations is the general neurophysiological principle that the impulse activity of a neuron within the central nervous system is not usually a reflection of the impulse activity in only one of its many afferent inputs; that is, a convergence of presynaptic activity is required before a postsynaptic neuron will generate an impulse (Eccles, 1964). It would be surprising, therefore, if an impulse in a postsynaptic neuron had exactly the same significance as

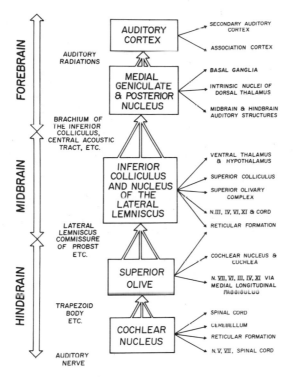

FIG. 8. Schematic summary of the central auditory system of mammals. Large boxes and connections between them constitute the classical or lemniscal auditory pathway. The arrows and structures on right include nonclassical pathways now known or suspected to exist in all mammals.

an impulse in a presynaptic neuron. Since the neurons in the auditory system are not unusual, it can be concluded that the significance of activity in any one structure is, for the most part, different from that in any previous structure in the system. If there are instances in which the code for a stimulus dimension is not altered by synaptic transmission, then such instances must be exceptions to the general rule.

Third, each structure in the auditory system serves to distribute its products to a variety of nonauditory structures. Some of these sensorimotor loops undoubtedly subserve unconditioned reflexes. But as will be seen below, other sensorimotor loops that also short-cut the forebrain subserve functions such as alerting, attending, orienting and learning that *cannot* be regarded as reflexes in the usual sense of this term (cf. Sherrington, 1906).

Fourth, each auditory structure serves to modulate its own input by efferent fibers that descend to lower auditory structures in feedback loops. Although the contribution of these "descending auditory" (or "efferent auditory" or "centrifugal") fibers is not yet understood, it is now known that activity in these fibers has a clear and obvious effect on the neural activity in structures lower in the pathway and consequently, eventually in the higher structures as well. Whether this effect is merely a gating of activity by facilitation and inhibition of lower brainstem centers is still a matter of debate.

It follows from these four general characteristics of the structures in the auditory system that a particular central auditory structure can be viewed in several ways: as a receiver, transmitter, analyzer, synthesizer, decoder, encoder, relay, sensorimotor linkage, distributor, or feedback controller. Therefore, in the description that follows, it would be misleading to suggest that the contributions of a particular structure are exhausted by the behavioral roles described. Undoubtedly, the various structures do many more things than are now known or even imagined, and in many cases, may make a contribution more subtle or more important than those already discovered.

Finally, because the present description relies heavily on the outcome of ablation-behavior experimentation, it is particularly important to note certain obvious consequences of removing one or another of the structures shown in Fig. 8. To begin with, each auditory structure from the cochlear nucleus "upward" can be properly thought of as the origin of a *motor* pathway—in the sense that part of its output is directed to other neural structures which project, in turn, directly or indirectly to effector cells. This "motor" role of auditory structures at every level of the system is the one that most often complicates the interpretation of ablation experiments. For example, the apparently simple task of choosing a behavioral response by which a particular auditory ability is to be measured becomes an important and complex decision. Because behavioral measurement requires a complex sequence of neural transformations from sense organ to response, any one link in the chain, including structures closer to the final common path, may prove to be the factor limiting performance. Thus, it is not impossible to obtain two apparently different outcomes from what would seem to be a simple test of sensory discrimination by using two different behavioral techniques (for example, compare Neff, Arnott, and Fisher [1950] where cats were required to find the source of a sound, with Thompson and Welker [1963] where cats indicated the direction of a sound source by reflexive orientation). This point will prove to be important in a later section.

With this general statement concerning the way in which centers are linked and interact, it is now possible to examine the results of ablation studies with an appreciation of the limitation and difficulties of this method. In the two subsections that follow, first the neural mechanisms of sound source detection and then, the mechanisms of sound source localization will be discussed.

B. The Role of the Auditory System in the Detection of Brief Sounds

Since brief sounds evoke responses throughout the auditory system and since there are many neural exits from the auditory system to motor systems (Whitfield, 1967; Goldstein, Hall, & Butterfield, 1968) (Fig. 8), it follows that it is virtually impossible to truncate the central auditory system in such a way as to make an animal completely incapable of responding to a brief sound. For if even a few fibers leaving one cochlear nucleus are left intact and the remainder are sectioned completely, auditory evoked activity can still reach motor structures throughout the central nervous system and an animal can use this activity either as a basis for an unconditioned or reflexive response, or via sensory feedback through other modalities, as a stimulus for almost any conditionable response in its normal behavioral repertoire.

Of course, this resilience to surgical disruption of sound-evoked or sound-elicited responses does not mean that destruction of one or another part of the auditory system does not always produce a deficit of some sort. On the contrary, the auditory system has gained the morphological form that it has as a result of relentless selective pressures on it. Consequently, a loss of part of the system cannot fail to produce some sort of behavioral deficit whether or not the deficit is obvious or yet discovered. But because auditory evoked activity is distributed so widely up and down the central nervous system beginning at the cochlear nucleus and then again and again in every higher structure, only an ablation that disconnects every auditory fiber from every motor mechanism renders an animal *completely* incapable of responding to a brief sound.

Since the production of complete unresponsiveness to all transient sounds requires either destruction of the ears or complete disconnection of the ears from the motor systems at or before the cochlear nuclei, it is almost trivial to point out that the detection of transient sounds is not affected by ablations confined to structures at still higher levels. Indeed, the higher the level of truncation or ablation of the auditory system, the more centers remain preserved so we might expect that a greater number of sensory motor pathways remain available, which is to say that the animal can exhibit its capacity in a greater variety of ways. This expectation is fulfilled at least in so far as removal of auditory cortex seems to result in little or no overt behavioral effect on the ability to detect sounds (cf., Kryter & Ades, 1943; Raab & Ades, 1946; Rosenzweig, 1946). In contrast, a lesion at a lower level, say between the superior olives and inferior colliculus, deprives the tectum of its auditory fibers and thereby removes whatever sensory-motor connections are achieved in the tectum. Precisely how this restricts the behavioral repertoire is not well documented.

In summary, the detection of brief sounds is not a fragile capacity of the auditory system. As long as the ear has ultimate access to muscles, behavioral responses to sound are possible. It is difficult to avoid the notion that this resilience is probably the result of the severe selective pressure for animal detection in natural environments. Still the variety of responses available to show this sensitivity to sound may be greater when more centers are left intact.

C. The Role of the Brainstem Tegmentum and Auditory Tectum in Sound Detection

A reticulated tegmentum extends throughout the length of the neuraxis from the diencephalon to the lowest segment of the spinal cord. Moruzzi and Magoun (1949) have shown that within the brainstem this tegmental core, or reticular formation, serves a widespread neural activating function that is clearly related to behavioral alerting responses. Further, it is known that the various sensory systems have access to this alerting mechanism and certainly, the auditory system is no exception (see Fig. 8). Many ascending fibers from the cochlear nucleus and superior olivary complex terminate in the tegmentum as do descending fibers from auditory structures at higher levels.

Although there has been little experimentation into the specific role of this activating system in audition, it seems likely that it provides a means of neural activation by sound quite apart from the lemniscal auditory system. Thus, disconnection of the lemniscal system at the level of the lateral lemniscus or higher does not entirely isolate higher structures from auditory evoked activity. Since this activation can serve as a conditioned stimulus, an animal deprived of its lemniscal connections alone is not incapable of learning conditioned responses to the presentation of a sound (Kelly, 1970). However, the observation that most neurons in the brainstem reticular formation are capable of being activated by more than one sensory system raises a further question of whether or not an animal deprived of its lemniscal auditory system could rely on the reticular system to discriminate either the occurrence of a sound from the occurrence of a nonauditory stimulus or one sound from another. Thus, the observation that the nonspecific activating system remains intact and functional after truncation of the lemniscal auditory system provides an adequate explanation of the observation that sound-detection ability remains despite massive lesions in the lemniscal auditory system. But the question remains whether or not the animal still perceives "sounds" as a natural class of stimuli discriminable from other classes of stimuli, and whether or not the animal can discriminate one quality of sound from another (Fisher & Harrison, 1962; Kelly, 1970; Kryter & Ades, 1943; Raab & Ades, 1946).

ATTENTION AND THE INTEGRATIVE ACTION OF THE AUDITORY CENTRAL NERVOUS SYSTEM

As Sherrington showed (1906), many stimuli impinge on the organism at once, and the main office of the central nervous system is to assure that only one of these is prepotent. In turn, the establishment of a hierarchy of stimuli permits the organism to do one main thing at a time. Thus, at any given moment, the detectability of a sound, insofar as this is determined by its effect on behavior, depends on factors other than the sensitivity of the ear to sound and the ability of the central nervous system to distribute auditory evoked activity to the motor systems. For the present purposes, it is convenient to lump all these factors, whether predispositions, motives, sets, etc., under the single term "attention." In its most general sense, attention refers to the means by which the central nervous system resolves the competition between stimuli for control of the motor system. Obviously, this one process alone includes the most fundamental functions of the entire nervous system. It is no wonder that it has proved to be one of the most perplexing problems confronting the neurosciences.

In the study of auditory attention itself, many experiments have dealt with the descending fibers in the auditory system, which, for obvious reasons, might be thought to modulate the system's activity and possibly its sensitivity. Since the descending system has now been shown to have both inhibitory and facilitatory effects on neural activity at all levels of the auditory system including the receptor organ itself, it remains a prime anatomic candidate (along with the more usual motor systems for somatic adjustment for listening) for the mediation of several of the processes often subsumed under the term "attention" (e.g., Galambos, 1956; Weinberger, 1971). However, it is also now clear that the descending auditory system is not, as was once thought, the sole substrate of attention (Worden, 1966).

We have already discussed one feature of sound (abruptness of onset) that probably renders an attention-demanding quality to sound for all animals. No doubt there are other features (for example, high intensity or high volume sounds) that produce similar effects on behavior. But it can be seen that each of these qualities is also directly related to the amount of neural activity leaving the ear per unit of time. That is, abrupt onsets, very loud, or very voluminous sounds each evoke a high rate of neural activity in the auditory nerve itself. Therefore, even though they are obviously attention-demanding, they are not attention-demanding because of some subtle or abstract psychological property extracted by the central auditory system. Indeed, it is more profitable to view these sounds as being so very important for the welfare of the animal, that the ear and the entire auditory system has evolved to a point that guarantees action by flooding the central nervous system with impulses (e.g., Hoffman & Searle, 1968).

With this class of stimuli set aside, another more tenuous and subtle class appears—sounds that are attention-demanding because of an animal's previous experience with them. Attention to these kinds of sound can be thought of as a conditioned or learned response. This learned or conditioned attention has been directly investigated by ablation-behavior methods in cats (Jane *et al.*, 1965). That study shows that normal cats, when exposed both to auditory and to visual stimuli for solving a shock-avoidance problem, select auditory stimuli over visual stimuli. Even cats with 95% of their second-order auditory neurons transected, and cats completely deprived of auditory cortex, continue to select a soft tone over a flashing light as a basis for avoiding shock. Cats with ablations of the inferior colliculus or sections of the brachium of the inferior colliculus, however, reverse their natural bias and select the light cue over the sound cue. Since this shift of attending from sound to light was not a secondary result of an elevation of the threshold for sound, it would seem that lesions in the auditory midbrain affect the attention-demanding qualities of sound without affecting either auditory sensitivity or the attentive or vigilant listening, required by a threshold determination procedure. From these results, it is difficult to avoid the notion that the auditory midbrain provides some sort of amplifying function for the neural activity in the auditory system—facilitating the effect of neural activity evoked by sounds recognized after their occurrence as important, and attenuating the effect of neural activity evoked by sounds recognized as unimportant.

Summarizing the sound-detection mechanisms of the auditory system, the ear allows abrupt or animate sounds to evoke a burst of neural activity in the auditory nerve. The central system provides for wide distribution of this activity to the motor systems throughout the central nervous system and to other auditory structures for analysis of its other salient attributes. The reticular formation contributes to the process by activating nonauditory structures and alerting the animal. The descending auditory system may contribute a modulation of sound-evoked activity in a manner which would seem to satisfy at least some of the requirements for the ability to pay attention to sound, although it is doubtful that this system will provide a full explanation of attentive processes. Finally, the midbrain and forebrain auditory structures may also be involved in assigning behavioral significance to certain sounds. Indeed, every opportunity for synaptic transmission is selective—and if this can be regarded as it was by Sherrington, as the neural counterpart of attention, then every center plays some part in this all important function.

D. The Contribution of Central Auditory Structures to Sound Localization

As described in an earlier section, sound localization depends on an animal's capacity to determine the azimuth, elevation, and distance of a sound source. Two of these three dimensions, elevation and distance, depend entirely on the frequency spectrum analysis achieved by the ear. Although azimuth is also partly dependent on frequency spectrum analysis, the two primary cues for azimuth, Δt and Δfi, obviously require binaural integration for their analysis. This means that the analysis of the cues for the synthesis of the azimuth dimension cannot be achieved by the ears alone and, therefore, the central auditory system must play an analytic as well as a synthetic role in this perceptual capacity. Because of the persistence of selective pressure on accurate sound localization, perhaps it is not a surprise that specialized structures for Δfi and Δt analysis have evolved within the central auditory system. A comprehensive review and bibliography of sound localization mechanisms can be found in Erulkar (1972).

E. Hindbrain

1. ΔFI ANALYSIS

All mammals, and possibly all tetrapods, can localize the azimuth of a sound source on the basis of frequency spectra differences at the two ears—that is, by utilization of Δfi cues. However, it is in mammals with their capacity for high-frequency hearing that this mode of sound localization has been perfected to the point where the source of a brief sound can be localized within a few degrees solely on the basis of Δfi cues alone.

The neural mechanism for Δfi analysis in mammals resides mostly, but not solely, in the superior olivary complex of the hindbrain, and within this complex, probably in the lateral superior olivary nucleus (Boudreau & Tsuchitani, 1970). Figure 9 shows the means by which binaural input arrives at the lateral superior olive (LSO). It can be seen that each lateral superior olive receives input directly from the ipsilateral cochlear nucleus and also indirectly from the contralateral cochlear nucleus via the main nucleus of the trapezoid body (Harrison & Feldman, 1970). Thus, the afferent fibers to the lateral superior olive are second-order neurons from the ipsilateral ear and third-order neurons from the contralateral ear.

The projection of the two ears onto each laterial superior olive is tonotopic (Boudreau & Tsuchitani, 1970). That is, the orderly spectrographic analysis achieved by the basilar membrane in the cochlea, and preserved in the auditory nerve, is also preserved by the synapses in the cochlear nucleus and the nucleus of the trapezoid body. By this means the cells of the lateral

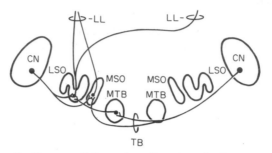

Fɪɢ. 9. Schematic diagram of the major afferents and efferents to the left superior olivary complex in cat. Abbreviations: CN, cochlear nucleus; LSO, lateral superior olive; MSO, medial superior olive; MTB, medial nucleus of the trapezoid body; TB, trapezoid body, LL, lateral lamniscus.

superior olive receive their stimulation from corresponding points of the basilar membranes in the two ears and are provided with the opportunity to compare the intensity of stimulation reaching the two ears at each frequency (Boudreau & Tsuchitani, 1970). Thus, the LSO allows the entire spectrographic analysis achieved by each ear to be compared frequency-by-frequency for relative intensity: a true spectrum difference or Δfi analysis.

The Δfi analysis from the lateral superior olive is passed on chiefly to the midbrain by way of the ipsilateral and the contralateral lateral lemniscus; but is is also probably distributed to many other nonauditory structures besides (Stotler, 1953). Certainly part of the output impinges on neurons in the reticular formation. Although the projections of the LSO may be confined to the midbrain, they have not yet been adequately studied. Until demonstrated otherwise, it is not impossible that part of its output is directed to the seventh nerve nucleus (just caudal to it) for directing the external ears toward the source of a sound, and to the eye and neck movement nuclei (III, IV, VI, and XI) via the medial longitudinal fasciculus for visual or olfactory orientation.

The idea that the LSO serves in a Δfi analysis is supported by the variation in its size among mammals. In mammals that depend on Δfi alone for azimuth localization, the lateral superior olive is large. In animals (such as man) whose ears are wide-set enough that Δt analysis provides an adequate cue for azimuth localization, the lateral superior olive is very reduced in size (Harrison & Feldman, 1970). Therefore, on the basis of species differences as well as on connections common to all mammals, it can be concluded that the lateral superior olive analyzes and encodes the spectral difference received by the two ears for transmission and distribution to other structures in the central nervous system.

2. Δt ANALYSIS

The second cue used for the determination of the azimuth of a sound source is the binaural time disparity, Δt. Δt analysis is also achieved by the superior olivary complex, and within this complex, almost certainly in the medial superior olivary nucleus (MSO).

The route by which the medial superior olive receives its input is also shown in Fig. 9. It can be seen that the MSO gains direct input from both cochlear nuclei via the trapezoid body and therefore its cells are third-order auditory neurons (Stotler, 1953). The neurons in the medial superior olive have two large dendrites oriented in a medial-lateral direction. It is these dendrites that receive the synapses of the fibers from the cochlear nuclei—the medial dendrite receiving fibers from the contralateral cochlear nucleus via the trapezoid body (Stotler, 1953).

The response characteristics of many, but not all, of the cells in the medial superior olive also indicate that they analyze Δt (Galambos, Schwartzkopff, & Rupert, 1959; Hall, 1965). Figure 10 shows the response characteristics of three of these cells. It can be seen from the figure that the cells are extremely sensitive to the small binaural time differences in the range required for the localization of the azimuth of a sound source (Masterton, Jane, & Diamond, 1967).

As has already been described, not all mammals are capable of Δt analysis because their ears are too close-set for that cue to have sufficient range. In these mammals, no medial superior olive exists (e.g., mouse, bat, hedgehog, dolphin) (Harrison & Irving, 1966). For example, the hedgehog has a lateral superior olive and a nucleus of the trapezoid body, but no medial superior olive. In contrast, the cat has a lateral superior olive, a medial superior olive, and a medial nucleus of the trapezoid body much like that illustrated in Fig. 9. In parallel to these differences in the structure of the superior olivary complex in hedgehog and cat, the cat is capable of localization either with spectrum differences or time differences, while the hedgehog appears to be incapable of using phase-difference (i.e., time-difference) cues (Fig. 11). Thus, data from comparative neurology and behavior, as well as from electrophysiology, also indicate that Δt analysis depends on the medial superior olive.

Since the medial superior olive gains its contralateral input via the trapezoid body, it is possible to deprive the nucleus of this part of its input by section of the trapezoid body. This deprivation of input by trapezoid body sections results in a loss of Δt-analyzing ability in the range normally used for the localization of the azimuth of a sound source. In a cat, for example, section of the trapezoid body results in an ability to distinguish binaural click pairs presented in the order left click–right click from identical

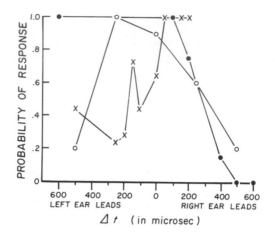

FIG. 10. Response of single units in medial superior olive of cat to variations in Δt (modified from Galambos *et al.*, 1959; Hall, 1965).

click pairs presented in the order right click–left click, if the clicks within the pair are separated in time (Δt) by 0.5 msec or less. Since this is exactly the range of Δt to which the MSO of a cat is normally exposed in sound localization, it is clear that the input to the superior olivary complex is necessary for the analysis. However, if the Δt is larger than 0.5 msec, a cat is able to perform Δt discrimination despite section of its trapezoid body. Therefore, there undoubtedly are binaural time-sensitive cells in the auditory system located elsewhere than in the superior olivary complex,

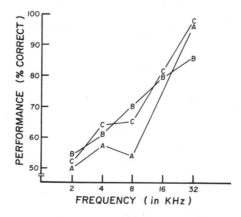

FIG. 11. Performance of MSO-less mammal (hedgehog) on localization of pure-tone pips. Note high level of performance at high frequencies when Δfi cues predominate and chance level of performance at low frequencies when phase-difference Δt cues usually predominate.

although these other cells are not sufficiently sensitive to analyze Δt in the range necessary for sound localization (Masterton et al., 1967).

To demonstrate that it is the superior olivary complex and not some higher structure in the auditory system that analyzes Δt, it is necessary to compare the deficits resulting from disruption of its output (the lateral lemniscus) from the deficits resulting from disruption of its input (the trapezoid). As already noted, lesions of the trapezoid body result in an elevation of Δt threshold. The more trapezoid body fibers that are interrupted, the wider the Δt must be before a cat can assess it accurately. In contrast, partial lesions of the lateral lemniscus do not produce this partial deficit in Δt discrimination. Lateral lemniscus lesions result in no obvious change in the Δt threshold, but instead, in an incommensurable deficit. With partial section of the lateral lemniscus a cat does not hear a sound to the left as being similar to another sound to the left, even though it can learn to discriminate a sound to the left from a sound to the right. Apparently, its normal ability to classify sounds on the basis of the locus of their source is lost, even though the ability to discriminate remains. Thus, lesions in the output of the superior olivary complex result in a behavioral deficit entirely different from the deficit resulting from lesions in its input. Therefore, several lines of evidence, neuroanatomical, comparative, physiological, and behavioral, suggest that the superior olivary complex encodes the binaural time disparities for the localization of the azimuth of a sound source, and furthermore, this evidence points most directly to the MSO (Masterton & Diamond, 1967).

The products of the Δt analysis by the MSO are directed towards the midbrain via the lateral lemniscus, but as in the case of the lateral superior olive output, the output of the medial superior olive may be directed to other motor and associative structures as well (Stotler, 1953). For example, Harrison and Irving (1966) have shown that, among mammals, the number of cells in the medial superior olive is closely correlated with the number of cells in the sixth nerve nucleus above it. Thus, the output of the medial superior olive may be directed to the sixth-nerve nucleus, especially in highly visual animals, and also to the other brainstem nuclei which control pinna, eye, and neck movements.

Therefore, from many lines of experimentation it can be concluded that the azimuth of a sound source based on either Δfi or Δt cues is performed primarily by the superior olivary complex and the products of this analysis are directed forward to the midbrain for further transformation and probably to the various motor (and associative) structures of the hindbrain, midbrain, and spinal cord either for expression in orienting movements of the eyes, ears, neck, and body, or for activation of the nervous system for behavioral alerting.

F. Midbrain

The analysis and utilization of Δfi and Δt cues for sound localization are not abolished by lesions in the inferior colliculus. The greatest part of the inferior colliculus can be ablated without any apparent change in the ability of a cat to localize the azimuth of a sound source, or to discriminate Δt or Δfi cues. However, if the ablation is deep enough to interrupt a large part of the lemniscal pathway, then the use of either Δt or Δfi is markedly affected (Masterton, Jane, & Diamond, 1968).

Since single units in the colliculus have been shown to be sensitive to the locus of a sound source, the lack of a behavioral deficit after relatively large lesions in the inferior colliculus that spare part of the lemniscal projection to the forebrain is puzzling (cf. Jane et al., 1965; Masterton et al., 1968; Altman, 1967; Rose, Gross, Geisler, & Hind, 1966). Nevertheless, it now appears that the inferior colliculus may have little to do with the strictly perceptual components of sound localization. But since deep lesions at the level of the brachium of the inferior colliculus abolish Δt and Δfi discrimination, it is also clear that the lemniscal pathway synapsing in the midbrain and continuing into the forebrain is absolutely essential for sound localization (Masterton et al., 1968; Strominger & Oesterreich, 1970). Lesions that section only the superficial brachium, but not the underlying fibers of the central acoustic tract (Galambos, Myers, & Sheatz, 1961; Papez, 1936) disrupt a cat's ability to discriminate Δt, but do not affect Δfi. Thus, the brachium itself seems to be necessary for the utilization of Δt cues while Δfi cues can be carried to the forebrain by deeper, more medial routes. Therefore, it would seem that the strictly lemniscal, superficial pathway from hindbrain to forebrain may be indispensable for Δt discrimination, but not necessary for Δfi discrimination. But apparently the neural activity evoked by both cues must gain access to the forebrain for their behavioral discrimination and for their use in sound localization (Masterton et al., 1968; Neff, 1968).

G. Forebrain

From the discussion presented so far, it would be surprising if the auditory cortex which is five or more synapses away from the ear would be necessary for simple sensory functions. Indeed, auditory cortex ablation does not disrupt amplitude or frequency discrimination (Butler, Diamond, & Neff, 1957; Kryter & Ades, 1943; Raab & Ades, 1946; Thompson, 1960). It might also be expected that the contribution of auditory cortex to sound localization is subtle. In order to begin to understand the contribution of auditory cortex, it is first necessary to distinguish among the techniques used to measure behavioral deficits.

To begin with, the most direct means of testing the azimuth localization ability of an animal would seem to be a task that requires the animal to find the source of a sound. Typically, an animal is first confined to a starting point until a sound occurs at one or another location. The animal is then allowed to proceed to the sound source, and if it does so correctly, receives a reward. This is the technique, used by Neff and his colleagues in many experiments (see review in Neff, 1968) and with a slight variation, also by Riss (1959). In this situation, cats demonstrate a total inability to localize the source of a brief sound when they are deprived of their auditory cortex. The localization deficit is so profound that cats without auditory cortex not only cannot localize the source of a brief sound (Riss, 1959), but they cannot reliably find the source of a loud buzzer, even when it is left on continuously (Neff et al., 1950). Thus, this behavioral technique, which seems to measure sound localization ability in the most direct way, suggests that an intact auditory cortex is an absolute necessity.

However, the idea that decorticate cats are suffering a purely sensory deficit in localization is probably not correct. For example, if cats are trained on a shock-avoidance task (double-grill box) in such a manner that clicks in the left ear designate "no shock" and clicks to the right ear designate impending shock, they can avoid the shock consistently (Masterton & Diamond, 1964). Thus, it is obvious that cats can discriminate sounds at their left ear from sounds at their right ear, even though they cannot find the source of a sound in space. Proceeding further, cats can also learn a shock-avoidance task when the "safe" and "warning" cues for shock are dependent solely on changes of Δt or Δfi. Thus, cats suffering a total disability for finding the source of a sound after an auditory cortex ablation are, nevertheless, still capable of discriminating the two cues for localization, Δt and Δfi, well above a chance level (Masterton & Diamond, 1964). Still sound lateralization is not the same as sound localization—the latter includes the attribute of the source being "out there" and this extra feature prohibits simple comparison of the two types of tasks.

Perhaps the most dramatic demonstration of the "nonsensory" contribution of auditory cortex to sound localization has recently been made in monkeys by Heffner (1973). In Heffner's experiment, monkeys with ablations of auditory cortex were trained and tested on three tasks that have markedly different *behavioral* requirements but closely similar perceptual requirements. In each case, the relevant cues were lateralizable or localizable sounds. In the first task, the monkeys were tested by means of "conditioned suppression" (Smith, 1970). In this technique, the monkeys sucked on a spout in order to obtain an occasional water reward while clicks emanated from a speaker on the left. On a test trial, the clicks shifted to a speaker on the right without, of course, any other correlated cue. Ten seconds after the clicks shifted to the right speaker, the monkey received an unavoidable shock to the foot. After a few pairings of right clicks with shock, the animal stopped sucking on the water spout whenever the clicks were shifted to the right speaker and would not begin sucking again until a shock had been received and the clicks had shifted back to the left speaker. In this test, monkeys without auditory cortex not only continued to *detect* the shift of the clicks from left to right, but in further testing they proved able to *identify* a single click as being either on the left or on the right.

In the second behavioral test, the monkeys were provided with two levers, one lever on the left and one lever on the right. Whenever the thirsty monkey placed his mouth on a water spout, a single click would emanate from either the left or the right speaker. If the animal pressed the left lever when the click had come from the left speaker, or if it pressed the right lever when the click had come from the right speaker, it received a water reward.

By this technique, monkeys with or without auditory cortex could also discriminate a click from the left versus a click from the right with almost the same acuity as normal monkeys (less than 5 degrees). From these two results, therefore, it would appear that sound localization ability might be entirely unaffected by ablation of auditory cortex.

However, in the third means of testing sound localization, this time by the direct technique used by Neff and his colleagues (1950), an entirely different result was obtained. In this case, the thirsty monkey was confined to a 10 by 15 foot room which had three water spouts arranged in a large triangle. One lick spout (the "start" lick spout) was at one end of the room. The other two lick spouts, with speakers just above them (the "goal" spouts), were located at the other end of the room. When the "start" spout was contacted, a single click emanated from the speaker at one or the other two lick spouts. If the monkey then proceeded to the lick spout from which the click had emanated, it received a water reward. It then had to return to the center lick spout to begin another trial by touching it and producing another click, etc.

In marked contrast to the other two means of testing sound localization ability, monkeys deprived of auditory cortex found this task impossible. At a 60 degree angular separation between the two click sources—an angle which would result in 100% correct performance by a normal monkey—monkeys without auditory cortex could not localize the source above a chance level even after thousands of training trials.

From a consideration of these several results in cat and in monkey, it becomes clear that auditory cortex ablation does not result in a simple sensory deficit. Indeed, the ability of monkeys to *indicate* the azimuth of a sound source, and to indicate the laterality of paired clicks on the basis of Δt or Δfi, is nearly, if not entirely, unaffected by auditory cortex ablation. On the other hand, if the cat or the monkey is required to *find* the source of a brief sound, it is incapable of doing so without auditory cortex. It is these results which form the basis of the conclusion that the primary contribution of auditory cortex to sound localization ability is not strictly sensory in nature. Because of the close relationship between the presence or absence of a deficit and the behavioral requirements of the task, it would appear that the contribution of auditory cortex to sound localization is somewhat more subtle than "sensory" as this term is usually used. That is, auditory cortex ablation seems to result in a deficit in what an animal can do in response to a localizable sound, rather than a deficit in perceiving the locus of the sound source itself.

The deficit is certainly not a strictly "motor" difficulty either. For example, if instead of an auditory cue, the correct locus is signaled by a flashing light, either a cat or a monkey without auditory cortex can promptly solve the problem at a very high level of performance. Thus, the deficit does not cross sensory modalities—it is confined to audition. Therefore, both a strictly sensory and a strictly motor deficit is ruled out. What seems to remain can now be specified only as an "audiomotor" deficit, that is, a deficit in the actions that an animal can take in response to a localizable sound source.

Up to now we have been speaking of the deficits produced by *bilateral* removal of auditory cortex. But there are also signs that the role of auditory cortex in sound localization may be revealed by unilateral ablations. In order to reveal a unilateral deficit, however, the perceptual requirements of the task must be complicated by presenting on any one trial either one or two sound sources (Whitfield, Cranford, Ravizza, & Diamond, 1972). In an apparatus similar to the one used by Neff, cats were trained to approach a food box on the left when the speaker on the left emitted tone pips (L) and to approach a food box on the right when *both* left and right speakers sounded (L+R). The two stimuli (i.e., L+R) were not simultaneous so what the animal heard was two trains of tone pips, one emanating from the left speaker and one from the right speaker. Normal cats learned the task easily; apparently they could ignore the left speaker when both left and right sounded. However, a left unilateral lesion of auditory cortex produced a profound deficit in this task, while a right lesion had no effect. When reciprocal training was given (i.e., R versus R+L), it was cats with lesions of the right side which suffered the loss, while cats with left lesions now learned the task with ease. Apparently, the discriminability of multiple stimuli is impaired by unilateral lesions, and the two hemispheres are symmetrical insofar as each plays a special part in selecting stimuli on the contralateral side. Whether or not the nature of this deficit is more one of "attention" or of "localization" is not yet clear.

Although by far the most complete and ingenious research into auditory cortex has been performed on cats and monkeys, there are several indications that the same sort of subtle deficit also results from auditory cortex ablation in the most primitive mammals. For example, opossums can *indicate* the locus of a click (by the conditioned-suppression technique) with or without auditory cortex (Ravizza & Masterton, 1972). Conversely, hedgehogs without auditory cortex cannot *find* the source of a brief sound (R. J. Ravizza & I. T. Diamond, unpublished observations). Thus, two facets of the cortical syndrome seen in the monkey and cat are duplicated in two of the most primitive mammals now extant. Therefore, the contribution of auditory cortex seen in monkeys and cats may not be a highly specialized or advanced function at all, but instead a relatively general and possibly, primitive one.

As Herrick (1933) has pointed out, the neocortical targets of the sensory systems are the site of neural mechanisms for identifying important objects and events in the vicinity. In this regard, it would appear that auditory cortex is part of a system for the identification of the attributes of sound sources. The import of this conclusion can be seen when it is placed in contrast with the contribution of the superior olivary complex in the hindbrain. Whereas the ear and the superior olivary complex analyze the physical cues contained in the stimulus for the localization of its source, it is the forebrain that seems to synthesize these analyses into a single coherent identity, location of the sound source itself. It is possible that auditory cortex may also allow the projection of the image of the sound source back into an organized "auditory space," perceptually isomorphic with a similarly organized "visual space" and "motor space" (Ravizza & Masterton, 1972). From this viewpoint, auditory cortex ablation may disrupt the isomorphism, at least between auditory space and motor space, even though it does not disrupt the organization of auditory space itself.

References

Altman, Y. A. Response in units of inferior colliculus in cats to unilateral change of intensity of a binaural stimulus. *Neuroscience Translation*, 1967, **3**, 239–247.
Ariëns-Kappers, C. U., Huber, G. C., & Crosby, E. C. *The comparative anatomy of the nervous system of vertebrates*. New York: Hafner, 1936.
Boudreau, J. C., & Tsuchitani, C. Cat superior olive S-segment cell discharge to tonal stimulation. In W. D. Neff (Ed.), *Contributions to sensory physiology*. Vol. 4. New York: Academic Press, 1970. Pp. 143–213.
Busnel, R. G. (Ed.) *Acoustic behavior of animals*. New York: Amer. Elsevier, 1963.

Butler, R. A., Diamond, I. T., & Neff, W. D. Role of auditory cortex in discrimination of changes in frequency. *Journal of Neurophysiology*, 1957, **20**, 108–120.

Capranica, R. A. Vocal response of the bullfrog to natural and synthetic mating calls. *Journal of the Acoustical Society of America*, 1966, **40**, 1131–1139.

Coleman, C. D. An analysis of cues to auditory depth perception in free space. *Psychological Bulletin*, 1963, **60**, 302–315.

Desmedt, J. E., & Mechelse, K. Corticofugal projections from temporal lobe in cat and their possible role in acoustic discrimination. *Journal of Physiology (London)*, 1959, **147**, 17–18.

Diamond, I. T., Jones, E. G., & Powell, T. P. S. The projection of the auditory cortex upon the diencephalon and brainstem in the cat. *Brain Research*, 1969, **15**, 305–340.

Diamond, I. T., Utley, J. D. Thalamic degeneration study of sensory cortex in opossum. *Journal of Comparative Neurology*, 1963, **120**, 120–160.

Eccles, J. C. *The physiology of synapses*. Berlin and New York: Springer-Verlag, 1964.

Erickson, R. P., Jane, J. A., Waite, R., & Diamond, I. T. Single neuron investigation of sensory thalamus of the opossum. *Journal of Neurophysiology*, 1964, **27**, 1026–1047.

Erulkar, S. C. Comparative aspects of spatial localization of sound. *Physiological Review*, 1972, **52**, 1, 237–360.

Fisher, G. L., & Harrison, J. M. Some functions of the superior olivary complex in auditory intensity discrimination. *Journal of Comparative Neurology*, 1962, **119**, 269–280.

Galambos, R. Suppression of auditory nerve activity by stimulation of efferent fibers to the cochlea. *Journal of Neurophysiology*, 1956, **19**, 424–437.

Galambos, R., Myers, R. E., & Sheatz, G. C. Extralemniscal activation of auditory cortex in cats. *American Journal of Physiology*, 1961, **200**, 300–315.

Galambos, R., Schwartzkopff, J., & Rupert, A. Microelectrode study of superior olivary nuclei. *American Journal of Physiology*, 1959, **197**, 527–536.

Goldstein, M., Hall, J. L., & Butterfield, B. O. Single unit activity in the primary auditory cortex of unanesthetized cats. *Journal of the Acoustical Society of America*, 1968, **43**, 3, 444–455.

Hall, J. L. Binaural interaction in the accessory superior olivary nucleus of the cat. *Journal of the Acoustical Society of America*, 1965, **37**, 814–823.

Harrison, J. M., & Feldman, M. L. Anatomical aspects of the cochlear nucleus and the superior olivary complex. In W. D. Neff (Ed.), *Contributions to sensory physiology*. Vol. 4. New York: Academic Press, 1970. Pp. 95–142.

Harrison, J. M., & Irving, R. Visual and nonvisual auditory systems in mammals. *Science*, 1966, **154**, 738–743.

Heffner, H. E. The effects of auditory cortex ablation on sound localization in the monkey (*Macaca mulatta*). Unpublished doctoral dissertation, Florida State University, 1973.

Herrick, C. J. The function of the olfactory parts of the cerebral cortex. *Proceedings of the National Academy of Sciences of the United States*, 1933, **19**, 7–14.

Herrick, C. J. *The brain of the tiger salamander*. Chicago, Illinois: Univ. of Chicago Press, 1948.

Hind, J. E. An electrophysiological determination of tonotopic organization in auditory cortex of the cat. *Journal of Neurophysiology*, 1953, **16**, 475–489.

Hoffman, H. S., & Searle, J. L. Acoustic and temporal factors in the evocation of startle. *Journal of the Acoustical Society of America*, 1968, **2**, 269–282.

Jane, J. A., Masterton, R. B., & Diamond, I. T. The function of the tectum for attention to auditory stimuli in the cat. *Journal of Comparative Neurology*, 1965, **125**, 2, 165–192.

Karten, H. J. The organization of the ascending auditory pathway in the pigeon. I. *Brain Research*, 1967, **6**, 409–427.

Karten, H. J. The ascending auditory pathway in pigeon. *Brain Research*, 1968, **11**, 134–153.

Kelly, J. B. The effects of lateral lemniscal and neocortical lesions on auditory absolute thresholds and frequency difference thresholds of the rat. Unpublished doctoral dissertation, Vanderbilt University, 1970.

Kryter, K. D., & Ades, H. W. Studies on the function of the higher acoustical nervous centers in the cat. *American Journal of Psychology*, 1943, **56**, 501–536.

Larsell, O. The differentiation of the peripheral and central acoustic apparatus in the frog. *Journal of Comparative Neurology*, 1934, **60**, 473–527.

Lende, R. A. Sensory representation in the cerebral cortex of the opossum. *Journal of Comparative Neurology*, 1963, **121**, 395–403.

Lende, R. A. Representation in the cerebral cortex of a primitive mammal: Sensorimotor, visual, and auditory fields in the Echidna. *Journal of Neurophysiology*, 1964, **27**, 37–48.

Lorente de No, R. Anatomy of the eighth nerve. III. General plan of structure of the primary cochlear nuclei. *Laryngoscope*, 1933, **43**, 1–38.

McGill, T. E. A review of hearing in amphibians and reptiles. *Psychological Bulletin*, 1960, **57**, 165.

Manley, G. A. Comparative studies of auditory physiology in reptiles. *Zeitschrift für Vergleichende Physiologie*, 1970, **67**, 363–381.

Manley, G. A. Some aspects on the evolution of hearing in vertebrates. *Nature (London)*, 1971, **230**, 506–509.

Masterton, B., & Diamond, I. T. Effects of auditory cortex ablation on discrimination of small binaural time differences. *Journal of Neurophysiology*, 1964, **27**, 15.

Masterton, B., & Diamond, I. T. Medial superior olive and sound localization *Science*, 1967, **155**, 1696–1697.

Masterton, B., Heffner, H. E., & Ravizza, R. J. Evolution of human hearing. *Journal of the Acoustical Society of America*, 1969, **45**, 4, 966–985.

Masterton, B., Jane, J. A., & Diamond, I. T. Role of brainstem auditory structures in sound localization. I. Trapezoid body, superior olive and lateral lemniscus. *Journal of Neurophysiology*, 1967, **30**, 341–360.

Masterton, B., Jane, J. A., & Diamond, I. T. The role of brainstem auditory structures in sound localization. II. Inferior colliculus and its brachium. *Journal of Neurophysiology*, 1968, **31**, 96.

Mohl, B. Auditory sensitivity of the common seal in air and water. *Journal of Auditory Research*, 1968, **8**, 27–38.

Morest, D. K. The neuronal architecture of the medial geniculate body in the cat. *Journal of Anatomy*, 1964, **98**, 4, 611–630.

Morest, D. K. The laminar structure of the medial geniculate body of the cat. *Journal of Anatomy*, 1965, **99**, 143–160.

Moruzzi, G., & Magoun, H. W. Brain stem reticular formation and activation of the EEG. *Electroencephalography and Clinical Neurophysiology*, 1949, **1**, 455–473.

Nauta, W. J. H., & Karten, H. J. A general profile of the vertebrate brain, with sidelights on the ancestry of cerebral cortex. In F. O. Schmitt (Ed.), *The neurosciences: Second study program.* New York: Rockefeller Univ. Press, 1970. Pp. 7–26.

Neff, W. D. Localization and lateralization of sound in space. In A. V. S. de Reuck & J. Knight (Eds.), *Ciba Foundation symposium on hearing mechanisms in vertebrates.* London: *Churchill,* 1968. Pp. 207–231.

Neff, W. D., Arnott, G. P., & Fisher, J. F. Function of auditory cortex: Localization of sound in space. *American Journal of Physiology,* 1950, **163,** 738.

Osen, K. K. Cytoarchitecture of the cochlear nuclei in the cat. *Journal of Comparative Neurology,* 1969, **136,** 543–489.

Papez, J. W. Evolution of the medial geniculate body. *Journal of Comparative Neurology,* 1936, **64,** 41–61.

Poggio, G. F., & Mountcastle, V. B. The functional properties of ventrobasal thalamic neurons studied in unanaesthetized monkeys. *Journal of Neurophysiology,* 1963, **26,** 775–806.

Pumphrey, R. J. Hearing. *Symposium of the Society for Experimental Biology,* 1950, **4,** 1–18.

Raab, D. H., & Ades, H. W. Cortical and midbrain mediation of a conditioned discrimination of acoustic intensities. *American Journal of Psychology,* 1946, **59,** 59–83.

Rasmussen, G. L. Anatomic relationships of the ascending and descending auditory systems. In W. S. Field & B. R. Alford (Eds.), *Neurological aspects of auditory and vestibular disorders.* Springfield, Illinois: Thomas, Springfield, Illinois, 1964. Pp. 5–19.

Ravizza, R. J., & Diamond, I. T. Projections from the auditory thalamus to neocortex in the hedgehog. *Anatomical Record,* 1972, **172,** 390.

Ravizza, R. J., & Masterton, B. Contribution of neocortex to sound localization in oppossum (*Didelphis virginiana*). *Journal of Neurophysiology,* 1972, **35,** 344–356.

Riss, W. Effect of bilateral temporal cortical ablation on discrimination of sound direction. *Journal of Neurophysiology,* 1959, **91,** 441–466.

Roffler, S. K., & Butler, R. A. Factors that influence the localization of sound in the vertical plane. *Journal of the Acoustical Society of America,* 1968, **43,** 1255.

Rose, J. E. The cellular structure of the auditory region of the cat. *Journal of Comparative Neurology,* 1949, **91,** 409–440.

Rose, J. E., Gross, N. B., Geisler, C. D., & Hind, J. E. Some neural mechanisms in the interior colliculus of the cat which may be relevant to localization of a sound source. *Journal of Neurophysiology,* 1966, **29,** 288 314.

Rosenzweig, M. R. Discrimination of auditory intensities in the cat. *American Journal of Psychology,* 1946, **59,** 127–136.

Schwartzkopff, J. On the hearing of birds. *Auk,* 1955, **72,** 340.

Sherrington, C. S. *The integrative action of the nervous system.* New Haven, Connecticut: Yale Univ. Press, 1906.

Smith, J. C. Conditioned suppression as an animal psychophysical technique. In W. C. Stebbins (Ed.), *Animal psychophysics: The design and conduct of sensory experiments.* New York: Appleton, 1970. Pp. 125–159.

Stotler, W. A. An experimental study of the cells and connections in the superior olivary complex. *Journal of Comparative Neurology,* 1953, **98,** 401–432.

Strominger, N. L., & Oesterreich, R. E. Localization of sound after section of the brachium of the inferior colliculus. *Journal of Comparative Neurology*, 1970, **138**, 1–18.

Thompson, R. F. Function of auditory cortex in frequency discrimination. *Journal of Neurophysiology*, 1960, **23**, 321–334.

Thompson, R. F., & Welker, W. I. Role of auditory cortex in reflex head orientation by cats to auditory stimuli. *Journal of Comparative Physiological Psychology*, 1963, **56**, 996–1002.

Tunturi, A. R. Audio frequency localization in the acoustic cortex of the dog. *American Journal of Physiology*, 1944, **141**, 397–403.

van Bergeijk, W. A. The evolution of vertebrate hearing. In W. D. Neff (Ed.), *Contributions to sensory physiology*. Vol. 2. New York: Academic Press, 1967. Pp. 1–46.

von Békèsy, G. *Experiments in hearing*. E. G. Wever (Transl. & Ed.). New York: McGraw-Hill, 1960.

Webster, D. B., & Webster, M. Adaptive value of hearing and vision in kangeroo rat predator avoidance. *Brain, Behavior, and Evolution*, 1971, **4**, 310–322.

Weinberger, N. M. Attentive processes. In J. L. McGaugh (Ed.), *Psychobiology: Behavior from a biological perspective*. New York: Academic Press, 1971. Pp. 130–187.

Whitfield, I. C. *The auditory pathway*. Baltimore, Maryland: Williams & Williams, 1967.

Whitfield, I. C., Cranford, J., Ravizza, R., and Diamond, I. T. Effects of unilateral ablation of auditory cortex in cat on complex sound localization. *Journal of Neurophysiology*, 1972, **35**, 718.

Woolsey, C. N. Organization of the cortical auditory system: A review and synthesis. In G. L. Rasmussen & W. F. Windle (Eds.), *Neural mechanism of the auditory and vestibular system*. Springfield, Illinois: Thomas, 1960. Pp. 165–180.

Woolsey, C. N., & Walzl, E. M. Topical projection of nerve fibers from local regions of the cochlea to the cerebral cortex of the cat. *Bulletin of the Johns Hopkins Hospital*, 1942, **71**, 315–344.

Worden, F. G. Attention and electrophysiology. In E. Stellar and J. M. Sprague (Eds.), *Progress in physiological psychology*. Vol. 1. New York: Academic Press, 1966. Pp. 45–107.

Young, J. Z. *The life of vertebrates*. London and New York: Oxford Univ. Press, 1962.

Chapter 19

AUDITION

DOUGLAS B. WEBSTER

I. NONMAMMALIAN AUDITORY SYSTEMS

Audition requires that sound waves be transduced into nerve impulses, which are carried to the brain where information is transferred to central nervous tissue. An old controversy about whether fish and certain other vertebrates can hear has apparently been laid to rest by new techniques, and all vertebrates recently tested have shown they can respond to some kind of sound stimulus.

A. Properties of Sound

This stimulus can be either of the two types of sound—near field or far field (van Bergeijk, 1967). Near field sound is most noticeable in water, where a vibrating object causes physical displacement of the water against which it vibrates. Since water has little elasticity or compressibility, it is forced alternately toward and away from the vibrating object. This displacement spreads out radially from the point of vibration, covering a broader area further from the source and thus decreasing as the square of the distance from the source. Were water totally inelastic and incompressible, this near field sound would be the only sound in water.

Water is however slightly elastic and compressible, and in addition to near field sound an object vibrating in it produces far field sound, also called a propagated sound wave. Although weaker, this wave travels much further, carried away from the vibrating source by the elasticity of the water molecules. This energy decreases as a first order function rather than as a square.

Both near field and far field sound are important in water. Most if not all fishes have some sense organs sensitive to near field but insensitive to far field sound, and other sense organs with the opposite characteristics.

In air as well a vibrating object causes both near field and far field sound. However, the density of air is so slight, and its elasticity and compressibility so great, that its near field sound can be for all practical purposes ignored; far field sound is what we investigate when we study audition in terrestrial animals.

B. The Hair Cell

Regardless of which type of vibratory energy is being received, or the permutations of the organ which receives it, the hair cell which transduces vibratory energy into nerve impulses is morphologically similar in all vertebrates (Smith, 1968a).

It is pear shaped to cylindrical, with a prominent nucleus and various unremarkable organelles such as mitochondria, endoplasmic reticulum, and Golgi apparatus. Most notably, the hair cell is polarized, both longitudinally and along its apical surface. On the apical surface are many cilia—long, thin cytoplasmic processes—extending out into extracellular fluids. These are the "hairs," and they may number from 40 or 50 up to over 200 on a single hair cell. On each hair cell, all but one of the hairs have little internal structure; they are called stereocilia. One cilium per hair cell has an internal structure and is called a kinocilium. Electron-dense filaments run the length of the kinocilium, in an orderly arrangement, with nine pairs around the periphery and two fibers in the center, just as is the case in mobile cilia and flagella (Wersäll, Flock, & Lundquist, 1965). The kinocilium is eccentrically placed, causing a polarization of the apical surface of the cell.

The cytoplasm of the hair cell is more electron dense at the apical portion, just at the base of the cilia, than it is in the remaining cytoplasm; this dense area is called the cuticular plate. In all cases, the cuticular plate surface lies against an extracellular, fluid-filled space, and although details are not known it seems that the cuticular plate has significant properties of differential permeability. The hairs, or cilia, lie within the extracellular fluid space, where their tips are usually attached to an acellular gelatinous mass. At the basal end the hair cell synapses with nerve fibers which lead to the brain (Fig. 1).

Basically, then, a sufficient stimulus causes the cilia to move, which initiates nerve impulses in the neurons synapsing upon the hair cell; this information is then carried to the brain. Different ways of stimulating the cilia have evolved in different vertebrate groups.

C. Diversity of Sound Transforming Apparatuses

Any specific sense organ must be particularly sensitive to one modality and relatively insensitive to all others. Were there hair cells all over the free surface of a fish they would be sensitive to near field sound, to touch, and, most likely, to chemical stimulation as well. They would carry mixed,

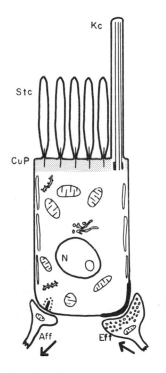

Fig. 1. Diagram of a generalized hair cell, with arrows indicating the direction of nerve impulses. Abbreviations: Aff, afferent nerve ending; CuP, cuticular plate; Eff, efferent nerve ending; Kc, kinocilium; N, nucleus; Stc, stereocilium.

unclear, and therefore essentially useless information to the central nervous system. An auditory receptor must be sensitive to sound but not to other modalities.

Fish and larval amphibians have a widespread network of canals, the lateral line system, near or on the body surface; these contain hair cells— here called neuromast organs—which respond to near field sound stimulation (van Bergeijk, 1967; Wersäll et al., 1965). They will not respond to far field propagated sound waves, because they are essentially the same density as the water and are thus transparent to such pressure waves. Being at the surface of the body, the neuromast cells of the lateral line system are also sensitive to nonsound disturbances of the water. They are thus more like "distance touch" receptors than auditory organs.

Fish also have aggregates of hair cells in their inner ears, or labyrinths. Lying deep within the skull, these are shielded from local water currents and disturbances and would thus be ideal for receiving far field sound, except that they contain fluid and therefore, like the lateral line, may be transparent to propagated sound waves. Many of the bony fish however have devices which can respond to propagated sound waves and then transmit these vibrations to the hair cells of the inner ear.

The organ which does this in many teleost fishes is the swim bladder, a gas-filled structure in the dorsal part of the peritoneal cavity just under the vertebral column, which may extend most of the length of the trunk. The swim bladder is primarily a hydrostatic organ, in which the gas can be increased or decreased to adjust the fish's specific gravity, enabling the fish to maintain a given depth without the use of metabolic energy. Because this "air bubble" has a different density than the rest of the body and the surrounding water, it and its walls are put into vibration by propagated sound waves. All that is needed for hearing, then, is a means of transferring these vibrations to the sensory epithelium of the inner ear.

In one group of fish, the Ostariophysii (catfish, carp, minnows, goldfish), the lateral processes of the three anterior vertebrae have become detached and modified into the Weberian ossicles which run between the anterior part of the swim bladder and the fluid spaces adjacent to the sensory epithelium of the inner ear (van Bergeijk, 1967). Experimental studies have shown that the Ostariophysii have acute hearing, which is vastly reduced after surgical interruption of the Weberian ossicles (Poggendorf, 1952).

A different coupling of the swim bladder to the inner ear is found in clupeid fish (herrings, sardines, etc.), in which there are anterior extensions of the swim bladder forward as far as the inner ear (O'Connell, 1955). These extensions enlarge around the labyrinth and transmit swim bladder vibrations directly to the fluids of the inner ear.

In a third group, the labyrinthine fishes (so named for their complex gill chambers, not their inner ears), diverticulae from the pharynx are filled with air and are closely applied to the surfaces of the inner ears, forming isolated "air bubbles" (Schneider, 1941) which are put into vibration by propagated sound fields and therefore act as transformer apparatuses to carry far field sound to the inner ear.

In still another group, the weakly electric mormyrid fishes of tropical Africa, anterior extensions of the forward extending air bladder are pinched off during development (Stipetić, 1939) and serve as paired isolated "air bubbles" next to the inner ear, responding to propagated vibrations in the water and stimulating the hair cells of the inner ear (van Bergeijk, 1967).

Tadpoles, the aquatic larvae of amphibians, also contain vibrating air chambers. These are the lungs, which have no respiratory function until the adult stage, but which vibrate in the tadpole stage in response to propagated sound waves in the water. Passing from the lung to the fluids of the inner ear is a bronchial columella (Witschi, 1949), which transmits vibrations to the fluids of the inner ear. These fluids then stimulate the hair cells of the inner ear.

Once the tadpole metamorphoses into an adult amphibian the lungs are used for respiration and the problem of hearing becomes quite different. Propagated sound waves in air are much weaker than those in water due to the greater density of water. In order for the hair cells to be adequately stimulated for perception of weak aerial sound to occur, a mechanism is necessary which can transform aerial sound waves into vibrations of the dense inner ear fluids (Webster, 1966). This transformation is effected by the middle ear apparatus, including a membrane—usually the tympanic membrane—which first receives the acoustical energy. Behind the tympanic membrane lies the air-filled middle ear cavity, and running through this cavity, carrying vibrations from the tympanic membrane to the fluids of the inner ear, are one or more small bones, the middle ear ossicles. In frogs, turtles, most lizards, crocodilians, and birds, the middle ear ossicle is the columella (a different structure than the tadpole bronchial columella). It is usually made up of two distinct portions—an outer extracolumella, frequently cartilaginous, and an inner columella proper. The extracolumella is attached to the tympanic membrane, and the columella proper inserts into the fluids of the middle ear in the oval window. Vibrations of the air set the tympanic membrane into motion; this causes the extracolumella and columella to vibrate, and they in turn cause vibrations in the perilymphatic fluids of the inner ear. Another membrane-covered window in the inner ear, the round window, allows for the resolution of the pressure caused by the columella.

Because of the relative sizes of the tympanic membrane and the footplate of the columella, there is an increase in force per unit area as this process occurs. If the diameter of the former is twenty times or more that of the latter, then an efficient transformation of air to fluid vibrations occurs, as the acoustical impedance in air is matched with that of the inner ear fluids. In all animals whose tympanic membranes have been measured, this ratio or better exists. The total force per unit area increase effected by the tympano-ossicular system is called the transformer ratio and is expressed as a whole number.

Some tetrapods—such as salamanders, snakes, and the rare limbless amphisbaenid lizards—have neither tympanic membrane nor middle ear cavity, yet functional studies have shown that they hear air-borne sounds. Recent work on the amphisbaenid lizards (Wever & Gans, 1970) has revealed the mechanism by which sounds are transmitted to the ear. The extracolumella in these forms is greatly expanded and runs just under the skin of the head; it covers a broad area of the face in a flat, thin, bony structure. Cutting the flat portion of the extracolumella causes a significant decrease in sound perception. This broad, thin, bony plate actually functions as a tympanic membrane, receiving sound stimuli and transmitting them to the inner ear. Current evidence suggests that the amphisbaenids have better hearing than either snakes or salamanders, whose precise sound-transmitting mechanism is still not known.

D. Diversity of Inner Ear and Auditory Brain

The sacculus and utriculus, along with the semicircular canals, comprise the membranous labyrinth of fishes and the vestibular (equilibratory) portion of the labyrinth of tetrapods. Within the sacculus and the utriculus are groups of hair cells, called maculae, whose hairs are embeded in a gelatinous membrane that contains also a calcified structure called the otolith. In fishes the otolith may be involved in hearing; in tetrapods its movements within the membrane stimulate the hair cells to send information only about tilt and acceleration—but that is another story.

In most fishes capable of hearing far field sound, it is in the macula of the sacculus that transduction occurs. In the Ostariophysii the macula is positioned to receive maximum vibrations from the Weberian ossicles, and the macula's otolith has a broad fluted surface at right angles to the movements which the ossicles cause in the perilymph (van Bergeijk, 1967).

In the frog, sound stimulates not the macula of the sacculus but two other areas of hair cells within the labyrinth: the amphibian papilla and the basilar papilla (Geisler, van Bergeijk, & Frishkopf, 1964). The membranes covering the hair cells of these sensory areas are gelatinous rather than otolithic, and are called tectorial membranes.

These structures have been extensively studied in the bullfrog, whose basilar papilla responds best to sounds between 1000 and 2000 Hz, and whose amphibian papilla responds best to sounds between 100 and 1000 Hz. The significance of these two auditory sensory areas to the life of the bullfrog has been demonstrated by Capranica (1968) in a group of ingenious experiments.

Amphibians have rich auditory connections to the brainstem, with most of the auditory information terminating in the deep part of the midbrain tectum (apparently the frog's most significant central auditory portion), in the area called the torus semicircularis (Potter, 1965).

Reptiles and birds have no amphibian papilla; as its name implies it is a structure found only in amphibians. However, the basilar papillae of both reptiles and birds are more extensive than the basilar papilla of amphibians, and are tremendously diverse in microscopic and ultrastructural detail (Baird, 1970).

The central auditory pathway in birds and probably also in reptiles extends past the midbrain, into the cerebrum itself. The tectum of the midbrain has a prominent torus semicircularis, whose specific auditory projection nucleus* is the nucleus mesencephalicus lateralis pars dorsalis. From this nucleus auditory information is projected to the nucleus ovoidalis in the thalamus. In birds at least it is projected from the nucleus ovoidalis to a very specific sensory region of the cerebrum, field L of the neostriatum (Karten, 1969).

II. MAMMALIAN AUDITORY SYSTEMS

A. External Ear

No fishes, amphibians, reptiles, or birds have a pinna, and in fact this is the most recently evolved portion of the mammalian auditory system. It is also the most variable, being completely absent in the mole and ranging through a multitude of intermediate stages to its extreme development in elephants. It is constructed of an inner core of elastic cartilage to which skin closely adheres, and of several muscles that move it independently of the head.

Its functional role is worth some speculation, which can probably be most fruitful in mammals other than man. This structure is certainly involved in sound collection and localization. The alerting, or pricking-up, response of

---

* In the central nervous system, an aggregate of nerve cell bodies is called a *nucleus*. Care must be taken to avoid confusion of this use of the word nucleus with its more common use as the nucleus of a cell.

the pinna to sound stimulation is obvious in dogs, deer, horses, and many other mammals. A large, erect pinna can surely act as an auditory funnel, collecting and directing sound waves into the external auditory meatus. Because the pinnae are mobile, they can also help localize sound. Even man, with a relatively immobile pinna, can localize sound better because of it (Batteau, 1968). In bats, the pinna is diversely specialized for echolocation (Pye, 1968); for instance, some of the echolocating bats rhythmically move their pinnae forward and backward in sequence with their echolocating calls. The echoes coming back to the external ear are thus modulated as a Doppler effect by the moving external ear, and can be utilized in locating the source of sound.

However, audition is apparently not the only function of the mammalian pinna. The elephant pinna for instance is a thin and highly vascularized structure, where the blood comes in close contact with the surrounding air. By rhythmically waving their "ears" (that is, their pinnae) in the air, elephants cool the blood there, which helps cool the entire body (Buss & Estes, 1971). It is possible that such a means of dissipating excess heat was an essential part of the development of homeothermy (warm-bloodedness), which occurred during the evolution of mammals, and that this, rather than auditory acuity, was the original adaptive value for the evolution of the pinna.

The pinna and the external auditory meatus, which leads to the tympanic membrane, comprise the mammalian external ear. The external auditory meatus is cartilaginous toward the outside, and bony in its deeper extent. It is completely lined with skin, within the deep layers of which are wax-secreting, or ceruminous, glands. These glands and associated hairs serve to protect the canal from dirt or other foreign matter which might occlude it or damage the tympanic membrane.

B. Middle Ear

In mammals a chain of three ossicles runs from the tympanic membrane to the inner ear; these are the malleus, the incus, and the stapes. The stapes is homologous to the columella of nonmammalian tetrapods; the malleus and incus are homologous to the articular and quadrate bones of nonmammalian vertebrates, in which they form the jaw articulation. When a new jaw articulation evolved in mammals these bones of the reptilian jaw became incorporated into the mammalian middle ear apparatus.

The mammalian tympanic membrane is shaped like a low cone. Along a dorsal radius of the tympanic membrane, and embedded within its tissue, runs the manubrium of the malleus, with its distal tip at the umbo (apex) of the cone. At the dorsal edge of the tympanic membrane the manubrium of the malleus gives way to its narrow neck, which leads to its large head. Coming off the neck anteriorly is the anterior process, with a ligament which attaches the malleus to the anterior wall of the middle ear. Posteriorly, the head of the malleus is articulated with the incus. To a posterior process of the incus is attached the posterior incudal ligament, which holds the incus onto the posterior wall of the middle ear cavity. These processes and their ligaments form the suspensions of the ossicles within the middle ear cavity, and the axis about which they vibrate when set into motion.

Coming off the head of the incus ventrally is an articulating process, which runs parallel to the manubrium of the malleus and then turns medially at a right angle to form the small lenticular process, which articulates with the head of the stapes. Two crura extend from the head of the stapes to the footplate of the stapes; this is held into the oval window of the inner ear by the annular ligament (Fig. 2).

The condensation portion of a sound wave moves the tympanic membrane medially, which moves the manubrium medially, and the articulating process of the incus medially; the articulating process of the incus pushes the stapes into the oval window of the inner ear, and this causes movement of the perilymphatic fluids. The rarefaction portion of the wave which follows reverses the process.

The mammalian middle ear functions as an efficient transformer largely because of two morphological features. First, there is an increase in force per unit area because of the considerable difference in size between the

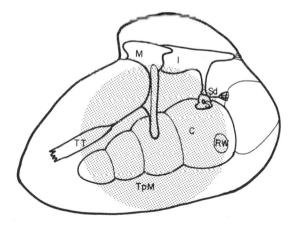

Fig. 2. Diagram of a ventrolateral view of a generalized mammalian middle ear. Abbreviations: C, cochlea; I, incus; M, malleus; RW, round window; S, stapes; Sd, stapedius muscle; TpM, tympanic membrane (stippled area); TT, tensor tympani muscle.

large tympanic membrane and the small footplate of the stapes. This is similar to what happens in nonmammalian ears.

Secondly, and unlike nonmammalian forms, the mammalian ossicles are articulated in such a way that they form a lever system, which further increases the force delivered to the fluids of the inner ear. The manubrium of the malleus is longer than the articulating process of the incus; the force resolved at the stapes is increased as the ratio of these two lengths.

In all mammals so far examined, the transformer ratio, calculated from these measurements, is 20 or more, and thus adequate impedance matching is accomplished. Acoustical energy from the air is theoretically transferred very efficiently to the fluids of the inner ear by way of the tympano-ossicular system (Webster, 1966).

In practice, however, the efficiency of the middle ear mechanism is somewhat less than calculated, because, despite its light, delicate suspension, some energy is lost through damping and friction in the system. Indeed, if there were no damping, resonance phenomena would predominate; vibrations would continue after the stimulus had ceased and the animal would not hear accurately.

Two of the smallest skeletal muscles of the body are attached to the tympano-ossicular system. In a canal of the temporal bone lies the belly of the tensor tympani muscle; its tendon attaches onto a muscular process of the manubrium of the malleus. When the tensor tympani contracts, it pulls the malleus and therefore the tympanic membrane medially; this increases the membrane's stiffness. Even smaller than the tensor tympani is the stapedius muscle. It runs from the posterior wall of the middle ear to attach high up on the neck of the stapes. Contraction of the stapedius muscle stiffens the stapes and its connection to the inner ear.

That both of these muscles contract reflexly in response to intense sound has been known for many years (e.g., Wiggers, 1937). It has also been postulated, and there is some supporting experimenal evidence, that these muscles can contract *partially,* thus adjusting the stiffness of the tympano-ossicular system in such a way as to facilitate reception of sounds within certain frequency ranges (Wiggers, 1937). Recently an increasing amount of evidence has suggested also that these middle ear muscles contract reflexly immediately prior to vocalization, remain contracted during it, and then relax; in this way the ear is most sensitive to hear any response (Salomon & Starr, 1963). Although reflex contraction to loud external sounds and to the animal's own vocalizations have been demonstrated, the precise neural connections of this acoustical reflex are not known. The tensor tympani is innervated by a branch of the trigeminal nerve, and the stapedius by a branch of the facial nerve; yet no anatomic connections between the central auditory nuclei and the motor nuclei of the trigeminal or facial nerve have yet been demonstrated.

In summary, the mammalian middle ear functions as a transformer mechanism which matches the impedance of air with that of fluid and in so doing efficiently carries vibrations from the tympanic membrane to the inner ear. It is a dynamic rather than a static system, adjusting its sensitivity by way of the middle ear (intraaural) muscles to prevent damage to the system and to control the vibrations so that they can eventually be decoded by the brain.

C. Cochlea

1. Gross Structure and Mechanics

The next step in the process occurs in the cochlea, where fluid vibrations are transduced into nerve impulses. The cochlea (Latin for snail shell) is a coiled structure, turning about a central bony core called the modiolus. Within the modiolus is the cochlear portion of the eighth cranial nerve, which transmits nerve impulses to the brain; here also are the cell bodies of the afferent cochlear neurons, collectively called the spiral ganglion.

Along the coiled length of the cochlea run two spaces filled with perilymphatic fluid (the scala vestibuli and scala tympani), above and below a space filled with endolymphatic fluid (the scale media) (Fig. 3). The two perilymphatic spaces are joined at the apex of the cochlea, at a hole called the helicotrema which functions as a "safety valve" to equalize pressure differences.

The outer surface of the scala media is bordered by a prominent vascular area, the stria vascularis; just below this is a smaller vascular area, the spiral prominence. Between the stria vascularis and the outer bony shell of the cochlea lies the spiral ligament.

Between the scala vestibuli and the scala media lies a thin epithelial structure, Reissner's membrane. Between the scala media and the scala tympani lies the basilar membrane. Resting partly on the basilar membrane and partly on a bony projection from the modiolus (the osseous spiral lamina) is the organ of Corti, where the actual transduction process occurs. The footplate of the stapes fits into the oval window at the base of the scala vestibuli and brings vibrations from the tympano-ossicular system into the cochlea. These vibrations set the fluids and the basilar membrane into motion and are finally dissipated at the round window at the base of the scala tympani.

2. Microscopic Structure of the Organ of Corti

If one imagines a section cut lengthwise through the center of the modiolus, the structure of the organ of Corti from the modiolus toward the outer edge of the cochlea are these (Fig. 4).

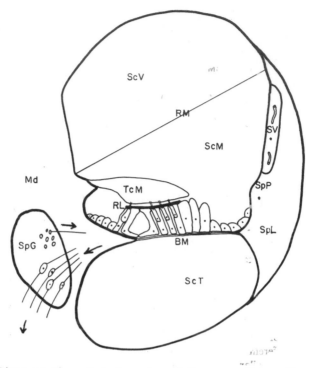

Fig. 3. Diagrammatic section of one turn of the mammalian cochlea, with arrows indicating direction of nerve impulses. (Details of the organ of Corti and its innervation appear in Fig. 4.) Abbreviations: BM, basilar membrane; Md, modiolus; RL, reticular lamina; RM, Reissner's membrane; ScM, scala media; ScT, scala tympani; ScV, scala vestibuli; SpG, spiral ganglion; SpL, spiral ligament; SpP, spiral prominence; SV, stria vascularis; TcM, tectorial membrane.

First, resting upon the osseous spiral lamina are the inner spiral sulcus cells, one inner sustentacular (supporting) cell, and the inner pillar cell; the outer pillar cell is the innermost structure on the basilar membrane. The pillar cells together form a roughly triangular shape, with an extracellular space between them from which they are separated by their plasma membranes; this space is called the tunnel of Corti. Beyond the outer pillar cell on the basilar membrane are three more sustentacular cells, called the cells of Deiters, and the border cells which include first rather large cells of Hensen and then smaller cells of Claudius. The cells of Claudius extend to the outer level of the basilar membrane and are then continuous with the external spiral sulcus cells, which abut against the spiral ligament.

The hair cells are supported by the sustentacular cells. There is a single row of inner hair cells—actually a single cell would appear in our hypothetical section. This is closely covered on all sides except the top by the

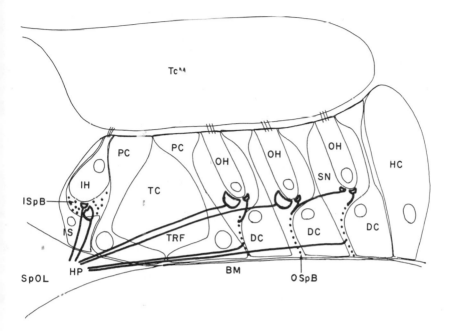

FIG. 4. Diagram of the organ of Corti, showing its innervation. The large nerve endings are from effe̶ ᷑t fibers and the small nerve endings from afferent fibers. Abbreviations: BM, basilar membrane; DC, Deiters' cell; HC, Hensen's cell; HP, habenula perforata; IH, inner hair cell; IS, inner sustentacular cell; ISpB, inner spiral bundle; OH, outer hair cell; OSpB, outer spiral bundle; PC, pillar cell; SN, space of Nuel; SpOL, ̶iral osseous lamina; TC, tunnel of Corti; TcM, tectorial membrane; TRF, tunnel radial fibers.

inner sustentacular cell and nerve endings. Only at the apical surface, where the stereocilia protrude into the scala media, is there any free cell surface. On the other side of the tunnel of Corti are the outer hair cells—usually three rows, or three cells in our section. Their bases are supported by the cells of Deiters, which also send phalangeal processes apically; these processes support the apex of the outer hair cells, but elsewhere there is between the hair cells and the phalangeal processes considerable extracellular fluid-filled space, the space of Nuel. The apical surface of the entire organ of Corti is somewhat thickened, and in electron micrographs it is electron-dense; it forms a cuticular surface, or reticular lamina, through which the stereocilia protrude into the endolymphatic fluid of the scala media.

Projecting from the modiolus above the osseous spiral lamina is the spiral limbus, which supports the tectorial membrane. This gelatinous structure is not actually part of the organ of Corti, but overlies it; in it are embedded the tips of the stereocilia. (A more detailed structural description of the organ of Corti can be found in Spoendlin, 1966.)

3. MOVEMENTS OF BASILAR MEMBRANE

The basilar membrane is narrowest at the base of the cochlea, and widest at its apex. The movements of the basilar membrane in response to intense sound have been studied by von Békésy (1952, 1953), with direct observation, and more recently by Johnstone and Boyle (1967), using the Mössbauer technique. Von Békésy's methods limited his observations to the apical coil of the cochlea, whereas Johnstone and Boyle observed the basal turn almost at the stapes. These studies show that with pure tone stimulation the greatest amplitude of basilar membrane vibration occurs in the basal part of the cochlea for high frequencies and in the apical part for low frequencies. Furthermore, only a small portion of the basilar membrane vibrates to any extent in response to a pure tone. At a point in the basal turn about 1.5 mm from the stapes, where Johnstone and Boyle measured, peak amplitude was in response to 18,000 Hz, whereas in the apical turn Békésy found the maximum vibrations in response to tones between 200 and 950 Hz, with the 200-Hz area being further apical than the 950-Hz area.

The stapedial footplate is large compared to the portion of the basilar membrane which responds to any given pure tone; therefore there is another increase in force per unit area, and the amplitude of movement of that small vibrating portion of the basilar membrane is greater than the amplitude of movement of the stapedial footplate. This difference in amplitude was measured by Johnstone and Boyle at about 50:1 (basilar membrane movement to stapedial movement) for an 18,000 Hz tone, with a measured movement of 500 Å in response to a 90 dB SPL (re. to 0.0002 dynes/cm^2) sound pressure. Working with lower frequencies, von Békésy found a 400-Å movement in the human cadaver ear in response to a 90 dB SPL (again re. to 0.0002 dynes/cm^2) sound pressure, with a ratio of only 10:1. The difference in these ratios is due to the fact that a smaller area of the basilar membrane vibrates in response to high frequencies than to low frequencies.

4. EXCITATION OF THE ORGAN OF CORTI

Given that sound sets the basilar membrane into motion, how does this cause the organ of Corti to function? Its geometry and that of surrounding structures must be considered. As basilar membrane vibrations push the organ of Corti toward the scala media, the stereocilia of the hair cells are pushed against the tectorial membrane. The tectorial membrane itself is firmly attached to the modiolus by way of the spiral limbus. Because of this firm attachment, pressures of the stereocilia against the tectorial membrane would tend to bend the stereocilia. It is believed that this bending of the stereocilia is the excitatory stimulus for the organ of Corti. This idea is experimentally justified by von Békésy's observations (1953) that mechanical vibration of the tectorial membrane will excite the organ of Corti.

Excitation of the organ of Corti causes transduction of mechanical stimuli to nerve impulses. In order to understand this we must consider the ultrastructure of the hair cells, the innervation of the organ of Corti, and the bioelectric properties of the cochlea.

5. Ultrastructure of the Hair Cells

Numerous investigators have described the organ of Corti's hair cells; the more extensive studies are those of Engström, Ades, and Andersson (1966), Iurato (1967), Smith (1968b), and Spoendlin (1966). The three-dimensional ultrastructural picture has been presented by the scanning electron microscopic studies of Bredberg, Lindeman, Ades, West, and Engström (1970) and Lim (1969).

The inner and outer hair cells differ morphologically. However, both are polarized apically to basally, and the apical surface itself is transversely polarized. Both also lack the kinocilium in the adult, even though it is present in the developing embryo (Hilding, 1969) and its position in the adult is indicated by a clear place with a centriole in the otherwise electron-dense cuticular plate of the apical cytoplasm.

On the columnar outer hair cells the three rows of stereocilia are arranged in a W shape, with the base of the W facing the stria vascularis where also is the centriole of the missing kinocilium. Only the uppermost tip of the stereocilium is embedded in the tectorial membrane. At its base, the stereocilium narrows and becomes electron-dense, with an electron-dense "rootlet" extending into the cuticular plate. Just below the cuticular plate there is an accumulation of mitochondria. Throughout most of the cytoplasm of the outer hair cell are a few organelles in addition to the large nucleus. Endoplasmic reticulum is largely restricted to the area adjacent to the outer plasma membrane, where there may be from one to seven or eight layers (depending on species) lying parallel to the plasma membrane. At the base of the outer hair cells there is more cytoplasmic specialization, with an accumulation of mitochondria and small vesicles, and thickenings of the plasma membrane in relation to the synaptic nerve endings.

The inner hair cells are more pear shaped. The stereocilia are coarser, but otherwise of the same morphology. They are arranged into three rows, in a flattened version of the W pattern of the outer hair cells. The cuticular plate is similar to that of the outer hair cells, as are the membrane modifications in relationship to the nerve fibers basally. Mitochondria and endoplasmic reticular membrane occur throughout the cytoplasm, rather than in the stereotyped arrangement seen in the outer hair cells.

The entire upper surface of the organ of Corti (facing the scala media) is tightly bound, with desmosomes between adjacent cells, and usually with thickenings represented by electron-dense material along the apical surfaces not only of hair cells but of all the cells. The thickenings and the tight junctions of the surface combine to form the reticular lamina, apparently a stout boundary area between the organ of Corti and the endolymph.

6. INNERVATION OF THE ORGAN OF CORTI

The cell bodies of all the afferent sensory neurons coming from the organ of Corti are located in the spiral ganglion, within the modiolus of the cochlea. Their dendrites reach the organ of Corti through the habenula perforata of the osseous spiral lamina, at which point they lose their myelin. Recent work by Spoendlin (1968) has shown that in the cat approximately 90% of these dendrites terminate in relationship to inner hair cells, with one dendrite per cell, and 10% of them in relationship to outer hair cells, with each dendrite branching and going to many hair cells.

The type of synapse is similar for outer and inner hair cells. An enlargement of the dendrite lies very close to the hair cell being innervated, but with a definite synaptic cleft between the two (Fig. 1). Mitochondria are observed within the nerve endings. On the hair cell side of the synapse is a synaptic bar of electron-dense material, usually at right angles to the plasma membrane of the hair cell, and surrounded by small vesicles in the cytoplasm.

After emerging through the habenula perforata, dendrites going to the outer hair cells travel along the bases of the pillar cells. At the level of Deiters' cells these dendrites turn at right angles, and then pass spirally along the organ of Corti between adjacent Deiters' cells; after traveling some distance they have moved up far enough to make synaptic junctions with the hair cells. This is in sharp contrast to the dendrites innervating the inner hair cells, which travel directly to the hair cell innervated.

In addition to this afferent innervation of the organ of Corti there is an efferent innervation, the olivocochlear bundle of Rasmussen, with cell bodies in the superior olivary complex of the brainstem. From there, some axons travel to the same side (uncrossed) and some to the opposite side (crossed). The uncrossed and crossed fibers of the olivocochlear bundle run with the vestibular nerve into the internal auditory meatus and at the base of the modiolus pass to the cochlear portion of the eighth nerve; then they spiral along the spiral ganglion, sending their axons finally out the habenula perforata (where they lose their myelin) to terminate on the hair cells.

The nerve endings of the efferent olivocochlear bundle are larger and have a quite different morphology than those of the afferent endings. The efferent endings contain large numbers of synaptic vesicles (Fig. 1). The entire postsynaptic plasma membrane is thickened, but there are no synaptic bars. Recent evidence (Fex, 1968) suggests that the crossed portion of the olivocochlear bundle sends its fibers to the outer hair cells and the uncrossed portion sends its fibers to the inner hair cells.

Most of the efferent endings in the outer hair cell region terminate directly on the outer hair cells, although a few terminate on afferent dendrites. The efferent fibers do not parallel the spiral course of the afferent dendrites; they cross the fluid space of the tunnel of Corti—where they are called the radial tunnel fibers—cross the space of Nuel, and pass directly to the outer hair cells.

In the inner hair cell region the efferent fibers have axo-dendritic endings in relationship to afferent fibers from the inner hair cells, and travel in an inner spiral bundle along the base of the inner hair cells, where a given efferent fiber may synapse with many dendrites of sensory neurons (Fig. 4).

Finally there is an adrenergic, very fine neural pathway to the cochlea which appears to terminate at the level of the habenula perforata or the initial segments of the afferent and efferent neurons (Lichtensteiger & Spoendlin, 1967). The functional significance is unknown.

7. BIOELECTRIC CHARACTERISTICS OF THE COCHLEA

Against this anatomic picture must be considered the bioelectric characteristics of the cochlea. A review by Wever (1966) covers most of this material very well.

The endolymph of the scala media is chemically more similar to cytoplasm than to other extracellular fluids, being high in potassium and protein and low in sodium. When there is no sound stimulus to the ear, this endolymph maintains a positive resting DC potential of about 80 mV; this is the endocochlear potential, and is restricted to the endolymph of the cochlea. In fact, microelectrode studies demonstrating that the endocochlear potential is bounded by the spiral ligament externally, Reissner's membrane superiorly, and the reticular lamina of the organ of Corti inferiorly (Tasaki, Davis, & Eldredge, 1954), have been interpreted as meaning that the endolymph itself is found only in the scala media and not in the extracellular spaces of the organ of Corti (e.g., tunnel of Corti or space of Nuel).

The endocochlear potential is oxygen-dependent, and is rapidly lost under anoxia. Both microelectrode studies and chemical inhibitor studies indicate that the stria vascularis actively maintains the endocochlear potential, which is evidently also dependent upon a potassium-ATPase-enzyme system within the stria vascularis (Kuijpers & Bonting, 1970a, 1970b).

A second cochlear resting potential is found within the organ of Corti, bounded by the reticular lamina and basilar membrane. There is no definitive evidence as to whether it is an extracellular or an intracellular potential. This resting potential is negative relative to the perilymph and other extracellular spaces throughout the body. It has been recorded between −15 and −90 mV; it is possible that the lower polarizations are extracellular recordings, and the higher, intracellular recordings.

The negative resting potential of the organ of Corti is separated from the positive resting potential of the scala media (the endocochlear potential) by the reticular lamina. The potential difference across the reticular lamina is therefore as much as 170 mV, an extremely large bioelectric resting potential.

When the ear is stimulated, however, there are additional bioelectric potentials in the cochlea. In 1930, Wever and Bray first demonstrated what is now usually called the cochlear microphonic. This can be recorded from an active electrode placed anywhere on or in the cochlea, although it is largest in the vicinity of the hair cells where it is undoubtedly produced. As the name implies, the cochlear microphonic response is analogous to that of a microphone. It is an AC potential that mimics the sound played to the ear, in wave form, frequency, and intensity: a 500 Hz sound played to the ear causes a 500 Hz cochlear microphonic to be produced in the vicinity of the hair cells. Within physiological limits (up to about 80 or 90 dB SPL relative to 0.0002 dynes/cm^2) the intensity function is linear. The cochlear microphonic has no threshold and its lower limit of detection is dependent only on the sensitivity of the recording instruments. If the cochlear microphonic is recorded while the active electrode is passed through the organ of Corti, a 180 degree phase shift occurs when the electrode penetrates the reticular lamina, suggesting that the microphonic is an alternating current running between the scala media and the organ of Corti (Tasaki et al., 1954). It is greatly depressed by anoxia; however, it persists, at a depressed level, for over an hour after death and therefore, unlike the endocochlear potential, is not completely dependent upon oxidative metabolism. Recordings from the scala tympani in reference to the scala vestibuli in various turns of the cochlea show that the cochlear microphonic is strongest in the apical turns in response to low frequency stimulation and in the basal turn in response to high frequency stimulation, thus at least roughly mimicking the movements of the basilar membrane.

A second bioelectric response to sound stimulation is the summating potential, which is recorded at higher intensity stimulation than is the cochlear microphonic, and appears as a shift in the base line of the cochlear microphonic during sound stimulation. It is thus a slow DC potential, sometimes positive and sometimes negative, depending on the type of stimulation. In mammals at least it is a significantly smaller potential than the cochlear microphonic. Dallos, Schoeny, and Cheatham (1970) simultaneously recorded the summating potential in the guinea pig cochlea from pairs of electrodes placed in the scala tympani and the scala vestibuli of a given turn, with each referred to an indifferent electrode in the neck musculature. They found that depending on the frequency and intensity of sound presented, as well as the location of the electrode along the cochlear turns, they could record a summating potential which was positive in one scala and negative in the other, or positive in both, or negative in both.

They analyzed their data in two ways. In the first, for a given response, they algebraically added the summating potential of the scala vestibuli to that of the scala tympani; this was called twice the average summating potential. In the second, they algebraically subtracted the summating potential of the scala tympani from that of the scala vestibuli; this was called twice the differential summating potential. By these mathematical manipulations they showed that the maximum average positive peak of the summating potential corresponds to the area of the basilar membrane maximally excited by the tone, and that the maximum negative differential summating potential coincides also with the area of the basilar membrane maximally excited by a given tone.

The final bioelectric potentials of the cochlea are the action potentials of the cochlear nerve; these may be recorded as individual spikes using microelectrodes, or as summed mass action potentials using gross electrodes. The major gross response is spoken of as the N_1 response, since to a tone or click stimulus a gross electrode records the summed potential of the firings of many neurons. The more intense the stimulus, the larger the number of auditory nerve fibers that fire, and therefore the larger the summed response. Thus there is no all-or-none phenomenon when recording with gross electrodes.

8. POSSIBLE TRANSDUCER MECHANISMS

How cochlear morphology and bioelectric potentials relate to actual neural transduction is still not known, despite masses of experimentation. It is apparent that the reticular lamina is a crucial boundary in the electrical excitation of the hair cells. If the endocochlear potential is experimentally increased by an external power source, the cochlear microphonic response to a sound stimulus is similarly increased in magnitude and the increase is linear. Furthermore, this increase in the cochlear microphonic is also linked with a change in the summating potential, and it is suggested that the two may play similar roles (Honrubia & Ward, 1969). Konishi, Teas, and Wernick (1970) reported that direct-current polarization of the organ of Corti causes an increase in both spontaneous and evoked firing rates of the eighth nerve if the current is running from the scala vestibuli to the scala tympani, whereas both spontaneous and evoked firing are decreased if the current runs from the scala tympani to the scala vestibuli. Pfeiffer and Molnar (1970) carried out a Fourier analysis of the nerve responses and found that frequency components of the cochlear nerve fibers show both phase and magnitude similarities to the cochlear microphonics; they therefore suggested that the cochlear microphonic is directly related to the firing of the cochlear nerve. Grundfest (1965), on the other hand, proposed that the cochlear microphonic is an epiphenomenon: that is, a real biological response to sound, but a byproduct rather than an essential part of the transduction of physical vibrations to nerve impulses.

All these results are consistent with the model presented by Davis (1965), that the cochlear microphonic is a receptor potential necessary for excitation of the cochlear nerve fibers, and is caused by a modulation of the potential difference of some 170 mV between the endolymph of the scala media and the hair cells of the organ of Corti. Davis did not believe that the cochlear microphonic directly excites the dendrites of the eighth nerve, for two reasons. The morphology of the synapses is characteristic of a chemical synapse rather than an electric synapse, in which pre- and post-synaptic fibers are continuous. Moreover, at threshold pressures of sound the cochlear microphonic is less than 0.005 μV, and it is difficult to conceive of any neurons being so sensitive as to respond to such minute voltage changes. Instead of direct excitation of the dendrites by the cochlear microphonic, Davis' model suggests that the cochlear microphonic triggers activity of the hair cells, which will then release a chemical transmitter at the synapse which in turn excites the sensory dendrites.

Various workers have demonstrated that under some experimental conditions the cochlear microphonic is not directly linked to the firing of the eighth nerve. For example, stimulation of the olivocochlear bundle augments the cochlear microphonic, yet depresses the N_1 response of the eighth nerve (Fex, 1968). Furthermore, both cochlear microphonic and summating potential are augmented while the N_1 response is depressed after perilymphatic increase in calcium ions (Moscovitch & Gannon, 1966). On the other hand, a deficiency of calcium ions in the perilymph causes depression of the N_1 response and a slight decrease in the cochlear microphonic, but no change in the endocochlear potential (Konishi & Kelsey, 1970). Xylocaine depresses the cochlear microphonic slightly, but has a much more profound effect on the N_1 response (Ward & Honrubia, 1969). Atropine depresses the N_1 response but not the cochlear microphonic; it also increases the latency time from cochlear microphonic to N_1 response but does not affect the latency time from sound stimulus to initiation of the cochlear microphonic (Gannon & Laszlo, 1968). Tetraethylammonium chloride depresses the endocochlear potential and the cochlear microphonic, but has only slight effect on the N_1 response, whereas tetrodotoxin depresses the N_1 response but not the cochlear microphonic (Katsuki, Yanagisawa, & Kanzaki, 1966). Acetylcholine depresses the cochlear microphonic, but has little effect on the action potential (Katsuki, Tanaka, & Miyoshi, 1965). Experimental cooling of the cochlea depresses the N_1 response and increases its latency but has little effect on the cochlear microphonic (Coats, 1965).

Since these various experimental manipulations of the cochlea can cause the cochlear microphonic and summating potential to be dissociated from the action potentials of the cochlear nerve, it is difficult to consider the cochlear microphonic as a necessary intermediate in the generation of action potentials. Grundfest's (1965) suggestion that the cochlear microphonic is an epiphenomenon is therefore the more believable.

It is possible that the bending of the stereocilia caused by the movement of the basilar membrane produces differential ion leakage—probably of potassium and sodium—across the reticular lamina, and that this excites the hair cells to release a still unspecified chemical transmitter substance which could in turn excite the dendrites of the cochlear nerve. Histochemical studies have shown that the hair cells possess large quantities of enzymes of oxidative respiration, of glycogen, and of various carboxylic esterases (Conti & Borgo, 1965; Nomura & Balogh, 1964; Plotz & Perlman, 1955; Vinnikov & Titova, 1964; Webster & Stack, 1968). It is therefore evident that these cells have a high metabolic capacity and may be mechanochemical transducers.

Another possibility is suggested by the report of Kaneko and Daly (1969) that with their electron microscopic histochemistry they can locate acetylcholine esterase on the endolymphatic surface—including the stereocilia—of the outer hair cells. Possibly this enzyme plays a role in the excitation of the hair cells. Spoendlin (1968) reports the presence of acid mucopolysaccharides between stereocilia.

The role of the olivocochlear bundle is masterfully discussed in a paper by Fex (1968) and in the lively (published) discussion which follows. Fex concludes that the olivocochlear bundle is a cholinergic system, acting as a feedback mechanism which helps sharpen the response of the cochlear nerve.

D. Central Auditory System

The central auditory system is summarized in Fig. 5. Once mechanical vibrations have been transduced into nerve impulses, they are transmitted by the cochlear portion of the eighth cranial nerve to the cochlear nuclear complex, composed of the dorsal cochlear nucleus and ventral cochlear nucleus, from which other fibers project to higher centers. Most fibers travel from the ventral cochlear nucleus in the trapezoid body, which leads to the superior olivary complex. Some fibers from the ventral cochlear nucleus, and fibers from the dorsal cochlear nucleus, leave in the dorsal and intermediate striae (stria of Monakow, and stria of Held, respectively). Some of the fibers in these striae go to the superior olivary complex, but others project to higher auditory centers, particularly on the opposite side (contralaterally).

The ascending pathway leading from the superior olivary complex on each side is the lateral lemniscus, which includes along its route a dorsal and ventral nucleus, and then terminates massively in the central nucleus of the inferior colliculus. From here, in addition to commissural fibers, there is a major projection to the medial geniculate body, which is the auditory nucleus in the thalamus, and from there a final projection to the auditory cortex in the temporal region. It must be emphasized that at every auditory nucleus in this ascending pathway both the complex fiber connections and the evoked auditory potentials indicate that auditory information is being processed, and not simply relayed toward the cortex. To demonstrate this, a more extensive (although by no means exhaustive) discussion of the major auditory nuclei and their connecting tracts is necessary.

As they enter the cochlear nuclei the cochlear nerve fibers bifurcate into an ascending and a descending branch. The ascending branch, with its collaterals, passes throughout the anterior ventral cochlear nucleus. The descending branch, with its collaterals, passes through the posterior portion of the ventral cochlear nucleus, and then continues into the dorsal cochlear nucleus. The arrangement of the fibers and their terminals is not haphazard; there is in effect a morphological and physiological "unrolling of the cochlea" three times, with fibers from each turn of the cochlea terminating in an orderly arrangement in each major part of the cochlear nuclear complex —once in the anterior ventral cochlear nucleus, once in the posterior ventral cochlear nucleus, and once along the dorsal cochlear nucleus (Powell & Cowan, 1962; Sando, 1965; Webster, 1970). Moreover, the cell populations of the cochlear nuclei are complex. The dorsal cochlear nucleus has three main regions: a deep central region, a single row of pyramidal cells, and a superficial molecular layer (Osen, 1969a). In the ventral cochlear nucleus five distinct but overlapping cytological areas have been identified

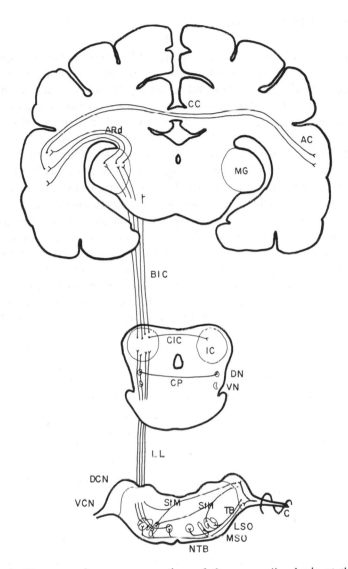

FIG. 5. Diagrammatic transverse sections of the mammalian brain at three levels, the medulla (lowest), the midbrain (center), and through the thalamus and cerebrum (highest). The major portions of the contralateral ascending auditory pathway are shown as well as auditory commissural connections. Abbreviations: AC, auditory cortex; ARd, auditory radiation; BIC, brachium of inferior colliculus; C, cochlea; CC, corpus callosum; CIC, commissure of inferior colliculus; CP, commissure of Probst; DCN, dorsal cochlear nucleus; DN, dorsal nucleus of lateral lemniscus; IC, inferior colliculus (central nucleus); LL, lateral lemniscus; LSO, lateral superior olivary nucleus; MG, medial geniculate body; MSO, medial superior olivary nucleus; NTB, nucleus of trapezoid body; StH, stria of Held; StM, stria of Monakow; TB, trapezoid body; VCN, ventral cochlear nucleus; VN, ventral nucleus of lateral lemniscus.

in the laboratory rat (Harrison & Irving, 1965, 1966b), in the cat (Osen, 1969a), and in the kangaroo rat (Webster, Ackermann, & Longa, 1968).

Evoked potentials from the primary neurons of the cochlear portion of the eighth nerve demonstrate that all fibers have certain similar firing patterns (Kiang, 1965). Each fiber has a characteristic or "best" frequency; it also responds, although with a higher threshold, to frequencies which are considerably lower, and to frequencies which are somewhat higher, although the cutoff for higher frequencies is reached more rapidly. Many low frequency fibers are phase-locked; that is, their firing patterns are correlated directly with the frequency of the tone presented. High frequency units are not phase-locked.

Recordings from cells in the cochlear nuclei demonstrate a greater diversity of physiological responses to acoustic stimuli. Some low frequency units will phase-lock, and others will not. Some units will fire only to the initiation of sound ("on units"); others fire in bursts throughout the length of a tone ("chopper units"); some will fire and then pause and then fire again ("pauser units") (Kiang, Pfeiffer, Warr, and Backus, 1965). Further, many cochlear nuclear fibers are either inhibited on facilitated by efferent neurons from the contralateral cochlear nuclei (Comis, 1970), or from the superior olivary complex or lateral lemniscus. Therefore the second order neurons of the cochlear nuclei carry quite different information than do the primary fibers. Unfortunately in most cases the physiological significance of these various firing patterns is still unclear. It has been suggested that especially units in the dorsal cochlear nucleus which are inhibited by stimuli on the contralateral cochlear nucleus could be coded to give very precise information about the localization of sound (Comis, 1970).

The largest fiber system leaving the cochlear nucleus is the trapezoid body, projecting to both the ipsilateral and the contralateral superior olivary complex. The posterior dorsal portion of the posterior ventral cochlear nucleus projects by way of the stria of Held to the superior olivary complex, and possibly to the lateral lemniscus and inferior colliculus (Warr, 1969). The dorsal cochlear nucleus projects partly to the superior olivary complex, but primarily to the contralateral nuclei of the lateral lemniscus and inferior colliculus (Fernandez & Karapas, 1967). There is now also some information about which cell areas of the ventral cochlear nucleus project to which nuclei of the superior olivary complex. These details will not be reviewed here; the interested reader is referred to Harrison and Irving (1966a), Osen (1969b), and Warr (1966, 1969).

The superior olivary complex is indeed a complex of discrete nuclear groups. The two largest nuclei are the medial superior olive and the lateral superior olive. Medial to the medial superior olive is the nucleus of the trapezoid body, and ventral to the lateral superior olive are two small cell groups, the lateral and medial preolivary nuclei. Finally, just dorsal and ventral to the superior olivary complex and included in it by some authors is a group of multipolar cells diffusely arranged, called the retro-olivary nucleus; these are probably the cells of origin of the olivocochlear bundle.

The medial superior olivary nuclei have a unique innervation and cell pattern. All their cells are spindle-shaped, with an anterior axon leading to the lateral lemniscus, and one dendrite laterally and another dendrite medially. In each medial superior olivary nucleus the lateral dendrites receive only from the ipsilateral cochlear nuclei, and the medial dendrites only from the contralateral cochlear nuclei. Therefore these cells, geometrically suited to receive information on very small time differences, could be important for sound-localization. And indeed, differences have been recorded in the evoked potentials in response to sound arriving at each ear at a different time.

Harrison and Irving (1966c; Irving & Harrison, 1967) have, in a comparative study of several mammalian species, shown that those with prominent visual systems—as indicated by the size of the eyeball and the abducens nucleus—have prominent medial superior olivary nuclei, whereas species with acute hearing but reduced visual centers have prominent lateral superior olivary nuclei; in fact, echolocating bats and porpoises, which have very small visual systems, lack medial superior olivary nuclei. They propose therefore that the medial superior olivary nucleus is related to sound localization which is coordinated with eyeball movements, while the lateral superior olive is related to sound localization which is independent of the visual system.

From the superior olivary complex the ascending projection is by way of the lateral lemniscus, which terminates primarily in the central nucleus of the inferior colliculus (Goldberg & Moore, 1967), with a few fibers terminating in the external nucleus and some in the ventral and dorsal nuclei of the lateral lemniscus. The commissure of the lateral lemniscus (commissure of Probst) originates from the dorsal nucleus of the lateral lemniscus, and projects to the contralateral dorsal nucleus of the lateral lemniscus and to the contralateral central nucleus of the inferior colliculus. Lesions restricted to the lateral lemniscus cause no degeneration in the brachium of the inferior colliculus, or in the pars principalis of the medial geniculate body. Therefore it appears that the inferior colliculus is an obligatory synaptic center for ascending auditory fibers (Goldberg & Moore, 1967).

Aitkin, Anderson, and Brugge (1970) have demonstrated in a microelectrode study a tonotopic organization in both the dorsal and ventral nuclei of the lateral lemniscus. The same authors (Brugge, Anderson, & Aitkin, 1970) have demonstrated that precise information regarding sound localization is transmitted in units of the dorsal nucleus of the lateral lemniscus.

Geisler, Rhode, and Hazelton (1969) reported units in the inferior colliculus whose firing patterns are dependent upon the times sound reaches the two ears. The most sensitive units demonstrating this sound-localizing ability respond independent of the frequency content and sound intensity. Other units were found which specifically code intensity information. Benevento and Coleman (1970) recorded single units of the cat inferior colliculus and their responses to binaural click stimuli. They found four types of units: (1) units responding to interaural intensity differences; (2) units responding to interaural time differences; (3) units not responding to differences in time or intensity; (4) units responding to both time and intensity parameters. Masterton, Jane, and Diamond (1968) carried out behavioral studies of sound localization following various lesions of the inferior colliculus and its brachium. They found that deep bilateral ablation of the inferior colliculus eliminates the cat's ability to localize sound from either time or intensity cues. If only the apical portions of the inferior colliculus were lesioned, thus sparing the lemniscal pathways, sound localization was not impaired. Lesions which severed the rostral projections of the inferior colliculus, but spared the inferior colliculus itself and the lemniscal pathway leading to it, abolished the cat's ability to localize sounds based on time differences, but not its ability to respond to intensity differences, thus giving behavioral evidence for the integrative ability of the inferior colliculus.

The fiber projections from the inferior colliculus have been studied by experimental anatomy (Moore & Goldberg, 1963, 1966; Powell & Hatton, 1969). Although there are minor differences in the results, they strongly indicate a rather wide projection of the inferior colliculus. Most fibers from the inferior colliculus project to the medial geniculate body by way of the brachium of the inferior colliculus. In the medial geniculate there are terminal endings throughout its magnocellular portion, and throughout the rostral and intermediate parts of its pars principalis portion; the caudal part of its pars principalis does not receive direct fiber projections from the inferior colliculus.

Some of the fibers from the inferior colliculus pass through its commissure and into the contralateral brachium of the inferior colliculus and thus to the medial geniculate body. There is some projection, both contralaterally and ipsilaterally, to the parabrachial region and to the interstitial cells of the brachium of the inferior colliculus. In the cat, but apparently not in the monkey, the inferior colliculus also projects sparsely to the lateral posterior thalamic nucleus. There are also projections to the superior colliculus, to the contralateral inferior colliculus, to the central gray, and to the pretectum. Powell and Hatton (1969) also reported a projection system to the anterior midline cerebellar cortex.

Descending paths from the inferior colliculus originate in the external nucleus and pass to the lateral pontine nuclei, the nuclei of the lateral lemniscus, the medial preolivary nuclei, the lateral preolivary nuclei, and the retro-olivary nuclei (Moore & Goldberg, 1966).

The medial geniculate body is the primary thalamic nucleus projecting auditory information to the cerebral cortex; it is made up of a large-celled portion (the pars magnocellularis) and a small-celled portion (the pars principalis). In addition Golgi preparations have revealed that the medial geniculate body is laminated, with a highly organized internal structure (Morest, 1965). Evoked potentials recorded from the medial geniculate body with microelectrodes show great diversity of response patterns, which in at least one recent study (Dunlop, Itzkowic, & Aitkin, 1969) are roughly divided into onset excitation units and onset inhibition units, depending upon whether the initial response to tone bursts is one of facilitation or inhibition. On physiological grounds, Love and Scott (1969) divided the magnocellular portion of the medial geniculate body into an anterior portion and a posterior portion; the former responds primarily to somatic sensory stimuli (although some units there respond to auditory stimuli), while the latter responds primarily to auditory stimuli (with some units responding to somatic sensory stimuli). A few cells were found to respond to both auditory and somatic sensory stimuli. Although much of the inhibitory information is probably ascending in the auditory pathway, some of it is descending from the cortex (Amato, LaGrutta, & Enia, 1970), for stimulation of the cat's auditory cortex causes inhibition in both the medial geniculate body and the inferior colliculus, particularly in their more peripheral portions.

The final ascending projection is from the medial geniculate to the temporal cortex. The precise portions of the temporal cortex vary with the species; in the cat, where it has been most extensively studied, these are the primary cortex (AI) and at least three secondary cortical areas (AII, EP, and IN,TE). With much longer latencies, evoked potentials can be recorded also from most of the somatic sensory, motor, and association cortex areas. By way of the corpus callosum there are commissural connections with the auditory cortex of the opposite side (Pandya, Hallett, & Mukherjee, 1969). There have been several reports that even after complete section of the brachium of the inferior colliculus, evoked potentials can be recorded from the auditory cortex. Most recent studies (e.g., Adrian, Goldberg, & Brugge, 1966; Majkowski & Morgades, 1969) show that complete section of the brachium of the inferior colliculus usually abolishes all evoked auditory potentials from auditory cortex, but does not affect the slower evoked potentials that can be recorded from association and sensory motor cortex.

Microelectrode studies have shown a wide variety of response patterns and best frequencies in the auditory cortex. Its tonotopic organization is nowhere near as precise as that in lower auditory centers (Goldstein, Abeles, Daly, & McIntosh, 1970); nor does the auditory cortex show the extreme columnar organization that is found in somatic sensory cortex and visual cortex (Abeles & Goldstein, 1970).

In the cat, both frequency and intensity discriminations can be made even after widespread bilateral lesions of the auditory cortex, including all the primary and secondary auditory cortical areas; such lesions do however abolish the localization of sound in space (Strominger, 1969). The ability to localize sound is also destroyed by complete section of the brachium of the inferior colliculus (Strominger & Oesterreich, 1970). Temporal patterns of sound are also cortical-dependent, for bilateral massive lesions of the auditory cortex disrupt the ability to respond to differing tonal patterns (Kaas, Axelrod, & Diamond, 1967, in the cat; Dewson, Cowey, & Weiskrantz, 1970, in the monkey).

III. SUMMARY

The one structure common to all vertebrate hearing organs is the hair cell. It is polarized on the apical surface by the pattern formed by the many stereocilia, and by the eccentric placement of the single kinocilium (lacking in the adult mammal but with an obvious position nevertheless). There is also apical-basal polarization, with the "hairs" apically and the innervation basally.

The structures surrounding the hair cells vary significantly among vertebrates, but in all they protect the hair cells from extraneous stimulation while providing maximum accessibility to sound energy. The mammalian pinna of the external ear (frequently quite mobile) can be significant in sound localization, and helps direct sounds into the external auditory meatus and to the tympanic membrane. The tympano-ossicular system of the mammalian middle ear acts as a dynamic transformer, changing weak aerial sounds into vibrations of the much denser inner ear fluids. The characteristics of this transformer can be varied by the contractions of the middle ear muscles.

The narrow basal turn of the basilar membrane of the cochlea responds best to high frequency sounds, and the wider, more apical turns to low frequency sounds. The movements of the basilar membrane push the hair cells against the tectorial membrane in a shearing action, which bends their stereocilia. This physical stimulus initiates the transduction of physical vibrations into nerve impulses. The exact mechanism of transduction is still not known; however, the ultrastructural morphology, bioelectric potentials, and biochemical characteristics of the inner ear all suggest that physical stimulation initiates chemical changes in the hair cell and that a chemical synapse exists between the hair cell and the afferent nerve endings. There is also a smaller descending auditory system, with efferent nerve endings synapsing upon the hair cells, which provides feedback from the brain.

In the central auditory pathway, each nucleus—from the cochlear nuclei of the medulla through the auditory cortex of the cerebrum—involves complex series of synapses, and the decoding and integration of auditory information as well as its projection.

Acknowledgments

Dr. Allen M. Schneider was kind enough to review the manuscript and make valuable comments. M. B. Webster generously assisted in all aspects of manuscript preparation including editing, typing, and execution of the illustrations.

References

Abeles, M., & Goldstein, M. H., Jr. Functional architecture in cat primary auditory cortex: Columnar organization and organization according to depth. *Journal of Neurophysiology,* 1970, **33**, 172–187.

Adrian, H. O., Goldberg, J. M., & Brugge, J. F. Auditory evoked cortical potentials after lesions of brachium of inferior colliculus. *Journal of Neurophysiology,* 1966, **29**, 456–466.

Aitkin, L. M., Anderson, D. J., & Brugge, J. F. Tonotopic organization and discharge characteristics of single neurons in nuclei of the lateral lemniscus of the cat. *Journal of Neurophysiology,* 1970, **33**, 421–440.

Amato, G., LaGrutta, V., & Enia, F. The control of acoustic input in the medial geniculate body and inferior colliculus by auditory cortex. *Experientia,* 1970, **26**, 55–56.

Baird, I. L. The anatomy of the reptilian ear. In C. Gans & T. S. Parsons (Eds.), *Biology of the reptilia.* Vol. 2. *Morphology B.* New York: Academic Press, 1970. Pp. 193–275.

Batteau, D. W. Role of the pinna in localization: Theoretical and physiological consequences. In A. V. S. de Reuck & J. Knight (Eds.), *Hearing mechanisms in vertebrates.* London: Churchill, 1968. Pp. 234–239.

Benevento, L. A., & Coleman, P. D. Responses of single cells in cat inferior colliculus to binaural click stimuli: Combinations of intensity levels, time differences and intensity differences. *Brain Research,* 1970, **17**, 387–405.

Bredberg, G., Lindeman, H. H., Ades, H. W., West, R., & Engström, H. Scanning electron microscopy of the organ of Corti. *Science,* 1970, **170**, 861–863.

Brugge, J. F., Anderson, D. J., & Aitkin, L. M. Responses of neurons in the dorsal nucleus of the lateral lemniscus of cat to binaural tonal stimulation. *Journal of Neurophysiology*, 1970, **33**, 441–458.

Buss, I. O., & Estes, J. A. The functional significance of movements and positions of the pinnae of the African elephant, *Loxodonta africana*. *Journal of Mammalogy*, 1971, **52**, 21–27.

Capranica, R. R. The vocal repertoire of the bullfrog (*Rana catesbiana*). *Behaviour*, 1968, **31**, 302–325.

Coats, A. C. Temperature effects on the peripheral auditory apparatus. *Science*, 1965, **150**, 1481–1483.

Comis, S. D. Centrifugal inhibitory processes affecting neurones in the cat cochlear nucleus. *Journal of Physiology (London)*, 1970, **210**, 751–760.

Conti, A., & Borgo, M. Activity of cytochrome oxidase in the cochlea of the guinea pig. *Laryngoscope*, 1965, **75**, 830–839.

Dallos, P., Schoeny, Z. G., & Cheatham, M. A. Cochlear summating potentials: Composition. *Science*, 1970, **170**, 641–644.

Davis, H. A model for transducer action in the cochlea. *Cold Spring Harbor Symposia on Quantitative Biology,* 1965, **30**, 181–189.

Dewson, J. H., III, Cowey, A., & Weiskrantz, L. Disruptions of auditory sequence discrimination by unilateral and bilateral cortical ablations of superior temporal gyrus in the monkey. *Experimental Neurology*, 1970, **28**, 529–548.

Dunlop, C. W., Itzkowic, D. J., & Aitkin, L. M. Tone-burst response patterns of single units in the cat medial geniculate body. *Brain Research*, 1969, **16**, 149–164.

Engström, H., Ades, H. W., & Andersson, A. *Structural pattern of the organ of Corti.* Baltimore, Maryland: Williams & Wilkins, 1966.

Fernandez, C., & Karapas, F. The course and termination of the striae of Monakow and Held in the cat. *Journal of Comparative Neurology*, 1967, **131**, 371–385.

Fex, J. Efferent inhibition in the cochlea by the olivo-cochlear bundle. In A. V. S. de Reuck & J. Knight (Eds.), *Hearing mechanisms in vertebrates.* London: Churchill, 1968. Pp. 169–181.

Gannon, R. P., & Laszlo, C. A. Effect of atropine on the latency of cochlear potentials. *Journal of Neurophysiology*, 1968, **31**, 419–427.

Geisler, C. D., Rhode, W. S., & Hazelton, D. A. Responses of inferior colliculus neurons in the cat to binaural acoustic stimuli having wide-band spectra. *Journal of Neurophysiology*, 1969, **32**, 960–974.

Geisler, C. D., van Bergeijk, W. A., & Frishkopf, L. S. The inner ear of the bullfrog. *Journal of Morphology*, 1964, **114**, 43–58.

Goldberg, J. M., & Moore, R. Y. Ascending projections of the lateral lemniscus in the cat and monkey. *Journal of Comparative Neurology*, 1967, **129**, 143–156.

Goldstein, M. H., Jr., Abeles, M., Daly, R. L., & McIntosh, J. Functional architecture in cat primary auditory cortex: Tonotopic organization. *Journal of Neurophysiology*, 1970, **33**, 188–197.

Grundfest, H. Discussion. *Cold Spring Harbor Symposia on Quantitative Biology*, 1965, **30**, 190.

Harrison, J. M., & Irving, R. The anterior ventral cochlear nucleus. *Journal of Comparative Neurology*, 1965, **124**, 15–41.

Harrison, J. M., & Irving, R. Ascending connections of the anterior ventral cochlear nucleus in the rat. *Journal of Comparative Neurology*, 1966, **126**, 51–64. (a)

Harrison, J. M., & Irving, R. The organization of the posterior ventral cochlear nucleus in the rat. *Journal of Comparative Neurology*, 1966, **126**, 391–403. (b)

Harrison, J. M., & Irving, R. Visual and nonvisual auditory systems in mammals. *Science,* 1966, **154,** 738–743. (c)

Hilding, D. A. Electron microscopy of the developing hearing organ: *Laryngoscope,* 1969, **79,** 1691–1704.

Honrubia, V., & Ward, P. H. Dependence of the cochlear microphonics and the summating potential on the endocochlear potential. *Journal of the Acoustical Society of America,* 1969, **46,** 388–392.

Irving, R., & Harrison, J. M. The superior olivary complex and audition: A comparative study. *Journal of Comparative Neurology,* 1967, **130,** 77–86.

Iurato, S. *Submicroscopic structure of the inner ear.* Oxford: Pergamon, 1967.

Johnstone, B. M., & Boyle, A. J. F. Basilar membrane vibration examined with the Mössbauer technique. *Science,* 1967, **158,** 389–390.

Kaas, J., Axelrod, S., & Diamond, I. T. An ablation study of the auditory cortex in the cat using binaural tonal patterns. *Journal of Neurophysiology,* 1967, **30,** 710–724.

Kaneko, Y., & Daly, J. F. Activity of acetylcholinesterase on the endolymphatic surface of outer hair cells. *Acta Oto-Laryngologica,* 1969, **67,** 602–610.

Karten, H. J. The organization of the avian telencephalon and some speculations on the phylogeny of the amniote telencephalon. *Annals of the New York Academy of Sciences,* 1969, **167,** 164–179.

Katsuki, Y., Tanaka, Y., & Miyoshi, T. Action of acetylcholine on cochlear responses. *Nature (London),* 1965, **207,** 32–34.

Katsuki, Y., Yanagisawa, K., & Kanzaki, J. Tetraethylammonium and tetrodotoxin: Effects on cochlear potentials. *Science,* 1966, **151,** 1544–1545.

Kiang, N. Y-s. Stimulus coding in the auditory nerve and cochlear nucleus. *Acta Oto-Laryngologica,* 1965, **59,** 186–200.

Kiang, N. Y-s., Pfeiffer, R. R., Warr, W. B., & Backus, A. S. N. Stimulus coding in the cochlear nucleus. *Annals of Otology, Rhinology, & Laryngology,* 1965, **74,** 463–485.

Konishi, T., & Kelsey, E. Effect of calcium deficiency on cochlear potentials. *Journal of the Acoustical Society of America,* 1970, **47,** 1055–1062.

Konishi, T., Teas, D. C., & Wernick, J. S. Effects of electrical current applied to cochlear partition on discharges in individual auditory-nerve fibers. I. Prolonged direct-current polarization. *Journal of the Acoustical Society of America,* 1970, **47,** 1519–1526.

Kuijpers, W., & Bonting, S. L. The cochlear potentials. I. The effect of ouabain on the cochlear potentials of the guinea pig. *Pflüegers Archiv,* 1970, **320,** 348–358. (a)

Kuijpers, W., & Bonting, S. L. The cochlear potentials. II. The nature of the cochlear endolymphatic resting potential. *Pflüegers Archiv,* 1970, **320,** 359–372. (b)

Lichtensteiger, W., & Spoendlin, H. Adrenergic pathways to the cochlea of the cat. *Life Sciences,* 1967, **6,** 1639–1645.

Lim, D. J. Three dimensional observation of the inner ear with the scanning electron microscope. *Acta Oto-Laryngologica, Supplementum,* 1969, **255.**

Love, J. A., & Scott, J. W. Some response characteristics of cells of the magnocellular division of the medial geniculate body of the cat. *Canadian J ology and Pharmacology,* 1969, **47,** 881–888.

Majkowski, J., & Morgades, P. P. Primary auditory evoked potenti of brachium of the inferior colliculus. *Electroencephalograph Neurophysiology,* 1969, **27,** 587–593.

Masterton, R. B., Jane, J. A., & Diamond, I. T. Role of brain-stem auditory structures in sound localization. II. Inferior colliculus and its brachium. *Journal of Neurophysiology*, 1968, **31**, 96–108.

Moore, R. Y., & Goldberg, J. M. Ascending projections of the inferior colliculus in the cat. *Journal of Comparative Neurology*, 1963, **121**, 109–136.

Moore, R. Y., & Goldberg, J. M. Projections of the inferior colliculus in the monkey. *Experimental Neurology*, 1966, **14**, 429–438.

Morest, D. K. The laminar structure of the medial geniculate body of the cat. *Journal of Anatomy*, 1965, **99**, 143–160.

Moscovitch, D. H., & Gannon, R. P. Effects of calcium of sound-evoked cochlear potentials in the guinea pig. *Journal of the Acoustical Society of America*, 1966, **40**, 583–590.

Nomura, Y., & Balogh, K., Jr. Localization of DPNH and TPNH diaphorase activity in the cochlea by various histochemical techniques. *Laryngoscope*, 1964, **74**, 1351–1367.

O'Connell, C. P. The gas bladder and its relation to the inner ear in *Sardinops caerulea* and *Engraulis mordax*. *United States, Fish and Wildlife Service, Fishery Bulletin*, 1955, **56**, 505–533.

Osen, K. K. Cytoarchitecture of the cochlear nuclei in the cat. *Journal of Comparative Neurology*, 1969, **136**, 453–483. (a)

Osen, K. K. The intrinsic organization of the cochlear nuclei in the cat. *Acta Oto-Laryngologica*, 1969, **67**, 352–359. (b)

Pandya, D. N., Hallett, M., & Mukherjee, S. K. Intra- and interhemispheric connections of the neocortical auditory system in the rhesus monkey. *Brain Research*, 1969, **14**, 49–65.

Pfeiffer, R. R., & Molnar, C. E. Cochlear nerve fiber discharge patterns: Relationship to the cochlear microphonic. *Science*, 1970, **167**, 1614–1616.

Plotz, E., & Perlman, H. B. A histochemical study of the cochlea. *Laryngoscope*, 1955, **65**, 291–312.

Poggendorf, D. Die absoluten Hörschwellen des Zwergwelses (*Amiurus nebulosus*) und Beiträge zur Physik des Weberschen Apparates der Ostariophysen. *Zeitschrift Luer Vergleichende Physiologie*, 1952, **34**, 222–257.

Potter, H. D. Mesencephalic auditory region of the bullfrog. *Journal of Neurophysiology*, 1965, **28**, 1132–1154.

Powell, E. W., & Hatton, J. B. Projections of the inferior colliculus in cat. *Journal of Comparative Neurology*, 1969, **136**, 183–192.

Powell, T. P. S., & Cowan, W. M. An experimental study of the projection of the cochlea. *Journal of Anatomy*, 1962, **96**, 269–284.

Pye, J. D. Hearing in bats. In A. V. S. de Reuck & J. Knight (Eds.), *Hearing mechanisms in vertebrates*. London: Churchill, 1968. Pp. 66–84.

Salomon, G., & Starr, A. Electromyography of middle ear muscles in man during motor activities. *Acta Neurologica Scandinavica*, 1963, **39**, 161–168.

Sando, I. The anatomical interrelationships of the cochlear nerve fibers. *Acta Otolaryngologica*, 1965, **59**, 417–436.

Schneider, H. Die Bedeutung der Atemhöhle der Labyrinthfische für ihr Hörvermögen. *Zeitschrift Luer Vergleichende Physiologie*, 1941, **29**, 172–194.

Smith, C. A. Electron microscopy of the inner ear. *Annals of Otology, Rhinology, & Laryngology*, 1968, **77**, 629–643. (a)

Smith, C. A. Ultrastructure of the organ of Corti. *Advancement of Science*, 1968, **24**, 419–433. (b)

Spoendlin, H. H. *The organization of the cochlear receptor.* Basel: Karger, 1966.

Spocndlin, H. H. Ultrastructure and peripheral innervation pattern of the receptor in relation to the first coding of the acoustic message. In A. V. S. de Reuck & J. Knight (Eds.), *Hearing mechanisms in vertebrates.* London: Churchill, 1968. Pp. 89–119.

Stipetić, E. Ueber das Gehörogan der Mormyriden. *Zeitschrift Luer Vergleichende Physiologie*, 1939, **26**, 740–752.

Strominger, N. L. Localization of sound in space after unilateral and bilateral ablation of auditory cortex. *Experimental Neurology*, 1969, **25**, 521–533.

Strominger, N. L., & Oesterreich, R. E. Localization of sound after section of the brachium of the inferior colliculus. *Journal of Comparative Neurology*, 1970, **138**, 1–17.

Tasaki, I., Davis H., & Eldredge, D. H. Exploration of cochlear potentials in guinea pig with a microelectrode. *Journal of the Acoustical Society of America*, 1954, **26**, 765–773.

van Bergeijk, W. A. The evolution of vertebrate hearing. In W. D. Neff (Ed.), *Contributions to sensory physiology.* Vol. 2. New York: Academic Press, 1967. Pp. 1–49.

Vinnikov, Ya. A., & Titova, L. K. *The organ of Corti: Its histophysiology and histochemistry.* New York: Consultants Bureau, 1964.

von Békésy, G. Direct observations of the vibrations of the cochlear partition under a microscope. *Acta Oto-Laryngologica*, 1952, **42**, 197–201.

von Békésy, G. Description of some mechanical properties of the organ of Corti. *Journal of the Acoustical Society of America*, 1953, **25**, 770–785.

Ward, P. H., & Honrubia, V. The effects of local anesthetics on the cochlea of the guinea pig. *Laryngoscope*, 1969, **79**, 1605–1617.

Warr, W. B. Fiber degeneration following lesions in the anterior ventral cochlear nucleus of the cat. *Experimental Neurology*, 1966, **14**, 453–474.

Warr, W. B. Fiber degeneration following lesions in the posteroventral cochlear nucleus of the cat. *Experimental Neurology*, 1969, **23**, 140–155.

Webster, D. B. Ear structure and function in modern mammals. *American Zoologist*, 1966, **6**, 451–466.

Webster, D. B. Projection of cochlear nerve fibers onto the cochlear nuclei in the kangaroo rat, *Dipodomys merriami. Anatomical Record*, 1970, **166**, 394.

Webster, D. B., Ackermann, R. F., & Longa, G. C. Central auditory system of the kangaroo rat, *Dipodomys merriami. Journal of Comparative Neurology*, 1968, **133**, 477–494.

Webster, D. B., & Stack, C. R. Comparative histochemical investigation of the organ of Corti in the kangaroo rat, gerbil, and guinea pig. *Journal of Morphology*, 1968, **126**, 413–434.

Wersäll, J., Flock, Å., & Lundquist, P.-G. Structural basis for directional sensitivity in cochlear and vestibular sensory receptors. *Cold Spring Harbor Symposia on Quantitative Biology*, 1965, **30**, 115–132.

Wever, E. G. Electrical potentials of the cochlea. *Physiological Reviews*, 1966, **46**, 102–127.

Wever, E. G., & Bray, C. W. Action currents in the auditory nerve acoustical stimulation. *Proceedings of the National Academy of United States*, 1930, **16**, 344–350.

Wever, E. G., & Gans, C. The ear and hearing in Amphisbae *American Zoologist*, 1970, **10**, 555.

Wiggers, H. C. The functions of the intra-aural muscles. *American Journal of Physiology*, 1937, **120**, 771–780.

Witschi, E. The larval ear of the frog and its transformation during metamorphosis. *Zeitschrift Luer Naturforschung B*, 1949, **4**, 230–242.

Numbers in italics refer to the pages on which the complete references are listed.

Tolman, E. C., 129, *138*
Tomita, T., 342, 343, 345, 346, *357*
Toraldodi Francia, G., 387, *403*
Torebjörk, H. E., 243, *247*
Torick, E. L., 276, *289*
Trehub, S. E., 103, *116*
Trevarthen, C., 94, 105, *113, 116*
Trircker, D. E. W., 287, *290*
Tsuchitani, C., 435, 436, *444*
Tucker, D., 188, 197, 201, 202, *205,* 209, *216, 218*
Tucker, T. J., 106, *117*
Tumarkin, A., 281, *290*
Tunturi, A. R., 415, *448*
Turk, A., 188, *204,* 214, *216*

U

Ueki, K., 106, *117*
Umrath, K., 240, *246*
Ungar, G., 49, *62*
Utley, J. D., 414, 415, *445*
Uttley, A. M., 174, *184*

V

Valenta, J. G., 215, *218*
Vallbo, Å. B., 231, 243, *248*
Van Bergeijk, W. A., 408, *448,* 449, 452, 453, 454, *478, 481*
Vance, W. B., 213, *218*
Vandenberg, S. G., 141, 145, 146, 147, *154, 155*
Vanderbelt, D. J., 210, *216*
Van Groenigen, W. B., 104, *115*
Vernon, M. D., 372, *403*
Verrijp, C. D., 377, *404*
Victor, J., 251, 254, *272*
Vigorito, J., 103, *111*
Vinnikov, Ya. A., 469, *481*
Vitelli, R., 267, *272*
von Baumgarten, R., 202, *205*
von Békésy, G., 253, *272,* 275, *290,* 411, *448,* 462, 463, *481*
von Campenhausen, G., 97, *114*
von Duering, M., 225, 227, 228, 231, 246, *247*
von Helmholtz, H., 394, *406*
von Holst, E., 102, *117*
von Senden, M., 82, *87,* 171, *184*

von Skramlik, E., 318, *325*
Voros, G. Y., 51, *62*

W

Waardenburg, P. J., 144, *155*
Waddington, C. H., 90, *117,* 150, *155*
Wagner, H. G., 74, *85,* 343, 349, *355, 357*
Wainwright, A. A. P., 107, *109*
Waite, R., 414, *445*
Walberg, F., 288, *289*
Wald, G., 329, 331, 332, *355, 356, 357,* 360, 362, 367, 369, *404, 406*
Walk, R. D., 171, *184*
Wall, P. D., 7, *20,* 43, 53, *61, 62,* 82, *87*
Wallace, J. G., 170, *182*
Wallach, H., 277, *290*
Walls, G. L., 71, *87,* 332, 336, *357*
Walraven, J., 396, *403*
Walsh, J. W. T., 328, *357*
Walzl, E. M., 415, *448*
Wapner, S., 297, 298, *315*
Ward, P. H., 468, 469, *479, 481*
Warr, W. B., 472, *479, 481*
Warren, D. H., 305, *314*
Warren, J. M., 162, *184*
Warren, R. M., 220, 227, 228, 234, 236, 242, *247*
Watanabe, K., 333, 334, 339, 340, 343, *355*
Waterbolk, H. T., 133, *135*
Watson, J. D., 143, *155*
Watson, W. E., 93, *111*
Watts, T. L., 179, *184*
Waziri, R., 40, *62*
Weale, R. A., 331, *357,* 370, *402*
Weaver, W., 130, *138*
Webb, A. D., 213, *216*
Webster, D. B., 427, *448,* 453, 458, 469, 470, 472, *481*
Webster, M., 427, *448*
Weddell, G., 6, 7, *20*
Weiler, I. J., 95, *117*
Weinberger, N. N., 433, *448*
Weinstein, M., 167, *182*
Weiskrantz, L., 476, *478*
Weiss, P., 91, 95, *117,* 292, *315*
Welker, W. I., 246, *246,* 430, *448*
Wells, M. J., 171, *184*

Subject Index

A

Acceleration detector, 240
Activity cycles, fetal rhythmic, 100
Action potential, 25
  encoding mechanism, 32, 33
Acuity, visual, 383
Adaptation, 15, 16, 222, *see also* Dark
  adaptation, Learning, Mechanore-
  ceptors, topics related to specific
  senses
Adaptation to environment, of population or individual, 120
Adapting stimulus, temperature, 323–324
After-images, *see also* Photopigments;
  Vision, psychophysics of
  dark adaptation, 370–372
  as stabilized images, 380–381
Ageusia, 207
Aircraft accidents, 287
Amacrine cell, 335
  retinal receptive fields, 342
  retinal responses, 346
Ambiguous figures in pattern recognition,
  159
Ampulla and crista ampullaris, 283, 284,
  285, 286
Amphibians
  auditory connections to brainstem, 455
  auditory termination in torus semicircularis, 455
  role in evolution of auditory systems,
  408, 409, 411, 412, 413
  metamorphosis, 97
  neuromast organs of larvae, 452
  pruning of receptor fields, 97
  sound transforming mechanisms, 453–
  454
Anableps microlepis,
  simultaneous aerial and aquatic vision,
  72–73
Anatomic pattern
  connections, 43–44
  by cell interaction, 90
Anatomic structures, *see* name of specific
  structure
Anatomy, importance of, 46–47
Animal experiments, *see* name of animal;
  Comparative animal studies

Anosmia, specific, 209
Appetites, specific, 211, 212
Aquatic animals, *see also* Fish; name of
  animal
  dermal photosensitivity, 68
  sound localization by Δ *fi* cues, 424
  vestigal olfactory system, 195
Areal summations, 386–388
Arthropods, compound eyes, 71
Artificial intelligence, 178–179
Atavism, 63–64
Attention, auditory, *see* Auditory attention
Aubert effect, 297
Audible fields, 416–419
  audiogram defined, 416–417
  brief sounds, significance of, 419–420
  comparisons for mammals, 418–419
  comparisons for tetrapods, 417
  philogenetic comparisons of audiograms, 418–419
  specialized, 419
Audiograms, 416–419
  basis of, and interpretation, 419
  comparisons, tetrapods, mammals and
  man, 418–419
  defined, 416–417
  long-duration pure tones vs. brief
  sounds, 419
Audiomotor function of auditory cortex,
  441–443
Auditory attention, 433–434
  ablation-behavior experiments, 434
  role of descending system, 433, 434
  role of midbrain and forebrain, 434
  role of reticular formation, 432, 434
Auditory central nervous system
  integrative action, 433, 434
Auditory cortex, 470, 471, 476
  ablation experiments for sound localization, 441–444
  audiomotor function of, 441–443
  mammalian variations in size and
  complexity, 414
Auditory discrimination, 160, 161, 168–
  170
  frequency changes and recognition,
  161

HANDBOOK OF PERCEPTION

EDITORS: *Edward C. Carterette and Morton P. Friedman*

Department of Psychology
University of California
Los Angeles, California 90024

Volume III: Biology of Perceptual Systems. 1973

IN PREPARATION

Volume I: Historical and Philosophical Roots of Perception.

Volume II: Psychophysical Judgment and Measurement.